American Government

ARMIN ROSENCRANZ J.D., Ph.D.
Lawyer and former lecturer on American Government
Stanford University, California
California State at San Francisco

JAMES B. CHAPIN, Ph.D.
Political Consultant and
Former Assistant Professor
Rutgers University, New Jersey
Yale University, Connecticut

SHARON WAGNER
Lawyer and former teacher
of American Government
Cubberley High School,
Palo Alto, California
Seattle Public Schools

BARBARA FINLEY BROWN
Teacher of Social Studies
San Leandro High School
San Leandro, California

HOLT, RINEHART AND WINSTON, PUBLISHERS
New York • Toronto • London • Sydney

ARMIN ROSENCRANZ is a lawyer, political scientist, writer, and foundation executive. He received his A.B. degree in political science from Princeton University and his M.A., J.D., and Ph.D. degrees from Stanford University, where he has served as a trustee. Dr. Rosencranz has taught American government at Stanford and at San Francisco State University. In the 1960's he served as a counsel to U.S. Senators Joseph Tydings and Robert Kennedy and was a staff member of the President's Task Force on Government Organization. Dr. Rosencranz is co-author of *Congress and the Public Trust*. He is a member of the District of Columbia and U.S. Supreme Court bars, a former fellow of the National Endowment for the Humanities, and a member of the Committee on Professional Ethics of the American Political Science Association. During 1979–80 Dr. Rosencranz directed the International Comparative Study of Transboundary Air Pollution at the Environmental Law Institute in Washington, D.C. He has written widely on law and public policy. Dr. Rosencranz is currently Executive Director of the Pioneer Foundation in Inverness, California.

JAMES B. CHAPIN is an author, historian, and political consultant. He received his B.A. degree from Hamilton College and his Ph.D. degree from Cornell University. Dr. Chapin has taught American history at Yale University and at Rutgers University. He is a member of the Academy of Political and Social Science and the Social Science History Association. Dr. Chapin has written articles for books, professional journals, magazines, and newspapers. He is a member of the Queensborough Library Board, acting Chairman of the board of World Hunger Year, Inc., and a member of the board of *Food Monitor* and the Food Policy Center.

ACKNOWLEDGMENTS: Grateful acknowledgment is made to the following sources for permission to reprint copyrighted material.

Thomas E. Cronin, for chart entitled "The White House Staff," adapted from **The State of the Presidency,** published by Little, Brown and Company. Copyright © 1975.

John E. Mueller, for chart entitled "Public Approval of President Johnson's Foreign Policy, 1965–1968," adapted from **War, Presidents and Public Opinion,** published by John Wiley and Sons, Inc., Copyright © 1973.

Prentice-Hall, Inc., for "Bureau Chiefs and Their World," "The Social Security System," "Formal and Informal Lines of Bureaucratic Organization," adapted from **Government by the People,** 9th edition, by James MacGregor Burns and J. W. Peltason with Thomas E. Cronin. Copyright © 1975.

Photo credits are on page 712.

ISBN: 0-03-059257-7

6 071 98765

CONTENTS

iv

ix

FEATURES

GRAPHS AND MAPS

CHARTS

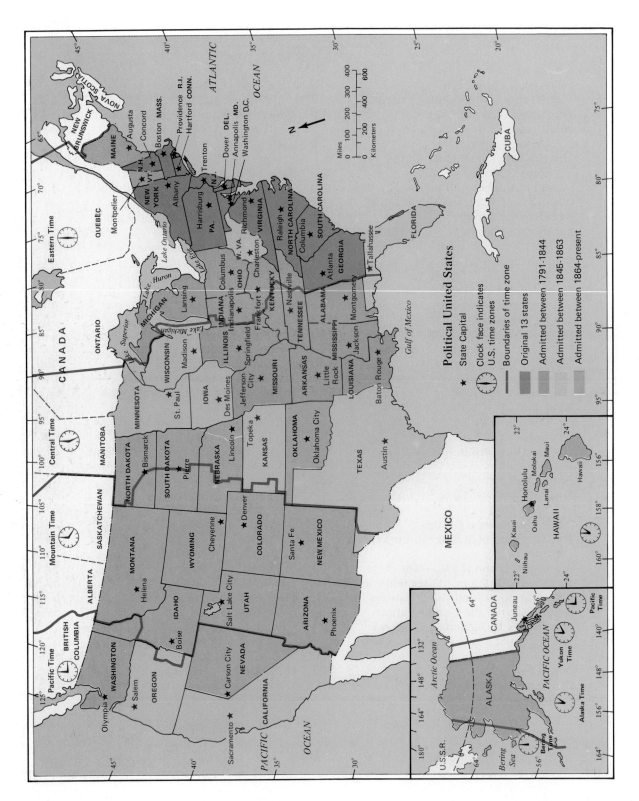

Political United States

★ State Capital
🕐 Clock face indicates
U.S. time zones
━━ Boundaries of time zone
Original 13 states
Admitted between 1791-1844
Admitted between 1845-1863
Admitted between 1864-present

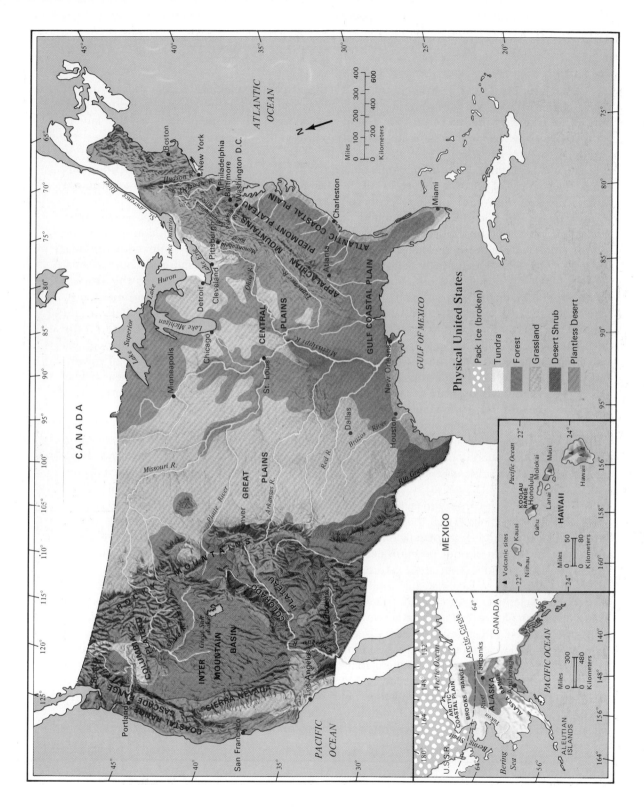

CANADA

ATLANTIC
OCEAN

Boston
New York
Hudson R.
Philadelphia
Baltimore
Washington D.C.
Charleston
Miami

St. Lawrence River

Lake Ontario
Lake Erie
Pittsburgh
Cleveland
Detroit
Lake Huron
Lake Michigan
Lake Superior
Chicago
Minneapolis

APPALACHIAN MOUNTAINS
PIEDMONT PLATEAU
ATLANTIC COASTAL PLAIN
GULF COASTAL PLAIN
Atlanta

Delaware R.
Potomac R.
Susquehanna R.
Monongahela R.
Allegheny R.
Ohio R.
Tennessee R.

CENTRAL
PLAINS
St. Louis
Mississippi R.
New Orleans
GULF OF MEXICO

Missouri R.
Platte River
Arkansas R.
Red R.
Brazos River
Rio Grande
Dallas
Houston
GREAT
PLAINS

ROCKY MOUNTAINS
COLUMBIA PLATEAU
INTER MOUNTAIN BASIN
COLORADO PLATEAU
Great Salt Lake
Snake R.
Colorado R.
Denver
Los Angeles
SIERRA NEVADA
CASCADE RANGE
COASTAL RANGE
Portland
San Francisco

PACIFIC
OCEAN

MEXICO

Physical United States

- Pack Ice (broken)
- Tundra
- Forest
- Grassland
- Desert Shrub
- Plantless Desert

Miles 0 100 200 300 400
Kilometers 0 200 400 600

N

HAWAII

KOOLAU RANGE
Honolulu
Oahu
Kauai
Niihau
Lanai
Molokai
Maui
Hawaii
Pacific Ocean
▲ Volcanic sites

Miles 0 50
Kilometers 0 80

22° 22° 24°
15.6° 15.8° 160°

ALASKA

Arctic Ocean
Arctic Circle
CANADA
BROOKS RANGE
ARCTIC COASTAL PLAIN
ALASKA RANGE
Fairbanks
Anchorage
Yukon River
Bering Strait
Bering Sea
ALEUTIAN ISLANDS
U.S.S.R.
PACIFIC OCEAN

Miles 0 300
Kilometers 0 480

132° 148° 140° 148°
164° 164° 156°
56° 64° 64°

XV

THE STUDY OF GOVERNMENT

Since the beginning of history, thinkers have been studying the government of society. But it is only in the last century or so that this subject has become a separate field of study.

In the beginning of the nineteenth century, the process of creating academic "disciplines" began. Law and political economy were among the first disciplines created. A *discipline* is the organization of scholarly inquiry that is distinguished from other fields of inquiry by the following criteria: its subject matter (what it is about), its method of inquiry (how one investigates the subject), and its goals (what people in the field want to learn.)

Most of the social sciences (particularly economics) emerged from the study of political economy. But the fields that eventually came to be known as government, or political science, emerged from two fields of scholarly inquiry: the study of history and the study of law. By the 1880's quite a number of colleges and universities offered political science or government as a course of study.

Political Science. Those who favor the term "political science" believe that the disciplines that study humanity (known collectively as the social sciences) should be equivalent to the physical sciences in their study of nature.

Social scientists assume that there are laws of human nature, just as there are laws of physical nature. These laws can be discovered, they believe, by using the scientific method—that is, by selecting a problem, making certain hypotheses (tentative laws) that explain the problem, and then testing the hypotheses against actual events. Eventually, it should be possible for social scientists to discern and explain the regularities in human organization, just as natural scientists have discovered such regularities as the law of gravity.

Government. Most secondary school curriculums offer a subject called government or civics.

This book on American government focuses on the legal foundations and the major institutions of the state: constitutions, laws, executives, legislatures, bureaucrats, and judges. It does not differ in this respect from the original works on government written a century ago by Woodrow Wilson and Lord Bryce. But this book also draws on the perspectives of political science through its sections on informal as well as formal governing institutions. It discusses political beliefs and behavior that were not considered in nineteenth-century textbooks.

Today we are aware of the many complexities of human behavior and organization that our ancestors did not understand. Their works were often moralistic and reflected their preferences for particular systems of government. Former President Woodrow Wilson, for example, thought that the British parliamentary form of government was superior to ours and his critical study of Congress reflected that point of view.

Nineteenth-century students of government generally did not use numbers very much. Today all the tools of investigation developed in the last century are at our disposal: psychology, archeology, computers, and statistics. Of these tools the most important is probably statistics. The use of numbers is very important, and at many places in this book they are presented in ways designed to help understand American government.

HOW TO USE STATISTICS

Why Numbers and Charts? We live in an age of numbers. Everything is tabulated. The pocket calculator is becoming as familiar to us as the slide rule was to past generations. There are a few subjects in school or in life in which one can function without using numbers.

Numbers are tools of measurement and thus of decision making. If you were going to build a house, you would have to decide on its size, determine its measurements, and calculate the amount of materials you would need to build it. Similarly, the government and those concerned with government action must collect a mass of statistics. No judgment in politics—whether about elections, budgets, taxes, congressional action, and even, in many cases, judicial decisions—is made without reference to numbers.

Charts and graphs visually illustrate the relationship among numbers. The ways in which numbers are presented may distort truth as well as demonstrate it.

There are four kinds of graphs: the pie graph, the line graph, the bar graph, and the pictograph.

Pie Graphs. Pie graphs always show divisions of a whole. The whole resembles a pie, with each part separated the way a piece of pie would be cut. A pie graph is always a percentage graph, with the whole pie equaling 100 percent of whatever is being measured.

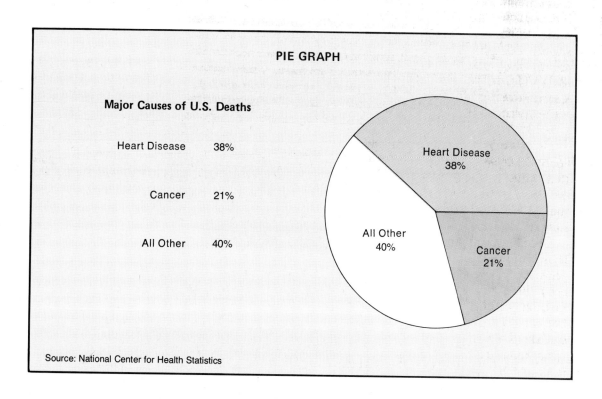

PIE GRAPH

Major Causes of U.S. Deaths

Heart Disease	38%
Cancer	21%
All Other	40%

Heart Disease 38%

Cancer 21%

All Other 40%

Source: National Center for Health Statistics

Line Graphs. To make a line graph, a horizontal base line is drawn, from which measurements are made. Usually this base line is zero, but it does not have to be. Numbers are indicated in ascending order on the vertical axis line on the left side of the diagram from the base line. A time scale is usually placed along the horizontal base line. The amount of what is being measured on the left axis is marked by a dot for each time interval on the horizontal axis. Then the dots are connected by a line. Line graphs are well suited to showing change over time.

Bar Graphs. Bar graphs are often made in the same manner as line graphs. But rather than connect the dots with a line, the marks stand alone and are filled in with a solid bar-shaped figure. Like the line graph, bar graphs are good devices for showing change over time. They can also be arranged horizontally rather than vertically.

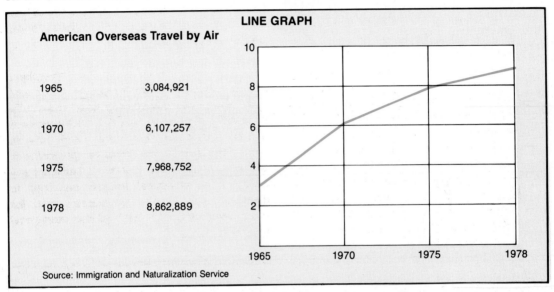

LINE GRAPH

American Overseas Travel by Air

1965	3,084,921
1970	6,107,257
1975	7,968,752
1978	8,862,889

Source: Immigration and Naturalization Service

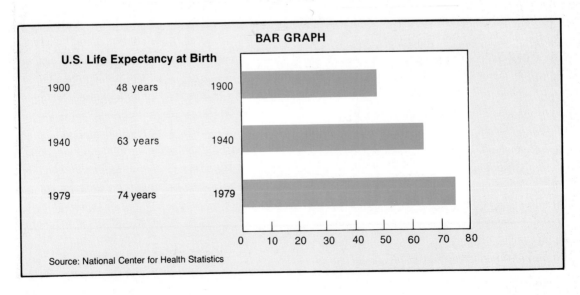

BAR GRAPH

U.S. Life Expectancy at Birth

1900	48 years
1940	63 years
1979	74 years

Source: National Center for Health Statistics

Pictographs. Pictographs replace the connected dots of a line graph or the solid bars of a bar graph with groupings of individual figures. Each figure in a group represents a given quantity of what is being measured. The advantage of a pictograph is that it shows individual units. Thus it is easy to tell from a pictograph that a given item has doubled or tripled.

Methods of Presentation and Choice of Numbers. Numbers look different when they are presented in different ways. For example, changing the base line changes the appearance of a graph; changing the scale of the numbers can change the graph even more. It is also possible to change the effect of a graph by shifting the beginning and ending dates on its horizontal base line.

The same numbers can be read in different ways. An example of this is the calculation of percentages. For example, although 92 percent of the Black population voted for George McGovern in 1972, they provided only 22 percent of his votes. However, although only 35 percent of the White population voted for him, they provided 78 percent of his votes. Clearly, different presentations would give different impressions of these data.

Categories. Information can give a variety of impressions, depending on how it is grouped, combined, or separated. What a piece of information is compared with makes a great difference. To return to the issue of race, one's impression of the status of American Blacks would differ greatly if they were compared with American Whites, with African Blacks, or with their own group during some period in the past.

Numbers Are Not Neutral. Numbers do not save one from having to think and make choices. Used correctly, numbers can be invaluable. One must pay careful attention to what questions should be asked, how to collect the information, how to categorize it, and how to compare it. But a mistake at any point of the statistical analysis can lead to disaster, both for the investigator and for those who act on the basis of this numerical misinformation.

PICTOGRAPH

U.S. Population Growth

1880	50,165,000	1880
1940	132,669,000	1940
1980	222,159,000	1980

Source: U.S. Bureau of the Census

Each symbol represents 10 million.

FACTS ABOUT THE UNITED STATES

STATE	YEAR ADMITTED TO UNION	CAPITAL	AREA IN SQUARE MILES	NUMBER OF COUNTIES	POPULATION*	NUMBER OF REPRESENTATIVES IN CONGRESS	NUMBER OF ELECTORAL VOTES	PER CAPITA INCOME	FARM LAND IN SQUARE MILES	NUMBER OF MANUFACTURING ESTABLISHMENTS
NORTHEAST										
Connecticut	1788	Hartford	5,009	8	3,096,951	6	8	6,564	687	5,836
Delaware	1787	Dover	2,057	3	594,779	1	3	5,883	985	567
Maine	1820	Augusta	33,215	16	1,123,560	2	4	4,627	2,380	2,075
Maryland	1788	Annapolis	10,577	23	4,193,378	8	10	6,561	4,115	3,579
Massachusetts	1788	Boston	8,257	14	5,728,288	11	14	5,826	940	10,770
New Hampshire	1788	Concord	9,304	10	919,114	2	4	5,365	790	1,434
New Jersey	1787	Trenton	7,836	21	7,335,808	14	17	6,492	1,502	15,069
New York	1788	Albany	49,576	58	17,557,288**	34	41	5,849	14,700	38,342
Pennsylvania	1787	Harrisburg	45,333	67	11,824,561	23	27	5,622	12,786	18,398
Rhode Island	1790	Providence	1,214	5	945,761	2	4	5,589	95	2,756
Vermont	1791	Montpelier	9,609	14	511,299	1	3	4,770	2,605	860
Washington, D.C.	—	—	68	1	635,233	—	3	7,074	—	564
SOUTH										
Alabama	1819	Montgomery	51,609	67	3,863,698	7	9	4,712	18,515	4,984
Arkansas	1836	Little Rock	53,104	75	2,280,687	4	6	4,443	22,871	2,897
Florida	1845	Tallahassee	58,560	67	9,579,495	19	17	5,761	20,617	10,275
Georgia	1788	Atlanta	58,876	159	5,396,425	10	12	5,071	21,677	7,627
Kentucky	1792	Frankfort	40,395	120	3,642,143	7	9	4,851	22,543	3,167
Louisiana	1812	Baton Rouge	48,523	64	4,194,299	8	10	4,790	14,266	3,657
Mississippi	1817	Jackson	47,716	82	2,503,250	5	7	4,120	22,337	2,727
North Carolina	1789	Raleigh	52,586	100	5,846,159	11	13	4,876	17,563	8,632
South Carolina	1788	Columbia	31,055	46	3,067,061	6	8	4,628	9,648	3,719
Tennessee	1796	Nashville	42,244	95	4,539,834	9	10	4,845	20,467	5,647
Virginia	1788	Richmond	40,817	95	5,321,521	10	12	5,883	15,117	4,837
West Virginia	1863	Charleston	24,181	55	1,928,524	4	6	4,851	5,462	1,734
MIDWEST										
Illinois	1818	Springfield	56,400	102	11,321,350	22	26	6,358	45,446	18,617
Indiana	1816	Indianapolis	36,291	92	5,454,154	10	13	5,751	26,218	7,345
Iowa	1846	Des Moines	56,290	99	2,908,797	6	8	5,439	51,616	3,387
Kansas	1861	Topeka	82,264	105	2,355,536	5	7	5,861	74,893	2,839
Michigan	1837	Lansing	58,218	83	9,236,891	18	21	6,130	16,920	14,467
Minnesota	1858	St. Paul	84,068	87	4,068,856	8	10	5,778	43,119	5,698
Missouri	1821	Jefferson City	69,686	114	4,901,678	9	12	5,493	46,549	2,305
Nebraska	1867	Lincoln	77,227	93	1,564,727	3	5	5,326	72,121	1,723
North Dakota	1889	Bismarck	70,664	53	652,437	1	3	4,856	66,208	482
Ohio	1803	Columbus	41,222	88	10,758,421	21	25	5,796	24,473	16,390
South Dakota	1889	Pierre	77,047	64	687,643	1	4	4,529	71,818	606
Wisconsin	1848	Madison	56,154	72	4,689,055	9	11	5,660	27,530	7,845
SOUTHWEST										
Arizona	1912	Phoenix	113,909	14	2,714,013	5	6	5,545	59,268	2,037
New Mexico	1912	Santa Fe	121,666	32	1,290,551	3	4	4,837	73,486	926
Oklahoma	1907	Oklahoma City	69,919	77	2,998,124	6	8	5,245	51,676	3,042
Texas	1845	Austin	267,338	254	14,152,339	27	26	5,633	209,597	14,422
MOUNTAIN										
Colorado	1876	Denver	104,247	63	2,877,726	6	7	6,118	56,079	2,841
Idaho	1890	Boise	83,557	44	943,629	2	4	5,072	22,296	1,190
Montana	1889	Helena	147,138	56	783,674	2	4	5,288	101,777	943
Nevada	1864	Carson City	110,540	17	800,312	2	3	6,533	16,891	447
Utah	1896	Salt Lake City	84,916	29	1,454,630	3	4	5,135	16,573	1,358
Wyoming	1890	Cheyenne	97,914	23	468,909	1	3	6,454	53,533	377
PACIFIC										
Alaska	1959	Juneau	586,412	11	400,331	1	2	9,170	2,551	342
California	1850	Sacramento	158,693	58	23,510,372	45	45	6,487	52,149	35,699
Hawaii	1959	Honolulu	6,450	4	964,624	2	4	6,005	3,310	770
Oregon	1859	Salem	96,981	36	2,617,444	5	6	6,018	28,492	4,670
Washington	1889	Olympia	68,192	39	4,109,634	8	9	6,394	26,026	5,345

*based on preliminary 1980 census figures
**estimated

UNIT
1

JAMES MADISON
"Founder of the Constitution"

James Madison probably had more to do with setting up our present form of government than any of the other Founding Fathers. Shorter in stature than any American President, Madison has continually been overshadowed by taller— and more famous—men, like Washington, Adams, Hamilton, Franklin.

Madison was born in Port Conway, Virginia, in 1751, the oldest of ten children. In three years at the College of New Jersey (now Princeton), he completed a rigorous course of history, government, Hebrew, and ethics that was normally expected to take at least five years.

In 1776 he was elected a delegate to the Virginia Convention. He played a leading role in its proceedings, particularly in areas concerning the basic rights of the people. In 1778 he was made a member of the governor's council, and in 1780 he became one of Virginia's delegates to the Confederation Congress. During his three years in Philadelphia, he became a national leader. He left the Congress at the end of 1783, but was returned as a delegate in 1784.

Madison was a dedicated nationalist. He believed the United States could not survive without a stronger central government. During the rest of the 1780's, he devoted himself to the advancement of this cause, both in the Congress and away from it. He played an active role in the Annapolis meeting that paved the way for the Constitutional Convention of 1787, and he helped persuade the Congress to approve the convention. Madison drafted large portions of the United States Constitution. It was he who wrote the so-called Virginia Plan for a strong national government.

After the convention, Madison led the Constitution's supporters at his own state ratifying convention against the formidable orator Patrick Henry. At the same time, he wrote key portions of "The Federalist," perhaps the ablest defense of our constitutional system ever penned. He was the logical choice to be sent to the new Congress by his state, and it was assumed that he would be the leader of the Constitutionalist forces in the House of Representatives. However, this group soon split over a host of new issues. You often hear that the early fight was between Hamilton and Jefferson, but in many ways it was really between Hamilton and Madison.

It was Madison who drafted Washington's Farewell Address in 1792,

PEOPLE IN
POLITICS

THE FOUNDATIONS OF GOVERNMENT

when Washington planned to retire after serving only one term. By the time the address was delivered four years later, Madison had been alienated from the President. Tired of doing battle in Philadelphia, he retired from the House in 1797, after eight years. But his unhappiness with Federalist policies brought him back into action. He wrote the Virginia Resolution — a strong "states' rights" expression of opposition to the Alien and Sedition Laws — in 1798. When Thomas Jefferson defeated John Adams for the presidency in 1800, Madison returned to national office in the new capital of Washington. There he served eight years as secretary of state and eight years as President. Although his performance as President is often criticized, it is worth remembering that he left the nation in 1817 in better condition than ever before. He died in 1836, having outlived the other Founders.

OVERVIEW

■ Governments are established to provide for the welfare and safety of citizens.

■ The concept of government has evolved gradually over many centuries.

■ There are many forms of government. Each reflects the specific views of those who govern and are governed.

■ American government is based on principles brought by English settlers.

■ The Articles of Confederation provided the first national government of the United States. However, it proved to be too weak.

■ In 1787 a constitutional convention was convened to revise the Articles. Instead, the new Constitution was created.

■ The government established by the Constitution is a federal system with power permanently divided between the national government and the states.

■ The Constitution created a system established on the following principles: representative government, based on popular sovereignty; separation of powers, with a system of checks and balances; and limited government.

UNIT
CONTENT

1

The Basic Concepts of Government

The strongest institutional expression of politics is government. This chapter focuses on the basic concepts of politics and economics with which you will be concerned as you read this book.

You will review basic definitions and concepts before you examine theories about how government originated. Then you will learn about the different kinds of governments that existed in the past and those that exist today.

You will also learn about one of the most important institutions in the modern world, the nation-state. Finally, you will learn about economic systems, particularly those that dominate the modern world—capitalism, socialism, and communism.

CHAPTER PREVIEW

1. THEORIES OF GOVERNMENT
2. KINDS OF GOVERNMENT
3. THE NATION-STATE
4. ECONOMIC SYSTEMS

1. THEORIES OF GOVERNMENT

Soon after civilization had developed, people began to ask themselves about the origins of their governmental institutions. The discussion of the origins of government has continued for more that 3,000 years. Origi-nally a question that concerned kings, queens, and holy persons, it became a matter of philosophical speculation for the Greeks and a question of politics and economics for the founders of the modern nation-state. It is an issue that contemporary social sciences deal with in specific ways.

Divine Right. Probably the most universally accepted theory of the origins of government was that of *divine right*. This theory attributed the creation of government to divine intervention in human affairs. This should not be surprising. In ancient societies such as Babylonia and Egypt, only priests and the educated members of the upper classes were able to read and write. Often the religious and the **secular** aspects of a society were so interwoven that religious leaders were able to hold governmental office. These leaders and their educated servants wrote histories that justified the existing social order. They proclaimed that the social order—particularly the government—had been created not by them but by the gods. Accordingly, people were far less likely to criticize a government they believed had been founded through divine intercession—an obvious advantage to governmental leaders.

> **Secular** means not specifically religious.

In the Christian civilization of western Europe that arose after the fall of Rome, monarchs asserted the right to rule based on the blessings given to them by the church. The church's blessing was considered the sign that God had given a king or a queen the authority to rule. If the church withdrew its blessing, the legitimacy of the monarch could be questioned. Rebels could then attack the government without provoking the church.

Britain's Queen Elizabeth and Prince Philip, dressed in the symbols of royalty, attend a ceremony in Australia.

The theory of divine right was reasserted most forcefully by the monarchs who ruled England in the seventeenth century. The theories of government that were inscribed in the Declaration of Independence were drawn from seventeenth-century philosophers such as John Locke, who opposed the theory of divine right. These theorists contended that government is legitimate only to the extent that it is based on the consent of the people being governed.

In modern times only a few monarchs— for example, the ruler of Saudi Arabia—claim divine right to rule.

The Social Contract Theory. A seventeenth-century English philosopher, Thomas Hobbes, advanced the social contract theory of government. In his book *Leviathan*, Hobbes wrote that humans originally existed in a "state of nature." This was not a state of well-being; rather, it was one in which human life was "nasty, brutish, and short." It was *anarchy*—that is, a state in which no rules exist to govern behavior.

In Hobbes' theory, the original contract between the people and the state was final. Consequently, Hobbes maintained, the state had absolute power to rule the people.

Hobbes' theory was considered harsh and pessimistic. Within a few years it was modified by John Locke, who said that the social contract between the people and the state could be renegotiated whenever the people found it unacceptable.

It is interesting to note that this concept of government as a social contract between the people and the state coincided with the rise of a new society in Europe. Whereas the older European society had been preoccupied with religious concerns, this new society was dominated by economic concerns. Thus a contractual rather than a divine origin of government was asserted.

A Theory of Force. Like religion and economics, violence has played a great role in history. As a result, a theory of force was proposed to explain the origins of government. This theory maintains that all governments were established through force. Governments have always forced the people within their reach to pay some kind of tribute, or tax, to them. This form of behavior became institutionalized, or sanctioned by custom, when groups that had imposed their will on their neighbors developed myths and legends to justify their rule. It does appear that the origins of many medieval baronies, or fiefs, followed the development implied in this theory.

The Evolutionary Theory. In the middle of the nineteenth century, Charles Darwin suggested that the earth had not been made in a single act. Rather, Darwin maintained, the earth was the result of a long process of evolution, or gradual development, from very simple to very complex forms of life. Social thinkers seized Darwin's theory and applied it to the development of human government.

First, claimed the Social Darwinists, came the family. The father became the head of the family, thereby establishing a simple form of government. Then a group of related families, called a clan, developed. Eventually a number of clans banded together to form a tribe. Methods of producing goods and services changed in similar ways over time. When agriculture developed, groups formed to coordinate and manage this enterprise. These managers became the rulers of the first agricultural society.

With the passage of time, the functions of maintaining internal order and protecting the society from external danger evolved into the governmental institutions that now characterize all states. Thus, the Social Darwinists maintained, the state evolved from an agricultural society that had evolved from the tribe, the clan, and the family.

section review

1. What is the basis for the "divine right" theory of government? What are its advantages and disadvantages?
2. What is the basis of government according to the "social contract" theory?
3. Define the "force" theory of government.
4. How was Darwin's theory applied to the development of governments?

2. KINDS OF GOVERNMENT

Monarchies still exist today. Pictured above is King Hussein of Jordan.

In theory, it is possible to have a society with no government; such a society is called *anarchy.* The term comes from the Greek *anarchos,* which means "without a ruler." Those who advocate such a society are called anarchists. They believe that humans are essentially good, and thus hold that government is an unnecessary evil.

In practice, all known societies have had governments. In the fifth century B.C., the Greek historian Herodotus maintained that there were three basic forms of government: monarchy, aristocracy, and democracy. A century later the Greek philosopher Aristotle classified governments into a much more complex pattern.

Aristotle's Pattern. *Monarchy* is the term used to describe a government headed by a single hereditary leader, usually a king, a queen, an emperor, or an empress. Some monarchies, such as the Roman Empire and the kingdom of Poland, provided for succession by appointment or by election, not through inheritance.

In modern usage the term *dictatorship* means what Aristotle and the ancients called *tyranny.* This form of government is ruled by an individual who has seized the power of the state in order to wield it for his or her own purposes.

Aristocracy, like monarchy, in modern usage means government based on heredity. It differs from monarchy in being ruled by a group of individuals or leading families rather than by a single monarch. Some governments that were monarchies in theory were aristocracies in practice. These aristocracies included the government of Great Britain during the period from 1688 to 1832.

Oligarchy resembles aristocracy in being the rule of a group of individuals rather than the rule of one person. Aristocracy differs from oligarchy in that it involves formal distinctions of rank. For instance, in an aristocracy the ruling group is divided into many subgroups—dukes, counts, earls, barons, and so forth—that designate different ranks. In an oligarchy the members of the elite share the same rank.

The term *democracy* originally applied to political systems in which all citizens made governmental policy at public meetings. This form of democracy reached its height in the Greek city-states of the fifth and fourth centuries B.C. It no longer exists at national levels of government anywhere in the world. However, this kind of democracy is still found at the local level in such forms as the New England town meeting. At the state level in the United States, it exists as the **initiative** and the **referendum.** This form of democracy is known as **direct democracy.**

Initiative is the procedure or device by which legislation can be introduced directly by the people.

Referendum is the practice of referring measures proposed or passed by the legislature to the people for their approval.

Direct democracy is the form of democracy in which citizens play direct roles in the formation of public policy.

In the modern world, the word "democracy" is usually used to denote government in which all the citizens, by voting in periodic elections, choose the representatives who are responsible for carrying out the day-to-day duties of running the government. This form of government is called *indirect democracy,* or *representative democracy.* The ancients did not call this form of government a democracy. They referred to it as a *republic.* As you will see in the next chapter, the founders of our nation agreed with the ancients about this classification. They regarded themselves not as democrats but as republicans. Many governments that we consider democratic are, in law, representative forms of government. Such governments include the constitutional monarchy of Great Britain and the federal republic of the United States of America.

Direct democracy is exercised as President Carter answers questions at a New England town meeting.

Margaret Thatcher is the first woman ever to become the Prime Minister of Great Britain. Thatcher's achievement is remarkable, for she rose within Britain's tradition-bound political system through leadership of its most moderate wing—the Conservative Party. Usually women have difficulty getting ahead in such systems, since they are excluded from the informal circles in which political power so often resides.

In England, the Prime Minister is not chosen in primary or general elections. When a party wins a majority in Parliament, the leader of that party becomes the Prime Minister. Party leaders are elected in Parliament by members of their own party. So when the Conservative Party won a majority in Parliament in 1979, the party leader, Margaret Thatcher, became Prime Minister.

Thatcher's first step in becoming Prime Minister came in 1974 when she challenged Edward Heath as Conservative leader. She campaigned as an outspoken supporter of conservative morals and economics. She paid tribute to the values of the English middle class, criticized those in England who "don't try," and promised a return to the policies of free enterprise. On the first ballot Thatcher led Heath by 130 to 119, with the other candidates far behind. One week before the second ballot, Heath dropped out and tried to find a candidate to beat Thatcher. But she was too close to victory, and the bandwagon effect took hold. Thatcher won easily on the second ballot, becoming head of the Conservative Party.

When the Labour government lost a vote of confidence in 1979, an election was held and Margaret Thatcher led the Conservatives to victory. As Prime Minister, she has continued to follow outspokenly conservative policies in economics, criminal law, and defense.

MARGARET THATCHER

Presidential Democracy and Parliamentary Democracy. Today most representative governments are either parliamentary or presidential democracies.

In a parliamentary democracy the executive branch of the government is composed of a prime minister or a premier, who heads the cabinet, and a cabinet of ministers. The prime minister and the cabinet must be members of the legislative branch. The prime minister is the head of the party that has won a majority in legislative, or parliamentary, elections. He or she selects a cabinet from among the members of the majority party or coalition of parties who have been elected to the legislative branch. The prime minister and the cabinet are responsible to the parliament for their actions.

The prime minister and the cabinet are called the government. They remain in power only as long as their policies have obtained parliamentary support. If the government loses a vote on an important issue—called a *vote of confidence*—the government is said to fall. This means that the prime minister and the cabinet must resign and a new government must be formed. Often the new government will include at least some of the same officials—including the prime minister—of the government that has fallen. If a new government cannot be formed, or if the defeated prime minister chooses to take the

Idi Amin Dada's dictatorship in Uganda ended with his overthrow in 1979.

elected separately and may represent different constituencies. Both France and the United States of America are considered presidential democracies.

Democracy Versus Dictatorship. In the language of politics, democracy and dictatorship are often perceived to be hostile to one another. However, this is a relatively recent way of looking at these terms. *Dictator* derives from a Roman term used to designate a citizen who had been chosen by the Senate to wield absolute power for a limited period of time. Dictators were chosen to govern during periods of crisis that threatened the survival of Rome. In the twentieth century the term *dictatorship* was revived, but with a meaning different from that originally denoted. Today it no longer describes a government selected to rule in a time of crisis. Instead, it is used to designate **authoritarian** or **totalitarian** types of **governments.**

Authoritarian governments are governments in which political power is concentrated in the hands of a few people who enforce obedience to their rule and permit no challenges to it.

Totalitarian governments are those governments that are similar to authoritarian governments in all but one crucial respect—they exercise much wider control over people than do authoritarian governments because they recognize no distinction between public and private life.

issue "to the people," a general election will be held. The party or coalition of parties that wins a majority of parliamentary seats in the election wins the right to form a new government. The government of Great Britain is a parliamentary democracy, as are the governments of the Republic of Ireland, Sweden, and West Germany.

In a presidential democracy like the U.S., the executive, legislative, and judicial branches of government are separate. Each branch exercises different powers. The party that controls the legislature in a presidential democracy does not automatically control the executive branch. The simultaneous control of the executive branch by one party and the dominance of the legislature by another party can happen because each branch is

When people use the term "dictatorship," they usually think of Germany under Hitler and the Soviet Union under Stalin. These regimes had different objectives and different sources of support, but they had one important thing in common. In both, unlimited power was exercised by a single person or a group of individuals who controlled the only mass party that was allowed to exist there.

In analyzing dictatorial governments a distinction is usually made between authoritarian and totalitarian regimes. Both systems are similar in that they permit no public challenge to or criticism of the regime. But totalitarian systems exercise much wider and tighter control over the societies that they rule. They recognize no difference between public and private life. Characteristics of totalitarian rule include the following: 1) a single mass political party, 2) a single leader or a small group of leaders, 3) a large, powerful, and terrorizing police force, and 4) monopoly over every aspect of life in a society.

Authoritarian regimes continue to be a common form of government in the world. Totalitarian regimes, historically quite rare, are recent phenomena.

section review

1. Define anarchy.
2. List the five basic types of government.
3. What is the difference between a direct and a representative democracy?
4. What is a parliamentary democracy? How does it differ from a presidential democracy?
5. How has the term dictator evolved from its Roman origin?
6. What is an authoritarian government? a totalitarian government? Compare their similarities and differences.
7. Describe the characteristics of totalitarian rule.

3. THE NATION–STATE

One of the most important institutions of our times is the nation-state. It has become so important that it is hard to envision a world in which it is not a major institution. But until recently the nation-state did not exist. It became a dominant institution of our civilization approximately 300 years ago. The modern nation-state has five basic characteristics: *territory, sovereignty, universality, hierarchy in government*, and *legitimacy*.

Territory. The modern nation-state is a territorially defined unit; that is, it is defined by the land that it occupies.

Sovereignty. The nation-state claims sovereignty, or supreme power, over all who reside in its territory. Before the emergence of the nation-state, many authorities claimed sovereign power that extended beyond the territories from which they ruled. For example, the medieval Church of Rome asserted sovereignty over all its nonresident clergy. Indeed, it even claimed sovereignty over all the inhabitants of Christendom, which meant the whole of Western civilization. Many ancient empires also claimed sovereignty over the inhabitants of various territories, who were at the same time governed by their own leaders according to authority conferred by the imperial rulers. For example, the Roman Empire claimed sovereignty over the inhabitants of territories as distant from each other as England and Persia. The inhabitants of those areas were governed by their own monarchs as well as ruled by Rome.

The modern nation-state claims *exclusive sovereignty*. This means that it alone has the right to govern those who live within its territory.

In the past, sovereignty was often split in a number of complicated ways. Sometimes it was divided between church and state, at other times between monarchs and the nobility, and at still others among various segments of a state.

Sovereignty and Geography. There are three kinds of geographical sovereignty—*unitary, federal*, and *confederal*.

In a government that asserts unitary sovereignty, that government has the sole right of exercising the power of the state. Local governments, or subdivisions of the unitary government, hold only as much power as the unitary government agrees to delegate to them.

Each of the state governments of the United States of America has the unitary sovereignty over its territory that is implied in the Constitution. For example, each state exercises unitary sovereignty over the creation of its educational system and its local subdivisions of government. Counties and cities within the state have only those powers that the state government specifically delegates to them. The state government can withdraw or limit those powers whenever it so decides.

In a federal government, power is divided between the central government and various geographically separated governments within the federation. This division of power is usually prescribed in a written document—like the United States Constitution. Such a document is legally binding on both levels of government and may not be changed by one of them without the consent of the other. In the United States the sharing of sovereign power regulates relations between the central government and the states. Federalism is also the dominant system in countries such as Canada, India, Switzerland, West Germany and Australia.

A confederal government is an alliance of sovereign states whose members have agreed to delegate certain powers to an administrative authority. Each state can withdraw from the confederation if it so chooses. The United States had a confederal system under the Articles of Confederation (1781–1789). During the Civil War, the southern states that became combatants united in a confederal alliance called the Confederate States of America. Modern international organizations such as the European Economic Community (the EEC, or "Common Market") and the North Atlantic Treaty Organization (NATO) are confederations. To those organi-

The first meeting of the Common market, held in 1957, had six member nations. How many nations belong to the EEC today?

zations member governments have delegated some of their national powers. Nevertheless, they retain their sovereignty and can withdraw from the alliance in accordance with the provisions set forth in the treaties that created the organizations.

Sovereignty Within Governments. Sovereignty can also describe the allocation of powers within the government itself.

In some governments power is unified in one part of the government. The House of Commons, which is part of the parliament of Great Britain, is an example of the concentration of power.

When a political party gains control of the House of Commons, it gains control of the entire government. It controls the executive branch of the government because the prime minister—the chief executive—is normally the leader of the party with the most members in the Commons, and is chosen for the office by that body. Because Great Britain has no written constitution, people who lack knowledge about its government may believe that the majority party can do anything that it pleases. English common law, operating through precedents and customs, restricts the powers of the House of Commons to those considered legitimate by the British people.

Within the central government of the United States, sovereignty is not concentrated in one part of the government. It is divided among the three branches of the central government. For example, one political party may be able to elect a majority of its members to the legislative branch but may fail to elect its nominee to the office of the President, who appoints federal judges.

Universality. As you have learned, the modern nation-state claims authority over all who reside within its territorially defined boundaries. Exempt from the jurisdictions of the nation-states in which they reside are the diplomatic representatives of other nation-states. By claiming a broad range of power, the nation-state is said to exhibit the quality of universality.

QUOTES
from famous people

"The government of the absolute majority instead of the government of the people is but the government of the strongest interests; and when not efficiently checked, it is the most tyrannical and oppressive that can be devised."

John Calhoun

Hierarchy in Government. Government in the modern nation-state is based on *hierarchies*, or ranks, of authority. There is usually an individual at the top of the governmental structure through whom the power of the state is expressed. This official may be a queen, a president, or another officer of the state. At the top there may also be an individual or a group of individuals who exercise state power. This power includes the power to wage war against other states and the power to preserve order within the state. In some governments, such as that of Great Britain, the two functions of expressing and exercising the power of the state are separated. The monarch performs the first function, and the prime minister exercises the second responsibility. In other governments, such as that of the United States, these functions are united in one person, the President. Within the hierarchy, below the officials who hold the highest power of the state, are the large staffs of people who perform all the many and varied functions of modern government.

Legitimacy. No other institution in the modern world has as much legitimacy as that accorded to the nation-state. A government is legitimate if the demands that it makes on its citizens seem appropriate to them. By complying with these demands, citizens give legitimacy to the government. A government loses legitimacy when its demands impress its citizens as being inappropriate. If a government loses all legitimacy, it will cease to exist. This was the case with the colonists' revolt against British rule in America.

The amount of legitimacy that a government has is not the same at all times. A government may have different degrees of legitimacy for different people within its boundaries. For example, the White government of South Africa has had a different degree of legitimacy for White South Africans than it has had for Black South Africans, who have been excluded from participation in the government and from society as well. A Palestinian Arab who has lived under the jurisdiction of Israel is likely to have different feelings about the legitimacy of Israel's government than an Israeli would have.

Legitimacy is also related to economics. Studies by political scientists have shown that people tend to believe in their governments when their economies are progressing and to lose faith in them when economic growth stands still or declines. When the Great Depression brought misery to the United States, many Americans lost faith in the administration of Herbert Hoover. They blamed him for the depression even though it had been caused by conditions beyond his control.

The dispute over rightful ownership continues in the twentieth century as Arabs and Israelis claim the same territory.

Who Is a Person? Although modern nation-states derive their legitimacy from the people, it is important to realize that no society has ever defined all its inhabitants as "the people." People in this sense mean those who are worthy of obtaining citizenship in the nation-state.

Ancient Athens, for instance, the first democratic city-state, considered fewer than 10 percent of its inhabitants people. The rest—women, the young, slaves, and foreigners—were not thought of as people in the political sense.

The measure of citizenship for democratic governments has always been competence, or the ability to perform the functions of citizenship and to share in the exercise of power. Throughout history most of the people of a state have not been considered competent to share in the exercise of power. Until recently sex was a barrier to citizenship. It is only within the last century that women have begun to attain full citizenship in most nation-states. Age continues to act as a barrier to citizenship. In every society a certain age has been defined as the age of majority, or the age at which young people are recognized as adults. Upon reaching this age, an individual becomes a citizen and thus one of "the people." Criminals and insane persons lose certain rights of citizenship. In many societies those who criticize the social order can be deprived of citizenship. In many societies that are called democratic, regulations with regard to race, religion, place of residence, and property ownership are used to prevent some individuals from being considered part of "the people."

section review

1. List and explain three characteristics of the nation-state.
2. What is sovereignty? List and explain three types of sovereignty.
3. What is meant by "the people"? How has this definition changed over time?
4. What are some historical bars to citizenship?

4. ECONOMIC SYSTEMS

Many of the forces that shape our society and our government are economic forces. But because economic questions so often produce strong political repercussions, some people confuse economic systems with political institutions.

"Our economic system is but an instrument of the social advancement of the American people. It is an instrument by which we add to the security and richness of life of every individual. It by no means comprises the whole purpose of life, but it is the foundation upon which can be built the finer things of the spirit."

Herbert Hoover

Capitalism. Some people confuse capitalism with democracy. Although the two are found together in many states, one can exist without the other.

Capitalism is an economic system, not a form of government. It is characterized by private ownership of the means of production and distribution, and the exchange of goods and services based on the operations of the market. In capitalistic economics, labor is a **commodity** that is to be traded on the open market. Those who own the means of production compete with other capitalists to hire labor, so goods and services can be produced and sold at a profit.

A **commodity** is something that is bought and sold.

On the floor of the New York Stock Exchange on Wall Street, stockbrokers trade bonds and securities of American and foreign businesses.

1. The Basic Concepts of Government   **13**

The focus of the capitalist system is competition. It is believed that out of the economic desires of individuals competing with one another will come benefits for the whole society. According to capitalist economists, the greatest benefits come not from carefully devised economic plans but from the competitive operation of the market.

Profit is the motivating force of the capitalist system. The capitalists—the owners of wealth—and the workers—those who seek to sell their labor—will each try to get the greatest return from investing their capital or their labor. Capital will tend to be invested where it is expected to yield the greatest return. The workers will seek employment in those businesses that will pay them the highest wages.

In a capitalist system, profit, or the difference between the cost of a product or a service and the price at which it is sold, represents the reward for innovation and enterprise. The post-World War II development of complex multinational enterprises reflects the continuous evolution of the capitalist system.

Laissez-faire. The idea of pure capitalism is often referred to as laissez-faire, the French expression for "to let alone." The concept of laissez-faire developed in the late eighteenth and early nineteenth centuries. Its foremost theorist was Adam Smith. His book *Inquiry into the Nature and Causes of the Wealth of Nations* was published in 1776, the year in which the *Declaration of Independence* was proclaimed. According to laissez-faire theory, the role of government should be limited. Government should perform only those economic functions that cannot be performed by private enterprise at a profit and those that enhance the success of the market. It was believed that government interference in the market would cause problems, for it would violate the laws of supply and demand. These laws, when left to themselves, were thought to result in "the greatest good for the greatest number." Like most theories, laissez-faire lost credibility over the course of time. It never explained the reality of any society.

FEATURES OF CAPITALISM

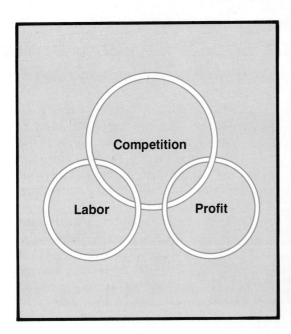

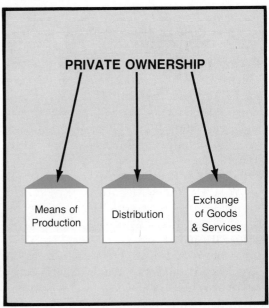

ADAM SMITH

Adam Smith, "the founder of capitalism," was accused of being an impractical intellectual who never had to meet a payroll. He did not develop his theory of free enterprise out of a love of business. Indeed, he believed that the merchants, more than any other class, wanted to interfere with his beloved "free trade." His chief concerns were the practical and moral benefits to be derived from a separation of the state from commercial enterprise.

Smith was born in Kirkcaldy, Scotland, in 1723. Between 1751 and 1764 he was a professor of logic and then of moral philosophy at the University of Glasgow. Among the subjects on which he lectured were theology, ethics, justice, and political institutions.

His first book, "Theory of Moral Sentiments," published in 1759, won him a nationwide reputation. His second, "An Inquiry into the Nature and Causes of the Wealth of Nations," published in 1776, became the "founding document" of capitalism.

Smith's sources for "Wealth of Nations" were not entirely academic. He had gone to England in 1764 as tutor to the family of Charles Townshend (whose Townshend Acts were instrumental in starting the American Revolution). On a two-year Continental tour with the family, he met the famous French philosophers of the day. Their ideas, which had some influence on the American Revolution, were later to inspire the French Revolution. Smith's work may have also been influenced by Benjamin Franklin, whom he met in London. In fact, in "Wealth of Nations" he cited the American colonies as closest in the world to his ideal social order. Many think it significant that this work was published in 1776. It was the economic expression of liberalism, just as the Declaration of Independence was its political expression.

In 1777 Smith was appointed Edinburgh's commissioner of customs. Ten years later he became lord rector of Glasgow University. He died in 1790. Although the events of his life were undramatic, the power of his ideas makes him one of the most important people who ever lived.

One important change in laissez-faire capitalism was the development of the *limited liability corporation.* This development changed the concept of ownership to a form that Adam Smith might not have recognized. These corporations became the dominant economic institution of capitalist states during the nineteenth century.

What is a limited liability corporation? It is a form of business in which the corporation assumes the rights of a person under the law. Because the corporation is a legal person, the owners of the business—those who invest in it—are not liable, or responsible, for debts that exceed their initial investments. Only the corporation—the legal person—is responsi-

ble for paying the difference between the debt and the sum of the original investments.

Limited liability corporations may have millions of investors. However, only a few of the owners—those who have invested the greatest amount of money—really control the corporation. Their interests are usually represented by the managers who run the corporation on a daily basis.

These corporations return part of their profits as dividends to their investors, who are also known as shareholders. The rest of the profits are reinvested in the corporation.

By 1900 these corporations had grown so large that many people began to think that they would close the competitive market

1. The Basic Concepts of Government   15

through sheer power. In some areas one company dominated the market. This kind of dominance is known as *monopoly*, or the rule of one company. In other areas a number of corporations shared control of the market. This arrangement is called *oligopoly*, or the rule of a few. (It is interesting to note that these terms are the economic equivalents of "monarchy" and "oligarchy" in politics.)

The Mixed Economy. Partly as a reaction against the development of the corporation, a second great change in laissez-faire capitalism slowly emerged. This change involved the growth of what is called the mixed economy. It began to develop when it became obvious that many functions of a society could be impaired by the free workings of the competitive market. These functions included social order, social justice, and the operations of the economy.

In a *mixed economy* the government regulates the market in various ways to ensure that its operations do not threaten the stability of society. It controls enterprises that produce public goods and institutions that offer public services—the postal system, public roads, some utilities, and educational and monetary systems. It oversees the conduct of the banks and the stock market, and it assists agricultural development. The entire economy is regulated through measures such as minimum-wage laws, antitrust laws, and environmental control and consumer protection laws. The government also supports substantial segments of the private economy through direct or indirect subsidies, loans, and various protective measures.

Socialism. Capitalism triumphed in America without much opposition. In Europe the forces that were hostile to capitalism—feudal monarchies, standing armies, and established churches—proved to be strong opponents. These forces never existed in the United States. The survival of what are sometimes called precapitalist forms, like feudalism, made it harder for Europeans to conceive of capitalism as the next stage of economic development.

The first form of socialism to emerge in Europe came to be called *utopian socialism*. Advocates of this system criticized the capitalist world for what they called its "war of all against all." In its place they proposed a voluntary system through which people would join together in communal groups, would hold their possessions in common, and would live together in happiness.

Marxism. Karl Marx and his collaborator, Friedrich Engels, took a different approach to socialism. Marxism dates from the publication of *The Communist Manifesto* in 1848. This book urged the workers of the world to unite and asserted that they had nothing to lose but their chains.

In their later writings, Karl Marx and Friedrich Engels outlined what they called *scientific socialism*. This theory was based on several main ideas.

The Class Struggle. To Marx all history was the history of the class struggle. Marx contended that there were two major classes in capitalist society: the *bourgeoisie*, or capitalists, who ruled society, and the *proletariat*, or workers, who were exploited by the capitalists. According to Marx, the class struggle would inevitably produce socialism as well as the dictatorship of the proletariat. When the dictatorship of the proletariat had triumphed, the state—the agent of the ruling class—would wither away, for it would not be needed in a society without class distinctions. At this stage—a communistic society—everyone would be equal in every respect.

The Contradictions of Capitalism. Marx thought that capitalism was the most successful economic system that the world had produced. But, he argued, like all previous systems, it created problems that would destroy it. These problems were what Marx called the contradictions of capitalism. These contradictions arose from the dependence of capitalism on profit. Like David Ricardo, the nineteenth-century English economist, Marx maintained that the value of any commodity was determined by the amount of labor needed to produce it. (This theory is known

MAJOR TYPES OF ECONOMIC SYSTEMS			
	CAPITALISM	**SOCIALISM**	**COMMUNISM**
Goal	Society in which individuals attain maximum achievement through competition	Society based on cooperation and mutual respect rather than on competition and self-interest	Society that provides equality and economic security for all
Features	Private ownership of most resources and technology Labor is allowed to choose where they will work	The government controls natural resources Technology is in private hands and labor operates independently	The government controls natural, technological, and labor resources
	Individual ownership of the means of production The government controls enterprises that produce public goods and services	Gradual assumption of major means of production by government, through nationalization Much property remains in private hands	The government owns, plans for, and decides the means of production
	The market place determines the exchange of goods and services The government regulates the market to insure the stability of society	Use of taxes and welfare payments to distribute wealth on the basis of equity and equality	The government controls the distribution of goods and services
	Regular elections in which citizens take part either directly or indirectly	Socialism is to be achieved gradually through democratic elections	The government is controlled by the dictatorship of the leaders of the Communist Party

as the labor theory of value.) The advocates of this theory contended that profit, or the surplus capital kept by the capitalist, was necessarily stolen from the workers. The workers were also consumers, who needed to buy what they had produced. But the desire of capitalists for ever greater profits competed against their need for ever larger markets and led to the production of commodities that could not be sold. The workers as consumers could not afford to buy the products of their own labor because the money that they could have used to buy them was being "stolen" from them by the capitalists in the form of profits. In denying the workers the value of what they produced, the capitalists, accord-ing to Marx, were undermining their own economic system.

Marx believed that the contradictions of capitalism would lead inevitably to the triumph of communism. This development would occur in the advanced countries in which capitalists had produced wealth but were unwilling to share it with the workers. Communism could not happen in backward, noncapitalist countries until they had at-tained capitalism—the first stage in the in-evitable transition to communism.

Communism in Practice. In the Soviet Union "the dictatorship of the proletariat" (a term that Marx never developed) has involved

Collective work is characteristic of Chinese Communist society. What are the advantages and disadvantages of working under these conditions?

both the dictatorship of one man, Stalin, the head of the party who ruled for almost 30 years, and the dictatorship of the top leaders of the Communist party. Fulfilling the predictions made by the critics of the Russian Revolution, Soviet leaders transformed their society by means more brutal than those used by the capitalists, which Marx and Engels had deplored. To this day the dictatorship of the proletariat is ruled in effect by the leaders of the Soviet Communist party.

In practice, the results of communism are less clear than Marx suggested they would be. Communism has spread to about one third of the world's people. The Soviet Union is now one of the world's most powerful states. But communism has not led, as Marx predicted, to a world free of nation-states. Instead, Communists cooperated with nationalist forces in establishing their dominance in countries such as China, Yugoslavia, and Vietnam. As communism spread, it splintered according to the distinctions that have historically separated nation-states. Communism, for example, is very different in China from what it is in Yugoslavia. At the same time, the concentration of economic and political power in one place—the state—has resulted in severe restrictions of personal freedom.

Socialism in Practice. *Socialism* is a term used to describe the economic system advocated by the Social Democratic parties of Western Europe. Social Democrats believe in evolutionary, or gradually achieved, socialism, to be brought about through the process of democratic elections. They also advocate the gradual assumption of control by the state over major enterprises such as transportation systems, banks, sources of energy, and public utilities. This process is called *nationalization*. None of the Social Democratic parties advocates the abolition of private property.

Almost all the major industrial nations of the Western world—with the exception of Japan, Canada, and the United States—have had Socialist governments for at least some periods of time since 1945. A totally socialistic economy does not exist. Even in Sweden, often considered the prime example of socialism in operation, 90 percent of the economy remains in private hands.

Social Democrats have not abolished capitalism. Through taxation and welfare payments, for example, they have tried to distribute wealth on the basis of equity and equality.

Capitalism Today. Capitalism today has proven to be a strong economic system. The world market, or world economy, is a capitalist economy, even though most of the world's leaders call themselves Socialists. Capitalism remains a source of innovation and prosperity in the world economy.

Those who oppose capitalism have not shown that their own economic systems are more just. Nor have they shown that they are more efficient than capitalists in distributing economic benefits to everyone. Although capitalism rests on a theory of competition that mirrors reality about as inaccurately as do theories of cooperation, the economy of the United States and the world economy are likely to remain capitalist for the foreseeable future.

section review

1. What are the characteristics of capitalism?
2. Define laissez-faire. What is the role of government in a laissez-faire economy?
3. How has the development of the limited liability corporation changed the economic concept of ownership?
4. Explain what is meant by the term "mixed" economy.
5. What is the basis of the class struggle, according to Marx and Engels?
6. What does Marx consider to be the contradiction in capitalism?

CHAPTER SUMMARY

1

Social theorists have developed four explanations of the origins of government: the divine right, social contract, force, and evolutionary theories. According to these theories, governments grew out of specific views of the people who governed and were governed.

Five basic types of government have developed over the centuries: monarchy, aristocracy, oligarchy, democracy, and totalitarianism. Each of these types may be found in the modern world. Democracies may be either direct or indirect (representative). Definitions of "the people," or citizens, have varied over time and from place to place.

Economic and political systems are closely interrelated. Capitalism, socialism, and communism are the three most commonly practiced economic systems today.

Capitalism, as practiced in the United States, has provided a source of innovation and prosperity in the world economy and is practiced at the world economic level even by countries who do not adhere to a capitalistic economic system.

REVIEW QUESTIONS

1. Why are territory, sovereignty, universality, hierarchy of authority, and legitimacy necessary for a nation-state?

2. Describe the four theories of government. What are the bases for these theories?

3. What are the major differences between capitalism, socialism, and communism?

4. Explain the essential differences between an aristocracy and an oligarchy.

ACTIVITIES FOR REVIEW

activity 1   Develop an ideal government, explaining your selection in terms of your theory of the function of government and how the type of government established fulfills those functions.

activity 2   Do research on obtaining citizenship in the United States and in one other country. How are the procedures similar? different?

activity 3   Do research on voting requirements in the United States and in the U.S.S.R. How are they similar? different?

political science DICTIONARY

anarchy—a state in which no rules exist to govern people's behavior.   p. 5

aristocracy—government by a select group of individuals or leading families. Selection of rulers may be based on birth or wealth.   p. 5

authoritarian government—government in which political power is in the hands of a few people who enforce obedience to their rule and permit no challenges.   p. 8

capitalism—an economic system characterized by private ownership of the means of production and distribution.   p. 13

democracy—government in which the people exercise supreme power, either through the direct formation of policy at public meetings or through the periodic election of representatives who govern by majority consent. p. 5

dictatorships—authoritarian or totalitarian governments of various kinds. p. 5

direct democracy—a form of democracy in which the citizens play a direct role in the formation of public policy. p. 5

divine right theory—theory attributing the creation of governments to divine intervention in human affairs. p. 3

exclusive sovereignty—the ultimate right of a nation-state to govern those who live within its territory. p. 9

force theory—the theory that governments were established through force. p. 4

indirect democracy—a form of democracy in which the people, through periodic elections, choose representatives to govern and make public policy for them (same as representative democracy). p. 6

initiative—a procedure in which citizens, by petition, can propose a law and have it submitted either to the voters or the legislature for approval. p. 6

limited liability corporation—a form of business organization in which the business has the rights of a person under law. Investors are not liable for debts that exceed their initial investments; the corporation must pay the debts. p. 15

mixed economy—an economy in which the government regulates the market in various ways to ensure that its operations do not threaten the stability of the society. p. 16

monarchy—government headed by a single hereditary leader, usually a king, queen, emperor, or empress. p. 5

nationalization—the process by which the state gradually takes over the major public services, such as transportation and public utilities. p. 19

oligarchy—like aristocracy in being rule by a group of individuals, but without aristocratic distinctions of rank. p. 5

parliamentary democracy—representative government in which power is concentrated in the legislature, which selects the executive branch from among its own members. p. 7

presidential democracy—representative government in which the functions of the executive, legislative, and judicial branches of government are separate. Powers are limited through a system of checks and balances. p. 8

proletariat—the workers. p. 16

referendum—the practice of referring measures passed or proposed by the legislature to the people for their approval. p. 6

republic—government by the elected representatives of the people. p. 6

scientific socialism—Marx's theory of economic and social equality in a classless society, achieved by the overthrow of the wealthy capitalists by the exploited workers. p. 16

totalitarian government—similar to authoritarian government, but exercising wider control over its citizens because it recognizes no distinctions between public and private life. p. 8

utopian socialism—first form of socialism to emerge in Europe; a voluntary system of group living in which all wealth, property, and goods produced are owned by the entire community and are distributed, by common consent, according to individual need. p. 16

vote of confidence—a vote by the parliament approving the prime minister's action on an important issue. p. 7

2

Origins of American Government

This chapter begins our discussion of the American governmental system. The roots of America's constitutional form of government are explored through examining the historic events that led to the birth of the new nation.

You will begin by reading about the revolutionary events in England that influenced the colonial origins of the United States and about how the 13 colonies were governed. You will then learn how different convictions about the nature of government held by the English and by the colonists led to the American Revolution.

You will examine the weaknesses of the first government and learn how that experience led some of the most active and intelligent members of the government to devise a new constitutional order. Finally, you will examine how this new government was created.

CHAPTER PREVIEW

1. THE COLONIAL PERIOD
2. A NEW NATION
3. THE ROAD TO THE CONSTITUTIONAL CONVENTION

1. THE COLONIAL PERIOD

The territory that eventually became the United States was explored, settled, and ruled by people from many nations. However, the English origin of the 13 colonies proved to be the most important influence in developing the government of the United States. By 1664 these colonies were under English rule. By 1776 more than 90 percent of the free inhabitants of the colonies could trace their ancestries to England.

A Troubled Century. The 13 colonies were established during one of the most troubled centuries in English history—the seventeenth century.

In the early seventeenth century, the monarch decreed that all English persons must join and pay tribute to the Anglican Church. Many religious groups were persecuted because of their refusal to obey the order, causing considerable turmoil in England. However, some of these religious minorities were granted charters by the king to establish themselves in America—the Puritans in New England, the Quakers in Pennsylvania, and the Catholics in Maryland. These charters, as well as others that were granted during the seventeenth century, formed the legal basis for establishing the colonies.

The struggle between the king and Parliament lasted for most of the century and was expressed in three major revolutions (1649, 1660, 1688) in England's government.

During the revolutionary period, the government was so preoccupied with its struggle for power that it allowed the colonies to develop without much supervision. This struggle was reflected in the colonies, where the legislatures sought to limit the power of the governors.

Eighteenth-Century England. After 1689 the turmoil of seventeenth-century England abated. The Anglican Church retained its status as the established church of England, but dissenters were tolerated. The monarchy remained, but its power was redefined and limited by Parliament. The aristocracy, or landed nobility, remained but had to share power with the monarch and with the middle class who dominated the House of Commons. The historic rights and guarantees accorded to the English people were reaffirmed. But suffrage, or the right to vote, was limited to male property owners. Throughout the eighteenth century, the House of Commons power was balanced by the power of the House of Lords, which consisted of all landed nobles.

Colonial Government. Although neither the English nor the colonists developed a theory of colonial government, they shared a belief in three principles: limited government, mixed government, and representative government.

The Mayflower Compact, signed by the Pilgrims in 1620, was the first example of self-government in American history.

Limited Government. The principle of limited government had become part of the unwritten constitution of England by 1689. Such rights as due process, trial by one's peers, religious freedom, and free speech were guaranteed under English common law. The colonists considered themselves English and, as such, entitled to exercise the rights of the English people.

QUOTES from famous people

"The emigrants who colonized the shores of America in the beginning of the seventeenth century somehow separated the democratic principle from all the principles that it had to contend with in the old communities of Europe, and transplanted it alone to the New World."

Alexis de Tocqueville

Mixed Government. English philosophers who sought to justify the government of eighteenth-century England stressed its mixed character. They asserted that the English had prevented the exercise of absolute power by incorporating the principles of monarchy, aristocracy, and democracy into their philosophy of government. The king represented the monarchical principle. The House of Lords represented the aristocratic principle. And the House of Commons represented the democratic principle.

Representative Government. Through the revolutions of the seventeenth century that established the supremacy of Parliament, the people obtained a voice in their government. The extension of this right reinforced the principle of representative government in England. Representative government is not the same as democratic government. The House of Commons, for example, represented the common people even though fewer than 7 percent of those people were allowed to vote.

The Royal Colonies. During the late seventeenth and early eighteenth centuries, the monarchs began to intervene in the colonial disputes. They established a system of government known as *royal colonies*—colonies ruled by the king. This system provided for a royal governor, appointed by the king; a council, or upper house (similar to the House of Lords), appointed by the governor; and a popular assembly, or lower house (similar to the House of Commons), elected by the people. Eight of the 13 colonies were ruled under this system by 1775.

The Proprietary Colonies. The three colonies that were established at the beginning of the seventeenth century—Pennsylvania, Delaware, and Maryland—continued to be ruled by their owners. The governments in these colonies resembled those in the royal colonies, except for one important difference. The governor was appointed by the proprietor rather than by the king.

The Charter Colonies. Several colonies were established through a written document called a grant, or charter. Through this document the king gave to an individual or to a company permission to control territory in North America. The *charter colonies* were given the right of self-government. They elected their own governors, councils, and assemblies every year. Their nominees for governor were subject to the king's veto. But their names were seldom submitted to him, and his veto was never imposed.

The governments of the two charter colonies—Connecticut and Rhode Island—were the most democratic of the 13 colonies. Their constitutions remained in effect for some time after independence was achieved—in Connecticut until 1818 and in Rhode Island until 1842.

England and the Colonies. The leading economic theory of the colonial period was that of mercantilism. According to this theory,

THE THREE TYPES OF COLONIES		
Corporate (Charter)	**Royal**	**Proprietary**
The king granted land to a company. The company governed this land. The charter companies were usually self-governed and the people retained their English rights.	The king and his ministers ruled the land.	The king granted land to a family, person, or group of people. These people (proprietors) had as much governing power as the king over their lands.
The governor was elected by those qualified to vote.	The king appointed a governor and a council of assistants. The governor had veto power.	The proprietor usually appointed a governor and a council of assistants.
Two-house legislature — the upper and lower houses were elected by the voters.	The governor and the council acted as upper house. The lower house was elected by voters.	The governor and the council were the upper house. The lower house was elected by voters.

the colonies existed solely for the benefit of the home country. This benefit was to consist of wealth derived from the profit gained by selling manufactured goods to the colonies and from the accumulation of precious metals and raw materials taken from the colonies. England's distance from the colonies made it difficult for the English government to pursue this policy.

Royal governors were expected to carry out the wishes of the English government. But they proved to be incapable of discharging their responsibilities. Most governors were not qualified to run the colonies. The English officials who selected them regarded the governorships as patronage posts, that is, as offices used to reward their less capable but faithful followers. Confronted with weak governors, the colonists took it upon themselves to run their own colonies and to make their own laws. They generally ignored the few orders that came to them from Parliament.

Toward Revolution. After 1760, when George III came to the throne, the English government changed its colonial policy. The king and his ministers discovered that a majority of parliamentary laws were not being carried out in the colonies. Their determina-tion to impose their will on the colonists coincided with the end of the Seven Years' War (1756–1763).

Growing Resentment. The Seven Years' War curtailed the power of the French in North America. Despite the benefits that the colonists gained from this victory, they refused to pay the taxes that the English imposed to pay for the war. They resisted orders designed to enforce parliamentary laws and refused to pay for English troops stationed in North America.

Over the years the colonists' conception of representation had changed. By the middle of the eighteenth century, it differed from that of the English government. Although property restrictions similar to those in England were in force in the colonies, half of the adult White males were eligible to vote in America. Representation in the colonies meant the right to vote; it also meant no taxation without representation. Under George III the English persisted in their blind determination to enforce rules in the colonies that they would never have tried to enforce in England. The Quartering Acts, which required civilians to shelter troops in their houses or in their towns, were examples of such rules. These policies provoked great resentment in the colonies. From 1763 to 1775 the colonies and England were on a collision course toward war.

American Confederation and Resistance. The idea of colonial confederation was not new. During the seventeenth century, union for specific purposes had been attempted, and other plans for union had been proposed. The New England Confederation (1643–1684) had been formed for defense against Indian attacks. As the threat of attack lessened, especially after the Dominion of New England had been established, interest in confederation ended for some time.

Two noted Pennsylvanians, William Penn, in 1696, and Benjamin Franklin, in 1754, proposed plans for colonial cooperation, but neither was accepted. Penn's plan focused on the problems of intercolonial trade and on the apprehension of criminals. Benjamin Franklin's Albany Plan of Union provided for a colonial council of representatives. The council would have the power to levy taxes, deal with Indian relations, and maintain an army. Both the colonial legislatures and Parliament rejected the plan. England believed that the proposed union would give the colonists too much power. The colonies rejected the plan because they were unwilling to give any power to an organization that could control each colony. The plan was important because it provided a model for the federal system of government that was to be established under the Constitution.

The Stamp Act. It was the English Stamp Act of 1765 that brought the first real colonial union into being. This act required that stamps be affixed to a variety of items before they could be considered legal.

THE POWHATAN CONFEDERACY

Confederate rule was not brought to North America by Whites. It was also a means of organization used by the Native Americans. Many of the famous groups were in fact confederacies, including the Iroquois, the Creek, and the Caddo. But the first native confederacy the English settlers encountered was the Powhatan confederacy.

The English at Jamestown discovered that all Native Americans in the area between the James and Potomac rivers—28 tribes comprising some 8,000 people—were under the leadership of a single chief, Powhatan, of the Pamunkey tribe. According to the stories the Pamunkeys told the settlers, Powhatan's father and his people had been driven out of Florida by the Spanish and had come north, conquering five other tribes. Powhatan had expanded his rule to include two dozen more tribes.

Unlike the Iroquois confederacy, Powhatan's confederacy was not a voluntary organization. It was the result of conquest. Having been conquered, a tribe was permitted to govern itself as long as it recognized the sovereignty of Powhatan. Jamestown's Captain John Smith wrote of Powhatan that the "laws whereby he ruleth is custome." Powhatan exacted a tribute from each subject tribe in "skinnes, beades, copper, pearle, deare, turkies, wild beasts, and corne." Beyond this he did not interfere with the power of the subchiefs to rule their own tribes. Smith believed that these chiefs "for good commanding, and their people for due subjection, and obeying, excell many places that would be counted very civill."

Boston colonists show their disgust for Great Britain's colonial policies by tarring and feathering a Tory tax collector.

A Stamp Act Congress, attended by delegates from nine of the colonies, met in New York. The Congress drafted a Declaration of Rights and Grievances and agreed to harass or boycott anyone who used the stamps. Confronted with this resistance, Parliament backed down and repealed the Stamp Act.

The English government continued to search for new means of raising revenue in the colonies. By 1773 Committees of Correspondence had been formed in the colonies to coordinate resistance to England's demands. When the citizens of Boston resisted the importation of English tea by dumping it into the harbor, the spark that they applied ignited the powder of revolution. Parliament responded by passing the so-called Intolerable Acts. These acts were designed to punish Massachusetts for the act of aggression committed by its citizens. Instead, they provoked the calling of the First Continental Congress.

section review

1. What was the cause of the turmoil in England during the seventeenth century?
2. Describe three principles of government considered essential by both the English and the colonists.
3. Name three types of colonial governments.
4. Define mercantilism.
5. What was the purpose of the Stamp Act?

2. Origins of American Government   **27**

2. A NEW NATION

The First Continental Congress. The First Continental Congress met in Philadelphia from September 5 to October 26, 1774. They responded to parliamentary actions by sending a declaration of rights to George III. They recommended a colonial boycott of English goods and scheduled a second congress to meet in May 1775 if conditions had not improved.

Conditions got worse. The English sent troops to Boston, and colonists in and around the city gathered arms. When the English sent a force to seize the arms, fighting broke out at Lexington and Concord on April 19, 1775.

The First American Government: The Second Continental Congress. The congress scheduled for May met on the tenth of the month at Independence Hall in Philadelphia. All the colonies were represented. Its actions suggested that the congress would soon become the governing body of an independent nation. An army was organized, and George Washington was appointed its commander in chief.

The Declaration of Independence was adopted toward the end of the congress. Although Benjamin Franklin, John Adams, Roger Sherman, and Robert Livingston contributed statements, Thomas Jefferson made the greatest contribution to the Declaration of Independence. The decision for independence was made on July 2, 1776, and the declaration was published two days later.

Transition. The revolutionaries of 1776 had one great advantage that enhanced their ability to build a nation: the adaptability of their government. In most of the colonies, the transition from colony to state was accomplished smoothly. Connecticut and Rhode

This engraving by John Trumbull, a famous American painter, shows the supporters of the Declaration of Independence. Can you identify some of these famous Americans?

Unit One: The Foundations of Government

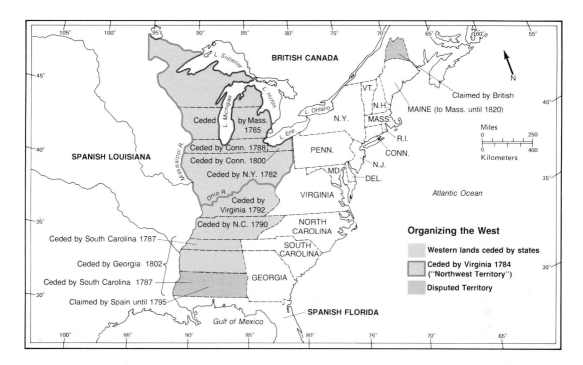

BRITISH CANADA

L. Superior

L. Michigan

L. Huron

L. Ontario

L. Erie

Ceded by Mass. 1785

Ceded by Conn. 1788

Ceded by Conn. 1800

Ceded by N.Y. 1782

Ceded by Virginia 1792

Ceded by N.C. 1790

Ceded by South Carolina 1787

Ceded by Georgia 1802

Ceded by South Carolina 1787

Claimed by Spain until 1795

SPANISH LOUISIANA

Mississippi R.

Ohio R.

VT.

N.H.

N.Y.

MASS.

R.I.

PENN.

CONN.

N.J.

MD.

DEL.

VIRGINIA

NORTH CAROLINA

SOUTH CAROLINA

GEORGIA

Claimed by British

MAINE (to Mass. until 1820)

Atlantic Ocean

Gulf of Mexico

SPANISH FLORIDA

Miles
0   250
0   400
Kilometers

N

Organizing the West

Western lands ceded by states

Ceded by Virginia 1784 ("Northwest Territory")

Disputed Territory

Island did not have to change their charters, and in several other colonies new constitutions had been adopted before the Declaration of Independence was proclaimed.

Transition proceeded relatively easily in Connecticut and Virginia. In these states support for the Revolution was almost unanimous, and the English troops posed no serious threat to either state. In New York, Pennsylvania, and Georgia, transition was difficult. These states had more *Tories*, or colonists who supported the English, and were occupied by the English for long periods of time.

Most of the constitutions under which the new states were to be governed had common features. These included the following:

Popular sovereignty. The belief that power derives from the people was recognized in the use of either assemblies or conventions to ratify state constitutions. Massachusetts was the first state to submit its constitution directly to the voters in 1780.

Legislative supremacy. Legislatures were empowered to be the representatives of the people. Governors were given little power. In its 1776 constitution, Pennsylvania proclaimed absolute legislative supremacy. It created a *unicameral*, or a one-chambered, *legislature*, to be elected each year, and declared that there would be no governor at all.

Limited government. The constitutions were short and specifically limited the powers of government. Great concern was expressed about protecting the rights of individuals against the state. No fewer than seven states included bills of rights in their constitutions.

QUOTES from famous people

"It seems indispensable that the mass of citizens should not be without a voice in making the laws which they are to obey, and in choosing the magistrates who are to administer them."

James Madison

The Articles of Confederation. When independence was decided upon, the Continental Congress began to debate a permanent plan of government for the new nation. That plan—the Articles of Confederation—was approved on November 15, 1777. However, it did not go into effect until the 13 states had approved it. Although 11 did so in 1778, Delaware delayed until 1779 and Maryland until 1781. Until March 1, 1781, the date on which the Articles of Confederation were considered ratified, the Continental Congress governed the nation.

The government established by the Articles was similar to that of Pennsylvania. It gave supremacy to the legislature, since it made no provision for establishing executive or judicial branches. Committees of the Congress were authorized to exercise these functions, and Congress was to appoint all civil servants.

Each state was allowed from two to seven delegates to Congress, but each state was given only one vote. The method of selecting or replacing delegates was left to the state legislatures.

The Articles established a "firm league of friendship" among the states. Each state retained "its sovereignty, freedom, and independence, and every power, jurisdiction, and right . . . not . . . expressly delegated to the United States in Congress assembled."

The powers delegated to Congress involved defense, foreign policy, the mails, and weights and measures. Its revenue raising powers, however, were limited.

The Critical Period. The period from 1781 to 1787 was a time of great difficulty for the country. Many leaders feared the collapse of the newly formed United States. Congress was burdened with financial problems and

| WEAKNESSES OF THE ARTICLES OF CONFEDERATION ||
Weaknesses	Results
No executive or judicial branch of government was provided for	The central government depended on the state governments to enforce the laws; there were no federal courts to settle disputes between the states
Congress lacked the power to regulate interstate and foreign commerce	States quarreled over common boundaries; there was no uniformity on interstate tariffs; foreign nations disregarded commercial agreement
Congress did not have the power to levy and collect taxes	States did not comply with Congress' requests for fund; as a result the government never had sufficient funds to operate efficiently
Both Congress and the states had the right to coin and regulate currency	Paper money lost its value
The agreement of nine states was necessary to enact a law, and a unanimous vote was needed on an amendment	It was difficult to enact laws and almost impossible to pass amendments since at no time were all states in attendance
Each state had only one vote in Congress regardless of population	States that were heavily populated disagreed with this method of representation

was unable to maintain law and order and to exercise authority.

Under the Articles of Confederation, the government was weak and failed to gain respect from foreign nations. American merchants and sailors grew angry when the government failed to prevent English goods from being dumped in American ports at low prices. The problem revolved around America's weak military position in the world. American sailors had traditionally been protected because they had sailed under the British flag—that of the world's greatest sea power. Without military force to protect them, they had to fend for themselves.

The confederacy failed to generate cooperation among the states. However, it did succeed in convincing the states to give up their western territorial claims through the Northwest Ordinance of 1787.

Three groups of individuals were most hostile to the confederation: merchants, creditors, and those who served or had served the nation abroad. These people were well aware of the weaknesses of the confederation. They wanted a strong government that could control commerce, finance the public debt, and suppress outbreaks of agrarian discontent such as Shays' rebellion in Massachusetts (1786).

section review

1. Describe three features that were included in most of the new state constitutions.
2. What were some of the weaknesses of the Articles of Confederation?
3. Which three groups of people were against the Confederation? Why?

3. THE ROAD TO THE CONSTITUTIONAL CONVENTION

Disputes between Maryland and Virginia over the navigation of their water bound-aries—the Potomac River and Chesapeake Bay—led to a meeting between representatives of the two states at Alexandria, Virginia, in March 1785. Based on the results of that successful meeting, the Virginia assembly in January 1786 proposed a meeting of all the states "to recommend a federal plan for regulating commerce." When the convention met at Annapolis in September 1786, only five states were represented. The delegates took it

The Annapolis convention was called to remedy some of the problems of the states under the Articles of Confederation. How many states attended the convention? Can you identify the representatives?

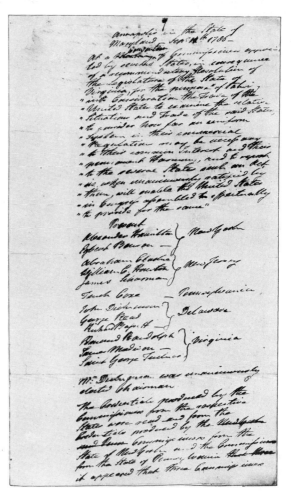

upon themselves to issue a call for a meeting of the states to be held in Philadelphia on May 14, 1787. The purpose of the meeting was to improve the national government.

On February 2, 1787, Congress endorsed the idea of a conference of all the states. The states were asked to send delegates to the convention for the "sole and express purpose of revising the Articles of Confederation" and for reporting suggested changes to the states and to the Congress.

All the states except Rhode Island elected 74 delegates to the convention that convened on May 25, 1787. Only 55 delegates attended the convention.

The Convention. The convention was supposed to begin on May 14. But it was not until 11 days later that a *quorum,* or the number— usually a majority—required to convene a meeting, arrived. Those in attendance at the convention did not reflect all the views that had emerged in the nation. The convention reflected general agreement.

George Washington was unanimously elected to preside. It was decided to keep the proceedings secret. The voting system of the Continental Congress—one vote for each state—was used, except that only a majority was required to pass a proposal. The disagreements at the Constitutional Convention were primarily disagreements about the extent to which the national government was to be strengthened.

The key figure at the convention was 36-year-old James Madison. His journals provide a full account of the private meetings, for he played a prominent role in creating the Constitution that was to be drafted by the convention.

The determination to create a central government was expressed by an early proposition of the convention "that a national government ought to be established consisting of a Supreme Legislative, Executive, and Judiciary."

All the debates of the convention were tactical debates—debates about means of achieving their common goals. They centered on two questions. First, which grouping of states (whether defined by size or by section) would benefit most from a new national government? Second, what concessions were necessary to ensure the people's approval of the new government?

The consensus of the delegates, who called themselves Federalists, was that the new government had to be given the powers to tax and to regulate interstate commerce. Within that consensus sharp divisions, perhaps best expressed in the so-called Virginia and New Jersey plans, were recorded. These plans differed in almost every detail, but the most important difference concerned principles of representation.

The Virginia Plan proposed a *bicameral,* or two-chambered, *legislature,* with representation proportionate either to a state's population or to the size of its financial contribution to the government. The New Jersey Plan proposed to keep the unicameral legislature, with its equal representation for the states, that existed under the confederation. The dispute was settled by the Connecticut Compromise proposed by Roger Sherman of Connecticut. This plan called for a bicameral legislature with membership in the upper house—the Senate—divided equally among the states and membership in the lower—the House of Representatives—divided according to population.

Both the Virginia and New Jersey plans proposed that the executive and judicial branches of the government be selected by Congress. Many members of the convention believed that the legislative power was already too great; they argued for some method of selection that would protect the independence of these branches. It was agreed that an electoral college system and presidential appointment of federal judges would achieve this objective.

Sectional Controversy. Sectional conflicts aroused the most serious disputes at the convention. Two major controversies between the North and the South arose during the meetings.

The first concerned the method of counting population to determine each state's quota of seats in the House of Representatives. Should slaves be counted? The final compromise was that all "free persons" and "three-fifths of all other persons" would be counted for purposes of both representation and taxation.

The second controversy was over the power of Congress to regulate trade. The North held a majority in both houses. The South was afraid that the North might unfairly discriminate against southern exports, or that it would interfere in the slave trade. The northern states were interested in maximizing the power of the national government over trade. They also wanted to end the importation of slaves. The eventual compromise gave Congress the power to regulate commerce, but it expressly withheld the power to tax exports or to favor one port over another. The slave trade was permitted to continue until 1808, when Congress could choose to end importation.

Many features of the Constitution reflect the ability of its framers to compromise. The states were left in charge of suffrage, since the convention could not agree on how extensive it should be. The four-year term for the President was a compromise between those who wanted a much longer term and those who wanted more frequent elections.

Article VII of the new Constitution stipulated that the approval of nine states would be enough to put the document into operation. This provision was in direct violation of the Articles of Confederation. Even so, the Congress agreed to the ratification procedure by formally sending the document to the states for their consideration on September 28, 1787.

Supporters and Opponents of the Constitution. Supporters of the Constitution were called Federalists. They were led by people whose experience had been that of national service—in the army, in the Congress, or in the diplomatic corps. James Madison and Alexander Hamilton played the greatest role. Those who opposed the Constitution were called Anti-Federalists. Some of the more famous Anti-Federalists included such figures as Patrick Henry, Richard Henry Lee, John Hancock, George Clinton, James Monroe, George Mason, Elbridge Gerry, and Sam Adams. Many had served at the state level of government.

Support for the Constitution was strongest in the cities and in the commercial areas of the nation. It was also strong in states that were too small or too weak to survive on their own: Delaware, New Jersey, and Georgia approved the Constitution unanimously. Support for the Constitution was weakest in the noncommercial areas of the stronger states (included in this category were upstate New York, backcountry Virginia, and western Massachusetts) and in exceptional states like Rhode Island that were doing quite well without a central government.

Criticism of the Constitution. Two major criticisms of the Constitution arose. The first objection was to the increased powers of the national government, particularly in the coinage of money and the regulation of trade. Debtors especially were opposed to the denial of money-printing powers to the states. The second objection was to the absence of a bill of rights. Several states endorsed the Constitution conditionally, insisting that a bill of rights be added. They were promised that amendments guaranteeing and protecting traditional liberties—such as freedom of speech, press, and religion, and guarantees of fair trial—would be drafted and passed by the first Congress under the new national Constitution.

As a leading opponent of the Constitution, Patrick Henry of Virginia argued that the central government would be too strong.

Ratifying the Constitution. Three key states were crucial to the adoption of the Constitution. In all three, the struggle was close. Massachusetts approved the document by a vote of 187 to 168 in February 1788. But the strongest opposition was in Virginia and New York. Without them the government could not succeed. In Virginia, Patrick Henry's fiery speeches against the Constitution nearly overcame the arguments of the Federalists, and Madison's forces won by only ten votes on June 25, 1788.

In New York the Anti-Federalist organization of Governor George Clinton won substantial victories in the elections for the ratifying convention. The tactic used by the Federalists was delay. They delayed until most of the other states had ratified, until

THE ORIGINAL 13 STATES RATIFY THE CONSTITUTION		
STATE	**DATE OF RATIFICATION**	**VOTE**
Delaware	December 7, 1787	30–0
Pennsylvania	December 12, 1787	46–23
New Jersey	December 18, 1787	38–0
Georgia	January 2, 1788	26–0
Connecticut	January 9, 1788	128–40
Massachusetts	February 6, 1788	187–168
Maryland	April 28, 1788	63–11
South Carolina	May 23, 1788	149–73
New Hampshire	June 21, 1788	57–46
Virginia	June 26, 1788	89–79
New York	July 26, 1788	30–27
North Carolina	November 21, 1789*	184–77
Rhode Island	May 29, 1790	34–32

*Second vote: North Carolina rejected the Constitution August 4, 1788 by a vote of 184–84

threats of New York City's secession from the state had stimulated support, and until inducements of various kinds had eroded the strength of the Anti-Federalist majority. In the end the tactic worked, and on July 26, 1788, New York ratified the Constitution by a very slim margin, 30 to 27. North Carolina remained outside the federation until November 21, 1789, and Rhode Island until May 29, 1790.

When 11 states had agreed to the new Constitution, the confederation Congress proceeded to finish its work. It provided for the selection of presidential electors who were to vote on the first Wednesday in February, 1789. New York City was selected as the nation's temporary capital. March 4 was the date on which the new government was to be inaugurated.

News spread very slowly in those days. Transportation was slow as well. Congress met on March 4, 1789, but there were not enough members present to conduct business. Congress had to delay the counting of electoral votes until April 6, and George Washington could not be sworn in until April 30. The system of government inaugurated on that spring day in New York City nearly 200 years ago is one of the most stable in the world. Although the United States of America for which the Constitution was written has changed, the governmental structure that the Constitution established has survived.

section review

1. What was the purpose of the meeting held in Philadelphia in 1787?
2. Why was the electoral college system proposed at the convention?
3. Name three Anti-Federalist leaders.
4. What were the two major criticisms of the new Constitution?
5. What three states were crucial to the adoption of the Constitution?

CHAPTER SUMMARY

2

The government of the United States evolved slowly over many centuries. Most of our political ideals were brought to the New World by English settlers during the seventeenth and eighteenth centuries. Three types of colonies were established by the English: royal, proprietary, and charter.

When George III became king after 1760, he and his ministers sought to bring the colonies under their control and to make them more profitable. This led to resentment from the American settlers, who argued that they were being deprived of their "rights as Englishmen." A series of confrontations between the American colonists and their British rulers finally led to the calling of a Continental Congress and the outbreak of the American Revolution.

The Articles of Confederation established Congress as the national governing body. Its powers were so limited that government almost ceased to function. Two major accomplishments of the new government were establishing national control over western territories and setting up a territorial system of government. The weaknesses of government under the Articles led to the calling of a convention, at which delegates wrote the U.S. Constitution.

REVIEW QUESTIONS

1. What were two major criticisms of the Constitution?
2. Describe the situation that prompted sectional controversy over regulation of trade.
3. What restrictions were placed on Congress by the Articles of Confederation?
4. Explain what was meant by "no taxation without representation."
5. How did the Connecticut Compromise satisfy the representatives of both the large and small states?
6. What attempts were made at colonial unification prior to the Constitution? Explain.
7. Why was the Stamp Act Congress opposed to the Stamp Act?
8. What was the function of the Committees of Correspondence?
9. Name the last two states to ratify the Constitution.
10. Tell how the weaknesses of the Articles of Confederation were corrected in the Constitution.

ACTIVITIES FOR REVIEW

activity 1   Research: Many of the famous Revolutionary leaders, such as Thomas Jefferson, Patrick Henry, and John Hancock, were not delegates to the constitutional convention and later opposed the Constitution. Read a biography of one of these men to determine the reasons for their opposition.

activity 2   Plan and stage a classroom debate on the following issue: RESOLVED, that the proposed U.S. Constitution be ratified. (The *Federalist* papers are a good source of information for your debates.)

activity 3   Chart the origins of important American concepts of government. Your chart should trace such concepts as limited government, mixed government, consent of the people, representative government.

political science DICTIONARY

bicameral legislature—a legislature that consists of two houses. p. 32
charter colonies (corporate)—self-governing colonies established by companies under grants from the king. p. 24
proprietary colonies—colonies with governments resembling those of royal colonies, but with governors appointed by each colony's proprietor instead of by the king. p. 24
quorum—the smallest number of a group or assembly that must be present to carry on business or legally make decisions. p. 32
royal colonies—colonies ruled by the king's appointed governor, a council appointed by that governor, and an elected assembly. p. 24
Tories—colonists who sympathized with the British and continued to be loyal to England. p. 29
unicameral legislature—a legislature that consists of one house. p. 29

3

Origins: The United States Constitution

This chapter concentrates on the basic principles by which the United States is governed, and how those principles have been changed or kept over time.

You will read first what the basic principles of our constitutional order are and what they mean. Then you will learn how these principles are kept even when the government changes. You will see the two methods of change in our Constitution that have developed over time: formal and informal change. Formal change takes place through the process of constitutional amendment. Informal change, which is at least as important as, but less obvious than, formal change, happens through the working of the years, as new realities outdate old formulas. You will read of some of the more dramatic informal changes that have taken place in the nearly two centuries since our form of government was set down on paper.

CHAPTER PREVIEW

1. THE PRINCIPLES OF THE CONSTITUTION
2. THE CHANGING CONSTITUTION: FORMAL CHANGE
3. THE CHANGING CONSTITUTION: INFORMAL CHANGE

1. THE PRINCIPLES OF THE CONSTITUTION

The founders of our nation devised a very complex structure of government. It has three main characteristics. It is a representative government, a divided government, and a limited government.

Representative Government. The government established by the founders is one in which the people govern through their elected representatives. In other words, they govern indirectly rather than directly. Thus our constitutional government is an indirect democracy, or republic.

Representative government reflects an important prinicple of the Constitution: the principle of *popular sovereignty.* According to this principle, power is vested in the people. "The people" means all members of the community, not just a particular person or ruling class. The principle operates when officials who act for "the people" as their elected representatives discharge their daily responsibilities.

QUOTES from famous people

"The constitutional convention of 1787 is supposed to have created a government of 'separated powers.' It did nothing of the sort. Rather, it created a government of separated institutions sharing powers.*"*

Richard Neustadt

Divided Government. As you recall, a parliamentary system of government concentrates power in the majority party or majority coalition of parties in the parliament. In the American presidential system power is divided among three branches of government. These three branches are the legislative (Congress), the executive (President), and the judicial (the Supreme Court).

No one branch has sovereignty, or supreme power.

The division of power is spelled out in the first three articles of the Constitution.

Article 1, Section 1, states that "all legislative powers herein granted shall be vested in a Congress of the United States. . . ." Article 2 Section 1, provides that the "executive power shall be vested in a President of the United States of America." Article 3, Section 1, says that the "judicial power of the United States shall be vested in one Supreme Court, and in such inferior courts as the Congress may from time to time ordain and establish."

James Madison defended this division of power in *The Federalist* (number 47) by saying that it was the only way to avoid "tyranny." He felt that such tyranny would arise if all power to govern were to be put "in the same hands . . . whether hereditary, self-appointed, or elective."

This division of power does not mean that the three branches of government are completely independent of each other. Each branch has its own area of power. However, the powers of each branch are related to the powers of the others in a system of checks and balances. Checks are limitations on the powers of one branch by the powers of others. Balances are ways of equalizing power so that no one branch can become supreme.

For example, all money bills must start in the House of Representatives. Since all funds for the executive branch must be appropriated by Congress, the President depends on the House to introduce such legislation. The President also depends on the Senate, which has the power to approve treaties entered into and appointments made by the President. The President can use the **veto power** to limit the legislative power of Congress. But by a two-thirds vote in both houses, Congress can overturn the President's veto and enact the legislation that has been rejected. The justices of the Supreme Court are appointed by the President and are confirmed by the Senate. However, the Supreme Court has the power of judicial review, that is, the power to decide whether the other two branches have acted constitutionally.

Veto power is the right of the President to reject a bill after Congress has approved it.

Limited Government. The government established by the Constitution is limited in the sense that it is prohibited from doing certain things. What it may not do is stated in the Constitution. If the Constitution states that the government does not have a certain power, then that power is assumed to be withheld by the people. Every government in the United States, not only the national government, is a limited one. The guarantees of personal freedom contained in the Bill of Rights flow from the concept of limited government. Freedom of speech, press, religion, assembly, and petition are some of the rights

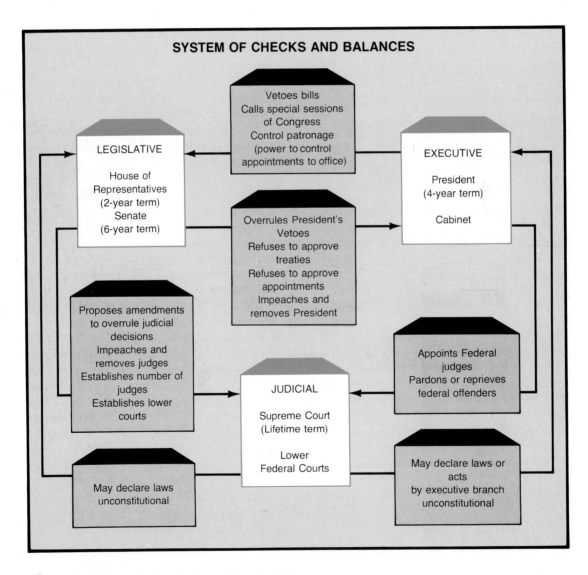

SYSTEM OF CHECKS AND BALANCES

Vetoes bills
Calls special sessions of Congress
Control patronage (power to control appointments to office)

LEGISLATIVE

House of Representatives (2-year term)
Senate (6-year term)

EXECUTIVE

President (4-year term)

Cabinet

Overrules President's Vetoes
Refuses to approve treaties
Refuses to approve appointments
Impeaches and removes President

Proposes amendments to overrule judicial decisions
Impeaches and removes judges
Establishes number of judges
Establishes lower courts

JUDICIAL

Supreme Court (Lifetime term)

Lower Federal Courts

Appoints Federal judges
Pardons or reprieves federal offenders

May declare laws unconstitutional

May declare laws or acts by executive branch unconstitutional

guaranteed by the First Amendment, which begins with the words "Congress shall make no law . . . ."

section review

1. List the three main characteristics of our system of government.
2. How are the powers of the federal government divided?
3. Define the term "veto power."
4. In what document are the guarantees of personal freedom contained?

2. THE CHANGING CONSTITUTION: FORMAL CHANGE

Any institution that lasts a long time must find ways of adapting to change. The Constitution is no exception.

Constitutional change takes place in two ways. There is a system of formal change that involves the passage of constitutional amendments. And there is informal change that takes place through the workings of time—change that goes on continuously.

The Eighteenth Amendment prohibited the sale, manufacture, and transportation of alcoholic beverages. Here a federal agent smashes kegs of whiskey during the Prohibition era.

Formal Change. Article 5 of the Constitution outlines a two-step method for amending the Constitution. The two steps are proposal and ratification. Each step can be accomplished in two different ways.

An amendment can be proposed in two ways. Two thirds of both houses of Congress can propose an amendment, or Congress can call a national convention at the request of two thirds of the state legislatures. All amendments that have been **ratified** have been proposed by the first method—a two-thirds vote of each house of Congress.

Amendments can be ratified by three fourths of the state legislatures or by conventions held in three fourths of the states. Twenty-five amendments have been ratified by state legislatures. The Twenty-first Amendment, which repealed Prohibition, was ratified by state conventions. Ratification was handled in this way because Congress believed that that method would give the amendment a better chance of being approved. The people would be more inclined to repeal Prohibition than would state legislators.

Ratified means approved.

The Amendments. Since 1789 over 4,000 amendments have been proposed to Congress. But Congress has sent only 33 amendments to the states. Of this number only 26 had been ratified as of 1980.

Constitutional amendments have been ratified in four historic clusters.

1. *1791–1804: Amendments 1–12.* The first ten amendments are the Bill of Rights. The Eleventh Amendment prevents a state from being sued in federal courts by the citizens of another state or of a foreign state. The Twelfth Amendment changes the method of electing the President and Vice-President.

2. *1865–1870: Amendments 13–15.* These amendments are called the "Reconstruction amendments." They abolished slavery, redefined American citizenship, asserted the civil rights of all against infringements by the states, and extended the vote to all male citizens.

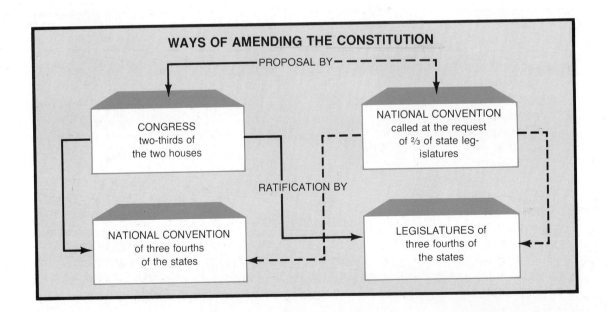

WAYS OF AMENDING THE CONSTITUTION

PROPOSAL BY

CONGRESS
two-thirds of
the two houses

NATIONAL CONVENTION
called at the request
of ⅔ of state leg-
islatures

RATIFICATION BY

NATIONAL CONVENTION
of three fourths
of the states

LEGISLATURES of
three fourths of
the states

"Believe it or not," wrote Robert Ripley in his popular newspaper feature, "the first President of the United States was . . . Peyton Randolph." Actually, Peyton Randolph was president of the First Continental Congress in 1774 and for two weeks served as president of the Second Continental Congress, resigning in May 1775 because the Virginia assembly, of which he was speaker, was called into session.

Randolph came from a prominent family that was part of the landed gentry of Virginia. He was admitted to the bar in 1744, at the age of 23. From 1748 to 1766 he was king's attorney for Virginia. In 1748 he served in the Virginia assembly. He was elected to the assembly in 1752 and in 1766 became its speaker, a position he held until his death.

Politically, Randolph was a conservative. After Patrick Henry's famous speech denouncing the Stamp Act, Randolph expressed regret that as speaker he had no vote to cast against Henry's anti-English resolutions. Gradually, however, his views began to change. His reputation for conservatism made his eventual opposition to the English significant.

By the 1770's Randolph was willing to participate in the colonial resistance to English authority. Since he was among the most respected citizens of Virginia, the revolutionaries quickly made him a leader. He became chairman of the Virginia Committee of Correspondence in 1773, and was the first of seven delegates elected by Virginia to the Continental Congress in 1774. As a noted representative of the most important colony, Randolph was a natural choice to chair the congress. But he considered his job as speaker in the Virginia legislature more important than the presidency of the Continental Congress.

Randolph died in October 1775. Had he lived, he would undoubtedly have continued to play a major role in the new American government.

PEYTON RANDOLPH, "THE FIRST PRESIDENT"

3. *1913–1933: Amendments 16–21.* These "Progressive era" amendments gave the government the right to impose an income tax, provided for the direct election of senators, gave women the vote, set new dates for the inauguration of the President and Vice-President and for convening Congress, and imposed and then repealed Prohibition.

4. *1951–1971: Amendments 22–26.* These amendments deal with the presidency and with presidential elections. They limited Presidents to two terms in office, gave the District of Columbia the right to vote in presidential elections, abolished the poll tax in federal elections, provided for selecting a successor to a President, stated how a vacancy in the vice-presidency is to be filled, established ways of deciding when a President is too disabled to serve, and lowered the voting age to 18.

Amendments that Were Not Approved. Five amendments that were proposed by Congress but were not ratified by the states were recommended during periods of change or crisis. Two of these amendments were to have been part of the original Bill of Rights. They dealt with the apportionment of the

House of Representatives and the payment of compensation to Congress. Another amendment was proposed in 1810, when the United States was having serious troubles with Great Britain and France. This amendment would have stripped citizenship from anyone who accepted a foreign title or honor. The fourth coincided with the outbreak of the Civil War. It would have prohibited the ratification of any amendment relating to slavery. The fifth, proposed in 1924, would have given Congress the right to regulate child labor. Two amendments were put before the states for their approval in the 1970's: the Equal Rights Amendment (proposed in 1972, deadline 1982) and an amendment giving Congressional representation to the District of Columbia (proposed in 1978, deadline 1985).

Women in America have been actively fighting for equality since the early 1900's. In this picture, women campaign for the right to vote. What reasons were given for denying the suffrage to women?

In November 1977 the National Women's Conference met in Houston, Texas, in support of the Equal Rights Amendment. American women are demanding equal economic, social, and political status.

section review

1. What are the two ways in which constitutional change can take place?
2. List the two steps necessary in amending the Constitution.
3. What ratification method has been used most often?
4. Describe the proposed amendment that was before the states for approval in 1978.
5. Why was the state convention method used for ratifying the Twenty-first Amendment?

3. THE CHANGING CONSTITUTION: INFORMAL CHANGE

Informal Constitutional Changes. Informal change has been more important in developing our government than has formal change. Apart from the 26 amendments, the Constitution today is the same document as that written almost 200 years ago—no words have been added or deleted. Yet the relationships of the various parts of the government are completely different from what the founders of our nation envisaged.

QUOTES from famous people

"Our Constitution professedly rests upon the good sense and attachment of the people. This basis, weak as it may appear, has not yet been found to fail."

John Quincy Adams

Informal Change: The Executive Branch. The Constitution grants to Congress the power to declare war. But since the Mexican War of 1848, Presidents have exercised this power. They have not assumed the formal power of declaring war, but they have committed the nation to war in accordance with the constitutional grant of power conferred on the President as the commander in chief of the armed forces. This presidential power was restricted in 1973, when Congress passed the War Powers Act.

The growth of the executive branch in the twentieth century has provided clear examples of an evolving Constitution. Woodrow Wilson was the first President to present Congress with a legislative program—an initiative that we now take for granted. The President's power to introduce legislation has been formalized in some areas in which Congress has consented to the so-called legislative veto. This device gives the President the power to do something unless one house of Congress disagrees within a specified period of time. For instance, the President may reorganize the executive branch unless either house of Congress vetoes his proposal within two months of its submission.

Informal Change: The Legislative Branch. The executive branch has assumed many powers that were originally defined as legislative. In turn, the legislative branch has assumed many executive powers. For instance, the Senate has restricted the President's power to appoint many federal officials—especially judges. It has done this by automatically rejecting a presidential appointee who is opposed by a senator from the appointee's state. What this means in practice is that senators are asked by the President to submit names to fill vacancies in federal offices in their states. The President either chooses one of the nominees or, if none is acceptable, he asks the senator to submit a new list. In effect, the Senate appoints, and the President confirms the appointment.

Congress now performs many other executive functions. For example, it passes legislation that specifies exactly how executive tasks are to be carried out.

Informal Change: The Judicial Branch. Change has taken place in the judicial branch, too. The Constitution does not state that the Supreme Court has the power to declare unconstitutional executive and legislative actions. But beginning with Chief Justice John Marshall's decision in *Marbury* v. *Madison* (1803), the Court has steadily widened its power to interpret the Constitution. Both the executive and the legislative branches have agreed with the Court's assumption of the power of judicial review. But as the ratification of the Sixteenth Amendment illustrates, Congress can limit the power of the Supreme Court by proposing amendments to the Constitution that can supersede the Court's decision.

The Constitution gives Congress the power to determine the jurisdiction of the Supreme Court. But Congress has used that power only once, more than a century ago. The size of the Supreme Court is not specified in the Constitution. Because the size of the Court is authorized in statutes, the number of justices can be changed simply by passing new laws. The traditional size of the court—nine justices—has become so sacred that changing it is considered improbable. Franklin D. Roosevelt tried to enlarge the Supreme Court in 1937, but he met such opposition that he quickly gave up the idea.

Chief Justice Charles Evans Hughes once said that "the Constitution means what the judges say it means." This view of its role has involved the Court in making decisions that might otherwise have been considered either legislative or executive.

Examples of the expanding role of the Court include the controversial 1977 abortion decision. The decision took on legislative overtones when the Supreme Court specified, month by month, the scope of the State's power over abortion. Another example involves the busing struggle in Boston. The federal district judge in the case finally drew school district lines—a decision that would otherwise have been made by the executive branch of the local government.

Other Informal Changes. The Constitution has been changed by the development of institutions that were not foreseen when the original document was written. The best example of this change is the emergence of the political party system. Political parties were considered an evil by the founders of our nation. But political parties developed within a few years after the ratification of the Constitution. By 1840 a two-party system and national party conventions had emerged. The presidency, which had been thought of as an office removed from everyday politics, became the center of the political system. Congress came to be dominated by two institutions—the system of permanent Congressional committees, chaired by members of the party that elects a majority in each house, and the party system. Neither institution is mentioned in the Constitution.

How the Changes Came About. Many informal changes came about through legislation. The Constitution provided only the basic framework for the government. It was left to Congress to add to this framework. The entire judicial system and the entire executive bureaucracy were created by congressional legislation. Congress, by the laws that it passes, defines what is in the Constitution. In other words, Congress defines such terms as interstate commerce, tax, and involuntary servitude.

The power to define what is in the Constitution is not reserved to Congress. The greatest power of definition is held by the courts—and most important, by the Supreme Court. In fact, Woodrow Wilson called the Court a "constitutional convention in continuous session." Among the Court's most important tasks of definition is that of applying to the modern world a document that is almost 200 years old.

Other sources of change are **precedents** and customs. One of the earliest examples involved George Washington. Article 2, Section 2, of the Constitution says that the President shall make treaties "with the advice and consent of the Senate." Taking the language literally, Washington went to the Senate and asked its advice concerning a treaty about which he had been thinking. He listened as the senators discussed minor matters for several hours. Then he became disgusted. He left and never returned. Washington's action became a precedent that has led to two customs. First, "advice and consent" are given only after a treaty has been signed. Second, Presidents do not go to Congress to seek the advice or the consent of its members.

> **Precedents** are actions, decisions, or practices that can be used as guides for later actions, decisions, or practices.

*"Do you ever have one of those days when every-
thing seems un-Constitutional?"*

The judicial branch checks Congress through its power of judicial review.

Precedents were begun by other Presidents as well. In 1841 John Tyler became the
first Vice-President to assume "the powers
and duties of the office" of President upon
the death of William Harrison. Tyler took his
succession to mean that he automatically
became President, not simply that he could
exercise presidential powers. This assumption was not incorporated into the Constitution until 1967 when the Twenty-fifth
Amendment was ratified. But Tyler's action
created a precedent that has been followed
by all Vice-Presidents who have succeeded
Presidents. Through the acquiescence of
Congress, twentieth-century Presidents have
established that "executive agreements" with
other nations have the status of treaties. This
precedent has enabled them to avoid the
time-consuming process of obtaining formal
approval from the Senate.

This process of change was necessary. It
has enabled the Constitution to survive the
many social, economic, and technological
changes that have swept the nation. The
flexibility of the Constitution has ensured its
durability.

section review

1. What is the traditional number of justices in
   the Supreme Court?
2. Why is the emergence of political parties considered an informal change to the Federal
   Constitution?
3. Define the term "precedent."

The Constitution of the United States and What It Means Today

(Portions of the text within brackets have been changed by amendment or are no longer in effect. The text of the Constitution appears in black; annotations appear in blue.)

Preamble

We, the people of the United States, in order to form a more perfect Union, establish justice, insure domestic tranquility, provide for the common defense, promote the general welfare, and secure the blessings of liberty to ourselves and our posterity, do ordain and establish this Constitution for the United States of America.

The Preamble. The opening is called the *Preamble*. It states the purpose of the Constitution. Note that it begins, "We, the people," not "We, the states. . . ."

Article 1. The Legislative Branch

Section 1. Congress

All legislative powers herein granted shall be vested in a Congress of the United States, which shall consist of a Senate and House of Representatives.

Section 1. This section states how Congress shall be organized and that it will have the power to make all federal laws. This clause has been modified in practice so that regulations made by certain federal agencies can function as federal laws.

Section 2. House of Representatives

1. Election and Term of Members. The House of Representatives shall be composed of members chosen every second year by the people of the several states, and the electors in each state shall have the qualifications requisite for electors of the most numerous branch of the state legislature.

Clause 1. Members of the House serve two-year terms. The term *electors* refers to voters.

2. Qualifications. No person shall be a Representative who shall not have attained to the age of twenty-five years, and been seven years a citizen of the United States, and who shall not, when elected, be an inhabitant of that state in which he shall be chosen.

Clause 2. A representative must be at least 25 years old, must have been a United States citizen for at least 7 years, and must be a resident of the state from which he or she is elected. The states are divided into congressional districts, each of which elects a representative.

3. Apportionment of Representatives. Representatives [and direct taxes] shall be apportioned among the several states which may be included within this Union, according to their

Clause 3. The number of members in the House of Representatives was to be determined by the number of "free persons" in each state, plus "three-fifths of all other persons." This meant that states could count only three-fifths of their respective numbers [which shall be determined by adding to the whole number of free persons, including those bound to service for a term of years, and excluding Indians not taxed, three fifths of all other persons]. The actual enumeration shall be made within three years after the first meeting of the Congress of the United States, and within every subsequent term of ten years, in such manner as they shall by law direct. The number of Representatives shall not exceed 1 for every 30,000, but each state shall have at least 1 Representative; [and until such enumeration shall be made, the state of New Hampshire shall be entitled to choose 3; Massachusetts, 8; Rhode Island and Providence Plantations, 1; Connecticut, 5; New York, 6; New Jersey, 4; Pennsylvania, 8; Delaware, 1; Maryland, 6; Virginia, 10; North Carolina, 5; South Carolina, 5; and Georgia, 3].

4. Vacancies. When vacancies happen in the representation from any state, the executive authority thereof shall issue writs of election to fill such vacancies.

5. Impeachment. The House of Representatives shall choose their Speaker and other officers; and shall have the sole power of impeachment.

Section 3. Senate
1. Number of Members and Terms of Office. The Senate of the United States shall be composed of two Senators from each state [chosen by the legislatures thereof], for six years, and each Senator shall have one vote.

2. Classification; Vacancies. [Immediately after they shall be assembled in consequence of the first election, they shall be divided as equally as may be into three classes. The seats of the Senators of the first class shall be vacated at the expiration of the second year, of the second class at the expiration of the fourth year, and of the third class at the expiration of the sixth year, so that one-third may be chosen every second year; and if vacancies happen by resignation, or otherwise, during the recess of the legislature of any state, the executive thereof may make temporary appointments until the next meeting of the legislature, which shall then fill such vacancies.]

Black slaves. This provision was overruled by the 13th Amendment (1865) and Section 2 of the 14th Amendment (1868).

Because representation is based on population, the Constitution provides for a national head count, or census, every ten years. The United States was the first nation to conduct a regular census. Every representative represents at least 30,000 people, but each state is entitled to at least one representative. In 1929, in order to prevent the House of Representatives from growing too large, Congress limited the membership of the House to 435.

Clause 4. If a member of the House of Representatives dies or resigns, the governor of the state orders a special election to fill the vacant seat.

Clause 5. By majority vote, the House can impeach, or accuse, officers of the executive branch or federal judges. The Senate tries all impeachment cases.

Clause 1. Each state legislature was to elect two members to the Senate. Senators represent states, not people. This system was changed by the 17th Amendment in 1913. Senators are now elected directly by the voters of each state.

Clause 2. Senators serve six-year terms. The paragraph defining "classes" of senators sets up a staggered system, whereby one third of the Senate comes up for reelection every two years. If a Senator resigns or dies, the 17th Amendment provides for the governor to call a special election to fill the vacancy or to appoint a temporary successor.

3. Qualifications. No person shall be a Senator who shall not have attained the age of thirty years, and been nine years a citizen of the United States, and who shall not, when elected, be an inhabitant of that state for which he shall be chosen.

4. The President of the Senate. The Vice-President of the United States shall be president of the Senate, but shall have no vote, unless they be equally divided.

5. Other Officers. The Senate shall choose their other officers, and also a president pro tempore, in the absence of the Vice-President, or when he shall exercise the office of the President of the United States.

6. Impeachments. The Senate shall have the sole power to try all impeachments. When sitting for that purpose, they shall be on oath or affirmation. When the President of the United States is tried, the Chief Justice shall preside; and no person shall be convicted without the concurrence of two-thirds of the members present.

7. Penalty for Conviction. Judgment in cases of impeachment shall not extend further than to removal from office, and disqualification to hold and enjoy any office of honor, trust, or profit under the United States; but the party convicted shall nevertheless be liable and subject to indictment, trial, judgment, and punishment, according to law.

Section 4.   Elections and Meetings
1. Holding Elections. The times, places, and manner of holding elections for Senators and Representatives shall be prescribed in each state by the legislature thereof; but the Congress may at any time by law make or alter such regulations, except as to the places of choosing Senators.

2. Meetings. The Congress shall assemble at least once in every year, [and such meeting shall be on the first Monday in December,] unless they shall by law appoint a different day.

Clauses 4 and 5. The Vice-President serves as the President of the Senate and votes only to break a tie. This is the only vice-presidential duty specified in the Constitution. If the Vice-President is absent or becomes President, the Senate elects a temporary president (pro tempore) to preside over its meetings.

Clauses 6 and 7. The trial of members of the executive or the judiciary accused by the House of Representatives is conducted by the Senate. A vote of two-thirds of the Senate is necessary for conviction. If convicted, the person is removed from office and is then subject to indictment and criminal proceedings according to the law. Andrew Johnson is the only President who was impeached (1868). He was not convicted. Conviction failed by one vote. Richard M. Nixon was the first President to resign from office. He did so in 1974, when the Judiciary Committee of the House of Representatives recommended that he be impeached. Following his resignation he was granted a presidential pardon, which spared him from possible prosecution.

Clause 1. The states set the conditions of congressional elections, determining who can vote. This was modified by the 15th Amendment (1870), which prevents the states from interfering with the right of Blacks to vote; the 19th Amendment (1920), which extends voting rights to women, the 24th Amendment (1964), which bans the poll tax as a condition for voting, and the 26th Amendment (1971), which lowers the voting age to 18.

Clause 2. The date for Congress to assemble was changed by the 20th Amendment (1933). Congress now convenes on January 3.

Section 5. Procedure

1. Organization. Each house shall be the judge of the elections, returns, and qualifications of its own members, and a majority of each shall constitute a quorum to do business; but a smaller number may adjourn from day to day, and may be authorized to compel the attendance of absent members, in such manner, and under such penalties, as each house may provide.

2. Proceedings. Each house may determine the rules of its proceedings, punish its members for disorderly behavior, and with the concurrence of two-thirds, expel a member.

3. The Journal. Each house shall keep a journal of its proceedings, and from time to time publish the same, excepting such parts as may in their judgment require secrecy; and the yeas and nays of the members of either house on any question shall, at the desire of one-fifth of those present, be entered on the journal.

4. Adjournment. Neither house, during the session of Congress, shall, without the consent of the other, adjourn for more than three days, nor to any other place than that in which the two houses shall be sitting.

Section 6. Privileges and Restrictions

1. Pay and Privileges. The Senators and Representatives shall receive a compensation for their services, to be ascertained by law and paid out of the Treasury of the United States. They shall in all cases, except treason, felony, and breach of the peace, be privileged from arrest during their attendance at the session of their respective houses, and in going to and returning from the same; and for any speech or debate in either house, they shall not be questioned in any other place.

2. Restrictions. No Senator or Representative shall, during the time for which he was elected, be appointed to any civil office under the authority of the United States, which shall have been created, or the emoluments whereof shall have been increased, during such time; and no

Clause 1.   Both houses have the right to refuse to seat members. A *quorum* is a majority of members of each house of Congress and is the minimum number required to be present to carry out business. In practice, however, business can be and often is transacted without a quorum as long as no member objects. Each house can compel the attendance of its members when their presence is needed.

Clause 3.   The framers of the Constitution wanted the voters to be kept informed of the activities of Congress. Such a record would also enable the people to find out how their representatives had voted on particular issues. Such openness in government was unknown in Europe at the time the Constitution was written. The *House Journal* and the *Senate Journal* are published at the end of each session of Congress. The *Congressional Record* is published for every day Congress is in session. It records the action of both houses.

Clause 4.   Once Congress is in session, the House and the Senate must remain at work until both agree on a time to adjourn. Because they work together, they must both work in the same place.

Clause 1.   This clause permits members to speak freely by providing *congressional immunity* from prosecution or arrest for things they say in speeches and debates in Congress. Members of Congress set their own pay.

Clause 2.   This clause underscores the principle of separation of powers. No member of Congress can hold any other government office. If Congress creates an office or raises the salary of an old one, no member of Congress may fill that office until his or her term expires. This provision was made to prevent the executive, or the President, from controlling Con-person holding any office under the United States shall be a member of either house during his continuance in office.

Section 7.   Passing Laws

1. Revenue Bills. All bills for raising revenue shall originate in the House of Representatives; but the Senate may propose or concur with amendments as on other bills.

2. How a Bill Becomes a Law. Every bill which shall have passed the House of Representatives and the Senate shall, before it becomes a law, be presented to the President of the United States; if he approves, he shall sign it, but if not, he shall return it, with his objections, to that house in which it shall have originated, who shall enter the objections at large on their journal, and proceed to reconsider it. If after such reconsideration two-thirds of that house shall agree to pass the bill, it shall be sent, together with the objections, to the other house, by which it shall likewise be reconsidered and, if approved by two-thirds of that house, it shall become a law. But in all such cases the votes of both houses shall be determined by yeas and nays, and the names of the persons voting for and against the bill shall be entered on the journal of each house respectively. If any bill shall not be returned by the President within ten days (Sunday excepted) after it shall have been presented to him, the same bill shall be a law, in like manner as if he had signed it, unless the Congress by their adjournment prevent its return, in which case it shall not be a law.

3. Presidential Approval or Veto. Every order, resolution, or vote to which the concurrence of the Senate and House of Representatives may be necessary (except on a question of adjournment) shall be presented to the President of the United States; and before the same shall take effect, shall be approved by him, or being disapproved by him, shall be repassed by two-thirds of the Senate and House of Representatives, according to the rules and limitations prescribed in the case of a bill.

gress. In Britain in the 18th century, the king and his ministers controlled Parliament by promising offices as bribes.

Clause 1.   Bills for raising money by taxes must be introduced in the House of Representatives. This was part of the compromise between the large states and the small states. The large states received proportional representation in one house, and that house was also given first authority over money and tax measures. This provision has little practical importance, however, because the Senate can amend such bills.

Clause 2.   Every bill that passes both houses of Congress is sent to the President. If the President approves the bill and signs it, it becomes law. The refusal to sign is called a *veto*. A vetoed bill is sent back to Congress with a written statement of the President's objections. If both houses can pass the bill by two thirds majority (usually very difficult to obtain), Congress can *override* the President's veto and the bill becomes law. If not, the veto is *sustained* and the bill dies. If the President receives a bill and keeps it ten days without acting on it, it automatically becomes law. If Congress adjourns within those ten days, the bill must be introduced again in the next congressional session. This is called a *pocket veto*.

The Presidential veto is an important check of the executive branch of the government on the legislative branch. Congress checks the President when it overrides a veto.

Section 8. Powers Delegated to Congress

The Congress shall have power

1. To lay and collect taxes, duties, imposts, and excises, to pay the debts and provide for the common defense and general welfare of the United States; but all duties, imposts, and excises shall be uniform through the United States;

2. To borrow money on the credit of the United States;

3. To regulate commerce with foreign nations, and among the several states, [and with the Indian tribes];

4. To establish a uniform rule of naturalization, and uniform laws on the subject of bankruptcies throughout the United States;

5. To coin money, regulate the value thereof, and of foreign coin, and fix the standard of weights and measures;

6. To provide for the punishment of counterfeiting the securities and current coin of the United States.

7. To establish post offices and post roads;

8. To promote the progress of science and useful arts by securing for limited times to authors and inventors the exclusive right to their respective writings and discoveries;

9. To constitute tribunals inferior to the Supreme Court;

10. To define and punish piracies and felonies committed on the high seas and offenses against the law of nations;

Section 8. This section lists the 18 *delegated* or *enumerated* powers granted to Congress. The first 17 specify areas in which Congress has authority and are called *expressed* powers. The 18th power is the elastic clause. The doctrine of *implied* powers developed from this clause.

Clause 1. Congress has the power to levy taxes to pay the nation's debts and to provide for national defense and for the general welfare of the people. All federal taxes must be the same throughout the country.

Clause 2. The Constitution sets no limit on the amount Congress can borrow—Congress itself sets the national debt.

Clause 3. Congress has the power to regulate trade with foreign nations. It also has direct control over interstate commerce. This phrase is so broad that it permits Congress to regulate transportation, the stock market, and the broadcasting industry.

Clause 4. Congress can decide how immigrants may become citizens. It can also make laws about procedures involved in business failures.

Clause 5. Congress can mint coins, print paper money, and set the value of both American money and foreign currency within this country. It can also set standard measurements for the nation.

Clause 6. Congress can make laws fixing the punishment for counterfeiting currency, bonds, or stamps.

Clause 7. Congress can designate which highways should be used to transport mail.

Clause 8. Congress can pass patent and copyright laws to give to inventors and artists sole rights to their works for a number of years. Anyone who uses patented inventions or copyrighted material without permission may be punished.

Clause 9. All federal courts except the Supreme Court are established by acts of Congress.

Clause 10. Congress can decide what acts committed on American ships are crimes and how such acts should be punished. It can also decide how American citizens who break international laws shall be punished.

11. To declare war, [grant letters of marque and reprisal,] and make rules concerning captures on land and water;

Clause 11. Only Congress may declare war. However, American forces have engaged in combat in some instances without congressional declarations of war—for example, in Korea and Vietnam. *Letters of marque and reprisal* refer to permission granted to American merchant ships to attack enemy ships, a practice common in early wars. This practice has been outlawed by international agreement.

12. To raise and support armies, but no appropriation of money to that use shall be for a longer term than two years;

Clause 12. All money for the army comes from Congress. However, Congress may not grant such money for longer than a two-year period. This is to make sure that civilians exercise financial control over the army.

13. To provide and maintain a navy;

Clause 13. There is no two-year limit on naval appropriations because the navy was not considered a threat to liberty.

14. To make rules for the government and regulation of the land and naval forces;

Clause 14. Because Congress can create the armed forces, it has power to make rules for the services. Such rules now include the air force.

15. To provide for calling forth the militia to execute the laws of the Union, suppress insurrections, and repel invasions;

Clause 15. Congress can call into federal service the state militia forces (citizen-soldiers now referred to as the National Guard) to enforce federal laws and defend life and property. Congress can empower the President to call out the militia, but only for the reasons named here.

16. To provide for organizing, arming, and disciplining the militia, and for governing such part of them as may be employed in the service of the United States, reserving to the states, respectively, the appointment of the officers, and the authority of training the militia according to the discipline prescribed by Congress;

Clause 16. The states may appoint officers for the militia, but Congress establishes rules for training the militia.

17. To exercise exclusive legislation in all cases whatsoever, over such district (not exceeding ten miles square) as may, by cession of particular states, and the acceptance of Congress, become the seat of government of the United States, and to exercise like authority over all places purchased by the consent of the legislature of the state in which the same shall be, for the erection of forts, magazines, arsenals, dockyards, and other needful buildings;—and

Clause 17. Congress has control over the District of Columbia as well as all forts, arsenals, dockyards, federal courthouses, and other places owned and operated by the federal government.

18. To make all laws which shall be necessary and proper for carrying into execution the foregoing powers, and all other powers vested by this Constitution in the government of the United States, or in any department or officer thereof.

Clause 18. The framers were very careful to ensure that Congress would be able to meet the needs of a changing society. Sometimes called the elastic clause of the Constitution, this clause enables Congress to frame laws that are related to specific powers listed in the Constitution. For instance, as part of its power "to raise and support armies,"

Congress can undertake the construction of roads. Such roads are "necessary and proper" for transporting, or maintaining, an army.

This elastic clause has enabled Congress to meet the changing needs of society over two centuries. The power that has become the most expandable is the power to regulate interstate trade and commerce. In the 20th century, Congress has used this power to pass Civil Rights Acts (protecting the free movement of people and trade) and labor legislation that guards the right of unions to organize (strikes interfere with interstate commerce).

Section 9. Powers Denied to the Federal Government

1. [The migration or importation of such persons as any of the states now existing shall think proper to admit shall not be prohibited by the Congress prior to the year 1808; but a tax or duty may be imposed on such importation, not exceeding $10 for each person.]

Clause 1. "Such persons" refers to slaves. This clause was the result of a compromise between northern merchants and southern planters. The Constitutional Convention gave Congress powers to regulate commerce and to tax imports, while also providing that the importation of slaves would not be prohibited prior to 1808 and that there would not be an import tax of more than $10 per person. The importation of slaves was prohibited in 1808.

2. The privilege of the writ of *habeas corpus* shall not be suspended, unless when in cases of rebellion or invasion the public safety may require it.

Clause 2. A *writ of habeas corpus* protects citizens from arbitrary arrest. It is an order demanding that a person who has been arrested be brought before a court so that a judge can decide if he or she is being held lawfully.

3. No bill of attainder or *ex post facto* law shall be passed.

Clause 3. A *bill of attainder* is a law that declares an individual guilty of a crime without a court trial. An *ex post facto* law makes an act a crime after the act has been committed.

4. [No capitation or other direct tax shall be laid, unless in proportion to the census herein before directed to be taken.]

Clause 4. Congress must allocate direct taxes among the states according to their populations. This provision was included to keep Congress from abolishing slavery by taxing slaves. The 16th Amendment (1913) makes it possible for Congress to levy a tax on individual incomes without regard to state population.

5. No tax or duty shall be laid on articles exported from any state.

Clause 5. Southern delegates to the Constitutional Convention opposed a tax on exports because they exported goods, such as tobacco and cotton, to Europe. The Constitution permitted Congress to tax imports for revenue, but not exports.

6. No preference shall be given any regulation of commerce or revenue to the ports of one state over those of another; nor shall vessels bound to, or from, one state, be obliged to enter, clear, or pay duties in another.

Clause 6. No port in any state is to have preference over any other. Ships going from state to state may not be taxed by Congress.

7. No money shall be drawn from the Treasury, but in consequence of appropriations made by law; and a regular statement and account of the receipts and expenditures of all public money shall be published from time to time.

8. No title of nobility shall be granted by the United States; and no person holding any office of profit or trust under them, shall, without the consent of the Congress, accept of any present, emolument, office, or title, of any kind whatever, from any king, prince, or foreign state.

Section 10. Powers Denied to the States

1. No state shall enter into any treaty, alliance, or confederation; grant letters of marque and reprisal; coin money; emit bills of credit; make anything but gold and silver coin a tender in payment of debts; pass any bill of attainder, *ex post facto* law, or law impairing the obligation of contracts, or grant any title of nobility.

2. No state shall, without the consent of the Congress, lay any imposts or duties on imports or exports, except what may be absolutely necessary for executing its inspection laws; and the net produce of all duties and imposts, laid by any state on imports or exports, shall be for the use of the Treasury of the United States; and all such laws shall be subject to the revision and control of the Congress.

3. No states shall, without the consent of Congress, lay any duty of tonnage, keep troops, or ships of war in time of peace, enter into any agreement or compact with another state, or with a foreign power, or engage in war, unless actually invaded, or in such imminent danger as will not admit of delay.

Article 2. The Executive Branch

Section 1. President and Vice-President

1. Term of Office. The executive power shall be vested in a President of the United States of America. He shall hold his office during

Clause 7. Only Congress can grant permission for money to be spent from the Treasury. This provision permits Congress to limit the power of the President by controlling the amount of money to be spent to run the executive branch of government.

Clause 8. This clause prohibits the establishment of a noble class and discourages bribery of American officials by foreign governments.

Clause 1. The clauses in this section limit the powers of the states. Most of these limitations stemmed from complaints the nationalists had made against the states during the Confederation period. The prohibition of laws "impairing the obligations of contracts" was intended to prevent the kind of relief laws the states had passed during the hard times of the 1780's (the time of Shays' Rebellion). These laws protected debtors against lawsuits. A debt or other obligation was a contract, and a state could not interfere with it.

Clause 2. States cannot interfere with commerce by taxing goods, although they may charge fees for inspecting such goods. Any such inspection fee must be paid into the Treasury of the United States. Also, all tariff revenue goes to the national government and not to the states.

the term of four years, and together with the Vice-President, chosen for the same term, be elected as follows:

2. Electoral System. Each state shall appoint, in such manner as the legislature thereof may direct, a number of electors, equal to the whole number of Senators and Representatives to which the state may be entitled in the Congress; but no Senator or Representative, or person holding an office of trust or profit under the United States, shall be appointed an elector.

3. Former Method of the Electoral System. [The electors shall meet in their respective states, and vote by ballot for two persons, of whom one at least shall not be an inhabitant of the same state with themselves. And they shall make a list of all the persons voted for, and of the number of votes for each; which list they shall sign and certify, and transmit sealed to the seat of the government of the United States, directed to the president of the Senate. The president of the Senate shall, in the presence of the Senate and House of Representatives, open all the certificates, and the votes shall then be counted. The person having the greatest number of votes shall be the President, if such number be a majority of the whole number of electors appointed; and if there be more than one who have such majority, and have an equal number of votes, then the House of Representatives shall immediately choose by ballot one of them for President; and if no person have a majority, then from the five highest on the list the said House shall in like manner choose the President. But in choosing the President the votes shall be taken by states, the representation from each state having one vote. A quorum for this purpose shall consist of a member or members from two-thirds of the states, and a majority of all the states shall be necessary to a choice. In every case, after the choice of the President, the person having the greatest number of votes of the electors shall be the Vice-President. But if there should remain two or more who have equal votes, the Senate shall choose from them by ballot the Vice-President.]

4. Time of Elections. The Congress may determine the time of choosing the electors, and

Clauses 2 and 3. The framers of the Constitution did not want the President to be chosen directly by the people. They thought the voters would not become familiar with the qualifications of leaders living in distant states. Therefore they devised an electoral college. The electors, it was hoped, would be prominent individuals acquainted with leaders in other states. They would thus be able to make a wise choice for President. Originally, the state legislatures chose the electors, but since 1828 they have been nominated by the political parties and elected by the people. The electors from all the states make up the electoral college. Each state has as many electors as it has senators and representatives.

This system provided that each elector vote for two candidates, with the person receiving the largest number of votes (provided it was a majority) becoming President and the one who was runner-up becoming Vice-President. In 1800 the two top candidates tied, making it necessary for the House to choose the President. The 12th Amendment (1804) was passed to prevent a situation of this kind.

Clause 4. Elections for President are held on the first Tuesday after the first Monday in November. The electors cast

the day on which they shall give their votes; which day shall be the same throughout the United States.

5. Qualifications for President. No person except a natural-born citizen [or a citizen of the United States, at the time of the adoption of this Constitution], shall be eligible to the office of the President; neither shall any person be eligible to that office who shall not have attained to the age of thirty-five years, and been fourteen years a resident within the United States.

6. Filling Vacancies. In the case of the removal of the President from office, or of his death, resignation, or inability to discharge the powers and duties of the said office, the same shall devolve on the Vice-President, and the Congress may by law provide for the case of removal, death, resignation, or inability, both of the President and Vice-President, declaring what officer shall then act as President, and such officer shall act accordingly, until the disability be removed, or a President shall be elected.

7. Salary. The President shall, at stated times, receive for his services, a compensation, which shall neither be increased nor diminished during the period for which he shall have been elected, and he shall not receive within that period any other emolument from the United States, or any of them.

8. Oath of Office. Before he enter on the execution of his office, he shall take the following oath or affirmation:—"I do solemnly swear (or affirm) that I will faithfully execute the office of President of the United States, and will to the best of my ability, preserve, protect, and defend the Constitution of the United States."

Section 2.   Powers of the President
1. Military Powers. The President shall be Commander in Chief of the Army and Navy of the United States, and of the militia of the several states, when called into the actual service of the United States; he may require the opinion in writing, of the principal officer in each of the executive departments, upon any subject relating to the duties of their respective offices, and

their votes on the first Monday after the second Wednesday in December.

Clause 6.   If the presidency becomes vacant, then the Vice-President takes the office. Congress may decide by law who will become President when neither the President nor the Vice-President is able to serve. In the present succession law, the Speaker of the House is next in line, followed by the President pro tempore of the Senate. The 25th Amendment (1967) deals with the inability of Presidents to discharge their duties.

Clause 1.   The President, who cannot be a member of the military, heads the armed forces. This clause places the armed forces under civilian control. The President can ask the heads of executive departments for written opinions about matters related to their departments. This clause provides the constitutional basis for the cabinet.

he shall have power to grant reprieves and pardons for offenses against the United States, except in cases of impeachment.

2. Treaties and Appointments. He shall have power, by and with the advice and consent of the Senate, to make treaties, provided two-thirds of the Senators present concur; and he shall nominate, and by and with the advice and consent of the Senate, shall appoint ambassadors, other public ministers and consuls, judges of the Supreme Court, and all other officers of the United States, whose appointments are not herein otherwise provided for, and which shall be established by law; but the Congress may by law vest the appointment of such inferior officers, as they think proper, in the President alone, in the courts of law, or in the heads of departments.

3. Filling Vacancies. The President shall have power to fill up all vacancies that may happen during the recess of the Senate, by granting commissions which shall expire at the end of their next session.

Section 3.   Duties of the President
He shall from time to time give to the Congress information of the state of the Union, and recommend to their consideration such measures as he shall judge necessary and expedient; he may, on extraordinary occasions, convene both houses, or either of them, and in case of disagreement between them, with respect to the time of adjournment, he may adjourn them to such time as he shall think proper; he shall receive ambassadors and other public ministers; he shall take care that the laws be faithfully executed, and shall commission all the officers of the United States.

Section 4.   Impeachment
The President, Vice-President, and all civil officers of the United States, shall be removed from office on impeachment for, and conviction of, treason, bribery, or other high crimes and misdemeanors.

Clause 2.   The President can make treaties with foreign countries, but they must be approved by two thirds of those present at a session of the Senate. Note that this is a power given to the Senate but not to the House and is a part of the checks and balances system.

The Senate must also approve the appointment of American representatives abroad, judges of the Supreme Court, and any other government official not provided for in the Constitution. However, Congress may make laws allowing the President, the courts, or heads of departments to appoint minor government officials.

Clause 3.   If vacancies occur in appointive federal offices when the Senate is not in session, the President may make temporary appointments.

Section 3.   The President must give Congress information about the condition of the country. It has become customary for the President to deliver a "State of the Union" message to Congress every January. If the need arises, the President may call either or both houses of Congress into special session. The President has the power to end a session of Congress if the two houses cannot agree on an adjournment date. The President is to receive foreign representatives, see that the laws of the federal government are carried out, and commission all officers of the armed forces.

Section 4.   (See annotation for Article 1, Section 2, Clause 5, and Section 3, Clauses 6 and 7.)

Article 3. The Judicial Branch

Section 1. Federal Courts

The judicial power of the United States shall be vested in one Supreme Court, and in such inferior courts as the Congress may from time to time ordain and establish. The judges, both of the Supreme and inferior courts, shall hold their offices during good behavior, and shall, at stated times, receive for their services a compensation, which shall not be diminished during their continuance in office.

Section 2. Jurisdiction of Federal Courts

1. General Jurisdiction. The judicial power shall extend to all cases, in law and equity, arising under this Constitution, the laws of the United States, and treaties made or which shall be made, under their authority; to all cases affecting ambassadors, other public ministers and consuls; to all cases of admiralty and maritime jurisdiction; to controversies to which the United States shall be a party; to controversies between two or more states; [between a state and citizens of another state;] between citizens of the same state claiming lands under grants of different states, and between a state or the citizens thereof, and foreign states, citizens, or subjects.

2. Supreme Court. In all cases affecting ambassadors, other public ministers and consuls, and those in which a state shall be a party, the Supreme Court shall have original jurisdiction. In all the other cases before mentioned, the Supreme Court shall have appellate jurisdiction, both as to law and fact, with such exceptions, and under such regulations as the Congress shall make.

3. Conduct of Trials. The trial of all crimes, except in cases of impeachment, shall be by jury; and such trial shall be held in the state where the said crimes shall have been committed; but when not committed within any state,

Section 1. The framers of the Constitution sought to control the power of the federal government with a system of checks and balances. Each branch of government—legislative, executive, and judicial—has certain checks against the other two. The President can veto acts of Congress, but Congress can override vetoes. In particular, the Senate must approve the President's appointments and consent to the President's treaties. The judiciary is an extremely important part of this system of balanced government.

Section 1 authorizes a Supreme Court and such lower courts as Congress shall establish. Both the President and Congress have checks on the courts. Congress determines the number of judges on the Supreme Court and creates by law all other courts. The President, with the consent of the Senate, appoints all federal judges. Federal judges hold office for life and may be removed only by impeachment.

Clause 1. Over the years the courts have defined their jurisdiction and established some checks of their own. In 1803 Supreme Court Chief Justice John Marshall asserted the power of the Court to determine the constitutionality of acts of Congress. If the Court finds a law unconstitutional, it is of no effect. Through Marshall's ruling, the Court made itself the interpreter of the Constitution. The Supreme Court has several times declared that the President is "under the law" as interpreted by the Court. Only once was there the threat of an open confrontation. In 1952 President Truman, acting in the emergency of the Korean War, seized the nation's steel mills. The Supreme Court, declaring that he had exceeded his constitutional powers, ordered him to return them to their owners. He did.

Clause 2. "Original jurisdiction" refers to the right to try a case before any other court hears it. Actually, very few cases come directly to the Supreme Court. Most federal court cases begin in the district courts. They can be appealed to the circuit courts and may finally be carried up to the Supreme Court. "Appellate jurisdiction" refers to the right to review cases appealed from lower courts. Most cases reaching the Supreme Court are taken to it on appeal. The Supreme Court has original jurisdiction in cases involving foreign representatives or in cases involving disputes between states. Congress determines appellate jurisdiction of the Supreme Court.

Clause 3. Except for impeachment cases, anyone accused of a federal crime has the right to a trial by jury. The trial must be held in the state where the crime was committed.

On July 23, 1788, a parade was held in lower Manhattan in celebration of the Constitution's ratification. The "federal ship," named in Hamilton's honor, was pulled along this New York street "with floating sheets and full sails."

the trial shall be at such place or places as the Congress may by law have directed.

Section 3. Treason

1. Definition. Treason against the United States shall consist only in levying war against them, or in adhering to their enemies, giving them aid and comfort. No person shall be convicted of treason unless on the testimony of two witnesses to the same overt act, or on confession in open court.

Clause 1. Treason is the only crime defined by the Constitution. Notice how strict the requirements are—there must be two witnesses to the same overt (open) act. The framers did not want anyone tried for treason merely for criticizing the government.

2. Punishment. The Congress shall have power to declare the punishment of treason, but no attainder of treason shall work corruption of blood or forfeiture except during the life of the person attained.

Clause 2. Congress has the power to fix the punishment for treason. But the families and descendants of a person found guilty of treason cannot be punished for his or her crime.

Article 4. Relations Among States

Section 1. Official Acts
Full faith and credit shall be given in each state to the public acts, records, and judicial proceedings of every other state. And the Congress may by general laws prescribe the manner in which such acts, records, and proceedings shall be proved, and the effect thereof.

Section 1. Each state must respect the laws, records, and court decisions of other states. If this were not the case, a person might move to another state to avoid legal punishment imposed by another state. The "full faith and credit" clause avoids much of the confusion arising from different state regulations.

Section 2. Privileges of Citizens
1. Privileges. The citizens of each state shall be entitled to all privileges and immunities of citizens in the several states.

Clause 1. This clause gives a person moving into a state the same rights the state gives to its own citizens. The state may still require a person to meet its own residency requirements for voting in elections and holding state office.

2. Extradition. A person charged in any state with treason, felony, or other crime, who shall flee from justice, and be found in another state, shall on demand of the executive authority of the state from which he fled, be delivered up, to be removed to the state having jurisdiction of the crime.

Clause 2. If a person charged with a crime flees to another state, the governor of the state where the crime was committed may request that he or she be returned. Sending back such persons for trial is called *extradition*. In the vast majority of cases, the return is automatic, but in a very few cases state governors have refused to return the fugitives.

3. Fugitive Slaves. [No person held in service or labor in one state, under the laws thereof, escaping into another, shall in consequence of any law or regulation therein, be discharged from such service or labor, but shall be delivered up on claim of the party to whom such service or labor may be due.]

Clause 3. This clause provided the constitutional basis for slave owners to have their escaped slaves returned to them. The 13th Amendment (1865) ended slavery, making this clause obsolete.

Section 3. New States and Territories
1. Admission of New States. New states may be admitted by the Congress into this Union; but no new state shall be formed or erected within the jurisdiction of any other state; nor any state be formed by the junction of two or more states, or parts of states, without the consent of the legislatures of the states concerned as well as of the Congress.

Clause 1. The Constitution specifically gave Congress power to govern the western territories. It can admit new states to the Union but cannot subdivide states without their consent. Subdivision has happened only three times. Kentucky was separated from Virginia in 1792. Maine was split off from Massachusetts in 1820. And during the Civil War (1863), West Virginia separated from Virginia and joined the northern Union.

2. Powers of Congress over Territories and Other Property. The Congress shall have power to dispose of and make all needful rules and regulations respecting the territory or other property belonging to the United States; and nothing in this Constitution shall be so construed as to prejudice any claims of the United States, or of any particular state.

Clause 2. Congress may govern and make regulations for the territories and properties of the United States. "Territories" here refers to lands not under the control of any state.

Section 4. Guarantees to the States

The United States shall guarantee to every state in this Union a republican form of government, and shall protect each of them against invasion; and on application of the legislature or of the executive (when the legislature cannot be convened) against domestic violence.

Section 4. In practice, Congress determines whether a state has a republican form of government. The Constitution also requires the federal government to protect a state against invasion and, upon request of the proper state authorities, to protect it against rioting and violence. Sometimes Presidents have ordered federal intervention without request from states when federal laws were being violated.

Article 5. Methods of Amendment

The Congress, whenever two-thirds of both houses shall deem it necessary, shall propose amendments to this Constitution, or, on the application of the legislatures of two-thirds of the several states, shall call a convention for proposing amendments, which, in either case, shall be valid to all intents and purposes, as part of this Constitution, when ratified by the legislatures of three-fourths of the several states, or by conventions in three-fourths thereof, as the one or the other mode of ratification may be proposed by the Congress; provided that [no amendments which may be made prior to the year 1808 shall in any manner affect the first and fourth clauses in the Ninth Section of the First Article; and that] no state, without its consent, shall be deprived of its equal suffrage in the Senate.

Article 5. The framers of the Constitution recognized that later generations would need to make some changes in the Constitution. However, they wanted to make the process of change difficult so that the Constitution would not be battered by every popular trend. According to Article 5, Congress can propose an amendment by a two thirds vote of both houses. Or, if two thirds of the state legislatures request it, Congress calls a convention to propose an amendment. So far, all amendments have been proposed by Congress. An amendment must be approved by three fourths of the state legislatures or by conventions in three fourths of the states.

Considering the enormous changes in American society, there have been remarkably few amendments to the Constitution. The first ten (known as the Bill of Rights) were approved within two years, but there were only two more amendments before the Civil War. There has been a total of 26 amendments.

Article 6. General Provisions

1. Public Debts. All debts contracted and engagements entered into, before the adoption of this Constitution, shall be as valid against the United States under this Constitution, as under the Confederation.

Clause 1. All debts and treaties made under the Articles of Confederation were recognized by the United States. This action was favored by Alexander Hamilton and was one of several steps taken by Congress to establish the credit of the new government.

2. The Supreme Law. This Constitution, and the laws of the United States which shall be made in pursuance thereof, and all treaties made, or which shall be made, under the authority of the United States, shall be the supreme law of the land; and the judges in every state shall be bound thereby, anything in the constitution or laws of any state to the contrary notwithstanding.

Clause 2. This clause is the basic, constitutional statement of national authority. It makes the Constitution and federal laws, rather than state laws, supreme. Many years—even a Civil War—intervened before the precise relationship between the federal government and the states was worked out.

3. Oaths of Office. The Senators and Representatives before mentioned, and the members of the several state legislatures, and all executive

Clause 3. All the officials listed must pledge themselves to support the Constitution. But such a pledge, or oath, cannot include any religious test or requirement that a person be-

and judicial officers, both of the United States and of the several states, shall be bound by oath or affirmation, to support this Constitution; but no religious test shall ever be required as a qualification to any office or public trust under the United States.

Article 7. Ratification

The ratification of the convention of nine states shall be sufficient for the establishment of the Constitution between the states so ratifying the same.

DONE in Convention by the unanimous consent of the States present the seventeenth day of September in the year of our Lord one thousand seven hundred and eight-seven and of the independence of the United States of America the twelfth. In witness whereof we have hereunto subscribed our names,
G. Washington—President and deputy from Virginia

long to a particular religious faith. This provision results from the principle of separation of church and state in the United States.

Article 7. The final article sets up the process of ratification. The framers knew they had to submit their document for popular approval. But they wished to avoid the state legislatures, which might resent the powers of the federal government. As a result, they provided for specially elected ratifying conventions, one in each state. And when nine states approved, the Constitution would be considered in effect. Of the 55 people who attended the Constitutional Convention in the summer of 1787, 39 signed the Constitution.

NEW HAMPSHIRE
John Langdon
Nicholas Gilman

NEW YORK
Alexander Hamilton

DELAWARE
George Read
Gunning Bedford
John Dickinson
Richard Bassett
Jacob Broom

NORTH CAROLINA
William Blount
Richard Dobbs Spaight
Hugh Williamson

MASSACHUSETTS
Nathaniel Gorham
Rufus King

NEW JERSEY
William Livingston
David Brearley
William Paterson
Jonathan Dayton

MARYLAND
James McHenry
Daniel of St. Thomas Jenifer
Daniel Carroll

SOUTH CAROLINA
John Rutledge
Charles Cotesworth Pinckney
Charles Pinckney
Pierce Butler

CONNECTICUT
William Samuel Johnson
Roger Sherman

PENNSYLVANIA
Benjamin Franklin
Thomas Mifflin
Robert Morris
George Clymer
Thomas FitzSimons
Jared Ingersoll
James Wilson
Gouverneur Morris

VIRGINIA
John Blair
James Madison

GEORGIA
William Few
Abraham Baldwin

Amendments to the Constitution

(The first ten amendments constitute the Bill of Rights. They became an official part of the Constitution in 1791. They limit the powers of the federal government but not the powers of the states.)

Amendment 1. Freedom of Religion, Speech, Press, Assembly, and Petition (1791)

Congress shall make no law respecting an establishment of religion, or prohibiting the free exercise thereof; or abridging the freedom of speech, or of the press; or the right of the people peaceably to assemble, and to petition the government for a redress of grievances.

Amendment 1. This amendment guarantees to Americans the most essential freedoms. Freedom of religion guarantees the right to worship as one chooses without interference from Congress. The Supreme Court has interpreted this amendment as a guarantee of the separation of church and state. Freedoms of speech and press are limited only when they involve slander and libel (false and malicious statements) or statements that might be injurious to the general welfare of the nation. The First Amendment also entitles the people to hold meetings and to request the government to respond to their grievances.

Amendment 2. Right to Bear Arms (1791)

A well-regulated militia, being necessary to the security of a free state, the right of the people to keep and bear arms shall not be infringed.

Amendment 2. The states have the right to maintain armed militias for their protection. However, the rights of private citizens to own guns can be, and are, regulated by federal and state legislation.

Amendment 3. Housing of Troops (1791)

No soldier shall, in time of peace, be quartered in any house, without the consent of the owner; nor in time of war, but in a manner to be prescribed by law.

Amendment 3. One source of bitter complaint in the colonies had been the British practice of housing their troops in American homes. The Third Amendment guarantees that no soldier will be quartered in a private residence during peacetime or in wartime without specific congressional authorization.

Amendment 4. Searches and Seizures (1791)

The right of the people to be secure in their persons, houses, papers, and effects, against unreasonable searches and seizures, shall not be violated; and no warrants shall issue but upon probable cause, supported by oath or affirmation, and particularly describing the place to be searched, and the persons or things to be seized.

Amendment 4. This amendment was proposed and ratified in response to the British writs of assistance—blanket search warrants permitting officers to search any house at any time. For an American home to be searched, a warrant must be issued by a judge, and it must state precisely what the official expects to find.

Amendment 5. Rights of Accused Persons (1791)

No person shall be held to answer for a capital, or otherwise infamous, crime, unless on a presentment or indictment of a grand jury, except in cases arising in the land or naval forces, or in the militia, when in actual service in time of war or public danger; nor shall any person be subject for the same offense to be twice put in jeopardy of life and limb; nor shall be compelled, in any criminal case, to be a witness against himself; nor be deprived of life, liberty, or property, without due process of law; nor shall private property be taken for public use, without just compensation.

Amendment 5. No person can be tried for a serious crime in a federal court unless indicted, or charged, by a grand jury. A grand jury is a group of 23 persons who hear in secret accusations against a person and then decide whether the person should be tried in court. "Twice put in jeopardy," or double jeopardy, means that no person can be tried twice in a federal court for the same crime.

People cannot be forced to give evidence against themselves that will help prove their guilt. This clause allows people on trial to refuse to answer questions, without paying penalties.

"Due process of law" has become quite complicated, but the framers wished to guarantee proper judicial procedures for a person accused of a crime (see Amendment 6). The taking of private property for public use is called the right of *eminent domain*. The government cannot take such property without giving owners fair prices for their property. The price is determined by a court.

Amendment 6. Right to a Speedy, Fair Trial (1791)

In all criminal prosecutions, the accused shall enjoy the right to a speedy and public trial, by an impartial jury of the state and district wherein the crime shall have been committed, which district shall have been previously ascertained by law, and to be informed of the nature and cause of the accusation; to be confronted with the witnesses against him; to have compulsory process for obtaining witnesses in his favor, and to have the assistance of counsel for his defense.

Amendment 6. This amendment defines the rights of the accused under due process of law. A person has the right to be informed of the charges against him or her and to a speedy and public trial by jury. Witnesses for and against the accused may be compelled to appear in court to give evidence. The accused is entitled to confront these witnesses and to be represented by a lawyer at all stages of the criminal proceedings.

Amendment 7. Civil Suits (1791)

In suits at common law, where the value in controversy shall exceed $20, the right of trial by jury shall be preserved, and no fact tried by a jury shall be otherwise reexamined in any court of the United States than according to the rules of the common law.

Amendment 7. If a sum of money larger than $20 is the object of dispute, the people involved may insist on a jury trial. However, in actual practice, cases do not reach federal courts unless much larger sums are involved.

Amendment 8. Bails, Fines, Punishments (1791)

Excessive bail shall not be required, nor excessive fines imposed, nor cruel and unusual punishments inflicted.

Amendment 8. The Eighth Amendment continues the enumeration of the rights of the accused. Before a criminal trial, the accused may remain free on payment to the court of a sum of money called bail. Bail is returned if the person appears for trial as ordered. Neither the amount of bail set nor the punishment inflicted should be excessive. The Supreme

Court has the final say in determining what is "excessive," "cruel," and "unusual" in any case.

Amendment 9. Powers Reserved to the People (1791)

The enumeration in the Constitution, of certain rights, shall not be construed to deny or disparage others retained by the people.

Amendment 9. This means that the rights listed in the Constitution are not necessarily the only rights that exist. Other rights shall not be denied to the people simply because they are not enumerated in the Constitution.

Amendment 10. Powers Reserved to the States (1791)

The powers not delegated to the United States by the Constitution, nor prohibited by it to the states, are reserved to the states respectively, or to the people.

Amendment 10. In the same vein as the previous amendment, the Tenth Amendment stipulates that those powers not given to the federal government are reserved to the states or to the people.

Amendment 11. Suits Against States (1798)

The judicial power of the United States shall not be construed to extend to any suit in law or equity, commenced or prosecuted against one of the United States, by citizens of another state, or by citizens or subjects of any foreign state.

Amendment 11. A state cannot be sued in any court other than the courts of the state. This amendment overruled a Supreme Court decision (*Chisholm* v. *Georgia,* 1793) that allowed two citizens of South Carolina to sue Georgia in a federal court.

Amendment 12. Electing the President and Vice-President (1804)

The electors shall meet in their respective states, and vote by ballot for President and Vice-President, one of whom, at least, shall not be an inhabitant of the same state with themselves; they shall name in their ballots the person voted for as President, and in distinct ballots the person voted for as Vice-President, and they shall make distinct lists of all persons voted for as President, and of all persons voted for as Vice-President, and of the number of votes for each, which lists they shall sign and certify, and transmit, sealed, to the seat of government of the United States, directed to the President of the Senate; the President of the Senate shall, in the

Amendment 12. This amendment nullifies Article 2, Section 1, Clause 3. At first the electors voted for President and Vice-President without specifying which person they wanted for each office. After the election of 1796, in which the people elected a Federalist President and a Republican Vice-President, and the election of 1800, which was a tie, the 12th Amendment was passed to require each elector to cast two ballots—one for President, one for Vice-President. Electors are nominated by the political parties and elected by the people. Each state has as many electors as it has senators and representatives in Congress. The electors of the party with the most *popular votes*—that is, votes cast by the people of the state—get to cast all the state's electoral votes for the party's candidates. The electoral votes are counted by the President of the Senate in the presence of both houses of Congress. Each candidate for President and Vice-President must receive a majority of electoral votes to be elected.

Political parties are not mentioned in the Constitution—the framers considered them unnecessary as well as harmful to national unity. The 12th Amendment recognized the fact that

presence of the Senate and House of Representatives, open all the certificates and the votes shall then be counted; the person having the greatest number of votes for President shall be the President, if such number be a majority of the whole number of electors appointed; and if no person have such majority, then from the persons having the highest numbers not exceeding three on the list of those voted for as President, the House of Representatives shall choose immediately, by ballot, the President. But in choosing the President, the votes shall be taken by states, the representation from each state having one vote; a quorum for this purpose shall consist of a member or members from two-thirds of the states, and a majority of all the states shall be necessary to a choice. [And if the House of Representatives shall not choose a President whenever the right of choice shall devolve upon them, before the fourth day of March next following, then the Vice-President shall act as President, as in the case of the death or other constitutional disability of the President.] The person having the greatest number of votes as Vice-President, shall be the Vice-President, if such number be a majority of the whole number of electors appointed, and if no person have a majority, then, from the two highest numbers on the list, the Senate shall choose the Vice-President; a quorum for the purpose shall consist of two-thirds of the whole number of Senators, and a majority of the whole number shall be necessary to a choice. But no person constitutionally ineligible to the office of President shall be eligible to that of Vice-President of the United States.

political parties had developed since the Constitution was ratified.

Amendment 13. Abolition of Slavery (1865)

Section 1. Neither slavery nor involuntary servitude, except as a punishment for crime whereof the party shall have been duly convicted, shall exist within the United States, or any place subject to their jurisdiction.

Section 2. Congress shall have power to enforce this article by appropriate legislation.

Amendment 13. The 13th, 14th, and 15th Amendments were passed after the Civil War. The 13th Amendment abolished slavery and gave Congress the right to enforce the law.

Amendment 14. Citizenship (1868)

Section 1. Citizenship Defined. All persons born or naturalized in the United States and subject to the jurisdiction thereof, are citizens of the United States and of the state wherein they reside. No state shall make or enforce any law which shall abridge the privileges or immunities of citizens of the United States; nor shall any state deprive any person of life, liberty, or property, without due process of law; nor deny to any person within its jurisdiction the equal protection of the laws.

Section 1. The main purpose of this amendment was to give Blacks equal rights. The first sentence, by definition, gives Black Americans citizenship. The second sentence prohibits the states from interfering with any citizen's right to equal protection under the law or with the right of due process of law. In recent years the Supreme Court has interpreted the phrase "due process" to mean that the states must respect the judicial rights guaranteed by the Bill of Rights.

Section 2. Apportionment of Representatives. Representatives shall be apportioned among the several states according to their respective numbers, counting the whole number of persons in each state, [excluding Indians not taxed]. But when the right to vote at any election for the choice of electors for President and Vice-President of the United States, Representatives in Congress, the executive and judicial officers of a state, or the members of the legislature thereof, is denied to any of the [male] inhabitants of such state, [being twenty-one years of age] and citizens of the United States, or in any way abridged, except for participation in rebellion, or other crime, the basis of representation therein shall be reduced in the proportion which the number of such [male] citizens shall bear to the whole number of [male] citizens [twenty-one years of age] in such state.

Section 2. This section nullified the three fifths compromise and declared every man over the age of 21 to be entitled to one vote. Notice that Indians and women were still excluded. This section provides for a punishment against any state preventing its eligible citizens from voting. This penalty has never been imposed.

Section 3. Disability for Engaging in Insurrection. No person shall be a Senator or Representative in Congress, or elector of President and Vice-President, or hold any office, civil or military, under the United States, or under any state, who, having previously taken an oath, as a member of Congress, or as an officer of the United States, or as a member of any state legislature, or as an executive or judicial officer of any state, to support the Constitution of the United States, shall have engaged in insurrection or rebellion against the same, or given aid or comfort to the enemies thereof. But Congress may, by vote of two-thirds of each house, remove such disability.

Section 3. This section was designed to punish the leaders of the Confederacy for breaking their oaths to support the Constitution. Many southern leaders were excluded from public office by this amendment, but by 1872 most were permitted to return to public life. In 1898 all the Confederates were pardoned.

Section 4. Public Debt. The validity of the public debt of the United States, authorized by law, including debts incurred for payment of pensions and bounties for services in suppressing insurrection or rebellion, shall not be questioned. But neither the United States nor any state shall assume or pay any debt or obligation incurred in aid of insurrection or rebellion against the United States [or any claim for the loss or emancipation of any slave]; but all such debts, obligations, and claims shall be held illegal and void.

Section 5. Enforcement. The Congress shall have power to enforce, by appropriate legislation, the provisions of this article.

Amendment 15. Right to Vote (1870)

Section 1. The right of citizens of the United States to vote shall not be denied or abridged by the United States or any state on account of race, color, or previous condition of servitude.

Section 2. The Congress shall have power to enforce this article by appropriate legislation.

Amendment 16. Income Tax (1913)

The Congress shall have power to lay and collect taxes on incomes, from whatever source derived, without apportionment among the several states, and without regard to any census or enumeration.

Amendment 17. Electing Senators (1913)

Section 1. Method of Election. The Senate of the United States shall be composed of two Senators from each state, elected by the people thereof, for six years; and each Senator shall have one vote. The electors in each state shall

Section 4. This section dealt a harsh financial blow to the South. The war debt of the Union was declared valid; the war debt of the Confederacy was declared void. There would be no reimbursement on Confederate bonds and no payment for the loss of slaves.

Amendment 15. This amendment prohibits federal or state governments from preventing any citizen from voting because of "race, color, or previous condition of servitude." It was designed to guarantee voting rights to Black American men.

Amendment 16. This amendment permits Congress to tax individual incomes without basing the tax on state populations. The income tax is now the major source of revenue for the federal government.

Amendment 17. This amendment gave the people the right to elect senators directly. Before this, senators were elected by the state legislatures. If a senator dies or leaves office during his or her term of office, the governor of the state can either order an election for a successor or appoint a temporary successor.

have the qualifications requisite for electors of the most numerous branch of the state legislatures.

Section 2. Filling Vacancies. When vacancies happen in the representation of any state in the Senate, the executive authority of such state shall issue writs of election to fill such vacancies: *Provided* that the legislatures of any state may empower the executive thereof to make temporary appointments until the people fill the vacancies by election as the legislature may direct.

[**Section 3. Not Retroactive.** This amendment shall not be so construed as to affect the election or term of any Senator chosen before it becomes valid as part of the Constitution.]

Amendment 18. Prohibition (1919)

[**Section 1.** After one year from the ratification of this article the manufacture, sale, or transportation of intoxicating liquors within, the importation thereof into, or the exportation thereof from, the United States and all territory subject to the jurisdiction thereof for beverage purposes is hereby prohibited.

Section 2. The Congress and the several states shall have concurrent power to enforce this article by appropriate legislation.

Section 3. This article shall be inoperative unless it shall have been ratified as an amendment to the Constitution by the legislatures of the several states, as provided in the Constitution, within seven years from the date of the submission hereof to the states by the Congress.]

Amendment 19. Women's Suffrage (1920)

Section 1. The right of citizens of the United States to vote shall not be denied or abridged by the United States or by any state on account of sex.

Section 2. Congress shall have power to enforce this article by appropriate legislation.

Amendment 18. This amendment forbade the manufacture, sale, and shipment of alcoholic beverages. It was repealed by the 21st Amendment.

Amendment 19. This amendment gave women the right to vote.

Amendment 20. "Lame Duck" Amendment (1933)

Section 1. Beginning of Terms. The terms of the President and Vice-President shall end at noon on the 20th day of January, and the terms of Senators and Representatives at noon on the 3rd day of January, of the years in which such terms would have ended if this article had not been ratified; and the terms of their successors shall then begin.

Section 2. Beginning of Congressional Sessions. The Congress shall assemble at least once in every year, and such meeting shall begin at noon on the third day of January, unless they shall by law appoint a different day.

Section 3. Presidential succession. If at the time fixed for the beginning of the term of the President, the President-elect shall have died, the Vice-President-elect shall become President. If a President shall not have been chosen before the time fixed for the beginning of his term, or if the President-elect shall have failed to qualify, then the Vice-President-elect shall act as President until a President shall have qualified; and the Congress may by law provide for the case wherein neither a President-elect nor a Vice-President-elect shall have qualified, declaring who shall then act as President, or the manner in which one who is to act shall be selected, and such person shall act accordingly until a President or Vice-President shall have qualified.

Section 4. Filling Presidential Vacancy. The Congress may by law provide for the case of the death of any of the persons from whom the House of Representatives may choose a President whenever the right of choice shall have devolved upon them, and for the case of the death of any of the persons from whom the Senate may choose a Vice-President whenever the right of choice shall have devolved upon them.

[**Section 5. Effective Date.** Sections 1 and 2 shall take effect on the 15th day of October following the ratification of this article.

Section 6. Time Limit for Ratification. This article shall be inoperative unless it shall

Amendment 20. This amendment moved the President's inaugural day from March 4 to January 20. Members of Congress take office on January 3 instead of the following December. The date of congressional sessions was also moved to January. Transportation and communication were so slow when the Constitution was written that it would have been almost impossible for officials elected in November to reach the capital in January. Hence newly elected representatives did not "sit" until the next congressional session began, 13 months later. The expression "lame duck" was used to refer to the defeated or retired officeholder still serving during the period between the election and the inauguration.

Section 3. This section provides for succession to the Presidency when a President-elect dies or fails to qualify.

have been ratified as an amendment to the Constitution by the legislatures of three-fourths of the several states within the seven years from the date of its submission.]

Amendment 21. Repeal of Prohibition (1933)

Section 1. The eighteenth article of amendment of the Constitution of the United States is hereby repealed.

Section 2. The transportation or importation into any state, territory, or possession of the United States for delivery or use therein of intoxicating liquors, in violation of the laws thereof, is hereby prohibited.

[**Section 3.** This article shall be inoperative unless it shall have been ratified as an amendment to the Constitution by conventions in the several states, as provided in the Constitution, within seven years from the date of the submission hereof to the states by the Congress.]

Amendment 21. This repealed the 18th Amendment.

Amendment 22. Two-Term Limit for Presidents (1951)

Section 1. No person shall be elected to the office of the President more than twice, and no person who has held the office of President, or acted as President, for more than two years of a term to which some other person was elected President shall be elected to the office of the President more than once. [But this Article shall not apply to any person holding the office of President when this Article was proposed by the Congress, and shall not prevent any person who may be holding the office of President, or acting as President, during the term within which this Article becomes operative from holding the office of President or acting as President during the remainder of such term.]

Amendment 22. This amendment was passed because many feared that President Franklin D. Roosevelt's four terms had set a dangerous precedent. Prior to his election to a third term in 1940, Presidents had followed the tradition of serving no more than two terms.

[**Section 2.** This Article shall be inoperative unless it shall have been ratified as an amendment to the Constitution by the legislatures of three-fourths of the several states within seven years from the date of its submission to the states by the Congress.]

Amendment 23. Presidential Electors for District of Columbia (1961)

Section 1. The District constituting the seat of Government of the United States shall appoint in such manner as the Congress may direct:

A number of electors of President and Vice-President equal to the whole number of Senators and Representatives in Congress to which the District would be entitled if it were a state, but in no event more than the least populous state; they shall be in addition to those appointed by the states, but they shall be considered, for the purposes of the election of President and Vice-President, to be electors appointed by a state; and they shall meet in the District and perform such duties as provided by the twelfth article of amendment.

Section 2. The Congress shall have power to enforce this article by appropriate legislation.

Amendment 23. This amendment gave the residents of Washington, D.C., three members in the electoral college and hence the right to vote for President and Vice-President.

Amendment 24. Poll Taxes (1964)

Section 1. The right of citizens of the United States to vote in any primary or other election for President or Vice-President, for electors for President or Vice-President, or for Senator or Representative in Congress, shall not be denied or abridged by the United States or any state by reason of failure to pay any poll tax or other tax.

Section 2. The Congress shall have the power to enforce this article by appropriate legislation.

Amendment 24. When this amendment was passed, five southern states used the poll tax as a means of discouraging Blacks from voting. This amendment applies only to national elections.

Amendment 25. Presidential Disability and Succession (1967)

1. In case of the removal of the President from office or his death or resignation, the Vice-President shall become President.

2. Whenever there is a vacancy in the office of the Vice-President, the President shall nominate a Vice-President who shall take the office upon confirmation by a majority vote of both houses of Congress.

3. Whenever the President transmits to the President pro tempore of the Senate and the Speaker of the House of Representatives his written declaration that he is unable to discharge the powers and duties of his office, and until he transmits to them a written declaration to the contrary, such powers and duties shall be discharged by the Vice-President as Acting President.

4. Whenever the Vice-President and a majority of either the principal officers of the executive departments or of such other body as Congress may by law provide, transmit to the President pro tempore of the Senate and the Speaker of the House of Representatives their written declaration that the President is unable to discharge the powers and duties of his office, the Vice-President shall immediately assume the powers and duties of the office as Acting President.

Thereafter, when the President transmits to the President pro tempore of the Senate and the Speaker of the House of Representatives his written declaration that no inability exists, he shall resume the powers and duties of his office unless the Vice-President and a majority of either the principal officers of the executive department or of such other body as Congress may by law provide, transmit within four days to the President pro tempore of the Senate and the Speaker of the House of Representatives their written declaration that the President is unable to discharge the powers and duties of his office. Thereupon Congress shall decide the issue, assembling within 48 hours for that purpose if not in session. If the Congress, within 21 days after receipt of the latter written declaration, or, if Congress is not in session, within 21 days after Congress is required to assemble, determines by two-thirds vote of both houses the President is

Amendment 25. This amendment clarifies Article 2, Section 1, Clause 6. The Vice-President becomes President when the President dies, resigns, or is removed from office. The new President then nominates a Vice-President, who must be approved by a majority of Congress. If a President is unable to perform the duties of the office, Congress must be informed of this fact in writing by the President or by the Vice-President and a majority of the cabinet. In this case, the Vice-President performs as acting President until the elected President is once again able to function.

This amendment was first used in a case in which Presidential disability was not a factor. In 1973 Vice-President Spiro T. Agnew resigned; President Richard M. Nixon filled the vacancy, according to Section 2 of this amendment, by naming Gerald R. Ford, a member of the House of Representatives, the Vice-President. Mr. Ford was approved by a majority of both houses of Congress. In 1974 Nixon became the first President to resign from office. Ford, in succeeding Nixon, became the first President not elected to that office or to the Vice-Presidency. To fill the Vice-Presidential vacancy, Ford appointed Nelson A. Rockefeller, who was then approved by a majority of both houses of Congress.

unable to discharge the powers and duties of his office, the Vice-President shall continue to discharge the same as Acting President; otherwise, the President shall assume the powers and duties of his office.

Amendment 26. Voting Age Lowered to 18 (1971)

Section 1. The right of citizens of the United States, who are 18 years of age or older, to vote shall not be denied or abridged by the United States or any state on account of age.

Section 2. The Congress shall have the power to enforce this article by appropriate legislation.

The Constitution was written at the Constitutional Convention in 1787. Delaware was the first and Rhode Island was the last of the original thirteen states to ratify the Constitution.

Amendment 26. This amendment lowered the minimum voting age to 18.

CHAPTER SUMMARY

3

The Constitution of the United States is the supreme law of the land. The Founders established the basic principles on which the government is based. They created a governmental structure and procedures that they believed would follow those principles. Representative government based on popular sovereignty, separation of powers with a system of checks and balances, and limited government are three basic principles of the government established in the Constitution of the United States.

The Constitution has proved to be a most flexible framework of government. It is capable of changing to meet the challenges of changing times. A formal amendment process is included in the original Constitution. This process has been used only 26 times in 200 years. Informal changes have occurred more frequently and have evolved gradually over the years. By allowing for flexibility in the Constitution, the founders set up a guideline for government that will be usable for many years to come.

REVIEW QUESTIONS

1. How have constitutional amendments been responses to historical circumstances?
2. Woodrow Wilson referred to the Supreme Court as a "constitutional convention in continuous session." What did he mean? Do you agree? Why or why not?
3. How has the system of checks and balances established in the Constitution fostered informal changes in the practical application of government?
4. Select one provision of the Constitution which illustrates one of the principles of the constitutional system. Why do you think this provision was included? Has it changed in its application since 1787? How was the change accomplished? (Was it a formal or informal change?)
5. How should the Constitution be further amended? What powers or practices do you think need alteration?

ACTIVITIES FOR REVIEW

activity 1   Create a wall chart illustrating the three basic principles underlying the government established by the Constitution: representative government based on popular sovereignty, separation of powers with a system of checks and balances, and limited government.

activity 2   Select one of the amendments to the Constitution and do research on the historical background that led to its passage. How did this particular amendment specifically relate to its historical period?

activity 3   Using current newspapers and periodicals, develop a bulletin board that illustrates the informal processes of amending the Constitution.

activity 4   Review recent new stories in which the Bill of Rights is at issue. Select one story that interests you. Do research on the story's background, and develop a judicial opinion on the issue based on your interpretation of the Bill of Rights.

political science DICTIONARY

limited government—government possessing only those powers specifically granted to it by the people in a constitution.   p. 40

popular sovereignty—government in which supreme power is held by the people.   p. 39

precedents—actions, decisions, or practices that may be used as guides for later actions, decisions, or practices.   p. 47

ratified—approved.   p. 42

veto power—the right of the President to reject a bill after Congress has approved it.   p. 40

4 *Federalism: Separated and Overlapping Powers*

You have already seen that division of power is characteristic of the American governmental structure. In this chapter you will see just what this phrase means.

First, you will see the meaning of divison of power. Then the division of power between the national government and the states will be outlined. You will read about the different rules for relations between the different states in a federal system. Finally, you will cover one of the more unique aspects of America's system—its ability to expand by the admission of new states.

CHAPTER PREVIEW

1. FEDERAL DIVISION OF POWERS
2. THE NATIONAL GOVERNMENT AND GUARANTEES TO THE STATES
3. RELATIONS BETWEEN THE STATES

1. FEDERAL DIVISION OF POWERS

The Federation. In a *federal system*, powers are permanently divided between a central government and a number of local governments. The United States, as a nation, is a *federation*. The individual states are not federations but are part of the larger federal unit.

One of the strongest characteristics of a federation, as opposed to other governmental systems, is that of allowing local units to assume power in local matters. In the United States, that basis is explicitly stated in the Tenth Amendment to the Constitution: "The powers not delegated to the United States by the Constitution, nor prohibited by it to the

The government's power to sell savings bonds is implied from its expressed power to coin and regulate money.

states, are reserved to the states respectively, or to the people." It is important to note that the powers of the United States as a whole are said to be *delegated*, or granted, to it by the people. Theoretically, the people could take back these powers if they wished. But this is unlikely to happen.

The Nature of the Government's Power. There are three kinds of delegated powers: *expressed powers, implied powers,* and *inherent powers. Expressed powers* are those that the Constitution actually describes. For example, an expressed power of the government is the power to coin money.

Implied powers are those that are not described by the Constitution in words but are suggested by powers that are described. The existence of implied powers is supported by Article I, Section 8, Clause 18, of the Constitution. This clause says that "Congress shall have the power . . . to make all laws which shall be necessary and proper for carrying into execution the foregoing powers, and all other powers vested by this Constitution in the Government of the United States, or in any department or officer thereof."

This clause is sometimes called the "elastic clause" because it is easily stretched to justify making new laws dealing with subjects covered by implied powers.

Inherent powers are those that the national government has just because it is the government. These powers are not expressed in the Constitution. It is assumed, however, that the writers of the Constitution meant the government to have these powers because they are necessary for a government to carry out its proper governmental functions. Inherent powers are usually inferred from expressed powers, and they are few in number. For example, the President's role as commander in chief is an expressed power. Based on this, he or she has the inherent power to send troops abroad to protect American lives and property.

The examination by customs officials of immigrants entering the United States at New York's Ellis Island exemplifies the inherent power of the national government.

The New York Times.

"All the News That's Fit to Print."

LATE CITY EDITION
Cloudy followed by clearing and colder today. Tomorrow fair and moderately cold.
Temperature Yesterday—Max. 44; Min. 25

Copyright 1941 by The New York Times Company

VOL. XCI. No. 30,638.   Entered as Second-Class Matter, Postoffice, New York, N.Y.   NEW YORK, TUESDAY, DECEMBER 9, 1941.   THREE CENTS NEW YORK CITY and Vicinity

U. S. DECLARES WAR, PACIFIC BATTLE WIDENS; MANILA AREA BOMBED; 1,500 DEAD IN HAWAII; HOSTILE PLANES SIGHTED AT SAN FRANCISCO

The power to declare war can only be exercised by Congress.

President Franklin D. Roosevelt asks Congress to declare war on Germany and Italy.

Our Declaration of War

Special to The New York Times.

WASHINGTON, Dec. 11—Following are the texts of the documents wherein the President asked a war declaration against Germany and Italy, and Congress acted:

The President's Message

To the Congress of the United States:

On the morning of Dec. 11 the Government of Germany, pursuing its course of world conquest, declared war against the United States.

The long-known and the long-expected has thus taken place. The forces endeavoring to enslave the entire world now are moving toward this hemisphere.

Never before has there been a greater challenge to life, liberty and civilization.

Delay invites great danger. Rapid and united effort by all of the peoples of the world who are determined to remain free will insure a world victory of the forces of justice and of righteousness over the forces of savagery and of barbarism.

Italy also has declared war against the United States.

I therefore request the Congress to recognize a state of war between the United States and Germany, and between the United States and Italy.

FRANKLIN D. ROOSEVELT.

The War Resolution

Declaring that a state of war exists between the Government of Germany and the government and the people of the United States and making provision to prosecute the same.

Whereas the Government of Germany has formally declared war against the government and the people of the United States of America:

Therefore, be it

Resolved by the Senate and House of Representatives of the United States of America in Congress assembled, that the state of war between the United States and the Government of Germany which has thus been thrust upon the United States is hereby formally declared; and the President is hereby authorized and directed to employ the entire naval and military forces of the United States and the resources of the government to carry on war against the Government of Germany; and, to bring the conflict to a successful termination, all of the resources of the country are hereby pledged by the Congress of the United States.

(An identic resolution regarding Italy was adopted)

QUOTES from famous people

"There is nothing stable but Heaven and the Constitution."

James Buchanan

Limitations on National Power. Each of these three powers has its limitations. There are expressed limitations on national power. The national government may not levy duties on exports, and it may not grant titles of nobility. Inherent limitations on national power exist in order to protect the existence of the federal system. They limit the national government's actions in order to safeguard the rights of the states.

State Powers. Under the federal system, vast areas of the nation's social and economic life are controlled by the states. They can decide what someone can drink or smoke, and where they can drink or smoke it. They can decide at what age people can marry, what they are taught, how that teaching is to be paid for, and how they can form a corporation.

Before the Fourteenth Amendment extended the guarantees of the Bill of Rights to the states, some powers of the states were even greater. For instance, the Constitution forbade the establishment of a national religion, but there was no such restriction on state

Demonstrators in the 1950's here demand abolition of the poll tax system, which prevented Blacks who could not pay from participating in elections.

religions. As a result, the Congregational Church was the state church of both Massachusetts and Connecticut until the mid-nineteenth century.

The states had the power to impose voting restrictions of all kinds. The poll tax was not abolished by the national government until 1964. Even today, various methods of voting and various ways of registering to vote are used in the states.

Limitations on State Power. The Constitution expressly limits the powers of the states in a number of ways. They are not allowed to coin or print money, make alliances with other states, grant titles of nobility, nor deprive their citizens of life, liberty, or property without due process of law.

There are also implied and inherent limitations on the powers of the states. They cannot tax the operations of the national government for the same reason that the national government cannot tax their operations. They cannot regulate interstate commerce because that would interfere with the power of the national government to regulate such commerce.

The states also have limited their own power by their state constitutions. Some state constitutions contain various versions of the guarantees of the Bill of Rights. This serves to limit powers further.

Concurrent Powers. Most of the powers of the national government are *exclusive*, which means that they can be exercised *only* by the national government. Some of the powers of the nation and the states, how-

WHO HAS THE POWER?	State Government	National Government
1. Power to enforce laws?	X	X
2. Power to declare war & make peace?		X
3. Power to decide at what age you can marry?	X	
4. Power to coin & issue money?		X
5. Power to grant titles of nobility?		
6. Power to regulate interstate commerce?		X
7. Power to collect an import tax?		X
8. Power to deprive citizens of life, liberty, or property without due process of the law?		
9. Power to establish a national religion?		
10. Power to establish lower courts?	X	X

ever, are *concurrent*, which means that they can be exercised by both the national and the state government. *Concurrent powers* are those that are not expressly or inherently denied to either the national or the state government. They include the power of taxation, the powers of criminal law, and the power to take private property for public use.

"Umpiring" the System. The courts, particularly the Supreme Court, have the job of "umpiring" the many undefined areas of the American legal system. This means that they serve as arbitrators. One of the most important tasks of the Supreme Court is to settle conflicts that arise between the states and the national government.

The basic guidelines for arbitrating such disputes are established in the Constitution. The "supremacy clause" in Article VI, Section 2, makes the Constitution the highest form of law. All laws and treaties are subject to the provisions of the Constitution. Thus a state law cannot conflict with the Constitution, with national law, or with a treaty. The Constitution, national law, and treaties take precedence over state constitutions. They are also above the individual laws of the various states.

QUOTES
from famous people

"The Government of the United States is one of delegated and limited powers, and it is by a strict adherence to the clearly granted powers and by abstaining from the exercise of doubtful or unauthorized implied powers that we have the only sure guaranty against the recurrence of those unfortunate collisions between the Federal and State authorities which have occasionally so much disturbed the harmony of our system and even threatened the perpetuity of our glorious Union."

James K. Polk

The key decisions of the Supreme Court in establishing this principle were made in two cases. In *Fletcher* v. *Peck* (1810), a Georgia land grant had been taken back by the state legislature. For the first time, the Supreme Court overturned a state law on the grounds that it violated the Constitution. In making its decision, it referred to the provision of Article 1, Section 10, Clause 1. This article prevents the states from "impairing the obligation of contracts."

In *McCulloch* v. *Maryland* (1819), an attempt was made by the state of Maryland to destroy the Baltimore branch of the Second Bank of the United States (established by Congress) by taxing its notes. McCulloch, the branch cashier, was convicted in Maryland for refusing to pay the tax and appealed to the Court. The Court ruled in his favor, resting its case on the supremacy clause of the Constitution. Chief Justice Marshall wrote that no state had the power "to retard, impede, burden, or in any manner control the operations of the constitutional laws enacted by Congress." Since then, the Court has overturned more than 800 other state laws.

section review

1. What is an inherent power?
2. Give two examples of expressed limitations on the states' powers.
3. Explain how the Supreme Court "umpires the system."

2. THE NATIONAL GOVERNMENT AND GUARANTEES TO THE STATES

Preservation of the States. The Constitution guarantees the geographic integrity of each state. Thus when a new state is to be created out of the territory of an existing state, the legislature of the existing state must agree (Article IV, Section 3, Clause 1). Three states were created in this way. Kentucky was

separated from Virginia in 1792. Maine was formed from the territory of Massachusetts in 1820. West Virginia broke away from Virginia and became a state in 1863.

Guarantee of a Republican Form of Government. Article 4, Section 4, of the Constitution guarantees every state the right to a "republican form of government." The Constitution does not define this form of government, nor have the courts ever defined it. But it is generally understood to mean a representative democracy.

This provision was tested only once in the nation's history—with regard to Dorr's Rebellion in Rhode Island (1842). At that time Rhode Island was the only state in the union still functioning under its prerevolutionary charter. This charter had given Rhode Island the most liberal government in the English colonies. After the creation of the Constitution, however, this charter gave the state the most conservative government in the new nation. For example, the right to vote was limited to larger property holders. The state government completely ignored requests for reform.

Finally, Thomas Dorr and his followers took matters into their own hands. They held their own elections, allowing all citizens to vote, proclaimed a new state constitution, and made Dorr governor of Rhode Island. When Dorr tried to put the new government into operation, the governor who held power under the old constitution appealed to President Tyler. Tyler threatened action against Dorr and his followers. The rebellion collapsed, and Dorr spent several years in jail. His revolution was not a complete failure, however. His opponents realized that there was still much discontent in the state. To prevent another uprising, they removed many of the limitations on voting.

In 1849 the Supreme Court had to rule on Tyler's decision in the Dorr Rebellion. In the case of *Luther* v. *Borden*, it ruled that the definition of "republican government" was actually a task for the President and Congress, not for the judicial branch. Thus they upheld Tyler's 1842 action in the Dorr incident.

Protection Against Invasion. The national government has the responsibility for protecting each state against invasion. This guarantee was necessary in order to get the states to give up their war-making powers. The national government pledged that an attack on one state would be seen as an attack on the whole nation.

Protection Against Domestic Violence. Article 4, Section 4, also states that on request of the legislature or the executive of a state, the national government must protect each state against violence within its own borders.

This provision had led to more controversy than any of the others. It was originally intended to put down uprisings such as Shays' Rebellion in Massachusetts. At first, the local militia had the responsibility for putting down such uprisings. But, in the case of Shays' Rebellion, even those who were in the militia were involved in the rebellion itself, so there was no one in the area to deal with the situation. The only alternative was to call in outside help.

Those who wrote the Constitution felt that, if states could not call in help from the outside, incidents such as Shays' Rebellion would tear the nation apart. In 1794, this constitutional guarantee was used in the Whiskey Rebellion—a massive national army was sent into western Pennsylvania to put down the uprising.

This guarantee was also used by Presidents Jackson, Taylor, and Lincoln against various forms of Southern dissent before the Civil War. In the late 1960's, it was used by President Johnson in three states—Michigan, Maryland, and Illinois—to put down riots. In these cases, action was taken at the request of the states involved. (Federal action to help states affected by natural disasters such as floods and tornados is also based on this provision.)

Presidents can and have acted against disturbances in a state against the wishes of the state leaders. The most important incident of this kind took place in 1894. Over the express objections of Illinois Governor John Peter Altgeld, President Cleveland sent federal troops to the Chicago rail yards to break the Pullman strike. In an 1896 case, the Supreme Court ruled that the action was justified because of the need to protect federal property, interstate commerce, and the mails.

The precedent set by this case was used in 1957 when President Eisenhower sent troops to Little Rock, Arkansas, to enforce school desegregation orders. It was also used by President Kennedy in 1962 and 1963 to protect Black students entering the University of Alabama and the University of Mississippi. In each case, the federal government took action against violence supported by the governors of the states involved.

Federal Aid to the States. Throughout history, the federal government has given aid to the states. Even under the Articles of Confederation (1785), Congress took such actions. For example, it directed that sections of public land in each township of the Northwest Territory be set aside for public schools.

Once the Constitution was adopted, federal intervention in the economy was justified under the "general welfare" clause (Article 1, Section 8, Clause 1). This clause gives Congress the power to "provide for the common defense and general welfare of the United States." The Morrill Land Grant Act of 1862 was passed under the authority of this provision. It formed the system of granting public lands for the construction of educational institutions such as state universities.

As the federal government grew larger in the twentieth century, such aid has generally

Federal troops from Fort Devens were sent to Massachusetts to aid state personnel during the worst storm disaster in that state's history.

taken the form of grants-in-aid. These grants are usually given for a specific purpose—highway construction, education, welfare, or urban renewal. The federal government now gives more than $80 billion a year to the states in this way.

Grants-in-aid are usually given on condition that the states getting them perform certain actions. For example, the states are required to set up certain agencies to administer the funds. They are forced to meet certain federal standards in order to receive the funds. They are required to *match* the grants with funds of their own. The states are able to accept or reject these grants as they choose. However, there is so much money available for these grants that the states find it politically difficult to refuse the grants.

Why are the states so inclined to accept the grants? First, since the money comes out of federal taxes, the states are already paying

for them, so they might as well get some of their own money back. Second, individual interest groups tend to think of federal money as "free" money.

The problem with these grants is that they allow the federal government to exercise authority in areas traditionally reserved to the states. Also, as a result of the "matching funds" requirement, states are often forced to spend money they don't have on programs they might not choose to have were it not for the federal funding.

In 1972 the Nixon administration tried to solve some of these spending problems with the General Revenue Sharing Act. The act was designed to help states and localities by giving them grants with no strings attached. Under this act one third of the federal aid goes to states and two thirds goes directly to counties and cities. The amounts involved in these grants are very large. About 12 percent of all federal aid to states and localities is distributed in this way.

Both types of aid—the grants with strings attached and those with no strings—have created a curious situation in the last 25 years. Nearly everyone speaks about the enormous growth of the federal government. Many believe the growth is too great, threatening the freedom of the states and the localities. Actually, the federal government is not growing as fast as people think it is. It is spending more money, but it is not employing more people. The real growth of government is taking place at state and local levels. Here, more and more government jobs are being created, more and more areas of life are coming under the supervision of the government, and more and more money is being spent.

Finally, it is important to note that aid does not go in one direction only. The states give aid to the federal government too. For example, federal elections and the naturalization of new citizens are both handled and paid for by the states rather than by the nation; yet each of these is a national, not a state, function.

section review

1. How does the national government protect the states against domestic violence?
2. What is the purpose of the "general welfare" clause in the Constitution?
3. Under what conditions does the federal government give grants-in-aid to the states?
4. Give two examples of how the states give aid to the federal government.

3. RELATIONS BETWEEN THE STATES

Agreements Among the States. In part, the Constitution began as an attempt to bring the quarrelsome states together under a common authority. To ensure the unity of the states, the Constitution says that no state can enter into a treaty, alliance, or confederation with another state. But it does give individual states the right to enter into **compacts** with each other and with foreign nations. This, however, can be done only with the permission of Congress.

Compacts are agreements.

The Supreme Court has interpreted this part of the Constitution. In doing so, it has ruled that the consent of Congress is not needed for compacts that do not "tend to increase the power of the states."

Until the early 1920's, the power to make compacts was rarely used. As late as 1900, only 19 compacts—all involving boundary disputes—had been approved by Congress. In 1921, New York and New Jersey agreed to create the Port of New York Authority. Its purpose was to manage and develop transportation facilities in the New York City area.

This compact set a precedent that changed the entire situation. The use of compacts grew considerably. There are now more than 200 such state compacts in existence. Most of them deal with the use of natural resources. The most extensive agreement is the Interstate Parole and Probation Compact, which involves all the states in a uniform system of supervising paroled criminals and people on probation. Other compacts cover such areas as regional economic development, pollution control, and civil defense.

Legal Separation. Each of the states is equal to all other states and separate from them in its powers. In addition, each state has jurisdiction only within its own boundaries. This jurisdiction can be given up by the state under certain circumstances. For instance, some states have so-called hot-pursuit agreements with neighboring states. These agreements were signed in order to make it possible for the police of one state to pursue fleeing suspects across state boundaries into another state. Without such agreements, suspected criminals would be safe once they had managed to get across the border into another state. When the police of one state catch a suspect in another state, however, they must turn him or her over to the local authorities.

Limitations on Separation. There are three important limitations on the separation of the states from each other's laws. These limitations are found in Article 4, Sections 1 and 2, of the Constitution. They are *full faith and credit, interstate rendition of criminals—*better known as *extradition—*and *privileges and immunities.*

Full Faith and Credit. According to the Constitution, "full faith and credit shall be given in each state to the public acts, records, and judicial proceedings of every other state." This means that a state must accept the laws, ordinances, licenses, records, deeds, contracts, and court decisions of other states. For example, one state is bound to honor a driver's license issued by another state. A contract legally made in one state is legally binding in another.

There are limitations on full faith and credit, however. First, it applies only to civil law and not to criminal law. This means that a state is not bound to enforce another state's criminal law. Second, not all states recognize child custody granted in other states.

Extradition. The Constitution says that a person charged with a crime in one state, who flees that state and is found in another state, shall be turned over to the state from which he or she fled, if the state's executive demands it. That person is then said to have been *extradited* from one state to another.

This is generally a routine matter. Sometimes, however, cases of extradition are more than routine. There have been a number of occasions in American history in which the governor of the state where the suspected criminal is found has refused to act. Usually, governors have done this for one of two reasons. First, the fugitive has become a respected citizen in his or her new home state. Second, the governor has questioned the fairness of the legal system in which the crime was committed.

In these cases, the Supreme Court has ruled that the word "shall" in the extradition clause of the Constitution is not an *imperative*, or order to act, but only a suggestion. If the governor of the second state decides not to extradite someone, then that is the end of the matter. The first state can do nothing about it.

Privileges and Immunities. In Article 4, Section 2, Clause 1, the Constitution states that the "citizens of each state shall be entitled to all privileges and immunities of citizens in the several states." This means that a state cannot discriminate *unreasonably* in favor of its own citizens. It still has the power and right to discriminate in their favor in a reasonable way.

Examples of reasonable discrimination include such things as residence requirements for voting, running for office, and practicing a profession like law, medicine, or dentistry in a state. They also include setting higher fees for out-of-staters in certain things like hunting and fishing licenses and requiring out-of-state students to pay higher charges in state colleges and universities.

Unreasonable discrimination would include such things as preventing someone from passing through or from residing in a state in pursuit of some lawful activity, limiting the rights of out-of-staters in state courts, limiting property rights, and limiting civil liberties. Corporations are not considered citizens, so a state may refuse to allow a corporation chartered in another state to operate within its boundries. But it may not interfere with interstate commerce.

Admission of New States to the Union. Only Congress has the right to admit new states to the Union. It has exercised this power 37 times, and the Union has grown from 13 to 50 states.

The states can be divided into the following seven groups on the basis of their road to statehood:

1. The 11 states that joined the Union and participated in the election of George Washington as the first President. These include Delaware, Pennsylvania, New Jersey, Georgia, Connecticut, Massachusetts, Maryland, South Carolina,

New Hampshire, Virginia, and New York.

2. The two states that were part of the 13 original English colonies but joined the Union after the Constitution had been ratified. Their admission to the Union required no congressional action. These are North Carolina and Rhode Island.

3. The three states that were formed from lands originally held by other states. The states that originally held these lands gave up their permission powers to the Confederation government before 1789. They are Vermont, Kentucky, and Tennessee.

4. The two states that were formed out of other states with the permission of the original states. These are Maine and West Virginia.

5. California, which was ceded to the United States by Mexico and became a state two years later.

6. Texas, which was an independent republic before it was admitted to the Union by a treaty. Since Texas was admitted by a treaty, it still has the right to break itself into as many as five smaller states whenever it chooses.

7. The 30 other states, all of which were territories before being admitted as states. The time during which these states were territories ranged from 2 years for Alabama to 62 years for New Mexico.

The following procedure for admission to the Union was used by these states. First, they applied to Congress for admission—sometimes several times over a number of years. This application is called a *petition*. When Congress accepted the petition, it passed an *enabling act*. This act directed the territory to formulate a constitution. When the constitution was approved by the people of the territory, Congress considered the matter again. If it still wished to admit the territory, it passed an *act of admission*. The territory then became a state. This procedure enabled Congress to make sure a state came into the Union with a state constitution that Congress had approved.

The method followed for admitting states led to great trouble during the 40 years before the outbreak of the Civil War. Most of the serious disagreements that led to the war were over whether to admit new states and territories as free or slave. The North did not want to admit the territory of Missouri as a state in 1819 with a constitution that allowed slavery. The South did not want to admit California in 1849 with a constitution that forbade slavery. And both sections were locked in struggle over Kansas in the years after 1854.

One other state had considerable trouble with its state constitution—Mormon Utah. Congress refused to admit Utah to the Union after the Civil War until it banned *polygamy*—the practice of having several wives—in its state constitution. Consequently, Utah spent 48 years as a territory until its leaders gave in and accepted Congress' terms.

The forty-ninth and fiftieth states—Alaska and Hawaii—also had problems getting admitted. First, questions were raised about the multiracial societies of each state. Second, concern was expressed about the two states not sharing any borders with the original 48 states. Both states adopted their constitutions without waiting for Congress to pass an enabling act. They were finally admitted to the Union.

section review

1. Define "full faith and credit."
2. Name three limitations on the separation of the states from each other's laws.
3. What are four examples of reasonable discrimination?
4. Why did Utah experience difficulty in getting admitted to the Union?

CHAPTER SUMMARY

4

The Constitution divides power between the national government and the states. All powers of the national government are delegated by the people. There are three kinds of delegated powers; expressed, implied, and inherent.

Most of the powers of the national government are exclusive, but some are held concurrently with the states. The federal court system serves as umpire in conflicts arising under the Constitution, the supreme law of the land.

The Constitution requires the national government to guarantee each state geographic integrity, a republican form of government, and protection against invasion or domestic violence.

Each of the states is equal to all other states and separate from them. There are three important limitations on this constitutional separation: full faith and credit, extradition, and privileges and immunities.

Only Congress may admit new states to the Union, and Congress may set conditions for admission.

REVIEW QUESTIONS

1. If a convention were called to revise the Constitution for the twenty-first century, what would you, as a delegate, propose be revised? Why?
2. Why is a federal system more practical for a nation like the United States than a unitary (one national government with sole power to rule) system?
3. Why, in the last century, has the power of state governments been limited more than the power of the national government?
4. If you were governor of a state, under what conditions would you refuse another state's request to extradite an accused criminal?
5. What are the advantages of a federal system? disadvantages?
6. Why must some powers be exclusively those of the national government? Cite specific examples.
7. What powers must be held concurrently by the national and state governments? Why?
8. Why did the Founders believe the national government had to guarantee each state a republican form of government and protection against invasion or domestic violence?
9. Why is it important for each state to guarantee equal treatment of all U.S. citizens?

ACTIVITIES FOR REVIEW

activity 1   Over a two-week period, read a national-coverage newspaper and collect examples of powers granted or denied the national and state governments.

activity 2   Do research on the evolution of the Supreme Court's power of judicial review.

activity 3   Stage a classroom debate on the following issues: RESOLVED, that the federal grants-in-aid, as an extension of control of the national government over local and state governments, should be eliminated.

political science DICTIONARY

UNIT SUMMARY

Governments have developed gradually over time from the specific views of the people who governed and who were governed. Economic and political systems are therefore closely interrelated.

The government of the United States has roots in the English system brought over by the English settlers. Although the governmental structure of the United States differs from the English model, they share basic principles.

The Constitution created a system established on the following principles: representative government, based on popular sovereignty; separation of powers, with a system of checks and balances; limited government; and division of powers between national and state governments.

All states, old or new, are equal under the Constitution. All United States citizens are entitled to equal treatment in every state in the Union.

Bibliography

Boorstin, Daniel. *The Genius of American Politics.* Chicago: University of Chicago Press, 1953.

Clough, S. B., and T. F. Marburg. *The Economic Basis of American Civilization.* New York: T. Y. Crowell, 1968.

Corwin, Edw. S., and J. W. Peltason. *Understanding the Constitution.* Hinsdale, Ill: Dryden Press, 1976.

Hofstadter, Richard. *The American Political Tradition and the Men Who Made It.* New York: Random House, 1954.

Madison, James, et al. *The Federalist Papers.* New York: Random House, 1964.

Mill, John Stuart. *Utilitarianism: Liberty and Representative Government.* New York: Dutton, 1976.

Orwell, George. *Animal Farm.* New York: Harcourt Brace, 1954.

———. *1984.* New York: Harcourt Brace, 1949.

Rossiter, Clinton L. *Seedtime of the Republic.* New York: Harcourt Brace, 1953.

Review questions

1. The Declaration of Independence and the Constitution comprise the basic philosophical beliefs of Americans about government. Are there any differences in the beliefs outlined in the two documents?

2. Select one amendment to the Constitution that changes the structure of the government. Explain how this amendment reinforces, extends, or modifies the basic principles upon which the government was founded.

3. Many people view the Constitution as a document too sacred to tamper with. Do you agree that the government established is perfect and should not be changed? Explain.

4. The Constitution has often been described as a "living document." Do you agree? Explain.

Skill questions

Based on the charts in Unit I, answer the following questions:

1. What two factors are most important in the perpetuation of the capitalistic system?
2. Compare and contrast a capitalist and socialist type of economic system.
3. Based on your knowledge gained from the chart, which type of economic system do you prefer? Why?
4. Outline a map of the United States in your notebook. Locate and label the 13 colonies. Using a key of three colors, classify the colonies according to type (corporate, royal, proprietary).
5. Which state ratified the Constitution first?
6. If an amendment is proposed by a national convention called at the request of two thirds of the state legislatures, how can it be ratified?

Activities

activity 1

You are a member of one of several domed colonies established on Venus. Because of the tremendous growth of these colonies and their great distance from Earth, you and the other colonists have decided that you need an independent government. A convention of representatives of all the Venusian colonies has been called for next month. What proposals would you offer for setting up the government? What are the basic principles upon which you will base your government? What governmental structure will most effectively carry out these principles?

activity 2

Select a nation other than the United States that has a democratic government. Briefly describe the structure of the government. Is it a federal, unitary, or confederal system? Upon what principles is it based? How is it similar to the government of the United States? How it is different? Can you explain why this nation chose its particular governmental structure?

activity 3

The United Nations is a confederal system of nations. Compare and contrast its structure with that of the United States government established by the Articles of Confederation. What is the purpose of the United Nations? Why is its central body so weak? Should it be stronger? Why or why not?

UNIT
2

JANET GRAY HAYES

Janet Gray Hayes is the mayor of San Jose, California, a city of over half a million citizens. Mayor Hayes won her office in 1974 with a campaign whose slogan was "Make San Jose better before we make it bigger."

PEOPLE IN POLITICS

Janet Hayes' career as a political activist began more than 30 years ago while she was a social worker in Chicago. While putting her husband through medical school and raising four children, she was actively involved in the life of her community. She worked for the PTA, the League of Women Voters, the YMCA, and other community groups. She says of those years as a volunteer, "I got to know more about the establishment—the power structure—and it was very interesting and challenging. I thought I'd move in. The time was ripe."

There were many changes in San Jose during Mayor Hayes' first term. San Jose added more industries and jobs than any other city in the United States. It redesigned its patchwork quilt of crowded roads, chopped-up housing tracts, trailer parks, industrial areas, vacant lots, and wrecking yards. Downtown San Jose was revitalized with urban renewal projects. A museum, a theater and convention center, a "restaurant row," and a four-block downtown park were built. City taxes were reduced and task forces were formed to work on city programs. Mayor Hayes eliminated many unnecessary city jobs. She also recruited many Chicanos, who make up one fourth of San Jose's population, into government service. In running her administration, Mayor Hayes has always had an open-door policy. Citizens have easy access to her and to her staff.

But Mayor Hayes has not been able to jump all the hurdles. The city still lacks major transportation routes. Because citizens refused to pass bond issues, public projects must be built on a pay-as-you-go basis. Many newer areas of the city are without parks, shopping centers, and other facilities.

By the end of her first term, Mayor Hayes was found to be the most admired elected official in the entire Santa Clara Valley. She was reelected in 1978 and she continues to face San Jose's tough problems and to find solutions for them before they become insoluble.

AMERICAN FEDERALISM AT WORK

OVERVIEW

■ States vary in wealth, population distribution, and the racial and ethnic backgrounds of their populations.

■ State constitutions are complex, detailed documents, but all share a similar structure.

■ State legislatures vary in structure and powers; lawmaking is the major function of all state legislatures.

■ The one-person, one-vote decisions of the U.S. Supreme Court have changed the nature of state legislative apportionment.

■ Each state has its own system of courts.

■ The United States is an urban, industrialized nation; many of its problems are those of urbanization.

■ City governments derive their authority and powers from the state.

■ Counties are basic geographic subdivisions of the state. Their principal purpose is to enforce and administer state laws.

■ Regional arrangements are cooperative ventures designed to solve areawide problems.

■ Decreased purchasing power and demands for new and better public services have produced one fiscal crisis after another in state and local governments.

■ State and local governments have two revenue sources: taxes and intergovernmental grants (federal aid).

5

State Government

The states occupy a middle position in the federal system. Sometimes this seems to be a handicap. Our news media tend to focus on local or national events, often ignoring the states. As a result, few of us are able to keep track of the specific activities and functions of state government.

But since World War II, the states have undergone a quiet revolution. Legislatures have been improved. Executive branches have been reorganized. Innovative laws have been passed. This revolution has made state governments better able to meet the challenges of the last quarter of the twentieth century.

States have steadily expanded their activities and services to meet the demands of their citizens. Between 1960 and 1980, the states increased their spending by more than seven times. The federal government only increased its spending by five and a half times during the same period. There are now more state and local employees than federal ones.

Many states have developed innovative solutions to problems long before the federal government has even begun to act on them. Some of these solutions have served as models for later federal legislation. For example, North Carolina is now bringing medical care to remote rural communities by opening clinics staffed by specially trained family nurses.

The states as a whole have shown that they can respond quickly to problems. The majority of the states have enacted some form of no-fault automobile insurance, but Congress is still debating the issue. Several states enacted energy conservation plans before the national government did. Many states formed consumer affairs and environmental protection agencies long before the federal government acted.

In this chapter we will explore this "quiet revolution" in state government, looking at the changes, the innovations, and the criticisms, too.

1. INTRODUCING STATE GOVERNMENT

Our national Constitution created a divided system of government. The national government has powers to deal with a specific list of tasks. These powers are delegated to it by the people under the Constitution. The states have reserved the power to carry out any other tasks that society believes government could or should perform.

Neither the national government nor the state governments by themselves can change the division of power outlined in the Constitution. A change can be made only if the national government and two thirds of the states agree to the change.

States and Localities. Although the states have specific powers, they do not usually keep all these powers for themselves. They delegate some of these powers to other governments within the state—cities, counties, townships, and special districts.

Unlike the division of power between national and state governments, the division of power between state and local governments can be changed by one side only—the state. It does not need the consent of the local governments to alter the distribution of powers. On its own, the state may take back completely, or modify, or grant to another locality, any of the powers it has delegated. This ability of the states to withdraw power is the reason some people say that local governments are nothing more than "creatures of the state."

QUOTES from famous people

"The partisans of centralization are wont to maintain that the central government can administer the affairs of each locality better than the citizens could do it for themselves. This may be true when the central power is enlightened and the local authorities are ignorant, when it is alert and they are slow, when it is accustomed to act and they to obey . . . But I deny that it is so when the people are as enlightened, as awake to their interests . . . as the Americans are."

Alexis de Tocqueville

Differences Among the States. There are basic differences among the states that should be kept in mind. First, the distribution of population within a state affects the political climate of the state. States with most of their population concentrated in large cities are very different from states where the population is scattered throughout rural areas. If the urban-rural breakdown is about even, both populations generally get the services they want from the state. But if there are more people in one area than another, one group tends to get more services.

Second, individual states vary widely in wealth. The **per capita** income of Alaskan residents is more than twice that of Mississippi residents. Such differences affect the ability of a state to meet the needs of its citizens. For example, states with low per

RANKING OF STATES BY PER CAPITA INCOME, 1977

State	1977 Per Capita Income	State	1977 Per Capita Income
Alaska	$9170	Rhode Island	$5589
Connecticut	6564	Arizona	5545
Maryland	6561	Missouri	5493
Nevada	6533	Iowa	5439
New Jersey	6492	New Hampshire	5365
California	6487	Nebraska	5326
Wyoming	6454	Montana	5288
Washington	6394	Oklahoma	5245
Illinois	6358	Utah	5135
Michigan	6130	Idaho	5072
Colorado	6118	Georgia	5071
Oregon	6018	North Carolina	4876
Hawaii	6005	North Dakota	4856
Virginia	5883	West Virginia	4851
Delaware	5883	Kentucky	4851
Kansas	5861	Tennessee	4845
New York	5849	New Mexico	4837
Massachusetts	5826	Louisiana	4790
Ohio	5796	Vermont	4770
Minnesota	5778	Alabama	4712
Florida	5761	South Carolina	4628
Indiana	5751	Maine	4627
Wisconsin	5660	South Dakota	4529
Texas	5633	Arkansas	4443
Pennsylvania	5622	Mississippi	4120

Source: U.S. Bureau of the Census

capita incomes cannot collect much tax money. Thus they cannot spend much money on basic services such as education, welfare, highways, and health.

Per capita is a Latin term meaning for or to each person.

Third, states differ greatly in the racial and ethnic backgrounds of their populations. In states with *heterogeneous* populations— populations composed of members of many different ethnic and racial groups—a great deal of political activity is focused on civil rights issues. These states also tend to have very competitive political parties. States with *homogeneous* populations—populations of citizens with a common or similar background—more often have one strong and one weak political party. And their political battles are over different kinds of issues.

Decentralized Government. State and local governments are excellent examples of our tradition of decentralized government. Many factors contribute to this. Political parties in the United States are organized on a state basis. The national Democratic and Republican parties are actually federations, or unions, of 50 independent state parties. Neither the Republican nor the Democratic National Committee has the power to control the nominations or the finances of state and local party organizations.

Most of the prizes of politics—known as *patronage*—are at the state and local levels. An elected state or local official is thus in a better position to reward followers with jobs and favors than an official of the national government. This is not only because there are so many jobs at state and local levels. It is also because state and local merit systems have fewer employment restrictions than the federal civil service system.

Other factors also contribute to decentralization. State and local governments are involved in a wide range of activities, and the scope of these activities is broad. These governments purchase thousands of different kinds of products and services. They provide hundreds of services to individuals and groups. They make decisions about taxation and control many areas of the local economy. These activities are handled by separate agencies of the state and local governments. The agencies are not usually supervised by a central power. Generally each is free to perform its job as it wishes.

section review

1. What are the differences among the states that affect the way their local governments are set up?
2. Define patronage.
3. Name two factors that contribute to decentralization.

2. STATE CONSTITUTIONS

Since 1776 the 50 states have had at least 144 different constitutions. Until the end of World War II, they had more experience in constitution-making than the rest of the world's nations combined. At that time, the new "third world" countries in Africa and Asia began their own period of extensive constitution-making.

Massachusetts has the nation's oldest constitution, adopted in 1780. Louisiana has the newest; it went into effect on January 1, 1975. The South leads all the other sections of the country in constitution-making. Each southern state has had at least six constitutions. The aftermath of the Civil War accounts for some of the constitutional changes in many southern states.

The Contents of Constitutions. Early state constitutions were short. As the nation grew and society became more complex, the role of the state government expanded, and ideas about what should be in a state constitution changed. Constitutions became longer and more detailed. And they began to require more amendments. Vermont's constitution, adopted in 1793, has 6,600 words. But Georgia's constitution, adopted in 1945, has over 600,000 words.

The Structure of State Constitutions. State constitutions follow a similar pattern. They have a preamble, a bill of rights, and a series of articles. These articles provide for separate branches of government, describe the form and powers of local units of government, outline the amendment process, and deal with different topics of concern to the state government.

State constitutions describe clearly the powers the government has and doesn't have. This has limited the freedom of public officials to act on many issues. And it has often prevented the state from taking action when action is needed.

In addition, state constitutions have become out of date. Thus they have undergone many formal revisions. These have been made either by amendment or by revision of the entire document.

This picture shows the Louisiana state constitution being signed in 1975.

Amending State Constitutions. Each state constitution has an article outlining amendment procedure. The amendment is first proposed and then ratified. Amendments may be proposed at a constitutional convention called for this purpose, in an initiative petition, or by the state legislature.

The Constitutional Convention. Amendments are rarely proposed by means of a constitutional convention. Usually, a convention is called only when a state wishes to revise an entire constitution.

Initiative Petition. Seventeen state constitutions allow citizens to use this method of proposing an amendment. It consists of writing and circulating petitions to get a certain number of voter signatures in support of the amendment or amendments. For example, California requires that such a petition be signed by 8 percent of the voters in the last election for governor. Nebraska requires that 10 percent of these voters sign the petition. And this figure must include 5 percent in each of two fifths of the counties in the state.

Legislative Proposal. A legislative proposal is the most common method of proposing amendments. It is permitted in all states. A majority or a two-thirds vote of members in each house of the legislature is required for this procedure.

Ratification. Once an amendment has been proposed, it must be ratified. In most states, an amendment is ratified if a majority of the people voting on the amendment approve it. New Hampshire requires a two-thirds vote. Minnesota and Wyoming require a majority of all those voting in the election, not just those voting on the amendment itself. Delaware allows its legislature to ratify as well as to propose amendments.

The Revision Process. To make changes, or revisions, in a constitution, the state usually calls a constitutional convention. It is the convention's task to rewrite the constitution.

Each state legislature can ask the voters to decide whether a convention should be called. Most states can put this question to the voters whenever they wish. However, fourteen state constitutions require that the legislature ask voters this question at specified times. For example, Alaska must ask its voters this question at least every ten years. Michigan must ask it every 16 years. Connecticut, Ohio, Missouri, Oklahoma, and several other states must ask it every 20 years.

Once the voters approve a convention, delegates must be elected to represent the people at the convention. Some state constitutions allow the legislature to decide when, where, and how the elections will be held. Other constitutions set forth detailed procedures for such elections.

After the convention has done its work, the rewritten constitution is submitted to the voters to accept or reject.

Revising State Constitutions: A Slow Process. In recent years, more than two thirds of the states have decided to rewrite their constitutions. They have called constitutional conventions or formed constitutional commissions to do the work. But only a few states

have approved the major changes made by these groups. Why?

State constitutions define the powers of the state. They assign these powers to certain groups and individuals. This distribution of power helps some groups get what they want from the state or local governments. But it keeps other groups from achieving their goals.

If a new constitution reassigns power, those losing power will oppose the change and vote against the new constitution. Those gaining power will favor the change. For this reason, most constitutional changes happen very slowly. No one group gains or loses power all at once.

section review

1. What similar features are included in all state constitutions?
2. What steps are involved in amending state constitutions?
3. Describe the process of revising a state constitution.

3. STATE LEGISLATURES

"I arrived at our new marble Capital to spend most of my time considering momentous issues—social security, taxes, conservation, civil liberties. Instead, we have devoted long hours to the discussion of the regulations for labeling eggs. We have argued about the alignment of irrigation ditches, the speed of motorboats on mountain lakes, the salaries of justices of the peace, and whether or not barbers and beauty parlor attendants should be high school graduates. For two days we wrangled about a bill specifying the proper scales for weighing logs and lumber. None of these questions concerns large numbers of people. Yet each question concerns a few people vitally."

This observation was made in 1941 by a young Oregon state legislator named Richard Neuberger—later Senator Neuberger. He was describing the difference between his expectations of the legislature and his experience there. Many legislators today still find that their expectations of public service are not fulfilled in the day-by-day activities of the legislatures. But in more and more states, legislators are turning their attention from issues affecting small groups. They are focusing instead on those that affect large numbers of citizens. Actually, they have no choice about this. The task of legislating has become so complex and demanding that they must devote their energies to the larger issues.

Comparing Congress and the State Legislatures. People often think of state legislatures as "little Congresses." But the differences between Congress and state legislatures are enormous.

State legislatures do not deal with foreign policy. They concentrate on matters that affect the state and its citizens.

Being a member of Congress is a full-time job. The salary and benefits members receive reflect this. But only a few states provide the salary and services that state legislators need to serve full-time. State legislatures are in session for many days out of the year. Nevertheless, most state legislators still earn most of their income as farmers, lawyers, educators, or business people.

Members of Congress stay in office longer than state legislators. There is also a high

This picture shows members of the Wisconsin state legislature in a meeting. Legislators need to be expert in many areas, as the sign on the assembly room door indicates. How do you think these demands affect the job of legislation?

turnover in state legislators. For some, serving causes severe financial burdens. One state legislator described the problem in this way: "Any way you look at it, the job means a sacrifice to you, your home, and your business. Most people don't realize that there are continual demands on your time outside the legislative sessions as well. I don't intend to make a career of politics." Some find that they do not like the job. Others regard their work in the legislature as a steppingstone to higher office.

The committee system of Congress is complex, well staffed, and central to the functioning of Congress. This is not true of many state legislatures. The committees of state legislatures rarely have large enough staffs. They often cannot conduct adequate investigations or hearings on bills being con-

sidered. In the state legislature, committee chairpersons often win their positions through friendship with the presiding officer. In Congress, seniority and length of service on a committee usually determine the selection of the chairperson.

The Organization of State Legislatures. Most legislatures are organized along similar lines. Forty-nine of the 50 states have bicameral (two-house) legislatures. Within each house of the legislature, all the members serve approximately the same number of voters.

But legislative districts vary in size across the country. A California state senator represents almost 500,000 persons and an assemblyperson (representative) 250,000. A Wyoming senator represents 11,080 persons,

The senate of the state of New Mexico is shown in session in this picture. A visitors' gallery is shown at the left. How does the membership of this senate compare in size to the average state senate?

and only 1,813 persons are represented by each New Hampshire representative.

State legislatures vary in size, term of membership, and length of the legislative session. Minnesota and New York have large senates of 67 and 60 members respectively. Alaska and Nevada have small ones, with 20 members each. The average membership of a state senate is 40; that of a state house of representatives, 100. Representatives serve two-year terms in all but four states. Three fourths of all state senators serve four-year terms. Forty-three states hold annual legislative sessions. The other seven states hold sessions once every two years, or biennially.

Reapportionment. Since World War II, the state legislatures have changed dramatically. Some of the greatest changes have resulted from the battle over reapportionment in the 1960's.

The word "apportionment" describes the way in which a state creates the districts senators and representatives will represent. In the past, some states used a federal plan to create these districts. Representatives for one house of the legislature were chosen from districts based on population. Each district supposedly had equal population. Representatives for the other house were chosen from districts based on geography. In other words, a certain area within the state would have at least one senator and representative regardless of its population.

The federal plan often gave the voters of one district an advantage over those of another district. For example, people living in a district with a population of 15,000 and one representative would have a greater vote on issues affecting them than would the people living in a district with 150,000 and one representative. Also, the voter in the district with the smaller population would have easier access to his or her representative. A representative with 15,000 constituents would be able to give more help and services than would a representative with 150,000 constituents.

Most state constitutions now give the state legislature the power to reapportion itself. Usually, the legislature can redraw legislative districts every ten years—after the national census has been taken. In this way, increases, decreases, and shifts of population can be accounted for.

Before 1962 many legislatures refused to reapportion themselves. Some legislators saw that they would lose their seats when districts were redrawn. Often it was the small-town and rural legislators who stood to lose their seats, because population had shifted to the cities.

By the 1960's most legislatures had become very unbalanced. For instance, Cook County, Illinois contained over half of Illinois' population. Its residents paid more than half the state taxes. But county residents elected fewer than half of the members of the state senate—24 out of 58. Dade County, Florida, had 20 percent of the state's population. But it elected only one of the state's 38 senators, and only 3 of the state's 95 representatives. At one time, the senator from Tulsa County, Oklahoma, represented 193,000 people. The senator from Logan County, Oklahoma, represented only 25,000.

Why didn't someone act to change the situation? Governors would not try to force legislatures to reapportion if their own political party was favored by the existing district lines. Individuals or groups often asked the state and federal courts to change unequal representation. But the courts ruled that fights about reapportionment were "political" fights and questions. Thus, they said, reapportionment was outside the scope of both state and federal judicial authority.

The deadlock was broken in 1962. The Supreme Court ruled in *Baker* v. *Carr* that federal courts could consider cases challenging representation in state legislatures.

Several other cases followed the case of

Baker v. *Carr.* These established the fact that the "one person, one vote" requirement covers all government units that have a legislative function. These units include congressional districts, state legislative districts, and local government units such as county commissions, city council districts, and junior college districts. Today, congressional districts across the country must be proportionately equal in population. However, states are allowed slightly greater freedom in drawing district lines. They are allowed to reapportion on the basis of individual political, historical, and geographical concerns. For example, in 1973, the Supreme Court approved a reapportionment plan that tried to reflect the state-wide political strength of the two major parties in the state legislature.

Local governments have even more freedom in drawing district lines. Population differences in local districts will be permitted if two conditions are present. First, there can be no deliberate attempt to discriminate against minorities. Second, each local district has traditionally been drawn in a certain way.

Even though state districts have been equalized, reapportionment fights are by no means over. Today, three other kinds of reapportionment fights are being waged in the courts. These involve *multimember districts, racially based reapportionment,* and *gerrymandering.*

Multimember Districts. A *single-member district* is one in which voters elect only one person to a legislative body. Twenty-eight states use this method to elect all their state representatives. And 38 states use it to elect all their senators. In the remaining states, legislators are elected from *multimember districts.* In this procedure, there are fewer, and larger districts. Each district elects several legislators.

Multimember districts are under attack for several reasons. First, it is argued that they make it harder for members of minorities to be elected. Second, it is claimed that these districts make it easier for certain groups or a certain political party to control elections. And third, some maintain that they violate the "one person, one vote" rule. Some multimember districts have been upheld by the courts. Others have been struck down.

Racially Based Reapportionment. This kind of redistricting involves two concerns. Some reapportionment plans have been struck down when challengers have been able to prove that districts have been redrawn to break up concentrations of minorities. They have argued successfully that reapportionment had been used to redraw a minority group district by splitting it up among different districts in order to dilute that minority's strength at the polls. Racially based reapportionment plans have also been challenged where district lines have been drawn in order to increase the political power of minorities.

Gerrymandering. *Gerrymandering* is the redrawing of district lines by members of the political party in control of the legislature in such a way as to give their own party as many representatives as possible. The practice has produced districts with senseless boundaries and populations varying widely in number and racial composition. However, no court has yet declared gerrymandering an unconstitutional practice.

California and New York provide good examples of gerrymandering. In 1971 New York adopted a redistricting plan in which one Bronx County district consists of two areas of that county completely separated by another district. Yet mapmakers said that the two halves of the district were adjoining because they were connected by means of the New York waterways.

This picture shows the original gerrymandered district in nineteenth-century Massachusetts. The practice of gerrymandering took its name from Elbridge Gerry, who, while governor of Massachusetts, had the state's legislative districts redrawn to favor his political party.

In California's 1972 redistricting plan, similar situations occurred. For instance, a senate district in the San Francisco Bay area consisted of parts of Marin County, part of San Francisco County, and part of San Mateo County. The only way a person could go from one part of the district to another without passing through other districts was by motorboat. California's redistricting plan was vetoed.

Reform. Since the 1930's legislatures have been concerned with legislative reform. Much of the reform has been aimed at simplifying the legislative process itself. A streamlined process would, it was believed, allow legislatures to compete with governors in shaping the policy of the state. Legislative reforms have been mainly in the following areas.

In the early 1940's only four legislatures met annually. By 1980 there were forty-three legislatures meeting annually. The change from holding a legislative session every two years to holding one every year became necessary so that legislators could deal with all of the pressing problems arising in their own districts.

Legislatures have operated much like Congress in their use of committees to perform a large part of their work. But the number of legislative committees grew, and the system became unwieldy and inefficient. Most legislatures have now reduced the number of committees in each house. They have also enlarged the scope of each committee's activities.

Facilities for legislative committees and their staffs have also been improved. And committee activities in over two thirds of the states are now governed by a set of rules— something unheard of a generation ago. The lack of such rules meant that each chairperson could run a committee as he or she liked.

According to one political scientist, a good legislative committee has several characteristics. It examines carefully the bills that are submitted to it. It frequently amends bills before sending them on to the entire house or senate. And it continues its work between legislative sessions. Committees also have staffs of legal experts and investigators. And the legislators serving on them devote their attentions to specialized areas.

Throughout the nation's history, state legislators' salaries have been low. This may have been more easily justified when most state legislatures met only every two years. However, campaigning for election, leaving their business or work during the legislative session, and, often, working long hours on committees between legislative sessions are very expensive for legislators.

Between 1965 and 1975, the average legislative salary rose from $7,167 to $18,216. But there are still big differences in salary and work schedule of legislators among the states. California pays its full-time legislators $56,220 over a two-year period. And New Hampshire pays its part-time legislators only $200 every two years.

section review

1. Describe two differences between state legislatures and Congress.
2. Define reapportionment.
3. What are some disadvantages that occur with reapportionment?
4. Define gerrymandering.

4. GOVERNORS

During colonial times, the governors of all the colonies except Rhode Island and Connecticut were appointed by the English king or by the proprietor of the colony. Their extensive powers included those of appointing civil officers, enforcing the laws, granting pardons, serving as head of the highest court in the colony, calling and dismissing legislative assemblies, and recommending and vetoing colonial legislation. In short, the governors controlled all legislative, executive, and judicial functions. They had supreme power and were fiercely hated by the colonists. After the Declaration of Independence, the new states tried to prevent the recurrence of their colonial experiences. They replaced executive supremacy with legislative supremacy. But the early legislatures abused their powers as much as the British governors had. They did not meet often. And soon they found that they could not effectively govern their states.

Governors Under the Constitution. The new national Constitution adopted in 1789, with its stronger executive branch and more balanced government, had an effect on the states. They revised their constitutions to bring the branches of the government into balance.

By 1850 the governors shared power with the other branches of state government. They were not subordinate to them. They were elected instead of being chosen by the legislature. And their terms of office were generally extended. But although governors gained independence from the legislature, they lost their power to appoint lower administrative officials. In most states by the mid-1800's, voters had the power to elect many state officials. These included lieutenant governor, secretary of state, state treasurer, and judges.

Nonetheless, the power of governors continued to expand. They became the majority-party leaders in their individual states. Some were given the power to call legislatures into special session.

But at the same time, more administrators were being elected directly by the voters. State regulatory agencies and commissions increased, and they were often independent of both the governor and the legislature. The result was that, by the early twentieth century, there was no central authority in most state governments. And governors were often in a tug-of-war with other executive agencies.

Reforming the Executive Branch. The Progressive movement that produced the initiative, the referendum, and the recall also generated the reform of the executive branch. For example, Illinois produced the Illinois Civil Administrative Code of 1917. This code was the first comprehensive plan to reorganize the structure of the state government. Other states followed Illinois' lead. They brought the executive branch under the governor's control. In each state hundreds of offices, boards, and commissions were abolished. Their functions were consolidated and assigned to a few departments. These were headed by a single director, who was appointed by, and directly responsible to, the governor.

Today most states have reorganized their executive branch in some way. But most governors still share their power with at least a few other elected officers—lieutenant governor, secretary of state, controller, treasurer, and attorney general. A governor has no power over these officials. If they are members of a different political party, they will not accept his or her leadership. They often make the activities of the agencies under their command difficult to coordinate.

Qualifications of Candidates for Governor. The legal qualifications of a candidate for governor are described in most state constitutions. Usually the minimum age for a candidate is 30. The candidate must be a United States citizen and must have lived within the state for a certain period of time. In practical terms, the candidate's most important qualification is the ability to get votes. He or she must have many supporters and must be able to raise money for the campaign.

Governors in 46 states serve four-year terms. In the other states they serve two-year

North Carolina's governor, James B. Hunt, Jr., is shown here giving a speech during his 1980 election campaign. Political leaders have always tried to make direct contact with voters in order to gain their support.

terms. Some states with four-year terms do not allow the incumbent governor to serve a second consecutive term. The average salary for governors is about $50,000 a year. New York has the highest salary at $85,000 and North Dakota the lowest at $27,500. In addition, some states provide allowances for expenses and an official residence.

Except in Oregon, a governor may be removed from office by impeachment. In 12 states the governor may be removed by popular recall. Rarely has either device been used.

The Job of Governor. The public tends to hold governors responsible for the legislative as well as the administrative performance of the state government. Most states require the governor to prepare the state budget and submit it to the legislature. This budget influences the course of debates and strategy in a legislative session. Studies have shown that the governor's budget recommendation is crucial in determining how much money a state agency finally receives from the state legislature.

Governors usually reduce an agency's request for money to conform to the budget they present to the legislature. A governor who succeeds in getting the legislature to approve his or her budget recommendations has an excellent chance of being reelected. But a governor whose party does not control the legislature is less likely to get his or her budget approved. In this situation, agencies tend to deal directly with the legislature. The governor's recommendations are likely to be modified or ignored.

Governors can call special legislative sessions. In 43 states governors have an *item veto*. This power permits the governor to delete any part of a bill before signing the rest of the bill into law. A governor can often win legislative support for his or her ideas by threatening to use the item veto.

Today most governmental growth occurs in the executive branch. The increasing complexity of state and local governments demands that priorities be set and legislative business determined largely by governors.

section review

1. What powers were given to colonial governors in America?
2. What was the function of the Illinois Civil Administrative Code of 1917?
3. What responsibilities do governors have at the present time?

5. THE STATE COURT SYSTEM

The most striking characteristic of the United States court system is its duality. In other words, one federal court system and 50 state court systems exist side by side. Most of the laws that govern our daily lives are state and local laws. Most of us will deal with a state court for our legal business. The quality of our state court system will determine whether or not we receive "justice."

Each state has set up its own system of courts. Although great diversity exists among them, we can place state courts into five classes, or grades: 1) justices of the peace and petty, or inferior, trial courts, 2) trial courts of intermediate jurisdiction, 3) trial courts of general jurisdiction, 4) intermediate appellate courts, and 5) the state supreme court.

Inferior Trial Courts. These courts are at the base of a state court system. They operate under various names—small claims courts; justices of the peace; justice, magistrate, municipal, traffic, and police courts; and in some states, district courts. Often the court divisions at this level are confusing. In some

A justice of the peace marries a couple. The speed and the informality of this wedding ceremony are typical of the procedures of inferior trial courts.

states there are justice courts in the counties and magistrate courts and police courts in some of the cities. Whatever their names, inferior trial courts have four things in common.

1. Their jurisdiction is limited to minor cases. In most states they cannot hear civil cases involving more than $1,000. And they cannot try criminal cases if the maximum jail sentence exceeds one year.
2. These courts are not generally courts of record. This means that no detailed record of their proceedings is kept on file. Only a brief entry with the names of the parties involved, their attorneys—if

there are attorneys—and the judge's decision is recorded.
3. The procedure is quick and informal.
4. A citizen who loses a case in this type of court normally has a right to appeal the case to a higher court. There he or she may obtain a new trial at a more formal proceeding.

Trial Courts of Intermediate Jurisdiction. In some states there are courts at a level between the inferior courts and the courts of general jurisdiction. They, too, are courts of limited jurisdiction. Typically there is one court at this level in each county or city. In some states these courts handle special types of cases—such as claims on estates, juvenile matters, or problems concerning legal incompetency.

Trial Courts of General Jurisdiction. These courts have authority to try all types of cases, civil or criminal. Some of these courts also have appellate jurisdiction. That is, a person losing a case in trial court may appeal to a court of general jurisdiction. A general trial court may be called a court of common pleas, a superior court, a district court, or a circuit court. In New York State the general trial courts are called supreme courts. This is confusing to non-New Yorkers, since most states call the highest appellate court the supreme court.

Multiple-judge general trial courts in large metropolitan areas often have criminal, civil-jury, domestic relations, juvenile, and probate divisions. The largest trial court of general jurisdiction in the world is the superior court of Los Angeles, which has 171 judges.

Intermediate Appellate Courts. These courts exist in 30 states. But there is no uniform pattern for their organization. Some are entirely separate from the trial court below and the state supreme court above.

Others are divisions of the trial courts of general jurisdiction. An appellate court consists of a "bench" of three or more judges. Appellate courts do not use juries. Their main function is to review the record of a trial court to determine if any errors were made during the trial.

The Supreme Court. At the top of every state judicial system is a "court of last resort." Most often it is called a supreme court. Maryland and New York call it a court of appeals. In West Virginia it is called a supreme court of appeals. Maine and Massachusetts call it a supreme judicial court. The function of all these courts is the same—to review the actions of the lower courts of the state. The court does this in two ways. One is to hear appeals at the request of losers—or sometimes winners—of cases tried in the lower courts. The court reviews the record to see whether a lower court has made errors in procedure or in applying the law to the facts in a particular case.

The second way of supervising lower courts is to direct their actions. The supreme court does this by issuing formal orders to the lower courts. The principal orders are the following.

1. *Mandamus.* The lower court is ordered to do something, such as grant a change of location for a trial or grant a jury trial.
2. *Prohibition.* The lower court is forbidden to proceed in a case in which it does not have jurisdiction or in which it is acting beyond its jurisdiction.
3. *Habeas corpus.* The lower court is directed to justify its action in holding a person in custody.

The supreme court may also control the lower courts by issuing rules of court procedure, which the lower courts must follow.

The Legal System in Action. Although the structure of a state court system is important, most Americans are probably more concerned with the operation of the courts. A

SELECTING JUDGES

States use one or more of the following methods in selecting judges.
1. **Gubernatorial appointment.** Selections are made directly by the governor for purposes of patronage or for professional or other types of considerations.
2. **Legislative election.** Selections are made by vote of the legislature, which may be influenced by the recommendation of the governor, the desire to confer patronage, or other factors.
3. **Nonpartisan election.** Judges are chosen in elections that formally exclude political parties from participation. Informal pressure from political leaders or bar organizations may influence the election results.
4. **Partisan election.** Judges are chosen in elections in which individual political parties participate. Party primaries are normally part of the election procedure.
5. **The Missouri plan.** This is the most complex selection system and has three essential parts. Slates of candidates are chosen by a nominating commission appointed by the governor. The governor then selects a judge from the list of names submitted by the commission. Finally, voters approve or reject the appointment.

COURT STRUCTURE FOR THE STATE OF CALIFORNIA

*SUPREME COURT

1 Chief and 6 Associate Justices

Appellate Jurisdiction:

Appeals from courts of appeal and cases transferred to itself from courts of appeal; appeals from superior courts if death penalty involved. Review of orders of Public Utilities Commission. Appeals go to U.S. Supreme Court.

*COURTS OF APPEAL

1st District	2nd District	3rd District	4th District	5th District
San Francisco	Los Angeles	Sacramento	San Diego	Fresno
4 Divisions with	5 Divisions with	7 Justices	Division 1,	4 Justices
4 Justices each	4 Justices each		San Diego: 4	
			Division 2,	
			S. Bernardino: 5	

Appellate jurisdiction: appeals from superior courts and quasi-judicial boards such as Workers' Compensation Appeals Board, Alcoholic Beverage Control Board. Appeals go to the Supreme Court.

*SUPERIOR COURTS
58 Courts (1 each county) 520 Judges

Original Jurisdiction:

CIVIL: All cases except those where municipal and justice courts have jurisdiction.

CRIMINAL: Felonies, juvenile cases.

Appellate Jurisdiction:

Appeals from municipal and justice courts. Appeals to go to appropriate court of appeal; to Supreme Court if death penalty involved.

MUNICIPAL COURTS
District of over 40,000 population
83 Courts   423 Judges

Original Jurisdiction:

CIVIL: $5,000 or less

CRIMINAL: All misdemeanors (if defendant over 18).

Sit as small claims court.

Conduct preliminary hearings for felonies.

Appeals go to Superior Court.

JUSTICE COURTS
District of 40,000 population or less
178 Courts   179 Judges

Original Jurisdiction:

CIVIL: $5,000 or less.

CRIMINAL: All misdemeanors (if defendant over 18).

Sit as small claims court.

Conduct preliminary hearings for felonies.

Appeals go to Superior Court.

*These courts have original jurisdiction for issuance of writs of habeas corpus and extraordinary relief.

person with a legal problem may have many questions. Are the courts fair? Will the judge be biased? Will I get better treatment if I am rich? Do "connections" count? How much money will it cost to go to court? How can I find a good lawyer? What should I do if I don't have the money to hire a lawyer?

In 27 states, trial judges are elected. In the states where they are appointed—often by the governor—local political leaders have a say in the selection process. Once elevated to the bench, judges often control the awarding of certain jobs—those of clerk and other court officials and trustees and appraisers for estates.

One study of trial courts concluded that citizens challenging local zoning ordinances had a better chance of winning when their lawyer was part of a law firm with a member who held county public office. When the officeholder from the law firm belonged to the same political party as the judge, the chances of winning were even greater.

Other studies have focused on state supreme courts. One national study of the voting behavior of judges found differences between that of Democratic and Republican judges sitting on the same court. Democratic judges tended more than the Republicans to favor the defense in criminal cases, the administrative agency in business regulation cases, the claimant in unemployment compensation cases, the tenant in landlord-tenant cases, the labor union in labor-management cases, and the debtor in creditor-debtor cases.

A study published in 1977 examined the kind and number of cases that state supreme courts handled between 1870 and 1970. The researchers found that case loads had declined during this 100-year period. Judges were now trying fewer cases and tending to write longer opinions. Case emphasis had shifted from debt collection and property disputes to personal injury, criminal, public law, and family law matters. This indicates that the state supreme courts are now deciding the legal problems of less wealthy people and people who are not members of the business community.

Reform. In reforming state governments, states have reorganized their court systems as well as their executive and legislative branches. They have tried to free the trial courts—the heart of a state judiciary—from the political control of small areas within the states. And they have tried to make them more responsive to the rules and policies of the highest state courts.

Court reforms have concentrated on three areas. First, many of the inferior trial courts have been abolished and their functions given to courts serving wider geographical areas. And reformers have also tried to achieve a greater uniformity in the administration of justice.

Second, 49 states now use court administrative officers. These officers collect detailed information on the workloads of all state courts. They also assist in the supervision of judicial budgets and personnel.

Third, many states have established judicial qualification commissions to maintain professional standards among judges. These commissions investigate charges of incompetence or misconduct against individual judges. After the commissions' investigations have been completed, they recommend action.

section review

1. Which courts are the base of the state court system?
2. Compare courts of intermediate jurisdiction with courts of general jurisdiction.
3. What is the function of the state supreme court?

CHAPTER SUMMARY

5

State constitutions follow a similar pattern: preamble, bill of rights, and a series of articles providing for separate branches of government, forms and powers of local units of government, the amendment process, and items of concern to the particular state.

Most state legislatures are organized along similar lines, and all have the same function: lawmaking. State legislatures vary in size, members' terms of office, and length of the legislative session. The one-man, one-vote decisions of the U.S. Supreme Court have changed the nature of reapportionment of state legislative districts, but conflicts still exist concerning multimember districts, racially based apportionment, and gerrymandering. Reform in the following areas has been characteristic of state legislatures in recent years: annual sessions, more efficient use of committees, improved staff and facilities, rules, and increased work loads and salaries.

Early state constitutions limited the governor's powers in order to prevent repetition of the colonial experience with royal governors. The separation of powers established in the federal Constitution became the model for state government after 1789. Candidates for governor, in most states, must be at least 30 years of age, must be U.S. citizens, and must have lived in the state for a certain length of time. They must also have the ability to get votes and to raise campaign money. In most states governors serve a 4-year term. They may be removed from office by impeachment or recall. The governor prepares the budget, calls special sessions, and, in most states, possesses the item veto power.

The experience of most Americans with the court system is at the state or local level. Each state has its own system of courts. There are four general classes of state courts: inferior trial courts of intermediate jurisdiction, courts of general jurisdiction, intermediate appellate courts, and the state supreme court.

REVIEW QUESTIONS

1. How may your state's constitution be amended? How often has it been amended? rewritten? Which amendment process has been used most often in your state?
2. The U.S. Constitution is a brief outline of the structure of the government. Most state constitutions are detailed and long. Which form do you favor? Why?
3. Review accounts of a recent legislative session in your state. Did the proceedings there resemble those described by Richard Neuberger of Oregon? How were they similar? different?
4. In New Jersey the governor is the only elected member of the executive branch. All other members of the executive branch are appointed by the governor with the consent of the legislature. Would you favor such a system in your state? Why or why not?
5. What qualifications, besides those discussed in the text, do you think the governor of your state should possess? Why?
6. If you had the power to appoint judges to your state's courts, what qualifications would you establish? Explain.
7. In some states judges are elected. Do you favor this practice? Why or why not?

ACTIVITIES FOR REVIEW

activity 1   Stage a debate on the following: RESOLVED, that the constitution of this state be replaced with one that reflects the needs of the twentieth and twenty-first centuries.

activity 2   Interview or invite a state legislator to speak on the duties and responsibilities of a state legislator.

activity 3   Write a brief biography of the governor of your state.

activity 4   Interview or invite a judge, district attorney, or public defender to speak to your class on the administration of justice.

political science DICTIONARY

gerrymandering—the redrawing of district lines by the legislature's majority party to give that party as many representatives as possible.   p. 107

heterogeneous populations—populations composed of members of many different ethnic and racial groups.   p. 100

homogeneous population—populations composed of citizens with a common or similar background.   p. 100

multimember districts—districts based on a reapportionment procedure in which fewer and larger districts are created. Each district elects several legislators.   p. 107

patronage—the power of an official to reward political supporters with government jobs, contracts, or special favors.   p. 101

per capita—a Latin term meaning "for or to each person."   p. 100

racially based reapportionment—a redistricting plan in which districts are redrawn to break up or increase concentrations of minority groups.   p. 107

6

Cities

During its history the United States has changed from a rural nation into a nation of cities. The economy has changed, too. Originally based on agriculture, it is now geared chiefly to heavy industry. The nation's once small population has grown to over 220 million people. Today three quarters of these people live in the cities and their suburbs. They occupy less than 10 percent of the total American land. This movement from the farm to the city, from agriculture to industry, is called urbanization.

Many of the major problems our society faces today are those resulting from urbanization. Supplying water, police and fire protection, streets, sewers, traffic control, housing, transportation, health care, welfare payments, land, and education to heavily populated areas is a complex task. The cities and their suburbs are continually faced with these problems.

Sometimes cities and suburbs work together. Sometimes they try to "pass the buck." Sometimes they fight bitterly, even taking one another to court. To meet their citizens' needs, they must constantly scramble and compete for money.

CHAPTER PREVIEW

1. THE URBAN SETTING
2. CITY GOVERNMENT
3. CITY PROBLEMS: LAND USE
4. CITY PROBLEMS: THE ELDERLY
5. CITY PROBLEMS: HOUSING

1. THE URBAN SETTING

Most of the American population is crowded into 282 metropolitan areas. A standard metropolitan area, as determined by the federal government, is a county or group of counties containing one city of 50,000 or more inhabitants or two cities with a combined population of at least 50,000. Each metropolitan area is usually a large city surrounded by smaller cities and towns called suburbs. Three fourths of all federal personal income tax collected comes from the 282 metropolitan areas. More than four fifths of the nation's bank accounts are located there. And almost four fifths of America's manufacturing is in metropolitan areas.

City Problems. America's metropolitan areas have many problems. Housing in cities is often inadequate, unsanitary, unsafe, and neglected. In the suburbs houses are frequently arranged haphazardly, without neighborhood planning. And in both places there is not enough housing of good quality.

Transportation poses another problem. Automobiles crowd streets and roads. The few mass-transit systems that exist are in financial trouble. It is becoming increasingly difficult and time-consuming to travel in metropolitan areas.

Cities and suburbs also face serious pollution problems. Their air and water are being contaminated. And they cannot dispose of the enormous amount of garbage they create.

Neighborhoods lack parks and other recreational facilities. Open spaces are rapidly decreasing. Crime is increasing, and juvenile delinquency continues. All school districts are in need of money. There is growing alarm about the lowering of educational standards and the inability of students to read. Unemployment is high in metropolitan areas.

RURAL AND URBAN DIVISIONS OF POPULATION BY STATE, IN THOUSANDS			
	Rural	Urban	Percent Urban
Alabama	1,432	2,012	58.4
Alaska	155	146	48.4
Arizona	362	1,409	79.6
Arkansas	962	961	50.0
California	1,817	18,136	90.9
Colorado	474	1,733	78.5
Connecticut	687	2,345	77.4
Delaware	153	396	72.2
Florida	1,321	5,468	80.5
Georgia	1,822	2,768	60.3
Hawaii	130	639	83.1
Idaho	327	385	54.1
Illinois	1,884	9,230	83.0
Indiana	1,822	3,372	64.9
Iowa	1,208	1,616	57.2
Kansas	762	1,485	66.1
Kentucky	1,535	1,684	52.3
Louisiana	1,235	2,406	66.1
Maine	488	504	50.8
Maryland	918	3,004	76.6
Massachusetts	879	4,810	84.6
Michigan	2,321	6,554	73.8
Minnesota	1,278	2,527	66.4
Mississippi	1,230	987	44.5
Missouri	1,399	3,278	70.1
Montana	324	371	53.4
Nebraska	571	913	61.5
Nevada	93	395	80.9
New Hampshire	322	416	56.4
New Jersey	795	6,373	88.9
New Mexico	307	709	69.8
New York	2,634	15,602	85.6
North Carolina	2,797	2,285	45.0
North Dakota	344	273	44.3
Ohio	2,626	8,026	75.3
Oklahoma	819	1,740	68.0
Oregon	689	1,403	67.1
Pennsylvania	3,363	8,430	71.5
Rhode Island	122	825	87.1
South Carolina	1,358	1,232	47.6
South Dakota	369	297	44.6
Tennessee	1,618	2,305	58.8
Texas	2,276	8,921	79.7
Utah	208	851	80.4
Vermont	301	143	32.2
Virginia	1,714	2,935	63.1
Washington	933	2,476	72.6
West Virginia	1,065	679	39.0
Wisconsin	1,507	2,910	65.9
Wyoming	131	201	60.5

Source: 1970 Census

Herblock Gallery (Simon and Schuster, 1968)

"Help!"

Herblock uses his skill as a cartoonist to make some points about problems currently facing many of the nation's cities.

City Government. These and other rapidly developing problems are facing the nation's local governments. Local government is complex, involving multiple levels of authority. The system's basic structure has changed little since it was designed two centuries ago. And because power at the local level is fragmented, action on problems is often frustrated.

Today a typical metropolitan area has some 90 units of general- and special-purpose government. The figure usually includes 2 counties, 13 townships, 21 cities, 18 school districts, 31 special districts, 3 or 4 federally supported planning districts, and one regional council. Each of these units of government has its own powers and its own special functions. But frequently the powers and functions of one unit conflict with those of another. Constitutional and legislative limits on the taxing and spending powers of these units also hamper their ability to perform their duties.

The federal government has tried to help metropolitan areas. But since so many local governments are eligible for aid, the federal government's financial help makes the continued fragmentation of power both desirable and profitable.

section review

1. Describe some of the problems of cities.
2. What kinds of government units exist within a city government?

2. CITY GOVERNMENT

A city is legally a municipal corporation. It can be a central city, a suburb of a larger city, or a city in a rural setting. The city government is the major local government for the resident of a metropolitan area.

Generally cities have more independence and greater flexibility in their activities than do other kinds of local government. But cities are, as you recall, "creatures of state government." They get their powers from the state and must perform certain state-ordered functions. They have only those powers of governing that the state grants them. Throughout the nation's history, state legislatures have been unwilling to give cities the powers they need to govern. Recently, however, governing cities has become a complex

TRENDS IN CITY GENERAL EXPENDITURE FOR SELECTED MAJOR FUNCTIONS: 1970–1979
(in billions of dollars)

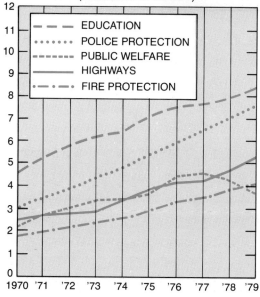

job. And states have been forced to give cities more independence and to supervise their activities less.

The Charter of a City. The state legislature drafts a charter for each city. The charter is like a constitution for the city. It establishes the form of the city's government and describes the powers the city has and how they may be exercised.

Some charters are complete documents. Others contain only part of a city's rules of government. The others are found in various state laws. Some states draft a special charter for each city. But most state legislatures give cities a *classified charter*. This means that there are general laws applicable to all cities within a certain classification. The laws are the equivalent of a charter. The cities are classified by population. When a city's population changes, it may move into a different

classification. It will then have a different kind of charter. However, a city does not automatically move from one classification to another when its population changes. To do this it must follow a formal procedure set down by the state.

A variation of the charter is a system called *municipal home rule.* Thirty-six states use this system. Municipal home rule allows a city to write, adopt, and amend its own charter with relatively little interference from the state legislature. The legislature does not have to approve every change in a city's charter, for example. Under home rule, a city has control over its local problems. It can make routine decisions without asking the legislature for permission to act. However, in so doing it may not violate the state's constitution or the general laws of the state.

Without home rule, governing a city can be difficult. For example, one North Carolina town without home rule had to have the state legislature pass a law to allow the town's city council to ban roller skating on the city sidewalks. A Nevada city had to get the state legislature's permission to buy a pump for the fire department. And an Iowa town could not purchase police uniforms without the state legislature's approval.

The Structure of City Government. There are three basic forms of city government in the United States: 1) the mayor-council system, 2) the commission system, and 3) the council-manager system. The mayor-council form of government separates legislative and executive power. The commission and council-manager plans do not separate these powers.

The structure of a city government is very important. It can determine who has access to influence and power in the city. For example, in cities where city council members are elected from districts instead of from the entire city, minority groups tend to be better represented on the councils. In 1977

NOTICE
CITY OF MADISON RESIDENTS

THE CITY OF MADISON IS NOW ABLE TO SEPARATE AND RECYCLE YOUR METAL AND GLASS CONTAINERS. ALL MATERIAL THAT YOU HAVE BEEN BRINGING TO OUR RECYCLING CENTER WILL NOW BE PICKED UP BY THE CITY ON YOUR REGULAR TRASH DAY.

FOR THOSE OF YOU LIVING OUTSIDE THE CITY OF MADISON, THE RECYCLING CENTER WILL REMAIN OPEN AS LONG AS YOU CONTINUE TO USE IT.

WE ALSO SUGGEST THAT YOU ENCOURAGE YOUR LOCAL GOVERNMENT OFFICIALS TO EXPAND THE ___Y OF MA___N'S OLIN AVENUE RECYCLING ___ THE RESIDENTS OF DANE

As part of its home rule, a city can take measures to solve a variety of local problems. In Madison, Wisconsin, for example, a glass- and metal-recycling center was set up. Do you have any such facilities in your area? How would you get one started?

San Francisco changed from a citywide election system for its board of supervisors, or city council, to a district election system. As a result, those elected to the board now represent a much wider cross section of the city's population than did the previous boards.

The Mayor-Council System.   The mayor-council system is used by over half of all city governments. Twenty-three of the 27 largest United States cities use this form of government. The mayor-council plan works in different ways, depending on how much power the mayor has.

The Weak Mayor-Council System.   Under this plan the council has both legislative and executive tasks. Members are usually elected by districts. Small cities have five to seven member councils. Large cities have from 11 to 50 member councils. The council appoints several administrative officers. Its members also serve on various boards, commissions, and committees. The council shares administrative responsibility with the mayor.

The mayor is weak because of this division of administrative power. The mayor's authority to appoint the officials of his or her own choice is limited. His or her power to remove people from office is even more limited. And the mayor does not prepare the budget.

No one individual is responsible for enforcing the laws or overseeing the operation of the government. Several of the most important city officials are elected by the voters. Each official heads a department, and each department operates independently. There is no one to coordinate activities of the departments. The city government becomes, in effect, a number of mini-governments.

The Strong Mayor-Council System. In this form of the mayor-council plan, the mayor and the council share the task of making city policy. But the mayor prepares the budget and supervises its administration. The council merely approves, or adopts, the budget.

Usually the mayor is the only elected administrator under this plan. She or he is free to appoint or dismiss heads of departments without the approval of the council. The mayor is thus ultimately responsible for carrying out city policy and coordinating the various city departments.

Under this plan the city council is generally small. It is usually elected at large, and it serves on a part-time basis. The mayor serves full-time. And because the mayor's position is so strong, she or he is often credited with the government's achievements or blamed for its failures.

The council does not share in administrative duties. It performs only legislative tasks. But it tends to be critical of the mayor's performance as chief executive. Like other legislative bodies, it often has the power to investigate any department within the city government.

Mayor-Council with Chief Administrative Officer. Many mayors are better campaigners and politicians than administrators. They lack the skills to run so complex an operation as a modern city government. The mayor often appoints a professional administrator to supervise the city's finances or its operations, or both.

The powers of these chief administrative officers vary. Most of them coordinate departments on a day-to-day basis, give advice to the mayor, and oversee the budget. Because they are appointed by the mayor, they can be dismissed by the mayor at any time.

San Francisco's chief administrative officer heads a group of city departments dealing mainly with public works. He or she is not involved in the budget and does not coordinate all city departments. The chief administrative officer of Los Angeles has broader responsibilities. But Los Angeles is basically a weak-mayor city. Its city council has many administrative duties. Many of its departments are controlled by five-member commissions appointed by the mayor. New York City had a chief administrative officer from 1953 to 1965 under Mayor Robert F. Wagner. Under his successor, John Lindsay, the powers of the chief administrative officer were eroded. In 1974 Mayor Abraham Beame abolished the office. He appointed a deputy mayor to supervise and coordinate city departments.

The Commission System. In 1900 a hurricane destroyed the city of Galveston, Texas. The city government was unable to cope with the problems of rebuilding the city. So the legislature suspended local self-government and appointed a commission of five local businessmen to govern and to oversee the rebuilding. The commission accomplished so much under such difficult conditions that the city kept the system of government.

Galveston's success with the commission plan attracted wide attention. Soon the plan had been adopted in other parts of the country. By 1917 over 500 American cities were using the system.

Under this plan the commission plays a

double role in city government. Each commissioner heads a city department. Together the commissioners make city policy. Thus they serve as both executives and legislators.

Most commissions have five members. Small cities may have only three, and larger cities may have as many as seven. The mayor is one of the commissioners. He or she performs ceremonial duties for the city and presides over commission meetings. In most cities with commissioners, the candidates for mayor appear separately on the ballot. The citizens thus select both the mayor and the other commissioners. In other cities the commission chooses the mayor. Often it selects the person who received the greatest number of votes in the election. Commissioners are generally expected to serve full-time. In most cities using this plan, no other administrators are elected.

Today about 175 American cities use the commission system. In the majority of these cities, a budget officer oversees the budget and reports to the commission. A professional administrator oversees each city department, providing the administrative skills the commissioners may lack.

The Council-Manager System. The basis of this plan is the belief that a manager experienced in all aspects of municipal operations is needed to help run the city. The manager system has spread rapidly across the country since World War II. Fifty percent of all American cities with populations between 10,000 and 50,000 use this system. It is most popular in suburban cities.

Under the council-manager plan, an elected city council makes policy. A city manager, hired by the council, heads a professional staff. The manager and his or her staff run the city on a daily basis.

There is no separation of power in this system. The legislative body—the council—appoints the executive—the city manager—who may be dismissed at the will of the

council. With a manager to administer city affairs, the council can devote itself to making policy. The execution of policy is the job of the manager.

Occasionally city managers do become involved in policy making. This happens mostly when the manager and the council are on good terms. Many councils do not make major policy decisions without advice from the manager and the manager's staff. Some managers even take the initiative and suggest policies to the council.

Under this plan city council members can also become involved in administering the city. If they are dissatisfied with the manager, they may bypass him or her and deal directly with heads of departments.

Studies of the council-manager plan show that it tends to be adopted in higher income communities with homogeneous populations. It is often supported by good-

Appellate Judge Ernest Morial was recently elected mayor of New Orleans—the first Black to be elected to that office. He is shown here with his wife Sybil and daughter Monique at the polls on Election Day, November 1977.

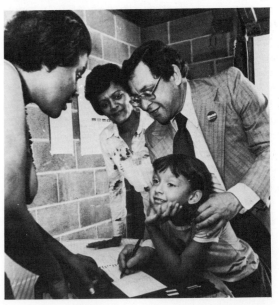

government groups and business groups who are interested in economical government and professionalism in city administration. Opposition to this form of government usually comes from organized labor, minority group leaders, politicians in office, and political party officials. These people fear the loss of their power and influence under the council-manager form of government.

section review

1. What is the function of a city charter?
2. Define municipal home rule.
3. List three basic forms of city government.
4. What is the commission system?

3. CITY PROBLEMS: LAND USE

Every modern city government faces a number of problems. These problems range from the complex and seemingly insoluble to the simple and easily handled. And they are different for different kinds of cities. Large central cities, for instance, face problems of growing street crime, police-community relations, and the decay of housing and other facilities. And behind these problems are those of poverty and tension between ethnic and racial groups.

Small-town problems are very different. They include dealing with the unplanned spread of housing developments, providing more recreational services, and modernizing downtown shopping and business areas.

Suburban cities face another array of problems. They are concerned with controlling commercial and industrial development, restricting low- and moderate-income housing and mobile home parks, preventing water pollution, and disposing of sewage. These cities also face the problem of land use. That is, they must decide how the private and public lands of the city are to be used—or not used.

The Land-Use Question. Historically, state governments have granted cities and counties the power to supervise and regulate land use. Land use has been considered a local responsibility. The effects of land use were thought to be limited to the locality itself. And local communities were believed to be better able to decide whether a certain use of land would help or harm the community.

In the early 1960's these ideas began to be questioned. Individuals and groups began to wonder whether the way a locality used its land really did affect only the local community. Studies were undertaken to investigate the problem. They revealed that while many local uses of land have limited effects, many do not. The land-use actions of one community may not have great impact outside the community. But the combined effect of many communities taking similar actions may change the region or the state.

QUOTES from famous people

"The legitimate object of government is to do for a community of people whatever they need to have done but cannot do at all, or cannot so well do for themselves in their separate and individual capacities. In all that the people can individually do as well for themselves, government ought not to interfere."

Abraham Lincoln

Land-Use Controls. Three land-use controls are common in the United States: subdivision regulations, zoning, and building-construction codes. *Subdividing* means dividing undeveloped land into lots. The subdivider has to present a *plat*, or map, to the local or county authorities. The plat usually shows projected sizes and shapes of lots, utility lines, soil types, street sizes and patterns, and topography. Many counties and communities have development plans that restrict and regulate subdivisions.

Whether a developer can divide a certain parcel of land for a particular purpose may depend also on the *zoning code* of the city or county. A city is normally divided into residential, commercial, and industrial zones. Each zone may be further divided into subzones. For instance, the residential zone may be divided into single-family homes, duplex-apartment buildings, small-apartment complexes, and so forth.

As shown here, land developers try to build as many housing units on as little land as possible. What must residents sacrifice in return for decent housing units?

A zoning code typically imposes other restrictions and standards. The height of buildings may be specified for each zone as well as the distance a building must be from the street. The total area of the lot that may be covered by a building may also be indicated.

Building-construction codes include regulations for the plumbing, electrical, heating, safety, and structural specifications of a building. All new buildings must follow these regulations. But building inspectors can undermine such codes by overlooking violations or granting exceptions. The cause of many fires in old apartment buildings in central cities can be traced to building-code violations that were not corrected or were purposely overlooked by inspectors.

Land-Use Control by States and Cities. Today many states have developed some form of regional or statewide land-use regulation. Two factors have encouraged this trend. Congress has made funds available for certain kinds of statewide planning. And the American Law Institute has created a model land development code, which includes provisions for state regulation.

Hawaii adopted state land-use regulations in 1961. But other states did not try to control the use of land by local governments until well into the 1970's. Hawaii's laws were designed to protect the state's agricultural lands from urban expansion. Montana, however, adopted state regulations to encourage expansion and economic growth. The major thrust of its legislation is to curb local or state interference with growth without damaging the environment.

Maine and Vermont regulate development activities rather than geographical areas. In Vermont, state control of city land use prevents cities from undertaking projects that may benefit the locality but harm the rest of the state. Other states have required that areas for parks, low or moderate income housing, and open space be shown on the zoning map of the city.

Arbitrary growth of cities and towns is no longer possible. In this picture, a city planner for Arlington, Massachusetts, examines a proposal for keeping some spaces open within his community.

Groups within cities are also fighting for different kinds of land-use codes. In a famous case, the city of Petaluma, California, passed a zoning rule that no more than 500 new houses could be built each year in subdivisions. Houses on single lots were not limited by the rule. Petaluma defended its action by stating that unlimited subdivisions were making it impossible for the city to provide needed services such as water, sewers, and schools.

Citizens in other cities have stopped major freeways from cutting their cities in half. Others have charged certain city council members with having a conflict of interests in approving certain developments. Often they have proved that a council member had a financial investment in the development.

There are often simple and inexpensive solutions to city problems. Here a "pocket" park for children has been created out of an empty lot.

Land-use control is likely to be a major cause of battles within cities and between city and state governments in the future. Such battles will affect the quality of our lives. The outcomes will not merely determine how much access to open spaces city dwellers will have. They will also touch nearly every aspect of city life.

section review

1. List three types of land-use controls that are common in the United States.
2. Name two factors that have encouraged regional or statewide land-use regulation.
3. Why is there opposition to land-use codes?
4. How did the city of Petaluma, California, defend its zoning rule?

4. CITY PROBLEMS: THE ELDERLY

Most large city populations include a substantial number of elderly men and women. Some live in extreme poverty in cheap, rundown hotels. They eke out their existence from one welfare or Social Security check to the next. Many do not leave their hotels, fearing that their rooms will be burglarized or that they will be mugged on the street. Other elderly people live in institutions—nursing homes or homes for the aged. The care they receive depends on the quality of the institution. Still others are financially secure enough to remain in their own homes.

The 1970 census showed that older Americans were moving into cities in increasing numbers. In 1975 a task force on aging was created by the U.S. Conference of Mayors. Its purpose is to focus attention on the problems of elderly people in cities. But in spite of federal, state, and local government action, as well as private programs, thousands of the elderly live in neglect and poverty. Somehow they slip through the network of programs designed to serve them.

Who are the elderly? Between 1900 and 1980 the percentage of United States citizens who were 65 or older more than doubled. It rose from about 4 percent of the population to over 11 percent. Today there are about 35 million people over the age of 60. This number will continue to increase as the average life expectancy in the United States is extended.

In 1980 about half the senior citizens of the United States lived in the seven most populous states—California, Illinois, New York, Ohio, Pennsylvania, Texas, and Florida. About 5 percent of these people live in some kind of institution. More than one third live alone or with nonrelatives. The rest live in a family setting. But the older they are, the less chance they have of living with a family. Since life expectancy is higher for women than men, there are many more elderly women than men in our society. There are more than five times as many widows as widowers in the world today.

The Problem of the Elderly. The elderly have a variety of problems. About 20 percent live on incomes at or below the poverty level. Many have limited or fixed incomes. That is, their incomes do not increase as the cost of food, housing, and other goods increase. These men and women are forced to buy less and less.

Many of the elderly are involved in volunteer programs in their communities.

Transportation is another problem. Once people lose the ability to drive, they must depend on some form of public transportation. Many cities have poor public transit services or none at all. And taxis are too expensive for the average elderly person.

Elderly people are often isolated. They need to socialize with other men and women. But senior citizen centers that provide a place for companionship and a hot meal are in short supply in most cities.

Many elderly people also suffer from a form of malnutrition. Some lack the desire or the ability to cook. Others pay so much for

ROSE KRYZAK

Rose Kryzak was born in 1900. She worked for 52 years but retired in 1972 "to do something different while still in good health." One day she walked into the senior citizens' center in her community of Sunnyside in the borough of Queens, New York City. She told the director of the center that she wanted to serve on the public affairs committee of the center. The director replied, "You're the chairman — so start the committee!" And so Rose Kryzak became a "senior citizen advocate."

Mrs. Kryzak started her committee. She was elected its representative to the Queens Council for Senior Citizens and was later elected vice-president of the council. She was appointed chairwoman of the borough president's Advisory Board on Aging, and was also elected vice-president of the New York State Senior Action Group. One day in March 1976 she learned that the Federal Power Commission was holding hearings in New York City for the first time. Mrs. Kryzak was concerned about the amount of her bills, so she decided to attend the hearings.

When she arrived she found the room was filled with "very impressive-looking men — lawyers and corporate presidents with fancy suits and briefcases — all ready to testify." The first speaker was a representative of a utility company that wanted a rate increase of $180 million in order to build a pipeline that would benefit consumers in 15 years. The second speaker wanted an increase of $200 million so that his company could build plants that would benefit consumers in 20 years. Rose Kryzak got angry. She thought, "I'm not even going to be alive in 20 years!" So she wrote a note to a commissioner, requesting time to testify. The commissioner replied that all the time allotted for testimony would be filled by lawyers, representatives of utility companies, and bankers, each of whom would be allowed 20 minutes. Rose Kryzak got angrier. She said, "All I need is one minute; let one of them talk for 19 minutes!" The FPC gave in and let her testify.

Kryzak complained that senior citizens, many of whom were living on fixed or limited incomes were being asked to pay for benefits they would not live to enjoy. The Federal Power Commission had never thought of this before. A new factor affecting power rates — the Kryzak problem — had been introduced. In October 1976 the FPC alerted Kryzak to read the next day's **New York Times.** The story said that as a result of Kryzak's eloquent pleas, the commission had rejected the proposed 15 percent rate hike on electricity rates, marking a victory for consumers. Rose Kryzak had become a nationally known figure. Although it was by chance that she became involved in the setting of power rates, she had now made herself an expert on the subject.

housing that they have little money left to buy the proper foods.

Opportunities to serve society are also limited for those over 65. They are excluded from the mainstream of the community—even though many have excellent skills and are able to do productive work.

Helping the Elderly. The picture is not entirely bleak, however. In the past few years, many government and private programs have focused on the problems of the elderly. In 1975 nearly 20 percent of the federal budget was devoted to older Americans. Each federal dollar spent on programs for the elderly is divided in the following way: more than 71¢ is spent on retirement benefits; more than 23¢ is spent on health services; more than 5¢ goes to all other purposes (such as income maintenance); with relatively small sums going to social services, employment services, and nutrition programs.

Communities, groups, and government agencies have also responded to the problems of the elderly in various ways.

The administration on aging within the Department of Health and Human Services has partially funded a television program that is seen on most Public Broadcasting Service stations. The series has three goals: 1) to foster positive attitudes about aging in our youth-oriented society, 2) to do away with myths and stereotypes about the realities and problems of aging, and 3) to encourage better communication between generations. Each half-hour program reports on such subjects as nutrition, health and medicine, housing, money management, legal rights, and other concerns of people who are retired or nearing retirement age.

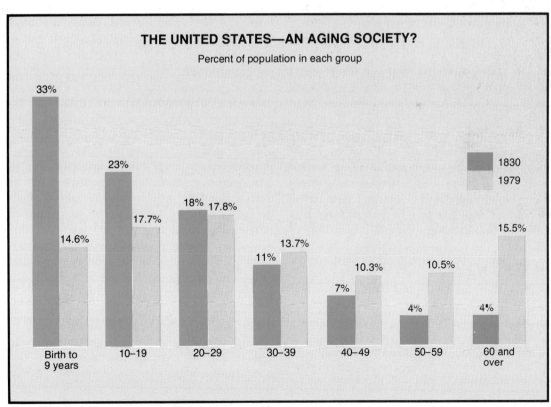

THE UNITED STATES—AN AGING SOCIETY?

Percent of population in each group

Source: U.S. Bureau of the Census, The New York Times

Many states have in-home services to provide housekeeping, homemaker, and chore assistance to low-income residents. These services allow many elderly individuals to remain in their homes and maintain as much independence as possible.

In Portland, Maine, a Postal Alert project operates for the seniors in the community. Participants put a sticker on their mailboxes to alert the mail deliverer that they are registered with Postal Alert. If the mail carrier discovers that the mail has not been picked up within a reasonable time, the carrier notifies his or her supervisor, who calls the Senior Citizens' Council. The council attempts to contact the person and summons help if necessary.

New Jersey's State Division on Aging maintains a senior citizen hotline. It provides assistance to elderly residents by answering questions about programs and services concerning senior citizens.

A lobby group, the Gray Panthers, actively works for legislation and programs that help the elderly.

In March 1977 the Supreme Court ruled it unconstitutional not to award survivor's benefits to widowers, since widows were already receiving those benefits.

Many cities with transit systems give senior citizens a discount on the fare or allow them to ride free at certain times of day, or both. Some cities have ordered new buses that have entrance and exit steps closer to the ground, so that the senior citizens have less difficulty in getting on and off.

section review

1. Why was the task force on aging created in 1975?
2. Name the seven states where the greatest number of America's senior citizens live.
3. Describe some of the problems of the urban elderly.
4. Describe some of the programs that have focused on the problems of the elderly.

5. CITY PROBLEMS: HOUSING

Since the end of World War II, the rise in individual income in the nation has allowed average Americans to improve their housing. But people with low incomes still face severe housing problems. The housing crisis is particularly acute in our cities, where there are many people on low or limited incomes. Much of the available housing is old and deteriorating. Much housing has been torn down for urban renewal projects. Property taxes rise higher and faster in cities than in suburban areas.

One serious cause of housing problems is racial discrimination. Certain ethnic and racial groups stake out territory and often actively discriminate in the sale or rental of housing to keep "those other people" out. Minority group members seeking housing may not even know that they have been discriminated against. Since the 1968 Civil Rights Act made discrimination in housing illegal, much of the discrimination has become hidden.

Attacking Discrimination in Housing. By the use of a process called auditing, fair-housing groups across the country have been able to document discrimination within communities and describe how that discrimination occurs. An *audit* is a procedure in which both a minority group member and a White person seeking housing visit the apartment or house advertised for rent or sale. The auditors are similar in educational background, sex, age, work experience, credit rating, and other characteristics that a landlord or real estate agent might find significant.

Each auditor visits the apartment or house within a short period of time. Neither consults the other. But each carefully records the rental or sales terms quoted by the apartment manager or house owner. Then a third person compares the reports of each auditor. If the reports reveal a significant

The south Bronx, in New York City, is an outstanding example of urban decay. With help from the federal and state governments, this area may once again prove a vital neighborhood for city residents.

difference in the treatment of the two auditors, it is determined that discrimination on the basis of race or ethnic origin has occurred. The same process is now used to document discrimination based on sex or life style. Below are some findings of a fair-housing group in California that conducted an audit of its community.

At an apartment complex, the Black auditor was told that no units were available, although two might open up in a few weeks. His name was put on a waiting list. The White auditor, who visited the apartment soon after the Black auditor, was shown an apartment that was available for occupancy that day.

At a single-family house, a non-Hispanic auditor was given an application to fill out in case she was interested. She was told that she and her husband could move in within several days. The Hispanic auditor was not offered an application and was given a move-in date of nearly a month later.

At a triplex, a Black auditor was told of an unusual rental agreement in which the tenant had to sign a one-year lease but the landlord could terminate the lease on 30 days' notice. The landlord explained that he was worried about loud music and about the possibility that another family would not move into the unit if he rented to the Black. The White auditor was not told of the landlord's worries and was offered a typical one-year lease.

Other Housing Problems. In addition to discrimination, other housing problems face cities today. The demand for housing in cities far exceeds the available supply. Some cities have made broad zoning revisions, changing neighborhoods from residential to industrial and from multi-family to single-family areas.

Lack of government loans for the rehabilitation of city housing has been a significant factor in the shortage of housing. But even more serious has been the practice of *red-lining*, or refusing loans, by local lending institutions, such as banks and savings-and-loan associations. These institutions see certain neighborhoods as poor investment risks. Consequently, they have refused to loan money either for rehabilitation of housing or for mortgage purposes. This practice contributes to the further decline of the neighborhood.

section review

1. What is one of the most serious urban housing problems?
2. Define auditing as it relates to housing.

CHAPTER SUMMARY

6

In 200 years the United States has changed from an agricultural nation into a nation of industry and cities. Many of today's major problems are those resulting from urbanization.

Nearly three quarters of the American population is crowded into 282 metropolitan areas. City governments have had most of the responsibility for problems involving housing, transportation, pollution, land-use reform, and care of the aging.

City governments are creatures of the state, deriving authority and power from the state government. States may withdraw power as well as give it. Generally, cities have more flexibility than other kinds of local government. A city's charter is its fundamental law and is granted by the state, either by law or by constitutional home rule. There are three basic forms of city government: the mayor-council system, the commission system, and the council-manager system.

REVIEW QUESTIONS

1. Should cities be given the right to frame their own charters? Why or why not?
2. Which of the three forms of city government do you believe could most effectively deal with the serious urban problems described in this chapter? Give reasons for your choice.
3. From the urban problems described in this chapter, select examples of the dual nature of federalism (i.e., power shared between local and national government).
4. Why is the structure of city government extremely important?

5. What are the characteristics of a weak mayor-council system? What are the characteristics of a strong mayor-council system?
6. Describe the event that attracted strong attention to the commission plan in Galveston, Texas (1900)?
7. What is meant by the term "zoning code"?
8. In what areas does the federal government allocate funds to senior citizens?
9. Who are the Gray Panthers?
10. What is one effort made by the state of New Jersey to help the elderly?

ACTIVITIES FOR REVIEW

activity 1 Attend a meeting of your city council, school board, or other local governmental agency. What problems are dealt with? How?

activity 2 Stage a debate on the following topic: RESOLVED, that my city should adopt a council-manager system of government.

activity 3 Review newspapers for examples of problems handled by your city government. Write a report on one problem and how the city government resolves it.

political science
DICTIONARY

audit—a procedure for detecting discrimination in housing. A minority-group member and a White person apply separately for an apartment or house advertised for rent or sale.   p. 132

classified charter—state laws that are applicable to all of the cities within a certain classification.   p. 121

municipal home rule—a system permitting a city to write, adopt, and amend its own charter with relatively little interference from the state legislature.   p. 121

plat—a plan or map of an area.   p. 126

redlining—the practice by banks of refusing to loan funds for city housing rehabilitation.   p. 133

subdividing—dividing undeveloped land into lots.   p. 126

zoning codes—regulations that impose restrictions and set standards for land developers.   p. 126

7

Local Governments

Local governments are divided in many different ways. These divisions may be made geographically, or they may be made according to the financial needs of an area.

In this chapter you will learn about the different types of divisions and how they operate. You will examine some of the problems experienced by each. You will also see how, over time, changes have occurred in local governments that reflect the growing demands of areas.

CHAPTER PREVIEW

1. COUNTIES
2. TOWNSHIPS AND SPECIAL DISTRICTS
3. REGIONAL ARRANGEMENTS

1. COUNTIES

Counties may differ in population, in form of government, in finances, and in the functions they perform. But they all share one characteristic. All counties are basic geographic subdivisions of the state.

Perhaps the greatest difference among counties can be seen when a metropolitan area county and a rural county are compared.

Los Angeles County, California, for example, is located in a metropolitan area. It has a population of seven million, its density measures 1,700 people per square mile, and it employs 107,800 people. Inyo County, California, is a rural county. Its population is 17,000, it has a density of two people per square mile, and it employs only 417 people. Compared to Inyo County, Los Angeles County has more people, who live closer

The law enforcement officer is vital to the operation of the county government.

together, and it employs many more people. Thus it may be able to raise more money to pay its employees and to provide services for its people.

In recent years it has become more difficult for heavily populated counties such as Los Angeles to provide services to its residents. This has brought about a crisis in county government as well as attempts to reform it.

County Governments. County governments are created by states. Their purpose is mainly to enforce and administer state laws. These laws determine their boundaries and forms of organization. They also grant counties their powers and delegate many administrative tasks to them.

County governments grew unsystematically. Most often they grew in response to local geographic, economic, political, and social pressures. They have resisted complete changes in function. Nevertheless, there have been some changes in their functions, although many of these came about in piecemeal fashion. For example, county governments have increased their activities and services. They have supported intergovernmental cooperation within a county and among counties.

In recent years some states have increased the powers of county governments, whereas others have chosen to decrease their powers. On the one hand, in 1975 the South Carolina supreme court abolished one of the five optional forms of county government. This left counties with one less alternative when deciding what form of government to adopt. Washington State voters rejected a proposed constitutional amendment that would have eventually created more home rule. These voters chose not to give counties more power over their government affairs.

On the other hand, Kansas increased the

County courthouses formed the hub of the community in the early days of the nation's history. This courthouse is typical of many such early government buildings.

length of terms of many county officials, which gave them more time in office to exercise their powers and carry out their programs. Maine gave county boards the power to hire a county administrator to administer all departments and offices that the board controls.

The Forms of County Government. There are three basic forms of county government—the commission, the council-administrator, and the council-elected executive. The commission form is the most widely used—77 percent of all county governments use it. In some states, one type of county government may be used more often than others. Yet in other states, a mixture of these forms can be found.

In Texas, all of the counties have a commission form of government. In Arkansas, all similar-size counties use the council-elected executive form. North Carolina counties with populations over 10,000 have a council administrator.

The Commission Form.

The *commission* form of county government has a governing board made up of several members. These members are generally elected by district. Members of the governing board act as the heads of specific departments. The board shares the administrative and some legislative responsibilities with other independently elected county officials. These include the county clerk, the treasurer, the sheriff, the coroner, and the recorder.

Usually, in this form of county government, there is no single administrator to supervise the county's activities. The lack of such a central administrator results in governmental authority being spread among elected officials. This makes it more difficult for the public to fix responsibility for poor county government. It also hinders the county's ability to carry out its increased duties and to deliver its services.

The Council-Administrator Form.

The *council-administrator* type of county government has an administrator appointed by and responsible to the elected council. The administrator is expected to carry out the council's directives. The county board establishes policy and makes various rules and laws. It also adopts a budget to carry out these rules and laws. The administrator develops the budget for the board, implements it after the board adopts it, hires and fires department heads, and recommends policies and laws to the board. The council must refrain from interfering with the administrator's functions.

The Council-Elected Executive Form.

In the *council-elected executive* form of government, there are two distinct branches of government—the legislative and the executive. The legislative consists of an elected county board, which develops policy, adopts the budget, and inspects county finances. It also has the power to veto the actions of the county executive. The executive branch is headed by an independently elected executive. He or she prepares the budget, supervises county operations, suggests policy to the board, and generally acts as the spokesperson for the county.

How Well Do Counties Do Their Job?

In the past, counties were created to provide a county seat and a county courthouse within a day's journey of all county residents. The residents of the county were mainly farmers. While the farmer attended to business at the courthouse and with local merchants, the family could shop, find out the local gossip, and visit with friends in town. Then the entire family could return home by wagon in time to do the evening chores.

Today, however, only a small percentage of the nation's population are farmers. Also, the modern farmer can drive to several county seats in one day by truck or car. Nonetheless, small counties remain, even though they may no longer serve the same purpose.

Because present-day counties were created to serve another age with other needs, they pose certain problems. For example, many counties are run very inefficiently. In addition, they are, in themselves, an inefficient way to run a state. To solve these and other problems, experts have decided that counties must be reorganized and consolidated. Proposals to do this have generally taken two forms. Some suggest consolidation of two or more counties into one. Others propose consolidating the county government with the major city in the county.

But voters have rejected most of these plans. County consolidations have been re-

Revenue of County Governments, by Source: 1978-79

Total: $50.1 Billion

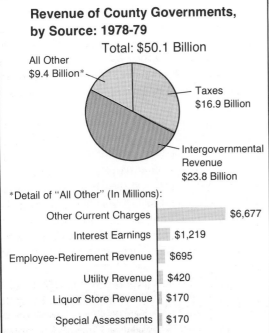

All Other
$9.4 Billion*

Taxes
$16.9 Billion

Intergovernmental
Revenue
$23.8 Billion

*Detail of "All Other" (In Millions):

Other Current Charges	$6,677
Interest Earnings	$1,219
Employee-Retirement Revenue	$695
Utility Revenue	$420
Liquor Store Revenue	$170
Special Assessments	$170
Sale of Property	$55

Expenditure of County Governments, by Character and Object: 1978-79

Total: $50.6 Billion

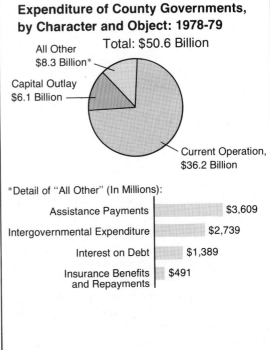

All Other
$8.3 Billion*

Capital Outlay
$6.1 Billion

Current Operation,
$36.2 Billion

*Detail of "All Other" (In Millions):

Assistance Payments	$3,609
Intergovernmental Expenditure	$2,739
Interest on Debt	$1,389
Insurance Benefits and Repayments	$491

General Expenditure of County Governments, by Function: 1978-79

Total: $49.1 Billion

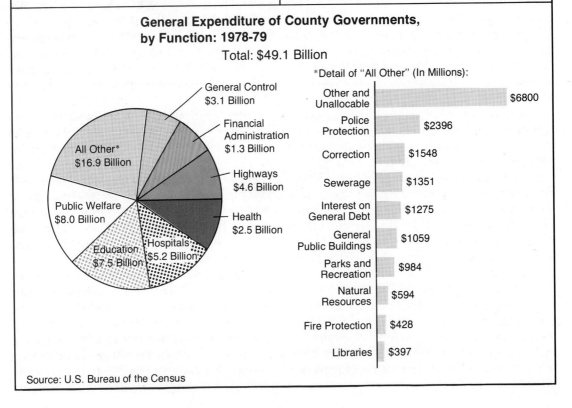

General Control
$3.1 Billion

Financial
Administration
$1.3 Billion

Highways
$4.6 Billion

Health
$2.5 Billion

All Other*
$16.9 Billion

Public Welfare
$8.0 Billion

Education
$7.5 Billion

Hospitals
$5.2 Billion

*Detail of "All Other" (In Millions):

Other and Unallocable	$6800
Police Protection	$2396
Correction	$1548
Sewerage	$1351
Interest on General Debt	$1275
General Public Buildings	$1059
Parks and Recreation	$984
Natural Resources	$594
Fire Protection	$428
Libraries	$397

Source: U.S. Bureau of the Census

jected in small, rural counties because the county government and the county seat provide a source of identity and pride for residents. Those who work for county governments want to retain their jobs in the local community. The usually small county seats are typically the largest local employers in their respective areas. The county seat depends on its employees and officeholders for patronage.

Since World War II, only 25 city-county consolidations have been successful. These consolidations have usually been between the largest city and the county, with smaller suburban municipalities permitted to remain outside of the consolidated government. These smaller municipalities have the option of joining at a later date.

City-county consolidations have failed for different reasons. First, the division between the usually Republican-dominated suburbs and the usually Democratic-dominated central cities has been a major obstacle to consolidation. Since the Democratic party controls both the cities and the rural areas in most southern states, there has been a lack of division in the South. Most of the city-county consolidations have occurred there.

Second, racial problems have played an important part in the disagreements about city-county consolidations. Both Blacks and Whites have opposed these consolidations, but for different reasons. Often White suburbanites (who previously left the central city) vote against consolidation to ensure that they will not be a part of the city again. Many Black leaders take the position that city-county consolidations are aimed at diluting Black voting strength.

Third, even though city and county governments may be inefficient, the dissatisfaction with this inefficiency is not enough to overcome the loyalty people have to the existing system. In order to maintain local control, many people are willing to tolerate inefficiency in their governments.

County Services. County reorganization has not been successful in most parts of the country. But counties and cities have, nonetheless, cooperated in many ways. They are working together today to provide a number of important services to a growing population.

Counties are given power by the state to provide their residents with a variety of services. Traditional county functions include tax assessment and collection, election administration, judicial administration, public record keeping, issuing licenses, running the sheriff's office, providing agricultural services, as well as health and welfare services, and maintaining and building roads and highways.

Rapid urban growth, especially in the suburbs, has put pressure on government to provide for a larger population. A shortage of money at all levels of government has pointed out the need to eliminate duplication of services and to provide more efficient services. Solving these problems has led to increased cooperation between local governments and counties. More and more counties are undertaking services that, in the past, were seen as the responsibility of city government.

During the 1970's, metropolitan county services increased by an average of about 20 percent. A 1975 survey revealed that an increasing number of services that used to be handled by small municipalities were now being handled by counties. The majority of these increasing county responsibilities were in the areas of elections, solid waste collection and disposal, public health, and law enforcement.

Counties are the leaders in seeking cooperation among the local government units within a county. This cooperation usually takes one of three forms. A county may perform functions for individual local governments on a contract basis. For example, King County, Washington, contracts out its public defender services to cities on a per-case

Mobile recreational units—in this case, a "skatemobile"—are a type of service counties often provide for their citizens.

basis. A county may work on a project with local governments within a county on a joint basis. For example, Santa Clara County, California, has developed a computer system that tabulates all crime-related data. Thirteen cities participate in the program. A county may work jointly or under contract with another county. For example, Clark County and Cumberland County, Illinois, have agreed to share the salary and services of a single highway superintendent.

section review

1. Name one characteristic that all counties share.

2. List three basic forms of county government.
3. Why have city-county consolidations failed?
4. How do counties cooperate with local governments that are under their jurisdiction?
5. List six traditional county functions.
6. Describe some of the pressures on city governments due to rapid urban growth.

2. TOWNSHIPS AND SPECIAL DISTRICTS

Townships, or towns, began with the earliest settlers, the Pilgrims. Today more than half the townships in the United States have fewer than 1,000 residents. A township consists basically of a number of rural and small urban areas organized under a single town government. The scope of powers granted to townships by the states varies widely. Some townships perform only a few services for rural areas, such as constructing and maintaining roads and bridges. Others may also provide libraries and relief for the poor. Still others perform services usually associated with municipal or county governments. Recently, however, counties and municipalities have been assuming tasks that townships once performed.

The Typical Township. Typical township officials include a board of supervisors, a justice of the peace, and a constable. In some townships, all the voters may attend an annual meeting to elect officers, levy taxes, and determine how the township spends its money.

New England is well known for its township system. Here the town is the principal government in rural areas. It performs most of the tasks that a county performs elsewhere. New England towns have annual meetings open to all voters. The voters may speak on any issue on the agenda and may help make the rules, pass new laws, and levy taxes. These annual town meetings are the best example of direct democracy in the United States. Everyone within the town boundaries may participate in the meeting and be elected as one of the town's officials.

In this picture citizens are shown attending a town meeting to discuss zoning. What topics do you think would draw the highest attendance at a meeting in your community?

DUTIES OF TOWNSHIPS BY STATE

State	Number of Townships	Description of Powers
Connecticut	149	The towns in Connecticut often serve heavily populated areas and perform functions ordinarily performed other places by municipal governments.
Illinois	1,436	Illinois townships have three main functions: They assess property for taxing purposes, maintain local roads, and support indigents. Some of them also operate libraries, cemeteries, and hospitals.
Indiana	1,008	Township functions have slowly been absorbed by the counties, and the principal task left to these units is administering relief for the poor.
Kansas	1,449	Most of the duties of Kansas townships have been taken over by the counties. Some still maintain local roads; a few provide fire protection, parks, libraries, water supply, and cemeteries. All help county assessors in assessing property for taxation.
Maine	475	The Maine towns and "plantations" perform many of the duties commonly associated with county governments and Maine towns and populous areas provide the same services as cities of corresponding size.
Massachusetts	312	Many Massachusetts towns serve heavily populated areas and perform functions performed other places by municipal governments.
Michigan	1,245	Some townships provide a variety of urban types of services, including police and fire protection and water and sewer services. Others perform only very minor governmental duties. Townships of 2,000 or more inhabitants may organize as "charter" townships and exercise considerably broader taxing powers and administrative flexibility than other townships.
Minnesota	1,792	The most important activity that townships now perform is maintenance of roads (if the county has not assumed this task). Some administer relief; a few provide fire protection.
Missouri	326	The main duty of these units is to build and maintain local roads and bridges.
Nebraska	471	The major township function is local road maintenance.

DUTIES OF TOWNSHIPS BY STATE

State	Number of Townships	Description of Powers
New Hampshire	221	Some provide limited services to rural areas, but towns in heavily populated areas perform functions ordinarily associated elsewhere with municipal governments.
New Jersey	232	Those townships in urban centers provide municipal types of services for their inhabitants.
New York	930	Some towns provide local road maintenance, but most handle a variety of functions and often provide urban types of services. Numerous kinds of improvement districts or special-service districts are associated with New York towns.
North Dakota	1,360	The primary function of these townships is to build and maintain local roads and bridges.
Ohio	1,319	The principal function of Ohio townships is maintenance of local roads. Some provide cemeteries, parks, libraries, hospitals, fire protection, street lighting, garbage collection, and land-use zoning.
Pennsylvania	1,549	Those townships with a population density of 300 or more per square mile are urban in nature and often perform functions similar to those of cities and boroughs.
Rhode Island	31	These towns perform various duties elsewhere commonly associated with county and municipal governments.
South Dakota	1,010	The primary function of these townships is to build and maintain local roads.
Vermont	237	These towns perform many of the duties commonly associated with county and municipal governments.
Wisconsin	1,270	These towns provide local road maintenance, and some provide a variety of services, including sanitation and utility services.

Source: U.S. Bureau of Census; 1977 Census of Governments

Special Districts. *Special districts* are formed to provide a particular service, such as schools and parks, water supply, or airport construction. These special districts can be classified into two categories—school districts and nonschool special districts. Since 1942, the number of school districts in the country has decreased dramatically. At the same time, nonschool special districts have increased at a surprisingly large rate. The growth rate of nonschool special districts has been higher than the growth of any other governmental unit.

Special districts are often favored as the least controversial means of solving problems. They are easy to create because they require only minor alterations in the existing system of local government. They are also a quick and often satisfactory method of delivering a visible public service or product. The special district is created under state law. It usually requires the consent of the people in the district. Since most districts are concerned with only a particular function, people view them as a method of delivering services rather than as another level of government.

Characteristics of Special Districts. Special districts vary greatly in size, number of employees, number of local governments served, and number and kinds of functions performed. Special districts are most often found in nonmetropolitan areas. More than 80 percent of all countrywide and multi-county districts are located in rural parts of the United States.

But all special districts have common traits. They always exist as a separate government and are responsible for providing a particular governmental service. They have legal power to perform their activities. They are run by a board of directors, trustees, or commissioners, but the selection process for these officials may differ. Special districts also have the power to raise revenue from one or more sources. Most often, special districts are supported by taxes or by the sale of bonds.

Special districts can be regional or local in character. Their boundaries frequently overlap other existing local government boundaries. A special district may serve an **unincorporated area,** only part of an **incorporated** municipality, or county, or any combination of these areas. Special district boundaries are adaptable. The district itself can often redefine its territorial bounds. Special districts established by an interstate compact or by parallel legislation in two or more states cross state lines. They are, in fact, the only governmental unit below the national level that can be interstate in nature.

Incorporated and **unincorporated areas** refer to the legal status of a local unit of government. Incorporated areas—also called municipal corporations—include cities, villages, and, in some states, towns and boroughs. Unincorporated areas—also known as quasi-corporations—include counties, townships, and school districts.

Dates of incorporation for many cities illustrate how fast regions of the country grew in population.

section review

1. What is a township?
2. What are common traits of special districts?
3. Why are special districts formed?

3. REGIONAL ARRANGEMENTS

Regional arrangements have increased since World War II because state and local governments have been unable to solve various kinds of problems by themselves. The earliest regional arrangements developed in metropolitan areas, where individual counties and cities were not able to cope with such problems as air and water pollution, sewage treatment, transportation, and housing. But since 1970 nonmetropolitan areas have been growing at a faster rate than metropolitan areas. As a result, their problems have been growing. They are finding that they too need to form cooperative arrangements to solve these problems.

There are five kinds of regional arrangements: area-wide special districts, federally encouraged and financed regional programs and institutions, state-mandated regional planning districts, "A-95" clearinghouses, and voluntary regional councils.

Areawide Special Districts. All three levels of government—federal, state, and local—have encouraged the growth of areawide special districts. The federal government funds about 50 percent of all large areawide districts in the 72 largest metropolitan areas of the country. States provide an incentive for creating special districts through limits on the taxes and debts of local governments. Local governments, in turn, promote the use of areawide special districts because they are unwilling or unable to perform a number of services.

Recently, some states have tried to curb the number of special districts. Five states—California, Nevada, New Mexico, Oregon, and Washington—permit state or local boundary commissions to review special districts. They determine if new districts are needed or whether old ones should be dissolved, consolidated, or expanded. There is much local opposition to changing special districts.

Federally Encouraged and Financed Regional Programs and Institutions. Federal agencies have established a wide new range of geographic regions that serve as special districts. There are at least 24 federal areawide programs that operate in over 4,100 special districts. The Department of Transportation and several other agencies have designated special districts that may cover a wide area for their programs.

The goal of each of these federal special districts is to improve regional communications. All of them are charged with preparing plans that consider both the civil rights and the environmental impact of various federal programs.

For the most part, federally encouraged areawide programs have added to the complexity of regional arrangements. Federal and state regional boundaries may be quite dissimilar. In fact, boundaries of federal programs match those of state regional planning districts only 35 percent of the time.

State-Mandated Regional Planning Districts. Forty-five states now have officially designated regional planning districts. These districts were created largely in response to federal assistance programs having a regional focus.

The federal government hoped that state regional planning districts would reduce the overlap created by the numerous federal programs. It expected the new state districts to provide a common framework for regional planning and programming across the nation. But these goals have not been realized in many cases.

Usually the states possess the major

responsibility for shaping federal grant programs. Therefore, many governors see state regional planning districts not only as a mechanism to bring order to the various federal-state programs but also as a way to get more federal grants.

Local governments look at state regional planning districts as a means of obtaining a larger voice in federal and state decisions in their areas. They are especially interested in doing this if such a voice helps them increase their share of federal grant money.

There are three sets of roles in the typical regional planning district—one for the state, one for the federal, and one for the local government. The state sets the boundaries of the regional districts. It establishes rules for the organization of such districts and helps local governments to implement them. Various federal agencies provide financial assistance for specific programs as well as guidelines for how to set up district organizations according to state and federal regulations and operate a variety of programs within the district framework.

"A-95" Clearinghouses.

The Federal Office of Management and Budget requires that state or regional clearinghouses review grants for many federal and federally aided planning and development projects. This review, called the A-95 process, is designed to coordinate federal and federally assisted projects with each other and with state, regional, and local programs.

Two types of clearinghouses handle the A-95 review. *State clearinghouses*, named by the governor, perform this function. These clearinghouses are usually, but not always, state planning agencies. In some cases, they are state budget or administrative offices. *Areawide clearinghouses* also handle the A-95 review. These are almost always planning agencies that cover one or more counties. Most of them are voluntary regional councils. Others are state regional planning districts.

There are some limits on the way clearinghouses manage the review process. They are limited in the time allowed for reviews. They must also inform any other government agency, at any level, if their plans or programs might be affected by that agency's proposed project.

Both types of area clearinghouses have eliminated some duplication in regional cooperation and coordination. In many cases, however, A-95 clearinghouse reviews have not been effective. The clearinghouse may have no areawide plan upon which to base its review. In some cases, clearinghouses have merely issued rubber-stamp approvals for federal grant applications. Rarely has a clearinghouse given a negative review of any application for federal funds. Occasionally the clearinghouses have been overloaded by unimportant regional projects and by environmental and civil rights impact statements. This is the result of not having turned down applications.

Voluntary Regional Councils.

Regional councils bring together local government officials at regular intervals on a voluntary basis. They discuss common problems, exchange information, and develop policy positions on matters of mutual interest. Regional council programs concentrate on physical developments. Most council programs deal with housing, water and sewage, land use, and open space. Some have health, manpower, and drug abuse programs. A member organization may withdraw at any time. In 1950 there were fewer than 25 of these voluntary regional bodies, but in 1977 there were 1,932 regional councils.

Regional councils have developed to meet federal requirements under the A-95 clearinghouses and the regional programs of various federal departments. The typical regional council membership in 1977 consisted of 31 municipalities, 5 counties, 3 school districts, and 3 special districts. Half of all councils operate under one-unit–one-vote representation formulas. About 25 percent

NUMBERS OF LOCAL GOVERNMENTS, BY TYPE, 1942–1977					
	1942	1952	1962	1972	1977
Counties	3,050	3,052	3,043	3,044	3,042
Municipalities	16,220	16,807	18,000	18,517	18,862
Townships	18,919	17,202	17,142	16,991	16,822
Special Districts	8,299	12,340	18,323	23,885	25,962
School Districts	108,579	67,355	34,678	15,781	15,174
Total	155,067	116,756	91,186	78,218	79,862

Source: U. S. Bureau of the Census.

base their voting formulas on the populations of the member governments. This formula makes the council more sensitive to the interests of the larger member governments. The rest of the councils use different voting formulas for different policy decisions.

Regional councils receive most of their funding from local and federal sources. In 1977, 87 percent of the funding for regional councils came from the federal government. Less than 6 percent of their support came from state funds. Local sources also contribute about 6 percent. The influence of federal funding is substantial. Sometimes it can be harmful. One study of regional councils found that most of these councils wait for federal grants to finance programs. Less than 5 percent of all councils adopted any program without federal assistance.

Problems with Regional Arrangements. When Michigan, Oregon, South Carolina, Utah, and Washington created their state regional planning districts, they incorporated existing metropolitan regional councils into larger state districts. The old districts either lost their identities or had their boundaries expanded to become the regional planning district. But in Arkansas, Kentucky, and Wisconsin, regional planning districts were superimposed on some metropolitan regional council districts. The two districts continued to operate separately. The competition that resulted between regional state planners

and metropolitan planners created severe problems.

As patterns of local government in the United States change, the need for regional arrangements will also change. One study showed that counties and special districts tended to receive funds for such services as solid waste collection and disposal or law enforcement. If local governments consolidate or if an existing areawide agency is assigned responsibility for all important areawide functions, the need for other kinds of regional arrangements lessens.

Regional arrangements today are complex, confusing, and overlapping. They are heavily influenced by federal funds and are most responsive to federal programs. The states have the power to redirect the emphasis of regional arrangements. They can refocus state regional planning districts and metropolitan districts toward more state-oriented programs and problems. But states can do this successfully only if they provide more funds and if they take leadership in consolidating the many regional arrangements that now exist.

section review

1. List three kinds of regional arrangements.
2. Why do local governments encourage the use of areawide special districts?
3. What did the federal government hope to gain by creating regional planning districts?

CHAPTER SUMMARY

7

Local governments are divided in many different ways. These divisions may be geographical or they may reflect the financial needs of an area.

Several types of local government serve the needs of diverse areas and populations. Many of the older divisions lost their original purpose as the United States changed from a rural to an urban nation.

Counties are basic geographic subdivisions of the state. Their principal purpose is to enforce and administer state laws. There are three forms of county government: the commission, the council-administrator, and the council-elected executive forms.

A township consists of a number of rural and small urban areas. Its functions are similar to those of large cities and counties. Special districts are formed to provide a particular service such as schools or sewage treatment. They are most often found in nonmetropolitan areas.

The newest level of local government is not really a government at all. Regional arrangements are cooperative ventures designed to deal with areawide concerns, such as pollution, federally encouraged and financed programs, state-mandated planning districts, federal aid clearinghouses, or voluntary regional councils.

Today's regional, county, or township governments are complex, confusing, and often overlapping.

REVIEW QUESTIONS

1. Should counties and townships be abolished? Why or why not?
2. What problems facing your community would be most effectively dealt with by county government? by a special district? by a regional arrangement? Why?
3. School districts are one form of special district. Do you think schools should be special districts or one department of city and county government? Explain your choice.

ACTIVITIES FOR REVIEW

activity 1   Attend a county board of supervisors meeting. What are the major problems discussed? How are they resolved?

activity 2	Invite a county official to speak to your class on the changing role of county government.
activity 3	Invite a representative of a special district (utility, transportation, schools) to speak to your class on the services provided by the district.
activity 4	Prepare an outline of the structure and services of your county government.
activity 5	Prepare a report on Canadian "metro" governments. How do they attempt to resolve some of the confusion and overlapping in local government today? Would you favor this kind of government in your area? Why or why not?
activity 6	Prepare a wall chart showing all the local governmental units (county, township, special districts) serving your community.

political science
DICTIONARY

areawide clearinghouses—planning agencies, covering one or more counties, which review grants for federal and federally aided planning and development projects. .... p. 148

incorporated area—the legal status of a local unit of government; also called a municipal corporation. It includes cities, villages, and, in some states, towns and boroughs. .... p. 146

state clearinghouses—agencies named by the governor to review grants for federal and federally aided planning and development projects, called A-95 review. .... p. 148

township—a number of rural and small urban areas organized under a single town government. .... p. 143

unincorporated area—the legal status of a local unit of government; also known as a quasi-corporation. It includes counties, townships, and school districts. .... p. 146

8

Financing State and Local Governments

During the Great Depression and World War II, state and local governments barely skirted bankruptcy. Since that time they have faced one fiscal crisis after another. These governments have borne the brunt of demands for new and better public services created by a growing and increasingly urban population with a rising standard of living. Newspaper headlines reflect the struggle to provide more services and programs as well as to keep taxes down: "Gallup Poll: Tax Relief Top Worry;" "School District Bonds Defeated;" "Medicare Spending Up 20 Percent;" "City Budget Increases 30 Percent."

State governments and local governments get revenue (money) from two main sources: taxes and intergovernmental grants. In this chapter you will learn how this is achieved.

CHAPTER PREVIEW

1. TAXES
2. STATE AND LOCAL GOVERNMENT TAX SOURCES
3. INTERGOVERNMENTAL TRANSFERS

1. TAXES

A *tax* is a compulsory contribution for the support of government. Generally, people cannot refuse to pay a tax simply because they, as individuals, do not receive a particular benefit from the tax.

Principles of Taxation. There are three systems of taxation in the United States—federal, state, and local. Two basic principles are associated with these tax systems. First, a preference exists for tax systems that are based on the ability to pay. People with the higher incomes are expected to pay progressively more taxes than those with lower incomes. Second, people who make the same amount of money should be treated equally under the tax system.

All tax systems are compromises, however, and principles are not always translated into systems. In 1953 the average family had an income of $5,000. It paid 11.8 percent of family income in direct federal, state, and local taxes. By 1977 the average family had an income of $16,000 and paid 22.5 percent of family income in taxes. The family's tax burden nearly doubled. Yet a high-income family paid taxes amounting to 20.2 percent of income in 1953 and 31.4 percent in 1977. This was an increase of only 46 percent. Clearly, this meant that the tax burden increased most for those who made less money, not for those who made more money.

Kinds of Taxes. Taxes fall into three broad categories. A *proportional tax* makes each person pay exactly the same percentage of his or her income. A *progressive tax* is one in which the tax rates increase as the ability to pay increases. A higher-income person pays not only a large income tax but also a progressively higher fraction of his or her income. A *regressive tax* is one in which the tax rate becomes proportionately lower as the tax base increases. It falls more heavily on

QUOTES from famous people

"The wisdom of man never yet contrived a system of taxation that would operate with perfect equality."

Andrew Jackson

Taxes paid by citizens to maintain roads should be paid back in services—in this case, improvement of highways.

low-income groups. A low-income person pays a greater percentage of his or her income in taxes than does a higher-income individual. Only 5 state and local tax systems fall in the progressive category, 15 are proportional, and the remaining 30 systems are regressive.

State Powers of Taxation. Within certain national and state constitutional limits, states may levy a variety of taxes on whomever they wish. The federal Constitution—under Article I, Section 10, Clauses 2 and 3—forbids the states to tax exports or imports or to levy tonnage duties without the consent of Congress. States cannot tax interstate and foreign commerce or the federal government (including military bases). States also cannot use their taxing power to deprive persons of

WHAT PART OF THE BUDGET WOULD YOU LIMIT?

Supposing the budgets of your state and local governments have to be curtailed, which one of these parts of the budget would you limit most severely?

	Percent of Total U.S. Public	Percent of Respondents by Region			
		Northeast	North Central	South	West
Public Safety (fire, police, criminal justice)	2%	1%	2%	3%	4%
Public Schools (K-12)	3	4	2	3	2
Tax-Supported Colleges and Universities	23	24	21	19	32
Aid to the Needy	8	3	9	11	6
Streets and Highways	11	15	10	7	16
Parks and Recreation	40	36	44	45	31
Don't Know	12	17	11	12	9

When 1980 national totals are broken down by income, they reveal the following:

	Percent of Total U.S. Public	Percent of Respondents by Income		
		Under $7,000	$10,000-14,000	$25,000 plus
Public Safety (fire, police, criminal justice)	2%	3%	3%	1%
Public Schools (K-12)	3	2	2	2
Tax-Supported Colleges and Universities	23	21	24	23
Aid to the Needy	8	7	6	10
Streets and Highways	11	10	12	15
Parks and Recreation	40	41	41	44
Don't Know	12	16	12	5

Source: Advisory Commission on Intergovernmental Relations—1980

equal protection of the law. Nor can states deprive persons of their property without due process of law.

Each state constitution may impose limits on the taxing power of the state government itself as well as on local units of government. Thus a state legislature may levy any tax that is not forbidden by the federal Constitution. But local governments may impose only those taxes that the states permit them to levy.

State and Local Tax Systems Vary. There are wide variations among state and local tax systems. Some states have income taxes. Some state constitutions set maximum tax rates that may be imposed on property. Most state constitutions exempt churches, schools, museums, cemeteries, and other similar properties from taxation. In recent years state-local tax burdens ranged from 9.51 percent of income in Ohio to 15.72 percent in New York.

When measured on a per capita—that is, per person—basis, state-local taxes also vary widely among regions and states. The 1975 state-local tax collections throughout the country averaged $666 per capita, with Arkansas at the bottom ($405) and New York at the top ($1,009).

The heavy reliance of states and local governments on tax resources located within their jurisdictions has fostered a competition for new sources of tax revenues. Attracting industrial development is the most common approach to boosting taxes. State and local officials offer a variety of inducements to persuade businesses to locate a new facility in their state or community. These inducements usually include publicly developed land, transport and utility improvements, low-cost loans, tax advantages, and a "friendly business climate."

The fear that their area will become uncompetitive is widespread among state and local officials. Thus a "friendly business climate" often means low taxes, a permissive attitude toward pollution, relaxed labor and safety standards, and sympathetic regulatory agencies. Every proposal at the state and local level to raise taxes, increase spending, enhance consumer protection, reduce air and water pollution, or upgrade labor benefits is attacked. People warn that the particular action will impose financial burdens that will scare off potential taxpaying businesses or cause existing ones to depart.

section review

1. Define the proportional tax.
2. What limits are there on state taxing power?
3. How do states or local governments compete for new sources of tax revenue?

2. STATE AND LOCAL GOVERNMENT TAX SOURCES

State governments have three major sources of tax revenue: general sales taxes, selective sales (or excise) taxes, and personal and corporate income taxes. The dominance of one tax source over another varies considerably from state to state. Recently income taxes have become increasingly important sources of state tax revenue.

The general sales tax is still the primary tax revenue source in most states. It accounts for more revenue than any other tax source in 31 of the 50 states. The individual income tax is the primary source of tax revenue in 16 states. In Alaska, new laws relating to oil and gas reserves have replaced individual income taxes with property taxes as the state's largest tax revenue source.

General Sales Tax. The largest single producer of funds for state government is the general sales tax. A *sales tax* is a tax levied upon the sale of goods, usually paid by the

8. Financing State and Local Government **155**

purchaser. It was born during the Depression, and 45 states now use some form of it.

Citizens in most states pay about a 4 percent sales tax. Some states exempt necessities such as food, medicine, and sometimes clothing. But the general sales tax is a regressive tax. It forces lower-income groups to pay a higher proportion of their income than wealthier groups must pay. That is, persons with small incomes spend a larger percentage of their income for food and clothing than do the wealthy. If these items are not exempt, then the sales tax falls most heavily on those least able to pay.

Despite their regressive nature, general sales taxes are popular. They are easy to administer. They produce large amounts of revenue. They are easy to increase. They also seem relatively painless, since only a few cents are paid with each purchase. Thirty percent of all state tax revenues were raised through the general sales tax in 1979.

Selective Sales Taxes.   Taxes levied on luxuries and on specific government services are called *selective sales taxes,* or excise taxes. They are levied most often on motor fuels, cigarettes, and alcoholic beverages. In 1979 these taxes produced 21 percent of the total tax monies collected by the states. In the same year, the general sales tax and selective sales tax combined produced 51 percent of the total state tax revenue.

Income Taxes.   An *income tax* is a tax levied on income received from profits, salaries, rents, interest, dividends, and other sources, less deductions permitted by law. In 1979 individual income taxes represented 26 percent of state government tax collections. Corporate income taxes represented 10.4 percent. Forty-four states have an individual income tax, which amounts to about 20 percent of each person's federal income tax. The income tax is a progressive tax. The rate goes up with the size of the income.

The tax automobile drivers pay on gasoline is an example of a selective tax. Many people try to avoid paying higher taxes on gasoline in their state by crossing the state line to fill their gas tanks.

Local Tax Sources.   Since colonial times, property taxes have been the main source of revenue for local governments. Over 80 percent of all local government tax revenues are from property taxes. The only source of tax revenue available to most school districts is the property tax.

Local governments across the country vary in their dependence on the property tax. One metropolitan county in northern California gets only 24 percent of its revenues from property taxes. It received 43 percent in aid from other government agencies and 33 percent from "other local funding" such as fines, penalties, other taxes, licenses, and permits.

Flaws in the Property Tax. The concept of a property tax implies that the owner of any type of property should contribute to the support of government in proportion to the total value of the owner's property. Property taxes, however, are now flawed because of the relation between the burdens they place on taxpayers and the ability of taxpayers to pay.

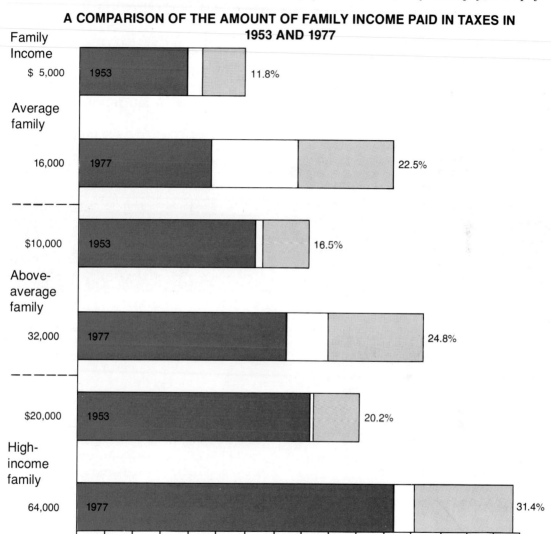

A COMPARISON OF THE AMOUNT OF FAMILY INCOME PAID IN TAXES IN 1953 AND 1977

Family Income

$ 5,000 — Average family

1953 ▮ 11.8%

16,000 — 1977 ▮ 22.5%

$10,000 — Above-average family

1953 ▮ 16.5%

32,000 — 1977 ▮ 24.8%

$20,000 — High-income family

1953 ▮ 20.2%

64,000 — 1977 ▮ 31.4%

0 2 4 6 8 10 12 14 16 18 20 22 24 26 28 30 32

Percentage of family income

1. The estimates are for a family of four and include only federal personal income tax, federal OASDHI, state and local personal income tax, general sales tax, and local residential property taxes.
2. OASDHI means old-age, survivor's, disability, and health insurance.

Use key to identify the following kinds of taxes:

▮ federal personal income tax   ☐ federal OASDHI   ▨ state and local taxes

Source: Advisory Commission on Intergovernmental Relations—1980

When the wealth of this nation was in land and improvements, the property tax was a reasonably fair means of raising local revenue. But the nature of wealth has changed in the twentieth century.

The property tax is flawed for other reasons. Most states leave the task of assessing property to local taxing districts. Part-time amateur assessors are commonly employed. Only 20 states require local tax assessors to be trained or certified. Consequently, assessment practices vary greatly within states and across the country.

Another flaw is revealed upon examination of the properties that are exempt from property taxation. Tax-exempt organizations, both private and public, have grown in recent years. This has resulted in the erosion of some local tax bases. Many groups are now clamoring for exemptions—the elderly and disabled, widows, veterans, nursing homes, and so on. Furthermore, tax exemptions for new industry are available as part of industrial development programs in some states.

Dissatisfaction with the property tax has

These people in Evanston, Illinois, are protesting the increase in their taxes. What sentiments are expressed by their signs?

increased in the 1970's because of inflation. The property tax is levied on any increase in the value of a home over the original purchase price. It does not matter that the increase is only on paper and not in the homeowner's hand unless the house is sold.

School Finance and the Property Tax. During the past few years, a major use of the property tax has been challenged. Suits have been filed in state and federal courts challenging the constitutionality of financing primary and secondary education from property taxes. The suits have charged that such a system violates the Fourteenth Amendment to the federal Constitution and similar provisions in state constitutions. They maintain that the system denies many people "equal protection of the law."

In 1971 the California supreme court held in the case of *Serrano* v. *Priest* that the California method of financing public schools discriminated against children in poor school districts. Under the existing system, two thirds of all school funds were locally provided and one third was provided by the state. The court said that this system unconstitutionally linked the quality of a child's education to the wealth of his or her parents and neighbors.

Supporters of school finance reform hoped that the *Serrano* decision would have an impact across the nation. But in 1973 the U.S. Supreme Court held that the Texas method of financing education from property taxes did *not* violate the federal Constitution, even though economic inequalities existed among school districts in Texas.

The Court held that education was not a fundamental right guaranteed "equal protection" under the federal Constitution. In the Court's view, the discrimination involved in unequal funding for education was directed at poor areas in general rather than at a particular class of people such as Blacks or Chicanos.

But school financing arrangements based on property taxes have remained vulnerable in many states because of specific state guarantees of equal educational opportunity. For example, Michigan's constitution requires that all citizens have access to an adequate education. The Michigan supreme court ruled in 1973 that the state's combination of local property taxes and state school aid resulted in unconstitutional inequalities among school districts. The constitution of New Jersey contains a mandate for a "thorough and efficient school system." In 1973 the New Jersey supreme court ruled that New Jersey's school financing system, which relied on local property taxes for almost three fourths of its funds, failed to meet this mandate. The court called for equality in all of New Jersey's schools.

In late 1976 the California supreme court reaffirmed its *Serrano* decision. It ruled that the legislature had failed to cure the unconstitutional features of the state's school financing system. But the California legislature still has not developed a plan that meets the court's requirements.

All across the country, states are grappling with the issue of school finance. Suits are still being filed. Some legislatures have

QUOTES
from famous people

"In exercising a sound discretion in levying discriminating duties . . . care should be taken that it be done in a manner not to benefit the wealthy few at the expense of the toiling millions by taxing lowest the luxuries of life—or articles of superior quality and high price, which can only be consumed by the wealthy— and highest the necessaries of life—or articles of coarse quality and low price, which the poor and great mass of our people must consume."

James K. Polk

WHICH IS THE WORST TAX?					
	Percent of Total U.S. Public				
	May 1980	May 1978	May 1975	April 1974	March 1972
Federal Income Tax	36%	30%	28%	30%	19%
State Income Tax	10	11	11	10	13
State Sales Tax	19	18	23	20	13
Local Property Tax	25	32	29	28	45
Don't Know	10	10	10	14	11

When 1980 national totals are broken down by region, they reveal the following striking contrasts:

	Percent of Total U.S. Public	Percent of Respondents by Region			
		North-east	North Central	South	West
Federal Income Tax	36%	31%	37%	39%	37%
State Income Tax	10	13	9	11	9
State Sales Tax	19	25	17	15	19
Local Property Tax	25	22	28	24	25
Don't Know	10	9	9	11	10

Source: Advisory Commission on Intergovernmental Relations—1980

attempted to change their state's financing system. But dependence on the local property tax for school financing still predominates in this country. The fights to change such systems will continue into the 1980's.

section review

1. Name three major sources of tax revenue for state governments.
2. What is the main source of revenue for a local government?
3. What are some flaws in the property tax?
4. What arguments support the suits claiming that primary and secondary education should not be financed by property taxes?

3. INTERGOVERNMENTAL TRANSFERS

If a state or local government needs to spend more money, it usually levies a new tax or raises the rates on existing taxes. But now it has another source of money—federal aid. Federal aid has become an increased source of funds for state and local governments. Between 1950 and 1980, federal assistance to these governments jumped from $2.3 billion to $91.4 billion. Federal aid for 1980 increased about 9 percent over 1979 aid, which had increased 13 percent over 1977. Federal aid now represents over 22 percent of state and local expenditures.

Problems with Federal Aid. Almost every major federal domestic program is designed to be put into action by state or local government. But the rapid expansion of federal assistance since the early 1960's has been a mixed blessing. Many federal programs overlap. Coordination among federal agencies has often been weak. In addition, the paper work needed to implement programs at the state and local level consumes increasing amounts of time and energy.

The increasing aid presents other problems. Some aid often bypasses state and local political executives and legislative bodies. This weakens the role of elected officials and increases that of specialized agencies—such as those responsible for road building and public housing. Also, some programs give money directly to local governments. This has made governors and other state officials very unhappy.

Probably the most serious criticism of federal aid has been its impact on the overall priorities, programs, and politics of state and local governments. Federal aid has helped to expand programs designed by state and local governments. But many federal programs represent efforts to impose federal priorities on programs at the state and local levels. The grant programs have set minimum national standards. They have fostered experimentation. They have helped state and local governments coordinate their efforts and improve their administrative capabilities. They have also helped progress toward certain social objectives such as nondiscrimination. But at the same time, the programs have caused conflict because many of them are aimed at controversial areas—welfare, poverty, housing, and education for the disadvantaged.

Despite all this, most state and local officials have eagerly accepted federal programs. The political cost to these officials of programs financed from state or local funds is much higher than the political cost of federally funded activities. Almost all at-

Clayton, New Mexico, became the first community in the United States to get windmill-powered electricity. The town's windmill-building project was funded partially by the federal government's Department of Energy. By taking advantage of the region's environment, the government was able to find a cheap method of providing energy to a community.

tempts to expand state and local revenues are subject to public debate and criticism. Also, use of federal money allows politicians to declare that no increases in state or local taxes will be necessary.

Categorical Grants. The biggest form of federal financial assistance to states and localities comes from categorical grants. This type of grant has been in existence for 90 years. *Categorical grants* provide funds for specific programs and projects. There are over 400 categorical grants for which state and local governments are eligible. There are four basic types of categorical grants. Some require the recipient government to provide matching funds.

1. *Project grants* are those designated for specific kinds of projects sponsored by various federal agencies. Recipients must submit specific applications for each proposed project. The actual awards are made on a competitive basis by the federal agency that supervises the program.
2. *Formula-project grants* require a specified formula to be used to determine the amount of money available for each state area.
3. *Formula-apportioned grants* are allocated by formula among recipients according to standards contained in the original law or in regulations made by the federal agency in charge of the grants.
4. *Open-ended reimbursement grants* involve a cost-sharing arrangement between federal government and the recipient government. The federal government reimburses a specified proportion of state and local program costs.

Over the years the focus of federal categorical grants has changed. In 1960 four fifths of the total grants were for transportation and social security. But by 1980 health, education, training, employment, social services, natural resources, and the environment took increasing amounts of dollars. In 1960 categorical aid was 55 percent urban and 45 percent nonurban. In 1980 it was 65 percent urban and 35 percent nonurban. The benefits received by various regions of the country have also fluctuated.

General Revenue Sharing. Revenue sharing was established in 1972 in response to criticisms of federal aid programs. Under *general revenue sharing*, the federal government gives money to the state and local governments to decide, within limits, how funds will be spent. Revenue-sharing funds have few strings attached. State governments get about one third of the money. Local governments get the other two thirds. Twelve percent of all federal aid money was classified as general revenue-sharing money in 1980.

Block Grants. Block grants accounted for 11.3 percent of federal aid in 1980. These grants fall between categorical grants and general revenue sharing in the federal aid system. They were created in response to the proliferation of categorical grants and the fragmentation that these often create. They are difficult to define.

The five existing block grant programs share these characteristics in varying degrees:

1. Federal aid is authorized for a wide range of activities within a broadly defined area like housing or health.
2. Administrative, planning, and other federally imposed requirements are kept to a minimum.
3. The funds are distributed on the basis of a formula that narrows the power of federal administrations.
4. The law that established the program says who shall be eligible for the grants. General-purpose governments are favored as recipients of these grants.

Based on these traits, *block grants* can be defined as federal aid programs in which money is provided mainly to general-purpose governments for use in certain broad areas and administered at the discretion of the government receiving the grant.

State Aid to Local Governments. The states aid local governments in three ways. They provide services directly to local governments. They initiate and distribute state grants-in-aid. They channel federal grants.

After many years of debate, Congress enacted the Housing and Community Development Act in 1974. The act was oriented toward cities, and consolidated a number of separate federal programs that had been administered by the U.S. Department of Housing and Urban Development (HUD). These programs included plans for urban renewal, neighborhood development, water and sewer facilities, neighborhood facilities, public facilities, open space, urban beautification, historic preservation, and rehabilitation loans. The federal funds for local programs that were consolidated under the 1974 law are called Community Development Block Grants (CDBG's).

The 1974 act does not define community development. It offers instead a series of objectives and a list of activities that qualify for funding.

Under the 1974 law, CDBG's are available to states and units of local governments of all sizes. The act establishes categories for applicants based on size, location, and type of government. These differences affect the amount and duration of the funding they receive. They also affect the degree to which applicants may decide which types of programs qualify for funding.

The CDBG guidelines list eligible community development activities. Certain areas related to community development cannot be funded under the grants. They include public works facilities and site improvements not specifically related to a particular neighborhood (a central library is not eligible, but a neighborhood library is); operating and maintenance expenses of community facilities; general government expenses not related to community development programs; and new housing construction.

As part of its application for funds, a local government must demonstrate that its proposals meet the specific objectives of the act: 1) elimination of slums and blight, prevention of property deterioration in neighborhood and community facilities; 2) elimination of conditions dangerous to health, safety, and public welfare; 3) conservation and expansion of the nation's housing stock, especially for low- and moderate-income persons; 4) expansion and improvement of the quantity and quality of community services, mainly for persons of low and moderate income; 5) better use of land and other natural resources and better arrangement of residential, commercial, industrial, and recreational activities; 6) reduction of the isolation of income groups within communities and geographical areas; and 7) restoration and preservation of properties of special value for historic, architectural, or esthetic reasons.

The CDBG encountered program problems during its first four years of existence. Local governmental officials have almost unlimited power in spending these funds, and the CDBG's bypass state government. As a result, challenges were entered in the courts both by local groups and other governments unhappy with the allocation of the funds. A case in Davenport, Iowa, illustrates these challenges. In 1976 a coalition of low-income Blacks, Mexican Americans, and Whites challenged the city of Davenport, Iowa, in federal court. The coalition challenged the city's plan to spend $337,000 of its total $925,000 allocation on parks and tennis courts in North Davenport,

CASE STUDY: COMMUNITY DEVELOPMENT BLOCK GRANTS (CDBG's)

CDBG's (continued)

the wealthiest section of the city. They won a decree requiring that Davenport spend over one third of its annual community development block grant on projects to benefit the poor.

The city agreed to several changes in its use of funds. Two housing staff members would be hired to put into action a housing program for the poor. A full-time "attorney-investigator" position would be created to combat housing discrimination. An inner-city development corporation would be created to find ways to expand the use of city land by low- and moderate-income citizens for both housing and business. The city would spend $225,000 to purchase land for multifamily housing and would create a land bank to supervise its distribution for this purpose.

This case demonstrates that local governments are not always responsive to the most pressing needs of their communities. They may also attempt to use block grant funds for purposes outside the scope of the law.

Federal aid programs have been criticized for not giving state and local governments real decision-making power. These governments now have such power in the block grant and revenue-sharing programs. It is not yet clear whether state and local governments will use that power conscientiously to help solve the problems of the poorest members of their communities.

In 1980 state aid totaled $61 billion. Channeled amounts represent 20 percent of state aid. Of this 20 percent, welfare and education aid accounted for more than 90 percent of total funds channeled to local government.

State assistance to local governments is split into two categories—general local government support (revenue sharing) and specific program support (categorical grants). General local government support is about 10 percent of total state assistance. Specific program support amounts to about 90 percent.

More than half of specific program support goes to one area—educational support. The great bulk of the rest goes to three other traditionally aided areas—highways, public welfare, and health and hospitals. Only about one dollar out of eight goes to all other areas. Most states use formula-based categorical grants to distribute their specific program support. Revenue-sharing funds are also distributed by formulas.

QUOTES from famous people

"We ought never to forget that true public economy consists not in withholding the means necessary to accomplish important national objects confided to us by the Constitution, but in taking care that the money appropriated for these purposes shall be faithfully and frugally expended."

James Buchanan

A Comparison: Federal Aid and State Aid. State and federal aid systems are very different. Federal aid is more diversified. The four largest state aid areas—education, highway, welfare, and health and hospitals—account for 87 percent of state aid funds.

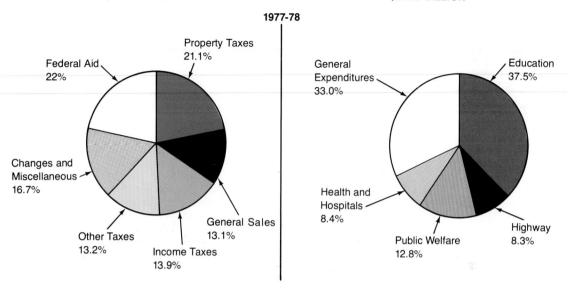

STATE AND LOCAL GOVERNMENT REVENUE
$316 BILLION

STATE AND LOCAL GOVERNMENT EXPENDITURE
$295.5 BILLION

1977-78

Federal Aid
22%

Property Taxes
21.1%

Changes and
Miscellaneous
16.7%

Other Taxes
13.2%

Income Taxes
13.9%

General Sales
13.1%

General
Expenditures
33.0%

Education
37.5%

Health and
Hospitals
8.4%

Public Welfare
12.8%

Highway
8.3%

Source: Advisory Commission on Intergovernmental Relations—1980

These same areas receive 60 percent of federal grants. The greatest difference between the two aid systems is their treatment of education. Education receives 59 percent of state aid. But it gets only 10 percent of federal aid.

Federal revenue sharing makes up about 11.6 percent of total federal aid. But state revenue sharing represents 10 percent of total state aid. The greatest contrast, though, between the two revenue-sharing programs is in the way they equalize resources among communities. Federal revenue sharing equalizes modestly *among* states and substantially *within* states. Central cities receive three to seven times as much as their affluent suburban neighbors. Conversely, more than 50 percent of state revenue-sharing dollars is returned to the area from which these funds are collected. Less than one percent is distributed on the basis of financial needs of the area.

Federal aid is oriented more toward urban needs than its state counterpart. Roughly 6 – 7 percent of all federal aid is directed

toward the needs of cities. State aid to cities is about 2.5 percent.

The federal government provides fewer direct services than do the states. Constitutional, political, traditional, and practical factors combine to keep the federal government from providing more and more services directly. It must therefore rely on grants in order to achieve domestic program goals.

Both systems have had problems managing their grants at the administrative level. But administrative reorganization, budgeting, and more planning have resulted in the improvement of both systems.

section review

1. List some of the problems that occur with regard to federal aid.
2. Name four basic types of categorical grants.
3. What three roles do the states play in the intergovernmental aid process?
4. What is the greatest difference between federal and state revenue sharing?

CHAPTER SUMMARY

8

Since 1945 demands for new and better public services—created by inflation and by the growth of an increasingly urban population with a rising standard of living—have caused state and local governments to move from one fiscal crisis to another. As demands for services have increased, a corresponding rebellion by taxpayers against higher taxes has occurred.

State and local governments get revenue from two sources: taxes and intergovernmental grants. A tax is a compulsory contribution for the support of government. There are three broad categories of taxes: proportional, progressive, and regressive. The three most common taxes levied by state governments are general sales tax, selective sales (excise) taxes, and personal and corporate income taxes.

Local governments depend primarily on property taxes for revenue. There are many disadvantages in using the property tax as a major source of revenue in an urban, industrialized nation. School financing by property tax has become a source of controversy since the 1971 *Serrano* v. *Priest* decision.

A second major source of revenue for state and local governments is federal aid: categorical aid for specific programs or groups, revenue sharing, and block grants. Although federal aid provides needed assistance, it often dictates priorities a local government might not otherwise wish to establish.

REVIEW QUESTIONS

1. Revenue sharing is the result of the desire of local governments to establish their own priorities for programs and services. Do you think federal aid should be allocated with no strings attached? Why or why not?

2. What are the major reasons for the increase in state and local governmental spending in the last 50 years? What sources of revenue have been most effective in dealing with some of these problems?

3. In 1976 New Jersey voters approved a plan to legalize gambling as a source of increased tax revenues. Several states have established state lotteries. Would you favor this type of revenue source for your state? Why or why not?

4. Some economists have proposed a unified income tax to be levied and collected by the federal government. Funds raised would be reallocated to state and local governments on a per capita basis. Do you favor such a plan? Explain.

5. Why has the property tax become such a controversial revenue source in recent years?

ACTIVITIES FOR REVIEW

activity 1   Stage a class debate on the following question: RESOLVED, that the property tax as a source of revenue should be abolished.

activity 2   Interview or invite the superintendent of schools, business manager, or school representative to your class to discuss funding sources for public education in your community.

activity 3   Interview or invite a representative from your city government to speak to your class on the extent of federal aid to your community and the advantages or disadvantages of this form of revenue.

political science DICTIONARY

block grants—federal aid provided mainly to general-purpose governments for use in certain broad areas and administered at the discretion of the governments receiving the grants.   p. 162

general revenue sharing—the granting of federal funds to state and local governments, which may decide, within limits, how the funds will be spent.   p. 162

income tax—a tax on personal income from profits, salaries, rents, interest, dividends, and other sources, minus deductions permitted by law.   p. 156

progressive taxation—a system in which individual tax rates increase with the ability to pay.   p. 153

proportional taxation—a system in which all people pay the same percentage of their income in taxes.   p. 153

regressive taxation—a system in which tax rates become proportionately lower as the tax base increases.   p. 153

sales tax—a tax on the sale of goods, usually paid by the purchaser.   p. 155

tax—a compulsory payment for the support of the government.   p. 152

UNIT SUMMARY

Division of power between the national and state governments places a major responsibility for serving the people and meeting the changing needs of the nation on state and local governments.

Most states, after 1897, adopted the constitutional model of government with three separate branches. The powers of the state legislatures and governors are by no means as great as those of Congress and the President. However, governors can exercise the item veto.

The United States today is a nation of cities. Urban concerns consume a major portion of the time and resources of state and local governments. Cities are created by the states and possess only as much power as the state legislature chooses to give them.

Many of the urban problems cannot be contained within city limits. County, township, and regional governments have been developed as means of dealing with the changing problems of local governments.

One major concern at all levels of local government is financing the increased services demanded by conditions and the people these governments serve. Property and sales taxes have provided the basic source of revenue for cities. Many urban problems cannot be resolved with these limited resources.

Bibliography

The Book of the States, published regularly by the Council of State Governments. Iron Works Pike, Lexington, Ky. 40511.

National Conference of State Legislatures (NCSL). 1405 Curtis Street (23rd floor), Denver, Colo. 80202, or 1150 17th Street NW (Suite 602), Washington, D.C. 20036.

U.S. Advisory Commission on Intergovernmental Relations (ACIR). 726 Jackson Place NW, Washington, D.C. 20575.

Adrian, Charles R., and Charles Press, *Governing Urban America*. New York: McGraw-Hill, 1977.

Jewell, Malcolm E., and Samuel C. Patterson, *The Legislative Process*. New York: Random House, 1977.

Palmer, Kenneth J., *State Politics in the United States*, 2nd edition. New York: St. Martin's Press, 1977.

Stedman, Murray S., *State and Local Government*. Cambridge, Mass.: Winthrop Publishers, Inc., 1976.

Review questions

1. Does federal aid to cities threaten the traditional division of powers between states and the national government?

2. Urban problems, such as housing, transportation, air pollution, unemployment, and care for the aged, have placed undue strain on the financial resources of cities. What sources of revenue do you consider most equitable and effective in assisting cities in resolving these problems? Explain.

3. In what ways are state governments similar in structure and powers to the national government? How are they different?

Skill questions

Based on charts in this unit, answer the following:

1. Which of the states has the median per capita income?
2. What kinds of cases are handled by the California superior courts? How many superior courts are there?
3. Is there any relationship between per capita income and the rural and urban distribution of the nation's population? Explain.
4. In 1977, what percentage of total income did a high-income family pay in taxes? What was the difference in the payments of an above-average-income family and a high-income family in 1977?

Activities

activity 1

Select one of the urban problems in this unit that affects your community. Write or visit the agencies that are attempting to resolve the problem. How many are local, state, or national governmental units? Have there been attempts to deal with the problem on a regional basis? Should there be? How effective is the present effort? What do you and those you interview believe needs to be done to resolve the problem? Prepare a report summarizing your findings.

activity 2

Prepare a series of wall charts illustrating your state's taxing and budget structure and process. How are decisions about taxes and budgets made? What agencies have the most control over fiscal affairs?

activity 3

Review the *Serrano* v. *Priest* and allied decisions. Might the principles advocated in these judicial opinions have an impact on future funding of other state and local government services? Report on the effects of this decision up to now on public education and other local services.

UNIT
3

BILL MOYERS,
Press Secretary

Bill Moyers was press secretary under President Johnson. Although he held this position for only a short time, from July 1965 to December 1966, he became known to journalists as the "best press secretary in memory."

PEOPLE IN
POLITICS

When Moyers was a sophmore at North Texas State College, he volunteered to work for Senator Johnson's 1954 reelection campaign. He started out addressing campaign literature and was quickly put in charge of handling Johnson's mail. In 1959, after finishing his schooling, Moyers decided to pursue a career in public affairs. When Johnson asked Moyers to rejoin his staff during the 1960 vice-presidential campaign, Moyers eagerly accepted.

Upon Johnson's election as Vice-President in 1960, Moyers resigned to work for the Peace Corps. Although he enjoyed his position there Moyers left in 1963, after Kennedy's assasination, to become a special assistant and key advisor on domestic affairs to President Johnson. In 1965 Moyers became press secretary.

President Johnson was ill-at-ease during press conferences. So Moyers, as press secretary, advised the President to hold small meetings in the Oval Office instead. Moyers showed the press many considerations. He gave informative daily briefings, anwered all questions possible, and arranged adequate lodging for the traveling press. Moyers, unlike other press secretaries, did not shield the President from unfriendly reporters. He set up many interviews with critics of the President.

Although Moyers wanted a more important position, Johnson insisted he remain as his press secretary. Because of this Moyers resigned in December 1966 to become publisher of the Long Island newspaper *Newsday.* Since leaving *Newsday* in 1970 he has written a book, *Listening to America; a Traveler Rediscovers his Country,* and has become a television figure with his own show on the Public Broadcasting Service. He has turned down offers to get involved in politics because he feels that "there is nothing as rewarding as being a good reporter in our society."

POLITICAL PARTICIPATION AND INFLUENCE

OVERVIEW

▪ Political parties serve four major functions: They mobilize public opinion, connect different levels of government, provide peaceful means of change, and convey information between the government and the governed.

▪ One key purpose of government is to translate the public's will into public policy.

▪ The most accurate measure of public opinion on a specific issue is scientific polling.

▪ Participants in the political system are generally wealthier, better educated, and more conservative than the general population.

▪ A pressure group is composed of people who share a common opinion or objective in matters of public policy.

▪ The media, particularly television, are effective in determining what issues are important.

▪ The right to vote is basic to representative democracy.

▪ Today the only requirements established for voting are minimum age, term of residence, citizenship, and registration.

▪ America has an increasingly low voter turnout for elections. Factors contributing to this trend are personal registration; the two-party, winner-take-all system; lack of issues in some elections; habit; and voter apathy.

9

Political Parties

Political parties are institutions that nominate and present candidates for office. As such they play a vital role in a representative democracy.

In this chapter you will learn about the history of the American party system, how parties choose candidates, how parties are organized, why people are willing to work in parties, and the role of money in the party system.

You will then examine how parties have functioned in elections and some of the special features in the two-party system, including the role that minor parties have played within it. Finally, you will explore questions about the future of American political parties.

CHAPTER PREVIEW

1. THE DEVELOPMENT OF POLITICAL PARTIES
2. PARTY FUNCTIONS
3. PARTY ORGANIZATION AND WORK
4. PARTY FINANCE
5. ISSUES AND ELECTIONS
6. THE FUTURE OF THE POLITICAL PARTY

1. THE DEVELOPMENT OF POLITICAL PARTIES

Approximately 90 million people in the United States are constitutionally eligible to become President. But in 1980 voters in most states could choose from among only four or five candidates. The real choice was between two: Jimmy Carter and Ronald Reagan. The

"*Oh-oh. Divisiveness.*"

Opinions were split on political issues during the late 1960's and early 1970's. Is friction one of the trademarks of political campaigns in a democratic society?

institution through which this choice was limited to these two candidates is the political party.

The modern political party is a comparatively new institution. It originated in the United States soon after the Constitution went into effect in 1789. Political parties did not develop in other countries until the second half of the nineteenth century. Today most countries do not have genuine, contested elections. But all except a few traditional monarchies—Saudi Arabia, for example—have political parties.

The party system in the United States developed at the highest level of government. It grew out of a conflict between two mem-

bers of George Washington's Cabinet over whether to establish a national bank. Secretary of State Thomas Jefferson opposed the formation of the bank that was advocated by Secretary of the Treasury Alexander Hamilton. The conflict spread to Congress, where Jefferson's allies, led by James Madison, opposed Hamilton's policies. It became a public issue when the Jeffersonians attempted to reverse their defeats within the government by appealing directly to the people.

The people were asked to choose between the policies of the Jeffersonians, who believed that the powers reserved to the states under the Constitution prevented the establishment of a national bank, and those of

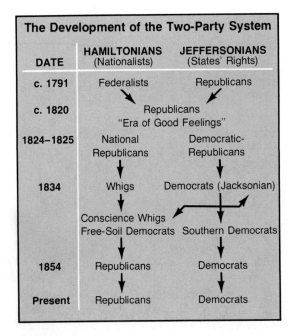

The Development of the Two-Party System

DATE	HAMILTONIANS (Nationalists)	JEFFERSONIANS (States' Rights)
c. 1791	Federalists	Republicans
c. 1820	Republicans "Era of Good Feelings"	
1824–1825	National Republicans	Democratic-Republicans
1834	Whigs	Democrats (Jacksonian)
	Conscience Whigs Free-Soil Democrats	Southern Democrats
1854	Republicans	Democrats
Present	Republicans	Democrats

the Hamiltonians, who favored a strong national government. In other words, the people were being asked to choose between the politics of one individual or the other. From these *factions*—small groups of individuals allied in coalitions to promote or oppose a policy, a program, or a cause—American political parties developed.

The Founding Fathers of the United States were hostile to factions and to parties. Madison wrote about the dangers of factions in *The Federalist*, No. 10, in which he claimed that the new Constitution would control the effects of factions. Washington devoted part of his farewell address to attacking the dangers of parties. But it was too late—America had begun to develop a party system.

The establishment of the party system in America was accomplished within 40 years. Hamilton's followers, who called themselves Federalists, disappeared from the political scene after the War of 1812. By the 1820's most of the American states had adopted one-party systems. But the single party developed several factions. In 1824 the House of Representatives had to decide which of four candidates from the same party to elect President.

The Unique Development of American Parties. Every system bears the marks of the time when it was instituted. Because the American party system was the first to emerge, it developed in ways that proved to be unique to the American experience. In 1789 the United States—the 13 states and the territories that it claimed—was a large land mass. When the closing of the American frontier in the 1890's prevented further continental expansion, the United States was larger than all the countries on the European continent except Russia.

QUOTES from famous people

"Party is organized opinion."

Benjamin Disraeli

In 1790 most Americans were small farmers of English background who owned their own land. Their political culture expressed the primacy of individual freedom in terms of personal liberty, free enterprise, and an overriding hostility to the centralizing directions of a distant government.

The spirit with which Americans settled the vast territory between the Atlantic and Pacific oceans and their distrust of any government that was distant from them reinforced the constitutional provisions that gave responsibility to the states for holding elections and required that elections for the executive and the legislative branches be held separately. The irony is that political parties that arose at the national level of government also developed at the state level of government.

The geographical size of the United States, its political culture, its federal system of government, and its separation of powers within the national government produced a *decentralized*, or locally based, party system that distinguishes American political parties from their counterparts throughout the world.

section review

1. How did the issue of establishing a national bank create a party system?
2. Define the term "faction."
3. Describe the political attitude of most Americans in the 1790's.

2. PARTY FUNCTIONS

Political parties are the only organizations that recruit, select, and nominate candidates for public office.

Parties mobilize public opinion, and they structure public choice. These functions are particularly important for states that use long ballots that contain the names of many candidates. For example, in 1964, as the result of a court decision, the entire Illinois General Assembly was elected at large—that is, every member of the assembly was to represent not one assembly district but the entire state. Every voter in the state was asked to vote for 177 members of the assembly. Each party agreed to run only 118 candidates. The Democrats won 118 seats, and the Republicans won 59. Clearly, without the means of identification suggested by party labels, the average voter would have had practically no other way of choosing 177 candidates out of the 236 who were running.

Parties serve to connect different levels of government in the complex American governmental system. Legislators are often elected because they are members of the same party as a popular President rather than because of their qualifications or achievements. The party responsible for their election can expect a high degree of loyalty to the party from individual legislators. Informal party organizations have been developed within legislatures to demand this loyalty.

In a competitive system parties offer alternatives to *coups d'état*, or illegal seizures of state power, for their representatives are entitled to oppose government leaders, to challenge them in elections, and to replace them in an office when they fail to win re-election.

Parties serve as conveyor belts of information between those who govern and those who are governed. The information that they transmit resembles public opinion polls that can inform those in power of current attitudes and concerns. This information can also serve to articulate and focus protest from those outside the center of political power.

Party Control Over Nominations: Early History. Before parties existed, nominations in colonial America were accomplished either by self-announcement or by nomination at a public meeting. *Self-announcement* means the act of nominating oneself by announcing one's candidacy. Today this method is used by candidates announcing for a party nomination and by minor-party and independent candidates for the presidency or other elected offices. John Anderson in 1980 is one example. Public meetings are rarely used, but they used to be a common way of calling on a candidate to run. Although usually described as spontaneous, such meetings were carefully planned by a candidate's supporters, who secured informal support for the candidate before the meeting convened.

The Caucus. When the term *caucus* was used to refer to the nomination process, it applied to a group of people who met to select candidates for public office. Before the

In 1980 John Anderson ran for the presidency as an independent. By running as an independent, Anderson was able to focus the voters' attention on issues he felt were not being given proper coverage by the main-party candidates.

establishment of the first party system in America, caucuses were informal meetings of local "notables," the elites of a town or a colony. But after party competition arose at the national level in the 1790's, caucuses were established in the form of the legislative caucus and the congressional caucus. By 1800 both the Federalists and the Jeffersonian Republicans selected local and state candidates at caucuses of their party members in the state legislatures and national candidates at caucuses of their members in Congress.

This system worked fairly well for two decades, but by the 1820's it was criticized as undemocratic and oligarchical. In the 1824 presidential election, three of the four major Democratic-Republican candidates for President (Andrew Jackson, Henry Clay, and John Quincy Adams) boycotted their party's caucus, which nominated the fourth candidate, William Crawford of Georgia. In the popular election that followed, Jackson, who made opposition to "King Caucus" a central point of his campaign, ran first, and Crawford finished third. The election of 1824, which had to be decided in the House of Representatives because no candidate had received a majority of the electoral college vote, discredited the caucus and led to the demise of congressional and legislative counterparts.

As candidate and President, Andrew Jackson was the first political figure in United States history to come into much contact with the voting public. Here he is shown on the way to his inauguration.

The Delegate Convention. The first delegate convention was held by the Anti-Masonic party in 1831. The procedure was adopted quickly by the major parties. Conventions continued to be the method of nomination until the twentieth century.

The *convention* is based on a pyramidal system of representation—that is, through a series of conventions, members at local levels of the party indirectly nominate candidates for national office. Party members meet at the local, or *precinct*, level to select local candidates and delegates to the county convention. At the county level delegates nominate candidates for county office and select delegates to the state convention. At the state

level delegates choose state candidates and delegates to the national convention, who in turn choose national candidates. There were variations of form in some states, but the basic pattern was nearly universal in late nineteenth-century America.

The collapse of two-party competition in the southern states as well as mounting hostility to the domination of the nomination process by "party bosses" led to an assault on the party convention in the 1890's similar to that waged against "King Caucus" nearly 70 years earlier. Primary elections have replaced the convention system as the most common method of nomination, although for the presidency the most common method involves primaries followed by national party conventions. The conventions are held in the nation's largest cities.

The Direct Primary. The *direct primary* is a uniquely American institution. It is an intraparty election—that is, an election that takes place within a party. Although direct primaries were held from time to time to nominate local candidates after the primary was introduced by the Democratic party in Crawford County, Pennsylvania, in 1842, the beginning of the modern primary system can be traced to the first statewide primary law passed in Wisconsin in 1902. The primary system spread with remarkable speed and is now used in every state.

The primary is regulated by the state, which sets dates on which primaries are to be held, furnishes ballots to be used by the voters in recording their choices, and provides officials to supervise the balloting, to count the votes, and to certify the results. As the agent entrusted with this responsibility, the state pays for the entire process. Thus American parties are unique, for they are recognized by law as the only organizations that are entitled to nominate candidates for public office.

There are two basic forms of the primary: open and closed.

The open primary. In an *open primary*, any voter, regardless of his or her party identification or nonpartisanship, can participate in either the Democratic primary or the Republican primary. In seven states (Michigan, Minnesota, Montana, North Dakota, Utah, Vermont, and Wisconsin), voters may cast their ballots in the primary of their choice. In two states (Alaska and Washington), there are *blanket*, or wide open, *primaries* in which voters may switch back and forth in casting ballots for candidates to be nominated by both parties. For example, a voter may vote in the Democratic primary for one of its candidates to be nominated for governor and may also vote in the Republican

primary for one of its candidates to be nominated for state senator.

The closed primary. Forty-one states use the *closed primary*—a primary that is closed to those who are not members of the party that holds the primary. In most of these states, party membership is established by enrollment in the party before its primary is held. Those who are not enrolled cannot vote in primary elections.

QUOTES
from famous people

"Let me . . . warn you in the most solemn manner against the . . . effects of the Spirit of Party. . ."

George Washington

The closed primary has become the predominant method of determining who will be permitted to vote because it prevents "raiding" by one party in the other party's primary. (In *Raiding*, members of one party attempt to ruin the other party's chance of success in the general election by voting in the primary for weak candidates who, they hope, will not only be nominated by the other party but also be defeated by the nominees of their own party in the general election.) A large number of votes for George Wallace in the Democratic presidential primaries in Wisconsin in 1964 and in Michigan in 1972 appear to have come from Republicans. The Democratic party has attempted to eliminate open primaries, but of course a party cannot by itself control state laws.

The runoff primary. In all of the states except Louisiana, only a *plurality*—that is, the largest number of votes, even if the total number is less than 50 percent—is required to win a general election. But in many southern states that have not developed two-party systems, runoff primaries are held whenever no candidate receives an absolute majority in the first primary. Because of the absence of a competitive system, the victor in the **runoff** wins party nomination and the election as well.

In two states (Iowa and South Dakota), candidates must get at least 35 percent of the vote to win party nomination. If none does, then state conventions make the choice. Localities sometimes have special rules. In New York City, for example, there are runoffs for the three citywide municipal offices—mayor, president of the city council, and comptroller—unless the top candidate for those offices secures 40 percent of the vote.

A **runoff** is a second primary that involves a contest between the candidates of the same party who have achieved the top two places in the balloting of the first primary.

The "double ballot" system, actually a runoff system, is usually used in nonpartisan local elections, such as those for school boards and judges.

The presidential primary. The presidential primary began in the same state that

This picture shows a handwritten tally of the returns during the 1980 New Hampshire primary.

initiated the statewide primary—Wisconsin. In 1905 Wisconsin provided for direct election of delegates to the presidential nominating conventions of each major party. The first state to institute a preference primary for specific presidential candidates was Oregon in 1910.

By 1916 more than 20 states used some form of presidential primary. But by 1968 there were presidential primaries in only 15 states. The reform movement that developed in the Democratic party after the 1968 convention led many states to adopt (or readopt) some form of presidential primary. By 1972, 23 states and the District of Columbia had presidential primary elections, and fifteen more states had adopted the practice by 1980.

Entering Primaries. States have established different procedures for entering party primaries. In many states the simple announcement of candidacy, coupled with the payment of a modest filing fee, fulfills the requirement for entry of a candidate's name on his or her party's primary ballot. At various times in various states, it has been possible for a candidate to enter the primary of more than one party.

In several states, in order to qualify to run, it is necessary to file nominating petitions signed by a specified number of duly enrolled voters in the district or in the state in which the election is to be held. This method is also used in general elections and in nonpartisan elections in order to qualify independent or minor-party candidates for office.

section review

1. Define the term *coup d'état.*
2. Discuss two functions of political parties.
3. How is an open primary different from a closed primary?
4. Why are runoff primaries held?

3. PARTY ORGANIZATION AND WORK

The organizational charts of American political parties do not differ in substance from those of the better-organized parties of Europe. American parties are organized in a pyramidal fashion that runs from precinct and election district committeepersons and ward captains, selected by the voters of 140,000 districts in the United States, to the national chairperson of the party.

The *national chairperson* is selected by the national committee of the party to serve a four-year term. (In practice this selection is determined by the incumbent President or by the presidential candidate.) In presidential election years the chairperson is supposed to act as the party's campaign manager and fund raiser. But in the last few elections, this role has been performed by the personal campaign committee of the candidate, such as President Nixon's Committee to Re-Elect the President in 1972.

The chairperson works out of headquarters in Washington, D.C., with a small staff of assistants. As "official spokesperson" for the party, his or her role differs according to personality and circumstance. For example, Paul Butler, who was chairperson of the National Democratic Committee during President Eisenhower's second term, concentrated on formulating positions, whereas Robert Strauss, elected chairperson by the anti-McGovern wing of the Democratic Party in 1973, acted as a conciliator and fund raiser rather than as an ideological spokesperson.

Until recently the national committees of both parties consisted of one man and one woman from each of the states and territories of the United States. Both parties have altered their representation in recent years.

Democratic party representation has changed dramatically. The party has added the chairperson and vice-chairpersons from each state's party organization, four members of Congress, 161 new members from the states selected according to population, Democratic governors, representatives of Young Democrats, Democratic mayors, and 25 members selected by the committee itself on the basis of their contributions to the party.

The Republican party changed the composition of its national committee slightly by adding the chairpersons of the party organization of all states that satisfied any of three criteria of electoral success. Those states, in the previous election, must have given their electoral votes to the Republican Presidential candidate, elected a Republican senator, or elected a majority of Republican representatives to Congress. Recently, all state chairpersons have been given seats. Members of each party's national committee are selected by a variety of methods that conform with state election laws.

Congressional Campaign Committees. Congressional campaign committees have assumed additional roles in recent years. There are four congressional campaign committees, two for each party, representing the Senate and the House, respectively. Their main function is fund raising, and they offer technical assistance as well. Most of the assistance goes to incumbents who seek reelection.

National Conventions. National conventions meet every fourth year to select candidates for President and Vice-President and to proclaim the party's platform. Beyond these functions they have had little or no authority. The 1972 Democratic convention mandated the holding of a midterm "miniconvention" in 1974. It met in Kansas City, adopted a national charter for the Democratic party, and recommended an economic program to Congress. The 1976 and 1980 conventions mandated that this "tradition" be continued. Some members of the Republican party, especially conservatives, have suggested that the Republican party should also try to hold midterm conventions.

This picture was taken during the 1980 Republican convention, which nominated Ronald Reagan for the presidency. How important a role do the delegates play in the nominating convention?

Although the effects of this innovation are not yet apparent, it seems reasonable to conclude that the convening of midterm conventions may well constitute an attempt by the Democratic party to create a policy-making role for its members—a role that has always been entrusted to the incumbent Democratic President or to the presidential candidate whom the party nominates every four years. Only the future will reveal whether this development represents a temporary response to a movement for reform or the first step in the evolution toward a system of party government.

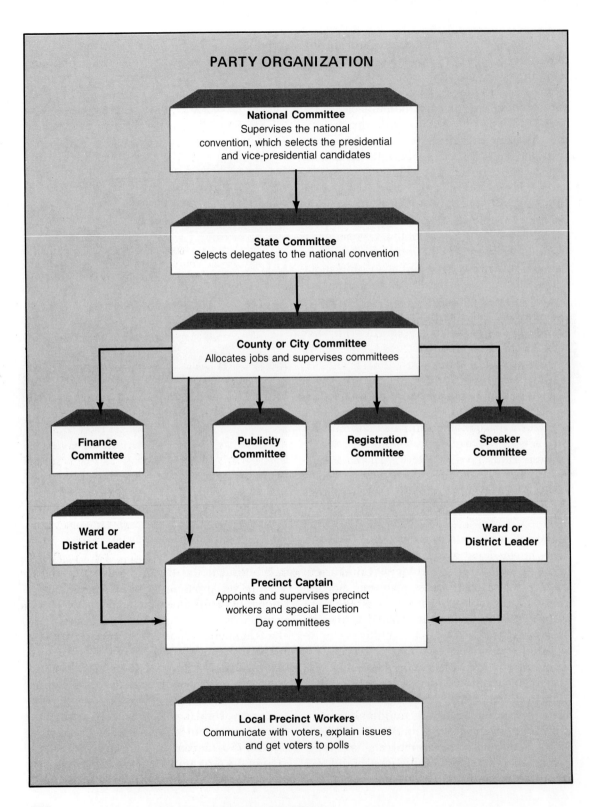

PARTY ORGANIZATION

National Committee
Supervises the national convention, which selects the presidential and vice-presidential candidates

State Committee
Selects delegates to the national convention

County or City Committee
Allocates jobs and supervises committees

Finance Committee

Publicity Committee

Registration Committee

Speaker Committee

Ward or District Leader

Ward or District Leader

Precinct Captain
Appoints and supervises precinct workers and special Election Day committees

Local Precinct Workers
Communicate with voters, explain issues and get voters to polls

State and Local Party Organizations.
State chairpersons are selected by the state committees of their party. Their powers vary from state to state. In some states they actually are independent forces who have influence over the distribution of certain offices to party faithfuls or members. In most states they are the lieutenants of leading state officeholders. State committees are sometimes chosen by county committees, sometimes by state conventions, and sometimes by primary elections. They are supposed to be the governing bodies of the state parties. But like the national committees, they have little actual influence.

County or city committees elect chairpersons. These chairpersons have often been powerful individuals, such as the late Democratic Mayor Richard Daley of Chicago and Republican Assemblyman Joseph Margiotta of Nassau County, New York. The chairpersons of county or city committees may be elected either by the voters or by their party in a convention.

Ward or *district leaders* are selected by the voters or by precinct captains. Their powers vary according to the areas represented and the individuals involved.

Precinct or district captains are selected by the voters. They represent the smallest electoral units—a few hundred voters in a neighborhood. In theory they represent the base of the party and do such work as "pulling out" voters to the polls on election days. In Chicago the job of a precinct captain is real, and its rewards are tangible. Elsewhere it is a paper job not often filled.

Levels of Party Activity. Party members are involved at three levels of activity: as leaders, as activists, and as followers. Leaders are the chief wielders of power within the party—those who are elected and appointed to office and those who play influential roles in electing and appointing party members to office. *Activists* are party workers who often believe that their time, effort, and money sustain the

political party to which they belong. Followers of a party identify with it for many reasons. Most are neither active nor concerned very much with issues. They often inherit their party memberships through fathers or mothers who have always voted for the same party. Traditionally they have not been willing to switch their votes.

QUOTES
from famous people

"The American party system contains major components that are the oldest large-scale partisan organizations in the world."

Walter Dean Burnham

Party Work: Rewards and Realities. Party work tends to be undervalued and inefficient. Harvard University political scientist James Wilson, in a study of the "economy of patronage," found that most precinct workers did not *canvass* (seek out individual voters to ascertain their preferences and to persuade them to support the party) frequently or vigorously. "Once they acquire a patronage job and become a member in good standing of the local political club or ward headquarters, they often concern themselves more with the social and fraternal advantages of membership. . . . Precinct workers canvass principally their friends and a small group of voters who are well known and can be relied upon."

In a study of 142 Detroit precinct workers in the early 1960's, Samuel Eldersveld found that less than half kept records of voters, and only 12 percent contacted these voters on election day. Fewer than one third met with campaign workers during a campaign, fewer than half distributed literature in a campaign, and even fewer telephoned or met with voters in their precincts. It is not surprising that the fabled "party organizations" have been defeated easily by enthusiastic "reform" movements. But the hard workers of one year's reform movement usually become observers the next year. Winning elections requires steady work, and there are fewer and fewer party members who are willing to work steadily.

Who Participates. The most underrated but most important political resource is time. Because most people do not spend much time in politics, those who do so exercise considerable influence. There are two major reasons that people devote time to politics: direct rewards and indirect benefits. The former category applies to candidates who run for office, workers who receive patronage jobs, and supporters who get government contracts. The latter category applies to all those who benefit indirectly from the adoption of policies that they support or through personal gratification.

Because party activism requires time, politically active people (other than full-time professional politicians) are likely to be in positions from which they can take time off or

Workers for political parties invest long hours during their candidates' campaigns. Here a Democratic party worker polls voters on their choice for the 1980 presidential election.

can control their own time. Groups that are likely to fall into these categories include lawyers, upper-middle-class homemakers, and college students. American politics has been dominated to an unusual degree by lawyers, for not only can they arrange their own time, but they also belong to one of the few professions that can benefit from time spent in politics.

Why do people participate at all? For the successful candidate and his or her immediate supporters, the rewards are still substantial. A member of Congress, as one incumbent testified, "lives like a prince." The young people around the President are collecting annual salaries of over $50,000 before they are 35. When they leave government service, many of them can expect to step into corporate jobs paying even more. To some degree, the same is true at the local level of politics. Soon after he was inaugurated mayor of financially troubled New York City in 1978, Edward Koch raised the salaries of his top assistants to between $45,000 and $57,000 a year.

Although the number of patronage jobs in government has been greatly reduced over the years and although the salaries for many of these positions are quite low, they still serve as incentives for many people.

For upper-income groups the far more important economic rewards are likely to be contracts of one kind or another. Federal, state, and local governments award contracts that attract lawyers, public relations specialists, contractors, bankers, and arrangers of every kind. Lawyers sometimes work in political campaigns because that may lead to judgeships, to exerting influence on the powerful, to becoming better known by potential clients, or to the possibility of getting influential support to run for office in the future.

The most important incentives, however, seem to be psychological rather than economic. A political activist has the opportunity to mix with a broad spectrum of social groups and with "celebrities." Most people who are active in politics for a while form friendships. There is the sense of belonging, the appeal of the game, the excitement of the struggle, a feeling of importance and self-worth, and the opportunity to advance one's ideas. The Eldersveld study showed that the most common motivations for precinct workers were social, with ideology a stronger secondary motivation for Republicans.

section review

1. Describe the organization of the national committees of the Democratic and Republican parties.
2. How are the state committees chosen?
3. What are the three levels of activity for party members?
4. What indirect benefits are derived from political participation?

4. PARTY FINANCE

Most Americans contribute nothing to the expenses of their parties. Therefore, parties have been forced to rely on other sources. These sources can be classified according to the following contributors:

1. *Candidates themselves.* Money contributed by candidates' families and their close friends can be quite important.
2. *Special-interest groups* with direct interests in the making of public policy. The biggest givers are labor unions, corporations, and medical and dairy associations. At the local level givers may be contractors, landlords, bankers.
3. *"Fat cats" or "angels."* Some of these contributors fall into the second category, but others are interested in politics either for

John F. Kennedy, shown here during the 1960 presidential campaign, spent a huge sum of money in his drive for the presidency.

ideological reasons, social associations, or because of a commitment to "civic responsibility." Their influence on national elections has been reduced by recent election reforms and campaign rules, but it is still extensive.

4. *"Cause" groups or individuals*, such as the liberal National Committee for an Effective Congress, the Conservative Caucus, and the League of Conservation Voters. Because these groups attract many small contributions and direct them to specific races for national office, their influence has been increased rather than reduced by the new rules that limit individual contributions.

5. *Government employees.* Before the reforms of the Progressive era early in the twentieth century, parties could expect to collect a certain portion of the salaries of government employees hired under their auspices. This practice no longer persists at the national level. But some of the stronger parties at the local level, such as the Democratic party of Chicago and the Republican party of Nassau County, New York, are said to carry on the practice.

Most of the money raised in politics goes directly to election campaigns. The largest of these expenses is for media, mainly in the form of newspaper advertisements and radio and TV commercials.

Money in Politics. The estimated spending for all political races has risen from about $155 million in 1956 to about $475 million in 1976, from about $2.50 per voter to somewhat less than $6.00 per voter. In the same period, however, the gross national product has risen more than four times. If inflation and the rise in national income are taken into account, the amount of money spent on politics has been decreasing relative to the amount of money spent on other things. Of every $4,000 spent annually in the United States, $1 goes to political campaigns.

Parties and politicians are always short of money, a fact that accounts for the prominence of politicians who command great fortunes. Recent campaign reform laws designed to reduce the amount of money spent in politics may result in protecting incumbents from being voted out of office. With the publicity of office, a large paid staff, the *frank privilege* (mail free of postage), and other such benefits amounting to an annual subsidy from the federal government of at least half a million dollars, an incumbent member

In an attempt to make political candidates more equal in the amount of money they spend on campaigning, the government uses a tax return form to poll the public's reaction to a presidential election campaign fund.

Form **1040**	Department of the Treasury—Internal Revenue Service **U.S. Individual Income Tax Return**	**1980**	

For Privacy Act Notice, see Instructions	For the year January 1–December 31, 1980, or other tax year beginning	1980, ending	19

Use IRS label. Otherwise, please print or type.	Your first name and initial (if joint return, also give spouse's name and initial)	Last name	Your social security number
	Present home address (Number and street, including apartment number, or rural route)		Spouse's social security no.
	City, town or post office, State and ZIP code	Your occupation ▶	
		Spouse's occupation ▶	

Presidential Election Campaign Fund

▶ Do you want $1 to go to this fund? . . . . Yes / No

If joint return, does your spouse want $1 to go to this fund? . . . Yes / No

Note: *Checking "Yes" will not increase your tax or reduce your refund.*

Requested by Census Bureau for Revenue Sharing ▶

A Where do you live (actual location of residence)? (See page 2 of Instructions.) State | City, village, borough, etc.

B Do you live within the legal limits of a city, village, etc.? ☐ Yes ☐ No

C In what county do you live?

D In what township do you live?

Filing Status

Check only one box.

1 ___ Single
2 ___ Married filing joint return (even if only one had income)
3 ___ Married filing separate return. Enter spouse's social security no. above and full name here ▶ ....
4 ___ Head of household. (See page 6 of Instructions.) If qualifying person is your unmarried child, enter child's name ▶ ....
5 ___ Qualifying widow(er) with dependent child (Year spouse died ▶ 19). (See page 6 of Instructions.)

For IRS use only

Exemptions

Always check the box labeled Yourself.

6a ___ Yourself   ___ 65 or over   ___ Blind
b ___ Spouse   ___ 65 or over   ___ Blind

Enter number of boxes checked on 6a and b ▶

c First names of your dependent children who lived with you ▶ ....

Enter number of children listed on 6c ▶

of Congress enjoys an advantage over his or her opponent.

Subsidies pose the problem of supporting single-issue or crank candidates. For example, the subsidy rules for presidential candidates enabled Lyndon La Rouche, head of a splinter group called the U.S. Labor Party, to collect federal funds to publicize his party's positions by running for President in the Democratic primaries in 1980.

Replacing private contributions with public subsidies raises serious problems. In general elections for national office, it confers benefits on the two major parties at the expense of all others. For example, third parties that did not receive 5 percent of the vote in the last general election are not eligible to receive federal matching funds during the election campaign. If financing reform is not extended to state and local primaries, private interests may shift their contributions to candidates who seek state-wide office. In the state of New Jersey, where general-election subsidies were introduced in 1977, several million dollars were contributed for the gubernatorial primaries.

The problem of money in politics relates to America's ambivalence about wealth and political power. The liberal creed asserts that government and society should be separate. But the history of the American political system suggests that government and society are interdependent, not separate, entities. If Americans are determined to limit the influence of money in the political system, they will have to resolve the contradictions between their acceptance of economic inequality and their belief in political equality.

section review

1. List the five main sources of financial contributions to candidates up for election.
2. What is the largest expense in an election campaign?
3. Define the term "subsidy."

5. ISSUES AND ELECTIONS

It is often asserted that the consensus of American society is reflected in its political system. The dominance of the two-party system in this country rests not only on agreement among Americans but also primarily on a definite series of constitutional and legal arrangements.

It has been suggested that if the United States were to change to a parliamentary system with *proportional representation*— that is, a system in which seats in the legislature are apportioned to parties on the basis of the total number of votes that they received in the last election—the two parties would break up into at least six. These parties could possibly be a single Black party and five White parties that would be representing the various political factions of the Republican and Democratic parties. When New York City used a proportional representation system to elect members to the city council (1937–1949), no less than seven parties won seats. The Democratic organization mounted a campaign against proportional representation on the grounds that Communists had been elected under it. Ever since the Democrats succeeded in eliminating it, they have always held at least 80 percent of the seats on the city council.

The two-party system is sometimes defended on the grounds that it "fosters competition." But in many areas and for most offices, there continues to be little competition between the parties. One party has tended to dominate the national political system, and the same process is evident as one moves from national to state to local offices.

For example, the Republican party was the predominant national party from 1860 to 1932. Only two Democrats, Grover Cleveland and Woodrow Wilson, were elected President in those years. Since 1932 the Democrats have been predominant. The only Republicans who have been elected President were Dwight Eisenhower, Richard Nixon, and Ronald Reagan, and the Republicans won control of Congress only twice (1946 and 1952) in the last 25 congressional elections. After the 1974 elections the Republicans were outnumbered three to one in 17 of the 49 states that provide for partisan legislatures.

Minor Parties. Candidates have run for office under thousands of different party labels, and only 16 parties have received as much as 5 percent of the vote in presidential elections. Six of these labels reflect the names adopted by the two major parties at different periods in American history: Democratic-Republican and Democratic, on the one hand, and Federalist, National Republican, Whig, and Republican, on the other. Another four were splinter groups that broke away from the great parties: American in 1856 and Constitutional Union in 1860 (both survivors of the Whig party in the South), Southern Democratic in 1860 (as a result of the Democratic split), and Progressive in 1912 (as a result of Teddy Roosevelt's disaffection from the Republican party).

The six minor parties that did not evolve from either of the major parties were as follows:

Anti-Masonic	1832
Free Soil	1848
Populist	1892–94
Socialist	1912
Progressive	1924
American Independent	1968

These minor parties succeeded in focusing on issues that had been ignored by the major parties. Eventually these issues influenced the politics of at least one of the major parties.

Each minor party marked a protest by some section of the population against an "elite" that the party claimed was misleading the nation and therefore had to be defeated. The elites attacked ranged from members of the Masonic order to slaveholders in the South to bankers in the East to "pointy-headed intellectuals."

Minor parties that have functioned on the national level can be divided into two types. The *single issue party* champions a specific issue. It vanishes as soon as its issue fades in importance or is addressed by one of the major parties. The *sect*, or *missionary* party is concerned not with winning elections but with changing beliefs and values. It is concerned not with winning elections but with winning converts.

Among the succesful minority parties all but one were flash parties. The Socialist party, a sect party formed in 1901, ran presidential candidates until 1956 (one of its factions began running candidates again in 1976). The other five parties lasted less than ten years. John Anderson took the antiparty tendency to its logical conclusion with his nonparty candidacy in 1980. Most of the sect parties that have survived on the local level are Marxist parties, such as the Socialist, Communist, Socialist Labor, and Socialist Workers' parties. But the minor party that has run third-party candidates for the longest time is the Prohibitionist party, which has run Presidential candidates since 1872. The two most successful minor parties in 1980 were the antigovernment Libertarians and the left-wing Citizens' party.

Minor parties have been weaker in the twentieth century than they were in the nineteenth. Only 47 minor-party candidates won in the more than 9,000 congressional contests that have been held since 1932, and most of these victories were in two states: the Progressive party in Wisconsin and the Farmer-Labor party in Minnesota. Since 1954 all members of the House of Representatives have been Republicans and Democrats. In the Senate Harry Byrd of Virginia was elected as an Independent in 1970 and 1976 (although he sits as a Democrat), and James Buckley of New York was elected as a Conservative in 1970 but lost in 1976.

Before 1920 minor parties ran full slates of candidates for offices. Beginning with Robert La Follette's campaign for President as a candidate of the Progressive party in 1924, minor parties have tended to run only for national office. In 1968, for example, the American Independent party ran only 18 candidates for the House of Representatives. These candidates received only 2 percent of the vote in districts where George Wallace got 13.3 percent.

Minor parties have served as innovators for the American political system. Among the concepts first advanced by minor parties that later found acceptance are the national convention, the abolition of slavery, the progressive income tax, women's suffrage, old-age pensions, and restrictions against child labor.

Some of the most successful minor parties have existed at the state level. The Farmer-Labor party in Minnesota (1920–1944) elected governors, senators, and members of the House of Representatives before finally merging with the Democrats to form the present Democratic–Farmer-Labor party. The Progressive party of Wisconsin (1934–1944), founded by the children of Robert La Follette, won many contests for state office.

Two minor state parties that have been most successful are the Liberal party and the Conservative party of New York. The existence of these two small parties in New York State shows the extent to which law can affect party survival. New York election law is one of the few in the country that allows *cross-filing*—that is, allows candidates to run on more than one party line.

Minor parties often have difficulty getting on the ballot. In 1976 two presidential candidates tried to get on the ballot in all 50 states—Eugene McCarthy as an Independent and Roger MacBride as a Libertarian. They succeeded in only 29 and 32 states, re-

spectively. In many states qualification procedures are complex, almost always time-consuming, and expensive; in all states the two major parties control the election process.

QUOTES from famous people

"The political parties created democracy and . . . modern democracy is unthinkable save in terms of the parties. As a matter of fact, the condition of the parties is the best possible evidence of the nature of any regime . . . Parties are not, therefore, merely appendages of modern government; they are in the center of it and play a determinative and creative role in it."

E. E. Schattschneider

Parties and Issues. It is often said that American parties stand for nothing, that they have no *ideology*, or comprehensive view of the world that enables them to formulate policies and positions. But any comparison with parties across the world would show that both American parties fall into the category of middle-class parties that have been traditionally liberal. The ideology of American parties is a liberalism that claims not to be an ideology. Instead it stresses the right of individual choice.

American parties are *broker parties*—that is, their leaders agree that life is a competitive game. The great difference between them is whether the results of the game are fair as they stand now (misnamed "conservatism") or whether the game needs to be started all over again. (The simile is usually a card game: New, Square, Fair Deals—one critic complained that the "liberals" were always dealing the cards but never playing the game!)

The parties accept the rules of the game and maintain that the best world is that of autonomous, competing individuals and parties. They seek electoral victory but never final victory over their opponents. They also seek balance among interest groups that are supposed to represent the "general good" that will grow out of competing private interests.

The Republican party has been the party of the northern, White, Protestant upper class. To some extent the Democrats have been the party of everyone else. As such, the Democrats had the potential for becoming the predominant party since the 1880's, but they did not achieve that status until the 1930's. Their problem was twofold. First, the Democrats, representing many "outgroups" in society, voted less frequently than did the Republicans. Second, the Democrats were a far more diverse group than were the Republicans—the Democrats recruited their members from different ethnic, racial, religious, regional, and economic groups.

Since the 1960's the American party system has been described as a one-and-a-half party system, to reflect that there are about twice as many Democrats as there are Republicans, or a three-party system, with two of the parties residing within the Democratic party. The University of Michigan poll of the electorate in 1972 showed that the two wings of the Democratic party disagreed with each other more often than either one did with the Republicans.

The consequences of this unusual development are interesting. Because Democrats at lower levels of public office can appeal directly to their constituents for support whereas Republicans have fewer constituents to whom they can appeal, Democrats have gradually increased their lead over Republican officeholders. But because the contradictions in the Democratic coalition are so great—for example, those between minority groups and women, who endorse affirmative action programs, and labor union leaders, who support the retention of seniority as the basis for protecting the security of their workers' jobs—the Republicans have been able to mount strong challenges at the national level, winning five of the last eight presidential elections.

In no other country in the world have the swings between elections been so great. Party identification in America is "looser" than elsewhere because the American political system is not a system of party government such as exists in parliamentary systems and because Americans vote so much more often and for so many more offices. It is possible to be an enrolled member of a party and not to have voted for any of that party's candidates.

Another practice that exists in America is *ticket splitting*, or voting for candidates of both parties, which has been increasing in recent years. The results are revealing. Statewide Republican percentages for different offices in Rhode Island in 1964 ranged between 19 percent and 61 percent. Democratic percentages in Massachusetts in 1966 ranged between 37 percent and 71 percent. In Arkansas in 1968 a majority of voters supported Democrat William Fulbright for senator, Republican Winthrop Rockefeller for governor, and American Independent George Wallace for President.

American parties, far more often than those in other countries, do not contest all available offices. Fifty-five members of the House of Representatives were elected in 1970 without contests; in Massachusetts in 1976 the Republicans ran candidates in only about half of the legislative districts.

Although the American parties are reluctant to read anyone out of their ranks for reasons of ideology, a number of interesting conversions since the mid-1950's suggests that party leaders detect some degree of ideological difference between the two parties. Those Republicans that became Democrats included the late Senator Wayne Morse of Oregon, Senator Donald Riegle of Michigan, and Mayor John Lindsay and Congressman Ogden Reid of New York. Those Democrats that became Republicans included Senator Strom Thurmond of South Carolina, Governor

Mills Godwin of Virginia, and Governor John Connally of Texas. The former group were well-known "liberal" Republicans; the latter, well-known "conservative" Democrats.

Individual conversions indicate something about party ideologies and interests. Journalist Samuel Lubell compared college students from Democratic families who were voting Republican with students from Republican families who were voting Democratic. He found that the former intended to go into private business, engineering, and medicine, whereas the latter were going into law, teaching, social service, and other government services. For these young people where they were going was more important than where their parents had been. They had fairly clear ideas about which party was the party of their future occupations.

Government, it has been suggested, is characterized by involuntary membership, authoritative rules, overwhelming force, and the monopoly of imposing sanctions that affect life and death. Elections can work as a means of controlling such a powerful institution only when the issues to be decided are considered legitimate. If anyone believes that his or her survival is at stake, that person will probably not accept the outcome of the election. The election of 1860, for example, showed that the United States had divided into two different sections over the issue of slavery. The Southern slaveholders would not accept the election of Lincoln because in their judgment his election meant the end of their way of life.

Moral issues such as slavery are what party leaders, campaign managers, candidates, and those concerned with the stability of the political system dread, for such issues involve "no-win" situations characterized by intense feelings on both sides and the fear that the official advocacy of any position will cause trouble.

During the 200 years that have elapsed since the founding of the American political

THE ELECTION OF 1860

	Popular Vote	Electoral Vote
Republican -Abraham Lincoln	1,865,593	180
Democratic (S) -John C. Breckinridge	848,356	72
Democratic (N) -Stephen A. Douglas	1,382,713	12
Constitutional Union -John Bell	592,906	39
		303

system, only one issue—slavery—threatened the existence of the United States. Despite the apathy that elections evoke—fewer than 50 percent of eligible voters vote in most elections—Americans who value their political system appear to be convinced that issues that generate debate about the means to be pursued in solving a problem, rather than those that provoke hostility about the nature of the system itself, enhance the stability of the political system. Americans, by and large, tend to be positive about their ability to meet issues and solve problems. Political candidates mirror this positive attitude in the way they appeal to the voters.

section review

1. How do minor parties influence the politics of major parties?
2. Define the term "cross-filing."
3. What are two problems experienced by the Democratic party in achieving its dominant status?
4. Why is party identification in America looser than elsewhere?

6. THE FUTURE OF THE POLITICAL PARTY

Is it possible to have a democratic system without parties that function effectively?

Some of the one-party states in Eastern Europe and Africa have experimented with contested elections but not consistently enough so that one can make judgments about their effects. In general it makes little difference whether there are contested elections in one-party states, for matters of public policy are not likely to be the center of political discussion.

In large areas of the United States, competitive party politics has been a rarity. In the state of Georgia, for example, competitive politics endured only for a few decades in the nineteenth century. Even in states such as New York and Illinois, in which party competition has been continuous, parties are considered competitive because these states contain "one-party" regions that balance each other (Democratic New York City and Republican "upstate"; Democratic Chicago and Republican "downstate").

Most American cities elect their leaders through a nonpartisan system of election, as does the state of Nebraska and until recently the state of Minnesota. Studies of nonpartisan systems show that they favor upper-status groups. The Progressive reform that established nonpartisan councils and city managers in cities after 1900 was often introduced to restore power to middle-class citizens and business people at the expense of Catholic immigrants and party leaders.

Systems that reject party identification have either a politics of "sound and fury, signifying nothing" that concentrates on "style" issues (such as the old-fashioned southern primaries) or a quiet "business-as-usual" politics in which well-off citizens govern without much debate. Studies of the nonpartisan legislature in Minnesota showed that "conservatives" who were actually Republicans were consistently elected, even though the state had been predominantly Democratic. When partisan identification was restored to the ballot, the Democrats won solid majorities. The restoration of party as a cue for the voters produced a direct political impact.

Every system limits competition for power to those who command certain kinds of resources and hold certain kinds of views. There is no such thing as a system that guarantees equal resources to everyone and abolishes power as a factor in government. The power of "party bosses" in a strong party system is not abolished by eliminating party. Rather, power is transferred to other groups or individuals who may be harder, not easier, for the public to reach.

Decline of Parties. In recent years many students of the political party have agreed that its influence is declining. Most of the public relations work traditionally performed by local party workers has shifted to the media. The average voter now knows more about the President than about elected officials at other national and lower levels of government. In the nineteenth century most people knew their local political leaders and considered governors distant figures. Now everyone knows who Ronald Reagan is, but few can identify their local party leaders and state legislators.

Party leaders once served as brokers between the government and individuals.

Much of this work has now shifted either to the bureaucracy or to members of Congress, who operate as individuals outside a party framework. Instead of contributing to the strengthening of party, the performance of this function outside the party structure now weakens that structure.

The rewards for working in political parties have diminished not only economically— that is, the number of patronage jobs has decreased—but also professionally—that is, the power to make decisions has eroded. With key decisions being made by unelected bureaucrats, or "experts," it is considered easier to influence policy by becoming an "expert" than by becoming a candidate for office.

Candidate-Oriented Politics. The center of American politics is increasingly shifting from the party to the candidate. Voting for office tends to fragment according to office and election. Increasingly each candidate runs his or her own campaign without reference to previous elections for the same office or to other elections occurring at the same time. This tendency is often praised, but it causes several problems.

Because a large segment of the population cannot identify their representatives, senators, and state legislators, and because the vast majority cannot name one thing that these individuals did during their terms of office, it is worth asking what voting for the candidate means. To vote for the candidate, not for the party, requires information that most voters do not possess. The ballot in many states lists only the candidate's name, party affiliation, and the office for which he or she is running. The voter often replaces the party cue with one based on ethnicity or sex—the only other information that can be inferred from the ballot.

The destruction of the party as a link between the people and the government would mean the elimination of the only political instrument that people who are weak can use to restrain the actions of those who are strong. It would mean that government would become increasingly responsive to "nonpartisan" interests that represent social and economic forces that are powerful in society—those groups that the political party was founded to fight.

Survival of Parties. Despite the decline of American political parties, polls show that the more committed that one is to a party, the more active, interested, and informed one is likely to be about the political system. Polls also show that an increasing number of voters—approximately 35 percent—classify themselves as independents. But further questioning reveals that approximately the same percentage of independents as that reported among partisan voters vote consistently for Democrats or for Republicans.

Party campaigns still mobilize voters, and on issues that they perceive to be important, these voters may well continue to make partisan discriminations between candidates. As the twentieth century draws to a close, the unresolved issue of inequality may well be decided by those who accord priority to ending inflation or by those who advocate full employment. If these issues generate the same kind of controversy as that provoked by the Great Depression, then the corresponding intensification of partisan political identification should strengthen American political parties and the political system as well.

section review

1. What status groups tend to be favored by a nonpartisan system?
2. How have the media relieved local party workers of some responsibilities?
3. How is the center of American politics shifting? Can you see any evidence of this shifting in recent elections?

CHAPTER SUMMARY

9

In *The Federalist*, No. 10, Madison voiced the attitude, shared by most of the framers of the Constitution, that parties and factionalism were dangerous to the Republic. Within ten years, however, political parties had developed.

The party system in the United States grew out of a conflict within Washington's Cabinet between Thomas Jefferson and Alexander Hamilton over the formation of a national bank.

Political parties have been part of American life since 1800. Parties are the only organizations that recruit, select, and nominate candidates for public office. They also perform four other major functions: They mobilize public opinion, help to connect different levels of government, provide the means for peaceful change and challenge, and transmit information between the government and the governed.

Methods of selecting candidates have become more democratic since 1800, when a caucus of legislators chose party candidates. Today the direct primary and political convention systems provide a greater opportunity for rank-and-file party members to participate in the selection process.

Each major party is organized on a national, state, and local basis. Most Americans contribute no money to the support of their party. Campaign funds are provided by candidates, special-interest groups, wealthy contributors, "cause" groups, and, in recent years, the government.

The two-party system has become a tradition in the United States. Minor parties arise every few years over specific issues. Usually these parties are short-lived—either the issues are rejected or they are adopted by one of the major parties. Minor parties have thus served as innovators in the American political system.

REVIEW QUESTIONS

1. What effect have campaign spending laws had on politics? What benefits have resulted from these changes? What problems?
2. What role have minor parties played in American politics? Why have they had such short-lived success?
3. Why do political leaders prefer to avoid moral issues? What might be the consequences of an election decided on a highly controversial moral issue?
4. Why does the author believe that the decline in party influence is unfortunate? Do you agree or disagree? Why?
5. What role do you think political parties should play in elections? Why?

ACTIVITIES FOR REVIEW

activity 1 Conduct a survey similar to that of the University of Michigan, discussed in the text. How many people identified themselves as Republicans, Democrats, other party, or no party preference? Of those who identified themselves as Democrats or Republicans, how many had a different party affiliation than their parents? Develop questions to help you identify the factors that contributed to this change. Report your findings to the class.

activity 2 Stage a debate on the following issue: RESOLVED, that political parties should be abolished.

activity 3 Obtain copies of the most recent political party platforms. Conduct a forum on the similarities and differences of the two major-party documents. Can you find evidence that the candidates of the two major parties considered themselves bound by the party platform? Cite specific examples of support or nonsupport.

political science DICTIONARY

canvassing—seeking out individual voters to ascertain their preferences and persuade them to support a particular party. p. 183

closed primary—a primary open only to members of the party holding the primary. p. 178

coups d'état—illegal seizures of state power. p. 175

cross-filing—procedure under New York's election law by which candidates may run on more than one party line. p. 189

factions—small groups allied in coalitions to promote or oppose a policy, a program, or a cause. p. 174

open primary—a primary in which any voter, regardless of party identification, can participate. p. 178

plurality—the largest number of votes for any candidate in a contest between three or more, but not more than 50 percent of the total votes cast. p. 178

proportional representation—the system in which seats in the legislature are apportioned to parties on the basis of the number of votes they received in the last election. p. 187

runoff primary—a second primary, to choose between candidates of the same party who have achieved the top two places in the balloting of the first primary. p. 179

self-announcement—the act of nominating oneself by announcing one's candidacy to office. p. 175

ticket splitting—voting for candidates of two or more parties running for different offices. p. 190

10

Political Opinion and Participation

One of the bases of democratic rule is the participation of the public in government. But a simple statement that the public participates in government does not really explain the nature of that participation. One of the ways that people are said to participate is through "public opinion."

In this chapter you will learn about the difficulty of defining public opinion. You will learn that public opinion can be expressed in many different ways. These expressions include a whole gallery of human actions, running from violent demonstrations to answering the questions of pollsters. Each expression can be used as a way of defining public opinion.

At the end of the chapter, you will learn about democratic models of government participation. There are many reasons that people participate. And there are many different kinds of resources available for their participation.

CHAPTER PREVIEW

1. THE DEFINITION OF PUBLIC OPINION
2. THE FORMATION OF PUBLIC OPINION
3. THE MEASUREMENT OF PUBLIC OPINION
4. PARTICIPATION

1. THE DEFINITION OF PUBLIC OPINION

In an indirect democracy such as ours, the representatives of the people are sup-posed to respond to public opinion. And our political dialogue is carried on as though public opinion actually exists. We read that the public wants the death penalty, or has become more conservative or more liberal, or has a certain opinion of the President.

What is Public Opinion? Many political scientists and philosophers have attempted to create a usable definition of public opinion. But none of them has been entirely successful.

"Public" implies "general." And the linkage of the word with opinion implies a "general" opinion. But opinion that is considered to be public is actually the sum of opinions held by a number of individuals and is seldom related to government. And most of the actions that government takes are on matters about which most of the public has no opinion.

Most of the public has opinions about matters that concern their own lives, for example, personal relations and self-images. It is true, of course, that personal matters may be greatly influenced by public policy. But few individuals are aware of how government affects their lives. Many people will say that politics is irrelevant to their lives even though their jobs, their children's education, or the health care that they receive, for instance, may be affected by decisions made by public officials. One thing that "radical" movements want to do is to politicize things, that is, to make people think of things as political. For example, the women's movement wants to convince people that questions generally thought of as nonpolitical, or unchangeable, are in fact political, or capable of being changed by public policy.

QUOTES from famous people

"Our government rests in public opinion. Whoever can change public opinion can change the government practically just so much."

Abraham Lincoln

A group of New Mexico citizens protest the use of nuclear energy. What alternatives do you think they might suggest?

Someone once wrote that "politics is organized opinion." But before organization can begin, opinions must be expressed. If an opinion is not expressed, it is neither public nor political. Richard Nixon's phrase "the silent majority" was catchy. But it is worth noting that he based his claim to majority support on the opinions of an active and far from silent minority—those who wrote him letters. As we shall see, those who write letters to politicians are as unrepresentative a group as are those who demonstrate. Judgments about the views of the passive majority should never be inferred from those of active minorities. Active minorities differ from passive majorities.

In theory, political opinion should be based on reasoned judgment. In fact, it often is not. The theorists of public opinion in democracies assumed that crucial decisions would be made by an informed public, acting in a disinterested manner. But fewer than 50 percent of Americans vote in elections, and of that number many vote for candidates whose images appeal to them or candidates who are members of a political party with which they identify.

Most of the issues that the government has to confront are so complex that few members of the general public can understand them. The government must decide such questions as the size of the appropriation for the coast guard, the exact legal definition of "new" and "old" oil, and what tariff should apply to Japanese machine tools. All these decisions could affect a great number of people. Japanese imports, for example, could well mean new jobs for some and jobs lost by others. It is unreasonable to believe that the public, or even its most intelligent members, can either understand any one of these questions or can obtain the necessary information on which to base opinions.

In fact, the ignorance of even the active members of the political system—those who vote—is monumental. Most people have almost no information on most public issues.

Terrorism is one of the most disturbing issues facing Americans and people throughout the world. This Florida airlines terminal was bombed by a Cuban terrorist group.

Michael Rappeport of the Opinion Research Corporation has pointed out that on many questions the responses of those who actually know something about the issue involved differ widely from the responses of those who know almost nothing. David Butler and Donald Stokes, two political scientists, conducted a massive panel study—interviews of the same people several times over several years—of the British electorate. They discovered that on most issues their interviewees changed their positions back and forth over time. The best explanation that they were able to arrive at was that only about 30 percent of the members of the panel had real opinions on the issues. The other 70 percent were giving essentially random, or chance, answers.

section review

1. On what should political opinion be based?
2. Why do radical groups want people to think of things as political?
3. Who are considered the active members of the political system?

2. THE FORMATION OF PUBLIC OPINION

In place of the concept of a general public, political scientists have arrived at the concept of issue publics. An *issue public* is that portion of the public that has real opinions on a given issue. The size of any issue public will vary, depending upon the significance of the issue and how many people believe that they are affected by it. Thus the issue publics on matters such as race and economic policy are relatively large. But those on foreign policy and animal care are much smaller. Issue publics overlap to some degree, and so there are some people—usually political leaders—who are members of many issue publics. Most people belong to only a few issue publics, some to only one, and some to none at all.

The size of an issue public varies over time as its importance, or salience, increases or decreases. Thus the issue public on foreign policy has tended to grow throughout this century as the role of the United States in world affairs became important. At times of war this issue public grows rapidly. But as peace returns, it shrinks.

Two Types of Issues. There are many ways of classifying issues. But there is an important distinction between two types of issues that should be noted—that between valence issues and position issues. The term "valence" comes from a Latin word meaning "to be strong," and it is used in chemistry to indicate the bonding capacity of an atom. *Valence issues* are those issues on which there is no disagreement. For instance, everyone, or nearly everyone, wants prosperity, honesty, cleanliness, and order. Studies of electoral behavior show that most voters are not particularly issue conscious. But they are likely to vote on the basis of valence issues. Thus they will vote against those in power in bad times and for them in good times. This may not match the ideal notion of the informed elector. But there is a certain rough-and-ready justice to this system of voting. And, as political scientist Anthony Downs has pointed out, it makes sense from the point of view of the average voter who does not have time, energy, or information enough to plumb the depths of the issues.

Position issues are issues about which there can be different positions—abortion, the death penalty, the minimum wage, policy toward Israel. Each of these issues influences several different issue publics. In every election and between elections politicians have to weigh the merits of each position and the power of those who advocate it.

The distribution of public opinion on a position issue is of great importance. (It is in the nature of a valence issue that opinion is not distributed.) And there are many possible distributions of opinion on an issue. Opinion can be divided into two opposed **blocs** with hardly anyone in the middle. If one bloc is far larger than the other, it will usually get its way. But if the two blocs are roughly equal in size, compromises may have to be made. Opinion could be spread out fairly evenly. Or it could fall into the common bell-curve distribution, with most people near the middle and relatively few at the extremes.

But the distribution of opinion on an issue is not the only factor that must be weighed. The strength of an opinion is as important as its direction. Politicians live in a world of many complex issues. And a minority that puts a premium on one issue will necessarily outweigh a majority that does not.

> A **bloc** consists of members of a legislative body, not necessarily of the same party, who have common aims or goals.

The most famous example of this phenomenon is the gun control issue. A large majority of the population favors gun control. An active minority—organized by the National Rifle Association and similar groups— opposes gun control so strongly that this single issue may well determine the way that they vote. If politicians support gun control, they will gain little from taking a position on the issue, for the votes of those members of the public who agree with them will not be determined by the issue. But they will be punished by those who disagree with them, whose votes will be cast against politicians who support gun control.

Opinion Formation. Modern social scientists are interested in the process of opinion formation. It is obvious, for example, that a large part of the political socialization of adults took place in their childhood. Thus social scientists have spent a great deal of time studying the political views of children at various ages. They have also studied other agents of opinion formation. For example, family, school, church, political party, work place, organizational membership, exposure to media, social contacts, neighborhood, and racial or ethnic identity have been studied extensively.

QUOTES
from famous people

"Public opinion consists of those opinions held by private persons which governments find it prudent to heed."

V. O. Key

Much has been learned. But there is much left to learn. In general it has been easier to explain the continuity of opinion than it has been to explain change. It is no surprise that most people follow in their families' footsteps. But that does not help to explain why some people deviate from the patterns. Explaining deviance has always posed a problem for social scientists. It is hard to explain and predict human behavior, especially how and why it changes.

The factors that influence a person's political opinions interact in complex ways. If they operate in the same direction, that interaction is called *issue reinforcement*. If they operate against each other, that opposition is called *issue dissonance*.

section review

1. What is an issue public?
2. How are valence issues different from position issues?
3. Define the term "issue reinforcement."
4. What is meant by issue dissonance?

3. THE MEASUREMENT OF PUBLIC OPINION

Since the days when the legendary caliph of Baghdad, Haroun al-Raschid, disguised himself as a commoner and went out to talk to the people in the marketplace, those who enact public policy have been concerned to find out the direction, the force, and the incidence of particular opinions. Over the years a number of methods have been developed. None of them is perfect, for each measures a different circumstance. But singly or together, they do give elected officials and the rest of us an insight into public opinion.

Elections. Democratic theory maintains that elections reflect public opinion on the issues debated by different candidates. This theory was credible before opinion polling showed that most people cast votes without much regard for specific campaign issues. This finding cannot be interpreted to mean that the voters do not care about issues. It simply means that the issues that they care about may not be those that the candidates stress.

A winning party will often claim a *mandate,* or authorization from the people, to carry out its program. Sometimes it is valid to interpret an election in that way. An example is the New Jersey gubernatorial election of 1977. Governor Brendan Byrne supported the state income tax and his opponent, Ray Bateman, campaigned against it. All parties in New Jersey treated Byrne's victory as having settled the tax issue.

In general, given the combination of interests that compete with one another in an electoral campaign and the general confusion of motives that are reflected in people's votes, a winning party is not always correct in considering victory to mean that it has been given a mandate to act on its programs. The use of referendums—in deciding on bond issues, constitutional amendments, and pro-

positions—may be a more accurate reflection of popular opinion. However, even when referendums are used, if a single issue is to be voted upon, the vote may or may not reflect strong opinion. And the vote may reflect the intensity of partisan advertising campaigns.

Demonstrations. One traditional way in which public opinion may be expressed is public demonstrations. Indeed, in predemocratic societies some sort of public action was the only kind of response to public policy that people could make.

A demonstration is useful in measuring the force of an opinion. If many people are present, it can be inferred that their opinions are strong, for most people are reluctant to engage in public demonstrations of any kind. But a demonstration tells little about how many nondemonstrators hold the opinions being expressed.

Editorial Comment. One measure of opinion that is considered to be influential is that of editorial commentary in newspapers. The broadcast media, regulated by the government and dependent upon it for the renewal of their licenses, have sometimes been reluctant to take strong stands on issues that may become controversial. Elected representatives are sensitive to editorial commentary. People sometimes assume that the editorials in a newspaper reflect the opinion of that paper's readership. But in fact they reflect the opinion of those who own the paper. The majority of newspapers in this country have supported the Republican candidate for President in every election held in this century except one—1964. But the Democrats won half of those elections.

Newspaper publishers are influential. But they do not control the readers of their papers. Studies have shown that the influence of newspapers has been greater on specific issues than it has been on elections. And newspapers have exerted greater influence on local elections than they have on

A group of Native Americans march near Reno, Nevada, on their way across the country to Washington, D.C., to voice their opposition to certain legislation before Congress.

national elections. Major media in an area can influence attitudes in the area over time. For instance, there is evidence that New Hampshire is more conservative than its neighboring New England states because of the views of its leading paper, the *Manchester Union-Leader*. And Arkansas is considered more liberal than its neighbors because of the great influence of its leading paper, the *Arkansas Gazette*.

The great influence of newspapers stems from the fact that they can make an issue salient by running stories about it. But they have proved to be inadequate measures of public opinion.

Polls. A method of measuring opinion that developed in the last few centuries is the *public opinion poll*. (The word "poll" comes from the Middle English *pol*, meaning "head." And in modern English it denotes the act of voting.) The accuracy of polls and the methods of polling vary widely. And it is important to note that modern opinion polling is less than half a century old.

Straw polls. Originally, polls were *straw votes*—unofficial votes taken to determine general group opinion on an issue. People were asked their opinions even though they had not been preselected in a scientific way. This practice originated in late nineteenth-century America. It exists today in the form of newspaper "clipout ballots" and responses solicited from audiences by radio or TV broadcasters. The problem with the straw poll method—as with all other methods that measure **self-selected public opinion**—is that it measures the force of the opinion but does not measure the number of people who hold it. Those who respond to the poll are likely to be elite groups in terms of social background, issue information, education, and income.

> **Self-selected public opinion** is the views of people who choose on their own to take positions on issues. Their opinions are not representative of the population at large. Self-selected public opinion may appear as letters, demonstrations, and so forth.

That this problem cannot be avoided was best demonstrated by the most famous polling failure of all time—the *Literary Digest* poll of the 1936 presidential election. Following the successful practice of previous presidential campaigns, the *Literary Digest* mailed out millions of sample ballots to people listed in telephone directories and in registries of automobile ownership. More than 2 million people returned their ballots. They voted overwhelmingly for Alf Landon, the Republican candidate. But when the actual election votes were tallied, the Democratic incumbent,

Truman fooled the pollsters and the media in snatching victory from Dewey in 1948.

Franklin Delano Roosevelt, won by a huge margin, carrying all but two states. (The *Literary Digest* folded shortly thereafter.)

Because about 5 percent of those who voted in the presidential election voted in the poll—a large proportion—the failure of the poll provoked an investigation. It was soon discovered that those who responded to the poll were members of a very high-status group, for at the height of the depression, the average American could not afford either a telephone or an automobile. And the self-selection factor increased this *bias*, or tendency to deviate from a true value. In previous years the upper-class bias in the sample had not mattered, because party lines in the United States had not yet come together along class lines. In 1936 party and class lines did intersect. The rich voted Republican, and the poor voted Democratic. It was this coming together that made the upper-class sample of the *Digest* poll so inaccurate.

Scientific sampling. A poll taken by George Gallup on the basis of fewer than 2,000 responses proved to be accurate. This result led to the sudden fame of the Gallup poll, and marked the first triumph of a new polling method—the scientific sample.

Many people wonder how a national poll that samples only 1,500 respondents can possibly reflect the behavior of hundreds of millions of diverse people. Perhaps an example will clarify the point. If 100 million marbles of different colors were stirred and shaken carefully and then 1,500 marbles were withdrawn at random, the percentage of marbles of each color in the 1,500 would be fairly close to those of the same colors among all the marbles.

Modern scientific polls usually use one of two methods.

1. They take a random, or *probability*, sample. Specific areas of the country are chosen in a random fashion that is mathematically correct. The poll taker is sent to one of these

clusters with orders to start at a certain place and then interview a predetermined number of people. This is the method used by most major pollsters, including the two most famous, the American Institute of Public Opinion (AIPO, better known as the Gallup poll) and Louis Harris & Associates.

2. A sample assigns quotas to various groups in the population. Then those who have designed the sample try to make sure that these groups are represented in the sample in the same proportion as they are represented in the general population. (Note that if a random sample is done correctly, the proportions of every group in the population should be accurately reflected.) The usual characteristics that samples try to match are sex, age, occupation, education, income, ethnic origin, and place of residence.

Strengths and Weaknesses of Polling. The greatest advantage of scientific polling is that it is the only method in which opinion is not measured by self-selection. As such, it is a reliable measure of the state of public opinion.

The disadvantages of polls can be analyzed on the basis of two categories.

The technical disadvantages of polling. It is hard to draw a sample. It is also difficult to write poll questions in a way that will not influence the answers. And it is almost impossible to ensure that the interviewers, whether purposefully (by falsifying results, for example, or emphasizing certain answers and omitting others) or unconsciously (through personal mannerisms and the built-in behavior patterns and responses of the interviewer and/or the interviewee) will not bias the results. Polls often underrepresent inner-city residents and those poor who live in rural areas. In recent years it has become harder to gain entrance into homes and harder to get some people to respond at all. More people deliberately lie to pollsters. Although telephone polls avoid some of these problems, they pose other difficulties (no phones and the increasing incidence of unlisted phones). Underlying the technical mathematics of polling, there is a very complex human reality.

And it should be remembered that the mathematic probability of polling is often not understood. The margin of error is greater when the sample drawn is smaller. And the margin of error will increase occasionally, for the average poll will be wrong one out of 20 times.

The Gallup poll is one of the most frequently used polls in the United States. In this photo a pollster asks a citizen her opinion.

THE POLLSTERS AND THEIR RECORDS, 1956–1980			
Predictions			
Harris	Gallup	Roper	Actual Outcome
1980		No	
Reagan 45%	46%	polling	51%
Carter 40	43	done	41
1976		No	
Carter 45%	48%	polling	50.1%
Ford 44	44	done	48.0
1972		No	
Nixon 59%	59%	polling	60.8%
McGovern 35	36	done	38
1968			
Nixon 40%	44%	No	43.4%
Humphrey 37	31	polling	42.7
Wallace 16	20	done	13.5
1964			
Johnson 64%	64%	67%	61.1%
Goldwater 36	36	28	38.5
1960			
Kennedy 49%	51%	49%	49.5%
Nixon 41	49	51	49.3
1956			
Eisenhower Not	51%	57%	58%
Stevenson determined	41	38	42

Basic disadvantages. The greatest problem of polling is the vagueness of what it purports to measure—public opinion. A poll does not measure reasoned judgment. And so it cannot predict what public opinion will be after the public has thought about an issue. Opinion polls are snapshots. They mean little unless they are viewed in the context of beliefs that develop and change over time.

Because attitudes about issues are often vague it is possible to elicit different answers in a poll by changing even slightly the wording of the questions. The order in which questions are asked can influence the answers to a given question. The built-in problem with polls is that they create the reality that they are attempting to measure.

Direct Communication or Lobbying. If

there is one thing to which congressional representatives are even more sensitive than polls and newspapers, it is their mail. This form of communication is, in effect, lobbying, although those who practice it do not think of it as such. They think of lobbying as something done by representatives of special interests. Their letters are simply expressions of citizen opinion.

Direct communication to elected or appointed officials generally falls into two categories: 1) communication from pressure groups on some general matter of public policy that they wish to affect, and 2) communication from individuals complaining about dealings with a particular government agency or from individuals supporting specific policies, issues, and so forth. The first is often considered lobbying. The second is consid-

GEORGE GALLUP, JR.

George Gallup escaped from the poverty into which he was born by developing a keen business sense at an early age. At the University of Iowa he became editor of the school magazine and then converted it into a daily newspaper. He also developed a method of measuring how many people were reading each item in the paper. After graduation he started his own business — that of sampling and evaluating public opinion. He won a national reputation in 1936 by predicting Franklin D. Roosevelt's presidential victory when the better known **Literary Digest** poll was forecasting a landslide defeat for Roosevelt.

Today Gallup and other major pollsters make most of their money working for major corporations. They predict sales, detect trends, and analyze the preferences of the consumer population. Their nationally known election polls are "prestige items" — projects by which their reputations, rather than their profits, are enhanced. However, the pollsters' high degree of success in predicting election results convinces private clients of the accuracy and value of their sampling methods and persuades others to use their services.

Most of the advanced techniques for measuring political opinion were developed in an attempt to measure buying opinion. For example, when the Gallup firm was hired by RKO Pictures — to measure the strength of movie stars at the box office, to test public reaction to different film titles, to predict audience response to stories from other media, and to determine how many people had heard of a film before its release — the firm employed the same methods now used in forecasting election outcomes.

Critics of political opinion polls argue that these polls are geared to a commercial model of politics. They object to the fact that the results of opinion polls are used in plotting campaign strategy and are thus helping to "sell" candidates in the same way they help to sell products.

---

ered a function of the officials' service to their constituents.

As measures of public opinion, these communications pose the disadvantages and advantages of other self-selected samples. They reflect the interests but not necessarily the opinions of the public.

section review

1. How are demonstrations an instrument for measuring public opinion?
2. Name three methods for measuring public opinion.

3. What are four of the technical disadvantages of polling?
4. What is meant by constituent service?

4. PARTICIPATION

The measures of public opinion that have been discussed are actually measures of political participation. It is possible to imagine a whole range of political participation, from people who don't participate at all (those who don't vote, write, or even pay attention) to the tiny but very important minority that participates in every available way.

A study of participation in America divided the population into five groups: 1) those who had never participated, 2) those who participated in both community and political activities, 3) those who participated in either community or political activities, 4) those who participated only by voting, and 5) those who participated only in constituent service activities (that is, those who made specific demands rather than general demands on government).

Those who participated in a variety of ways (with the exception of the last group) were better educated, richer, and more conservative than the population as a whole. In effect, as in other methods of self-selection, participation produced a distorted picture of the entire population.

Resources. Different people have different resources available for participation. The most important—and most often over-looked—is time. Without time, other resources yield few results. Therefore political participation is heavily weighted in favor of those who have free time or can make it for themselves—that is, those who can control their own time.

Money buys other people's time. Money also buys two other important commodities—attention and information. People with money get more attention from other people, and they are therefore encouraged to participate. People with information have something to say and are generally listened to when they say it.

These factors are interrelated with an individual's sense of his or her own effectiveness. Those who feel that their presence in politics will make a difference participate more than those who do not. This judgment can be both objective and subjective. Participants generally belong to groups and to

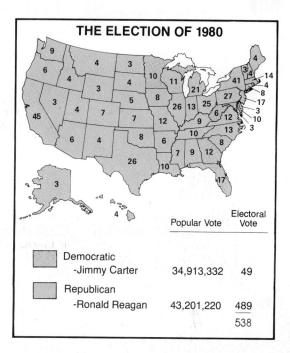

THE ELECTION OF 1980

	Popular Vote	Electoral Vote
Democratic -Jimmy Carter	34,913,332	49
Republican -Ronald Reagan	43,201,220	489
		538

classes that are more effective politically. The environment is very important to participation. People participate more when their personal acquaintances expect it of them and less when they do not. Clearly, all these factors intersect.

section review

1. How is the American population classified according to political participation? Can you make any generalizations about American voters from this information?
2. Why is time an important factor in political participation? Give a few examples from recent political events to support your answer.
3. Explain how environment influences political participation.

CHAPTER SUMMARY

10

One of the basic beliefs of a democratic society is that government should translate the public's will into policy. Public opinion is difficult to define, determine, and measure.

There are many public opinions. The concept of issue publics comes from the fact that various groups may have firm opinions on specific issues, but the general public does not. There are two types of issues: valence and position issues.

A variety of factors shape opinion. Specific factors and their relative importance are still being studied.

The most common measures of public opinion are elections, demonstrations, editorial comment, and polls.

Public opinion polls that call for self-selection are the least accurate. Those that depend on scientific sampling are more accurate than other measures, but because of their potential margin of error they are not very useful in a close election.

Direct communication with elected or appointed officials is sometimes used to measure public opinion. This method has the same disadvantages as other self-selection methods, with the added problem of special-interest group lobbying.

Public opinion has been a measure of participation. Generally those who participate and shape public policy are richer, better educated, and more conservative than the population at large. This group usually has the resources—time, money, and information—that allow for greater political participation.

REVIEW QUESTIONS

1. On election night major TV networks predict, on the basis of computerized polls, the winners of an election even before the polls are closed in western states. Do you think that these kinds of polls pose a threat to the success of representative government? Explain.

2. Why are election results considered a poor measure of public opinion?

3. Why is it important to determine public opinion? Why is it so difficult to do so?

4. Why do people participate in politics? Do you think these reasons would encourage you to participate? Why or why not?

5. Do you consider participation important in a democratic society? Why or why not?

ACTIVITIES FOR REVIEW

activity 1   Develop a questionnaire to poll your community on a current issue. Write a report that includes your questionnaire, how you selected respondents, and your findings.

activity 2   Look through newspapers and periodicals of the last six months for articles on various opinion polls. What kinds of questions were asked? Were questions repeated during this period? Are most of the questions about valence issues or position issues? Do you find any significant changes in public attitudes? Do the pollsters cite possible reasons for changes?

activity 3   Stage a classroom debate on the following issue: RESOLVED, that the Federal Communications Commission should prohibit televised predictions of national election outcomes before all the polls in the country are closed.

political science DICTIONARY

bloc—members of a legislative body, not necessarily of the same party, who have common aims or goals.   p. 200

position issues—issues on which the public takes different sides.   p. 199

self-selected public opinion—the views of people who choose on their own to take positions on issues. Their opinions do not reflect those of the population at large.   p. 203

valence issues—issues on which there is no disagreement.   p. 199

11

Pressure Groups and the Mass Media

Two of the key influences on American politics are pressure groups and the mass media. They serve as instruments of communication and information between the people and their elected officials.

In this chapter you will learn about some of the types of pressure groups that attempt to influence public policy. Then you will find out what these groups do in their attempts to alter the government policies.

You will next examine the question of the growing role of the media in our political life. Finally, you will explore the problem of agenda setting in public issues. How do new issues reach the public?

CHAPTER PREVIEW

1. PRESSURE GROUPS: DEFINITION AND TYPES
2. WHAT PRESSURE GROUPS DO
3. THE MEDIA
4. AGENDA SETTING

1. PRESSURE GROUPS: DEFINITION AND TYPES

A *pressure group* (sometimes called an *interest group*) is a group of people who share a common opinion or objective on matters of public policy and attempt to influence that policy. Parties often begin as pressure groups. But there are important differences between parties and pressure groups. Parties nominate candidates for office and are primarily concerned with winning control of public offices. Pressure groups are primarily concerned with affecting public policy. In America most pressure groups are concerned with specific areas of policy. However, there are ideological pressure groups with a wider scope.

Pressure groups come in a variety of shapes and forms. Some are organizations which speak for millions of members and employ hundreds of people. Others are groups of only a few people, with perhaps no more than a single spokesperson. Some have endured for a century. Others may last for only months. They are organized in a variety of ways for a variety of purposes. But what they all have in common is the attempt to influence public policy. Many organizations are not pressure groups when they are founded. But they become such after they find that their goals require some help from the makers of public policy.

Types.   There are a number of possible ways in which pressure groups can be distinguished from one another. One way is by their purposes. They can be distinguished according to whether they focus on economic or more general interests and whether they are single- or multiple-issue groups. These distinctions are not absolute by any means. But they do serve as a useful place to begin discussion.

Economic-Interest Groups.   Most of the better organized and longer lasting pressure groups in this country have at their base economic interest. That is, they represent their members according to how they earn their living. The most effective of these groups are organized on an occupational basis— business, labor, agriculture, and professional groups.

Business.   Business leaders were involved with national policy from the very beginning of the nation. Many businesses wanted tariff protection, economic subsidies, and financial stability from their national government.

Business leaders have often spoken against government intervention in the economy and have violently opposed the organization of other interests in society. But business itself was the earliest and best organized of the pressure groups. In the business community, as in other groups we will be discussing, one must make a distinction between the *single-issue groups* and the *multi-issue groups*. (The latter are often *peak associations*, combining the interests of many different kinds of business.)

The single-issue groups are far more common. They can include everything from brewers to truckers to land developers to utility companies. Specific examples might

ORGANIZED INTEREST GROUPS

Economic Groups	Noneconomic Groups
National Federation of Business and Professional Women's Clubs	John Birch Society
American Bankers' Association	Federation of the Blind
National Council on the Aging	National Conference of Christians and Jews
Airline Pilots' Association	National Society, Daughters of the American Revolution
National Association of Retail Druggists	National Abortion Rights Action League
Communication Workers of America	Diabetes Association
Brotherhood of Locomotive Engineers	Moral Majority
Disabled American Veterans	Americans for Democratic Action
United Steelworkers	
Dairy Industry Committee	
See the textbook for other examples.	

include the National Association of Real Estate Boards or the American Petroleum Institute. Depending upon the power and wealth of the businesses they represent, these groups can be influential or unimportant. They lobby for the particular interests of their industry group. In the case of the regional business associations, they lobby for the interests of business in a certain area of the country. They may often be pitted against one another. Railroads may be pitted against trucking companies, oil companies against coal companies, and different communications industries against one another.

The behavior of multi-issue groups, or peak associations, is quite different. These try to combine the interests of business as a class. The two largest traditional multi-issue groups have been the National Association of Manufacturers (NAM) and the Chamber of Commerce of the United States. The NAM tends to represent the larger industrial corporations. The Chamber of Commerce is dominated by hundreds of local chambers of commerce representing smaller businesses. Just recently a new group, the Business Roundtable, has come into existence. It speaks for the very largest corporations, and it has proved to be perhaps the single most powerful business representative at the present time.

Agriculture. Agriculture was slower to organize than business. It did so only when it became obvious that the once dominant position of farmers in the economy was vanishing. The oldest and now most conservative of the three multi-issue farm groups, the National Grange, dates back to 1867. The largest (about 1.8 million members) and most effective of the agricultural pressure groups is the American Farm Bureau Federation. The Farmers' Union is smaller and more militant and favors government programs more than the other two. Unlike the situation in business, in which the large associations are

In 1979, farmers marched in Washington to show their dissatisfaction with government policies on agriculture.

usually on the same side on key issues, the Farmers' Union often stands in opposition to the other two groups.

Smaller farmers' groups are organized on a single-product basis—for example, the National Wool Growers' Association and the

During the war in Vietnam, these Chicago businessmen tried to bring pressure from the business community on the government to stop the war.

American Cattleman's Association. Like business groups of the same type, these may take opposite positions on an issue. Intraproduct fights are also quite common. Arkansas rice growers can be pitted against California rice growers, or beet sugar producers against cane sugar producers.

Professional Groups. Most of the major professions organized around the turn of the century. Originally they focused largely on their professional interests and problems. But many of them came to realize that control of their professional lives depended on influencing the government. However, the degree of influence and power they developed varied more widely than that of other economic groups. The professional pressure groups include such powerful groups as the American Medical Association and the American Bar Association and such relatively power-

less groups as the American Historical Association.

Labor. The peak association for the labor movement is the American Federation of Labor-Congress of Industrial Organizations (AFL-CIO). It includes nearly 17 million members belonging to about 130 separate unions. Although the history of the unions belonging to the AFL-CIO goes back more than a century in some cases, the real power of the unions as a lobbying force began during the Great Depression of the 1930's.

It should be noted that two of the largest unions, the United Automobile Workers (UAW) and the International Brotherhood of Teamsters, as well as important smaller unions such as the United Mine Workers (UMW), do not belong to the AFL-CIO. And, while the entire labor movement can unite on certain economic issues, such as the right to collective bargaining and higher minimum wages, the unions often find themselves on opposite sides of many questions. The UAW, for example, has been considered a liberal union; many of the building trades' unions are conservative on most issues. Specific economic issues such as tariffs or automobile-emission controls may set union against union.

Other Economic Groups. There are a number of groups organized around the promotion of the economic interests of people defined by means other than productive relation to the economy. These would include veterans' groups, lobbies for the poor or welfare groups, senior citizens' lobbies, and consumers' groups.

Noneconomic Groups. These pressure groups are usually smaller and more tran-

sient than the economic-interest groups just discussed. Yet they also are capable of arousing great numbers of people when the issues seem relevant. Thus, at various times, prohibition groups, environmental groups, good-government groups, religious groups, and groups asserting racial or ethnic identity have been able to affect our history significantly.

Some of these groups are organized around a single issue or group of issues—preservation of the environment, advancement of a particular ethnic or racial group, promotion of legislation for or against abortion, or campaigns against a particular disease. Some single-issue groups are involved in issues that become multiple issues. For example, the American Civil Liberties Union's concern with the protection of the Bill of Rights involves it in many different arenas. The "citizens' lobby," Common Cause, attempts to bring "good government" into our

Many handicapped Americans have recently formed organizations to force government to take notice of their special needs. Do you have any government-supported services for the handicapped in your community?

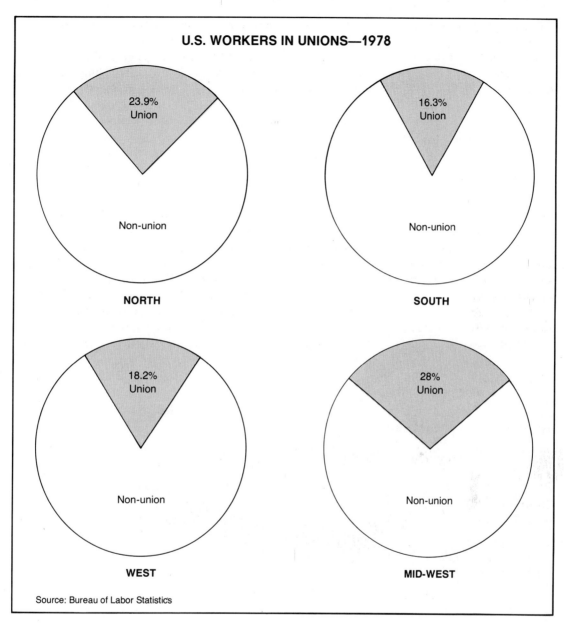

U.S. WORKERS IN UNIONS—1978

23.9%
Union

Non-union

NORTH

16.3%
Union

Non-union

SOUTH

18.2%
Union

Non-union

WEST

28%
Union

Non-union

MID-WEST

Source: Bureau of Labor Statistics

system and thereby involves itself in a host of different issues. Some ideological groups, such as the Americans for Democratic Action or the Conservative Union, are multi-issue groups by definition. Church groups also often find themselves in this last category. Church groups are sometimes more outspoken on certain issues than other multi-issue groups.

section review

1. What are the two key influences on American politics?
2. What is the primary concern of pressure groups?
3. Define the term "peak associations."
4. How can single-issue groups affect government policy?

11. Pressure Groups and the Mass Media   **215**

2. WHAT PRESSURE GROUPS DO

In the long run, a policy that does not have the support of the people will not survive. Therefore, any pressure group that wants to influence policy has to reach out for public support.

Economic pressure groups, especially, spend vast sums in trying to convince the American people to favor policies that they want. Most of this money is spent by business since money is business' greatest asset. You see advertisements by oil companies or savings banks on your TV screen or in your newspaper that do not sell the corporation's products or services. They argue in favor of a particular policy, such as deregulation of natural gas.

Noneconomic pressure groups seek not only issue support, but also membership and financial support. Most of these groups have to spend so much time in just surviving that they are not as effective as they might be. Their most common weapon is the form letter sent out in great numbers to potentially sympathetic people. Every year an organization such as Common Cause sends hundreds of thousands of letters appealing for funds and support for its positions. Many of these letters ask people to write congresspersons on controversial issues. For instance, groups on both sides of the Panama Canal issue sent out millions of pieces of mail in 1977–1978. As a result, Congress received great numbers of letters on the issue.

Influencing Candidates and Elections. One of the easiest ways to influence public policy is to get people favorable to a particular policy elected to office. Thus Lyndon Johnson's legislative triumphs in 1965 were largely a result of his landslide win in 1964, which brought in liberal Democrats with him. Blacks and labor groups found themselves with a very favorable Congress.

But when Republicans made substantial gains in the 1966 elections, conservative groups had a reason to be pleased.

There are built-in links between some pressure groups and some parties. In general, labor has found a friend in the Democratic party and business in the Republican party. But some unions will cooperate with Republicans and some Republicans will work with unions. And there are major business interests that are close to the Democrats. Certain lobbies can generally be expected to support Democratic candidates—the UAW, the ADA, the National Committee for an Effective Congress (NCEC), and so on. But other groups have closer ties to the Republicans.

Many economic pressure groups "hedge their bets" by contributing to the campaign funds of candidates from both parties. The idea behind many pressure groups' contributions to candidates is not to buy the vote of a victorious candidate, but to win access to him or her. As one lobbyist put it, "All a contribution does is get your foot in the door."

Influencing Public Officials. Since public policy is, in the end, made by public officials, pressure groups spend most of their time on this task. Public opinion and elections are simply ways to reach the ear of power.

It is important to remember that lobbying is not limited to legislative bodies. In fact, the really effective and powerful lobbies exert a great deal of influence on the executive branch. This is especially true of the economic lobbies. But it is increasingly true of all lobbies. Much congressional legislation now consists of general mandates to the executive branch to do something about some area of policy. This means that the key details of regulation writing and enforcement procedures are left to the executive branch. This also applies to noneconomic lobbies. For example, issues such as busing and abortion depend a great deal on how the executive departments, influenced by congressional legislation on these matters, interpret their mandates.

An effective lobbyist, then, must be vitally concerned with Congress, with the executive branch, and with the courts which have the final say on many American policy questions. Any major lobbying operation will be staffed in all these areas. As a result of the growing involvement of the national government with so many areas of our national life, an ever larger private community of consultants, lawyers, lobbyists, technical specialists, and public relations experts has grown up around Washington. The salaries for these specialists are high. They can earn as much as $500,000 or more per year.

Bribery is much rarer than it used to be. Modern lobbyists spend most of their time working with those who are already favorable to their cause. Studies have shown that their function often is not so much to convince people to be on their side as to provide information to those who are already committed. Direct contact by the lobbyist with undecided congresspersons is less important than you might think. What lobbyists do to influence other people is orchestrate campaigns from the "grass roots" of the districts and from their colleagues in Washington. During the struggle over oil policy a few years ago, one undecided congressman found himself being lobbied in favor of an oil company's position by a rabbi who had been a childhood friend.

The fragmented character of the American government increases the role of the lobbyist. Since execution and coordination of policy requires cooperation from otherwise competitive branches of government, it is often the case that a lobby provides the coordination. An industry or even a single group can coordinate, not only the congressional committees in charge of the area with which they are concerned, but also those relevant parts of the bureaucracy.

Of course, in fields in which there are strong forces on both sides of a question, the opposing groups may focus their efforts on different agencies or branches of the government in order to achieve their specific goals.

Regulating the Lobbyists. Lobbying rests on one statute, the Federal Regulation of Lobbying Act. This law was passed in 1946 as part of the Legislative Reorganization Act of that year.

The act required registration of persons and organizations that collect or spend money for the "principal purpose" of influencing congressional activity. They have to register with the clerk of the House and with the secretary of the Senate. They also are required to file quarterly reports listing funds received and expended. They must supply the names and addresses of major ($500 or more) contributors, of those who received money ($10 or more), and of publications in which articles have been printed.

All of the data reported are published quarterly in the Congressional Record. There are stiff penalties (fines up to $10,000, prison terms up to five years, suspension of lobbying rights up to three years) for failure to comply with the law. The law was attacked in the courts as a violation of the First Amendment and overturned by the District Court. But it was upheld by the Supreme Court (*United States* v. *Harris*, 1954).

More than 6,000 different individuals and groups, spending more than $5 million a year, have registered with the House clerk. Nonetheless, the law is remarkably ineffective. Congress did not establish an agency to enforce the law. Thus there is no check on the reports that are filed. Lobbying before executive agencies—which may be the most important kind—is not covered, nor is testimony before congressional committees. And the "principal purpose" definition of lobbying is a giant loophole. It allows many organizations to claim that their lobbying is insignificant or that they are engaged in research or in giving out information that should be shared with the public.

Pressure groups such as the National Council to Control Handguns use the mails to communicate with their supporters.

HOW YOU CAN HELP WIN THE FIGHT FOR EFFECTIVE HANDGUN CONTROL

An Action Guide for NCCH members

CONTROL HANDGUNS National Council to Control Handguns

section review

1. How can the public help pressure groups to survive?
2. Explain what is meant by pressure groups' "hedging their bets."
3. Which two branches of government are influenced by lobbyists?
4. Why is it necessary to regulate the activities of lobbyists?

3. THE MEDIA

Communication is a central factor in politics. Communication and information are clearly linked. Who controls communication? Who controls information? These are basic questions that are asked when one analyzes the politics of any society.

A "Mediacracy"?   In recent years a number of sociologists, political scientists, and writers have suggested that America is becoming a society dominated by a knowledge industry, or a communications/information complex. They have suggested that the dominant companies of the Industrial Revolution were those of energy and transportation, but that the dominant companies of our "post-Industrial Revolution" are those concerned with the creation and spread of information. Political theorist Kevin Phillips even coined the term "mediacracy" to describe the dominance of this new social order.

The Power of the Media.   Few doubt that the media now have great power. But the exact nature of that power has yet to be fully explored. TV news reporters are among the best-known people in the country—indeed, in the world. As one person put it, "There is hardly any story in the world to which we could send Walter Cronkite without his attracting more attention than the story." The mere presence of cameras changes events. It

Printing in the eighteenth century was a slow process. Using the hand-operated presses of the period, even the fastest printers could produce no more than a few hundred sheets of newsprint a day. As a result, newspapers were usually available only to the wealthy and educated members of the population.

Nevertheless, newspapers gained popularity in colonial cities. In 1760 Philadelphia had six newspapers (as many as London had) and Boston had five. About 40 colonial newspapers survived the Revolution. By the year 1790 nearly 100 newspapers were being published in the United States and by 1800 there were over 230.

The year 1800 was an election year, and both the nation and its newspapers were becoming increasingly partisan. The Republican press addressed the average citizen more and more by lowering prices, using more illustrations and cartoons, and writing in a more popular style on political affairs. Politics in America was a popular concern, and the press was influential in shaping public opinion. By 1810 the American press had a larger circulation than that of any country in the world.

The invention of the steam-powered cylinder press revolutionized printing and the newspaper industry. With the new invention thousands of papers could be printed in a day and the price of a paper could be lowered to a penny. The resulting increase in readership greatly affected American thought.

The first penny paper was the **New York Sun,** begun in 1833 by Joseph Pulitzer. Joseph Pulitzer introduced the comics page, scandals, crime, and the exclusive story, or "scoop," to journalism. The penny papers were a huge success. Pulitzer's format was soon imitated by William Randolph Hearst, the publisher of the **San Francisco Examiner** and the **New York Journal.** The two publishers entered into fierce competition for the biggest scoop. What developed from this was some excellent investigative reporting.

Many investigative reporters turned their attention to corruption in government. One of the first major scandals concerned William Marcy "Boss" Tweed, whose political machine controlled New York City. In 1871 the **New York Times** revealed how Boss Tweed's organization was stealing the taxpayer's money through false accounting and inflated bills relating to public works, municipal services, and administrative expenses. One famous receipt was for $170,730 of municipal funds spent for 40 tables and chairs! Inspired by newspapers and periodicals, the cries for reform eventually led to reorganization of the civil service and general cleanup of certain municipal governments. Reform movements were responsible for establishing model governments in both Cleveland and Toledo, Ohio, for electing a reform mayor of Chicago, and for overthrowing New York City's corrupt "Tammany Hall" politicians.

Investigative reporting continues today. A recent example is Bob Woodward and Carl Bernstein's persistent probing of the Watergate break-in. Their discoveries led to the resignation of President Nixon and the arrest of several of his top aides.

The struggle over freedom of the press goes back in American history to 1734, when Peter Zenger, a printer and newspaper owner, was arrested for

NEWSPAPERS AND THEIR INFLUENCE ON AMERICAN THOUGHT

publishing seditious libel. Alexander Hamilton came to Zenger's defense. Hamilton admitted that Zenger had in fact published articles opposing the government. But he argued that, since Zenger's charges were true, no crime had been committed. The jury found Zenger not guilty amid cheers from the crowd in the courtroom. A precedent was set for freedom of the press in America.

Since then there have been many attempts to restrict this freedom. John Adams' administration passed the Sedition Act, which made it a crime to write or publish anything "scandalous" or "malicious" against either house of Congress, the President, or the government. This measure was passed by the Federalists in an attempt to silence the popular Republican press. The measure expired in two years and was never reenacted.

There have even been attempts to suppress political cartoons. In 1902 a political cartoon in the **Philadelphia North American** portrayed Pennsylvania's Governor Pennypacker as a parrot. The governor was so outraged, he had a legislator introduce a bill prohibiting "the depicting of men . . . as birds or animals." The newspaper responded by having another cartoonist depict him as a beet.

may even create them. Modern politicians shape their campaigns and their administrations to fit the needs of TV network news. Short, dramatic, filmable events that will fit into 30 seconds of air time are now standard features of political campaigns. And campaign managers are willing to spend money to buy air time.

But do the media shape attitudes? They have been able to focus attention on a person or issue. They have been able to destroy politicians by sustained attacks on their capability. However, it is possible that politicians and social scientists alike have been mesmerized by the media—particularly by television—and have overlooked evidence that it is difficult to shift or change attitudes through television alone. They also may not realize that in most cases voters get little

information affecting their voting choice from TV news programs.

The media did however, influence voter turnout on election day 1980. In mid-afternoon the media began predicting a Reagan landslide, and President Carter's concession was broadcast before the polls closed. This reduced voter turnout, especially in the west.

section review

1. How can the media create or destroy a candidate?
2. What companies emerged as dominant after America's industrial revolution?
3. Why do politicians shape their campaigns to fit the needs of TV network news?
4. How do TV programs affect voters?

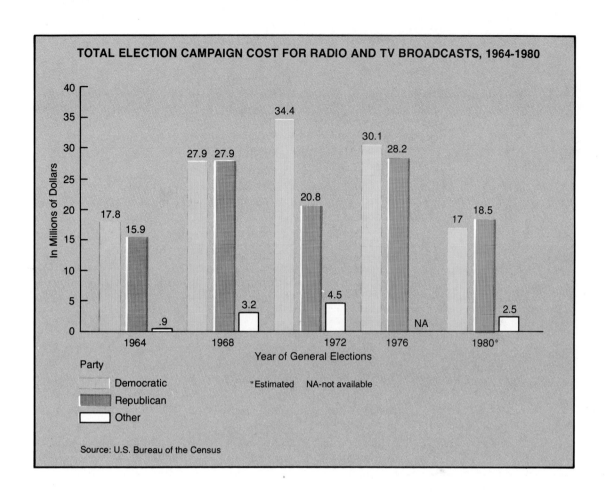

TOTAL ELECTION CAMPAIGN COST FOR RADIO AND TV BROADCASTS, 1964-1980

In Millions of Dollars

Year of General Elections

Party

Democratic

Republican

Other

*Estimated   NA-not available

Source: U.S. Bureau of the Census

4. AGENDA SETTING

Who Asks the Questions? It is sometimes said that the person who asks the questions has more power over a situation than the one who gives the answers. In political terms the practice of defining a situation is often called *agenda setting,* after the practice in meetings of writing an agenda for the business of the meeting.

In terms of modern American politics, we might consider agenda setting the ability to define a problem. Every pressure group has some problems that are of major concern to

them. They would like to have other people share that concern. One of the goals of most pressure groups is to get their problems and issues on the national agenda.

Who Writes the Agenda? It is obvious that the President has great power in this respect. Lyndon Johnson could focus attention on poverty and the Vietnamese war as major problems of the mid-1960's. Jimmy Carter was determined to emphasize energy and management of government bureaucracy as primary problems of the late 1970's. It is important to note that the power to present a problem is not the power to solve it, just as the power to get a bill on the legislative

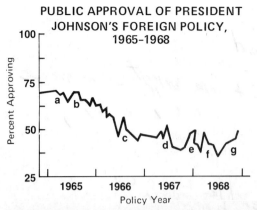

PUBLIC APPROVAL OF PRESIDENT JOHNSON'S FOREIGN POLICY, 1965–1968

a. February 1965	Bombing of North Vietnam begins
b. April 1965	United States troops sent to Dominican Republic
c. June 1966	Extension of American bombing in North Vietnam
d. June 1967	Glassboro, N.J., summit with Russian leaders
e. January 1968	Tet offensive by North Vietnamese
f. April 1967	North Vietnam agrees to begin peace talks after partial bombing halt
g. October 1968	Full bombing halt, peace talks advance

agenda is not the power to pass it. Most of the problems Presidents have identified in recent years have not been solved; they have just been ignored.

Creating an Issue. Even Presidents cannot create an issue by themselves. What other factors are involved? One inspiration for Lyndon Johnson's War on Poverty was Michael Harrington's book *The Other America*. It made many Americans aware that there were still many pockets of poverty in this affluent nation. Another was the President's own Great Depression and New Deal experiences. But there were deeper causes. In the 1960's people saw the possibility that poverty could be eliminated. Previously, poverty had been

regarded as a problem with no solution.

For an issue to be a political problem, a solution not only must exist, it must also be attainable through political action. Although the Declaration of Independence guarantees us the right to "the pursuit of happiness," unhappy people do not generally think of their emotional condition as a matter to be cured by political action.

It is possible for people to see something as a problem but to disagree on the nature of the problem. Cows are considered sacred in India. An Indian Hindu looking at America might see a problem in a system that feeds cattle to human beings. An American Christian looking at India might see a problem in the presence of so many cattle at the same time that people are going hungry.

Generally the discovery of a problem depends upon several factors. There must be an intellectual analysis of some situation as a problem. There has to be an idea that a solution might be attainable. And there must exist a group that agitates to focus attention on the problem. If a solution is thought to be unacceptable for some reason, a problem can remain low on the agenda even if there seems to be a solution.

The Media and Issue Creation. The major role of the media is giving emphasis to an issue, not shifting positions on that issue. A classic case was demonstrations at the Democratic convention in Chicago in 1968. Since some of those who were beaten by police were reporters, the coverage of the incidents was generally favorable to the demonstrators and hostile to the police. Despite this, public opinion, already hostile to anti-Vietnamese War protesters, was heavily in favor of the police. Public opinion then turned against the media. If it were really so easy for the media to shape the opinions of people, reporters most certainly would not have been exposed

Abused children need the protection of community organizations and pressure groups such as the National Council for the Prevention of Child Abuse. One of their advertisements is shown here.

to the hostility they met during the turbulent period of the late 1960's. It should be remembered that the media are a pressure group. Like other pressure groups, they have been more successful in protecting their interests than in affecting popular opinion concerning themselves.

As a powerful and visible social institution, the media are blamed by society for troubles of society's own making. In any event, it is clear that there remains much to be learned about the role of the media in politics. Recently, writers and observers of the national scene have focused their attention on the role of the media in political life. We have not seen the last of controversy on the subject.

section review

1. Define the term "agenda setting."
2. State one of the goals of most pressure groups.
3. How effective have presidents been in recent years in solving the problems they have identified?
4. What factors are needed to discover a political problem? Once discovered, how can the problem be brought to the government's attention?
5. What are some of the concerns of those who criticize the media?
6. What is the major role of the media in regard to important issues?
7. What are some of the factors that cause an issue to be a political problem?

CHAPTER SUMMARY

11

Two of the key influences on American politics are pressure groups and the mass media. They serve as instruments of communication and conveyors of information between the people and their elected representatives.

A pressure group is a group of people with a common opinion or objective on matters of public policy. They share several characteristics with political parties but are different in their basic functions. They do not nominate candidates. They seek to affect public policy rather than to control political offices.

Pressure groups generally have an economic interest. The most successful represent the interests of business, agriculture, professional groups, and labor. General-interest groups are usually smaller and more transient and focus on a single issue or cluster of issues. They are successful when they can arouse general support.

Pressure groups, or lobbies, seek to affect public policy both by increasing the public's awareness of and support for their causes and by influencing candidates, voters, and public officials. Because a great deal of authority is delegated by Congress to the executive branch, much of a lobbyist's work focuses on bureaucrats.

Concern over the influence of pressure groups and their lobbyists led to the passage of laws regulating lobbying activities. A number of loopholes still exist, and Congress continues to investigate the problem of new regulations for lobbyists.

The media, particularly television, have become important in determining what issues will be discussed and when. The power of the media is great, but recent studies indicate that their influence is limited to the focusing of attention on people and issues. Shaping public opinion is more complex than was earlier thought, and other factors seem to have a greater influence on opinion than the media.

REVIEW QUESTIONS

1. Why do people organize into pressure groups?
2. What makes an organization become a pressure group?

3. Why do you think that economic-interest groups are longer-lived than other pressure groups?

4. Do you think that pressure groups should be permitted to function in a democratic society? Give reasons for your position.
5. What qualities should a lobbyist possess?
6. Congress is currently considering lobbying reform. What items do you think should be included in the law?

7. The media help determine which issues will be discussed. Do you think the media, particularly television, are too powerful in setting the national agenda and shaping public opinion? If so, why? What regulations would you wish to see placed on the media? If none, why not? Give specific reasons.

ACTIVITIES FOR REVIEW

activity 1   Write to the national office of a pressure group listed in this chapter or to another that interests you. Ask for current materials on issues important to the interests the group represents. On what issues is the group working? What methods are being used?

activity 2   Prepare a position paper on lobbying and its regulation, and present it to the class. Send your statement to your congressperson.

activity 3   If you were setting the agenda for America in the next decade, what problems and/or solutions would you include? Why?

activity 4   Do research on a recent presidential campaign. What evidence can you find of media influence on the outcome? What role did the media play in identifying the critical issues of the campaign? Present your findings to the class.

political science DICTIONARY

agenda setting—defining of a situation in political terms.   p. 221
pressure group—a group who share common opinions or objectives on matters of   p. 210
    public policy and who attempt to influence that policy.

12

Voting and Elections

The most important right in a representative democracy is the right to vote. In the beginning of American history, this right was controlled by the states and was limited in a number of ways. Over the years it has become more a matter for the national government and has been extended to most of the population.

In this chapter you will deal with the steps by which the suffrage, or the right to vote, was extended to new groups. Then you will review limitations on the right to vote that still exist in the United States. You will find out how the civil rights movement led to a great extension of national power over the suffrage. You will also examine the way in which people cast their ballots. Finally, you will review the problem of nonvoters in our American society.

CHAPTER PREVIEW

1. THE EXTENSION OF THE SUFFRAGE
2. LIMITATIONS ON THE RIGHT TO VOTE
3. CIVIL RIGHTS AND THE RIGHT TO VOTE
4. THE ACT OF VOTING
5. NONVOTING IN AMERICA

1. THE EXTENSION OF THE SUFFRAGE

The right to vote is basic to a representative democracy. The term for this right is *suffrage*. But under United States law, the right to vote is not a *civil right*—that is, a right belonging to all persons. It is a *political right*—one limited to those who meet the requirements of law. It is sometimes described as a privilege.

The Constitution left the power to determine suffrage qualifications to the individual states. But there was one exception. The electorate for the House of Representatives had to be the same as that permitted to vote for the "most numerous branch of the state legislature" (Article 1, Section 2, Clause 1). This meant that those qualified to vote for the lower houses of the state legislature, would also be permitted to vote for the national lower house. The upper houses of the state usually had tighter property limitations on voting.

The Drive to Extend the Suffrage. The history of the suffrage in this country reflects the same pattern found in the constitutional amendments. There was a simultaneous extension of individual rights and of national power. This is not surprising, since so many of the amendments were concerned with questions of suffrage. In effect, the idea of America as a national democracy slowly replaced the idea of America as a federal republic.

In the new nation suffrage was limited on any or all of the following grounds— religion, property, race, sex, citizenship, residence, and age. Step by step the direction of change was abolishing or reducing these

Susan B. Anthony was a leader of the woman's suffrage movement in the late nineteenth century. She helped to organize the National Woman Suffrage Association in 1869.

restrictions. Now only the last three—citizenship, residence, and age—have any legal effect.

Religion was the first requirement to go. The various voting tests that were required by some states were finally abolished in 1810. Even the concept of established state churches was gone by 1835. Property and tax requirements followed. By the 1850's universal adult male suffrage was the norm.

Race was a far more difficult issue. The Reconstruction amendments were intended to settle this problem. For a generation following their passage, Blacks were allowed to vote. But a series of legal decisions and laws at the turn of the century, coupled with massive violence against the southern Black population, disenfranchised southern Blacks once more in the years 1882–1904. By the beginning of the twentieth century, less than 5 percent of the Blacks in the former Confederate states—which still included about 90 percent of the nation's Blacks—were allowed to vote. Literacy tests administered in a discriminatory way, voting laws, "grandfather clauses," "White only" primaries, and poll taxes were used for this purpose.

At almost the same time that Blacks were being removed from the electorate, the largest disenfranchised group in the country was being added to it—women. Women first got the vote in the Wyoming territory in 1869. State by state they gained ground until World War I. Then things changed with a rush. In 1920 the Nineteenth Amendment took effect giving women the right to vote everywhere. The question of Black voting was reopened during the aftermath of World War II. Beginning in the courts and then spreading to the streets and to the Congress, the civil rights movement took shape. As Blacks became a growing part of the electorate of the northern cities, their cause met with more sympathy than it had at the turn of the century. It was not until the Voting Rights Act of 1965, however, that southern Black voting became general.

Three other amendments to the Constitution had the effect of helping minority voting. The Twenty-third Amendment, adopted in 1961, added the Black-majority District of Columbia to the presidential electorate. The Twenty-fourth Amendment, adopted in 1964, ended poll taxes or other taxes as a condition for voting. The Twenty-sixth Amendment, adopted in 1971, set the minimum voting age at 18 instead of 21. Since the minority population of the U.S. is younger than the white population, this too aided minority voting.

The Reconstruction amendments also extended the national guarantees in the Bill of Rights to the states. The federal courts have used these amendments to limit the grounds on which people can be excluded from the electorate.

THE EXTENSION OF SUFFRAGE IN THE UNITED STATES

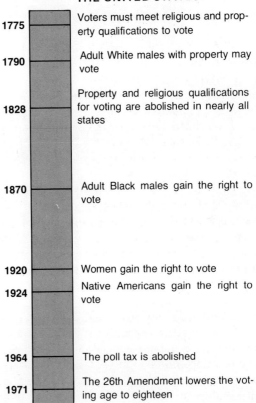

1775	Voters must meet religious and property qualifications to vote
1790	Adult White males with property may vote
1828	Property and religious qualifications for voting are abolished in nearly all states
1870	Adult Black males gain the right to vote
1920	Women gain the right to vote
1924	Native Americans gain the right to vote
1964	The poll tax is abolished
1971	The 26th Amendment lowers the voting age to eighteen

section review

1. What kind of right is the right to vote?
2. Who has the power to determine suffrage qualifications?
3. When and where did women first get the vote in the United States?
4. How did Amendments 23, 24 and 26 aid Blacks in exercising their right to vote?

2. LIMITATIONS ON THE RIGHT TO VOTE

Remaining Suffrage Limitations. Despite the extension of the suffrage and of national power over the suffrage, a number of limitations remain. The individual states continue to control the right to vote as long as they do not violate federal rules. These limitations generally fall into four classes—age, citizenship, residence, and registration.

Age. Before the adoption of the Twenty-sixth Amendment, all but four states had set 21 as their voting age. The exceptions were Georgia (1943) and Kentucky (1955) with age 18, Alaska (1959) with age 19, and Hawaii (1959) with age 20. Here again a war sparked a change. It seemed unfair that 18-year-olds could be sent to die in Vietnam without having the right to vote.

The Twenty-sixth Amendment simply states that the right of citizens 18 years or older to vote "shall not be denied or abridged . . . on account of age." This amendment does not prevent a state from enfranchising those under 18. Nevertheless, no state has done so thus far.

Citizenship. One area in which legislation has become more restrictive is citizenship. At present no noncitizen is allowed to vote in any election. But in the past a dozen states permitted noncitizens who had applied for citizenship to vote. Generally these were states with few immigrants, states that needed labor and wanted to attract it. Those states in which immigrants were a large percentage of the population were the most restrictive in immigrant suffrage. Arkansas, however, one of the states with the fewest foreign-born residents, permitted noncitizen voting until 1926. All states except Minnesota now put naturalized and native-born citizens on the same legal footing. Minnesota requires 90 days of citizenship before a person can vote.

Residence. Until the 1970's state control over residence requirements went largely unchallenged. Most states required a year's residence in the state, several months residence in the county, and a month's residence in the local election district. The justification for these rules was that they kept candidates from bringing in outside voters to swing elections.

In the Voting Rights Act of 1970 and in two Supreme Court cases (*Oregon* v. *Mitchell*, 1970, and *Dunn* v. *Blumstein*, 1972), the national government extended its power over this area of the suffrage. In the 1970 act Congress provided that no state could deny the right to vote in presidential elections to anyone who had lived in a local election district for 30 days immediately before the election and was otherwise qualified to vote in the state. States were still allowed to exclude *transients*—those who were living in the state for a limited time for a specific purpose, such as students or soldiers. But the courts have more recently ruled that students can vote on campus if they claim it as their legal residence. In *Oregon* v. *Mitchell* the Court upheld this law on the basis of Congress' "broad authority to create and maintain a national government."

The Court extended the limitation on state residence requirements to state elections in *Dunn* v. *Blumstein.* It found the Tennessee requirement of a year in the state and three months in the county to be a violation of the Fourteenth Amendment on the ground that it discriminated against new residents. It suggested that 30 days' residence in the state was more reasonable. As a result many states took the hint. At present about half the states—mostly the smaller ones—have no fixed residence requirement. The other half have a 30-day requirement. A few states have fixed odd time periods, between 10 and 60 days.

As late as 1968 state residence requirements were a major limitation on American voting because the average person moves every seven years. This is no longer a serious problem.

Registration. Perhaps the most important and effective remaining limitation on voting deals with registration requirements. Only North Dakota does not require registration before voting. Several states put the responsibility for registration on the state itself. But in most of the states the individual voter is required to register before he or she is allowed to vote.

Registration is a feature relatively unique to America. In most nations the government registers its voters. But here it is a private responsibility. This requirement grew up at the turn of the century. It was clearly aimed at reducing voting by immigrants and lower-income groups in urban areas. Indeed, many states limited registration only to urban areas. Other states allowed permanent registration in rural areas but required periodic registration in urban areas.

Registration by individuals—particularly when they were required to register some months or even a year before an election—greatly reduced participation in elections. In theory these requirements were aimed at fraudulent voting. In practice they resulted in a smaller electorate rather than a purer one. Every survey of fraudulent voting has shown that this practice requires the cooperation of election officials.

Types of Registration. Originally the states required *periodic registration*. This meant that a voter had to reregister at stated intervals. In southern states this was coupled with a *cumulative poll tax*. This required the payment of several years' tax if a voter had skipped a year. This practice greatly limited Black participation.

Most states now use a *permanent registration* system. Under this system a voter stays on the rolls until something happens to void his or her registration. Registration lapses only with a change in citizenship status, or residence—through death, crime, insanity, or a move—or with the person's failure to vote at least once within a specified period of time.

Usually officers of the state, often called *registrars*, must register voters. In some states party officials, candidates, or even other citizens can register voters. Voters may also register by mail in some states. In 1977 President Carter proposed national legislation that would have permitted instant voter registration on a nationwide basis. Such a program had been started in 1976 in Minnesota and Wisconsin. Most active politicians and political scientists felt that such a program would greatly favor the Democrats, the party with greater support among the poor. The proposal died in Congress when conservative Democrats and Republicans united to oppose it. In referendums in November 1977, instant voter registration was defeated by voters in two states—Ohio and Washington.

Besides serving to prevent fraud, registration is also important in states that have closed primaries. These primaries limit voters to participating in their own party's primary. For example, a registered Republican cannot vote in the Democratic party's primary. Clearly registration is necessary to identify the voter's party preference. On the day of the election, however, voters may revise their decision.

Voter registration is the first step to be taken before voting in any election.

section review

1. What are the limitations on the extension of suffrage?
2. How did the Supreme Court case of *Dunn* v. *Blumstein* challenge residency requirements?
3. What effect does individual registration have on participation in elections?
4. Why was instant voter registration opposed in Congress?

3. CIVIL RIGHTS AND THE RIGHT TO VOTE

Several types of suffrage limitation that were once quite common have been eliminated in recent years. They have been abolished on the grounds that they were intended to be discriminatory. These include literacy tests and taxes.

Literacy Tests. The first literacy tests were adopted in some of the New England states in the 1850's as anti-Catholic measures. But they became widespread only in the 1890's when the southern states added them to their repertoire of anti-Black measures.

In the south they usually included an *understanding clause*. This meant that, in case of doubt of literacy, a clause of the state constitution was read to the voter. Somehow it developed that Black Ph.D.'s could not "understand" the clause, but White school dropouts could.

To make sure that the literacy test excluded only Blacks, southern states used the *grandfather clause*. This provided that anyone whose ancestor could vote before 1870 could

Blacks were guaranteed the right to vote by the Fifteenth Amendment. This sketch was done in the post-Civil War period.

vote without regard to tax or literacy requirements. The Supreme Court, in *Guinn* v. *Oklahoma* (1915), held that these clauses violated the Fifteenth Amendment. South Carolina had a different method—it exempted property taxpayers from the literacy requirement. This was effective since hardly any Blacks owned property.

In the Voting Rights Act of 1970, Congress suspended the literacy requirements of all the states—18 had them—for five years. In *Oregon* v. *Mitchell* the Supreme Court upheld this provision of the law as well. In 1975 Congress made the ban on literacy tests permanent.

Taxes. A few states retain tax or property restrictions for voting on bond issues. Otherwise there are no taxes permitted in American elections. These requirements, once nearly universal, had generally expired by the time of the Civil War. They were revived in the 11 southern states between 1889 and 1902 in the form of the poll tax.

Beginning in 1920 most of these states abolished their taxes—North Carolina in 1920, Louisiana in 1934, Florida in 1937, Georgia in 1945, South Carolina in 1950, Tennessee in 1951, and Arkansas in 1964, after the Twenty-fourth Amendment. Alabama, Mississippi, Texas, and Virginia—the four remaining states—kept their taxes on the state level until the Supreme Court, in *Harper* v. *Virginia State Board of Elections* (1966), ruled them incompatible with the Fourteenth Amendment. "Wealth, like race, creed, or color," said the Court, "is not germane to one's ability to participate intelligently in the electoral process."

Civil Rights and the Suffrage. Most of the extension of national power over the suffrage in recent years was related to the civil rights issue. The major congressional legislation (as distinct from amendments) on the issue of the suffrage since the mid-1950's can be summarized as follows.

1957. The Civil Rights Act of 1957, sponsored by the Eisenhower Administration, created a Civil Rights Commission. It had the power to inquire into cases in which it was claimed that suffrage had been abridged because of race. These cases would be tried in federal courts instead of state courts. It forbade public officials or other persons to intimidate or coerce people in their right to participate in federal elections. It also empowered the attorney general to seek court rulings against such practices. Registrars could not evade the law by hiding the records or resigning suddenly when faced with an investigation by the attorney general's office.

1960. The Civil Rights Act of 1960, also sponsored by the Eisenhower Administration, provided that a federal court that found a "pattern or practice" of infringement on suffrage rights could appoint federal "voting referees." They would help people in the

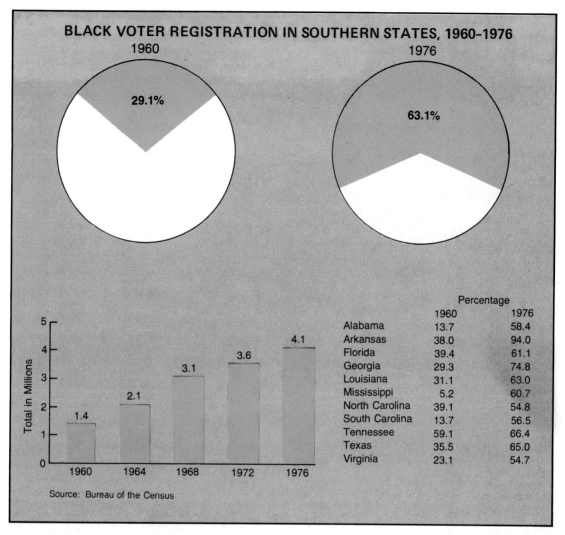

BLACK VOTER REGISTRATION IN SOUTHERN STATES, 1960–1976

1960

29.1%

1976

63.1%

	Percentage	
	1960	1976
Alabama	13.7	58.4
Arkansas	38.0	94.0
Florida	39.4	61.1
Georgia	29.3	74.8
Louisiana	31.1	63.0
Mississippi	5.2	60.7
North Carolina	39.1	54.8
South Carolina	13.7	56.5
Tennessee	59.1	66.4
Texas	35.5	65.0
Virginia	23.1	54.7

Total in Millions

1.4 (1960) · 2.1 (1964) · 3.1 (1968) · 3.6 (1972) · 4.1 (1976)

Source: Bureau of the Census

affected areas to exercise their suffrage rights. In other words, the referees were to serve as watchdogs for the public.

1964. The Civil Rights Act of 1964 was sponsored by the Johnson Administration, civil rights groups, and bipartisan congressional leadership. It focused on a provision stating that no state or local registration requirement could be applied in a discriminatory way. It had several clauses dealing with literacy rules. It also dealt with the integration of public facilities. All areas of the country were now answerable to federal laws.

1965. Unlike the earlier three acts, the Voting Rights Act of 1965 dealt exclusively with the right to vote. Also unlike earlier laws, this one was effective. It applied to elections at all levels and set up the following voting procedure.

If a state or county had a literacy requirement in 1964 and less than 50 percent of its voting-age residents were registered or voted in that year, then the literacy requirement was automatically suspended. Federal voting examiners could be sent in to supervise elections. Also, no change in the suffrage laws could take effect until approved by the Washington, D.C., District Court. The coverage of the act would be ended only when the district court found that the affected area had not discriminated at any point during the previous five years.

The provisions of this act brought six states—Alabama, Georgia, Louisiana, Mississippi, South Carolina, and Virginia—and part of a seventh—North Carolina—under the law. It was upheld by the Supreme Court in 1966 in *South Carolina* v. *Katzenbach* as a "rational and appropriate" means of carrying out the Fifteenth Amendment.

1968. The Civil Rights Act of 1968 included a provision making it a federal crime to interfere in any way with a voter or candidate in any public election.

1970. The Voting Rights Act of 1970 extended the 1965 Act for an additional five years. It also added several amendments. The voting age was lowered to 18. Literacy requirements were suspended in all states. Residency requirements were set at 30 days in all states. In addition the provisions of the 1968 law were substituted for those of the 1964 law. This last change extended the effects of the law to parts of six more states—Alaska, Arizona, California, Idaho, New York, and Oregon.

1975. Once more the provisions of the 1965 laws were extended, this time for seven years. Once more there were several significant changes. The ban on literacy tests was made permanent. The coverage of the federal-examiner section was extended to states and counties in which the following three conditions existed: more than 5 percent of the residents were of a single "language minority" (Hispanic, Native American, Asian, or Alaskan), election materials were printed only in English in 1972, and less than 50 percent of the residents were registrants or voters in that year.

These provisions extended the reach of the law to the entire states of Alaska and Texas, as well as to parts of 24 other states.

The states were required to print election materials in both English and the minority language in question. This led to some interesting problems in a few American Indian counties where the local language group had a language that had never been put into written form.

section review

1. Define the term "grandfather clause."
2. List the names of the states that kept election taxes at the state level until 1966.
3. What are three provisions of the Voting Rights Act of 1970?

4. THE ACT OF VOTING

Federal Power. Previous sections in this unit have demonstrated the ever-increasing reach of the national government over the election process. The Constitution gave Congress the power to set "the times, places, and manner of holding elections" for its own members and for presidential electors (Article 1, Section 4, Clause 1, and Article 2, Section 1, Clause 4). It has set the date in this century as the first Tuesday following the first Monday in November. Until 1960 Maine held its elections in September.

But Congress had gone on from here to regulate the finances, the right to the suffrage, and corrupt practices in elections, as well as requiring the use of secret ballots. At one time all these provisions were left to the individual states. The actual administration of elections is still left to the states, however, as long as their procedures do not violate federal statutes.

State Power. The states remain in charge of the time of elections in two ways. First,

VOTER PARTICIPATION, 1934–1980

Year	Estimated[1]	Votes Cast for President		Votes Cast for Representatives	
		Number	Percent	Number	Percent
1934	77,997,000	X	X	32,256,000	41.4
1936	80,174,000	45,642,503	56.9	42,886,000	53.5
1938	82,354,000	X	X	36,236,000	44.0
1940	84,728,000	49,840,443	58.8	46,951,000	55.4
1942	86,465,000	X	X	28,074,000	32.5
1944	85,656,000	47,794,819	53.1	45,103,000	52.7
1946	92,659,000	X	X	34,398,000	37.1
1948	95,573,000	48,794,432	51.1	45,933,000	48.1
1950	98,134,000	X	X	40,342,000	41.1
1952	99,927,000	61,551,118	61.6	57,571,000	51.6
1954	102,075,000	X	X	42,580,000	41.7
1956	104,515,000	62,027,372	59.3	58,426,000	55.9
1958	106,447,000	X	X	45,818,000	43.0
1960	109,674,000	68,838,950	62.8	64,133,000	58.5
1962	112,958,000	X	X	51,261,000	45.4
1964	114,085,000	70,645,510	61.9	65,895,000	57.8
1966	116,638,000	X	X	52,908,000	45.4
1968	120,285,000	73,212,875	60.9	66,288,000	55.1
1970	124,498,000	X	X	54,173,000	43.5
1972	140,068,000	77,719,590	55.5	71,270,000	50.9
1974	145,034,000	X	X	52,391,000	36.1
1976	150,041,000	81,551,918	54.4	74,262,000	49.5
1978	151,600,000	X	X	69,600,000	45.9
1980	160,000,000	86,495,678	53.9	Not available	Not available

X–Not applicable

1–Population 18 and over in Georgia, 1944–1970, and in Kentucky, 1956–1970; 19 and over in Alaska; and 20 and over in Hawaii, 1960–1970

Source: Federal Election Commission

they can set whatever dates they wish for their own elections. Second, they can define the voting hours for all elections, including those for President.

Most of the states have chosen to hold their own elections at the same time as national elections—in November during even-numbered years. But there has been an increasing tendency to shift these elections to the so-called off years between presidential elections. Throughout American history the terms of state officials have tended to grow longer. Often, they were elected for one-year terms in the last century. Gradually these were extended to two-year terms. Now four years is the general length.

Holding elections in off years is usually justified as avoiding the *coattail effect*, in which strong candidates at the "top" of the ticket bring in other candidates behind them. The idea is that it is better that local elections be decided without reference to national ones. This argument has seemed persuasive. But since fewer people vote in off years and since these voters tend to be wealthier and better educated, this pattern contributes to having a smaller and richer electorate select state and local officials. It also encourages and contributes to the splintering of the various levels of government.

Several states still have their elections in off years. Four—Kentucky, Mississippi, New Jersey, and Virginia—have them in November of odd-numbered years. Louisiana has its elections in April. Many local elections are also held at odd times. New York City, for example, is also an odd-year city.

The states can also decide how long their elections will be in terms of hours. That is why on presidential election nights some states, such as Kentucky or Connecticut, report their results much earlier than others. Shorter hours reduce turnout. Longer hours increase it.

The state can also determine the number and size of their voting districts. These districts are usually called precincts, wards, or election districts. These decisions are usually left to counties or cities, however.

The supervision of polling places in these districts, which includes the actual conducting of elections, is left to *election boards.* These are generally bipartisan, consisting of equal numbers of Republicans and Democrats. The theory is that the two parties will watch each other and ensure an honest election. This works better in general elec-tions than in primaries. In the latter the ruling forces in the two parties may cooperate to freeze out rebels. Sometimes this leads to problems in general elections when a strong independent candidate is running.

Usually candidates or parties are permitted to have *poll watchers.* These officials watch the process of voting to make sure that unqualified voters do not vote, to see that the election is conducted fairly, and to help get their own voters to the polls. Modern American elections are generally pretty tame affairs when compared either to past elections or to those in other countries. But every year some instances of violence or fraud occur, marring the elections in some locality.

The Ballot. In its origin voting was a public process. In the colonies even those that used paper ballots had them signed. Public voting remained common even as late as 1850. (In Great Britain it was abolished only in 1872.) Citizenship was considered to be a public

Monitoring election returns has become a highly complex operation. This picture shows the headquarters of a major TV network during the 1980 presidential election.

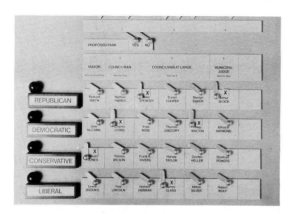

This picture shows a hypothetical roster of names in a typical voting machine.

thing. But by the nineteenth century it became obvious that intimidation and corruption were built into the public process.

When the private vote began, it did so informally, with slips of paper prepared by the voters themselves. Soon the parties took over this function. By the middle of the nineteenth century, the party ballot was the norm. These ballots were printed on distinctively colored paper. Thus it was easy to tell how people voted. Since there was no requirement specifying party color, some of the most spectacular vote swindles of the century came from printing one party's slate on another party's color.

The Australian Ballot. A new system of balloting was introduced into Australia in 1856. It spread to Great Britian and from there to the United States. It was first introduced here in 1888, and it covered all the states within less than 20 years. The Australian ballot was prepared by the state and listed all the candidates. It was distributed only at the polls and was voted secretly there.

The introduction of this ballot was part of a series of moves aimed at purifying elections by reducing both party influence and the number of participants (low-income and illiterate voters found it harder to use the Australian ballot). It immediately made "split-ticket" voting easier because now all the candidates were on the same ballot. Before, a voter had to take a party ballot, cross out some names, and then substitute new ones.

There are two basic forms of the Australian ballot—the *office-block*, or *Massachusetts*, *ballot* and the *party-column*, or *Indiana*, *ballot*. In the Massachusetts ballot, which was the first to be used, the names of all candidates for a particular office are grouped together. Originally they were printed in alphabetical order. But this was found to favor the *A*'s over the *S*'s. Now the names are generally rotated in different election districts. This voting system leads to split-ticket voting because there are no political party distinctions on the ballot itself.

In the Indiana ballot, which is used in slightly more than half the states, all the candidates for a given party are arranged in a row one way, and all the offices to be filled are arranged in a row the other way. Often a box or lever is included, making it possible to vote a "straight ticket" with one mark or motion. Not surprisingly the states using this system, such as Connecticut or Indiana, have stronger party systems than those using the Massachusetts ballot.

Sample Ballots and Voter Information. In most states sample ballots are printed in the newspapers or mailed to the voters. In a number of states, such as Oregon, voter pamphlets are mailed to each voter. These list all candidates and resolutions. They also give the candidates and spokespersons for and against the resolutions free space to state their cases. It is hoped that voters will read these pamphlets before going to the polls to cast their ballots.

1948 and the Polls

After the collapse of the **Literary Digest** poll in 1936, the most famous error in the public opinion polls came in 1948. In that year Democratic incumbent Harry Truman, who during most of his time in office had had the lowest poll rating of any President, seemed in desperate trouble. His party was split not once, but twice: left-wing Democrats, led by Henry Wallace ran on the Progressive party ticket; right wingers, led by Governor Strom Thurmond of South Carolina, ran on the States' Rights, or Dixiecrat party, ticket. By October all the polls showed the Republican candidate, Governor Thomas E. Dewey of New York, more than ten points ahead. Hardly anyone except Truman himself seemed to believe that he could win the election. And yet he did. The result astonished the nation and left the pollsters reeling.

How did the pollsters make such an error? This type of sampling had begun in 1936 and was still relatively new. So the pollsters were essentially inexperienced. They stopped polling several weeks before the election, confident that Dewey's lead was insurmountable. Thus they missed the late swing of "undecideds" to Truman. They also missed the steady swing of voters from minor parties back to the majority party. Their weighing of factors affecting the number of people who would vote was inaccurate — the 1948 election had one of the lowest turnouts in American history. In short, pollsters didn't yet know how to assess voting trends for an election lacking in voter interest and participation.

Is this kind of upset likely to happen again? The pollsters are careful to continue sampling until the last possible minute, and they are very attentive to such factors as voter turnout and motivation. But they still have problems in very close elections. When an election is decided by a margin of 2 percent—as were the elections of 1960, 1968, and 1976—public opinion polls can only tell us that the result is going to be very close. They cannot predict who is going to win. Occasionally pollsters are not even close to their predictions. For example, pollsters predicted that the 1980 election would be very close. It was, in fact, a landslide for Reagan. Apparently voter sentiment switched drastically in the final hours of the campaign, too late for the pollsters to change their predictions.

Length of Ballot. The *bed-sheet ballot* is a typically American institution. In most countries the voter is required to vote for only a few offices at the most—generally just one at a time. But in America voters are asked their opinion on everything from judges to dogcatchers, not to mention a host of bond issues, amendments, and propositions.

The length of state ballots still varies a great deal, however. It depends upon how many offices are to be filled and on whether or not the state allows the initiative, referendum, and recall. Some states, such as New Hampshire, have relatively short ballots. Others such as California, are notorious for the length of their ballots. Generally, the tendency in America from the 1820's to the 1920's was to lengthen the ballot in the name of "democratic control." This took place particularly in the Jacksonian era and the Progressive era. Since then the trend in the United States has been to attempt to shorten the ballot in the name of "responsibility."

The Physical Act of Voting. Voting began with the *viva voce*, or voice, vote. Paper ballots were introduced at first as a permanent record, and then as a means to the secret ballot. At the same time as the Australian ballot was introduced, the first voting machines were invented. The first American voting machine was developed by Thomas Edison and used in an election in Lockport, New York, in 1892.

Today voting machines are used in every state, especially in the larger urban areas. There are several different types of voting machines. The most common type has separate levers that the voter pulls in order to vote for each office. This prevents voting more than once for the same office. This type of machine has an automatic counter that records the votes secretly while they are being cast. At the end of the day, the machine is opened, and the tallies are read off the front or back of the machine. With these machines the closing of the polls takes just a few minutes.

In recent years electronic data processing has been introduced into the voting process. Some states issue computer-card ballots, which the voters punch. Others issue paper ballots, which the voters mark with special pencils. In either case the ballots are then collected and read by high-speed computers or optical scanners.

All these machines are expensive. Consequently there has been a tendency for voting machines to be used most in richer and more-populated areas. But, in general, more and more local areas are using some sort of machine-voting procedure.

Special Ballots. A number of special provisions have been made for groups of citizens who cannot get to the polls on election day. These include the *military ballot* and the *absentee ballot*. Under these provisions members of the armed services and civilians who, for reasons of occupation or health, cannot be physically present at the polling place are allowed to cast their votes by mail before the election if they have properly applied for these ballots.

The types and use of these ballots vary widely from state to state and in different types of elections. Generally, they are used more by wealthier and better-educated citizens. They are also used more in states with strong political organizations.

section review

1. How are elections held in off years justified?
2. Define the term "precincts."
3. Describe the difference between the Indiana ballot and the Massachusetts ballot.

5. NONVOTING IN AMERICA

One of the special features of the American system that has drawn much comment both at home and overseas is the relatively low turnout of American voters. America has one of the smallest turnouts of any democracy in the world. Almost half the potential voters do not participate in presidential elections. Even smaller percentages turn out in other elections.

Patterns. Nonvoting takes several forms. There is *drop-off* or *fall-off* from national elections every four years to the state elections and congressional elections that are held in the intervening years. In these off years the electorate is perceptibly smaller. There is *roll-off* within each election, since a varying percentage of those who actually vote at the top of the ticket don't make it all the way to the bottom. This figure runs anywhere from 5 percent to 25 percent, and sometimes more, in every election.

Among those counted as *nonvoters*

Practically every means of communication is employed in reaching the voting public. Billboards are still among the most frequently used forms of visual communication.

—that is, those who do not choose to go to the polls—are the following: noncitizens, the insane, and criminals, who are not eligible to vote; travelers and sick people, who are physically unable to vote; and members of certain religious or political groups, whose beliefs prevent them from voting.

The most common factors influencing people not to vote are the following: the individual's opinion of the race before him or her; people opposed to all candidates in a particular election; people who think it makes no difference; and, above all, those who lack interest in the political process. This last group is heavily concentrated in certain segments of the population. It is not surprising that the same factors that operate to increase or decrease voting participation in general operate to affect voting choices—sex, residence, income, education, occupation, issues, ease of participation, and so on.

What IS Different About America? Although the above factors affect turnout throughout the world, they do not have the same overall effect elsewhere that they do in America. That is to say, in most other countries uneducated, poor workers vote at levels not greatly different from those of better-educated, upper-income groups.

Personal Registration. Since the United States puts the responsibility for registration on the individual rather than on the state, far fewer people register here than elsewhere. Nonregistration is the greatest single reason for nonvoting. It should be noted, however, that in most countries the number of eligible voters is considered to be those registered by the state. Consequently, those voters missed by the government are not included in turn-out calculations. This increases turnout figures in Europe as compared to the United States by several percentage points.

Voting System and Number of Parties. A *winner-take-all election system* operates to limit the number of parties. This often means that one party consistently wins certain districts. But a *proportional-representation system* tends to increase the number of parties. This means that no vote is wasted. In Switzerland, for example, the turnout in cantons that elect just one representative averages around 50 percent. But in areas that elect a number of representatives through proportional voting, the turnout runs close to 80 percent.

In other words a two-party system will tend to lead to a smaller turnout. Since there is a one-party system in large areas of America, turnout is reduced further.

Factors that Influence Voter Behavior

Factors	Voting Tendency	
	Republican	Democratic
Age:		
Under 35		X
Over 55	X	
Sex:		
Male		X
Female	X	
Religion:		
Catholic		X
Protestant	X	
Jewish		X
Race:		
White	X	
Black		X
Education:		
Grade School		X
High School		X
College	X	
Income:		
Low		X
High	X	
Occupation:		
Business Professional	X	
Other White Collar	X	
Skilled Semiskilled		X
Unskilled		X
Labor Union Affiliation:		
Member		X
Nonmember	X	
Type of Community:		
Urban, Metropolitan		X
Rural, Small Town	X	

Issues. American parties do not differ very much on the issues. Since the voters are faced with only two parties that both read the same opinion polls, many voters are forced to choose what to them are "the lesser of two evils." In the European system there are not only more parties but also more issue-oriented parties. Almost everyone can find a party to his or her taste and expect a vote for that party to show some effect.

This pattern has a reinforcing effect as well. European parties appeal to a minority of the voters with strong platforms. American parties appeal to a majority of the voters with vague ones.

History and Habit. American history went in a different direction from that of other countries. America granted the suffrage to every adult male before any other country did so. But then participation in its elections diminished at the same time as it began to rise in other countries.

Nonvoting, like voting, becomes a habit. There is substantial evidence that the non-voting that began at the turn of the century has now become habitual for large chunks of the American population.

Attempts to Solve the Problem. Since the 1960's the prevalence of nonvoting in America has come to be identified as a problem. At first, many people felt that it was simply a sign of discontent with the system. More recently the attitude has been one of greater concern. For example, attention is being given to the role of former nonvoters in bringing the Nazi party to power in Germany. Some people have felt that the real danger of nonvoters is their lack of commitment to the present system. This might mean that, in a moment of crisis, such voters could be led to support extreme solutions outside the normal limits of democratic politics.

section review

1. Why is there party concern over a light voter turnout in an election?
2. What are the most common factors that influence people not to vote?
3. What is the single greatest reason for not voting?

CHAPTER SUMMARY

12

The right to vote is basic to a representative democracy. Suffrage is a political right subject only to requirements established by law. The Constitution gives states the power to determine suffrage requirements, with some exceptions. In 1787 states were required only to use the same standards for electors for the House of Representatives as they had for the lower house of the state legislature.

Restrictions were eliminated one by one during the nineteenth and twentieth centuries. Religion, property, race, sex, citizenship, residence, and age were frequent bases of restriction. Today, only citizenship, residence, age, and registration requirements remain.

Literacy tests and poll taxes were banned by a series of civil rights acts and court decisions in the last two decades.

The power of the national government over elections has grown considerably in the last century. Today Congress regulates election finances, ensures voting rights, investigates corrupt practices, and requires the use of the Australian (secret) ballot.

America has the fewest restrictions on voting of any country in the world. It also has one of the smallest voter turnouts. Some nonvoters are those who by law or because of disability are unable to vote. The most common reasons for not voting are opposition to all the candidates, lack of interest, and a belief that voting doesn't make any difference.

There are specific factors in the American system that also contribute to the low voter turnout: personal registration, the voting system and number of parties, issues, and habit and history.

REVIEW QUESTIONS

1. Why was the Voting Rights Act of 1965 more effective than previous civil rights legislation?
2. Some people have proposed that voting be mandatory. Would you favor such a law? Why or why not?
3. Recent legislation permits voter registration by mail. What effect do you think this will have on voter turnout? on voter participation? What are the advantages of this system? What are some potential problems?
4. Should voting be considered a right or a duty? Why?
5. What voting restrictions have been eliminated during the past two centuries?

ACTIVITIES FOR REVIEW

activity 1   Request a copy of a sample ballot and voter's handbook (if your state prints one) from the registrar of voters. Outline the basic structure. Does your state use the Massachusetts or the Indiana ballot form? Does your state have the initiative and referendum? If so, how are these handled in the voter's handbook? Present your findings to the class.

activity 2   Stage a classroom debate on the following issue: RESOLVED, that all state documents, including the ballot, be printed in the majority language (English) only.

activity 3   Interview or invite a local election official or a representative from the League of Women Voters to speak to your class on your state's suffrage requirements and registration system.

activity 4   Plan a voter registration drive for 18-year-olds in your school.

political science DICTIONARY

civil rights—rights belonging to and able to be exercised by all persons.   p. 226

grandfather clause—a clause in the constitutions of some southern states, which   p. 231
    permitted anyone to vote, without paying a poll tax or meeting literacy
    requirements, if their ancestors were eligible to vote before 1870.

office block ballot—a form of general election ballot in which names of all   p. 237
    candidates for a particular office are grouped together. Also known as the
    Massachusetts ballot.

party column ballot—a form of general election ballot in which various offices are   p. 237
    arranged in one column under their respective party names and symbols. Also
    known as the Indiana ballot.

political rights—rights limited to persons who meet certain requirements of the   p. 226
    law.

suffrage—the right to vote.   p. 226

UNIT SUMMARY

Political parties, pressure groups, the media, and elections are key elements of the American political system. Each has contributed to the growth of a broader based, better informed electorate.

Political parties were not favored by the nation's Founders, who believed that the factionalism parties created was unhealthy for a representative democracy. Yet by 1800 parties had developed and were selecting candidates, identifying issues, and mobilizing public opinion.

The two-party system is based on a broad consensus of the American people. American pressure groups have assumed the role still played by many European political parties—that of advocating single issues or interests.

Because public opinion is so difficult to measure, parties and pressure groups are important in identifying and clarifying issues of public policy. Most measurement of public opinion is really a measure of political participation. Those who participate are better informed and more influential in shaping public policy.

Voting is a political right basic to representative democracy. Restrictions on suffrage have decreased since 1787. Today only minimum age, citizenship, registration, and residence are usually required. Low voter turnout is a serious concern. Many fear that disaffected nonvoters may prove susceptible to radicals and dictators proposing apparently simple solutions to complex problems.

Bibliography

Blumenthal, Sidney. *The Permanent Campaign: Inside the World of Elite Political Operatives.* Boston: Beacon Press, 1980.

Crouse, Timothy. *The Boys on the Bus.* New York: Random House, 1973.

Greenfield, Jeff. *Playing to Win: An Insider's Guide to Politics.* New York: Simon and Schuster, 1980.

Key, V. O. *Public Opinion and American Democracy.* New York: Knopf, 1964.

Kirkpatrick, Jeane J. *Political Woman,* New York: Basic Books, 1974.

Ladd, Everett Carl, Jr. *American Political Parties.* New York: W. W. Norton, 1970.

——. *Where Have All the Voters Gone?* New York: W. W. Norton and Company, Inc., 1978.

Polsby, N. W. and Wildavsky, A. B. *Presidential Elections: Strategies of American Electoral Politics,* 4th edition. New York: Scribner, 1976.

Witcover, Jules. *Marathon: The Pursuit of the Presidency 1972–1976.* New York: Viking Press, 1977.

Review questions

1. The nineteenth century has been called an age of democraticization in America. What evidence of broader based election laws and public participation in government can you find to support this contention?
2. Do you think that political parties should be reorganized on an issue and ideology basis?
3. The media have an important effect on twentieth-century American politics. What role do they play in selecting candidates, identifying issues, setting national priorities, and influencing voting behavior? What role do you think they should play? Why?
4. What factors seem to influence political participation—voting, campaigning, communicating with representatives—in America? What should be done by the government to increase public participation? Explain.

Skills questions

Using the charts in this unit, answer the following questions:

1. What is the job of precinct captains? Who are under their direct supervision?
2. Which states voted for Abraham Lincoln in the election of 1860?
3. List the names of the southern states with the lowest percentage of Black voter registration in 1960. In at least two paragraphs, explain what factors might have influenced the percentage increase between 1960 and 1976.
4. Which organized interest groups exist in your state? Consult your phone book.
5. Compare the Harris and Gallup poll predictions for 1964. What was the outcome of that presidential election?
6. Trace the development of the Democratic party.

Activities

activity 1   Trace the effect of third parties on the U.S. political system.

activity 2   Conduct a survey to determine the attitudes of students in your school toward voting and other types of political participation. Are 18-year-olds more interested than others in political participation and voting? Try to identify the factors that separate participants and nonparticipants.

activity 3   Interview a local representative of your community (a city council member, for instance) to determine areas available to citizens in your community for participation in government and policy making. Report your findings to the class.

UNIT 4

ROBERT McNAMARA

Robert McNamara has been a leader in three policy arenas of American life: private business, national security, and international finance. He is effective in all three areas.

During World War II, when McNamara was in the air force, he and some close friends decided to work together after the war ended. In 1945 they wrote to Henry Ford II, who had just taken over the failing Ford Motor Company from his famous grandfather. Ford jumped at the chance to hire the ten Whiz Kids, as they came to be known by the business community.

When the group joined Ford, the business was losing money. The total value of the company was only about 600 million dollars. They initiated a series of financial and statistical controls that turned the company around. Within five years Ford had several billion dollars in assets and was earning more than $200 million annually as a result of the group's innovations.

Only one of the Whiz Kids is still with Ford. Several became corporation presidents and one is the dean of the University of Stanford Business School. But none went as far as Robert McNamara.

By 1960 McNamara, then president of the Ford Motor Company, had won a reputation as an efficient and socially conscious businessman. In 1961, when President John Kennedy needed someone to establish cost and management controls in the sprawling Pentagon bureaucracy, he appointed Robert McNamara secretary of defense. The country had never seen anyone like him. He quickly became the most powerful member of the Cabinet and a symbol of the new efficiency of President Kennedy's New Frontier and President Johnson's Great Society programs.

But after 1965 McNamara and the Democratic administration he served were bogged down in the endless problems of the war in Vietnam. McNamara's national popularity diminished, and he became increasingly doubtful about the goals and morality of the war. Johnson grew unhappy over the uncertainty of his defense secretary and in 1968 nominated him to head the International Bank for Reconstruction and Development (better known as the World Bank). He served in this position until 1981.

The World Bank was created in 1944 to aid in restructuring international economy after World War II. Its role is to help finance the economic

POLICY ARENAS IN AMERICA

development of nations—in 1977 it had more than $7 billion in outstanding loans. The bank is an international institution, with over 110 countries as members, but the United States controls about one quarter of its votes.

When McNamara took over, the bank was under attack for its elitist emphasis. McNamara attempted to shift from the financing of "prestige" projects to projects that help the world's poor. Whether he succeeded in this attempt is a matter of some controversy. That he tried is not.

OVERVIEW

UNIT CONTENT

■ Government outputs may be tangible or symbolic.

■ Two major areas of government are foreign policy and domestic policy arenas.

■ A nation has final authority over domestic affairs.

■ In order for a nation to have authority in the foreign policy arena, it must have the cooperation and respect of other nations.

■ The major goal of foreign policy is national survival.

■ Foreign policy in the United States is dominated by the executive branch, which enjoys the broad support of the citizenry in this arena.

■ Domestic policy has many and diverse issue publics.

■ Domestic policies overlap, interact, and respond to scientific, technological, and social changes.

13

External Policy Arenas

This chapter introduces you to the question of government outputs—what government does. You will survey different aspects of policy and learn about the difference between the domestic and the foreign policies of a nation.

Then you will examine how foreign policy decisions are made and review the goals of American foreign policy, past and present. Finally you will survey some of the international organizations and treaties to which the United States is a party.

CHAPTER PREVIEW

1. GOVERNMENT OUTPUTS
2. SPECIAL FEATURES OF DOMESTIC AND FOREIGN POLICY
3. FOREIGN POLICY DECISION MAKING
4. THE GOALS OF AMERICAN FOREIGN POLICY
5. THE UNITED STATES ON THE INTERNATIONAL SCENE

1. GOVERNMENT OUTPUTS

The last unit concentrated on what political scientists sometimes call the *inputs* of government—the supports and the demands within a society that influence government. Now the *outputs* of government will be discussed—that is, what government does.

What does government do? What should government do? Many of the ideological issues discussed in the first unit focused on what output the government should produce. *Normative questions*—those about what the government should do—usually set capitalists against Communists, democrats against totalitarians, liberals against conservatives.

Kinds of Outputs. Government scholar Murray Edelman has divided the outputs of government into two kinds: tangible and symbolic. A *tangible output* is something that the government actually does to or for its people. A *symbolic output* is something that the government does that is not real but is a sign of its expectations. Loyalty oaths are examples of the symbolic output of government. For both sides in the debate over loyalty oaths, the oath served more as a symbol of the allegiance that the government expected its citizens to affirm than as a code of behavior that it would enforce.

Symbolic outputs are not necessarily less important than are tangible outputs. Many of the most *polarizing*, or divisive, political issues in American history have been those that involved symbols. Unlike tangible issues that are generally subject to compromise, symbolic issues cannot be negotiated. A very large part of a government's legitimacy is symbolic, and a government that loses its symbolic value soon loses its legitimacy as well as its power.

Many issues may be symbolic for the groups that advocate them but tangible for those to whom they are applied. For example, during the prohibition controversy the opponents of the law were deprived of a tangible substance and the advocates of the law, nonusers of alcohol, received symbolic rewards.

To some degree politics is always tangible for politicians because it involves their employment. For the general public, however, politics is more often symbolic, for they often do not make connections between political

events and their own lives. This may explain why activists (who are mobilized by symbolic issues) are so often unhappy with "compromising" politicians, who must always think about reelection.

History of Government Outputs. In the past the claims of a state over its citizens were unlimited, but its ability to enforce those claims was very limited. Absolute rulers of ancient times, whatever their claim to power, had little ability to enforce their rule beyond the territory controlled by their troops. The average inhabitant of such a society usually met a government official only when the tax collector arrived once a year.

Historically the main (and often the only) function of government was security, and almost all government expenditures were directed toward foreign security (armies and navies) or domestic security (police forces).

With the rise of new technologies, forms of communication, and ways of controlling people, there also arose the need to limit the power that governments claimed. New ideologies, such as religious freedom and liberal capitalism, developed in response to that need.

But even in democratic political systems, the power of the modern state is far greater in reality than it was 500 years ago. With social security, the personal income tax, major state intervention in the economy, and a complex set of impersonal economic relations requiring government intervention, functions once considered the responsibility of individual citizens have been assumed by the government.

Internal and External Power. All governmental outputs rely on the use of internal and external power. The most important difference between these powers is that in domestic matters the nation-state makes the final decision. All decisions and laws can be enforced by the state within its own territory. But in external matters the nation-state is not the final arbiter, for it must survive in a world where other states exist. There is no sovereignty, or final power, in the world as a whole.

section review

1. Define the concept of tangible output.
2. Compare and contrast tangible outputs and symbolic outputs.
3. How has the function of government changed?

2. SPECIAL FEATURES OF DOMESTIC AND FOREIGN POLICY

What is the difference between foreign policy and domestic policy? First, because foreign policy concerns the survival of the whole nation, national leaders represent all the people. In domestic policy, in which choices are made among the various competing interests of Americans, Presidents may appear to be the representatives of only some of the people.

This perception is strengthened by the public's lack of information about foreign affairs. Most Americans are more likely to have strong opinions on race relations, taxes, crime, urban problems, wages, and prices than they have on NATO, the Middle East, international trade, or the United Nations' law of the sea conferences. Information is necessary to the formation of opinion.

As a result of the lack of information about foreign affairs, government policy on such issues is likely to be accepted without question. By contrast, most domestic issues are likely to divide the public.

The Rallying Effect. Studies have shown that any strong action by a President in foreign affairs is likely to result in a favorable increase in that persons' rating by the public. This is a result of the *rallying effect*. In foreign affairs, which evoke images of America versus the world, the public usually rallies behind the President. The President gains by appearing before the public and appealing for the support of all Americans.

The Iron Law of Specificity. In domestic affairs, however, any strong action by a President is likely to produce an unfavorable rating. This result is associated with the *iron law of specificity*, which means that the opponents of a position are likely to increase their opposition whenever the position is discussed in public.

War. Wars generally start with universal public support. If a war lasts very long, however, the public is increasingly affected. Wars draw directly on individual resources through the draft, rationing, shortages, and so on, and eventually provoke the iron law of specificity.

Most American wars have been marked by sharp domestic divisions about their wisdom and morality. World War II, which provoked American belligerency because of a direct attack on the United States, was an exception. But other wars generated much internal conflict.

In 1972 President Richard Nixon took strong action in foreign affairs by visiting the People's Republic of China.

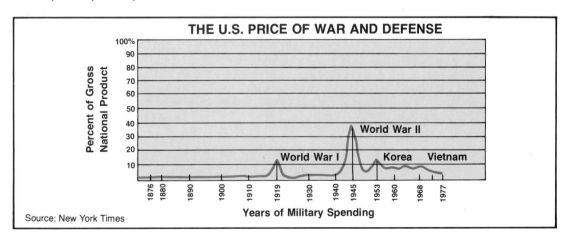

Operation of the Foreign Policy Arena. In traditional monarchies kings controlled the army and conducted foreign policy. In the United States these functions are performed by the executive branch of the national government. Under the Constitution the President's primary responsibility for conducting foreign policy comes from the role of the Chief Executive as the commander in chief of the armed forces, together with the authority to appoint ambassadors and other diplomats and to enter into treaties with sovereign states with the advice and consent of the Senate.

In addition to this broad grant of constitutional authority, the President's control over the flow of information necessary to the operation of the foreign policy arena—information supplied by executive departments and agencies such as the Department of State, the Department of Defense, the National Security Council, and the Central Intelligence Agency—makes it possible for the Chief Executive to limit the power of Congress in the foreign policy arena.

The Role of Congress. Under the Constitution Congress has the authority to

The President relies on staff and advisers for information on foreign affairs. President Carter is shown in the late 1970's with Zbigniew Brzezinski (left), an advisor on foreign affairs, and Stuart Eisenstadt (center), a staff member.

declare war and to appropriate funds. In addition the Senate has the power to approve the appointment of ambassadors and diplomats and to ratify treaties. But recognizing that the separation of powers has given the legislature the power only to check the President's foreign policy-making power, Congress has intervened in the foreign policy arena only in matters pertaining to appropriations and in periods of crisis.

In connection with its power of appropriation, Congress allocates specific defense contracts. Even during the Vietnamese War dovish members of Congress from antiwar districts fought to get defense contracts for their districts. Congress has assumed the right to act as the advocate of veterans, often overriding presidential vetoes on veterans' benefits—indeed, Congress has overriden more vetoes by more Presidents on this subject than on any other. Also, when a war goes on for a long time, Congress is likely to be the arena where objections are raised.

In 1973, in response to the Watergate crisis and to what many members of Congress considered presidential abuse of power in conducting the war in Vietnam, Congress passed, over the President's veto, the War Powers Act, which limited to 60 days the power of the President to send troops abroad without the consent of Congress.

In matters of war it seems reasonable to conclude that executive-legislative relations will be characterized by conflict as each branch struggles to preserve its power over this most important aspect of foreign policy.

section review

1. How does the public's lack of information on foreign affairs affect government policy?
2. How do wars affect the iron law of specificity?
3. When has Congress intervened in the foreign policy arena?

3. FOREIGN POLICY DECISION MAKING

Graham Allison, a political scientist who had alternated between teaching at Harvard University and serving in Washington, D.C., has suggested in a major work on the Cuban missile crisis (*Essence of Decision*) that there are at least three models that offer explanations about how the executive branch reaches foreign policy decisions.

Rational Actor Model. The first is what he calls the *rational actor model.* This model assumes that nations are rational game players, actors who make decisions. One hears, for example, that Russia does one thing and that France does another. Allison suggests that explanations about foreign policy events usually start with the event to be explained. The analyst then reasons backward by saying, "If I were Russia, why would I have put missiles in Cuba?"

Almost all explanations of foreign policy, whether made by democrats or totalitarians, liberals or conservatives, are based on the rational actor model. But, as Allison suggests, the model rests on a false analogy, for a nation is not a single entity but a vast collection of human beings. The rational actor framework is merely a *model*—that is, a shorthand way of thinking about reality. There are other models, based on assumptions that offer different conclusions about how nations act.

Organizational Politics Model. Allison proposes a second model, that of organizations. Governments are not single entities but collections of organizations with different goals and different ways of making decisions. These ways are called *standard operating* *procedures* (SOP's)—regular ways of doing things. Organizations do not make decisions in a "rational" way but through a search procedure of examining alternatives one at a time until a satisfactory one is reached. The procedure may not be the best method, but it is the way that organizations work.

Organizations defend their "turf" against other organizations. Each sees the world from its own vantage point, not from the imagined position of a rational decision maker who acts for the whole nation. Usually people in organizations do not know what the executive wants them to do. They simply follow standard operating procedures.

Governmental Politics Model. A third model developed by Allison grows out of the work of another Harvard political scientist, Richard Neustadt. This model explains politics as a contest among individuals who hold different offices and act from different personal and policy perspectives. Each looks at policy from his or her own point of view. Thus policy is subjective rather than objective.

Every decision is perceived in the context of continuous bargaining because so many different bureaucratic games are being played, and each decision is considered to lay the groundwork for the next decision. Government decisions are therefore reached by a series of internal bargains negotiated by the political actors involved. A policy that satisfies the interests of each of these bargainers may very well not be the best policy for the whole nation.

section review

1. Define the concept of the rational actor model.
2. How do organizations make decisions?
3. List the three kinds of models suggested by Graham Allison.

4. THE GOALS OF AMERICAN FOREIGN POLICY

The central concern of foreign policy is survival. Although the same statement could be made about domestic policy, government is very rarely subjected to an ultimate domestic test such as the Civil War posed for the United States. In foreign affairs survival is always in question. Nuclear bombs can be dropped if wrong decisions are made.

In the past, before the advent of nuclear weapons, foreign policy did not possess so destructive a potential. But its conduct was always crucial to the survival of the nation. The United States won its independence in a war in which foreign aid—French, Spanish, and Dutch—was absolutely essential. The majority of the troops and all of the ships at the crucial battle of Yorktown were French.

The Attributes of Foreign Policy. The foreign policy of every nation is shaped by its attributes. Among the most important are physical, socioeconomic, and governmental characteristics. The *physical attributes* of a nation include such features as its population, natural resources, geographical location, and the strength of its neighboring powers. The *socioeconomic attributes* include its technology, communications, strength of its armed forces, and so on. The *governmental attributes* include the strength of its legitimacy, civil-military relations, political structure, and decision-making processes. Some attributes are permanent; others can change quite rapidly.

American Attributes. American attributes include the great size and richness of its natural resources, its distance from other powerful nations, its high standard of living, its advanced level of education, and its decentralized and democratic decision-making

Henry Kissinger was secretary of state under Presidents Nixon and Ford. What ideas are represented in this cartoon?

A CHAMP IN HIS FIELD!

structures. America's relations with its neighbors are outstandingly friendly.

Attributes that have changed are the size and concentration of its population (from small and dispersed to large and concentrated in geographical regions), the size and capacity of its armed forces (from small and weak to large and technologically superior), and the speed of its communication process (from three months for ships to cross the Atlantic to seconds for messages to be transmitted and minutes for missiles to be launched).

Early American Foreign Policy. When the Republic was founded, the United States was small and weak but separated geographically from other nations. The founders hoped to establish relations with other nations that would promote foreign commerce. But Americans wanted to expand to the country's "natural limit," the Pacific Ocean, and so were eager to eliminate the presence of European powers on the continent.

In a world that was divided between "revolutionary" France and "status quo" Great Britain, America's founders were afraid that foreign conflicts would lead to civil conflicts among partisans in the United States. Like the leaders of the Third World today, they urged neutrality. George Washington, in his farewell address of 1796, warned against "permanent alliances." Thomas Jefferson restated that warning in 1801 when he opposed "entangling alliances."

Isolationism. A policy of neutrality is often called **isolationism**. In many ways the word is misleading when applied to American foreign policy, for America was never isolationist in the sense that such nations as Japan or Tibet were—nations that closed their borders to the world. The United States engaged in world trade, fought a war to protect that trade (the War of 1812), conquered and purchased

most of a continent through negotiations with other nations, accepted immigrants from across the world, and proclaimed its interest in the cause of freedom everywhere. The United States did, however, participate in international conferences and ratified a number of treaties.

> **Isolationism** is a policy of abstaining from alliances and other international political and economic commitments.

Monroe Doctrine. In his annual message to Congress of 1823, President James Monroe proclaimed what came to be known as the Monroe Doctrine. It set forth the attitude of the United States government toward interference in the Western Hemisphere. The Monroe Doctrine included two important provisions: 1) The United States would protect any independent nation in the Americas against European interference. 2) The United States would not tolerate any future attempts by European countries to establish colonies in the Americas.

The original reason for this message was fear that European powers would intervene in the revolutions that were then sweeping Latin America. At the time the doctrine was announced, it had no legal force. Latin Americans soon found that it meant little, and no U.S. President mentioned it for more than 20 years. But as the United States grew stronger, the doctrine became a central part of American foreign policy. It served as a justification of America's special role as the most powerful country in the hemisphere.

Imperialism and World Power. As the United States grew to be a great power, its ambitions became expansive. Before the turn of the century, it became an **imperial** power.

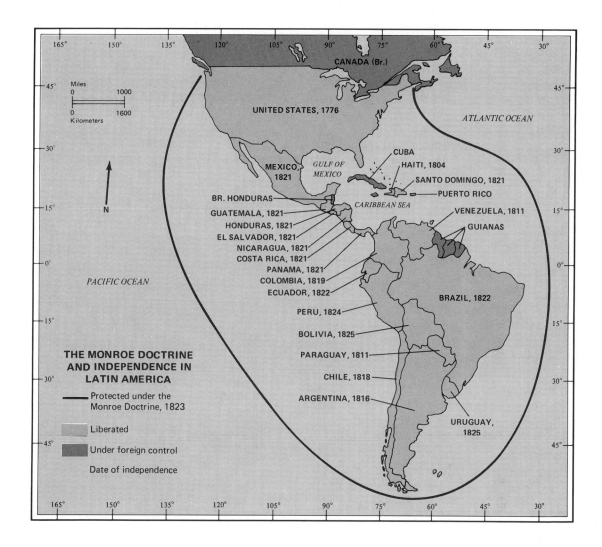

THE MONROE DOCTRINE AND INDEPENDENCE IN LATIN AMERICA

—— Protected under the Monroe Doctrine, 1823

Liberated

Under foreign control

Date of independence

Map labels:

CANADA (Br.)

UNITED STATES, 1776

ATLANTIC OCEAN

GULF OF MEXICO

MEXICO, 1821

CUBA

HAITI, 1804

SANTO DOMINGO, 1821

PUERTO RICO

BR. HONDURAS

GUATEMALA, 1821

HONDURAS, 1821

EL SALVADOR, 1821

NICARAGUA, 1821

COSTA RICA, 1821

PANAMA, 1821

COLOMBIA, 1819

ECUADOR, 1822

CARIBBEAN SEA

VENEZUELA, 1811

GUIANAS

PERU, 1824

BOLIVIA, 1825

PARAGUAY, 1811

CHILE, 1818

ARGENTINA, 1816

BRAZIL, 1822

URUGUAY, 1825

PACIFIC OCEAN

Miles
0   1000
0   1600
Kilometers

N

It fought the Spanish-American War in 1898 and annexed the Philippines, Guam, and Puerto Rico. It also assumed a protective role over newly independent Cuba and annexed Hawaii as a territory of the United States.

Imperialism relates to the practice of extending the power and wealth of a nation through acquisition of territory or through indirect economic or political control of other areas.

Open Door Policy. In 1899 and 1900 Secretary of State John Hay sent declarations to the European powers insisting that an "open door" be maintained for all nations that wanted to trade with China. This was done in order to protect American commercial interests in that country. Hay affirmed United States interest in the preservation of Chinese unity and sovereignty over its own territory. Like the Monroe Doctrine, the Open Door Policy became more important in later years. It helped influence future relations between the United States and China.

Protector of the Western Hemisphere. In 1903 America intervened in a revolt in Colombia, recognized the insurgents as the new government of Panama, and eventually built the Panama Canal. Within a few years the United States assumed the role of protector of the Western Hemisphere by intervening militarily in nations that did not maintain order and pay their debts.

In 1917 America secured protection for the Panama Canal by purchasing the Danish Virgin Islands. By that time the United States had bases and troops in a number of Latin American countries and had acquired territory that extended beyond the continental United States.

World War I. A major conflict that began in Europe in 1914 involved the United States in war three years later. The triggering factor was the German submarine campaign against British vessels carrying American passengers. In 1917 America entered the war, proclaiming it "the war to end all wars."

The Versailles Treaty incorporated a number of ideas proposed by President Woodrow Wilson, most notably the League of Nations. But in the disillusionment brought on by the failure of the war to end the rivalries of the world powers, the Senate rejected the treaty.

The Twenties. American foreign policy in the 1920's has often been called isolationist. But that description is considered an overreaction to the United States' unwillingness to join the League of Nations. America continued to be deeply involved in Europe, for it entered into cooperative agreements with the League, and its officials drafted various plans that carried their names—for example, the Young Plan, the Dawes Plan, and the Kellogg-Briand Pact.

The United States also entered into cooperative agreements with the rest of the world, most notably the Nine-Power Pact and the Four-Power Treaty negotiated during the Washington Conference of 1921–1922. In addition, during the 1920's the United States began to withdraw from the various Latin American nations that it had occupied from time to time during the preceding 20-year period.

The Great Depression. The structures of the 1920's—the League of Nations, economic agreements covering the repayment of war debts and reparations, and treaties that limited naval armaments—collapsed in the years that followed the Great Depression of 1929. Hitler came to power in Germany, and the military rose to power in Japan. In America there developed a reaction against involvement overseas, and a series of laws called the Neutrality Acts was passed.

President Franklin Roosevelt proposed a Good Neighbor Policy of cooperation with Latin America that formed the basis for the Organization of American States (OAS), founded in 1948.

World War II. In the late 1930's, as the dictators in Germany, Italy, and Japan moved toward war, America began to reverse its neutralist course. In 1941, two years after war broke out in Europe, the U.S. government disregarded the Neutrality Acts and passed legislation such as the Lend-Lease Act and the draft. When the Japanese attacked Pearl Harbor on December 7, 1941, the United States entered the war.

The four years of World War II ended any thought of American nonparticipation in international forums. The United States was the key power in the war and the key power in the peace. International structures that have provided the framework for relations throughout the world for more than three decades are American structures.

American troops and supplies arrived by ship to invade Normandy, France, during World War II. The United States was the key power in the war and the key power in peace.

QUOTES from famous people

"Any man and any nation that seeks peace—and hates war—and is willing to fight against hunger and disease and ignorance and misery will find the United States of America by their side, willing to walk with them—walk with them every step of the way."

Lyndon B. Johnson

The Cold War. For almost two decades after the end of World War II, the central feature of American foreign policy was the Cold War between the western nations and those of the Communist bloc. Hopes for a peaceful world after the defeat of the Axis in 1945 soon proved ill-founded. By 1948 these groups of powers aligned themselves against each other.

Since 1949, when the Soviets acquired the atomic bomb, the two powers that dominate the world have had the capability to inflict destruction on each other and on the rest of the world. This fact seems to have prevented the United States and the Soviet Union from engaging in actual warfare, but they have contended in indirect conflict (cold, as distinct from hot, war).

During those years the concerns of American diplomacy were containment, collective security, deterrence, and world order through law. Each of these concerns was conservative—that is, each of these concerns was geared toward maintaining the world order that developed in the years immediately following World War II.

Containment. As a way of preventing communism from spreading to other countries, the United States developed the policy of containment in 1947. The idea involved *containing,* or confining, Soviet expansion to the states that it already occupied or controlled in Eastern Europe.

As an expansion of the policy of containment, President Truman announced that the United States would help any government that asked for assistance to deter Communist aggression or subversion. Under what became known as the Truman Doctrine, the United States government gave millions of dollars of military and economic aid to foreign nations and fought two wars in Asia—the Korean War and the Vietnamese War. Much to the dismay

of America and its leaders, neither war seemed to accomplish its aim.

Collective security. The nations of the West united in alliances against the Communist bloc for *collective security.* According to this doctrine, an attack against one member of the alliance is considered an attack against the alliance as a whole. Such an attack will provoke collective retaliation—the unleashing of the might of all.

Deterrence. Deterrence developed in response to the failure of the democracies to deter, or prevent, Hitler's aggression. It is based on the belief that the development of sufficient military strength will convince an expansionist power that its aggression will provoke retaliation.

With the development of the "balance of terror" that resulted from the buildup of nuclear weapons, the doctrine of *mutual*

Secretary of State John Foster Dulles (center) was critical of the policy of containment. Here he is shown on his way to a conference in London in 1956.

deterrence was advanced. According to this doctrine, the *equivalent strength* of the Soviet Union and the United States—that is, their capabilities of destroying in a nuclear holocaust—will prevent both world powers from launching nuclear attacks against each other.

World order through law. The search for world order through international law has produced a variety of international organizations since the end of World War II. The North Atlantic Treaty Organization (NATO) and the Southeast Asia Treaty Organization (SEATO) are examples of these organizations.

section review

1. What are the most important attributes that shape foreign policy?
2. Why did the United States develop the policy of containment?
3. On what is the doctrine of deterrence based?

5. THE UNITED STATES ON THE INTERNATIONAL SCENE

The domestic institutions of American foreign policy will be examined elsewhere in this book. Here some of the international institutions that serve as arenas for the conduct of American foreign policy will be surveyed. These organizations include the United Nations and its specialized agencies, the military alliance systems, and the institutions of international finance.

The United Nations. During World War II the United States invited its allies to draft a treaty that would create a more effective successor to the League of Nations. Twenty-six nations signed the Declaration of the United Nations on January 1, 1942, and in 1943 Congress passed resolutions urging the formation of a new international organization. The founding conference of the UN was held in San Francisco from April 25 to June

Pictured below is the first conference session of the UN, on April 25, 1945.

26, 1945. Although its first session opened in London on January 10, 1946, the headquarters of the organization was eventually established in New York City.

The structure of the UN reflects American ideas. Among the six principal organs of the UN are two key bodies: the General Assembly and the Security Council. Both these bodies perform specific functions.

The General Assembly. The General Assembly is organized on the principle of one nation, one vote. It originally had 51 members. Now it has almost tripled in size. The General Assembly meets in regular session once a year. It usually acts by majority vote, but on an important issue a two-thirds vote is required. However, a majority of the Assembly may decide whether or not a question is important. In this case a resolution may be passed by a simple majority. Consequently, seemingly important resolutions have been passed by simple majority votes.

The General Assembly does not have the power to make decisions that bind member states or the Security Council of the UN. It does have the power to adopt the budget and to allocate shares among member states. It alone can propose, but not adopt, amendments to the UN Charter, and it shares with the Security Council the power to admit,

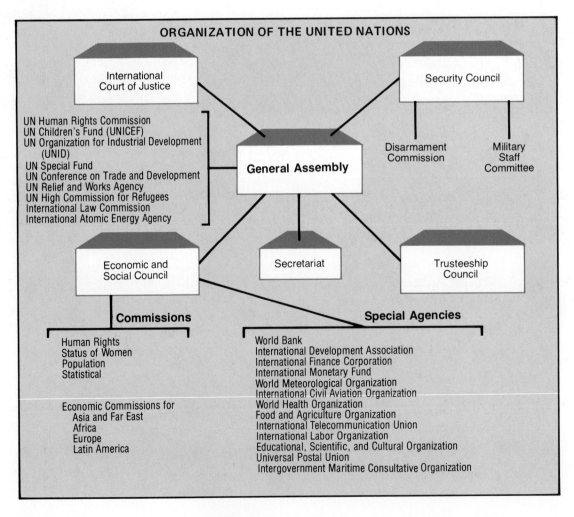

ORGANIZATION OF THE UNITED NATIONS

International Court of Justice

Security Council

UN Human Rights Commission
UN Children's Fund (UNICEF)
UN Organization for Industrial Development (UNID)
UN Special Fund
UN Conference on Trade and Development
UN Relief and Works Agency
UN High Commission for Refugees
International Law Commission
International Atomic Energy Agency

General Assembly

Disarmament Commission

Military Staff Committee

Economic and Social Council

Secretariat

Trusteeship Council

Commissions

Special Agencies

Human Rights
Status of Women
Population
Statistical

Economic Commissions for
Asia and Far East
Africa
Europe
Latin America

World Bank
International Development Association
International Finance Corporation
International Monetary Fund
World Meteorological Organization
International Civil Aviation Organization
World Health Organization
Food and Agriculture Organization
International Telecommunication Union
International Labor Organization
Educational, Scientific, and Cultural Organization
Universal Postal Union
Intergovernment Maritime Consultative Organization

MEMBERSHIP OF THE UNITED NATIONS

Charter Members (in alphabetical order)

Argentina	Cuba	Guatemala	New Zealand	Turkey
Australia	Czechoslovakia	Haiti	Nicaragua	Ukranian S.S.R.
Belgium	Denmark	Honduras	Norway	Union of Soviet
Bolivia	Dominican Republic	India	Panama	Socialist Republics
Brazil	Ecuador	Iran	Paraguay	United States
Byelorussian S.S.R.	Egypt	Iraq	Peru	Uruguay
Canada	El Salvador	Lebanon	Philippines	Venezuela
Chile	Ethiopia	Liberia	Poland	Yugoslavia
*China	France	Luxembourg	Saudi Arabia	
Colombia	Great Britain	Mexico	South Africa	
Costa Rica	Greece	Netherlands	Syria	

Admitted Since 1945

Afghanistan	Cyprus	Jamaica	Nepal	Sudan
Albania	Dahomey	Japan	Niger	Surinam
Algeria	Djibouti	Jordan	Nigeria	Swaziland
Angola	Dominica	Kampuchea	Oman	Sweden
Austria	East Germany	(Cambodia)	Pakistan	Tanzania
Bahamas	Equatorial Guinea	Kenya	Papua-New Guinea	Thailand
Bahrain	Fiji	Kuwait	Portugal	Togo
Bangladesh	Finland	Laos	Qatar	Trinidad and Tobago
Barbados	Gabon	Lesotho	Romania	Tunisia
Benin	Gambia	Libya	Rwanda	Uganda
Bhutan	Ghana	Malagasy	Saint Lucia	United Arab Emirates
Botswana	Grenada	Republic	São Tomé	Upper Volta
Bulgaria	Guinea	Malawi	and Príncipe	Vietnam
Burma	Guinea-Bissau	Malaysia	Senegal	Western Samoa
Burundi	Guyana	Maldives	Seychelles	West Germany
Cameroon	Hungary	Mali	Sierra Leone	Yemen
Cape Verde I.	Iceland	Malta	Singapore	Zaire
Central African	Indonesia	Mauritania	Solomon Islands	Zambia
Republic	Ireland	Mauritius	Somalia	
Chad	Israel	Mongolia	South Yemen	
Comoros	Italy	Morocco	Spain	
Congo	Ivory Coast	Mozambique	Sri Lanka	

*Nationalist China was expelled from the UN in 1971. The General Assembly voted to seat The People's Republic of China.

suspend, and expel members. It elects the ten nonpermanent members of the Security Council, appoints members to the other principal UN organs, and supervises the work of those organs in their day-to-day administrative functions.

The Security Council. The Security Council consists of 15 members: five permanent members (the United States, the Soviet Union, Great Britain, France, and China) and ten nonpermanent members selected to serve two-year terms. Unlike the Assembly, this body is in permanent session.

Like the Assembly, the Security Council makes a distinction between **substantive** and **procedural questions.** Nine votes are required for passage in either case, but on substantive questions any one of the five permanent powers can cast a veto, or negative vote, that will prevent Security Council action.

Substantive questions deal with what is to be decided.

Procedural questions deal with how decisions will be made.

The 15 member nations of the UN Security Council are shown meeting at the UN in New York City.

The Veto. The veto has an ironic history. The United States expected to control the General Assembly when the UN was founded, for almost all of its 51 members were either Western European or Latin American nations allied with the United States. (The Soviet Union had used the veto 105 times when the United States cast its first veto on March 17, 1970.)

Since 1957 the admission of newly independent countries to the UN has shifted control of the General Assembly away from the United States and its allies to Afro-Asian countries known as the Third World. The United States has become increasingly unhappy with the General Assembly and concentrates its major efforts in the Security Council, where its use of the veto can prevent decisions that it considers hostile to its interests.

According to the UN Charter, the Security Council is entrusted with the primary responsibility for maintaining peace and security by conciliation if possible or by boycott or military action if necessary. The use of the veto has generally prevented military action in situations that involve direct conflict between the United States and the Soviet Union.

ANDREW YOUNG, Former UN AMBASSADOR

Andrew Young was one of the more controversial members of Jimmy Carter's administration. As UN ambassador, Young attracted support for U.S. foreign policy from Third-World nations that had not always been friendly in the past. At the same time, however, he aroused more opposition from other political groups than did any previous ambassador.

Young was born into a prosperous New Orleans family in 1932. After graduating from Howard University, he attended Hartford Theological Seminary to study for the ministry. His first job was with the National Council of Churches, as associate deputy director of youth work. But the civil rights movement was getting under way, and Young quickly became involved.

Young went to work with Martin Luther King's Southern Christian Leadership Conference, first as a staff member (1961–1964), then as executive director (1964–1967) and later as executive vice-president (1967–1972). He was among those in the marches, the picket lines, and sometimes even the jails.

In 1972 Young made the transition to conventional politics. He ran for Congress from the Fifth District of Georgia, which had a large Black vote but a White Majority. His victory made him the first Black to be elected from the Deep South in the twentieth century.

He became familiar to the national liberal community by serving as national co-chairperson of the disarmament group SANE. He gained national attention in 1976, when he supported his fellow Georgian, Jimmy Carter, for the presidency. His support helped Carter gain the trust not only of the Black community but also of White liberals. After Carter's victory Young was offered the post of UN ambassador.

Andrew Young's background helped him become the first UN ambassador in years to be influential in the General Assembly. He tended to apply his experiences in the civil rights and anti-Vietnam War movements to the UN. Young was perhaps the first American ambassador to the UN who was automatically sympathetic to the Third-World nations. While this established relations with those nations, some who were less sympathetic to the Third World felt his policies were naive or misguided.

In the end, Young's attempts to be close to Third-World interests went too far. In 1979 he had a secret meeting with a representative of the Palestinian Liberation Organization. When others found out about the meeting, he claimed it was a chance encounter. The truth, however, came out. Under fire from those Americans particularly sensitive to Israeli interests, Young was forced to resign. He left behind him some excellent political work and an extremely controversial reputation.

The only exception was the intervention of UN forces in the Korean War, which was approved on June 25, 1950, because the Soviet Union happened to be boycotting the session that day.

Other principal organs. The Economic and Social Council is responsible for promoting world progress in the matters of economics, health, culture, education, and human rights. ECOSOC consists of 27 members elected for three-year terms. It maintains several commissions and, under the supervision of the General Assembly, coordinates the work of 13 specialized agencies.

Although all of the specialized agencies perform important and valuable work, the most important are those involved in international finance. The International Bank for Reconstruction and Development (better known as the World Bank) and the International Monetary Fund helped to rebuild the economy of the postwar world, finance economic development in the Third World, and promote the stability of international payments necessary to the continuance of world trade.

The International Court of Justice and the Trusteeship Council have become ineffective as principal organs of the UN. For example, in 1980 the Court ruled unanimously for Iran to release the American hostages, but Iran ignored the ruling. The Court's ineffectiveness and the fact that few trust territories are left, may cause these organs to disband.

The Secretariat, the administrative branch of the UN, has played an important role as a principal organ through its chief administrative officer, the secretary general. So far four people—Trygve Lie of Norway, Dag Hammarskjöld of Sweden, U Thant of Burma, and Kurt Waldheim of Austria—have held this office. Each has been able to use the office as a vehicle for the settlement of international disputes.

The UN's Role. Although the UN has failed to satisfy the hopes of its founders for a lasting peace and solutions to the problems of a troubled world, it serves many useful purposes. The UN's specialized agencies have spearheaded worldwide assaults on such diseases as smallpox and malaria and have promoted literacy, nutrition, and economic development throughout the world.

Because some disputes have not involved direct confrontations between the United States and the Soviet Union, the UN has sent peace-keeping forces to some of the world's "hot spots," such as the Middle East, Cyprus, and the newly independent Congo (now Zaire).

Military Treaties. As was previously noted, during World War II the United States took a leading role in establishing the United Nations. When the Cold War prevented the resolution of conflict between the Soviet Union and the United States in the UN, the United States entered into a number of regional security treaties, which are authorized under the UN Charter.

Rio Pact. The first of these treaties, signed in 1947, was the Inter-American Treaty of Reciprocal Assistance, better known as the Rio Pact. It gave the Monroe Doctrine the force of international law, for it bound each of the signatories (the United States and the nations of Latin America) to mutual defense against outside intrusion into the hemisphere. It provided the legal basis for United States action against the placement of Soviet missiles in Cuba in 1962.

North Atlantic Treaty Organization. The most important of the regional security treaties is the North Atlantic Treaty Organization (NATO), established in 1949. NATO was formed to deter Soviet aggression in Western Europe through the use of military forces contributed by the member states and through the protection of the United States nuclear deterrent. It is comprised of the United States, Canada, and 13 Western European nations.

NATO has been weakened by the withdrawal of French troops from the alliance command and by the withdrawal of NATO troops from French soil in 1966 (although France remains a member). Greece and Turkey, two important members, have been engaged in conflict with one another over

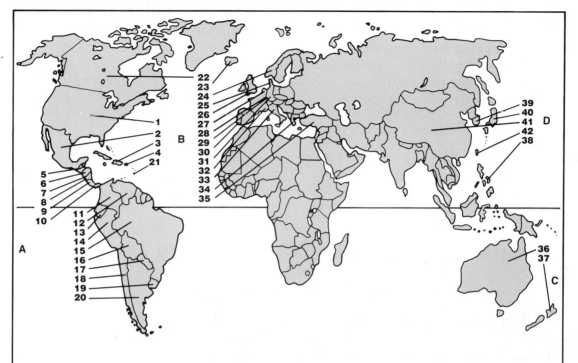

THE UNITED STATES AND ITS ALLIES

A. Rio Pact

1 United States	6 Honduras	11 Colombia	16 Bolivia
2 Mexico	7 El Salvador	12 Venezuela	17 Paraguay
3 Haiti	8 Nicaragua	13 Ecuador	18 Chile
4 Dominican Republic	9 Costa Rica	14 Peru	19 Uruguay
5 Guatemala	10 Panama	15 Brazil	20 Argentina

21 Trinidad and Tobago

B. North Atlantic Treaty (NATO)

1 United States	25 Denmark	29 Luxembourg	32 France
22 Canada	26 United Kingdom	30 Portugal	33 Italy
23 Iceland	27 Netherlands	31 Federal Republic	34 Greece
24 Norway	28 Belgium	of Germany	35 Turkey

C. Anzus Pact

1 United States	36 Australia	37 New Zealand

D. Individually Allied with U.S.

38 Philippines	40 Japan	42 Republic of China
39 Republic of Korea	41 People's Republic of China	(Taiwan)

Cyprus and the Aegean Islands, a conflict that has further weakened the alliance.

Other agreements. The United States has entered into a number of security agreements with small groups of nations and with individual nations—for example, the Anzus Pact (1951), with Australia and New Zealand, as well as pacts with the Philippines (1951), Japan (1951), South Korea (1953), and Formosa (1954). It has also concluded a number of agreements with countries such as Israel and Saudi Arabia, although none of these agreements is embodied in a treaty.

Foreign Aid. Since 1945 the United States has distributed nearly a quarter of a trillion dollars in foreign aid. Much of this aid has been in the form of military assistance. Substantial portions of nonmilitary aid have been loans made through such agencies as the **Export-Import Bank** and through **multilateral agencies** such as the World Bank. Most of the money has flowed back into the

On September 7, 1977, the Panama Canal Treaty was signed at a gathering of the OAS. Can you identify any of these diplomats?

ESTADOS UNIDOS   SECRETARIO GENERAL   PANAMA

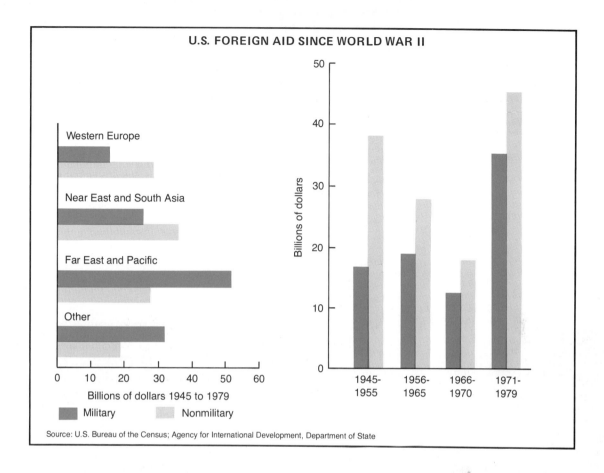

U.S. FOREIGN AID SINCE WORLD WAR II

Western Europe

Near East and South Asia

Far East and Pacific

Other

Billions of dollars 1945 to 1979

■ Military   ▨ Nonmilitary

Billions of dollars

1945-1955   1956-1965   1966-1970   1971-1979

Source: U.S. Bureau of the Census; Agency for International Development, Department of State

United States for the purchase of U.S. goods and services.

The granting of foreign aid suggests the dramatic change that has occurred in American foreign policy in the past 200 years. From a weak, small nation that was suspicious of entangling alliances, the United States has evolved into a superpower whose nuclear deterrent and military and economic aid sustain many nations throughout the world.

The **Export-Import Bank** makes loans to American exporters and importers and to foreign governments who are trying to build up their resources.

Multilateral agencies are those that involve more than two nations.

section review

1. Name the two key bodies of the United Nations.
2. List the powers of the General Assembly.
3. Who is the present UN secretary general?
4. Why was NATO established?
5. Who are the permanent members of the UN Security Council?
6. Between what kinds of questions does the Security Council make a distinction?
7. How many votes are required to veto an action recommended by the Security Council? Is this a negative or positive factor?

CHAPTER SUMMARY

13

Outputs are those things a government does. There are two types of governmental outputs: tangible outputs, which are actions for its people, and symbolic outputs, which are a sign of the government's intentions. The government increasingly touches all aspects of a citizen's life through health and safety regulation, welfare benefits, and supervision of industry and the economy.

In domestic affairs the nation has final sovereignty. In foreign affairs it depends on cooperation from other sovereign nations. Power is the key element of sovereignty.

Foreign policy usually has the support of the whole nation because it 1) addresses the question of survival of the nation, 2) is an area concerning which the public has less information and, therefore, fewer opinions, and 3) evokes images of America versus the world.

Foreign policy is the one arena completely dominated by the executive branch. In America this means that Presidents make foreign policy. Defense budgets, tariff rates, and decisions to enter or leave wars are largely the preserve of the executive branch, with the consent of Congress.

The foreign policy issue public is rather small, with a greater concentration of people of wealth, education, and social standing than other issue publics.

Three models of decision making in the foreign policy arena are the rational-actor model, the organizational politics model, and the governmental politics model.

The central concern of any nation's foreign policy is survival. The early American policy of unilateralism was modified with the Monroe Doctrine, the expansion of American economic concerns, two world wars, and the Cold War. Since World War II, deterrence, containment, and collective security have been the goals of American foreign policy.

World War II awakened America to the importance of international cooperation. In succeeding years the United States has fostered the development of several international structures for mutual protection and the prevention of another world war. Military treaties, usually regional or multilateral, and foreign aid are also expressions of America's recognition of its role in international affairs.

REVIEW QUESTIONS

1. How do the United Nations and regional security treaties illustrate the post-World War II foreign policy of the United States?
2. The United States refused to join the League of Nations after World War I. Yet it spearheaded the drive to establish the United Nations after World War II. How do you account for this change?

3. What do you consider to be the major successes of the United Nations? failures? Explain your answer.
4. Modern governments control or regulate many activities of their citizens. Do you favor this trend? Why or why not? (Be sure to cite specific advantages and disadvantages of increased governmental involvement.)
5. Foreign policy is identified by the authors as the preserve of the executive branch. What are the advantages of this situation? the dangers? Do you favor this delegation of power? Explain your answer.
6. List and explain what you believe should be the goals of American foreign policy for the twenty-first century.

ACTIVITIES FOR REVIEW

activity 1   Prepare a brief report to present to the class on a current problem in American foreign policy.

activity 2   Prepare a recommendation to the President on means and methods of preventing World War III.

political science DICTIONARY

Export-Import Bank—an agency of the UN that makes loans to American exporters and importers and to foreign governments.   p. 269

imperialism—the practice of extending the power and wealth of a nation through acquisition of territory or through indirect economic or political control of other areas.   p. 257

isolationism—a policy of abstaining from alliances and other international political and economic commitments.   p. 256

multilateral agencies—agencies that work with and assist more than two nations.   p. 269

procedural questions—questions in the Security Council concerning how decisions will be made. Nine votes are required for their resolution.   p. 263

socioeconomic attributes—a nation's technology, communications, and military strength.   p. 254

substantive questions—questions in the Security Council concerning what issues are to be decided. Nine votes are required for their resolution.   p. 263

14

Domestic Policy Arenas

This chapter investigates the domestic policies of the American government. First you will examine three kinds of government output: regulations, subsidies, and services. You will also learn about three models that try to explain how the government makes decisions on domestic policy: the pluralist model, the power elite model, and the model developed by Theodore Lowi. Then you will review different policy arenas, or sectors, of the American government in domestic matters. You will learn how issues, arenas, and interest groups interrelate and change over time. Finally, you will see that defining a problem may be the first step toward changing government policy.

CHAPTER PREVIEW

1. DOMESTIC GOVERNMENT OUTPUTS
2. DOMESTIC POLICY ARENAS
3. THE IMPORTANCE OF POLICY ARENAS

1. DOMESTIC GOVERNMENT OUTPUTS

Domestic policy is far more varied than foreign policy is, both in the nature of the problems that are confronted and in the way that they are resolved. Foreign policy tends to involve relatively few people and is centered in the executive bureaucracy. Domestic policy arenas are many and varied, ranging from small arenas to those that are very large.

Government output in domestic policy

tends to be of three kinds: regulations, subsidies, and services.

Regulations. Regulations are rules specifying not only what things cannot be done but also how things should be done. They include rules covering such government functions as criminal justice, traffic control, and inspection of the quality of food and drugs.

Subsidies. Subsidies are direct sums paid to citizens by the government. They include farm support payments, social security checks, and aid to dependent children.

Services. Services are special provisions or facilities with which the government meets the needs of the public. They include the postal service, education, and police protection.

People's needs and wants vary widely. But we can make at least one general observation: Almost everyone wants the government to provide subsidies and services,

This meat inspector puts the USDA stamp on carcasses at a meat-packing plant. What type of government output would meat inspection be?

but almost no one wants to be regulated or taxed by the government.

Lowi's Model. Political scientist Theodore Lowi has proposed a model relating the type of decision made by government to the way that the decision is made. His model grew out of his attempt to reconcile the conflicting views advanced by pluralist and power elite theorists.

Pluralist theorists maintain that various groups participate in government decisions; that is, that decisions are made by compromise through negotiations with contending groups. *Power elite theorists*, on the other hand, argue that government decisions are made by a small number of self-selected individuals, that is, that decisions are dictated through the use of power.

Lowi suggests that there are three different types of government policy. He considers all three types historically as well as functionally distinct.

Distribution. From 1789 to 1890 the domestic policy of the United States government can be classified as *distributive.* Distributive policies involve the payment of government subsidies to specific individuals and small groups. All government actions transfer resources from some people to other people. But in distributive policies those who receive subsidies benefit from special government grants of preference that are not paid for by other citizens. Thus there are winners but no apparent losers. Patronage policies, land grants, tariffs (import taxes on certain products from foreign countries), and *pork barrel* purchasing (the buying by the government of goods and services from certain suppliers) fall into the category of distributive policies.

This policy of government is *co-optation.* It is a policy in which the government is willing to add to the number of people who receive grants by creating new categories of preferences, rather than by making the grants on the basis of conflict and compromise (the pluralist model) or dictation (the power elite model).

Regulation. In the late 1880s the American government began to concern itself with *regulation.* Regulatory policies involve decisions by the government about matters that affect producers and consumers. Thus, for example, in setting railroad rates the government had to decide between the conflicting claims of those who owned the railroads and those who used them.

For understanding regulatory policies the pluralist model makes more sense than does the power elite model. Decisions of a regulatory nature are reached through a process of conflict and compromise. Often this process results in the establishment of a regulatory agency of some kind. After a while a pattern of behavior develops among the regulatory agency or agencies, the conflicting outside interests (that is, the producers and the consumers), and the congressional committees assigned to oversee the regulatory activities of the agency.

Redistribution. In the 1930's the American government's policies took a different direction—of *redistribution,* or taking from one class in order to give to another, through such measures as the social security tax, the progressive income tax, and welfare payments. For understanding policies of redistribution the power elite model seems to be closer to reality than does the pluralist model. Policy tends to be made in the executive branch of government. The role of Congress is limited to ratifying agreements that were made by leading members of the executive bureaucracy. For example, the Social Security system was formulated in the executive branch by a committee on economic security.

In redistributive issues there is a direct clash between money-providing and service-demanding groups. According to Lowi, since such confrontations may upset the political balance, they are usually handled at the top level of the executive branch.

The Growing Role of Government. One way to understand what we often call the 'growing role of government' is to plot the movement of government policies by observing that issues tend to shift from distribution to regulation to redistribution. American land policy, when land seemed abundant, was largely a matter of distribution. But as the conservation movement began early in the twentieth century, policies began to shift toward regulation. In recent years, as land has become a scarce and valuable resource, a policy of regulation has begun to shift to a policy of redistribution. Marsh land and land classified as coastal zones have recently been transferred to the public domain through the *power of eminent domain.*

Power of eminent domain is the government's right to set a price for land and then to purchase it without the owner's consent. This is an example of redistribution.

section review

1. List the three kinds of governmental output in domestic policy.
2. Define the term 'services' and give two examples.
3. Who is affected by regulatory policies?
4. Why has American land policy shifted to redistribution?
5. Define the term 'subsidies.'
6. When did the American government become concerned with the regulation of business matters?

2. DOMESTIC POLICY ARENAS

Domestic policy arenas involve those sectors of American society that concern the President's domestic cabinet—that is, all executive departments except State and Defense.

Some issues, such as civil liberties, have existed for as long as the Republic. Others have ceased to exist or else have changed their forms. For example, in the early nineteenth century, canals were a major means of transportation in this country; therefore, a great deal of transportation policy was concerned with canals. Transportation policy is still important today, although its focus has shifted from canals to more modern forms of transportation—trains, automobiles and trucks, and airplanes. Race relations have always been a matter of policy. But at various times the struggle over race has centered on slavery, segregation, desegregation, integration, and now on affirmative action.

New issues or policy arenas arise in response to scientific and technological change. The environmental movement did not emerge as a political force until the 1960's, when pollution began to affect the ecology of the entire planet.

In the early nineteenth century, canals were a major means of transportation. This woodcut shows canal boats in their winter quarters.

The Development of a Policy Arena. A policy arena develops when a generation begins to view different aspects of the complex world as connected and important. For example, the nutritional value of food and the therapeutic value of drugs was always a concern. But it was not until the 1960's and 1970's that concern began to grow, and people began to express the need for a policy to remove harmful substances from food and drugs. A policy arena is often developed when a concerned group attempts to define a problem in a new way. Typically, such a group wants the government to respond by regulation, control, or subsidy.

From the perception that government action is required grows a demand for legislation to deal with the problem. The problem then becomes an issue. Legislation creates executive agencies, and congressional committees are formed to oversee their activities. And so a policy arena has developed.

The definition of a problem is the key not only to how an issue will be decided but also by whom. Survey after survey has shown that the manner in which a problem is posed influences its outcome.

The Environmental Movement. The rise of the environmental movement reflects a perception that is beginning to affect our policy arenas. This perception is a growing awareness of how issues overlap. In the past there was a strong tendency to treat issues one at a time. For example, when the post-World War II veterans' housing programs were developed and when the National Defense Highway Act of 1956 was passed, no one thought that these government subsidy programs could contribute to the decay of the cities. But by subsidizing suburban homeowners and automobile users, they encouraged the growth of the suburbs at the expense of the cities.

More recently a greater awareness of overlap has developed. In some ways this broader view can be more of a problem than a

Which aspect of the environment is this bike rider concerned with?

help, for policy-making has become more difficult. When some groups pushed for a policy and very few opposed them, it was relatively easy to get a new policy enacted. Now everyone is aware that new policies may influence him or her, so veto groups arise to oppose them.

section review

1. What factors contribute to formation of new policy arenas?
2. When does a policy arena develop? Give an example.
3. Why is the definition of a problem important?

3. THE IMPORTANCE OF POLICY ARENAS

One of the most important recent examples of policy overlap can be seen in the complex fields of transportation, energy, the environment, urban policy, and foreign trade. Indeed, it affects almost all aspects of American life.

At its center is the private automobile. The car is the primary means of transportation in America. It is, however, the most inefficient user of energy, as well as one of the most serious polluters of the environment.

Our urban environment is greatly affected by the car. Its use by city residents as well as by commuters not only has led to the decline of mass transportation, such as subways, trams, trains, and buses, but also has increased serious pollution and traffic problems in inner cities.

The recent American deficit in the *balance of payments*—the amount by which our payments for goods and services purchased abroad exceed our revenue from foreign purchases made here—stems from the importation of oil from the Middle East. Ironically, another part of the deficit results from the importation of foreign automobiles. Without

This electric car is one possible solution to the air pollution caused by gas-burning cars.

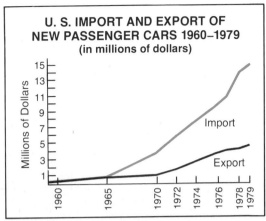

U. S. IMPORT AND EXPORT OF NEW PASSENGER CARS 1960–1979
(in millions of dollars)

Millions of Dollars

Import

Export

Source: Bureau of Economic Analysis

of automobiles and the services and industries that are related to it and are lost if cars are not produced in the United States.

From the perspectives of the government policy maker, of those representing private interests, and of the average citizen, the importance of the automobile in American society creates a complex set of problems. The automobile is too important to our economy to eliminate, but it is at the center of many of the problems that we face.

the importation of oil and cars, we would have a foreign payments surplus. The deficit in our balance of payments leads to a loss of confidence in the American dollar and creates confusion in the international monetary system. The interrelationships go much further. Employment policies are also affected. Jobs are generated by the production

QUOTES from famous people

"The principle of our government is that of equal laws and freedom of industry."

Andrew Johnson

It involves many powerful interests: giant corporations, huge unions like the United Auto Workers, and very powerful consumer

Why are these garment workers protesting importation of clothing?

movements and people such as Ralph Nader. At the same time it involves questions of foreign policy.

Changing Policy Arenas. If one side of an issue "wins," that does not bring the contest to a close. Usually a new struggle will begin in the same arena, or the interest group will try to move to a new arena. For example, as we have already suggested, the policy arena of race relations has been an issue since the colonies began. For some 250 years two problems were important in the arena of race relations: one concerning Black-White rela-

tions and centering on the policy of slavery; the other concerning Native American-White relations and centering on the issue of Native American policy.

Although there were free Blacks from the beginning of our history, the central concern of the political system was working out the relation between the slave system and the rest of the economy. And the Native American question until 1871 was, according to law, a matter of foreign policy.

In the years immediately after the Civil War, the policy focus in this arena changed. The Black slaves were freed in 1865, and the

RALPH NADER—A FIGHTER FOR JUSTICE

Ralph Nader always wanted to be a lawyer. "A lawyer to me meant someone fighting for justice," he explains.

Ralph Nader was born in 1934 to Lebanese parents. He grew up in a middle-class factory town in Connecticut. One of his earliest memories is of visiting the New York World's Fair when he was five years old. "I saw fantastic models of automobiles. Cars with spectacular shapes—magical forms—cars of the future. I was told how clean and efficient and fast and safe they were supposed to be."

Twenty-six years later, after graduating from Harvard Law School, Nader began investigating a car being sold by General Motors. The car was a new model with its engine mounted in the rear. The design still contained several "bugs" when GM decided to put it on the market. Ralph Nader exposed the dangers that could result from these bugs in his book "Unsafe at Any Speed" (1964). The book probably would not have received national attention if GM had not overreacted. The president of that company hired detectives to uncover anything about Nader that could be used to discredit him. When Nader discovered that he was being investigated, he complained to Congress and filed suit against GM. A Senate committee forced the president of GM to apologize, and in his suit Nader won $500,000 in damages.

With this money and the proceeds of his now famous book, Nader established his own law firm. What made it an unusual law firm was that its "client" was the American consumer. Reflecting the crusading spirit of the late 1960's, many eager law students volunteered to aid Nader in his efforts to expose fraudulent claims and inferior products. The staff soon became known as Nader's Raiders.

Presidents of the United States have not encouraged Nader. Johnson was cool to him, Nixon openly disliked him, and Ford merely avoided him. Nader supported Carter in 1976 when he was a Presidential candidate, and some of his aides were appointed to posts in the Carter administration; but within a few years Nader turned against Carter and attacked some of his former aides for "selling out."

Native Americans protest violations of their land rights in a demonstration at Alcatraz in 1969.

problem of Native American relations was made a domestic issue by Congress in 1871. The crucial questions for both groups became that of civil rights, since the legal rights won by both groups were trampled upon through the practice of segregation.

In the third quarter of this century there has been another change. In the new atmosphere that followed World War II, there developed a movement against segregation. The vast structure of segregation was dismantled in slightly more than twenty years. And the effects of the Black civil rights movement that led to this change spread into related policy arenas.

The effect of this movement was to create a new issue within the policy arena of race relations—the issue of affirmative action. Desegregation is no longer an issue; now the debate concerns whether the government should make a positive effort to help the victims of past or present discrimination in the fields of employment and professional education.

The Black campaign for an equal place in American life has gone on for centuries, but the nature of the issues within the policy arena has changed. Among other Black leaders, Frederick Douglass campaigned for an end to slavery; Martin Luther King, Jr., for an end to segregation; Vernon Jordan for an end to economic inequality. Although each sought the same end—an equal place for Black people—the changing nature of the issue changed the allies that each individual won and the tactics that each individual used.

Groups. If interest groups go from one policy arena to another, policy arenas will be occupied by different interest groups. Civil liberties is an example of a policy arena that has been occupied by several interest groups. Covering the broad range of liberties enumerated in the Bill of Rights, the arena of civil liberties has been occupied by different groups such as lawyers, teachers, civil servants, writers, publishers, and members of various religious groups. Journalists have been in this arena since colonial times.

Creating a New Policy Arena. When interest groups want to create a new policy arena (and that is easier than changing an existing one), they try to re-define a problem.

The importance of definition can be understood by reviewing the problem of starvation. A nineteenth-century English economist defined starvation as being the result of too many people. He argued that the problem could be solved only by reducing the number of people. American society defines starvation as a problem of too little or badly distributed food. Society tries to solve the problem by producing more food and distributing it in a more efficient way.

There are many times when scientific and technological change leads to political change. This is not because science and technology are powerful in themselves but because they make it possible to re-define problems. Definitions are extremely crucial to the creation of policy arenas.

section review

1. How has the automobile affected the urban environment?
2. Define the term "deficit."
3. Explain how the policy arena of Native American relations has changed.
4. Give an example of a policy arena that has been occupied by several interest groups.
5. How does American society define starvation?
6. How did Ralph Nader attempt to help the American consumer?
7. What prompted the creation of affirmative action?
8. What various issues have Black leaders campaigned for?

CHAPTER SUMMARY

14

Domestic policy is more varied than foreign policy, both in the nature of the problems confronted and in the way they are resolved. Government output in domestic policy tends to be of three kinds: regulation, subsidies, and services.

Political scientist Theodore Lowi's model of domestic policy making relates the type of decision made to the way that decision is made. He identified three historically and functionally distinct types of government policy: distribution, regulation, and redistribution.

Sectoral issues are parts of policy arenas of concern to the President's Cabinet officers, who head the Justice, Transportation, Energy, Agriculture, Commerce, and Labor departments.

Policy arenas develop when a generation begins to view different aspects of a complex world as connected and important. Policy arenas develop from the definition of a problem by a group seeking governmental regulation, control, or subsidy. The demand for resolution transforms a problem into an issue. The manner in which the problem is posed influences its outcome.

If one side of an issue wins, a new struggle may begin in the same arena, or the losing interest group will move to a new arena. When interest groups want to create a new policy arena, they try to redefine a problem.

Scientific and technological changes lead to political change. These two factors make it possible to redefine problems, and definitions are crucial to the creation of policy arenas.

REVIEW QUESTIONS

1. How is government land policy an example of the growing role of government?

2. Apply Lowi's model to the automobile in American society.

3. Why do the authors contend that defining a problem may be the first step toward changing government policy? Do you agree? Explain.

ACTIVITIES FOR REVIEW

activity 1 Select a current issue about which some groups are asking government to establish policy. How does each group define the problem? Is this issue part of a previously defined problem in another policy arena? What type of solution does the problem definition seem to call for?

activity 2 Collect newspaper items concerning domestic issues for a period of two weeks. What are the major policy arenas? Are the same interest groups involved in more than one arena? Prepare a report to the class.

activity 3 Investigate the role of various domestic policy interest groups such as Nader's Raiders, Common Cause, People's Lobby, NAACP, Urban Coalition, or the American Civil Liberties Union. What domestic arena is the present focus of their attention? What was it five years ago? ten? How do you account for this change?

---

political science DICTIONARY

balance of payments—the amounts by which the nation's payments for goods and services purchased abroad exceed its revenue from foreign purchases of American goods and services. p. 277

co-optation—a policy in which the government agrees to add to the number of people who receive grants by creating new categories of preference. p. 273

power of eminent domain—the government's right to set a price for land and then to purchase it without the owner's consent. p. 274

redistribution—the practice of taking from one group to give to another, through social security and income taxes or welfare payments. p. 274

UNIT SUMMARY

The major policy arenas in American government involve foreign and domestic policy. In domestic affairs the nation has final authority. In foreign affairs the nation depends on recognition of its authority by other nations.

Foreign policy generally has broader national support than domestic policy because of its specialized nature and its focus on national survival.

Domestic policy arenas have narrower support because of shifting issues, groups, and understanding of the interrelationships of various arenas.

Bibliography

Allison, Graham. *Essence of Decision.* Boston: Little, Brown, and Company, 1971.

—— and Peter Szanton. *Remaking Foreign Policy: The Organizational Connection.* New York: Basic Books, Inc., 1976.

Destler, I. M. *Presidents, Bureaucrats, and Foreign Policy*, 2nd edition. New Jersey: Princeton University Press, 1974.

Harrington, Michael. *The Other America.* New York: Penguin, 1962.

Huntington, Samuel P. *The Common Defense: Strategic Programs in National Politics.* New York: Columbia University Press, 1961.

Kolko, Gabriel. *Wealth and Power in America.* New York: Praeger, 1962.

Kolodziej, E. A. *The Uncommon Defense and the Congress 1945–1963.* Ohio University Press, 1966.

Newhouse, John. *Cold Dawn: The Story of SALT.* New York: Holt, Rinehart and Winston, 1973.

Rosenau, J. N. *Domestic Sources of Foreign Policy.* New York: Free Press, 1967.

Wilcox, Francis O., and Richard A. Frank. *The Constitution and the Conduct of Foreign Policy.* New York: Praeger, 1976.

Review questions

1. Why do you think foreign policy decisions are likely to be supported by a majority of the people? Do you think this should be the case? Explain.

2. How do the decision-making models used in the foreign and domestic policy arenas differ? Why? Could the same model be used in both? Explain.

3. Foreign policy tends to be dominated by the executive branch; domestic policy by the legislative. What are some reasons for this distinction? Do you agree with it? Explain.

4. Apply Lowi's decision-making model to a foreign policy problem. Does it work? Why or why not?

Skill questions

Use the charts in this unit to answer the following questions.

1. What percent of the GNP was spent on World War II? the Vietnamese War?

2. List the names of the countries that belong to NATO. Which of these countries were admitted to the UN since 1945?

3. Since World War II, what nation has received the most American military aid? Give the amount in billions of dollars.

4. Between which years did the United States show a significant increase in imported cars? Compare the amounts spent on imports and exports during that period.

Activities

activity 1   President Franklin D. Roosevelt was a major architect of foreign and domestic policies of the United States government in the middle years of the twentieth century. Analyze his approach to problems in both arenas. Was his approach to the two areas similar or different? Explain. Report your findings to the class.

activity 2   Select a current problem in the foreign policy arena. Try to identify its roots and the decision-making models that seem to have been applied at various points. Which was most effective? Why?

activity 3   Select a current domestic issue and trace its history. What groups have defined and redefined the nature of the problem? How has the issue changed over time? Why do you think the nature of the issue and proposed solutions have changed?

UNIT
5

NANCY LANDON KASSEBAUM

Nancy Landon Kassebaum became the first woman to be elected to the Senate from the state of Kansas, and the first woman elected to the Senate without first having been preceded in Congress by her husband. She won her office in 1978 with the campaign slogan "A Fresh Face, a Trusted Kansas Name."

Born in 1932, Kassebaum grew up in Kansas and was surrounded by politics from birth. Her father was Al Landon, governor of Kansas from 1932 to 1936, and he was the 1936 Republican presidential nominee. Following his defeat to FDR he never again ran for public office, but he still remained active in politics. Kassebaum took an interest in politics at an early age but never dreamed that she would become involved in a political career.

Kassebaum received her B.A. in Political Science from the University of Kansas and a Masters degree in Diplomatic History from the University of Michigan. After completing her education she returned to Kansas with her husband and raised a family. Her political career was limited to local politics. She was on the Kansas Committee for the Humanities, the Kansas Governmental Ethics Committee, and a member of the Maize School Board in Kansas.

In 1975 she got to see the mechanics of national government by working on the staff of Senator James B. Pearson of Kansas. When the Senator announced that he would not seek another term in 1978, Kassebaum decided to run. She won the election 407,907 to 315,582. Following her victory she rushed off to Washington to get a head start.

Senator Kassebaum is a member of the Banking, Housing, and Urban Affairs Committee and its International Finance and Rural Housing Subcommittees; the Commerce, Science, and Transportation Committee and its Surface Transportation Subcommittee, and is the ranking Republican member of the Committee's Aviation Subcommittee. She is also a member of the Budget Committee and the Special Committee on Aging, and served as Temporary Chairperson for the 1980 Republican Convention in Detroit.

PEOPLE IN
POLITICS

THE LEGISLATIVE BRANCH

OVERVIEW

■ A bicameral legislature with coequal houses was set up in the Constitution to give equal legislative power to both large and small states. Representation in the House of Representatives is determined by state population; each state is equally represented in the Senate.

■ The two houses of Congress have different organizational structures and powers. The enumerated powers of Congress are listed in Article 1, Section 8, of the Federal Constitution. Political parties assist in achieving cooperation between the executive and legislative branches on legislative programs.

■ The nonlegislative functions of Congress blur the separation of powers of the three branches of government. Congress possesses, in its investigative and appointive powers, some elements of judicial and executive functions.

■ Running for Congress is a difficult and expensive task, especially for new and unknown candidates. Incumbents have many advantages that help them get reelected: name recognition, service to constituents, access to constituents through the media, and the franking privilege. Members of Congress are usually White males from upper- and middle-class backgrounds, with professional training in the law.

■ A wide variety of factors influences final legislation: the committee system and seniority, presidential support or opposition, special-interest groups, the values of individual legislators, constituent mail, party goals, and national priorities.

15

Legal Authority and Organization of Congress

The first article of the Constitution deals with Congress. It lists all the powers that the Constitution gives to the legislative branch. The Founding Fathers thought that Congress would create national policies, whereas the President would carry them out. The Constitution gives the President the power to veto laws, but it also provides that Congress can override a presidential veto with a two-thirds vote in each house.

The Consitution establishes two houses of Congress. The House of Representatives represents the general population—that is, the number of representatives from each state depends on the state's population. The Senate represents the individual states, and each state has two senators. The powers of Congress include the power to pass, amend, or reject legislation, to appropriate money, and to serve as a check on the executive branch.

CHAPTER PREVIEW

1. CONSTITUTIONAL PROVISIONS
2. POWERS AND FUNCTIONS
3. THE ORGANIZATION OF CONGRESS

1. CONSTITUTIONAL PROVISIONS

Congress is a unique institution, for it is an independent and coequal branch of government. In parliamentary democracies, such as Canada, Great Britain, and the Federal Republic of Germany, the executive and legislative powers are combined.

The Capitol Building in Washington, D.C., serves as the home of Congress.

Another unique feature of the American Congress is that it consists of two houses rather than one. Neither the U.S. Senate nor the House of Representatives can act without the other.

Congressional Representation. The Constitution entitles each state to elect two senators. When it was adopted in 1789, there were 26 senators from the original 13 states. Today there are 100 senators representing 50 states. The House of Representatives originally consisted of 65 members, but its size has been increased several times since 1789.

Since 1910 the size of the House of Representatives has remained at 435 members, who are elected in 435 districts throughout the nation. Each district has approximately 500,000 constituents. Congress reapportions its 435 seats among the states after each census. (Censuses are taken every ten years.) In each reapportionment some states may lose seats, and others may gain seats, depending on how the population shifts across the country.

Constituencies. Senators have larger constituencies than do representatives in all but the six least-populous states—Alaska, Delaware, Nevada, North Dakota, Vermont, and Wyoming—which have one representative each.

Terms of Office. Representatives are elected for two-year terms, whereas senators are elected for six-year terms. Every two years the terms of one third of the senators expire. Many people believe that the longer term for senators enables them to take a broader national view of issues. They claim that representatives, who must seek reelection every two years, are more likely to focus on the problems and the needs of the people in their districts.

Qualifications for Office. The Constitution

CONGRESS AND ITS MEMBERS

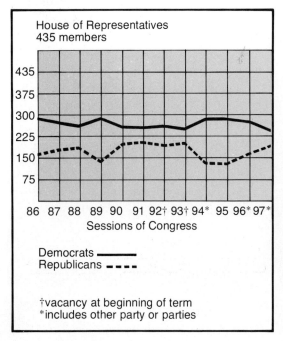

House of Representatives
435 members

Democrats ———
Republicans ▬ ▬ ▬

†vacancy at beginning of term
*includes other party or parties

Sessions of Congress
86 87 88 89 90 91 92† 93† 94* 95 96* 97*

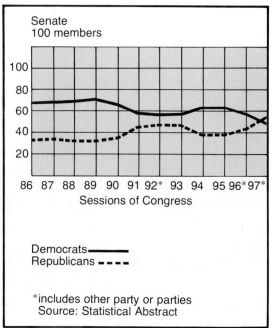

Senate
100 members

Sessions of Congress
86 87 88 89 90 91 92* 93 94 95 96* 97*

Democrats ———
Republicans ▬ ▬ ▬

*includes other party or parties
Source: Statistical Abstract

requires that representatives be at least 25 years of age and that senators be at least 30. A candidate for the House of Representatives must be a citizen of the United States for seven years, and a candidate for the Senate must be a citizen for nine years. Furthermore, both representatives and senators must reside in the states from which they are elected.

Congressional Elections. The Constitution leaves elections to the individual states unless Congress chooses to intervene in national elections. Before the passage of the Seventeenth Amendment in 1913, senators were elected by state legislatures rather than by the direct vote of the people. Different states held elections for representatives at different times of the year. In 1872 Congress provided that representatives be chosen by secret ballot throughout the nation on the first Tuesday after the first Monday in November. Every

United States citizen over the age of 18 is entitled to vote.

Each session of Congress lasts for two years and is numbered consecutively from the beginning of the American Republic. The First Congress was elected in 1788, and the Fifty-first Congress was elected in 1888. The Congress elected in 1980 was the Ninety-seventh Congress.

Reapportionment. Until 1964 state legislatures drew the lines of congressional districts within their states as they saw fit. As a result some districts contained ten times as many people as did other districts. In 1964, in *Baker v. Carr*, the U.S. Supreme Court decided that all districts must be roughly equal in population. This decision incorporated the "one man, one vote" principle.

It is still possible for a determined state legislature to underrepresent a significant part of the population. For example, a predominantly Black community can be included in one district, which would give the voters in that community a chance to elect a Black representative. But a legislature can also place the community into two different non-Black districts, which may prevent the election of a Black representative.

The party that controls a state government at the time of reapportionment may attempt to draw district lines that concentrate supporters of the opposition party in certain districts and thus give the majority party the opportunity of continuing to control the same number of seats. For example, a Democratic legislature could create one district that was 80 percent Republican and three districts that were each 60 percent Democratic, rather than creating four districts that were all equally balanced between Republicans and Democrats.

Racial and partisan criteria are only two of a number of factors that state legislators consider in reapportioning districts. Other factors include natural boundaries (rivers, lakes, mountains, plateaus), city and county boundaries, and the predominant urban, suburban, or rural character of an area. Weighing these factors often makes reapportionment a difficult process, subject to extensive bargaining and compromise.

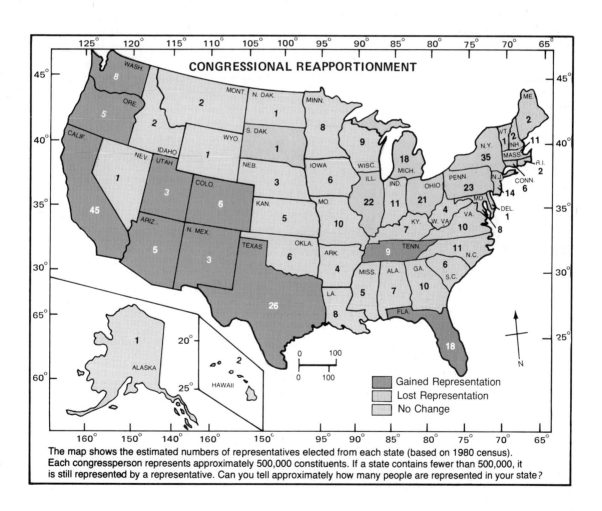

CONGRESSIONAL REAPPORTIONMENT

Gained Representation
Lost Representation
No Change

The map shows the estimated numbers of representatives elected from each state (based on 1980 census). Each congressperson represents approximately 500,000 constituents. If a state contains fewer than 500,000, it is still represented by a representative. Can you tell approximately how many people are represented in your state?

section review

1. Explain two unique features of the Congress of the United States.
2. Explain the basis of the apportionment of the House of Representatives.
3. List the qualifications for members of the Senate and the House of Representatives.
4. Why is the term of a member of the House shorter than that of a member of the Senate?

2. POWERS AND FUNCTIONS

Over the years Congress has gradually lost much of its power. The President initiates most legislation. Power in Congress is widely distributed among party leaders, committee chairpersons, and subcommittee chairpersons, making it hard for Congress to act quickly or to speak with a strong voice on most national issues.

From time to time Congress reasserts itself and regains some of its lost power. This reassertion of power usually occurs after a rapid expansion of executive power. The 1970's illustrated this pattern. Individual members of Congress reflected public opposition to the war in Vietnam and helped to end it. Faced with a President who had abused the power of his office, the Senate responded with an investigation, and eventually the House Judiciary Committee voted articles of impeachment. Many people believe that the Watergate crisis showed the strength of Congress. But it remains to be seen whether Congress will exercise its power and recover its historic role as a coequal branch of government.

Enumerated Powers. Article 1 of the Constitution lists the powers of the national government that are delegated to Congress. The most important of these powers are the power to appropriate money and the power to regulate interstate commerce.

All money bills must originate in the House of Representatives. Money bills include those designed to raise revenue from

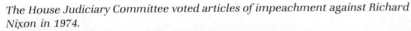

The House Judiciary Committee voted articles of impeachment against Richard Nixon in 1974.

taxes and tariffs as well as those dealing with appropriations to run the national government.

The commerce power has been broadly interpreted both by Congress and by the Supreme Court to include a variety of subjects. It enables Congress to fix minimum wages and maximum hours, to prohibit the shipment of certain goods, to regulate banks, to prohibit discrimination, and to provide for

THE POWERS DELEGATED TO CONGRESS

I. Peace Powers

Enumerated Powers

1. To lay taxes.
2. To borrow money.
3. To regulate foreign and interstate commerce.
4. To establish naturalization and bankruptcy laws.
5. To coin money and regulate its value; to regulate weights and measures.
6. To punish counterfeiters of federal money and securities.
7. To establish post offices and postal roads.
8. To grant patents and copyrights.
9. To create courts inferior to the Supreme Court.
10. To define and punish piracies and felonies on the high seas; to define and punish offenses against the law of nations.
11. To exercise exclusive jurisdiction over the District of Columbia; to exercise exclusive jurisdiction over forts, dockyards, national parks, federal buildings, and the like.

II. War Powers

12. To declare war; to grant letters of marque and reprisal; to make rules concerning captures on land and water.
13. To raise and support armies.
14. To provide and maintain a navy.
15. To make laws governing land and naval forces.
16. To provide for calling forth the militia to execute federal laws, suppress insurrections, and repel invasions.
17. To provide for organizing, arming, and disciplining the militia, and for its governing when in the service of the Union.

Implied Powers

18. To make all laws necessary and proper for carrying into execution the foregoing powers.
    For example:
    To establish national banks.
    To acquire land by eminent domain.
    To put restraints on freedom for the sake of public welfare and the social good.
    To punish federal law breakers.
    To promote agriculture.

the construction of dams. In the name of interstate commerce, Congress supervises the regulation of radio and television broadcasting, the telephone and the telegraph, railroads, ships, planes, cars, trucks, buses, bridges, ferries, rivers, harbors, canals, pipelines, food, drugs, and cosmetics.

Implied Powers. Those powers not specifically denied to Congress or to the national government can be exercised by Congress within the scope of the doctrine of implied powers. This doctrine applies to Article 1, Section 8, Clause 18, of the Constitution, which empowers Congress "to make all laws which shall be necessary and proper for carrying into execution the foregoing powers, and all other powers vested by this Constitution in the Government of the United States." This clause is called the elastic clause or the "necessary and proper" clause.

Electoral Power. Congress has several nonlegislative functions including the electoral power to choose the President and the Vice-President if the electoral process becomes deadlocked. Deadlocks for President have happened twice: the House of Representatives elected Thomas Jefferson in 1800 and John Quincy Adams in 1824. The Senate elected Richard M. Johnson Vice-President in 1836. This was the only deadlock for Vice-President.

Since 1967 Congress has had an additional electoral function granted to it by the Twenty-fifth Amendment. Whenever there is a vacancy in the office of the Vice-President, the President nominates a Vice-President, who takes office after a majority of both houses of Congress **confirms** the nomination. Gerald Ford was appointed to the vice-presidency in 1973 under this provision. When Ford succeeded to the presidency the following year, he, in turn, appointed Nelson Rockefeller Vice-President.

Congress confirmed Gerald Ford's choice of Nelson Rockefeller for the vice-presidency in 1974.

Impeachment Power. Another nonlegislative function of Congress is its impeachment powers. This special judicial function permits Congress to remove a federal official from office for wrongdoing. The Constitution forbids Congress from imposing any punishment other than removal from office and a prohibition against holding future office. The established judicial system imposes any additional punishment.

When Congress seeks to remove a federal official from office, the House of Representatives may by majority vote *impeach* that official—that is, the House holds a hearing and if a majority decides that sufficient evidence exists to warrant a trial, the official is presented with a list of charges against him or her that may be answered during the course of a trial. The Senate then tries the official on the specific charges brought by the House. A two-thirds vote is required for conviction and removal from office.

There have been only 12 impeachment trials since 1789. The most famous was the trial of President Andrew Johnson in 1868. The Senate failed to convict Johnson by one vote.

Executive Power. The Senate has the exclusive right to ratify treaties and to advise on and consent to presidential appointments. The Senate can reject by a two-thirds vote a treaty that the President has negotiated with a foreign government. It can also reject a President's nominee to high office. Normally the Senate gives the President freedom in making appointments to the executive departments. With nominees to the Supreme Court, however, the Senate is more inclined to make its own judgments. Two of President Nixon's and one of President Johnson's nominees to the Supreme Court were rejected by the Senate.

By the unwritten rule of *senatorial courtesy*, the Senate has often rejected a President's nominee from a particular state—such as a federal judge—if the senators from that state disapprove of the nomination. Thus the President consults with senators before making federal appointments in their states. This custom increases the senators' power to control federal appointments within their states.

Amendment Power. Congress plays an important role in amending the Constitution. A proposed amendment requires a two-thirds vote by both houses of Congress. The amendment becomes law when it is ratified by three quarters of the states.

Congressional Self-discipline. The Constitution empowers each house of Congress to expel its own members by a two-thirds vote. From time to time Congress has disciplined its members by voting resolutions of **censure.** In 1980 several members of Congress were censured for conspiring to take bribes from FBI agents posing as Arab oil sheiks.

Investigative Power. The power of Congress to conduct investigations is important in obtaining information to be used in drafting legislation, developing public opinion, supervising regulatory agencies, and exposing corruption.

section review

1. Explain the difference between enumerated powers and implied powers.
2. List two peace powers and two war powers.
3. Give four examples of powers derived from a broad interpretation of the commerce power.
4. What is the elastic clause?

5. Explain the nonlegislative congressional power of impeachment.
6. Which house of Congress must confirm a presidential choice for a vice-presidential vacancy?
7. How does the Senate check the President on the making of foreign policy?

3. THE ORGANIZATION OF CONGRESS

At the beginning of each session of Congress, the members of each party in each house meet in *caucus*, or private conference, to choose their leaders. Members of the majority party in the Senate choose the president pro tempore, a majority leader, and a majority whip, or assistant leader. The minority party chooses a minority leader and a minority whip. In the House of Representatives, the majority party chooses the speaker of the House, a majority floor leader, and a majority whip. The minority party in the House elects a minority floor leader, who acts as a public spokesperson for his or her party, and a minority whip.

In neither house are leaders chosen according to seniority. LBJ became his party's leader after four years in the Senate.

Party Leaders. Leaders are expected to respect the customs and the traditions of Congress. They are usually moderates who are more interested in reaching agreement than in defending ideological positions. Senator Everett Dirksen, when he was Senate Republican leader, observed, "I am a man of principle, and one of my basic principles is flexibility." Other leadership qualities include the art of persuasion, the ability to command respect, patience, tolerance, and sympathy for other members' views and political needs.

Majority leaders in both houses assume responsibility for enacting the majority party's program, particularly when the majority party also controls the presidency. Minority leaders have similar functions, but their usual aim is to resist programs submitted by the majority party.

Whips inform members when important bills are scheduled to be voted on. They exert pressure on their party members to vote with the party, and they try to secure maximum attendance for important votes.

Senate leaders. In the Senate the majority and minority leaders work closely in scheduling debates. The majority leader has the right to be the first to speak. He or she also has influence over assigning members of the majority party to committees.

House leaders. House Democratic party leaders tend to be promoted one step at a time. The majority whip may succeed to majority leader when that post is vacant, and the majority leader may succeed to the speakership. Among House Republicans leadership contests have tended to be open and quite competitive.

The Speaker of the House. The Speaker is the most important member of the House of Representatives. Although the House formally elects its presiding officer, the Speaker is actually chosen by the majority party. Thus the Speaker of the House is not only the presiding officer but also the leader of the majority party.

The Speaker directs business on the floor of the House, assigns bills to committees, appoints select and conference committees, and influences legislation being processed in the House. In the case of a Democratic majority in the House, the Speaker serves on the **Steering Committee** and appoints 9 of its 24 members, who assign other Democrats to committees.

The **Steering Committee** appoints Democratic members to standing committees of the House of Representatives.

The Speaker is elected by the House of Representatives. Although the Constitution does not require this, every Speaker has been a member of the majority party in the House. The position is one of prestige and power. It usually goes to a senior member of the House who has demonstrated legislative ability. The Speaker is both the presiding officer of the House and the head of the majority party. The Speaker conducts all meetings of the House, recognizes members who wish to speak on an issue, assigns bills to the appropriate committees, and applies the rules of the House in all procedures.

During Carter's administration Thomas P. "Tip" O'Neill was elected Speaker. O'Neill was born in 1912 in a poor section of Cambridge, Massachusetts, and attended Boston College. He is married to Rose Anne Tolan. One of their six children became lieutenant governor of Massachusetts. O'Neill entered public service at the age of 24 as a member of the Massachusetts state legislature. He remained there until 1952, when he took over the national House seat vacated by John F. Kennedy, who was running for the U.S. Senate.

O'Neill developed a reputation in the House for being a skillful compromiser and a representative of all the people rather than those of Massachusetts alone. O'Neill was one of the first representatives to come out publicly against the Vietnamese War. He has also been a strong supporter of civil rights. He was one of the first representatives to call for the impeachment of Richard Nixon.

In 1971 O'Neill was elected majority whip, the third-ranking position in the House. When the majority leader was killed in an airplane accident, O'Neill took over that position. In 1977 O'Neill was elected Speaker, replacing Carl Albert (D-Okla.), who retired. His election reflected the sentiment in the House that O'Neill was an astute politician.

One of the early tests of the new Speaker was the Ethics Bill. Congressional representatives had voted themselves a pay increase in 1976 to compensate members for income they would lose when a stricter code of ethics went into effect. But when the time came to vote on the Ethics Bill, support for it had waned. O'Neill had to call in some of the favors members owed him. He also reminded members that behavior of the congressional officials had to be above reproach. The Ethics Bill passed and has become law.

The Speaker can do more than simply make appeals to members or try to influence them. The Speaker influences the assignment of members to committees and influences the distribution of the majority party's national campaign funds to individual candidates for Congress.

The Speaker can therefore exert considerable influence over legislation. Carter and O'Neill became the first President and Speaker from the same party since 1968. Their alliance brought the introduction of some major legislation into Congress. President Reagan, however, must cooperate with Speaker O'Neill to get his programs through the Democratic-controlled House.

THOMAS P. "TIP" O'NEILL, JR., SPEAKER OF THE HOUSE

The Speaker is in a powerful position to aid the majority party's legislative program. Assisted by the majority leader, the Speaker handles the scheduling of legislation once a bill has been reported out of committee and sent to the Rules Committee. This scheduling function gives both the Speaker and the majority leader the opportunity to influence legislation. They know what bargains are possible and negotiate compromises whenever possible. They can and do use their influence to gain a member's vote, but they cannot give orders to other lawmakers.

Presiding Officer of the Senate. The president of the Senate is the Vice-President of the United States. Unlike the speaker of the House, the Vice-President does not have the right to participate in debates and votes only in the case of a tie.

In the absence of the Vice-President, the *president pro tempore*, or temporary president, presides over the Senate. Although formally elected by the Senate, he or she is actually selected by the caucus of the majority party.

The Two-Party System. The two-party system has become an important element in the organization of Congress. Party caucuses have increased their control over committee assignments and the selection of committee chairpersons. Members who actively support another party's candidate for President or who refuse to support their party's candidate for speaker of the House are likely to lose seniority or committee assignments as a penalty. During the 1960's several southern Democrats in the House were stripped of seniority after they supported Republican presidential candidates.

Presidents do not control their party in Congress, but they do propose its legislative program. If the program receives congressional support, both the President and the party are likely to get credit for the passage of popular legislation. Similarly, leaders of the minority party in Congress will claim credit for defeating unpopular legislation.

The Power of Committees. Committees have the power to delay bills, to amend them either slightly or drastically, and to recommend their rejection or enactment. Members of interest groups realize the power that committees have in areas of special interest to them. They try to persuade committee members to accept their points of view and often contribute to the reelection campaigns of important committee members.

Party Representation on Committees. The ratio of Democrats to Republicans on each committee is roughly equal to the ratio elected to each house. When Democrats outnumber Republicans by two to one, there will be twice as many Democrats as Republicans on each committee.

The Committee Structure. Over the years Congress has done an increasing amount of its work in committees. In 1789 the first Senate had no *standing*, or permanent, committees, the House had one standing committee, and there was one joint committee. In 1981 during the Ninety-seventh Congress, the Senate had 15 standing committees, the House had 22 standing committees, and there were 4 joint committees.

The House and the Senate each adopts rules of organization at the beginning of each new Congress. With some modifications each body usually retains the rules, procedures, and committee structure of the preceding term. In 1977 the Senate completely reorganized its committee structure. This reorganization was the first major change in the Senate in 30 years.

The Senate reorganization act reduced the number of committees from 31 to 21, restricted the number of committee and subcommittee assignments that a senator may accept to a maximum of 11, and granted the minority party's demand that it appoint a proportionate number of the committees' staff.

Most committees deal with particular areas of policy—for example, the Agriculture committees deal with farm problems, and the Foreign Relations and Foreign Affairs committees deal with foreign policy. In a typical day an average of 30 committee or subcommittee meetings are held in each house.

Senate Standing Committees. The Senate's 15 standing committees contain over 100 subcommittees. Among the most important Senate committees are Foreign Relations, Finance, and Appropriations. The Committee on Foreign Relations is important because of the Senate's power to ratify treaties.

Unlike the House, the Senate has no standing committee that sets rules governing the conduct of debate. Instead the Senate observes unlimited debate, which sometimes means that senators can talk a bill to death. The specific use of this device—known as the *filibuster*—will be discussed elsewhere in this unit.

House Standing Committees. The House's 22 standing committees are divided into more than 148 subcommittees. The most important of the House committees are the Ways and Means Committee, which has power over taxation, and the Appropriations Committee, which has power over all federal spending. All bills introduced in the House are referred to one of the standing committees.

After bills are reported out of the standing committees, they must be sent to the Rules Committee, one of the most powerful committees in the House. The Rules Committee sets rules under which bills must be debated, amended, and considered by the House.

The Committee of the Whole. The House of Representatives transacts much of its business when it sits as a *committee of the whole.* This device streamlines business by restricting all members' speeches to five minutes or less, eliminating roll call votes, and minimizing delaying tactics. The House has become so large and unwieldy that it is now unusual for a bill to be amended on the floor.

Select Committees. *Select committees* are temporary committees created for special purposes. In the House members are selected by the Speaker. In the Senate the president of the Senate makes appointments. Often select committees are formed to investigate specific situations. One of the most famous select committees came to be known as the Watergate Committee. There will be more about the Watergate Committee and how Congress uses its investigative power elsewhere in the unit.

Joint Committees. *Joint committees* are composed of members of both houses. They are sometimes select committees, but most of them are standing committees organized to promote cooperation between the House and the Senate on broad aspects of public policy—for example, the Joint Economic Committee and the Joint Committee on Taxation.

Joint committees can be traced to the first Congress in 1789. Those who favor the establishment of joint committees contend that they are efficient because they eliminate the wasteful duplication that the dual committee structure sustains. Their use today, however, is not nearly as widespread as their advocates recommend.

Conference Committees. After a bill has passed in both houses, *conference committees,* made up of members of both bodies, are formed to reconcile differences between the House and Senate versions of the bill.

Committee Chairpersons. By custom and tradition the longest-serving committee member of the majority party most often

THE UNITED STATES CONGRESS AND ITS COMMITTEES

U.S. SENATE

Standing Committees	Select or Special Committees	Joint Committees
Agriculture, Nutrition, and Forestry(7)*	Aging	Economic(5)
Appropriations(13)	Ethics	Taxation
Armed Services(6)	Indian Affairs	Library
Banking, Housing, and Urban Affairs(8)	Intelligence(4)	Printing
Budget	Nutrition and Human	
Commerce, Science, and Transportation(7)	Needs	
Energy and Natural Resources(5)	Small Business(6)	
Environment and Public Works(6)		
Finance(11)		
Foreign Relations(7)		
Governmental Affairs(7)		
Judiciary(7)		
Labor and Human Resources(7)		
Rules and Administration		
Veterans' Affairs(3)		

U.S. HOUSE OF REPRESENTATIVES

Standing Committees	Select or Special Committees	Joint Committees
Agriculture(10)	Aging(4)	(same as above listing under U.S. Senate)
Appropriations(13)	Congressional Operations	
Armed Services(8)	Ethics	
Banking, Finance, and Urban Affairs(9)	Intelligence(4)	
Budget(9)	Narcotics Abuse and Control	
District of Columbia(4)		
Education and Labor(9)		
Foreign Affairs(8)		
Government Operations(7)		
House Administration(8)		
Interior and Insular Affairs(7)		
Interstate and Foreign Commerce(6)		
Judiciary(7)		
Merchant Marine and Fisheries(5)		
Post Office and Civil Service(7)		
Public Works and Transportation(6)		
Rules(2)		
Science and Technology(7)		
Small Business(6)		
Standards of Official Conduct		
Veterans' Affairs(4)		
Ways and Means(6)		

*For each committee, the number of subcommittees or task forces is indicated in parentheses.

becomes chairperson of that committee. The same procedure is usually followed to select subcommittee chairpersons. The chairperson and the ranking minority member of a committee or subcommittee usually become the most influential members of the committee or subcommittee. Each member of a committee or subcommittee moves up in rank as those above him or her resign, retire, or are defeated for reelection.

"...And while I may be ignorant about the subject, Gentlemen, don't
forget that my seniority on this committee makes me an authority!"

*Many top congressional positions are occupied by
members having the most seniority.*

Although there was a great deal of committee switching during the nineteenth century, when members did not stay in Congress for long, members today generally remain on the same committees year after year. Switching usually takes place when vacancies occur on especially important committees, such as the Appropriations committees.

In the Senate the chairperson of each committee appoints the members of that committee's subcommittees. Once appointed, a senator may serve as long as he or she chooses. In the House all Democratic members of a committee ratify the selection of subcommittee chairpersons. Because of rules adopted by the House Democratic caucus during the 1970's, no member of the House can chair more than one committee or subcommittee. The 13 subcommittees of the House Appropriations Committee are so powerful that their chairpersons must be confirmed by the House Democratic caucus, just as the caucus confirms all committee chairpersons.

Between 1975 and 1980 the House Democratic caucus refused in four instances to install the most senior Democratic member of a committee as its chairperson. The person passed over in each instance had lost the confidence of other members of the committee. The principle of seniority operated, however, because even in each of those instances one of the next three senior members of the committee was selected chairperson.

Committee Members and Elections. In making assignments to the most important committees, selectors try to appoint members who not only are capable and hard working but also understand the art of compromise. Because congressional leaders want the members of their own party reelected, they try to assign them to committees that will benefit their constituents.

In the House of Representatives, hardly anyone who is appointed to the Rules, Ways and Means, or Appropriations committees ever leaves the committee. This observation applies to the Senate Appropriations and Finance committees as well. The incidence of tenure is hardly surprising, for members of those committees are very influential and can usually serve the direct interests of their constitutents.

Committee power can be translated into votes on election day. One powerful Senate committee chairperson sent out campaign literature to remind his constituents how much federal tax money was being spent in their state: "This does not happen by accident," he wrote; "it takes power and influence in Congress." In the next chapters of this unit, both the power and the influence of Congress will be examined.

section review

1. What powers make the Speaker the single most important person in the House?
2. What is a caucus?
3. What are the functions of the majority whip, minority whip, majority leader, minority leader, and speaker of the House?
4. Who presides over the Senate? What is that person's role in Senate affairs?

CHAPTER SUMMARY

15

In providing for separation of the powers of the legislative and executive branches of the government, the Founders tried to distinguish between enumerated and implied powers. Both the nation and most of the states have bicameral legislatures. Although the executive and legislative branches of the federal government both have the power to defeat legislation, there are compelling reasons for Congress and the President to work together to pass a legislative program. Political parties help to bring this kind of coordination into the legislative process. Power in Congress is generally concentrated in party leaders and committee chairpersons. Committees in Congress tend to disperse power through subcommittees, whereas political parties tend to centralize power because members vote with their party most of the time. Hoping to claim credit for specific legislation, political parties try to exert control over the votes of individual members.

REVIEW QUESTIONS

1. What role does Congress play in amending the Constitution?
2. Give an example of how the reapportionment of 1980 changed representation in the House.
3. What effect does a two-year term of office have on members of the House?
4. Where does the Constitution place responsibility for most electoral matters? What are Congress' electoral powers?
5. What are Congress' judicial powers?
6. Why are investigative powers necessary in enabling Congress to function as a legislative body?
7. What are the most important of the delegated (enumerated) powers of Congress?
8. Explain why the "necessary and proper" clause has also been called the elastic clause.
9. Explain the function of the Rules Committee.
10. What are some of the exclusive powers of the Senate? the House?
11. Explain how the seniority system works in Congress.
12. What powers do standing committees have in the legislative process?

ACTIVITIES FOR REVIEW

activity 1   Study the enumerated powers of Congress in Article 1 of the federal Constitution. Go through the newspaper for one week and list all congressional legislative programs proposed during that period. Indicate whether the basis of each program is an enumerated or implied power. Explain.

activity 2   Look at the results of your voting district's House or Senate elections over the past decade. Did reapportionment change your district? How? Did it change the number of representatives in Congress from your state? Explain the changes, if any.

activity 3   Using these same statistics, determine how many senators and representatives in your state were Republicans, Democrats, or members of a third party. Were many districts in your state solidly Republican or Democratic? How can you account for this trend?

activity 4   Find statistics showing how members of Congress voted on party-supported issues. Did your senator and representative vote with their party on these issues? How do you account for this?

activity 5   Do research on the development of the Speaker's role in the House of Representatives. Using specific examples, compare the power of one Speaker of the past with the present Speaker's power.

political science
DICTIONARY

caucus—a private conference of members of Congress who belong to the same political party.   p. 296

censure—strong disapproval.   p. 295

conference committees—committees to reconcile differences between the House and Senate versions of a bill. They are composed of members of both houses.   p. 299

confirm—to approve.   p. 295

impeachment—the act of bringing charges of wrongdoing against a federal official. The House of Representatives has the power to impeach the official, but the Senate has the power to try the charges.   p. 295

joint committees—sometimes select, but usually standing, committees organized to promote cooperation between the House and Senate. They are composed of members of both Houses.   p. 299

president pro tempore—the temporary president of the Senate, in the absence of the Vice-President.   p. 298

select committees—temporary committees created for special purposes.   p. 299

senatorial courtesy—the policy of presidential consultation with Senators before federal appointments are made within their states.   p. 295

speaker of the house—the House's presiding officer and majority party leader; the most important member of the House.   p. 296

steering committee—committee responsible for assigning congresspersons to other congressional committees.   p. 296

16 *Lawmaking and Influence of Party Membership*

In this chapter you will review the shaping of legislation; that is, you will learn who proposes and who sponsors legislation. Next you will examine the role of congressional committees in the lawmaking process and survey the steps that must be followed before a bill can become law. Then you will learn how Congress—especially through Appropriations subcommittees—influences public policy by appropriating funds to carry out laws.

Finally, you will examine the role that political parties play in influencing the behavior of lawmakers.

CHAPTER PREVIEW

1. THE SHAPING OF LEGISLATION
2. THE ENACTMENT PROCESS
3. THE INFLUENCE OF PARTY MEMBERSHIP

1. THE SHAPING OF LEGISLATION

The President has come to be called the chief legislator. This title reflects the fact that the President plays a central role in setting legislative goals for Congress. Most bills are drafted in executive departments and agencies. The executive department must persuade a representative and a senator—preferably influential ones—to introduce administration bills.

Other bills are drafted by special interest groups whose purposes are usually apparent in the substance of their bills. Apart from noncongressional sources, some bills are drafted and introduced by individual members of Congress who act on their own

President Carter is shown signing the Synthetic Fuels Bill (1980) as members of the Senate look on.

initiatives. To assist members and their aides in drafting legislation, each house has a staff of lawyers.

The Role of Congressional Committees
After a bill is introduced in the House, the speaker assigns it to a particular committee. This assignment is important because most bills cut across the jurisdiction of a number of committees and the speaker can choose to send the bill to any one of them. Some committees will be more receptive to the bill than others would be. The speaker's knowledge about the policy preferences of individual committees and his ability to choose the most receptive committee can ensure passage of the bill.

In the Senate the Vice-President usually assigns a bill to whichever committee the bill's sponsor prefers. Often it will be the sponsor's own committee.

In 1965 Vice-President Humphrey referred a civil rights bill to the Commerce Committee, whose chairperson was considered liberal, rather than to the Judiciary Committee, whose chairperson was considered conservative. In the House, Speaker McCormack sent the bill to the Judiciary Committee instead of the Commerce Committee for exactly the same reason.

Committees hold public hearings on all important bills. Those interested in the legislation—executive department representatives who usually testify in support of or in opposition to legislation, representatives of special interest groups, and private citizens—are invited to testify. Most hearings and an increasing number of all committee sessions are open to the public. This development reflects a trend away from secrecy and in favor of freedom of information.

Most committees specialize in particular subjects. The Commerce Committee specializes in transportation, communications, and interstate commerce; the Agriculture Committee specializes in farm problems; and the Interior Committee specializes in conservation and the environment. But a few powerful committees range across several fields: Appropriations (both houses), Ways and Means (the House), Finance (the Senate), Government Operations (both houses), Rules (the house), and Budget (both houses).

Some committees are less influential than others because their members are perceived by other representatives and senators as the spokespeople for special interest groups. For example, the Agriculture committees have a disproportionate number of members from farm states. These committees are in effect special pleaders for farmers. Similarly the House Education and Labor Committee is overrepresented by supporters of labor. When bills emerge from House committees, they are usually subjected to few amendments on the floor. But bills emerging from the Agriculture Committee and the Education and Labor Committee tend to be amended extensively. For example, over a 12-year period only 59 percent of the bills reported by the Education and Labor Committee passed the House. By contrast, 94 percent of the Ways and Means Committee's bills were passed, suggesting that this broad-purpose committee exerts considerable influence.

A member of Congress who serves on the same committee for many years becomes an expert in the legislation handled by that committee. A senior member of the Armed Services Committee, for example, could know

more about certain military conditions and problems than would a Defense Department official who testified before that committee.

After a while a senior committee member may not only become an expert and an advocate but may in fact determine public policy in a particular area.

section review

1. What are the three most common sources of proposed legislation?
2. Why are some committees more influential than others? Give examples.
3. Why is the assignment of a bill to a specific committee important to its eventual enactment?

2. THE ENACTMENT PROCESS

After hearings are held, the committee meets to discuss, revise (mark up), and vote on the bill.

If the vote is favorable, the bill goes to the full House or Senate, where it is debated and voted on. During the debate amendments are often proposed. Sometimes these amendments drastically change the original intent of a bill.

Once a bill is passed in one chamber, the whole process must be repeated in the other chamber. Important bills are often considered in both houses at the same time to speed the process of passage. If different versions of a bill are passed by the House and the Senate, the two versions must be **reconciled** by a conference committee.

Reconciled means made to conform, or made the same.

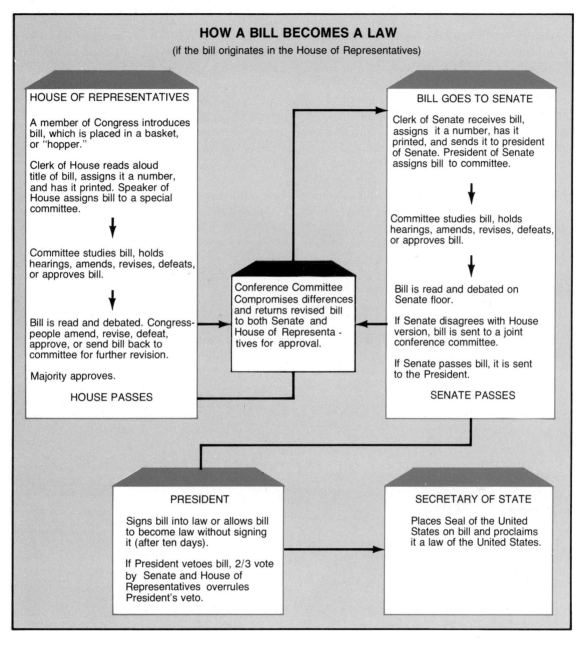

HOW A BILL BECOMES A LAW

(if the bill originates in the House of Representatives)

HOUSE OF REPRESENTATIVES

A member of Congress introduces bill, which is placed in a basket, or "hopper."

Clerk of House reads aloud title of bill, assigns it a number, and has it printed. Speaker of House assigns bill to a special committee.

Committee studies bill, holds hearings, amends, revises, defeats, or approves bill.

Bill is read and debated. Congress-people amend, revise, defeat, approve, or send bill back to committee for further revision.

Majority approves.

HOUSE PASSES

Conference Committee

Compromises differences and returns revised bill to both Senate and House of Representatives for approval.

BILL GOES TO SENATE

Clerk of Senate receives bill, assigns it a number, has it printed, and sends it to president of Senate. President of Senate assigns bill to committee.

Committee studies bill, holds hearings, amends, revises, defeats, or approves bill.

Bill is read and debated on Senate floor.

If Senate disagrees with House version, bill is sent to a joint conference committee.

If Senate passes bill, it is sent to the President.

SENATE PASSES

PRESIDENT

Signs bill into law or allows bill to become law without signing it (after ten days).

If President vetoes bill, 2/3 vote by Senate and House of Representatives overrules President's veto.

SECRETARY OF STATE

Places Seal of the United States on bill and proclaims it a law of the United States.

Floor Debate. For most bills the committee or subcommittee determines the text of a bill. When bills are important or controversial, however, committee debate is only the first step in the process of passing a bill. The next and critical step is debate on the floor of each house of Congress.

In the Senate it is the responsibility of the majority leader to determine the order in which bills are to be debated. Once the schedule is established, the majority leader permits debate.

The House of Representatives has a different system. In the House the Rules Committee—now under the influence of the speaker and the majority leader—determines the order of debate. In addition, the Rules Committee establishes the rules for debate on each bill. It can vote a *"closed rule,"* which means that the House must accept or reject the bill in its entirety. If amendments are allowed, the Rules Committee controls the extent to which amendments will be allowed. Toward the end of a session, when there are more bills awaiting action than can possibly be debated, the Rules Committee decides which bills will be considered and which must die.

In both chambers debate on each bill is organized by floor managers. The floor manager is usually the chairperson of the subcommittee from which the bill was submitted to the floor. His or her job involves lining up supporters for the bill. Some of the most influential members of both chambers will be encouraged to speak on behalf of the bill.

If the floor manager does not expect a majority to vote for a bill, he or she may agree to amendments. Negotiating amendments is part of the process of compromise. The object is to give away as little as possible and still achieve passage of the bill. Working with the party leaders and whips, the floor manager of an important bill will take continuous head counts—polling the members to determine variations in their positions. If polls suggest the development of a trend against the passage of a bill, the leaders may decide to negotiate further concessions.

The Filibuster. In the Senate the rule of unlimited debate makes a filibuster possible. A *filibuster* is a device, used by a minority of senators, by which a bill is "talked to death." Typically a senator gains recognition to speak, yields time to his or her supporters, and refuses to yield time to his or her opponents. Thus a small group of senators can suspend all proceedings—including the passage of crucial appropriations bills—until their conditions are met. A filibuster or the threat of one is most effective toward the end of a session when the pressure of other business is most likely to force the rest of the

Senator Henry M. Jackson (D-Wash.) gets some rest during a Senate filibuster.

Senate to yield. Thus a minority may win otherwise unacceptable amendments as a price for withdrawing its obstruction.

Until recently the filibuster was used almost exclusively by southerners who opposed civil rights legislation. During the seventies it was used by senators from other parts of the country on a wide variety of issues. For example, in 1977 a group of liberal Democratic senators filibustered against energy legislation because they believed that at least one of the provisions of the bill would prove damaging to the interests of consumers.

The only way to end a filibuster is by a procedure called **cloture.** Until 1975 cloture required a two-thirds vote. It now requires a three-fifths vote of the entire Senate. More than half of all cloture motions have been voted on since 1971.

> **Cloture** is a technique that is used to end debate in order to vote on the question that is under consideration.

Voting is completed much faster in the House than it is in the Senate. The Senate takes a *roll call vote;* that is, each member votes orally when his or her name is called in alphabetical order. The House used oral roll calls until 1973 when it installed an electronic voting machine—following the example of several state legislatures. Each member presses a "yes" or "no" button, and the tally is recorded in seconds.

As we have seen, there are numerous opportunities to delay and obstruct the passage of a bill. Usually these tactics do not postpone indefinitely a bill that has broad national support. But a determined minority can, if it chooses, delay action for a year or two, or sometimes longer.

In times of national crisis, Congress generally cooperates and follows the President's lead in shaping policies to deal with the emergency. Delaying bills in times of crisis would be harmful to all involved.

Conference Committees. Because of the different pressures and interests that operate in each house, the Senate and the House of Representatives usually pass different versions of a bill. The conference is in effect a supercommittee, for conference bills are not subject to amendments in either house. In other words, each house must accept or reject the conference bill in its entirety. After so much time, effort, and compromise, most members are inclined to accept the bill— even if it is only a pale reflection of the original bill.

The House and the Senate are equally represented in the conference committee. The chairperson of the committees and subcommittees that first considered the bill are usually appointed to the conference committee. Amendments that the leaders of one chamber failed to defeat are often dropped in the conference committee when the bill from the other chamber contains no such amendments.

Presidential Action. After passing both houses a bill goes to the President. If the President signs it within ten days, it becomes law. But if Congress adjourns during the 10-day interval and the President does not sign the bill, the bill does not become law. This device is known as a *pocket veto.*

If the President vetoes a bill, each House can override the veto by a two-thirds vote. Only then will the bill become law.

The President is under great pressure to accept a bill that has gone through this elaborate process of consideration, amendment, and compromise. The President must sign or veto the entire bill. Sometimes the President tolerates unwanted provisions in order to save the bill.

The power to veto bills gives the President considerable bargaining power with

CONGRESSIONAL BILLS VETOED, 1913–1980

Period	President	Vetoed Bills			Vetoes Sustained	Vetoes Overridden
		Total	Regular	Pocket		
1913–1921	Wilson	44	33	11	38	6
1921–1923	Harding	6	5	1	6	–
1923–1929	Coolidge	50	20	30	46	4
1929–1933	Hoover	37	21	16	34	3
1933–1945	F. Roosevelt	635	372	263	626	9
1945–1953	Truman	250	180	70	238	12
1953–1961	Eisenhower	181	73	108	179	2
1961–1963	Kennedy	21	12	9	21	–
1963–1969	Johnson	30	16	14	30	–
1969–1974[1]	Nixon	42	24	18	36	6
1974–1977	Ford	72	53	19	60	12
1977–1980	Carter (through 11/4/80)	25	12	13	23	2

[1]Nixon resignation effective August 8, 1974
Source: Statistical Abstract of the U.S.

Congress. The difference between the majority required to pass a bill originally and the two thirds needed to override a veto is great enough to give the President considerable sway over the passage of legislation.

The Appropriations Process. Suppose a program to vaccinate everyone against flu is enacted. This program will not actually go into effect unless the Department of Health and Human Services (HHS) gets an appropriation. The Appropriations Subcommittee on Labor, Health, Education, and Welfare must be persuaded to make an appropriation for the new program as part of the annual appropriations bill for HHS. That subcommittee is one of 13 subcommittees of the House Appropriations Committee. Each subcommittee has a counterpart on the Senate Appropriations Committee.

Many of the same members serve on the Appropriations subcommittees year after year. The subcommittees accumulate considerable knowledge about the operations of the executive departments for which they must appropriate funds.

The Appropriations committees in both houses tend to be relatively **nonpartisan**—Democrats and Republicans on each committee seem to think alike and vote alike. Most of them are committed to saving the government money.

> **Nonpartisan** means not bound by party ties.

Members of the House Appropriations Committee work especially well together. House Appropriations subcommittees routinely cut most of the President's budget requests.

On the Senate side, Appropriations subcommittees usually include members from the corresponding legislative committees. If

C. Schultze, former Director of the Office of Management and Budget, is shown testifying before the Senate Appropriations Committee.

For each policy area there are two units of the committee system that are very important. One is the subcommittee that deals with the legislative programs—and the other is the Appropriations subcommittee that is responsible for funding a particular policy area. If a member is chairperson of both the legislative subcommittee and the Appropriations subcommittee for a particular subject, the member is bound to have decisive influence.

During the 1950's and 1960's Senator Lister Hill (D-Ala.) was chairperson of three key committees that were concerned with public health and medical research: the Senate Committee on Labor and Public Welfare, its subcommittee on health, and the Senate Appropriations Subcommittee on Health. On the House side, Representative John Fogarty (D-R.I.) was chairperson of the House Appropriations Subcommittee that dealt with the same subject. Both men worked together to expand national health programs. The year after Senator Hill took over the Appropriations Sub-committee on Health, funds for the Public Health Service increased 56 percent. Within ten years Hill and Fogarty had increased funds for the Public Health Service eightfold. Spending for the National Institute of Health had grown twelvefold. Whereas most Appropriations subcommittees tried to trim department budgets, Hill and Fogarty regularly gave the administration more than it asked for in the health field.

they supported programs in the legislative committees, they will probably support reasonable appropriations. Agencies that have been treated roughly by the House Appropriations Committee may lobby for more funds in the Senate Appropriations Committee.

section review

1. List the steps a bill must pass through to become law.
2. What are some of the ways by which a bill's progress may be impeded? moved ahead?
3. How can the House Rules Committee determine the fate of proposed legislation?
4. What is the role of the floor manager?
5. Define cloture.

3. THE INFLUENCE OF PARTY MEMBERSHIP

How does a member of Congress decide to vote for or against a bill?

Sources of Influence. First, a member may defer to the chairperson and to the members of a committee on which he or she serves. A member may defer to the political judgment of other party leaders. If the President or a Cabinet secretary contacts a member and urges him or her to vote a certain way, that appeal may be decisive. A member may also consider the views of constituents and major supporters. Finally, a member may look for guidance to influential members of Congress

REPRESENTA-TIVE BARBARA MILKULSKI

Representative Barbara Milkulski (D-Md.), elected to Congress in 1976, was born to Polish American parents. She now represents the district in Baltimore where she grew up. Representative Milkulski attended local Catholic girls' schools from nursery school to college. After graduation she began working as a social worker and teacher at Loyola College.

Representative Milkulski's political career began in 1971, when she ran for the city council. Her parents, who owned a grocery store, helped campaign for her by sending out weekly grocery-special notices, which also advertised, "Please vote for our daughter." However, she did not win.

Barbara Milkulski was a determined person. Losing the city council election made her work even harder during her congressional campaign. In the primary she managed to beat ten opponents with 76 percent of the vote and went on to win the election. She was again elected in 1978 and 1980.

Representative Milkulski advocates legislation on behalf of ethnic groups, senior citizens, and women. She is interested not in impressing anyone but only in doing the best job she can. "I don't know if we'll eliminate all unemployment or unfair taxation or sex discrimination, but I do know we'll eliminate some of it or make the people doing it pretty uncomfortable."

She believes in making herself available to the people she represents. She does not use a desk because "it would be setting up a barrier between me and the person I'm trying to help."

Representative Milkulski keeps close ties with her district. She commutes by car from her 180-year-old federal-style house in Baltimore to Washington, D.C. During the long drive, she operates her CB radio under the name of "White Eagle," the Polish symbol of valor.

whose judgment he or she has grown to trust and respect. This group often includes experienced members of the same party from a member's home state.

Another factor that influences a member is *reciprocity.* Members of Congress are expected to help one another and to be repaid in kind. This kind of mutual-assistance pact reflects the principle of reciprocity. In the context of Congress, it means, "You vote for my dam, and I'll vote for your highway"; or "You help me with my housing project, and I'll help you with your farm subsidy." Another name for this particular kind of reciprocity is *logrolling.*

A third influential factor is the mood of the country. When people are especially worried about inflation, for example, members of Congress are likely to cut the President's budget and refuse to pass welfare legislation.

Lobbyists—representatives of interest groups—may influence members of Congress. They frequently visit members and their staffs, giving them specialized information and offering to assist them in drafting bills. Lobbyists are very likely to influence a member, especially if their points of view do not appear to conflict with the interests of the member's constituents. For example, oil and gas lobbyists are likely to have no trouble persuading a member from an oil- or gas-producing state but may have more trouble with a member who represents oil and gas consumers.

Party Voting. No member of Congress is compelled to vote with his or her party. Nevertheless, as we have seen, there is a remarkable degree of party voting in Congress. Members of parties vote together for a variety of reasons. They tend to share certain views on what the government's role should be in regulating the economy. They relate in the same way to the President, who is either the leader of their party or the leader of the other party.

Party **solidarity** is lowest—and consti-

tuency influence is highest—in the policy arena of civil rights. This arena includes the issue of busing children to achieve racial balance in the schools. Party voting is also relatively weak in the policy arenas of defense and foreign policy. The two parties do not usually take fixed stands on these issues.

> **Solidarity** is the perception of or the feelings of togetherness.

There is considerable *party cohesion,* or party voting, in the policy arena of social welfare. This arena includes public housing, federal aid to education, social security, and minimum wage laws. Party voting is quite high on the issue of *farm subsidies,* or higher prices given to farmers for their crops than they could get in the open market. In the policy arena relating to government regulation—including tax reform, the regulation of business, conservation, and public works—party solidarity is very strong.

The President and other leaders of his party try to take advantage of the natural tendency of members of their party to vote together. They can get votes through persuasion, granting of special favors, the impact of their personalities, and the influence of their offices. The President can arouse public opinion through the news media. His appeal can bring constituents' pressure to bear on a member's vote. Because the main objective of the member of Congress is to achieve reelection, this arousal of constituent pressure may encourage more party voting.

section review

1. Describe the reciprocity factor.
2. How does the mood of the country affect congressional legislation?
3. Why do congressional representatives of the same party tend to vote together?

CHAPTER SUMMARY

16

The task of proposing legislation and drafting bills is awesome and complex. The President is actually the chief legislator, since the President's leadership influences Congress in determining financial priorities and passing legislation. Special-interest groups, political parties, congressional chairpersons, and members' constituents, all help to shape legislation. Legislative power is dispersed through the committee system, but it is also centralized through party controls. The committee system was set up to deal with the complexity of the lawmaking function. Committee members become specialists in their fields and can devote their time to these areas. Political parties work for party unity in Congress to help pass the legislation they support.

REVIEW QUESTIONS

1. Explain the power of the Speaker in the legislative process.
2. Explain the importance of the choice of committee in referring a bill.
3. List four ways in which a bill can be impeded.
4. On what kinds of issues does a political party show solidarity?
5. What are the duties of a floor manager in the legislative process?
6. Explain the President's veto power.
7. What is the purpose of the Senate filibuster?
8. How does a Congress member decide to vote for or against a bill?
9. What is a "closed rule" on a bill?

ACTIVITIES FOR REVIEW

activity 1

Send for a copy of a bill relating to some aspect of government that could affect you, such as the lowering of minimum wages for those under 18 years of age. Have the class set up a committee to "mark up" the bill. Hold a mock hearing, inviting persons in the community whose knowledge would be helpful. Have the committee decide the fate of the bill.

activity 2   Send for the Conference Committee report on a piece of legislation meaningful to you and your class. Analyze opposing views in the report. Explain the eventual compromise adopted by the committee. Do research on the outcome of the bill.

activity 3   Visit or write to the district office of your representative in Congress. Ask to be put on the mailing list. Invite the congressperson to speak to the class. Prepare questions ahead of time that will help the class understand the legislative process.

political science
DICTIONARY

closed rule—the rule in debate that the House must accept or reject a proposed bill in its entirety.   p. 308

cloture—a technique used to limit or end debate in order to vote on a question under consideration.   p. 309

filibuster—a strategy, used by a minority of senators, in which a bill is "talked to death."   p. 308

lobbyists—representatives of interest groups, whose attempts to influence members of Congress include providing information and assistance in drafting bills.   p. 313

logrolling—a form of reciprocity.   p. 313

mark up—the final step by a committee in preparing a bill for consideration by the entire chamber.   p. 306

nonpartisan—not representative of any political party.   p. 310

party cohesion—the show of unity by members of a political party in voting as a bloc on important issues   p. 313

pocket veto—procedure by which the President can defeat a bill by ignoring it. If Congress adjourns within ten days after a bill has been sent to the President, and the President has not taken any action, the bill does not become law.   p. 309

reciprocity—mutual assistance. Members of Congress help one another and expect to be repaid in kind.   p. 313

reconciled—made the same or brought into harmony.   p. 306

roll call vote—an oral vote by each congressional member, called in alphabetical order.   p. 309

solidarity—unity; community of interests.   p. 313

17 *Constitutional Checks and Congressional Reform*

In this chapter you will trace the history of congressional investigations. You will also examine how Congress exercises its constitutional power of checking the executive branch of government. In this context you will survey legislative-executive relations in the policy arenas of foreign affairs, defense, and government operations. Finally you will examine the nature of congressional reform in the context of the development of party control.

CHAPTER PREVIEW

1. CONGRESSIONAL INVESTIGATIONS
2. CONGRESS AND THE EXECUTIVE BRANCH
3. CONGRESSIONAL REFORM

1. CONGRESSIONAL INVESTIGATIONS

One power of Congress that can sometimes be effective is its power to conduct investigations. In the 1970's two investigations captured headlines and produced shock waves throughout the country.

The first was conducted in 1973 by a special Senate committee that was empowered to investigate election practices and campaign finances. This committee, known as the Watergate Committee, unraveled the story of the burglary of the headquarters of the Democratic National Committee and other improper or illegal campaign activities connected with the 1972 presidential election. Eventually the investigation led to the resignation of President Richard Nixon and the indictment, conviction, and imprisonment of his top aides.

President Carter's brother Billy faced a Senate Judicial investigative subcommittee hearing in 1980. The panel was investigating Billy's ties with the Libyan government.

Two years later another special Senate committee investigated the government's various intelligence-gathering activities. The investigation uncovered a wide range of abuses by the Central Intelligence Agency (CIA), including various attempts to assassinate foreign leaders. As a result of this investigation, legislation was enacted not only to strengthen the President's control over the CIA but also to expand the power of Congress to oversee the operations of the agency.

The Purpose of Investigations. For many years congressional investigations have served as important channels of communication and influence. In the 1920's the congressional investigation of the Teapot Dome scandal exposed corruption among high gov-

ernment officials. It led to the disgrace of several members of President Harding's inner circle of advisers.

Senator Joseph McCarthy's investigation of Communist sympathizers in the army ended by exposing the senator as an irresponsible agitator. The investigation led to his downfall, but not before many reputations had been severely damaged.

Other important investigations in recent years have probed organized crime, labor racketeering, unsafe drugs, unsafe automobiles, unsafe mines, and mismanagement of the Vietnamese War.

By giving publicity to a particular issue, investigative committees of Congress can create a climate of opinion, both within the government and among the public at large,

Some investigations, like the one conducted by Senator Joseph McCarthy, seem to have been primarily motivated by publicity seeking on the part of the investigators. Some have denied witnesses their constitutional rights by forcing them to testify against themselves. Some have clouded witnesses' reputations and jeopardized their livelihoods by accusing them falsely.

Rights of Witnesses. The main protection of witnesses is their right to refuse to answer a question on the grounds that they may incriminate themselves. This privilege against self-incrimination is guaranteed by the Fifth

This is a copy of the subpoena issued by the House Judiciary Committee to Richard Nixon on April 11, 1974. He was asked to produce all tape recordings that were relevant to his case.

Senator Joseph McCarthy is shown leading the investigation of Communist sympathizers that resulted in his own downfall.

that favors action to bring about reform and change.

The Scope of Investigative Power. The scope of the congressional power to investigate is broad. Committees have the power to carry out inquiries, to **subpoena** witnesses, to compel the production of papers, and to cite uncooperative witnesses for contempt of Congress—a citation that carries a jail term.

A **subpoena** is a written order of Congress that requires a witness to testify. If the witness refuses, he or she can be charged with contempt of Congress.

ORIGINAL

BY AUTHORITY OF THE HOUSE OF REPRESENTATIVES OF THE CONGRESS OF THE UNITED STATES OF AMERICA

To _Benjamin Marshall, or his duly authorized representative:_

You are hereby commanded to summon _____

Richard M. Nixon, President of the United States of America, or any subordinate officer, official or employee with custody or control of the things described in the attached schedule,

to be and appear before the _Committee on the Judiciary_

Committees of the House of Representatives of the United States, of which the Hon. _____

Peter W. Rodino, Jr. _is chairman, and to bring with_

him the things specified in the schedule attached hereto and made a part

hereof.

in their chamber in the city of Washington, on _or before_

April 25, 1974 at the hour of _10:00 A.M._

produce and deliver said things to said Committee, or their then and there to ~~summon witnesses and testify before said Committee and there~~ duly authorized representative, in connection with the Committee's investi- ~~gation as will appear in the attached Schedule~~ gation authorized and directed by H. Res. 803, adopted February 6, 1974.

Herein fail not, and make return of this summons.

Witness my hand and the seal of the House of Representatives

of the United States, at the city of Washington, this

_11th_ day of _April_, _1974_.

Peter W. Rodino, Jr. _Chairman._

Attest: _Trad Jennings_ _Clerk._

Amendment to the Constitution. The main problem with using the Fifth Amendment, however, is that many people infer that whoever claims the privilege must be guilty.

The courts and Congress have tried to remedy abuses by developing procedural safeguards to protect witnesses. The Supreme Court case of *Watkins* v. *U.S.* (1957) declared that no committee has the power to "expose for the sake of exposure" and that Congress must leave it to the courts to conduct trials and punish wrongdoers.

section review

1. What was the result of the investigations held by the Watergate Committee?
2. What have been some of the pitfalls of congressional investigations?
3. How have the courts tried to remedy investigation abuses?
4. What are the chief purposes of congressional investigations?

2. CONGRESS AND THE EXECUTIVE BRANCH

The Constitution gives the executive and legislative branches a number of checks with which to keep the other branch in proper balance. The operations of the checks-and-balances system have been detailed elsewhere in this book. But to illustrate the changes that have occurred in legislative-executive relations, the effectiveness of that system will be examined in the policy arenas of foreign affairs, defense, and government operations.

Foreign Policy and Defense. Congress has lost power to the President in the important arenas of foreign policy and defense. The issues involved in these fields are technologi-cally complex or secret or both, and the style and the organization of Congress do not allow for secrecy or speed.

But Congress has not relinquished all of its power over foreign and defense policy. In addition to its reassertion of power in connection with the War Powers Act, which is discussed elsewhere in this book, Congress began to reassert its checking power during the 1970's.

For example, as the American people became more critical of the Vietnamese War, Congress began to scrutinize Pentagon spending proposals—particularly requests for new weapons. By 1970 Congress began to slash these requests and in some cases refused funds for new weapons systems.

In 1973 Congress attempted to check President Nixon's bombing of Cambodia by prohibiting his use of appropriated funds for that campaign. In 1975 Congress withheld military aid to Cambodia.

The Senate took no action in 1979 and 1980 to ratify the Strategic Arms Limitation Treaty (SALT II) despite its sponsorship by President Carter.

The President strongly disagreed with these actions. Whoever was right, one thing seems clear: Congress demonstrated that it could still exercise power over foreign policy and defense.

Legislative Oversight. *Legislative oversight* is the implicit power of Congress to assess how the executive branch spends the money that it appropriates and administers the laws that Congress has passed.

As you have already seen, the 26 Appropriations subcommittees in both houses exercise tight control over federal spending in most areas. They examine each year's budget requests after they have determined how efficiently money was spent during the previous year.

Congressional capacity for legislative oversight in budgeting and appropriations

Senator Strom Thurmond (left), Chairman of the Senate Judiciary Committee, is shown meeting with Senator William S. Cohen (R-ME.) and Senator Mark Hatfield (R-OR.) prior to the opening of the 97th Congress.

was significantly enlarged by the establishment of budget committees in each house in 1975. These committees now have the power, staff experts, and information necessary to review budget requests and hold hearings on them.

The budget committees are authorized to act as bridges between committees that raise money through taxes—the House Ways and Means Committee and the Senate Finance Committee—and committees that spend money through appropriations—the House and Senate Appropriations committees. All of these committees and their staffs have accumulated a considerable amount of expertise and information. They check the executive branch by changing tax proposals, evaluating budget requests, and reducing appropriations.

Differences between presidential re-quests and congressional appropriations reflect different reactions to the demands of various groups in American society by the President and by Congress. They may also reflect different assessments of the same information and different preferences about what policies are best for the country.

Committees that Oversee the Executive Branch. Various congressional committees oversee executive branch operations through investigative hearings. Two standing committees that perform this function almost exclusively are the House and Senate committees on Government Operations. The Permanent Investigations Subcommittee of the Senate Committee on Government Operations has a staff of 40.

The General Accounting Office (GAO), which reports directly to Congress, helps

Congress to perform its oversight function. It has the authority to examine the legality and the efficiency of all executive branch spending, including military spending by the Pentagon. The GAO has revealed monumental delays, waste, and incompetence in defense spending and in other programs.

Congress and the Organization of the Executive Branch. The Constitution empowers Congress to determine how the executive branch is organized. In practice, however, all proposals for new organizations or reorganizations of the executive branch have come from the President. In 1979, for example, President Carter proposed the creation of a new Cabinet-level Department of Education. The new department was fashioned from the education-related units of the Department of Health, Education, and Welfare.

The President set up the new department subject to the right of Congress to reject it. In effect, though, Congress seems to have delegated to the President the initiative to reorganize the executive branch.

Confirmation. All senior federal officials, including Cabinet officers, ambassadors, and judges, are appointed by the President subject to the advice and consent of the Senate. The Senate must confirm these appointees before they take office. Confirmations are sent to committees. These committees usually hold hearings. After the hearings they issue favorable or unfavorable reports.

Generally the Senate approves executive-branch nominations as a matter of course. Sometimes it may raise questions about proposed appointees' possible conflicts of interest if their own business interests overlap the interests of the executive department with which they will be associated.

For example, if the president of a major aircraft company is about to be appointed secretary of the air force, the Senate may demand assurances that the appointee will not favor the company with government con-

tracts. Sometimes the appointee may be required to sell all of his or her stock in the company. This process is far from foolproof, but it puts the appointee on notice that Congress has the power to demand compliance with its regulations.

All of the President's nominees for the Supreme Court are examined very carefully by the Senate Judiciary Committee. The Senate is much less inclined to ratify these nominations routinely, for Supreme Court justices are not members of the President's team. The judicial branch is a separate and coequal branch of government. Usually, however, the President nominates people of integrity and competence to the Supreme Court, and it is rare for the Senate to refuse to confirm such nominations. It is a serious blow to a President's prestige to have any nominee rejected.

The Senate can also require the President to submit names of appointees for offices that have never been subject to Senate confirmation. This can happen when, for example, the powers and functions of a presidential assistant expand greatly over time. The Director of the Office of Management and Budget used to be part of the President's personal White House staff and thus not subject to Senate confirmation. Recognizing the great power that has been given to this official, however,

QUOTES
from famous people

"Congressmen interviewed generally indicate that they have little tendency to raise . . . questions of military policy. . . . In fact, during the 1946–57 period, few examples could be found where congressional committees created any impression of . . . evaluating decisions about weapons, appropriations, personnel, missions, organization, or administration in terms of national or international goals. . . ."

Lewis Dexter

Congress now requires both the director and his or her deputy to be confirmed by the Senate.

section review

1. Which two standing committees are responsible for overseeing executive-branch operations?
2. In what ways can Congress check actions of the President?
3. What are the reasons for the increase of presidential advantage over Congress?
4. Explain the importance of Congress' power over appropriation of funds.
5. What causes differences between presidential requests and congressional appropriations?

3. CONGRESSIONAL REFORM

Some critics of the legislative branch contend that members of Congress come from upper- or upper-middle-income backgrounds and cannot understand—much less meet—the needs of lower-income groups. Moreover, the operation of Congress by the seniority and the committee systems put actual control in the hands of a relatively small number of mostly conservative members.

Others argue that the procedures of Congress work to guarantee minority rights and to check majority abuse. Most people agree that minorities should have the right to publicize an issue and to delay action on it until everyone has had time to consider the question. But they also maintain that minorities should not have the power to stifle the will of the majority.

Despite the assertions of congressional critics, reapportionment and redistricting are making Congress a little more representative of all segments of the population. Congress has also shown the ability to reform itself. The Senate cloture rule seems to have weakened the power of the filibuster. Congress is getting more and better staff. The Congressional Research Service, the GAO, and the new Congressional Budget Office are giving Congress more and better information.

The main reforms have taken place in four areas: the growth of party control in the House of Representatives, a new capacity for budget review, the increased power of subcommittees, and new ethics codes in both houses of Congress.

Party Control. This unit has traced the movement of power away from committees to party leaders, particularly in the House of Representatives. This development reverses a trend that began at the beginning of the twentieth century.

During the first decade of this century, Speaker of the House Joseph Cannon controlled his party's committee appointments, the Rules Committee, the floor schedule, and the House Republican caucus. With these powers he was able to dominate the House and stamp his own views on legislative policy. In 1910 the Republican rank and file in the House of Representatives rebelled against Speaker Cannon and greatly diminished the role of the Speaker. Most of the Speaker's powers were dispersed to the committees.

In the early 1970's liberals in the House turned to the speakership to check the excessive power of committee chairpersons. The House Democratic caucus invested its Steering and Policy Committee with power over all committee assignments, including the nomination of chairpersons. The Speaker heads the Steering and Policy Committee and names almost half of its members.

In addition, the Speaker has increased power to choose which committees will review major bills. The Speaker now nominates the majority party members of the Rules Committee. As a result, the Speaker now

Pictured from left to right are Senate Minority Leader Robert C. Byrd, Vice-President George Bush, Senator Paul Laxalt, Senate Majority Leader Howard H. Baker Jr., and President Reagan. This picture was taken in 1981 prior to President Reagan's inauguration.

speaks for the majority party with a stronger voice and has a greater opportunity to fashion and direct the party's legislative program.

The majority whip is the third-ranking officer of the majority party in the House of Representatives. The Speaker and majority leader choose the majority whip. During the 1970's the office of the majority whip grew dramatically. The whip's office has now become an information center. It summarizes all legislation for members and highlights the controversial points of a bill. This new system has enabled the party leaders to become the major sources of information for their members in the House.

The recent changes, like the changes of 1910, seem to be part of a cyclical pattern of reform and change. Decentralized committees and subcommittees are now counterbalanced by party direction, coordination, and publicizing of major legislation. The result is a stronger Congress that is better able to fulfill its role in the political system.

CASE STUDY ON PARTY CONTROL: THE STORY OF THE OIL DEPLETION ALLOWANCE

For years the oil depletion allowance was one of the biggest loopholes in the American tax structure. Under the allowance oil companies could claim huge tax deductions. The deductions were based on the theory that the oil that the companies were pumping out and selling at a profit was a shrinking resource for which they deserved compensation. Critics considered it a device to increase the profits of the oil companies by reducing their tax liabilities.

In 1975 liberals on the Ways and Means Committee attempted to reduce the oil depletion allowance. They were defeated by a coalition of Republicans, conservative Democrats, and Democrats from oil-producing states. The same coalition controlled the Rules Committee. But the liberals used a tactic made possible by the development of party control. They successfully petitioned for a meeting of the House Democratic caucus. By a majority vote of the caucus, all members of the Rules Committee were compelled to vote a rule on the bill that permitted floor amendments on oil depletion allowances.

The liberals then took their fight to the House floor. There they were able to obtain an amendment that reduced oil depletion tax writeoffs.

New Capacity for Budget Review. In the early 1970's many members of Congress perceived that the presidency had gotten out of control and that the balance of power between the President and Congress had to be restored. President Nixon had refused to spend billions of dollars that Congress had appropriated for farm programs, clean water projects, and housing programs. Many members of Congress began to think that President Nixon was using *impoundment*—that is, refusing to spend funds—in order to disregard Congress and weaken its constitutional power over spending.

The Budget and Impoundment Control Act of 1974 not only established the House and Senate Budget committees but also requires that appropriated funds be spent unless both houses approve a presidential proposal that funds be set aside. Congress must vote such approval within 45 days after the President proposes it.

At the same time that the Budget committees were being formed, changes were being made in the two other House committees that deal with money. The House Ways and Means Committee was increased from 24 to 36 members, diluting its power. The power of the House Appropriations Committee shifted to its 13 subcommittees.

Increased Power of Subcommittees. In the late 1950's the House had 83 subcommittees. Today it has more than 148. More complex issues have led to more specialization within committees. This development, in turn, has led to the addition of subcommittees and their growth in power.

Subcommittee chairpersons are usually not as powerful as the strong committee chairpersons of the past. Problems have arisen with the growth of subcommittees. Legislation sometimes fails to reflect the broad view that a full committee ordinarily takes. There are disagreements over jurisdiction. With so many subcommittees, chairpersons struggle to protect their limited jurisdictions.

The main benefit flowing from the growth of subcommittees is that the House of Representatives is a more active place than it used to be. More hearings are being held, more issues are being considered. More bills are being introduced, and more members are actively participating in the lawmaking process. What counts now is expertise rather than seniority. It is much harder for a few individuals who are bent on obstruction to undercut the majority of the House.

New House and Senate Ethics Codes. In the wake of Watergate and in response to the urging of the press, both the House and the Senate adopted rules that limit a member's outside income to 15 percent of his or her official salary. Both the House and the Senate require full financial disclosure of all sources of income. The House code also prohibits the acceptance of speaking fees above $1,000 and gifts valued at more than $100.

Some members of Congress believe that the new ethics rules are too severe. One member recently complained, "The pendulum has swung too far since Watergate." Notwithstanding such complaints, it seems clear that standards of ethics and financial disclosure are here to stay.

Consequences of Reforms. Congressional reforms have made that institution more representative. Influence is now distributed more broadly inside Congress. For example,

Former Rep. Barbara Jordan of Texas became a noteworthy speaker during the 1974 Watergate hearings.

congressional proceedings—including most committee sessions and some House-Senate conference committees—are open to the public. These reforms stem from a variety of pressures. The net effect is that Congress seems to be more responsive to the will of the people. As responsiveness grows, the people's respect for Congress as an institution is likely to grow as well.

section review

1. What have been some positive steps taken by Congress to reform itself?
2. How has the power of the Speaker increased in recent years?
3. What are some of the problems resulting from the increase in congressional subcommittees?

CHAPTER SUMMARY

17

Congress' power of investigation is great. The purpose of this power has been to serve as a channel of communication and influence. Congress can affect public and governmental opinion through this power.

The Constitution has set up a system by which the legislative, judicial and executive branches check each other. This system of checks and balances has undergone changes, especially in the areas of foreign policy and defense.

Major reforms have enabled Congress to strengthen itself and to carry out its legislative duties more effectively.

REVIEW QUESTIONS

1. Explain what you believe to be legitimate functions of legislative investigations.
2. In what ways does Congress still maintain some control over foreign policy and national defense?
3. Explain the system of checks and balances in the legislative process.
4. What are the rights of a witness in a congressional investigation?
5. How was Congress' power of legislative oversight enlarged?
6. What is the function of the General Accounting Office (GAO)?
7. Describe the confirmation process.
8. List the four areas of congressional reform.
9. How was the oil depletion allowance a tax loophole?
10. How does Congress create a climate of opinion about issues through its investigations?
11. What problems does one encounter when pleading the Fifth Amendment?
12. What was the result of the *Watkins* v. *U.S.* case?
13. Which congressional committees oversee the executive branch of the government?
14. How is the majority whip chosen?

ACTIVITIES FOR REVIEW

activity 1   Do research on the Rules Committee in the House of Representatives. Explain how new congressional reform measures have helped to make the legislature more responsive to the needs of the people.

activity 2   Do research on the Senate's Watergate investigation. Write a report describing the abuses of the legislative process by the executive branch.

activity 3   Construct a time line of events that were the focus of congressional investigation.

activity 4   Do research on new issues that have required Senate investigations. In chart form, give the issue, the persons involved, the year, and the outcome of the Senate's investigation.

political science DICTIONARY

impoundment—refusal to spend appropriated funds.   p. 324

legislative oversight—Congress' implicit power to assess the spending of congressional appropriations by the executive branch and the administration by the executive of laws passed by Congress.   p. 319

subpoena—a written order of Congress requiring a witness to testify. A witness who refuses can be charged with contempt of Congress.   p. 318

18

Congressional Representatives

Members of Congress perform a wide variety of jobs. They must service the people they represent and try to carry out the wishes of these people. They are responsible for making laws that affect millions of people.

Getting elected to Congress is a difficult feat to accomplish. Congresspersons must perform their duties well if they wish to be reelected. Once in office they have not only the prestige of holding an office but also the many tools and resources available to a member of Congress.

In this chapter you will deal first with the means by which candidates are elected to Congress. Then you will look at how members of Congress stay in office. You will find out what kind of people become members of Congress. You will learn what they have in common with one another and with their constituents. You will examine the increasingly heavy work load of members of Congress and discover how the time of a typical member is spent.

Finally, you will see how Congress has expanded in recent years. You will explore the ways in which different members represent their constituents, and you will see how members respond to the many people who ask for their help in dealing with the government.

CHAPTER PREVIEW

1. RUNNING FOR CONGRESS
2. GETTING REELECTED
3. THE BACKGROUNDS OF MEMBERS OF CONGRESS
4. THE JOB OF A MEMBER OF CONGRESS

1. RUNNING FOR CONGRESS

A recent poll showed that 60 percent of the voters sampled had not heard or read anything about any of the candidates campaigning for Congress in their districts. Of those who went to the polls, 46 percent said they voted without knowing anything about the candidates in the race. **Incumbents** are usually twice as well known as challengers, but—if this poll is an indication—even incumbents are unknown to more than half the voters.

> An **incumbent** is a person who holds an office and seeks reelection.

Most voters identify themselves as either Democrats or Republicans. When they go to the polls, they are likely to vote their party's ticket. Incumbents, because they are better known and have had many chances to help their constituents, usually have no difficulty in getting reelected. In the last 20 years, over 90 percent of the incumbents who sought reelection were successful.

A congressional seat becomes vacant when an incumbent retires or dies, or when reapportionment after a census results in the creation of a new district. When this happens, the contest is likely to be interesting. Typically, a variety of people are waiting in the wings. This group may include state legislators, mayors, and district attorneys. These people are aware of the difficulty of challenging an incumbent. So they usually wait for a congressional seat to become vacant.

Sometimes an incumbent looks "beatable." The incumbent may have won the last election by a slim majority, or the incumbent's party may have lost favor among the voters. The incumbent may be receiving bad publicity because of a scandal. In such instances there are likely to be a number of contenders in the race.

Incumbent Senator Gary Hart of Colorado is shown here giving a speech after his reelection.

The Primary Election. The first hurdle is usually the primary election. In primaries, the enrolled voters of each party are asked to choose from among two or more people seeking the party's nomination to Congress.

Once nominated, candidates have support—the blocks of votes of those who automatically support their party's nominee. Candidates will gain the attention of the press and their party's state and national leaders.

REPRESENTATIVE MARY OAKAR

Mary Rose Oakar (D-Ohio), elected to Congress in 1976, wasn't always in politics. She was born in Cleveland, Ohio, and is of Syrian descent. After receiving undergraduate and graduate degrees in English and drama, she directed and acted in various local theatrical productions. She taught high school English for a while and then became an assistant professor of English at Cuyahoga Community College. It was at this time that she began her political career as a member of the city council.

As councilwoman in Cleveland, she worked to get things done by reducing delays and simplifying routines of government agencies. She was also involved in inner-city renewal and programs for senior citizens. She works for the same causes now, but on a national level. "A Social Security payment has to go through a maze of agencies before it reaches the person who needs it," she says.

Her first campaign for national office was tough. She had to beat 11 opponents in the primary. With a campaign staff of 80 volunteers, she managed to win the general election with 81 percent of the vote. She became the second woman Ohio has sent to Congress. Representative Oakar was reelected in 1978 and 1980.

Representative Oakar now sits on the Banking, Finance, and Urban Affairs Committee and the Select Committee on Aging. Under the auspices of the Committee on Aging, Representative Oakar chaired a task force on Social Security and Women. She has introduced six pieces of legislation aimed at relieving the inadequacies found in the Social Security system's coverage of women.

The Campaign. A popular candidate for President or governor who heads the party's ticket may be a boost on Election Day to all other candidates on the ticket. Aside from this, candidates must sell themselves on their own merits. The party will be of little further help.

In most cases candidates must raise their own funds. Local and state parties usually have very limited funds with which to help new candidates for Congress.

The candidates' main problem is making themselves known to enough voters to make a difference at the polls. Television advertising is too costly for most candidates and often covers a wider area than a congressional district. So candidates usually rely on personal appearances, door-to-door campaigning, and direct appeals to voters through the mails.

The public does not think of individual candidates for the House or Senate in terms of party programs. Those voters without strong party ties, or those who do not belong to a party, are much more likely to base their choices on factors having nothing to do with policy. They may be influenced by a candidate's family, by his or her appearance, or by a campaign style that inspires their trust.

Campaign Costs. In the early days of the United States, modest sums, if any, were spent in campaigning for election. In 1838, when Abraham Lincoln ran for Congress, he raised only $2.00 in campaign funds. He spent $.50 on a keg of cider and returned the remaining $1.50.

Campaign costs are high and increase every year. Incumbents from "safe" seats do not need to spend much money to get reelected. But contenders usually need large sums to run successful campaigns.

"Mama, come on up here and say hello."

Family members often help candidates in their campaigns.

Today it is not unusual for a congressional candidate to spend more than $200,000 for a contested House race. One mailing to every family in a candidate's district costs about $20,000 in postage alone. Senate contests are often much more costly, sometimes running well over $1 million in states with large populations.

This money is raised from the candidate's own funds, from local contributions, and from the contributions of special-interest groups. The national party will probably give only partial financial support to congressional candidates. National organizations, particularly those representing the labor movement, often give campaign support to candidates who are likely to help them when they get to Congress. Most campaign money comes from within candidates' districts. It is raised by campaign organizations, consisting of family, friends, and other loyal supporters of the candidate.

When John Anderson—the independent candidate for President in 1980—was a member of Congress he observed, "Campaign costs have become very large compared to what they used to be, and a lot more special-interest money has come our way as the result of the public financing of presidential campaigns. Because of inflation and the increased cost of campaigning, it's easy to rationalize—to say, 'I'm not going to be compromised, and I do need the money.' So it becomes easy to take it."

section review

1. Why is victory in the primary important for a congressional candidate?
2. What is an incumbent? What advantages does he/she have in an election?
3. Name two situations that may cause a congressional seat to become vacant.
4. How do candidates raise money for their congressional campaigns?

2. GETTING REELECTED

One senator has observed, "I start running for reelection on the first day of my new term." Why is this necessary? You have already seen that most voters pay little attention to their representatives and senators in Congress. The typical voter, in fact, does not even know the name of his or her congressional representative or senators. Moreover, most seats in Congress are "safe" year after year. Sometimes age or a shift in the population of a district will cause a senior member to leave office. More often members stay in office as long as they like.

Nonetheless, many members of Congress—even those who have every reason to feel secure—become uneasy. They can always point to some senior and respected member who was unexpectedly brought down by an unknown challenger. They may recall the story often told by former Senator (and later, Vice-President) Alben Barkley, who learned that one of his old supporters was about to vote for his opponent. "How can you do this," asked Senator Barkley, "after all I've done for you?" "Yeah," came the reply, "but what have you done for me lately?"

The Unpopularity of Congress. Congress has always been a favorite target of journalists and humorists. With 535 public targets, any enterprising journalist is bound to find some wrongdoing somewhere. Congress has been the object of fun and criticism since the early days of the Republic.

Congress as a whole is unpopular, but this is not true of individual members of Congress. In a recent Harris poll, two questions were asked:

1. "How would you rate the job done by Congress this year?" About half the people responding had a positive impression of Congress. The other half had negative feelings.
2. "How would you rate the service your representative gives to your district while he or she is in Washington?" Favorable responses outnumbered unfavorable responses by three to one. In the words of one observer, "We love our congressperson but not our Congress."

Another interesting inconsistency is that, although public approval of Congress is generally low, more Representatives of Congress are reelected now than ever before. Incumbent Representatives have won reelection in about 90 percent of the contests since 1960.

Campaigning. It is no surprise that most members of Congress want very much to be reelected. Staying in office means keeping their power and privileges.

Campaigning is a major drain on members' time and energies. They must make considerable efforts to raise campaign funds. At the same time, they must fulfill their official duties without being influenced by campaign contributors.

Many members of Congress believe campaigning to be an important part of public life. It keeps them in touch with their constituents and gives them first-hand understanding of the problems of the people they represent.

Members of Congress do all sorts of favors for their constituents, favors that challengers cannot perform. This practice usually wins incumbents the enthusiastic support of grateful constitutents and often that of their relatives and friends. The ability to do favors also makes it easier for members to raise campaign funds.

Representatives or senators can get coverage in the local press. Local television stations also report what members of Congress say and do. Such free publicity is rarely available to challengers. Recognition is the "name of the game." Unless they automatically vote a straight party ticket, voters are likely to choose the candidate whose name they recognize.

Communicating with the public is part of the job of a member of Congress. The staff and services available to all members for this purpose are not intended for use in campaigns. Nevertheless, the office help, stationery, printing, and radio and television facilities to which they have access enable members to stay in close communication with voters, at government expense, as part of their congressional duties. This, of course, pays off in voter recognition on Election Day.

The most important advantage available to incumbents is the **frank.** With the franking

Pictured is a congressional mailing. The signature in the upper right-hand corner—the frank—enables the letter to travel postage-free.

privilege, members can keep constituents informed on issues, voting, and other business throughout their terms. One representative, who was about to be succeeded in the House by his son, said, "Son, I have three pieces of advice for you if you want to stay in Congress. 1) Use the frank. 2) Use the frank. 3) Use the frank." However, a member who uses the frank to distribute campaign materials is abusing the privilege.

> The **frank** is the privilege of sending mail postage-free. Members of Congress substitute facsimiles of their signatures (franks) for postage.

Additional Advantages. Any challenger is bound to be hard pressed to make up for the incumbent's built-in advantages. Raising campaign funds is a problem for the incumbent, but it is even more of a problem for the challenger. The incumbent is a tested winner, and who wants to back a probable loser? The challenger is disadvantaged further when his or her opponent has seniority,

power, and influence. In that case, even the President may agree to appear at a fundraising dinner or a campaign rally on the incumbent's behalf.

Through skillful campaigning and service to constituents over the years, members of Congress have been able to develop strength at the polls that is unconnected with their party's programs or their voting records. Ironically, recent research reveals that the behavior of voters is almost unaffected by the policy positions of candidates. Factors like conscientiousness, hard work, and a "**down home**" style weigh more heavily at the polls than does a member's legislative record.

> A **"down home" style** is a manner conveying an impression of frankness, concern, and friendliness to the voters in a candidate's district.

Mayhew's Analysis. Political scientist David Mayhew agrees with the widely held view that reelection is a congressperson's chief goal. Mayhew focuses on three activities announcing federal allocations or programs directly benefiting their own states or districts) enable members to take credit publicly for governmental action.

Committee and subcommittee hearings provide platforms for position taking, particularly for senior members

> Doing **casework** is helping constituents with their problems.

Continual concern with their public images and the probable effects of their actions at the polls cause members to drag their feet, in Mayhew's view. Legislation is delayed until everyone involved has something for which to claim credit at election time. Special-interest groups, who keep track of laws and insist on action, are rarely satisfied. "Symbolic" laws like the Humphrey-Hawkins Employment Bill—which influence voters

Vice-President Mondale rides in a horse-drawn carriage with Daniel P. Moynihan (D-N.Y.) during Moynihan's campaign for the Senate in 1976.

Recognition is one factor that helps congressional representatives get reelected.

designed to help incumbents reach this goal. These are advertising (getting favorable name recognition); credit claiming (taking credit for governmental actions, especially those that benefit constituents); and position taking (taking a stand on policy questions).

The organization of Congress, according to Mayhew, lends itself perfectly to all three activities. With office staffs from which to recruit campaign workers, congressional resources for doing **casework,** and the franking privilege for free mailings, a great deal of "advertising" is possible. Traditional use of the media (press releases, interviews, news conferences) and the cooperation of the executive branch (which normally permits senators or representatives to be first in

"Well, Senator, we've sharpened your image, and your recognition factor is way up. Unfortunately, they're all against you."

Drawing by Stevenson © 1976; The New Yorker, Inc.

HOW WELL DO AMERICANS KNOW THEIR REPRESENTATIVES?								
	Age Group*			Size of Community*				
	21 -29	30 -49	50 and Over	Under 2,500	2,500- 49,999	50,000- 499,999	500,000- 999,999	1,000,000 and over
Name of Congressional Representative	44	55	54	51	60	55	57	44
Party Affiliation of Congressional Representatives	54	63	64	59	68	62	62	60
Name of State Senator	17	30	31	31	42	22	23	23
Name of State Representative	14	26	28	26	43	16	17	18
Name of Mayor	57	72	73	55	74	76	74	84
Name of County Clerk	18	30	32	44	49	20	11	8

*Numbers are in percent.

and permit position taking by members but have little effect otherwise—are slow to be approved because such bills do not always increase the popularity of the legislators.

One weakness of Mayhew's analysis is that it does not take into account the fact that many members of Congress—especially those from safe seats—care about public policy and want to improve it. Nevertheless, Mayhew's argument that concern over reelection interferes with the work of legislators is probably valid. No seat is so secure that the member who holds it can afford to forget about public relations.

Candidates for the Senate are generally better known than are candidates for the House. They have probably served either in the House or in state office. They are therefore known to at least some of the voters. As a result, the advantage of incumbency in the Senate is somewhat less than the advantage in the House. Incumbent senators, for example, are sometimes beaten by governors running for the Senate—either in their party's primary or in the general election.

Still, the majority of senators who run for reelection are successful. Indeed, members of both houses of Congress are usually reelected, nearly all of them by comfortable margins of votes.

section review

1. What factors are most important in influencing voters to reelect an incumbent congressperson to office?
2. Name three activities that are commonly used by congresspersons seeking reelection.
3. What is a "safe" seat?
4. On the basis of Mayhew's analysis, name the three activities that help incumbents get reelected.

3. THE BACKGROUNDS OF MEMBERS OF CONGRESS

Lawyers have always predominated in Congress. The tie between lawyers and legislators is a natural one. Both professions are concerned with laws. Moreover, lawyers, more than members of other professions, have flexible work schedules. With the help of their partners, lawyers are able to leave their practices for months or years at a time. Today over half the members of Congress are lawyers—47 percent of the House and 65 percent of the Senate. Most of them no longer practice law, although a few still draw incomes from their law partnerships.

Business and banking are the professions

from which the next largest groups in Congress are drawn (29 percent). Education is 12 percent and politics or public service is next with 10 percent. Hardly any members of Congress were manual laborers before they entered politics. (The figures add up to more than 100 percent because some members list more than one occupation.)

The educational level of Congress members is far above the national average. Most members have college degrees. They are also much wealthier than the average citizen. Several are millionaires. Many, however, must rely on their salaries alone for support.

There are disproportionately few women and minority group members in either house of Congress. In 1981 there were only 19 women in the House and 2 in the Senate, even though women constitute half the nation's population. In that same year there were only 16 Blacks in the House and none in the Senate, although Blacks numbered 11 percent of the population.

Senators and representatives come largely from upper- and middle-class families. Their parents have more often been business people or members of professions than laborers or other types of wage earners.

SENATE MINORITY LEADER ROBERT BYRD

Senator Robert Byrd (D-W. Va.), the Senate minority leader, was born Robert Sale. His mother died before his first birthday, and he was later adopted by his aunt and uncle, named Byrd. The family was poor. Byrd grew up in a coal-mining town in Stotesbury, West Virginia. He became the valedictorian of his high school class. At the age of 19 he married Erma Ora James, a miner's daughter.

Senator Byrd began his working career as a butcher in Crab Orchard, West Virginia. "Working hard was not a matter of choice," he says. "It was a necessity." In 1946, having become known to voters by playing the fiddle during his campaign, he won a seat in the state legislature. He went on to be elected to the House of Representatives. In 1958 he made it to the Senate. Up to this point he had never received an undergraduate degree. So while he was in the Senate, he attended law classes at American University at night. In 1963 he graduated with academic honors.

Byrd's early years in Congress reflect his conservatism. For example, when he was chairman of the District of Columbia Appropriations Subcommittee, he attempted to remove from welfare rolls women of whose life styles he disapproved. However, beginning in the late 1960's, he tried to change his conservative approach. He has accomplished this by supporting liberal legislation and campaigning for Democratic candidates of all political beliefs. In 1967 Byrd became secretary of the Democratic Conference. Because of the tedious duties connected with this position, he earned the title "the Senate's garbage man."

Now in his early 60's, Byrd is one of the most powerful people in the Senate. He attributes his success to his experience.

Byrd is a very hard worker. He arrives at his office at 7:30 every morning and works long hours in the Senate. In the evenings he returns to his home in McLean, Virginia, and spends time with his family. In his spare time he likes to jog and play his fiddle for his daughters and grandchildren.

How does Senator Byrd's background differ from that of the typical member of Congress discussed in this chapter?

Two Misconceptions. There are two popular misconceptions about members of Congress. One misconception is that they are much older than the people who elect them. The average age of members of Congress is 48. Because the average citizen of voting age is 43, the age difference between the voters and their representatives is not vast.

The other misconception is that most members of Congress come from rural areas. Actually, most of them were born or grew up in towns or cities in the states or districts from which they were elected.

Prior Governmental Experience. Most senators and representatives have had prior governmental experience. Senators, on the average, have devoted about ten years to governmental service before being elected to the Senate. Often they have served in the House of Representatives before their election to the Senate. Many representatives, as noted earlier, have previously been state legislators or district attorneys.

Members of Congress tend to be much more active than the average citizen is in such service associations as the Rotary and Lions' clubs, the Masons, the Knights of Columbus, and veterans' organizations.

Summary. Whatever their backgrounds, most members of Congress are dedicated to one occupation. They are professional politicians. They are public people who receive great satisfaction from public attention and acclaim. They are sometimes ambitious for higher office—representatives may want to be senators and senators may want to be President—but their main ambitions are to do a good job, gain the respect of their colleagues, and leave some mark on history.

section review

1. What is the most common occupational background of members of Congress?
2. What is the age of the average member of Congress?
3. What are the two misconceptions about members of Congress?
4. What political experience does a senator usually have?

4. THE JOB OF A MEMBER OF CONGRESS

The Congress of 1789 was composed of 26 senators and 65 representatives. The largest state, Virginia, had a population of 950,000. Congressional constituencies averaged about 33,000 persons, enabling a congressperson to know many constituents.

There was no question of a member's commuting back and forth, since sessions were short and distances were great. Congress had comparatively few matters on which to legislate.

The framers of the Constitution expected members of Congress to be citizen-legislators. That is, members were expected to spend a few weeks each year making laws and to devote the rest of their time to a variety of occupations such as farming, banking, and commerce.

Congress Expands. The enormous expansion in the work load of Congress dates from World War I, the depression of the early 1930's, and the recovery efforts following the depression. World War II imposed vast new responsibilities on both Congress and the executive in the conducting of national and international affairs.

QUOTES from famous people

"Most congressmen are neither heroes nor villains, but well-meaning men caught in an almost impossible job. Half the congressman's time is spent on trivial inquiries for his constituents, the other half in a desperate effort to keep up with

the heavy volume of mail, with committee assignments which are far too burdensome, and in an anxious absorption with personal political tactics and fence-mending . . . his thinking is likely to be that of the interest groups with which he has spent his life. Some have charged Congress with being either delinquent or defective, and others have felt that it could do no wrong. But the fact is that Congress is neither an assembly of gods, nor a pack of rascals, but a fairly accurate mirror of the strengths, weaknesses, and tensions of American middle-class life, and the average congressman is only an ordinary man under extraordinary pressures."

Max Lerner

Since the 1940's, letters to members of Congress have been arriving at an ever-increasing rate. More and more constituents write to demand help from their representatives and senators, and many also visit and telephone them in the hope of getting faster service.

Over 25,000 bills are introduced in each two-year session of Congress. Nearly 1,300 of these are enacted into law. Members of Congress must appropriate money to operate the federal government. State and local governments depend on federal grant-in-aid programs. The annual federal budget now approaches $500 billion. Money must be raised by Congress to finance this enormous level of spending. Members must oversee the process by which nearly 3 million federal employees carry out the laws Congress passes.

Today's members of Congress respond to time, work, and financial pressures in ways the eighteenth-century citizen-legislators could not have imagined.

Congress has grown to 100 senators and 435 representatives. The typical member represents more than 500,000 constituents. Congress and its committees are in session for most of the year. Virtually all members, except those from areas within commuting distance, maintain residences in both Washington and their home states or districts.

A Demanding Profession. Congressional service has clearly become a full-time job. Many members work a six-day week of from 60 to 80 hours.

Even the most conscientious members cannot meet all legitimate demands upon them. No matter how hard they try, it is unlikely that they can devote most of their time to the process of legislation—which includes committee hearings, floor debate, and homework on legislative issues—and still serve their constituents effectively.

Each member normally has to supervise a Washington staff, numbering at least 18 for a representative and 25 for a senator. If he or she heads a committee or subcommittee, the number of personnel employed may be much greater. By mail and telephone, each member must also operate a home district office.

Members must greet countless visitors to their offices. They listen to the legislative demands of constituents, lobbyists, and executive branch representatives. They entertain important visitors at lunch or dinner, and they may be asked to arrange tours or other meetings for some of them. Members carry on a steady stream of telephone conversations with constituents, executive branch officials, fellow legislators, and representatives of special-interest groups. Their staffs frequently struggle to gain a moment of their time, either to brief them or to get something approved.

The Ombudsman Function. Legislation and committee work obviously take up a substantial part of a member's time. Somehow, members must also find time to serve their constituents. Part of this service has come to be called the *ombudsman* function. An ombudsman is a government official, especially in Scandinavian countries, who investigates complaints by citizens against the government or its functionaries.

In the United States most people turn to their representative in Congress for this kind of help, and at least 10 percent of a member's time is spent in providing it.

HOW REPRESENTATIVES SPEND THEIR TIME

PERCENT OF WORK WEEK	ACTIVITY	HOURS
25.8%	Attending sessions of the House of Representatives	15.3
12.1%	Legislative research and reading	7.2
12.0%	Committee work on legislation	7.1
12.1%	Answering mail	7.2
8.6%	Handling constituent problems	5.1
7.4%	Visiting with constituents in Washington	4.4
5.9%	Committee work outside of committee meetings	3.5
4.0%	Leadership and party functions	2.4
4.6%	Writing chores, speeches, magazine articles, etc.	2.7
3.9%	Meeting with lobbyists and lobby groups	2.3
3.5%	Working through the media	2.1
99.9%		59.3

Source: *Congress and the Public Trust* James G. Kirby, Jr., and Armin Rosencranz

Members and Their Constituents. Another important congressional function is to serve as a link between the government and the people back home. The typical representative makes 35 trips home every year and spends about 20 percent of the year in his or her district. (Of these trips, 32 are paid for by the taxpayers as part of the member's travel allowance. The costs of the other 3 come out of the member's own pocket.)

In addition to this personal contact, members learn what their constituents want from the letters and telegrams that pour in every day. Congressional offices receive hundreds of letters every week, mostly from constituents. Some senators, particularly those from states with large populations, routinely get over 2,000 letters a day.

Many letters tell a member how constituents view recent or pending legislation or current issues. All constituency mail—even letters that are angry or abusive—receives an answer. The volume of mail jumps when a particular issue captures public attention or when an interest group organizes a letter-writing campaign.

Another kind of letter is the request for assistance. This relates to the ombudsman and service functions mentioned earlier. These functions have become a major responsibility of members of Congress today. Some consider them the basis of all the work that members of Congress perform.

Individual cases—requests for help—vary widely. They can involve the member in obtaining a federal contract for his or her district, interceding on behalf of a veteran, inquiring why a constituent's Social Security check has not arrived, setting up a meeting with a federal official, or arranging a tour of the White House for a constituent.

A special appropriation from Congress enables members to publish and mail to their constituents two newsletters a year. A typical newsletter describes a member's activities and points of view on current issues. A questionnaire may also be included in the newsletter. Congresspeople are kept informed of their constituents' views on certain issues by reviewing their responses to questionnaires.

Many members, particularly representatives, establish office hours during which they are available to constituents when they visit their districts. Constituents are invited to drop in, meet their representative, and discuss any problems they have with the federal government.

A member must find time to make numerous ceremonial appearances and speeches. At graduation time and around the Fourth of July, members are likely to be unusually busy.

Serving as the link between the government and the voters is a basic part of the function of representatives in a democracy. It is through activities like the ones mentioned above that this function is carried out.

Salaries and Allowances. Salaries of senators and representatives passed the $60,000 mark by 1979 and are expected to rise to $75,000 by 1985. Most members of Congress spend all their salary on work-related or campaign-related expenses. Under recent legislation, congressional salaries will be increased automatically as the cost of living rises. This will spare members the embarrassment of voting themselves a pay raise and will reduce the criticism from opponents and angry constituents after each salary hike.

Members now have a very good pension plan. A veteran legislator may retire with as much as $48,000 a year. These provisions were designed to induce senior representatives to retire. They were successful. A record number of older members have retired since the new pension plan went into effect.

Fringe Benefits. Other fringe benefits include 32 paid trips home each year, $67,000 for office-related expenses (excluding office space and telephones), and a paid staff of about 18 people for representatives and 25 or more for senators. Many representatives and senators also use the services of committee and subcommittee staffs.

Each representative is given an office suite of at least three rooms, and each senator has a suite of five. Senior senators and representatives also have "hideaways"—special offices in the Capitol Building, in which they can work uninterrupted by visitors, telephones, and other daily pressures. All members also receive free office space in a federal building in their home states or districts and an allowance for staff to run the local office.

Many members take trips abroad in connection with their committee assignments. These trips enable members to gather information on foreign political and economic conditions. Because some members have abused their travel privileges by using them for recreation rather than research, journalists have had a field day attacking congressional "junketing"—the practice of taking pleasure trips at public expense.

The House and Senate maintain several restaurants, various barber shops and a beauty parlor, some radio and television studios, a medical staff and laboratory, two swimming pools, two gymnasiums, and an indoor paddle tennis court.

Members are entitled to free publication and distribution of their speeches. They also have unlimited free use of the mails except during the 60 days before a primary or general election. The congressional majority and minority offices print, fold, and mail a variety of political items, such as newsletters and questionnaires. The Library of Congress, which is the largest library in the United States, maintains the Congressional Research Center, with 360 specialists who do non-partisan research for members of Congress.

Outside Income. Members of Congress have traditionally supplemented their congressional salaries with income from a variety of sources. This income includes honoraria for speeches, royalties from books, fees from law practices, profits from real estate and other business investments, and income from family businesses and trusts.

Over the years many senators and representatives have been able to earn as much as their official salaries in honoraria and legal fees. Most speaking fees come from colleges and universities. A few are paid by special-interest groups whose legislative interests coincide with those of the congressional committees on which their chosen speakers serve. Because critics regard some of these congressional speaking engagements as improper, journalists have urged that all honoraria be subject to public scrutiny. In 1977 both the House and Senate adopted codes of ethics that required members to make full public disclosure of their personal income and assets—including all the sources of their money and the amount from each source. The codes also limited annual earnings from all outside activities to 15 percent of a member's official salary. Fees for a single speech may not exceed $1,000. Many congressional leaders believe that people in public life should meet high standards of ethical conduct. The new ethics codes have been designed to ensure that they do so.

section review

1. How has the job of a congressperson changed since 1789?
2. What are the principal fringe benefits for members of Congress?
3. What kinds of requests do members of Congress receive from their constituents?

CHAPTER SUMMARY

18

Getting elected to Congress is difficult for a challenger. It is hard to defeat an incumbent whose seat is "safe." Many times, a challenger either must wait for a seat to become vacant or must hope that the incumbent is losing favor among the voters. The high cost of campaigning is another factor that makes victory hard to achieve.

Campaigning for reelection is important to members. It keeps them in touch with the needs and desires of the people they represent. Incumbents possess the resources to help supporters. They have media attention, staff and support services, and the franking privilege. These resources are not intended for use in campaigns. However, if an incumbent has used these resources to communicate with people throughout his or her term in office, the voters are sure to remember this at election time.

Congress has disproportionately few women and minorities. The typical congressperson is a White male, age 48, from the upper middle class. He has a degree in law, banking, or business, prior political experience, and a record of active participation in service associations. He is usually a native of the state or district he represents.

The work load of Congress has expanded greatly over the last 50 years. It now includes more than the increasingly massive legislative responsibility. A member is an ombudsman, a supervisor of a district and Washington staff, and a link between constituents and the federal government. The long hours that a congressperson puts in reflect the job's change from a part-time to a full-time occupation.

REVIEW QUESTIONS

1. List in priority order the tasks of a member of Congress.
2. Describe the typical congressperson.
3. If you were elected to Congress, how would you apportion your time?
4. What do you consider the most important responsibility of a member of Congress?
5. Do you agree with Mayhew's view on how reelection affects the Congress? Give reasons to support your viewpoint.
6. What are the basic provisions of the codes of ethics adopted by Congress? Do you think these are sufficient? Explain the reasons for your position.
7. Distinguish among three types of representation as described in this chapter. Which type should have priority, in your opinion?
8. What effect do you think increasing the number of women and members of minorities in Congress would have on public policy?
9. Explain the inconsistency between the way voters feel about Congress and the way they feel about their own congresspersons.

ACTIVITIES FOR REVIEW

activity 1   In your library or career center, do research on a career in which you have some interest. Compare that career with that of a congressperson in terms of training/education, salary, fringe benefits, retirement, and hours of work.

activity 2   Write to your representative and senator, and ask them to send you their mailings to their constituents. Analyze these mailings and point out any statements that appear to you to have been written for reelection purposes.

activity 3   Write letters to your senator and representative, expressing your point of view on some national issue of importance to you. Analyze their responses and explain either your satisfaction or dissatisfaction with the replies.

activity 4   Do research on your senator's or representative's background. Is he or she a typical member of Congress? If so, how? If not, how?

activity 5   Stage a debate on the following issue: Should senators receive higher salaries than representatives?

political science DICTIONARY

casework—the helping of constituents with their problems. p. 334
"down home" style—a manner conveying an impression of frankness, concern, and friendliness to the voters from a candidate's district. p. 333
frank—the privilege of sending mail postage-free. p. 333
incumbent—a person who already holds an office and is seeking reelection. p. 329
ombudsman—a government official, especially in Scandinavian countries, who investigates citizens' complaints against the government or its functionaries. p. 338

UNIT SUMMARY

A bicameral legislature with co-equal houses was created in the Constitution to give equal representation to both large and small states.

The two houses of Congress have different structures and powers.

The powers of Congress are listed in Article 1 of the federal Constitution.

Congress possesses nonlegislative as well as legislative functions.

Incumbents have a distinct advantage over challengers because of name recognition, access to media, and the franking privilege.

Members of Congress are usually White males from upper- and middle-class backgrounds, with professional training in the law.

Final legislation is affected by many factors: the committee system and seniority, constituent reaction, party goals, national priorities, and the personal values of individual legislators.

Bibliography

Barone, Michael, Grant Ujifusa, and Douglas Matthews. *The Almanac of American Politics, 1976 Edition Who's Who in Congress.* New York: Dutton, 1978.

Congressional Directory, 96th Congress, First Session. Washington, D.C.: Government Printing Office, 1979.

Congressional Quarterly Weekly Report. Congressional Quarterly, Inc. (See each one from 1945 to present.)

Dodd, Lawrence C., and Bruce I Oppenheimer, eds. *Congress Reconsidered.* New York: Praeger, 1977.

Fenno, Richard F., Jr. *Congressmen in Committees.* Boston: Little, Brown, and Company, 1973.

Green, Mark, et al. *Who Runs Congress?* New York: Bantam, 1972.

Oleszek, Walter J. "Congressional Procedures and the Policy Process." *Congressional Quarterly,* 1978.

Polsby, Nelson W. *Congress and the President* (3rd Edition). Englewood Cliffs: Prentice Hall, 1976.

Review questions

1. List the major differences between the House and the Senate in composition, procedures, and powers.
2. Explain how the two-party system operates within the structure of Congress.
3. Explain how having to run for office every two years in the House and every six years in the Senate affects members of Congress.
4. What factors do you believe influence legislators most? Do you agree that these factors should have a high priority? Explain.
5. Explain how Congress and the President check each other.

Skills questions

Using the charts in this unit, answer the following questions:

1. List the states that have the largest number of representatives in Congress.
2. Find the longitude and latitude of North Dakota, California, South Carolina, and your own state.
3. What Senate standing committees are not common to the House standing committees?
4. According to the chart "How Congress Members Spend Their Time," what activities take up the largest percent of the work week?

Activities

activity 1
Select a current member of the House of Representatives and of the Senate. Using the *Congressional Directory, Readers' Guide,* or other current biographical sources, find your selected members of Congress and determine how they compare with the "typical" Congressperson described in this unit in terms of Constitutional requirements and "informal" or traditional requirements such as participation in voluntary associations, previous political experience, education, and occupation.

activity 2
Write a letter to your school principal and class adviser explaining why a trip to the nation's capital would be a valuable experience.

activity 3
By using a written questionnaire approved by your teacher, interview approximately 100 students from all class levels at your school to learn what changes could be made in order to improve life for teenagers in your community. Submit your findings to your Congressional and state legislature representatives.

UNIT 6

HUBERT H. HUMPHREY

Hubert Humphrey was born in the small town of Wallace, South Dakota, in 1911. During his early years he studied to be a pharmacist. Later he graduated from the University of Minnesota and became a professor in its air force training program.

PEOPLE IN
POLITICS

Humphrey's career in politics began in 1945, when he was elected mayor of Minneapolis. At the state level, Humphrey helped unite the Farmer-Labor party with the much weaker Democratic party in the late 1940's. The Democratic-Farmer-Labor party (DFL) attracted scores of talented men and women. In 1948 the DFL swept the Minnesota election, and Humphrey, its candidate, became a United States senator. The DFL has dominated Minnesota politics ever since.

Humphrey became a national figure in 1948 when he led the pro-civil rights forces at the Democratic National Convention. He succeeded in passing a strong civil rights resolution. Throughout his Senate career, Humphrey was a strong civil rights advocate. He was the author and prime strategist of the Civil Rights Act of 1964. Humphrey was deeply involved in shaping farm policy, economic policy, and the foreign aid program. The Peace Corps was his idea.

In the Senate Humphrey served as majority whip from 1961 to 1964. In 1964 President Johnson selected him as his running mate. The Johnson-Humphrey ticket won by a landslide. But the next four years were unhappy ones. The nation was immersed in, and very much divided by, the Vietnamese War. Humphrey swallowed his misgivings and supported the President's policies. In doing so he lost many of his old liberal friends and supporters. Because of this, he narrowly lost the presidency in 1968 to Richard Nixon.

Humphrey returned to the Senate in 1970. There he continued his career as an inspirational leader of the senate, the Democratic party, and the American people.

Even in his last months, Hubert Humphrey never lost his exuberance, his zest for life, or his interest in everything around him. Many national and international leaders, as well as thousands of ordinary people, attended memorial services for Humphrey following his death from cancer in 1978. Vice-President Mondale, who had been brought into political life by Humphrey, observed, "He taught us all how to hope and how to love, how to win and how to lose. He taught us how to live, and finally, he taught us how to die."

THE EXECUTIVE BRANCH (Part I)

OVERVIEW

- The powers and responsibilities of the President have expanded greatly in the last 100 years.

- The Constitution assigns to the President the major responsibility for administering the government and executing the laws.

- Constitutional and practical requirements for the presidency have produced able candidates.

- The President is nominated by his or her political party and elected by the electoral college.

- The President is chief of state, commander in chief, chief executive, chief legislator, director of foreign, domestic, and economic policy, and party leader.

- Management of the vast governmental structure has become more difficult and time-consuming as the nation has become more powerful and more complex.

- In recent years, the President's Cabinet has declined in influence and the White House staff has assumed greater responsibility and authority in executive branch decisions and operations.

19

Presidents and the Presidency

At noon on January 20, 1981, Ronald Reagan placed his left hand on a Bible held for him by his wife Nancy. He raised his right hand and repeated these words of the oath of office administered by the Chief Justice of the United States: "I do solemnly swear that I will faithfully execute the office of President of the United States and will, to the best of my ability, preserve, protect, and defend the Constitution of the United States." These words, first uttered by George Washington and repeated by each of his 39 successors, made Ronald Reagan the fortieth President of the United States.

The powers and responsibilities of the Presidency are extensive. The President is the Chief Executive, commander in chief of the armed forces, party leader, economic planner, sponsor of legislation, and national and world leader. The President directs an administration with some 5 million employees and oversees the spending of $500 billion a year.

The nation continues to ponder the President's power and leadership. What should be the limits on the powers of a President? What are those special qualities of leadership that make certain individuals great Presidents?

CHAPTER PREVIEW

1. THE GROWTH OF PRESIDENTIAL POWER
2. PRESIDENTIAL CHARACTER
3. NOMINATING AND ELECTING A PRESIDENT AND SELECTING A VICE-PRESIDENT
4. TAKING OFFICE

1. THE GROWTH OF PRESIDENTIAL POWER

The eighteenth century was the age of the legislature. Article 1 of the Constitution goes into detail about the powers of Congress. Article 2, which deals with the presidency, is much shorter. The President's specific powers are few: commander in chief, the veto, plus authority to conduct foreign relations, to appoint people to executive and judicial offices, and to take care that the laws be faithfully executed. From this brief constitutional recitation of responsibilities, a powerful institution has grown.

The first President of the United States, George Washington, expanded the President's authority to conduct foreign policy by wielding broad power in that policy arena. Thomas Jefferson, despite his modest view of presidential power, expanded that power during his presidency. He nearly doubled the size of the country with the Louisiana Purchase, even though no specific provision in the Constitution authorized the President to acquire territory. To justify the purchase Jefferson relied on the first sentence of Article 2: "The executive power shall be vested in a President of the United States." The executive power that the Constitution failed to define is considered the inherent power of the President.

Abraham Lincoln strengthened the presidency at the expense of Congress and the Supreme Court. When the Civil War began,

Ronald Reagan is shown delivering his inaugural address. Can you identify anyone else in this picture?

Lincoln, on his own authority, raised and supplied an army, suspended **habeas corpus,** and blockaded Southern ports.

> **Habeas corpus** is the right of every person to be informed in writing by a judge of the legal basis for confining that person against his or her will.

The Modern Presidency. Theodore Roosevelt and Woodrow Wilson were the designers of the modern presidency. Roosevelt believed that the President could do anything not forbidden by the Constitution or by national law. He seized millions of acres of western lands for conservation as national parks and forests. He pursued an aggressive foreign policy, sending American troops and ships to various parts of the world to show the strength of the United States.

Wilson was a forceful President. He often succeeded in bending Congress to his will. During his direction of World War I (1917–18), the President assumed sweeping emergency powers over the wartime economy—powers that the Congress reluctantly agreed to endorse.

Franklin D. Roosevelt (FDR), who led the nation during the height of the worst depression in history and later led it through World War II, expanded presidential power. With the help of Congress, FDR created a host of new federal agencies and programs designed to end the Great Depression and recharge the economy. FDR's economic programs led people to expect the President to play a continuing role in stabilizing the economy.

Work programs were instituted to ease the economic situation during the Great Depression. Here WPA workers make copper utensils.

"I acted for the public welfare, I acted for the common well-being of all our people, whenever and in whatever manner was necessary, unless prevented by direct constitutional or legislative prohibition."

Theodore Roosevelt

During and after World War II, the United States was drawn further into the arena of foreign policy. Confronted with the pre-1941 refusal of Congress to renounce the United States policy of **neutrality** toward the **belligerents** in World War II, FDR negotiated an exchange of unused American warships for British naval bases by **executive agreement.**

Neutrality is the legal status of a nation-state that does not participate in a war. To retain its neutrality a nation-state may not engage in action that could favor one side in a war.

Belligerents are nation-states that are engaged in a war.

Executive agreement is an international agreement made on the President's authority alone.

Presidential power under FDR has often been considered the standard for measuring the use of power by his successors.

Symbolic Leader of the People. Poll takers regularly ask people throughout the world whom they most admire. The President of the United States is usually at or very near the top of the list. The President is not only the head of government but also the head of state. As head of state the President is the symbolic leader of the country. As a symbol the President is larger than life.

Although only a small number of people in the United States can name their representative, senator, or governor, almost all Americans know who the President is. Most of the time the American people approve of what the President does simply because the person is the President. When a President becomes ill, people usually respond with anxiety. When a President dies in office, there is an outpouring of grief and sorrow.

Moral Leader. Presidents are expected to provide a sense of purpose, a vision of the nation's destiny, a tone of moral leadership. Americans want their President to give character to the government, to symbolize national unity, and to be concerned with their welfare. The President symbolizes the American dream.

Americans want and need to believe that the ordinary people they elevate to the presidency are leaders who are committed to doing good. That is how they perceive the presidential candidates for whom they vote on election day. From that point on a President's popular esteem falls, except for times of crisis. At such times most citizens rally to support the President, the symbol of national unity.

section review

1. Which articles of the Constitution deal with the President's powers?
2. Define habeas corpus.
3. What two Presidents are considered the designers of the modern presidency?
4. What is an executive agreement?

2. PRESIDENTIAL CHARACTER

The President presides over the national government. The President is a world leader who exercises extensive powers. But these powers are checked and balanced at many points by Congress, the Supreme Court, and the Federal bureaucracy. Despite the restrictions imposed upon the presidency, personal qualities of style and character play a central role in determining the effectiveness of a President.

Personality. A President's personality may determine how that person reacts to crises. A President who is secure and self-confident may act in one way. A President who needs to appear strong and tough may act in another way. A President's personality may also affect management of the White House and the executive branch. A President's style of authority can open or close channels of communication with associates and aides. The President sets the tone and the boundaries that govern the discussion of policy recommendations. Associates learn quickly whether they can speak frankly or whether they must say only what the President wants to hear.

In order to determine what personality traits make politicians suitable for election to the modern presidency, some political scientists have developed personality profiles of past Presidents that they have used in constructing models of presidential leadership. James Barber believes that a politician who shapes his or her environment and enjoys the give and take of political life is best suited to be President.

According to Barber, Franklin D. Roosevelt, Harry S Truman, and John F. Kennedy were happy, well-adjusted, self-confident, and open people who were capable of growing and developing. By contrast, Woodrow Wilson, Herbert Hoover, Lyndon Johnson, and Richard Nixon lacked self-esteem and strove ceaselessly for power and deference.

Counteracting Images. Presidents try to counteract the images that they project. For example, Eisenhower, a former general, made huge cuts in the military budget. Lyndon Johnson worked to counteract his image as a compromiser on civil rights by sponsoring the strongest civil rights bills in history.

The style and character of a President may determine how well and how democratically that person will use the power of the presidency. A dictatorial style of leadership tends to drain the initiative of the President's aides. It also blocks the flow of information. A democratic style, however, is likely to free the energies of the White House staff and permit them to respond to new situations.

Presidents' and Presidential Candidates' Backgrounds. Most modern Presidents have been professional politicians. They have spent most of their adult lives in politics. Presidents Reagan and Carter are exceptions to this rule. Reagan was a movie actor and president of the Screen Actor's Guild prior to serving two terms as governor of California. Carter served one term as governor of Georgia after a brief career as a state legislator. The four preceding Presidents—Ford, Nixon, Johnson, and Kennedy—were all elected to Congress in their twenties or early thirties. They served there continuously until elevated to the vice-presidency or presidency.

Ronald Reagan, who was 69 at the time of his inauguration, is the oldest person ever to serve as President.

Abraham Lincoln was born in a log cabin, and several recent Presidents—Eisenhower, Johnson, and Nixon—came from poor families. Most of America's Presidents, however, have come from the upper-middle-income groups.

It is not possible to predict a President's actions from that person's social or economic background. FDR and Kennedy were rich, but they sponsored programs to help the poor and the disadvantaged. Hoover and Nixon came from poor families, but they were

BACKGROUND CHARACTERISTICS OF TWENTIETH-CENTURY PRESIDENTS

PRESIDENT	HOME STATE WHEN ELECTED	AGE ON TAKING OFFICE	ANCESTRY	RELIGION	FAMILY BACKGROUND	EDUCATION	OCCUPATION	POLITICAL EXPERIENCE
Theodore Roosevelt	New York	42	Dutch	Dutch Reform	Wealthy, urban	Harvard	Rancher, soldier, politician	Vice-President Governor
William H. Taft	Ohio	51	English	Unitarian	Wealthy, professional	Yale	Lawyer	Cabinet Officer
Woodrow Wilson	New Jersey	56	Scotch-Irish	Presbyterian	Ministry	Princeton	University professor	Governor
Warren G. Harding	Ohio	55	English	Baptist	Farm	Ohio Central College	Newspaper publisher	Senator
Calvin Coolidge	Massachusetts	51	English	Congregational	Small merchant	Amherst	Lawyer	Vice-President Governor
Herbert Hoover	California	54	Swiss-German	Quaker	Farmer, small merchant	Stanford	Engineer	Cabinet Officer
Franklin D. Roosevelt	New York	51	Dutch	Episcopalian	Country squires, wealthy, small town	Harvard	Politics	Governor
Harry Truman	Missouri	60	Scotch-Irish, English	Baptist	Small town, poor	Kansas City School of Law	Politics	Vice-President, Senator
Dwight D. Eisenhower	New York	62	Swiss-German	Presbyterian	Small town, poor	West Point	Soldier	None
John F. Kennedy	Massachusetts	43	Irish	Roman Catholic	Wealthy, business	Harvard	Politics	Senator
Lyndon B. Johnson	Texas	55	English, French, German	Christian Church	Small town, modest means	Southwest Texas State Teachers College	Politics	Vice-President, Senator
Richard M. Nixon	New York	56	Irish	Quaker	Small town, merchant	Whittier College, Duke	Politics	Vice-President, Senator
Gerald R. Ford	Michigan	61	English, Scotch	Episcopalian	Business	Yale	Lawyer	Vice-President, U.S. Representative
Jimmy Carter	Georgia	52	English	Baptist	Small town, merchant	Ga. Institute of Technology, U.S. Naval Academy (Annapolis)	Farmer, engineer	Governor
Ronald Reagan	California	69	Irish, Scotch	Presbyterian	Small town, modest means	Eureka College	Actor	Governor

conservative in their approaches to welfare programs.

Only two Presidents, William Howard Taft and John Kennedy, were born and raised in large cities. Others came from small towns and "made good." Several were able to take advantage of their small-town backgrounds and manners to appeal to the "average" American.

Until recently it was assumed that a presidential candidate had to come from a populous state in the north or west. But the election of Lyndon Johnson from Texas and Jimmy Carter from Georgia seems to have disproved that notion. Recently several of the leading presidential contenders have come from sparsely populated states: Hubert Humphrey and Eugene McCarthy from Minnesota, George McGovern from South Dakota, Barry Goldwater from Arizona, and Edmund Muskie from Maine.

Presidential candidates are usually moderates whom both liberals and conservatives can support. The most recent candidates have been governors or senators. Senators have more opportunities than governors to become knowledgeable about foreign policy. They can leave their posts and travel abroad more easily than governors can. Unlike governors—who raise taxes, cut budgets, and reduce public services—senators are not held accountable to the public for program failures. Former governors, like Reagan and Carter, have one advantage—more free time to campaign for the presidency than senators have.

section review

1. What type of person is best suited to the presidency, according to James Barber?
2. How did Eisenhower counteract his image as a military general?
3. What effect would a dictatorial President have on the people he or she works with?

THE "GREAT PRESIDENTS"

Most historians agree that any list of "great" American Presidents should include five people—George Washington, Thomas Jefferson, Abraham Lincoln, Woodrow Wilson, and Franklin Delano Roosevelt.

Except for Washington, these Presidents were practicing politicians. They worked hard to gain the presidency. Once in office, they granted and took away political favors. They used the influence of their office to persuade or bargain with members of Congress. They knew when to compromise and when to stand firm. These "great" Presidents pursued their policies forcefully to achieve the goals they believed were in the best interests of the country. In the judgment of history, they were largely successful.

Today presidential "greatness" can be measured by additional standards: the appointment of talented people to staff and Cabinet posts, leadership through reason and persuasion rather than through confrontations, and coolness under pressure or in a crisis.

3. NOMINATING AND ELECTING A PRESIDENT AND SELECTING A VICE-PRESIDENT

To be eligible for the presidency under Article 2 of the Constitution, a person must be a natural-born citizen, at least 35 years old, and a resident of the United States for at least 14 years.

Under the Twenty-second Amendment, ratified in 1951, no President can be elected to more than two terms. Vice-Presidents who move up to the presidency after the middle of their predecessors' terms may be elected twice (for a maximum of ten years), but if they become President before the middle of their predecessors' terms, they can be elected only once. Franklin Roosevelt is the only President who served more than two terms. He died a few months after the beginning of his fourth term in 1945.

Franklin Delano Roosevelt served as President of the United States for four consecutive terms, 1933 – 1945. FDR did not live to complete his fourth term or see the end of World War II. He died suddenly on April 12, 1945.

Campaigning for the Nomination. Every fourth year Americans engage in a remarkable ritual. Beginning in the early spring of election years, almost all candidates for each party's nomination for President follow a well-worn route starting in New Hampshire, which has the first primary. They court members of their parties by identifying with their concerns and values. Their campaign workers make great sacrifices, endure the discomforts of wintry weather, eat bad meals on the run, sleep very little, and work very hard, all in the hope of building a bandwagon that will carry their candidate into the White House.

Winning the nomination. In presidential election years 35 states and the District of Columbia hold presidential primary contests during the winter and spring preceding the November election. A good showing in the primaries suggests how candidates will do in November. Jimmy Carter came to national prominence principally by winning several important presidential primaries.

Nominating Conventions. Presidential nominating conventions are scenes of much color, pageantry, and drama. The major television networks devote much of their news programming time to convention happenings, because political parties really come to life at conventions. Ronald Reagan won the 1980 Republican nomination by virtue of his primary victories. But often there are enough uncommitted delegates from the nonprimary states to give the convention the unpredictability and suspense of a race. A leading candidate may have to woo delegates, trade favors in return for votes, and negotiate skillful compromises in order to build a winning coalition.

Each state delegation sits together on the convention floor surrounded by its banners and signs. The chairperson of each state delegation has a microphone that he or she uses to announce the results of the delegation's ballot for President and subsequently for Vice-President. Journalists, broadcasters, technicians, and spectators crowd into the convention centers. Despite the turmoil caused by the participants, the reporters, and the audience, the convention adopts a party **platform** and nominates a President and Vice-President.

> A **platform** is a statement of principles, a program, or a plan that a party pledges its candidates will put into effect after he or she has been elected.

A majority of all votes cast is necessary to nominate a President in each party. If the first ballot does not produce a winner, successive ballots are cast until one candidate receives the required number of votes.

Nominating an Incumbent. Each time in this century that incumbent Presidents have sought their party's nomination, they have been successful—although President Gerald Ford narrowly won nomination in 1976 over his opponent, Ronald Reagan. An incumbent has many advantages over the opponent, including the prestige of the office; control over most factions of the party; the newsworthiness of any presidential activities, announcements, actions; and the recognition that the President's name evokes.

When President Nixon ran for reelection in 1972, he took advantage of his incumbency. His campaign slogan was "Reelect the President," and his campaign was run by the Committee to Reelect the President.

In a presidential election campaign, the candidates need their parties, and their parties need them. A party's success in mobilizing its voters may prove to be its candidate's margin of victory. A popular presidential candidate may sweep in other party candidates on his or her coattails. Most presidential candidates form their own campaign organizations. These organizations coordinate strategies and activities with state and local party organizations.

THE ROAD TO THE PRESIDENCY

CANDIDATE
A candidate takes two main paths to win delegate votes at the party's national nominating Convention. One in States that choose delegates in primary elections, the other in States that choose delegates in party conventions.

LOCAL CONVENTIONS
Precinct or township meetings in a State choose delegates to county conventions, which in turn elect delegates to congressional district and State conventions.

DISTRICT CONVENTIONS
Conventions of congressional districts select the bulk of State's delegates to the National Convention.

PRIMARIES
Voters in primary States choose delegates to the National Convention in two general ways—in some States, by electing delegates directly; in others, by showing a preference for a presidential candidate.

STATE CONVENTIONS
A State convention or committee chooses the State's remaining delegates to the National Convention.

NATIONAL CONVENTIONS
Delegates choose the nominee of each major party. The conventions of both major parties are held in July and August.

ELECTION DAY
Voters, in choosing between candidates, actually pick presidential electors, known as the Electoral College—people expected to support a specific candidate. Election Day is Tuesday following the first Monday in November.

ELECTORAL COLLEGE
Presidential electors meet in State capitals on the Monday following the second Wednesday in December to cast their electoral votes, to be officially counted in Washington on Jan. 6. A majority of electoral votes—270 out of 538—is needed for election as President. The winner will be sworn in on Jan. 20.

Note: The above outline indicates general procedure; variations occur in many States.

During the three months between the convention and election day, the candidates campaign continuously. Exposure in the media (as seen in Chapter 11) is thought to be the most important aspect of the campaign.

The Electoral College System.

Each state has as many electors (and electoral votes) as it has representatives and senators in Congress. The electors of all the states constitute the electoral college. There are 538 members of the electoral college, which is equivalent to the 535 members of Congress plus three representatives from the District of Columbia (whose residents are not citizens of any of the 50 states but have been given special representation by the Twenty-third Amendment).

The history of the electoral college. The framers of the Constitution expected the members of the electoral college to use their discretion in choosing the President from among candidates who led in the popular vote. They intended the runner-up to be the Vice-President.

George Washington was chosen unanimously. John Adams, the second President, was the only person who was actually chosen independently by members of the electoral college. Adams' major opponent, Thomas Jefferson, ran second in the electoral college balloting. Thus Jefferson became Adams' Vice-President. This association led to conflict because Jefferson and Adams were leaders of rival political parties.

The original format of the electoral college ended with the presidential election of 1800. Thomas Jefferson, who was running for President, received 73 electoral votes, and his running mate, Aaron Burr, also received 73 electoral votes. The tie between these two members of the same party had to be settled by the House of Representatives.

In order to prevent such a situation from happening again, the Twelfth Amendment was ratified. From 1804 to the present, presidential elections have been characterized by two or more major parties contending for the presidency; party nominations for President and Vice-President on the same ticket; and people voting for presidential electors committed to particular nominees.

Electors. Article 2 of the Constitution, as modified by the Twelfth Amendment, describes how the President shall be chosen.

According to custom the winning candidate in each state, represented by a slate of party electors, receives all the electoral votes of that state. Because of this "winner take all" system, it is possible for a candidate to win the popular vote but lose the electoral vote—and thus lose the presidency.

For example, suppose candidate A wins 70 percent and candidate B wins 30 percent of the popular vote in both Illinois (26 electoral votes) and Ohio (25 electoral votes); and candidate B wins 51 percent and candidate A wins 49 percent of the popular vote in both Pennsylvania (27 electoral votes) and Texas (26 electoral votes). Candidate A would have a large majority of the total popular vote but would have won only 51 electoral votes, whereas candidate B would have received less than a majority of the popular vote but would have won 53 electoral votes.

This pattern of voting could occur throughout the country, although it has not happened since 1888. In that year President Grover Cleveland ran for reelection against Benjamin Harrison. Harrison lost the popular vote by a significant margin but won the electoral vote and thus was elected President. Interestingly, Cleveland ran again four years later, defeated Harrison in both the electoral and the popular votes, and returned to the White House for a second nonconsecutive term.

The election of 1888 was the third presidential contest in which the winner received fewer popular votes than did the loser. There were two other instances where this occurred. In the election of 1824, Andrew Jackson received the most popular votes but lost to John Quincy Adams when the election was decided in the House of Representatives. In

1876, Republican Rutherford B. Hayes won over his Democratic opponent, Samuel Tilden, even though Tilden received not only a majority of the popular votes but a majority of the electoral votes. Democratic electors from the South were disqualified by an appointed electoral commission that had a Republican majority of one vote. Republican electors were chosen, and they awarded the election to Hayes.

For almost a century the country has been lucky in having electoral college votes confirm the results of popular votes. Nevertheless, the electoral vote rarely matches the popular vote. Jimmy Carter won 41 percent of the popular vote in 1980 but only 9 percent of the electoral vote. Ronald Reagan won 51 percent of the popular vote and 91 percent of the electoral vote.

The electors meet in their state capitals in mid-December to cast their ballots. The candidate receiving the majority of electoral votes in the entire electoral college is chosen President. If no candidate receives a majority of electoral votes, the House of Representatives chooses the President from among the three candidates who have received the highest number of electoral votes. In the selection by the House of Representatives, each state's congressional delegation—no matter how large—has only one vote.

If no candidate for Vice-President receives a majority of the electoral votes, the Senate chooses between the two candidates who received the highest number of electoral votes. The House of Representatives has chosen a President twice, in 1800 and 1824. The Senate has elected a Vice-President only once, in 1836.

Although there has not been a deadlock in the electoral college since 1824, a strong third-party candidate (such as George Wallace, who won 46 electoral votes in 1968) could deprive the two major candidates of a majority in the electoral college and thus shift the election to the House of Representatives.

Because of this possibility, leading critics of the electoral college system have called for direct popular election of the President and Vice-President. They advocate that the electoral college be modified or eliminated by constitutional amendment.

Supporters of the electoral college system contend that a direct popular vote could produce unforeseen political consequences. Conservatives fear that it would benefit liberals. Liberals fear that it would benefit conservatives. Small states fear that large states would benefit. Large states fear that small states would benefit. People of all political persuasions fear that a direct popular vote would encourage minor parties and thereby undermine the two-party system.

Given these fears, it seems reasonable to conclude that the country will coast along with the electoral college system until the winner of the popular vote loses the election.

1976

	Popular Vote	%	Electoral Vote	%
Carter	40,831,000	50.1	297	55
Ford	39,148,000	48.0	240	45
Other	15,780,000	1.9	0	0

1980

	Popular Vote	%	Electoral Vote	%
Reagan	43,201,220	51	489	91
Carter	34,913,332	41	49	9
Other	6,684,074	8	0	0

Presidential Campaign Financing. Presidential campaigns are extremely costly. The total amount spent in the 1980 race has been estimated at $200 million. Television advertising is the largest single expense. In some large metropolitan areas a half hour of prime TV time may cost $250,000 or more. Other large expenses include radio, newspaper, and billboard advertising, as well as staff, travel, direct mailings, and printing.

Until 1976 presidential campaigns were financed entirely from private sources—wealthy individuals; political action committees of special-interest groups (especially labor unions and business groups); candidates' committees organized primarily to raise campaign funds; fund-raising activities such as direct mail solicitations, telethons, and testimonial dinners (whose attendants paid as much as $1,000 each); and the candidates themselves.

These sources are still important. But they are gradually being replaced by the presidential election campaign fund financed by voluntary "checkoffs" on personal income tax returns.

Under the Federal Elections Campaign Act of 1971, as amended in 1975, candidates in presidential primaries may get matching public funds provided that they raise at least $5,000 in contributions of $250 or less in at least 20 states. No person may contribute more than $1,000 to an individual candidate. Candidates who use the fund may spend no more than $10 million on all primary races leading to a general election and no more than $20 million in the general election. However, in 1980 a cost of living increase provision was added giving both Carter and Reagan $29.4 million for their general election campaign.

In the general election, a major-party candidate could choose to raise no money from private contributors but, rather, rely exclusively on public financing. Candidates have thus far refrained from doing so for fear of offending taxpayers.

Minor-party candidates in the general election are entitled to public financing in proportion to their party's vote either in the previous presidential election or in the current election. (In the latter case, of course funds are distributed after the election.) In either case the minor party must have received (or receive) at least 5 percent of the vote.

In 1980 the leading primary candidates and the final nominees—Carter, Reagan, and Anderson—obtained large sums from the Presidential Election Campaign Fund. The fund is administered by the Federal Elections Commission, whose six members are appointed by the President and confirmed by the Senate. The constitutionality of public financing of campaigns was upheld by the Supreme Court in *Buckley v. Valeo* in 1976.

Selecting Candidates for Vice-President. Presidential candidates traditionally choose their running mates. Until the 1960's most candidates used the selection of vice-presidential candidates either to win over important state delegations at presidential nominating conventions or to build winning tickets by naming vice-presidential candidates with strengths different from their own.

For example, northerners choose southerners. In the Democratic Convention of 1960, a candidate from the liberal, urban East (Kennedy) chose a running mate from the conservative, rural South (Johnson).

Since the assassination of President Kennedy in 1963, presidential candidates have seemed to pay more attention to their running mates' fitness to be President than to the need to balance their tickets.

The national conventions allow little time between the presidential and vice-presidential nominations for careful selection. Richard Nixon could not have examined Spiro Agnew's background when he chose

Lyndon Baines Johnson was sworn in by federal Judge Sarah T. Hughes as the nation's 36th President.

him as his running mate in 1968. After Agnew had served as Vice-President for five years, it was revealed that while he was governor of Maryland Agnew had required contractors to pay him *kickbacks,* or illegal fees. He resigned as Vice-President in October 1973.

Jimmy Carter was not subject to the usual time pressures because his primary victories guaranteed him the presidential nomination well in advance of the 1976 convention. This enabled Carter to spend many weeks interviewing and closely examining the qualifications of a number of potential vice-presidential candidates before choosing Senator Walter Mondale, a liberal from the Midwest, as his running mate.

In 1980, Ronald Reagan chose George Bush, the runner-up in the Republican primaries, as his running mate. Bush, who had held several high offices in the Nixon and Ford administrations, appealed to the eastern liberal wing of the Republican party.

Succession. The Twenty-fifth Amendment, ratified in 1967, provides for the appointment of a Vice-President in the event of a vacancy in that office. The President nominates an individual who must be confirmed by majority vote of both houses of Congress. This procedure has been used twice—in 1973, when Gerald Ford was nominated to succeed Spiro

Agnew, and in 1974, when President Gerald Ford nominated Nelson Rockefeller to the vice-presidency.

This method allows for a much more careful examination of the nominee (by House and Senate committees) than is possible at nominating conventions. But it makes possible a situation not conceived of by the drafters of the Twenty-fifth Amendment—a nonelected President and Vice-President holding office at the same time.

section review

1. Describe the nominating convention.
2. What advantages does an incumbent President have over opponents?
3. What problems arose when Thomas Jefferson became John Adams' Vice-President?
4. What is the purpose of the electoral college?
5. What was the traditional strategy used for selecting vice-presidential candidates?
6. What is the purpose of the Twenty-fifth Amendment?
7. What is the disadvantage of the Twenty-fifth Amendment?

4. TAKING OFFICE

Between the day of election in early November and the day of inauguration on January 20, a President-elect must choose and appoint Cabinet members and other executives of the administration, become familiar with procedures and policies in the executive branch, and develop a program to guide the administration during the coming months.

No President begins with a clean slate. That person inherits the social and economic conditions confronted by the previous President. If the nation is at war, as it was when both Eisenhower and Nixon assumed office, the new President will not be able to stop the war overnight.

Selecting a Cabinet. During the transition public attention focuses on the President-elect's Cabinet choices. Frequently a President-elect will appoint to the Cabinet a few individuals who played leading roles in the election campaign. The President may seek persons who have demonstrated management capability to head large executive departments like Defense. The secretary of the treasury generally comes from the business and financial world. The secretary of the interior often comes from the West, where the work of the department is concentrated. The Agriculture and Labor departments require secretaries who are acceptable to the communities involved (farmers and labor unions). Members of Congress who are knowledgeable about special subjects may be leading candidates for appropriate Cabinet posts. People with previous service in high-level positions are often considered.

Recent Cabinets have usually reflected the increased influence of women and Blacks in politics. President Carter's original Cabinet included two women—Commerce Secretary Juanita Kreps and Secretary of Housing and Urban Development Patricia Harris, a Black. President Reagan appointed one Black to his original Cabinet—Samuel R. Pierce Jr., Secretary of Housing and Urban Development and one woman—Jean J. Kirkpatrick, ambassador to the United Nations. (The UN ambassador is not officially a member of the Cabinet but is usually given Cabinet rank.)

Personal Style. During the first months of a new administration, before a President has had a chance to influence programs or policies, much attention is usually paid to the personal manner of the President. Almost everything that the President does is newsworthy, because personal style and preferences may reveal that person's values.

For example, during his first few months in office, President Carter did several newsworthy things. He announced that his eight-year-old daughter Amy would attend public school in Washington. He set the White House thermostat at a maximum of 65 degrees to conserve energy. He reduced the number of limousines used by the White House staff. He specified that his grown children who lived in the White House would clean their own rooms. He appointed a triple amputee as head of the Veterans Administration. He conducted a radio program in which the public was invited to ask questions.

The Presidential Context. No matter how much a new President may have read about the presidency, that individual knows amazingly little about the job. It may take a year or longer to learn. Some of the most important decisions must be made when the President is least experienced to make them.

A new President's most trusted advisers are usually people who held positions of major responsibility in the election campaign. They are likely to assume governmental responsibilities, for a President tends to give assignments to those who have proved loyal.

Overconfidence has led to astonishing mistakes following election victories—FDR's attempt to "pack" the Supreme Court (1937), Kennedy's Bay of Pigs invasion (1961), Johnson's decision to escalate the Vietnamese War (1965), and Nixon's Watergate coverup (1973).

Most of the people with whom the President deals—members of Congress, Supreme Court justices, journalists, and representatives of interest groups—held their positions before the President was inaugurated and will retain them after the President leaves office.

The President did not appoint them and so cannot dismiss them. To leave a mark on history, the President must rely on the ability to persuade them and on their sense of responsibility to cooperate with the Chief Executive.

The President learns that a person can do much less than one would think to bring about change. Change depends on the support of Congress and the cooperation of the bureaucracy.

QUOTES from famous people

"People talk about the powers of a President . . . let me tell you something from experience! The President may have a great many powers given to him in the Constitution and may have certain powers under certain laws which are given to him by the Congress of the United States. But the principal power that the President has is to bring people in and try to persuade them . . . that's what I spend most of my time doing. That's what the power of the President amounts to."

Harry Truman

Midway through a President's first term, that person may begin to feel that many programs are stalled. It becomes clear that any necessary action may have to be initiated by the President—relying on the White House staff to carry it through. Priority programs are placed directly within the Executive Office of the President. More and more of the President's time begins to be spent on foreign policy, an arena in which there are fewer people to thwart the President's efforts.

As the fourth year of the President's term begins, the Chief Executive's attention returns to domestic issues. The distribution of social benefits—such as housing programs, educational subsidies, welfare programs, medical benefits, and veterans' programs—becomes essential as the election approaches.

QUOTES
from famous people

"The problems are more difficult than I had imagined them to be. The responsibilities placed on the United States are greater than I imagined them to be, and there are greater limitations placed on the ability to bring about favorable results than I had imagined there to be."

John F. Kennedy

If reelected, the President may devote much of the second term to international events. As this term begins to wane, the media will begin to focus on potential successors. To get the nation's attention, the President may have to resort to summit meetings, foreign travel, and other highly visible activities. Foreign leaders may postpone important negotiations until the next President comes into office. Many legislative programs will probably have to be postponed during a President's last year because most members of Congress will be out campaigning for their reelection.

Persuasion, Public Opinion, and Popularity. Modern Presidents pay considerable attention to public opinion. Public opinion polls are taken almost every week on issues of national importance and on attitudes toward the President. These polls may not stop the President from taking unpopular action, but they are certain to interest the Chief Executive. Abraham Lincoln reportedly said that with public opinion on his side he could do

anything; but with public opinion against him, he could do nothing. All Presidents since Kennedy have held periodic televised press conferences. In these conferences they have communicated their views not only to the journalists involved but also to the American people. The President grants interviews, issues public statements, and communicates with the press corps through the White House press secretary's daily news briefing. The President accepts invitations to speak before sympathetic or influential audiences, relying on the press coverage of the reception to present a favorable image.

From time to time a President will appear on television to inform the public about a major decision or policy. FDR used to address the American people periodically on the radio in his famous "fireside chats." President Carter adapted this same technique to television. In all public appearances a President may inspire confidence by coming across open and relaxed and may lose public confidence by appearing tense and ill at ease.

Public support fluctuates. A President's popularity is usually extremely high when the person first takes office. All modern Presidents have experienced at least one sharp decline in popularity during their tenure. People may expect the President to do more than is possible and are disappointed when their expectations fail to be met. The longer a President is in office, the more likely people are to become dissatisfied. Interest groups grow restive, the President's programs run into trouble on Capitol Hill or within the bureaucracy, and people tend to blame the President when things go wrong.

Still, as discussed earlier, there is a hard core of loyalists—perhaps 25 percent of the general public—who support any President no matter what that person does. They give that support not because of party loyalty or shared political viewpoints but simply because that person is the President—the symbolic leader of the nation.

President Ronald Reagan is shown here meeting with the press to discuss his plans for 1981.

section review

1. How long does it take for a President to become accustomed to the position?
2. Name some of the problems experienced by a new President.
3. How might the fourth year of a President's term be different from the first three?
4. What is the function of a presidential press conference?

CHAPTER SUMMARY

19

The powers and responsibilities of the President have expanded greatly since Washington was inaugurated in 1789. Washington, Jefferson, Lincoln, both the Roosevelts, and Wilson all expanded the President's powers in both domestic and foreign policy.

Great Presidents share an ability to attract talent, to lead through reason and persuasion, and to act effectively under pressure or during a crisis. Due to the increasing influence of the media, especially television, the President serves as a focus of national goals, aspirations, and decision making. The President must provide reassurance in times of trouble and convey a sense of progress and action. The President is seen as a moral leader, above politics and, at the same time, as a "super-politician" who can work effectively with Congress and other decision makers. Personality and character determine a President's effectiveness as a leader.

Constitutional requirements for the presidency are few. The candidate must be at least 35 years of age, a natural born citizen and resident of the United States for at least 14 years.

Presidents have tended to be White males from upper- or middle-class families of Northern European ancestry. In general, Americans want a President who is a happily married, self-made man with a "common touch." Until recently, political scientists believed Americans also wanted the President to be a Protestant from a populous state. Most Presidents have been political moderates with previous political experience, usually in the Senate.

Selection of the Vice-President has changed greatly since the first elections. The vice-presidency is now viewed as a major office because of the assassination, death, or resignation of several Presidents. The Twelfth Amendment requires the separate election of President and Vice-President. The Twenty-fifth Amendment provides for the appointment of a Vice-President in the event of a vacancy in that office.

REVIEW QUESTIONS

1. How have the character and powers of the presidency changed since Washington?
2. Do you agree with Barber's analysis of the qualities a good President needs? Explain.
3. Should the electoral college system be modified or abolished? Why or why not?
4. What roles have the media—especially television—played in the election of Presidents and the administration of the presidency?
5. How has the office of Vice-President changed since 1960?
6. According to the authors, what qualities do great Presidents have in common? What would you add to the list? Why?

7. What is the role of the political party in the selection and election of a presidential candidate?

8. What presidential campaign reforms have been instituted in the last decade? Why do you think these reforms came about?

ACTIVITIES FOR REVIEW

activity 1 Select one of the "great" Presidents and do research on his life. Did he possess all the qualities Barber contends are necessary?

activity 2 Find instances of presidential "grace under pressure" or the lack of it. (Possible examples are Lincoln, upon the secession of South Carolina; F. D. Roosevelt, after the bombing of Pearl Harbor; Kennedy, during the Cuban missile crisis.)

activity 3 Analyze a recent presidential campaign to determine the importance of television in the final outcome. How significant was television? How did it shape and mold public opinion? Did it affect the final results? Why do you think so?

activity 4 Read about televised presidential debates in 1960 and 1976. What role did they play in the final results? How effective were they in revealing the qualities the authors of this text say are necessary for effective leadership?

political science DICTIONARY

belligerent—a nation-state that is engaged in a war.   p. 351

executive agreement—an international agreement made on the President's authority alone.   p. 351

habeas corpus—the right of every person to be informed in writing of the legal basis for his or her confinement.   p. 350

kickbacks—the covert return of portions of payments received because of prior agreement or coercion.   p. 361

neutral—legal status of a nation that does not actively participate in an armed conflict.   p. 351

platform—a statement of principles, or a program or plan that a party pledges its candidates will put into effect after election.   p. 356

20

The Office of the President and Vice-President

The American presidency is probably the most powerful office in the world, not only because the United States is extremely powerful, but also because its President is given a unique combination of powers. The President may play a decisive role in foreign and military matters and in domestic emergencies. When acting in those areas, the President enjoys broad popular support.

The President's powers are derived from the Constitution, congressional authorizations, customs, and precedents (the acts of former Presidents). The powers of the President include executive powers, foreign relations powers, military powers, legislative powers, and judicial powers.

The flow of power to the President seems to be slowing down. The Vietnamese War and the Watergate scandal have made many people wary of presidential power. Widespread opposition to Johnson's war policies forced him to reverse his decision to run for reelection in 1968. Nixon was forced to resign in disgrace in 1974. Future Presidents may learn important lessons from recent history about the limits of presidential power. Nevertheless, much of what the President does may not be done by anyone else. As Lyndon Johnson used to say, "I'm the only President you've got."

CHAPTER PREVIEW

1. FUNCTIONS OF THE PRESIDENT
2. IS THE PRESIDENT TOO POWERFUL?
3. THE VICE-PRESIDENT'S DUTIES

1. FUNCTIONS OF THE PRESIDENT

It is possible to classify the President's many functions. The six functions or roles that seem most important are those of chief of state, commander in chief of the armed forces, director of foreign policy, chief executive, chief legislator, and director of domestic policy.

Chief of State. As chief of state, the President bestows medals on the nation's heroes, unveils monuments, and receives foreign dignitaries. The President tosses out the first baseball of the season, buys Christmas and Easter seals, and serves as honorary president of the Red Cross. As chief of state, the President also pays tribute to Washington and Lincoln on their birthdays, lays a wreath at the Tomb of the Unknown Soldier on Memorial Day, and congratulates astronauts for their feats in outer space.

The functions of the chief of state are symbolic of the President's leadership of the nation.

Commander in Chief. The Constitution designates the President as commander in chief of the armed forces of the United States. Congress has the constitutional authority to declare war, to tax for the common defense, to raise and support armies, and to provide and maintain a navy. But Congress has never declared war except at the request of the President. By contrast, the President has often sent troops, planes, and warships to various parts of the world without first seeking the permission of Congress.

The *Federalist* papers justify the President's broad powers over the armed forces and foreign policy on the grounds of unity (a single executive compared with two houses of Congress), secrecy, superior sources of information, decisiveness, and speed. Most

As head of state the President's responsibilities are diverse. Here President Kennedy throws the first ball at the opening of the 1963 baseball season.

people believe those justifications apply with even greater force today.

Full-scale declared wars either have been started by Presidents who brought about the conditions of war, or they have resulted from Presidents' responses to belligerent acts against the United States. Some of those responses involved asking Congress for declarations of war (the War of 1812 and World Wars I and II are examples).

The power to create conditions of war was demonstrated by President Polk, who ordered American troops into disputed border territory in 1846. When Mexico resisted Polk told Congress that war existed because of that resistance. Congress then formally declared war on Mexico. In 1898 President McKinley dispatched the battleship *Maine* to Cuba (then a Spanish possession). The battleship was blown up, and then Congress responded to the resulting war fever by declaring war against Spain.

Lincoln was faced with a condition of war when the Confederates opened fire on Fort Sumter. He acted swiftly to meet the emergency. Believing that Congress would only hinder the mobilization for war, Lincoln did not call it into session until ten weeks after the Civil War began. During those ten weeks he readied the militia, enlarged the army and navy, summoned volunteers for service, spent unappropriated money, used his own friends to dispatch money from the treasury to pay arms and ammunition makers, censored the mail, imprisoned persons of suspected loyalty, suspended habeas corpus, and blockaded Southern ports. Lincoln recognized that he was exceeding presidential authority, but he justified his excesses "under what appeared to be a popular demand and a public necessity, trusting then as now that Congress would readily ratify them."

In wartime political power is centered in the President. The President makes secret agreements with foreign leaders, decides how to spend the vast sums appropriated by Congress, and directs the overall strategy of the war. There is a strong push for the nation to close ranks in wartime. Even leaders of the minority party ordinarily will not obstruct a President's war program. During World War II Congress authorized the President to ration food, regulate wages and prices, and control war-related industries.

In 1794 President Washington led federal troops to suppress the Whiskey Rebellion in western Pennsylvania. No President since Washington has actually commanded troops in battle. But all wartime Presidents have been involved in military strategy. Lincoln visited the battlefields to talk things over with his generals. Truman decided to drop the atomic bomb.

The power of the commander in chief implies the power to remove field commanders. Accordingly, Lincoln removed several generals during the Civil War.

Undeclared Wars and Other Military Action. In 1798 President Adams ordered the American navy to fire on French vessels that were interfering with American merchant ships. Adams carried on an undeclared war with France between 1798 and 1801. That action was supported by Congress. Congress passed at least 20 laws to encourage Adams' response to hostile foreign action.

Since that time Presidents have ordered the armed forces into more than 150 separate military actions. Some lasted minutes. Others, like the Vietnamese War, lasted many years. Although most of those military actions were supported by Congress, all were taken on the President's authority as commander in chief.

President Franklin Pierce demonstrated the President's power to threaten a sovereign nation when he sent a naval squadron to open Japan to the West in 1854. President McKinley sent 5,000 American troops to China to help suppress the Boxer Rebellion against foreigners. Theodore Roosevelt, William Howard Taft, and Woodrow Wilson sent American forces into Mexico and countries in the Caribbean. They even installed provisional governments without authorization from Congress.

In 1941 Congress came within one vote of disbanding the American army. FDR could not have expected Congress to support his peacetime defense of British ships against German submarines in the North Atlantic. FDR chose to ignore congressional opposition to American involvement in World War II. As commander in chief he ordered the navy to escort British convoys of goods and arms across the Atlantic and to torpedo any ships that attacked those convoys. On his own authority Truman ordered American troops to resist the North Korean invasion of South Korea on June 25, 1950. Eisenhower relied on presidential authority to send 14,000 troops to Lebanon in 1958. He also delegated authority over foreign security operations to the Central Intelligence Agency (CIA) throughout his administration. The CIA helped overthrow

President Franklin Roosevelt (seated center) discusses military war strategy with two of his naval commanders. What role is he exercising?

governments in Iran (in 1953), Guatemala (1954), and Laos (1959), and it organized an expedition of Cuban refugees against Castro's rule in Cuba (1960).

Acting to ensure domestic peace, Eisenhower sent federal troops to Little Rock, Arkansas, in 1957 to help enforce school desegregation. Kennedy did the same in Montgomery, Alabama, five years later. Kennedy's military actions included ordering a naval blockade of Cuba in 1962 and sending 10,000 military advisers to Indochina (Vietnam, Laos, and Cambodia).

Johnson sent troops to the Dominican Republic in 1965 to protect American lives and interests. His critics maintained that the troops were sent to intervene in the country's domestic affairs. They also maintained that troops were often sent abroad to prevent the take-over of a country by a party or group that would end America's influence there.

Johnson and Nixon relied on the inherent powers of the presidency and on their powers as commanders in chief to fight and expand the war in Vietnam from 1964 to 1974.

Checks and Balances. An international crisis almost always brings the people—and Congress—together to back the President. Any President who wants to enlist congressional support in such circumstances would undoubtedly succeed. In practical terms, Congress acts to check the President when things go wrong and when popular opposition grows.

In the wake of public disillusionment with the Vietnamese War, the War Powers Act was passed in 1973. Had the War Powers Act been in effect in 1941, it would have prevented President Roosevelt from responding to Hitler's attacks on British ships. But it could not have prevented President Johnson from escalating the war in Vietnam, because Congress supported that war in its early stages.

President Nixon, however, did encounter growing congressional opposition to his war policies. As the Vietnam war was drawing to a close, Congress began using its appropriation powers and rejected further war spending.

Remembering the bitter conflict over the war in Vietnam and the threat Nixon posed to the preservation of constitutional government, future Presidents may well decide to consult Congress before, not after, they commit troops abroad. In 1980, President Carter was criticized for not consulting Congress or America's foreign allies in his unsuccessful military attempt to rescue American hostages in Iran.

The President's ability to persuade through consultation, and Congress' willingness to support the President during a crisis, should not only strengthen the system of checks and balances but should also enhance the commander in chief's power to fulfill the military commitments of the United States.

Director of Foreign Policy. As long ago as 1823, President Monroe demonstrated the President's power to make foreign policy. This was done when he proclaimed the Monroe Doctrine. With the constitutional power to deal with foreign nations and the power as commander in chief, the President dominates American foreign policy.

The President's dominant position was upheld by the Supreme Court in the Curtiss Wright decision in 1936. That case described the President's "exclusive" power as "the sole organ of the federal government in the field of international relations—a power which does not require as a basis for its exercise any act of Congress."

Since World War II the United States and the Soviet Union have been the world's leading powers. Both countries have very large military forces and weaponries. Both countries have alliances, treaties, agreements, and aid programs with many countries. The direction of the United States' vast network of commitments around the world belongs to the President.

In foreign policy, unlike domestic policy, there are few influential interest groups. The general public and most members of Congress are much less interested in foreign affairs than in domestic matters. Lack of interest and knowledge make most people willing to yield to the President in foreign policy, especially when the President seems to base action on information and intelligence.

Noted political scientist Aaron Wildavsky asserts that Franklin Roosevelt, Truman, Eisenhower, and Kennedy prevailed on every foreign policy issue. By contrast, only 40 percent of all presidential proposals dealing with domestic policies were passed by Congress during the presidencies of Truman, Eisenhower, and Kennedy. Presidential failure and congressional denials on foreign policy were more common during the 1970's. But their overall success is still impressive.

The State Department is exclusively concerned with foreign policy and relations with other countries. President Eisenhower relied on his secretary of state, John Foster Dulles, and gave him broad authority to conduct negotiations with other countries. He followed Dulles' judgments and recommendations with few exceptions. Presidents Nixon and Ford relied on Secretary of State Henry Kissinger's diplomacy and advice.

Other Presidents, such as FDR and Kennedy, preferred to conduct their own foreign policies. FDR frequently bypassed the secretary of state to consult with his subordinates in the State Department. He also used members of the White House staff as representatives to foreign leaders and conducted extensive correspondence with some leaders. Kennedy relied on his special assistant for national security affairs. When he wanted advice on foreign policy, he relied on his secretary of defense and his brother, the attorney general, as much as or more than he relied on his secretary of state.

A President's personal style, interest in foreign policy, and capacity for diplomacy determine how that administration will conduct foreign relations.

By tradition the President is responsible for initiatives in foreign policy. Congress may act in a negative way by withholding appropriations and treaty approvals and by trying to limit the President's war-making powers. But the President, not Congress, has command over two major instruments of foreign policy making: *the diplomatic service*

Secretary of State Henry Kissinger (right) was valued by two Presidents for his expert advice. Here Kissinger, seated with President Ford is discussing Middle Eastern affairs.

—ambassadors and their staffs—and the armed forces.

When there is widespread disagreement over the President's foreign policy, Congress can play a major role by offering a forum for those who disagree. The possibility of such criticism may sometimes be enough to restrain a President from taking a particular action. A President's policies are most effective when the nation seems to be united.

Of course, American foreign policy is not created by the President only when problems arise. The President is bound by two centuries of treaties, agreements, traditions, rules, and influences. The interests of the State Department, the Defense Department, the Joint Chiefs of Staff, and the CIA must also be taken into account. Each department and agency tends to support policies that will give it greater influence in executing foreign policy. The President must decide which combined recommendations will serve the nation's interest.

Recognition. The President may grant diplomatic recognition to or withhold it from foreign governments. Prompt recognition of a new government may help sustain it. President Truman recognized the new state of Israel within hours after its creation in 1948. This act gave an important boost to the young nation, which was being attacked on all sides by opposing armies. Over the years Presidents have chosen not to recognize some governments, such as those of the Soviet Union, the People's Republic of China, and North Korea. Withholding recognition means the suspension of diplomatic relations, trade, and tourism.

Treaties. Until FDR's presidency began in 1933, most understandings with foreign governments were formalized into treaties. The constitutional requirement that two thirds of the Senate advise on and consent to treaties has sometimes affected the ratification of a treaty that a President considered essential to conducting foreign policy. After World War I President Wilson helped draft the Treaty of Versailles, which created the League of Nations. Although two thirds of the Senate would have approved the treaty without the League of Nations provision, President Wilson refused to separate it from the rest of the treaty. The Senate voted 49 to 35 in favor of the treaty. But because that was 7 votes short of the necessary two thirds, the treaty, including the League of Nations provision, was rejected.

Despite the Senate's exclusive vote in the ratification process, the President is usually wise to consult House leaders. Without the House's willingness to appropriate funds, most treaties could not be carried out. George Washington learned that the House could be sensitive when it was not consulted about a treaty. When Washington failed to inform the House about the circumstances surrounding the Jay Treaty (1795), the House decided not to appropriate funds for the treaty. When Washington persisted in withholding documents concerning the treaty, the House threatened to impeach him. Washington's successors have been more careful of the House's sensitivity.

Executive agreements, which the Supreme Court holds to have the same authority as treaties, may be made by the President without the requirement of consultation. Under this power President Franklin D. Roosevelt recognized the Soviet Union in 1933 and exchanged American destroyers for British naval bases. When FDR and Churchill met at sea in 1941 to draft the Atlantic Charter, Churchill consulted his Cabinet 30 times by telegraph. FDR, however, acted entirely on his own authority and did not consult Congress.

Executive agreements are much more common today than treaties. When the government of Israel, at the President's urging, makes a concession to Egypt, it is likely that the President—by executive agreement—has

THE CONVEN-IENCES OF THE PRESIDENCY

The framers of the Constitution wanted the President to be an elected statesperson who could exercise considerable power and act above parties and groups. The framers knew that the President would have to have certain privileges because of the nature of the office. However, these privileges were not expected to be lavish displays of wealth. It was believed that such excesses would remind the people of the monarchy from which they had just freed themselves.

George Washington exercised his powers wisely. He seemed to reassure most leaders of the Republic that the Chief Executive would not misuse the powers of the office. Thomas Jefferson was even less authoritarian than Washington. Even after his inauguration Jefferson did not object to waiting in line for a place at his boardinghouse table. Most other Presidents have not been so modest.

Even though the White House is an imposing structure, it was neither guarded by police nor surrounded by a fence until 1913. Before that time, anyone who wished to walk on its lawns could do so. Things are very different today. A huge fence wired with electronic detectors surrounds the White House. Secret Service agents patrol the entire area. They check everyone who enters and leaves the White House grounds. The Oval Office is surrounded by 2-1/2 inch-thick bulletproof glass. The President moves in and out of the White House by helicopter or with an armed motorcade.

Besides these elaborate security precautions, the addition of regal formalities, special services, and luxurious accommodations have permanently altered the simpler presidency of the past. On official occasions or visits, for example, a 21-gun salute is sounded in the President's honor. At the President's disposal are a fleet of jet airplanes, chauffeured limousines, and uniformed guards.

The President receives an annual salary of $200,000 plus a $50,000 tax-free expense allowance. The presidential family resides in the White House, which is a 132-room mansion on 18 acres. The White House is provided with a swimming pool and a movie theater. A weekend house at Camp David, in the Maryland mountains, and a 60-foot cruiser are also available to the President. The President has a paid personal staff, including a doctor, a barber, and a cook.

The President can talk by telephone or wireless radio to any leader in the world. A special telephone hookup, called the hot line, enables the President to talk almost instantly to the leader of the Soviet Union. Whenever the President travels this communications network also goes.

given the Israeli prime minister guarantees to offset the concession's effects. There were as many executive agreements concluded between 1975 and 1980 as there were in the first 150 years of United States history.

In the early 1970's Senator J. William Fulbright, (D-Ark.) who was the chairman of the Senate Foreign Relations Committee, noted that most important understandings with foreign governments were negotiated through executive agreements rather than treaties. He noted, "We get many treaties dealing with postal affairs . . . recently we had an extraordinary treaty dealing with the protection of stolen art objects. These are treaties. But when we put troops and take on commitments in Spain, it is an executive agreement."

Secrecy and National Security. Since World War II, America's intelligence-gathering networks have grown. Secrecy on matters related to war and national security is thought to be essential in wartime. With the agreement of each President since 1945, wartime conditions of secrecy have been imposed—in the name of national security—on most matters dealing with foreign and defense policy. Documents are classified with such labels as "secret," "top secret," "Q [atomic] clearance," and "President's eyes only."

This system has produced at least two effects. First, Presidents have started believing that their information is reliable and that decisions based on such information can withstand public challenge. Second, only people with security clearance can take part in decision making that affects national security. This provision screens out most members of Congress, the press, and other potential critics.

One loophole in this tight system of secrecy is the *"executive leak"* whereby information is published against the President's wishes. The leaker may act from a variety of motives, ranging from patriotism to self-interest.

The most famous leak in recent times was Daniel Ellsberg's release to the press of the top-secret Pentagon Papers. Ellsberg was a former Defense Department consultant. These documents revealed that the American people had been told a series of untruths about the Vietnamese War. The Supreme Court upheld the freedom of the press to publish these documents and struck down the executive branch's claim that the documents were *privileged* (not subject to disclosure) on national security or any other grounds.

Some leaks may signal the President's intentions and thus weaken his negotiating position with a foreign power. Other leaks may merely embarrass the administration and delight its political opponents. Presidents are offended by leaks, although they vary widely in their responses to them. Nixon created the "Plumbers" unit to plug up leaks within the White House staff. This unit played a major part in the Watergate scandals.

Theodore Sorensen, counsel to President Kennedy, observed that "secrecy adds to a President's aura of knowing everything, shrouds his mistakes, protects his surprises and deters his critics." In Sorensen's view secrecy prevents well-informed debate. Whatever the disadvantages, leaks act as checks on excessive presidential secrecy and ill-advised plans by bringing them out into the open.

Executive Privilege. Throughout history Presidents have argued that their communications were entitled to remain private and should not be examined by Congress. This claim is known as *executive privilege.*

President Nixon's claims of executive privilege exceeded the bounds of what previous Presidents had claimed. He argued that executive privilege prevented any member of his staff from testifying about anything, even criminal matters. Nixon's sweeping claims were struck down by the Supreme Court in the landmark case of *United States* v. *Nixon.* The Court acknowledged the privileged nature of presidential communications, especially those dealing with national security. But the Court found that the privilege must yield to the need for criminal evidence. Nixon was then required to turn over to the special Watergate prosecutor tapes of conversations in his office.

Executive privilege is a vague area that is likely to bring Presidents into conflict with other branches of government.

Chief Executive. The Constitution empowers the President to "take care that the laws be faithfully executed." This power enables the Chief Executive to control the executive branch of government.

The executive branch is composed of almost 3 million civil servants, and 2 million members of the armed forces. Only about 3,000 of the 3 million civilian employees are exempt from the civil service system. They therefore are appointed by the President. Fewer than 600 of these appointees are actually involved in policy making at the executive level.

All modern Presidents have struggled—with only limited success—to get the executive departments to do what they wanted. President Kennedy asked the State and Defense departments many times to negotiate for the removal of United States nuclear missiles in Turkey. The departments did nothing.

Presidents follow different strategies in filling executive posts and in establishing control over the executive branch. Some Presidents, including Truman, Eisenhower, Ford, and Carter, have been inclined to select their Cabinet members with considerable care. They then delegated to them the responsibility for appointing their subordinates. Others, including Kennedy, Johnson, and Nixon, have played active roles in appointing undersecretaries, assistant secretaries, and other sub-Cabinet officials. They assumed people appointed directly by them would be loyal to them and to their policies.

Appointees are chosen for at least one of four reasons: 1) They are personally loyal to and have worked with the President in the past; 2) they represent important segments of the President's constituency, including the President's party; 3) they have proved their capabilities in certain areas; or 4) they are highly competent professional bureaucrats who have moved up through the ranks.

Sometimes the President must use considerable influence to persuade highly qualified men and women to accept federal appointments. If they are lawyers or business leaders, they must take cuts in pay. They must disclose their financial holdings and may be compelled to sell those holdings, since such holdings may affect the way they carry out their federal responsibilities. The Senate usually respects the President's executive branch appointments. But some of the nominees have been rejected. In 1959 President Eisenhower's nominee for secretary of commerce was rejected by the Senate when a senior senator claimed he personally disliked the nominee. More recently, President Carter's choice for director of the CIA was withdrawn at the nominee's request after several senators promised a fight over his possible confirmation.

Senate approval is unnecessary when the President decides to fire an appointee. This kind of decision is often politically difficult for the President to carry out, especially if the individual represents an important party faction or interest group. Some officials have been in office so long and have so many friends in Congress that a President might lose political support by trying to remove them. J. Edgar Hoover, the controversial head of the FBI for almost 50 years, enjoyed this kind of job security, although a number of Presidents thought about replacing him.

Members of regulatory commissions and agencies are appointed by the President for fixed terms of office. They may not be removed during those terms. Congress intended for these commissions to be independent of the Chief Executive.

The most important appointees of any administration are the Cabinet members. The *Cabinet* is simply a term used to designate the heads of the 13 executive departments. As Chief Executive, the President regularly consults with each Cabinet secretary. The President may choose to consult with the Cabinet collectively, although the last one to hold regular and frequent Cabinet meetings was Eisenhower.

THE EXECUTIVE DEPARTMENTS AND THEIR RESPONSIBILITIES

DEPARTMENT AND YEAR ESTABLISHED	RESPONSIBILITIES
Agriculture (1889)	**Promotes and Assists Agriculture** 1) Aid to farmers 2) Inspection of foodstuffs 3) Rural development 4) Food stamp program 5) Soil, forest, and water conservation 6) International trade
Commerce (1903)	**Promotes Industry and Business** 1) International trade 2) Assistance to depressed areas 3) Weather Bureau 4) Census Bureau 5) Oceanic and Atmospheric Administration 6) Merchant Marine
Defense (1947)	**Provides for the National Defense** 1) Joint Chiefs of Staff 2) Army, Navy, Air Force, Marines 3) Overseas troops and military bases 4) Military aid programs 5) Research, design, and developing of weapons 6) Arms sales
Education (1979)	**Promotes Aid to Education** 1) Aid to elementary and secondary schools 2) Aid to colleges and universities 3) Educational research 4) Education of military dependents abroad
Energy (1977)	**Implements a Coordinated National Energy Policy** 1) Allocating oil and natural gas supplies 2) Energy conservation 3) Research and development of alternative energy sources 4) Nuclear weapons and energy research
Health and Human Services (1979)	**Promotes Human Concerns** 1) Public health 2) Welfare 3) Social Security Administration 4) Special programs for the elderly, children, handicapped 5) The Headstart program
Housing and Urban Development (1965)	**Provides for Housing and Community Development** 1) Housing programs 2) Urban restoration 3) Mortgage insurance 4) Relief from natural disasters

THE EXECUTIVE DEPARTMENTS
AND THEIR RESPONSIBILITIES
(CONTINUED)

DEPARTMENT AND YEAR ESTABLISHED	RESPONSIBILITIES	
Interior (1849)	**Is Custodian of the Nation's Resources**	
	1) Leasing of federally owned land 2) National Park Service 3) Bureau of Indian Affairs	4) Mining technology and safety 5) Fish and wildlife conservation
Justice (1789)	**Provides Lawyers for the Government and the People**	
	1) Administration of federal prisons 2) Civil Rights Division 3) Antitrust Division	4) FBI 5) Immigration and naturalization
Labor (1913)	**Promotes the Welfare of American Wage Earners**	
	1) Administers federal labor laws 2) Job training 3) Unemployment insurance	4) Collective bargaining 5) General economic policy
State (1789)	**Implements Foreign Policy**	
	1) Foreign Service (ambassadors, embassies) 2) Economic aid	3) International trade 4) Negotiates treaties 5) Cultural exchanges
Transportation (1966)	**Implements Federal Transportation Policy**	
	1) Federal highway system 2) Urban mass transit 3) Air safety standards	4) Coast Guard 5) Experimental programs
Treasury (1789)	**Implements Monetary and Economic Policy**	
	1) Taxes (Internal Revenue Service) 2) Minting of coins, currency, stamps 3) International trade	4) Secret Service 5) Customs Service 6) Alcohol, tobacco, and firearms control

At various times Presidents have given certain senior officials Cabinet rank. The director of the Office of Management and Budget and the ambassador to the United Nations are among those who now have Cabinet rank. In recent years the Vice-President has attended all Cabinet meetings.

Patronage. At one time Presidents appointed all federal officials, including post masters. In practical terms, most federal appointees in local areas were made by Congress or state and local party officials. These posts are now mostly covered by civil service regulations. Selection is based on merit rather than patronage.

Patronage still survives. Today favors are more often in federal programs and public works rather than jobs. President Johnson was quite frank about exchanging political favors for political support. Johnson chose to reward several of his supporters by awarding large model-cities grants to 63 cities. These cities received grants only because they were represented by influential members of Congress. Smithville, Tennessee (population 2,300), received one such grant. Smithville was represented by the chairman of the House Appropriations subcommittee in charge of model-cities grants. Johnson also awarded a grant to Pikeville, Kentucky (population 5,000). Pikeville's representative was the chairman of the House Education and Labor Committee, which rescued LBJ's antipoverty program.

As head of the executive branch, the President may favor members of Congress by ordering funds to be spent in a member's district, locating government installations in a member's district, and helping cooperative members at campaign time.

Presidents Kennedy and Johnson always announced local federal appointments and projects through Democratic members of Congress or Democratic party officials. Democrats in Congress were ruffled when President Carter was slow in resuming this practice. He soon learned to give them advance notice of any public announcements affecting their states or districts. Kennedy's special assistant for congressional relations arranged for members of Congress to take the credit for federal grants and contracts in their districts. He also managed to blame the federal bureaucracy when expected grants and projects did not materialize.

Executive Orders. President Truman used an executive order to integrate the armed forces. Kennedy distributed surplus food to the poor by executive order, and LBJ issued executive orders guaranteeing minorities equal access to federally supported housing and jobs.

Congress lets the executive branch spell out how laws are to be implemented. The details are specified in rules and regulations issued under executive orders.

Impoundment. President Nixon impounded more than $10 billion that Congress had appropriated for a wide variety of domestic programs. These impoundments were challenged in the courts. Nixon was judged to have overreached his authority. The Courts held that the President's obligation to carry out the laws required that he spend funds appropriated by acts of Congress. Following these Court decisions, Congress passed a law forbidding impoundment unless it specifically granted an exemption.

Reorganizing the Executive Branch. Under the Reorganization Act of 1949, Congress granted the President power to establish, rearrange, and eliminate executive agencies. This power was subject to Congress' right to reject any plan within 60 days of its issuance.

It takes an act of Congress to abolish, create, or merge whole executive departments or regulatory commissions. Moreover, the President may not abolish any function authorized by statute. Career bureaucrats have independent ties to Congress. They use those connections to ensure that no President will abolish their functions.

One use of the President's reorganizing authority was President Carter's 1979 separation of the Agency for International Development from the State Department and creation of a new International Development Cooperation Agency.

Chief Legislator. Presidents Washington and Adams delivered their State of the Union messages in person before Congress. Most nineteenth-century Presidents sent written messages to Congress. Woodrow Wilson restored the practice of delivering these messages personally. Presidents since Franklin Roosevelt have addressed not only both houses of Congress but—because of radio and television—the entire nation.

The State of the Union message, delivered each January, has become a state occasion. At that time, the front rows of the large House of Representatives chamber are occupied by the members of the Cabinet and justices of the Supreme Court. Foreign ambassadors are seated at the side. Senators and senior representatives occupy front seats. Other members of Congress are seated in all parts of the crowded chamber. Special guests, including the President's family, sit in the gallery.

The State of the Union message normally contains outlines of the President's legislative program for that session of Congress. It is followed by the President's budget message and economic report.

Once legislation has been introduced on the President's behalf by members of the President's party in Congress, the President and the presidential staff generally take active roles in persuading members to pass those bills.

Theodore Roosevelt and Woodrow Wilson were the first Presidents to take active roles in recommending legislation and in gaining its passage. Woodrow Wilson re-

marked that if a President does not get the recommended legislation approved by Congress in the first two years, it will not be approved at all.

Franklin Roosevelt was sworn in as President during the depths of the depression. He found that Congress at that time wanted to be led, and he responded vigorously. During the first 100 days of FDR's presidency, Congress passed a host of major programs designed to bring about economic recovery. Throughout his first two terms, FDR proposed legislation and used persuasion to enlist the support of Congress.

Lyndon Johnson took an even more active personal role in securing congressional passage of his Great Society programs. Although history will probably deal harshly with President Johnson's war policies, he will be remembered as a great legislative architect. Johnson had been the majority leader in the Senate and was a master in legislative bargaining and compromise. He seemed to know how to get a hesitant senator or representative to support him.

The rapid growth of popular support for Johnson after Kennedy's assassination, his landslide victory in 1964, his rapport with Congress, the overwhelmingly Democratic Congress swept into office with him, and his own mastery of legislative strategy combined to enact the most ambitious legislative program in 30 years.

How does the President get Congress to support a program? First, the President's program automatically becomes the program of the President's party in Congress. Congressional party leaders tend to be party loyalists as well as practical legislators. Consequently they usually give the President the needed support. Some members of the President's party, who might not be inclined to support a bill, may be won over when a party leader or a member of the presidential staff says, "The President needs your help on this bill." Some legislators are reluctant to incur the President's displeasure. Others hope to receive presidential favors, still others go along out of respect for the presidency. All Presidents since Kennedy have assigned to key members of their staffs the responsibility of maintaining a working relationship with Congress. These members work with their party's leaders in Congress to assess support, identify undecided members, and work out compromise amendments to build a majority.

The President's points of influence with members of Congress include public flattery, White House breakfasts with key members, the pressure generated by constituents and the press in response to a President's public appeal for support, and the threat of a veto. In

Having formerly been an influential and senior member of Congress, President Lyndon B. Johnson was able to institute many new domestic programs during his administration.

"Did The Music Man Say When Our Instruments And Uniforms Are Coming?"

from The Herblock Gallery (Simon & Schuster, 1968)

really tough fights the President may resort to patronage.

The President also has the constitutional power to call Congress into special session. This device was used by President Truman after Congress had adjourned in the spring of 1948. Truman referred to the Republican-controlled Congress as a "do nothing" Congress and called members back to enact needed legislation. Truman was running for President that fall. And his act may have been politically motivated. In any case, he was successful. He was not only elected, but he also brought a Democratic Congress into office with him.

Veto Power.   From Washington's first day in office to the 1980 election, Presidents have vetoed 2,390 bills passed by Congress. The difference between a majority and a two-thirds vote is so great that Congress has been able to override only 92 of the 2,390 vetoes.

Presidents may not veto one part of a bill with which they disagree. They must accept or reject the entire bill. Modern Presidents have frequently used the threat of veto to persuade Congress to change or delete certain amendments. Because the veto is the power to say no, it is of only limited use to a President who wants to enact a program.

Director of Domestic Policy.   In 1921 Congress acknowledged that it needed the President's help in controlling the finances of an expanding national government. Congress created the Bureau of the Budget (now renamed the Office of Management and Budget). This office was designed to help the President prepare an annual budget for the executive branch. Since that time Congress has used the President's annual budget for the executive branch as a guideline for formulating appropriations and tax measures.

The Employment Act of 1946 requires the President to send Congress an annual economic report describing the state of the nation's economy. Under the act the Council of Economic Advisers was created to help the President analyze the state of the economy. Under this act and successive acts of Congress, the President has played a growing role in shaping federal tax policy and in determining the level of federal spending. At critical times Congress has also given the President broad powers over the regulation of wages and prices.

Americans have come to expect the President to initiate action that reduces unemployment and inflation, lowers taxes, and promotes economic growth. Programs to reduce unemployment often require increased federal spending. More spending means more taxes. The very complexity of economic problems tends to give initiation—and power—to the President.

Today all new programs of the federal government must be cleared by the Office of Management and Budget (OMB) before they may be submitted to Congress. OMB is now part of the Executive Office of the President.

Congress, through its committees (especially its budget committees), analyzes the budget. It then tries to reconcile the President's priorities with its own priorities. The Federal Reserve Board also plays a role. The Federal Reserve Board determines how much money will be in circulation at any given time. The chairperson and other members of the Federal Reserve Board are appointed by the President for fixed terms. They may not be removed during those terms. Since the board members' terms do not coincide with the President's term in office, a President may have to work with a board that was chosen by predecessors.

The President influences the economy but hardly controls it. America's economic system is based on free enterprise. For that reason, Congress resists giving the President control over wages and prices in the absence of serious inflation or depression.

Domestic Policy Making. In making domestic policy the President and the presidential advisers are likely to clarify the major issues and decide what can be accomplished. The President then decides how to use the federal bureaucracy, Congress, and public opinion to achieve those policy goals. The President must try to allocate limited federal resources in ways that help the people and groups who most need help—people who are unemployed, disadvantaged, hungry, poor, or sick. Whatever action the President takes or does not take, it will always disappoint some people.

So-called new initiatives in domestic policy generally have been considered before. "Most good ideas have already been thought of," comments political analyst Richard Scammon. "You don't really come into the presidency with a totally new concept. You improve this, polish up that."

Presidents Kennedy and Johnson may be remembered for their domestic achievements in civil rights and for their fights against poverty. Between 1966 and 1976, however, domestic issues were overshadowed by national security issues. Wars and crises help to justify what most Presidents would like to do anyway—leave domestic matters to the bureaucracy.

Presidents get little political credit for tackling such difficult domestic questions as income maintenance for the poor, tax reform, school busing, and clean water and air. Moreover, domestic policy requires coordination with Congress, always a difficult task. Foreign affairs, by contrast, give the President immediate political rewards. This is because the President controls the necesssary resources (the defense establishment) and may act decisively. It is no wonder that domestic policy runs a poor second to foreign policy.

Party Leader. Except for Washington, every President has been the leader of a political party. Most often, the President appoints members of that party to administrative spots. Through appointments and patronage the President tries to reward members of that party for their faithful service during the election campaign.

The President will usually also try to strengthen that party while in office. Sometimes the President will assist that party's candidates for Congress and state and local offices by personal appearances and statements of support. Some Presidents have tried to stay out of party politics and have assigned party responsibilities to their Vice-Presidents. Eisenhower delegated the role of campaigning for Republican party candidates to Vice-President Nixon. When Nixon became President eight years later, he delegated party responsibilities to Vice-President Agnew.

The party needs the President's leadership, prestige, and patronage. The President needs the party's backing to enact a program. The President's program becomes the party's program, even if it varies from the platform adopted at the party's national convention.

Presidents have limited powers over their parties. They choose the chairpersons for the national committees, but national committees have few functions except during presidential election years. Presidents have very little influence over the selection of candidates for congressional, state, and local office. It is more the exception than the rule for candidates to receive active campaign help from the President. It is equally exceptional for a President to seek publicly the defeat of a party member. In 1938, two years after his reelection by a landslide, President Franklin Roosevelt campaigned in Democratic primaries against several Democratic members of Congress who had opposed his New Deal programs. All but one of Roosevelt's targets were reelected. None of FDR's successors is likely to repeat his mistake.

Being party leader can enhance the President's legislative goals. Democrats in Congress, for example, tend to be favorably inclined toward the legislative program of a Democratic President. Republicans in Congress behave similarly toward a Republican President. The leaders of the President's party in Congress generally work hard to pass the President's program. But a Democratic majority in Congress is no guarantee that a Democratic President's program will pass.

The executive and legislative branches of government are independent. Their policy views and political interests often diverge. When a Republican President must work with a Democratic Congress, as in 12 of the years between 1956 and 1976, conflict between the two branches is likely. Nonetheless, compromises are frequently reached. And the essential functions of government are carried out.

Judicial Powers. In prerevolutionary America, the pardoning power was a prerogative of the king or queen of England or the colonial governors acting on the sovereign's behalf.

President Ford used his pardoning power to grant a "full, free, and absolute pardon unto Richard Nixon" for his alleged misuse of presidential powers. By accepting the pardon before he was brought to trial, Nixon in effect admitted wrongdoing.

In 1977 President Carter granted pardons to all Americans who had refused to serve in the Vietnamese War. By this act Carter hoped to help heal the division in American society brought about by the unpopular war.

section review

1. What are the six most important roles of the President?
2. Give four examples of how past Presidents have exercised their power as commander in chief.
3. Explain why there are fewer influential interest groups in foreign policy than in domestic policy.

4. What is meant by executive privilege? executive order?
5. Describe the relationship of Presidents to their own political party.

2. IS THE PRESIDENT TOO POWERFUL?

The President's Impact. A recent series of interviews with White House aides found that only 10 percent described the President as having a "very great impact over public policy." Clearly there is a gap between the view from within the White House and the view from outside.

There is no doubt that presidential power is extensive in the areas of foreign and defense policy. A President may act alone for a limited time, but only at the risk of losing the democratic consensus on which the system of government rests. Without support and funds from Congress, without the energetic participation of the career bureaucracy, and without the ultimate approval of public opinion, the President can accomplish little of lasting importance.

During much of the twentieth century, Congress got into the habit of delegating broad powers to the President. Sometimes Congress delegated its power because a situation required rapid decisions, and Congress acts too slowly to assume responsibility for most emergencies. At other times Congress was unwilling to suffer the political consequences involved in making unpopular decisions. When there is a need to reallocate scarce resources—such as gasoline during an energy shortage—Congress is likely to "pass-the-buck" to the President. Whatever the reason, Congress has encouraged the growth of presidential power more than it has checked such growth.

The complexity of domestic and foreign policy and the need to confront crises will continue to require strong presidential leadership. But to preserve the constitutional system of government, the system of checks and balances must be used to hold the President accountable to Congress and the people.

Excess, Limits, and Safeguards. In a tape of a conversation held in his office on September 15, 1972, Nixon talked about his so-called enemies: "They are asking for it and they are going to get it. We have not used the power . . . the FBI . . . the Justice Department. But things are going to change now."

Without the Watergate burglary and the tapes, this abuse of power might have gone undetected. Bureaucrats can check the President's power by endlessly delaying or resisting presidential directives that upset them. But apparently Nixon's senior bureaucrats did not get very upset.

Other measures against hidden abuses of power operate uncertainly. Very few members of the press are willing to ask questions that might lose them standing with the White House. Courts can only punish crimes after they are detected. The general public cannot be counted on to check a President for misusing his power: Nixon's disposition toward imperial presidency was widely publicized, but 49 of the 50 states cast their electoral votes for him in 1972.

Nor was Nixon the only President to have exceeded his powers. Most of the modern Presidents have engaged in Nixon's excesses. Such excesses have included managing the news, punishing enemies, ignoring the letter of the law in election campaigns, impounding funds, invoking executive privilege, lying to the people, deceiving Congress, and choosing aides more loyal to the President than to the democratic system. Several Presidents have disregarded the public's opinion and the need to get congressional consent either in time of crisis or the heady aftermath of successful election campaigns.

The Constitution provides no sure safeguard against flaws in a President's character. As Justice Jackson observed, "The chief restraint on those who command the physical forces of the country in the future, as in the past, must be their responsibility to the political judgments of their contemporaries and to the moral judgments of history."

Checks on Presidential Power: The Courts. One of the most important Supreme Court cases, *Marbury* v. *Madison* (1803), established the principle that an act of the President was subject to judicial review.

Over the past 50 years, the Court has limited the President's powers in a number of ways. It has prevented the President from: seizing an industrial plant as commander in chief, dismissing an independent agency commissioner, stopping newspaper publication of leaked government documents, suspending the provisions in the Bill of Rights on wiretaps or burglaries, impounding certain funds appropriated by Congress, blocking pay raises passed by Congress for federal employees, and claiming absolute executive privilege for all forms of presidential communications.

Despite having made decisions limiting the President's powers, the Court has rarely made a President account for presidential acts. When FDR violated the civil rights and liberties of 100,000 Americans of Japanese ancestry by confining them in relocation centers during World War II, the Court upheld his authority to do so. After the war ended and the relocation camps were disbanded, the Court acknowledged the injury done to these Americans.

Another indication that the Court may be a weak defense against an overreaching President is the opinion contained in *U.S.* v. *Nixon* (1974). Although denying Nixon's claim of absolute executive privilege, the Court suggested that if a President invoked national security as a foundation for the claim, the judiciary might either decide not to review the action or might allow it to continue.

Checks on Presidential Power: Congress. During the presidency of Richard Nixon, many people charged that the President had become less accountable than ever before to Congress, the Courts, and public opinion for executive actions. The irony here, of course, is that Nixon was ultimately driven from office by the Congress, which was about to impeach him; the Supreme Court, which forced him to release his incriminating tapes; and the opinion of the public, which massively withdrew its trust in him.

The problem was that Nixon had abused his power and had exceeded constitutional limits for quite some time before the constitutional balance was restored. People began believing that the system of checks and balances was not working.

"Congress has all the controls it could ever need. All it lacks is the guts to use them," commented Representative Don Fraser (D-Minn.) during the Nixon presidency. Instead of using their controls, most members of Congress went along until the abuses could no longer be overlooked.

Impeachment is a drastic response to a drastic condition. For many years people believed that impeachment was an outdated practice. Its sudden revival as a workable process may remind future Presidents of the disgrace that can come—to the nation as well as to the President—when excessive power is finally checked.

section review

1. How have the courts limited the President's powers?

2. Discuss why judicial limitations are placed on the President's exercise of authority.
3. How can bureaucrats check the President's power?
4. What are some other measures that could be used to check presidential power? Why do these other measures operate uncertainly?

3. THE VICE-PRESIDENT'S DUTIES

The constitutional duty assigned to the Vice-President is to preside over the Senate and to vote only in the event of a tie. The Vice-President actually spends little time presiding over the Senate, for the role of presider carries little influence in the Senate.

Several Vice-Presidents have been irritated about their ineffectual roles. John Adams called the office of Vice-President "the most insignificant that ever the mind of man did conceive." Truman once told FDR's press secretary to tell the President to stop treating him like an office boy.

Incoming Presidents usually announce that they intend to use the Vice-President fully. President Carter was no exception. He declared that Mondale's role would be "unprecedented in American history for a Vice-President. I look on him as my top staff person." Carter, a stranger to Washington before becoming President, depended on Mondale's 12 years of Washington experience as a senator, as well as on his judgment.

No government official besides the President earns more than the Vice-President, whose annual salary is $79,000. The speaker of the House and the Chief Justice of the Supreme Court earn the same amount.

The Vice-President takes on whatever duties the President assigns. The President is likely to share some ceremonial and political duties with the Vice-President. A Vice-President may be sent on goodwill tours abroad or may represent the United States at the funeral of a foreign leader. Recent Presidents have emphasized their own symbolic leadership and have preferred to remain aloof from party politics. Accordingly, they have sent their Vice-Presidents to campaign for party candidates, particularly at midterm congressional elections.

A President would find it intolerable for the Vice-President to disagree with presidential policy in public. President Johnson's liberal Vice-President Hubert Humphrey was widely criticized for supporting Johnson's war policies. He answered his critics by saying that a Vice-President must be a firm supporter of the President's policy.

When Vice-Presidents speak in public, they are usually covered by the media. Thus they become well-known figures. Visibility and recognition have made Vice-Presidents serious contenders for the presidency. Even today, when the Vice-President is taking on important public relations functions for the administration and seems to be involved in presidential decisions, the function of that office is still advisory. There are no management responsibilities and little opportunity to gain administrative experience. The limitations of the vice-presidency are especially unfortunate, since through succession to a presidential vacancy or through their own elections, four of the most recent eight Presidents have served as Vice-Presidents.

section review

1. What is the constitutional duty assigned to the Vice-President of the United States?
2. How effective is this role?
3. Why do Presidents find it intolerable for Vice-Presidents to disagree publicly with presidential policy?
4. Why is having little administrative or managerial responsibility a disadvantage to some Vice-Presidents?

Acting as President Carter's emissary in foreign affairs, Vice-President Walter F. Mondale (left) converses with President Valéry Giscard d'Estaing of France.

SALARIES OF FEDERAL OFFICIALS IN 1980

POSITION	SALARY
President	$200,000
Vice-President	79,000
Speaker, House of Representatives	79,000
Chief Justice, Supreme Court	79,000
Associate justice, Supreme Court	76,000
Cabinet member	69,500
President pro tempore, Senate	68,500
House and Senate majority and minority leaders	68,500
Congressperson	60,500
Court of Appeals justice	60,500
Undersecretary, Senior White House Aide	60,500
District Court judge	57,500
Assistant department secretary	55,500

Source: *Congressional Quarterly*

Pictured here are two former Vice-Presidents, Charles Fairbanks (l) and Charles Curtis (r). Under which Presidents did they serve? How has the role of the Vice-President changed since these men were in office?

CHAPTER SUMMARY

20

The American presidency is probably the most powerful office in the world—not only because the United States is extremely powerful, but also because the President can exercise sole authority in foreign and military matters and in domestic emergencies.

The President's powers are derived from the Constitution, custom, congressional authorization, and the acts of previous Presidents. As America's chief of state the President is the world's single most widely recognized national leader.

The President is chief of state, commander in chief, director of foreign policy, chief executive, chief legislator, director of domestic and economic policy, and party leader. Both the legislative and judicial branches check and are checked and balanced by the executive.

The major functions of the Vice-President are to preside over the Senate and to assume the presidency if the President dies or is incapacitated. Historically, the Vice-President has had little to do except stay out of the way. Recent Presidents have sought to include Vice-Presidents in governmental operations, but more as an aide than as a full-fledged member of the administration.

REVIEW QUESTIONS

1. Why has the President been given such broad powers over the armed forces and foreign policy? Do you agree with this policy? Explain.
2. Why have recent Presidents devoted more time and energy to foreign and military matters than to domestic questions? Do you agree with this allocation of time and attention? Explain.
3. What effects has the extension of wartime secrecy had on the conduct of foreign policy?
4. Why does Theodore Sorensen believe that

secrecy is practiced by Presidents? Do you agree? Why or why not?
5. Why is it difficult to persuade highly qualified men and women to accept federal appointments? What do you think could be done to encourage their participation?
6. Why has the President's power to initiate economic policy increased during the twentieth century? Do you favor this increase in the President's power? Why or why not?

ACTIVITIES FOR REVIEW

activity 1   Prepare a research paper on secrecy and executive privilege as factors contributing to the resignation of Richard Nixon as President of the United States.

activity 2   Select a Vice-President who has succeeded to the presidency on the death of the Chief Executive. What preparation had he had for his presidency? What problems were caused by his lack of involvement in the administration before assuming the presidency?

activity 3   Try to find information about George Washington's concept of the presidency. How does it differ from that of today? Compare and contrast Washington with a twentieth-century President. Report your findings to the class.

political science DICTIONARY

executive leak—disclosure of information against the President's wishes.   p. 376

executive privilege—limited right of members of the executive branch to refuse to give certain information (documents, testimony) to Congress.   p. 376

21 *Presidential Management*

In the early years of this century, the President's staff consisted mainly of housekeepers, gardeners, and cooks. President McKinley answered his own telephone, and President Wilson typed his own speeches and some of his letters. President Franklin D. Roosevelt's staff was larger than those of his predecessors. He needed a larger staff to meet the new economic responsibilities caused by the Great Depression. Many of FDR's principal aides were paid by executive agencies rather than by the President's office.

Government grows more complex each year. There are more interest groups, more regulatory agencies, more programs—many of which overlap—and there is more work to be done. Today the executive office of the President has a staff of over 5,000 people, including 600 aides who work within the White House itself. Answering the White House mail occupies 220 people.

The modern presidency has been characterized by the increasing influence of the White House staff and the declining influence of the Cabinet; the Presidents' increasing distrust of the bureaucracy, leading to the creation of a series of managerial units within the White House; and the expectation that special groups will be represented on the White House staff.

CHAPTER PREVIEW

1. HOW MUCH CAN THE PRESIDENT GET DONE?
2. PRESIDENTS' WORK STYLES
3. THE CABINET
4. THE BUREAUCRACY
5. THE EXECUTIVE OFFICE OF PRESIDENT AND THE WHITE HOUSE STAFF

1. HOW MUCH CAN THE PRESIDENT GET DONE?

In 1801, when Jefferson was President, 2,120 persons held jobs in the national government. Today the national government employs 3 million civilians in 2,000 executive agencies. The President, who is responsible for this huge establishment, needs a lot of help to make it function efficiently according to presidential goals.

Large governments are not known for their efficiency. Any president of a business corporation is likely to have greater power over his or her subordinates than the President of the United States has over the executive branch.

To establish control over so many people in so many agencies, a President would have to be a manager without peer. In fact, most Presidents are not managers in the usual sense of the word. It is a mistake to expect them to be. The President is the nation's chief political officer rather than its chief exec-

The job of the President has grown because of the constant advancement and complexity of society.

"PAGE ONE"

utive manager. Managers in the business world are usually concerned with producing resources. The political process is concerned with distributing resources—deciding who gets how much of what is available.

Recognizing that the presidency is a political rather than a managerial office, Congress gives most statutory powers directly to agency heads rather than to the President. This delegation of managerial authority, in the words of analyst Stephen Hess, enables the President to devote his time and energies to the essentially political tasks of

1. making policy that will ensure the security of the country, with special attention to situations that could involve the nation in war;
2. formulating a legislative program that presents specific recommendations for new initiatives;
3. preparing the annual budget, through which changes in the size of existing programs are recommended;
4. sharing responsibility for adjustments of the economy;
5. selecting noncareer government officials;
6. informing the people and Congress of actions proposed or carried out, and offering assessments of the state of the nation and of the world;
7. resolving conflicts between departments, and seeking coordination of departmental policies;
8. sharing authority for promoting social service programs within the executive branch.

In the day-to-day life of the President these political tasks or decision areas do not come before the President on any regular basis. The President spends a fair amount of time dealing with what Richard Neustadt calls "action-forcing" deadlines—documents awaiting signature, vacant positions to be filled, officials seeking hearings, news reporters probing for answers, interest groups requesting audiences, intelligence reports requiring responses.

Neustadt believes that to do the job a President's first need is information. Many scholars agree that one of the great dangers in the presidency is being dependent on a single source of information.

It is hard for most Presidents to believe that they have achieved their goals, at least on domestic issues. One aide to Lyndon Johnson remarked, "Except in times of emergencies, Presidents cannot get much accomplished."

Some, like a senior Kennedy aide, blame Congress: "The annual Congressional appropriations process made long-range presidential planning difficult. The biannual congressional election process made consistent support of presidential proposals doubtful. The quiet web of relationships between powerful committee or subcommittee chairmen and career bureau chiefs made many budget and policy decisions meaningless."

Others blame the political environment. They feel that there are many powerful people and interests pulling in different directions and sometimes neutralizing the President.

section review

1. How has the job of the President changed since Jefferson's time?
2. According to analyst Stephen Hess, to what essential political tasks should the President devote time?
3. What is meant by action-forcing deadlines?

2. PRESIDENTS' WORK STYLES

Presidents organize their staffs to help with their work. The amount of tidiness or chaos that Presidents choose depends on their work habits. They decide how much advice to get from the government and how much to get from outside. They decide whether to give competing assignments and overlapping jurisdictions (FDR), or to assign each aide to a clearly defined area (Ike), or to have the staff work as a team (Kennedy). They decide whether the staff will have direct access to the President (FDR, Kennedy) or will have to petition through a chief of staff (Ike, Nixon). They decide whether to rely on specialists or on generalists.

Relations with Staff. Truman presided over morning meetings of his whole staff. Eisenhower sought to organize the White House more efficiently by adding a chief of staff and staffing the National Security Council. Kennedy's staff was organized less formally. He preferred to deal directly with whoever was handling an important matter. Johnson tended to overpower people and wanted to be at the center of routine operations. Nixon relied on a few loyal aides and preferred to have detailed recommendations submitted in writing so that he could consider them in solitude. Ford tended to arrive at his own position while engaging in oral give and take rather than by selecting from a sheet of opinions.

Energy Levels. Presidents vary in their levels of physical energy. Dwight Eisenhower, who was 70 when he left office and had two major illnesses during his two terms, undoubtedly had a lighter schedule than did his successor, John Kennedy, who became President at the age of 43. Lyndon Johnson had vast energy. He worked steadily from seven in the morning until midnight. Thus he got almost two normal working days out of every 24 hours.

Getting Information. "I sit in the White House, and what I read and see is the sum total of what I hear and learn. So the more people I can see, or the wider I can expose my mind to different ideas, the more effective I can be as President," remarked Kennedy. In his drive for facts, Kennedy intervened in every stage of the policy-making process. Sometimes he phoned subordinates far down the line to get information. He also read a lot. LBJ preferred to deal with a small number of people and to read a stack of one-page policy memos that typically ended with "yes" or "no" and "want more information."

Outside Advisers. Many Presidents have sought advice outside their Cabinets and White House staffs. Andrew Jackson's informal group of advisers came to be known as the Kitchen Cabinet. President Franklin Roosevelt similarly had his Brain Trust, consisting largely of unpaid advisers from outside the government. Kennedy, Johnson, and Carter relied on contacts outside the White House. Nixon, by contrast, sought isolation.

Diversity and Openness. Presidents vary greatly in their abilities to carry on freewheeling discussions with their advisers and to tolerate disagreements with their points of view. Presidents Roosevelt and Kennedy sought to expose themselves to wide varieties of viewpoints. In contrast, most other recent Presidents disliked conflict and competition. They preferred to let ideas and recommendations filter up through a few key staff people.

Kennedy deliberately chose people with diverse views to work in his administration. He frequently assigned the same task to more than one person to make sure that he received a diversity of viewpoints. During the Cuban missile crisis, Kennedy absented himself from most discussions of the EXCOM, or Executive Committee (his group of top advisers who explored all possible courses of action), to make sure that disagreement would be voiced. In the Kennedy White House, diversity did not mean intense rivalry and competition for influence (as it did in FDR's White House).

A President whose mind is open to several views is likely to reach different decisions from those of a President whose mind is closed to all but one view. For example, during the Cuban missile crisis, the early discussions in the EXCOM focused on an air attack on Cuba. A majority favored that view. But Kennedy's insistence on considering alternatives led eventually to the effective and much less risky blockade.

FDR and Ike: Two Extremes. FDR's work style was to stay flexible, to work informally— often outside regular channels—to give competing assignments, to shift his inner circle so that no one got too powerful, and to keep himself at the center of the action.

FDR stayed informed, and his system of staff competition promoted creativity. He cast himself as the final judge between feuding factions.

FDR was freewheeling and played aides off against one another. FDR's aides helped him to shape public opinion. They moved from one assignment to another as the President directed. He also established a host of new agencies that reported directly to him. Some of these agencies overlapped the jurisdictions of the regular departments.

Eisenhower expected his Cabinet secretaries to run their departments and used his staff experts for advice on matters that he thought were not adequately handled by the departments. Ike disliked the give and take of politics and rarely intervened in Congress. He delegated to his army friend, General Lucius Clay, the job of selecting his Cabinet, and each Cabinet member chose subordinates.

Whereas most Presidents want their aides to provide alternatives to choose from, Ike wanted recommendations to ratify. He accepted uncritically almost anything that his advisers proposed. Sherman Adams, his chief of staff for six years, screened the flow of information and people to the President. Ike delegated authority to his Cabinet and to Adams. He disliked reading anything over one page, rarely wrote notes or memos to his staff, and did not like to talk on the telephone.

Three Approaches to Organizational Leadership. FDR's style of organization has been called the competitive approach. This approach keeps the President informed and stimulates creativity at the cost of some duplication of effort and many insecure aides. The approach breaks down when the President cannot give it continual attention.

Ike's formalistic approach, consisting of a hierarchical staff and the delegation of responsibility, emphasized order and analysis. Technical considerations prevailed over political considerations. But with this approach information tends to be incomplete and distorted, and decision making is slow.

The formalistic approach seems to work best in dealing with the bureaucracy. The competitive approach is best suited to dealing with Congress. The competitive approach embraces conflict, bargaining (including the trading of certain political favors for votes), and compromise.

Kennedy used a third style that some analysts have called the *collegial approach.* In

THE THREE APPROACHES TO ORGANIZATIONAL LEADERSHIP		
	Strengths	**Weaknesses**
Formalistic Approach	Orderly decision process results in more thorough analysis. Conserves the decision maker's time and attention for the big decisions. Emphasizes the optimal.	Hierarchy that screens information may also distort it. Tendency of the screening process to wash out or distort political pressures and public sentiments. Tendency to respond slowly or inappropriately in crisis.
Competitive Approach	Places the decision maker in the mainstream of the information network. Tends to generate solutions that are politically feasible and bureaucratically workable. Generates creative ideas, partially as a result of the "stimulus" of competition, but also because this unstructured network is more open to ideas from the outside.	Places large demands on decision maker's time and attention. Exposes decision maker to partial or biased information. Decision process may overly sacrifice optimality for viability. Tendency to aggravate staff competition, with the risk that aides may pursue their own interest at the expense of the decision maker.
Collegial Approach	Seeks to achieve both optimality and viability. Involves the decision maker in the information network but somewhat eases the demands upon him by stressing teamwork over competition.	Places substantial demands on the decision maker's time and attention. Requires unusual interpersonal skills in dealing with subordinates, mediating differences, and maintaining teamwork among colleagues.

Source: "Managing the White House," Richard Tanner Johnson

this approach the President's subordinates work together as a team to shape policy out of divergent viewpoints.

The collegial approach may be best for the White House itself. It stimulates conflict but avoids feuding and any attempts on the part of the staff to undercut one another. However, it makes great demands on the President's time and energy. Also the collegial approach does not seem to work especially well on the federal bureaucracy or on Congress.

President Reagan seems to have profited from the experience of his predecessors. He uses the formalistic approach in dealing with the bureaucracy. He delegates much responsibility to his department heads. Reagan relies on a chief of staff and key aides to transmit his wishes to the White House staff.

section review

1. How did FDR's style of working differ from that of Ike?
2. What is meant by Kitchen Cabinet? Brain Trust?
3. Which approach to organizational leadership seems to work best in dealing with the federal bureaucracy?

3. THE CABINET

In America the Cabinet does not function as a decision-making body. The President is individually responsible for executive decisions. Some Presidents have not held regular Cabinet meetings. Kennedy preferred to reach decisions by conferring informally with two or three Cabinet officers in the presence of some of his own staff members. The Cabinet is composed of the heads of the major executive departments—the secretary of state, the secretary of defense, and so on. Sometimes the President will include in his Cabinet such senior officials as the ambassador to the United Nations or the director of the Office of Management and Budget.

Cabinet members take office eager to help and ready to support the President. The career civil servants who staff the departments on a permanent basis, however, are often strongly dedicated to the programs that they administer. The main pitfall for a secretary (department head) is being "captured" by his or her career subordinates. A "captured" department head becomes more committed to the interests and morale of the department than to the President's interests. Over time the secretary may find himself or herself at odds with the President because the secretary is responsible for only one department of the government whereas the President is responsible for the entire executive branch and must balance a much broader range of interests.

Moreover, secretaries must build alliances in Congress in order to receive legislative authority and funds. They depend on the interest groups served by their departments—farmers, unions, builders, business people—for public and political support. These allies pull the secretary in the same direction as do the department's civil servants and further separate the secretary from the President.

The Cabinet serves as a consultative group to the President. Here President Reagan is shown meeting with his Cabinet members.

The President's top aides now seem to have at least as much influence over presidential decisions as the department heads have. Presidents are inclined to trust their own aides to view problems from the President's perspective. Cabinet secretaries may be less reliable. Presidents may see their top aides every day and not see a department head for weeks. President Nixon's first Secretary of the Interior, Walter Hickel, once reported that he had not seen the President for three months. Although it is desirable for a Cabinet secretary to have direct access to the President, it is not necessary to the operation of his or her department. The secretary's leadership is generally enough to ensure the smooth functioning of a domestic department.

Some political scientists have distinguished between "inner" and "outer" Cabinets. The "inner" Cabinet consists of the secretaries of defense and state, the attorney general, the secretary of the treasury, the director of the Office of Management and Budget, the special assistant for national security affairs, and a handful of ranking White House aides. The "outer" Cabinet is composed of all the other Cabinet members.

President Johnson gave enormous responsibility for domestic policy to two White House officials: his budget director, Charles Schultze (chairman of the Council of Economic Advisers to President Carter); and his chief domestic policy assistant, Joseph Califano (President Carter's secretary of health, education and welfare). This arrangement screened the domestic Cabinet secretaries from direct access to the President.

Cabinet Versus White House Staff. Cabinet members have long resented the influence of the President's inner circle of aides. They believe that these aides do not possess needed experience. One scholar familiar with the ways of the White House observed the rise of the aide and the decline of the Cabinet secretary: "I have seen Cabinet members, top brass, and big-city mayors cooling their heels for half an hour waiting to see a young presidential aide and no one batting an eye."

The youth of many White House aides tends to separate them from members of Congress and the bureaucracy. Top-flight Cabinet members who participate in presidential decision making can work for the President's interests with the bureaucracy and Congress far more effectively than can the White House staff. This is especially true of Cabinet members who have built their own political bases and reputations and can stand up to a President with more confidence than can White House aides or Cabinet secretaries who are wholly dependent on the President.

One Kennedy-Johnson domestic Cabinet member observed, "A good Cabinet member can be an excellent corrective to the White House hothouse staff who are confined there and are virtually locked up fourteen hours a day. . . . the President needs to hear from his Cabinet."

section review

1. What is the Cabinet?
2. What is the main pitfall for the head of a federal department?
3. What people belong to the inner and outer Cabinets? Why do Cabinet members resent the President's inner circle of aides?

4. THE BUREAUCRACY

Federal bureaucrats—the almost 3 million civil servants who staff the executive departments and agencies—have gotten a very bad press from those who are interested in presidential management. Many bureaucrats leak stories to the press to serve their own personal careers or the interests of their particular bureaus. Generally the leaker has an ulterior motive, although the press never indicates what that motive might be—what policy may win if the policy being disclosed loses, what individual keeps his job, what bureau retains its jurisdiction.

A President may be elected to office for a maximum of eight years. Many career civil servants stay at their posts all of their adult lives. They see many bold new presidential pro-

grams rise and fall. They can use their knowledge, their contacts in Congress, and their allies among the interest groups served by their agencies to delay or undermine any presidential action with which they disagree. They can be a President's worst enemies unless they can be persuaded to share the President's ideas and beliefs.

Cabinet secretaries are too occupied with policy matters, new initiatives, public relations, Congressional hearings, and interagency coordination to run their departments. Day-to-day decisions are made by assistant secretaries and top-level civil servants. FDR and Kennedy knew this and frequently established communications with subcabinet personnel. This approach made senior agency people more responsive to the Presidents' wishes.

These Presidents did not excel at management techniques but rather at political leadership. They capitalized on one important political resource. During the last 50 years, the majority of civil servants have been progressive Democrats who shared the goals of a progressive Democratic President.

Rather than attempt to gain control over the existing bureaucracies and make them work for the goals of the Chief Executive, several Presidents have chosen easier courses. They set up new agencies and transferred important policy development and monitoring activities to the Executive Office of the President to counter the threat that their new programs would be buried in the old-line bureaucracies.

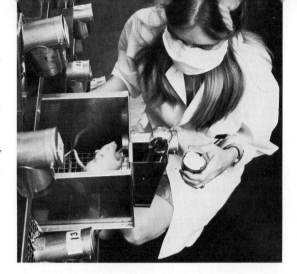

This woman works for the USDA. What other agency would use research scientists?

QUOTES from famous people

"The Treasury is so large and far-flung and ingrained in its practices that I found it almost impossible to get the action and results I want. But the Treasury is not to be compared with the State Department. You should go through the experience of trying to get any changes in the thinking, policy, and action of the career diplomats and then you'd know what a real problem was. But the Treasury and the State Department put together are nothing compared with the Navy. The admirals are really something to cope with—and I should know. To change something in the Navy is like punching a feather bed. You punch it with your right, and you punch it with your left, and then you find the damn bed just as it was before you started punching."

Franklin D. Roosevelt

Moreover, many governmental problems overlap the jurisdictions of several agencies. An interagency unit, centered in the Executive Office of the President, can overcome built-in agency biases, weaken alliances with interest groups, and analyze problems from a broader perspective. In the Nixon administration, units were established in the Executive Office of the President to deal with pollution, civil rights, drug abuse, cancer research, and telecommunications.

Bureaucrats tend to be more accountable to Congress, which appropriates their funds, than to their nominal director, the President. There are some bureaucracies, however, that seem not to have been accountable to either Congress or the President. Recent presidential and congressional investigating committees have revealed that some government agencies, including the CIA and the FBI, have spied on American citizens and have hatched plots to kill foreign leaders. The revelation of this secret and illegal activity has troubled many members of Congress and the general public. It remains to be seen whether measures to make these agencies accountable will prove effective.

section review

1. Why are some civil servants more loyal to their agency than to the President?
2. Explain how some Presidents have attempted to deal with the above situation.
3. Why do bureaucrats tend to be more accountable to Congress than to the President?
4. How did John Kennedy and Franklin Roosevelt make bureaucrats more responsive to their wishes?
5. Why are day-to-day bureaucratic decisions often made by assistant secretaries?

5. THE EXECUTIVE OFFICE OF PRESIDENT AND THE WHITE HOUSE STAFF

The Executive Office of the President was created by Congress in 1939 on the recommendation of President Roosevelt's committee on administrative management. Since 1939 the President has been able to use the Executive Office of the President (EOP) to help coordinate the enormous executive branch. By Washington agency standards the EOP is relatively small, for it consists of fewer than 5,000 people.

The main unit of the Executive Office of the President is the Office of Management and Budget (OMB). The director of OMB is one of the most important persons in government. That person also has Cabinet rank. OMB devises techniques for improving the efficiency of government agencies, evaluates the effectiveness of government programs, and determines the amount of money that each agency and program should request from Congress. It coordinates the planning and management operations of the entire executive branch.

Agency officials are often inclined to serve their own interests rather than conform to the President's priorities. Presidents use their budgets to impose their own priorities over the diverse elements of the executive branch. In carrying out the President's wishes, OMB may support some agencies or programs by requesting additional funds and thwart others by reducing their requests.

The Executive Office of the President has grown steadily over the past 40 years. Congress enlarged the EOP by adding the Council of Economic Advisers (1946), the National Security Council (1947), the Office of the Special Representative for Trade Negotiations (1963), the Council on Environmental Quality (1970), and the Office of Science and Technology Policy (1976).

The budget for the White House office staff alone increased from $3.6 million in 1970 to more than $21 million in 1980. This growth reflects the modern Presidents' preference for working with assistants committed to their goals rather than to the interests of the individual executive departments.

EXECUTIVE OFFICE OF THE PRESIDENT—1980

Council of Economic Advisers	Office of Management and Budget
Council on Environmental Quality	Office of Science and Technology Policy
Council on Wage and Price Stability	Special Representative for Trade Negotiations
Domestic Policy Staff	Vice-President's Office
National Security Council	White House Office
Office of Administration	

The White House Staff. The main part of the White House was built during the presidency of John Adams at the end of the eighteenth century. The east and west wings, which contain the offices of the White House staff, were built during the early part of the twentieth century, as was the Oval Office, where the President does much of his work.

Aside from the director of OMB, the people closest to the President and of most help in the day-to-day work are the several dozen members of the White House staff. During the Truman administration, the President met daily at 10:00 A.M. with a dozen staff members. Kennedy's White House staff was considerably larger: His top aides had staffs of their own to assist them. Johnson's White House had 20 people working on domestic

EDWIN MEESE III

Edwin Meese III is the chief public spokesman on policy for the Reagan administration. His official title is counselor to the President. Meese is generally acknowledged to be the senior and foremost member of the White House staff. President Reagan gave Meese Cabinet rank—unprecedented for a member of the White House staff. Meese is responsible for Cabinet administration, which consists of overseeing both the National Security Council and the domestic policy staff. In addition he has been designated a member of the National Security Council by the President.

Meese's association with Reagan began when Reagan was governor of California. Meese served as legal secretary to the governor and as chief of staff. He left state government in 1975 to become vice-president of an aerospace and transportation firm. Upon his return to politics in 1980, Meese was active in Reagan's presidential campaign and became the director of the Reagan transition team from November 1980 to January 1981.

Meese received a degree in public administration from Yale University in 1953 and a law degree from the University of California at Berkeley Law School in 1958. Since then he has held positions such as law professor, Director of the Center for Criminal Justice Policy and Management at the University of San Diego School of Law, and deputy district attorney in Alameda County, California. Meese is a retired lieutenant colonel in the military intelligence branch of the army reserve.

Meese is married and has three children. He is active in numerous civic, legal, and educational organizations and serves on the board of directors of both the California Journal and the Institute for Contemporary Studies, a public policy research organization. Meese's hobbies include listening to police radios and collecting small statues.

Those who have worked for Meese describe him as disciplined, organized, self-effacing, and a "patient-doer." He reportedly is calm and a model of efficiency. The press, however, complains that he seldom makes himself available to them and when he does he is very guarded in what he says.

policy alone. Nixon increased the domestic policy staff to 28 and the national security staff to 50.

The White House staffs are service units that assist Presidents in performing their daily work, in scheduling their time, in preparing speeches and correspondence, in planning trips, and in communicating with the press. Recent Presidents have relied on their staffs for advice on major issues of policy and have given them responsibility for operating government programs.

The President's principal aides include a press secretary, an appointments secretary, a legal counsel, a special assistant for domestic affairs, and a special assistant for national security affairs. Most of the President's major staff members used to be *generalists*—gatherers of information who served as troubleshooters in a variety of areas. Although a number of the President's key aides still handle a variety of matters, most White House staff members are primarily involved in one of six policy arenas:

1. foreign and military policy (primarily the national security council staff);
2. domestic policy and legislative programs;
3. budget and economic policy;
4. congressional relations;

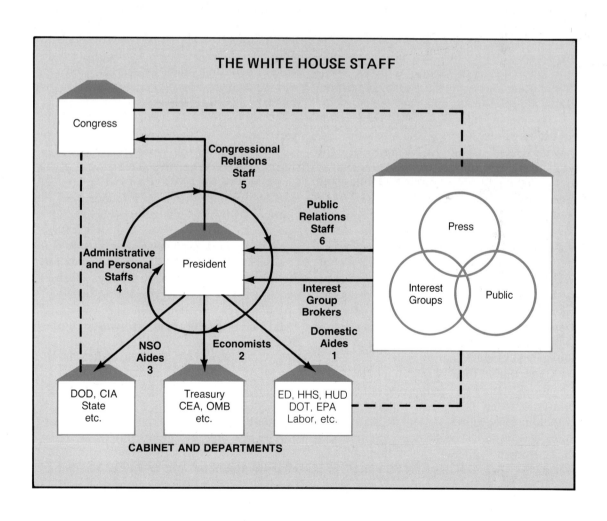

THE WHITE HOUSE STAFF

5. press and public relations;
6. personnel and management, including appointments, schedules, and trips.

White House aides tend to be relatively young and to keep low profiles. They have no special ties to parties or interest groups. Few are well known outside the White House. Henry Kissinger, an exception, became prominent on the White House staff because of his bold initiatives toward China in the President's behalf. He later became secretary of state.

Members of the White House staff are viewed as extensions of the President. In keeping with the principle of the separation of powers, they are not subject to confirmation by the Senate. Thus they are accountable only to the President. Correspondingly, Presidents alone are responsible for the conduct of their White House staffs.

Presidents Johnson and Nixon made strong attempts to bring the executive departments under White House control. By the early 1970's President Nixon had transferred to the White House responsibility for proposing policy, had given the White House staff the power to oversee the operations of government, and had used the White House staff to operate programs of high presidential priority. This transfer of power posed a challenge to the constitutional power of Congress, through which authority for federal programs had traditionally been delegated to department heads. President Ford reinstated that policy and confined the role of the White House staff to coordination only.

John Ehrlichman, Nixon's chief assistant for domestic policy, epitomized the White House staff view of the rest of the executive branch in these words: "There shouldn't be a lot of leeway [for Cabinet officials] in following the President's policy. . . . When he says 'jump,' they [should] only ask how high."

Most people who work on the White House staff find that they have a heady amount of power and influence. One former presidential aide observed, "I had more power over national affairs in a few years in the White House than I could if I spent the rest of my life in the Senate."

Life in the White House, however, is not a series of dramatic crises. It consists mainly of long days spent in helping the President to "keep the machinery of government running without too many breakdowns or explosions," as one staff member expressed it.

Former Kennedy aide Theodore Sorensen believes that the sole function of the White House staff is to advise and assist the President on political matters. Those who direct administrative agencies and have operating responsibilities should not be in the White House at all. This view would have stopped Henry Kissinger, for example, from serving simultaneously as secretary of state and as the President's special assistant for national security affairs.

New Initiatives. One aide observed that the main business of the White House is to get things started: "You only have a year at the most for new initiatives, a time when you can establish some programs on your own in contrast with what has gone on before. After that, after priorities are set, and after a President finds he doesn't have time to talk with Cabinet members, that's when the problems set in, and the White House aides close off access to Cabinet members and others."

National Security and Domestic Policy Staffs. One of the most important units of the White House staff is the Office of the President's Special Assistant for National Security Affairs. The office provides staff to the National Security Council (NSC), of which the President, the Vice-President, the secretaries of state and defense, among others, are members, or to the President directly, and makes recommendations on a range of matters pertaining to national security, including both domestic and foreign policy. The NSC

Political scientist Theodore Sorensen, author of Decision Making in the White House, served as special counsel to President Kennedy.

deals only with immediate and overriding issues of national security rather than with general matters of foreign policy that are routinely administered by the State Department bureaucracy and the members of its foreign service.

The office as run by Henry Kissinger became President Nixon's model for staff organization. Kissinger and his staff gathered and analyzed information and presented choices that helped Nixon to make decisions. Nixon found Kissinger's method so useful that he organized his Domestic Council along the same line as the Office of the President's Special Assistant for National Security Affairs.

The Domestic Council worked through subcommittees consisting of White House staff and agency officials. Its functions were to clarify the President's policy choices and to make many decisions that were considered not important enough to be referred to him. The staff devoted a significant portion of its time to emergency activities. It also maintained checks on the domestic departments and recommended that reforms be made in specific departments.

The Domestic Council survived under President Ford but was disbanded by President Carter. Its work was taken over by the smaller and more flexible domestic policy staff.

Drawbacks and Pitfalls. There are pitfalls in the mutual dependence of the President and his staff. The staff can become insulated from reality and can insulate the President in turn. This atmosphere is more likely to develop when a President is not open to criticism and dissent. White House aides who think like the President may fail to provide him with fresh insights and may tend to emphasize rather than offset his weaknesses. If Presidents surround themselves with people who agree with them or who are afraid to disagree, they will receive misleading or false viewpoints, proposals, and recommendations that can lead to bad decisions and grievous mistakes.

A frequent criticism of the White House staff is that its members focus primarily on immediate problems and short-term consequences. Once they have instituted an action or solved an immediate problem they tend to put the matter aside and focus on the next problem. There is a "rush" atmosphere in the White House that does not promote long-range thinking and planning.

Members of the White House staff may see issues from a broader perspective than do Cabinet members. But they often know less about management, Congress, and organized groups. If Presidents become cut off from the workings of the executive branch, it is because they allow their staffs to stand between them and the rest of the government. There is the danger, too, that Presidents may come to rely on the supposed expertness of their staffs to the exclusion of important advice and contacts outside the White House itself.

Accountability. White House aides exercise great authority even though—unlike other important leaders of the executive branch—their acts are not subject to congressional review. Moreover, White House staffs often shield Presidents from their own chosen department heads, depriving them of an opportunity to question presidential policies.

Furthermore, the National Security Council staff and top military staff advisers are beyond the control of Congress and the public and therefore are not accountable to them.

The White House Staff Under Nixon. It is possible for White House staff members to become too loyal to the President and neglect their loyalties to the Constitution, democracy, civil liberties, and a government of shared responsibilities and balanced powers. In the case of President Nixon, his staff members not only insulated him from reality, but they began to think that they alone knew the President's thoughts, needs, and purposes. They tyrannized the rest of the government in the President's name and helped to bring down his administration.

Nixon centralized power in the White House as never before. During the Nixon presidency, Senator Hollings of North Carolina observed, "It used to be that if I had a problem with food stamps I went to see the secretary of agriculture, whose department had jurisdiction over that program. Not anymore. Now if I want to learn the policy I must go to the White House. If I want the latest on textiles I won't get it from the secretary of commerce, who has the authority and responsibility. No, I am forced to go to the White House staff. I shouldn't feel too badly. The secretary (of commerce) has to do the same thing."

Alexander Butterfield, assistant to Nixon's chief of staff H. R. Haldeman, testified that 60 percent of the time that Nixon spent with any staff member was spent with Haldeman and for 90 percent of that time they were alone. The discretion that Haldeman used in transmitting information to the President, the priorities that he established in setting the President's daily schedule, and his decisions on what appointments would be granted produced an impact on policy. By screening the President's reading material, clearing visitors, and helping to assess the mood of

Former President Nixon's aides played a key role in White House management. Above are two of Nixon's top aides, Chief of Staff H. R. Haldeman (front) and John Ehrlichman (rear), the adviser for domestic affairs. Both were indicted in the Watergate conspiracy.

the public, Haldeman served to insulate Nixon from the country.

Decision Making in the White House. The President's major function is to make decisions. Many people can be of help by gathering information. Staff members may work through the night to present the President with recommendations or options. But only the President can make the final decision.

Most of the matters that come to the President for a decision are difficult to resolve. President Eisenhower told President Kennedy as the latter was about to assume office, "There are no easy matters that will come to you as President. If they are easy, they will be settled at a lower level."

Often Presidents decide issues dealing with the economy. For example, a President may consider how to settle a coal strike or how to meet an unexpected rise in the cost of steel. Sometimes the President has to make decisions affecting the peace and security of the nation and the world. President Truman decided to commit our nation's resources to rebuild war-torn Europe after World War II. President Kennedy decided to blockade Cuba to force the Russians to dismantle the missile sites that they had installed there. President Johnson chose to commit massive American troops to aid South Vietnam.

Every President makes mistakes. President Kennedy, according to Theodore Sorensen, regretted three major decisions: authorizing the Bay of Pigs invasion, encouraging the defense establishment by talking about an imaginary "missile gap," and sending military advisers to Vietnam.

The White House Staff Under Carter. With the bad experience of President Nixon as a reminder of how the White House staff should not be organized, President Carter announced that his White House aides would serve in a staff capacity only and would have no responsibility for administering government programs. In 1977 Carter announced that he had reduced the White House staff by 28 percent, saving $6 million in payroll costs. The purpose of the reduction was to strengthen Cabinet government. "I am very much opposed to having a concentration of large numbers of people in authority in the White House staff," said Carter. By 1980, however, such Carter figures as Zbigniew Brzezinski and Hamilton Jordan clearly had power to rival that of any Cabinet officer.

The controversial Taft-Hartley Act injunction halted striking miners in 1978. The act, passed in 1947, forbids undesirable labor practices.

QUOTES from famous people

"The President's entire existence is a continuous process of decisions—including decisions not to decide and not to take action—decisions on what to say, whom to see, what to sign, whom to name, and what to do, as commander in chief and diplomatic chief, as legislative leader and political leader, as moral leader and free world leader, and in taking care that the laws be fully executed. Every policy announcement is the sum of many decisions, each made in a different mold and manner."

Theodore C. Sorensen

Presidents can only do their best and try to learn from their own mistakes. Unless the costs of a decision vastly outweigh the ap-

parent benefits, the American people are very likely to support it and to support the President who makes it.

The most significant political decisions that Presidents make—the decisions for which, in Kennedy's phrase, they earn their salaries—involve:
1. setting national priorities, through the budget and legislative proposals; and
2. making policy that will ensure the security of the country, especially in situations that could involve the nation in war.

Many presidential decisions in foreign and military policy are made in an atmosphere of crisis. Conditions for making the right decision are far from ideal: Time is short, the stakes are high, and it is impossible for the President to study all of the options in detail. The President must depend on partial information and cannot predict the result of each course of action.

The biggest problem for every President is that there are not enough hours in a day to fulfill the many obligations of the office. Presidents from the time of George Washington to the present have found the tasks of the office to be almost overwhelming. President Polk said, "In truth, though I occupy a very high position, I am the hardest-working man in this country."

A typical day in the life of President Carter started at 5:30 or 6:00 A.M. After a light breakfast he tackled the mountain of reading material awaiting his attention. His appointments started at 8:15. The entire morning was occupied in holding meetings, reading documents, and answering memos.

After eating lunch alone at the office, President Carter spent the early afternoon dealing with ceremonial affairs. If there were no afternoon meetings, he caught up on more reading. Occasionally the President played tennis with his aides in the late afternoon.

Carter usually had dinner with his family and then returned to the Oval Office, where he worked alone for much of the evening.

Truman had a schedule similar to Carter's. Truman, an early riser, would wake up at 5:30 A.M. and work for several hours in his study before joining his family for breakfast. At nine o'clock the President would arrive at his office and spend an hour dictating letters and reading documents. At exactly ten o'clock his appointments would begin. A President's appointments are usually kept as short as possible, and they follow one another without a break.

At one o'clock Truman would go home for lunch and a half-hour's rest. At 2:45 he would return to the office for more appointments and more documents. In a single day Truman would often sign his name to more than 400 documents.

Truman would not usually leave his office till 6:00 P.M. Unless there was a White House function in the evening, he would generally have dinner and then return to his study. There he would work until midnight on more documents.

A few Presidents have tried to make their work days less hectic. President Eisenhower was one of these. His day started at 7:00 A.M. Eisenhower liked to do business over meals, so he often began with a breakfast meeting at 7:30. By eight o'clock he would be in his office scanning documents, letters, and newspapers. His appointments were scheduled in an unbroken series from 8:30 through 4:30, including an appointment for lunch. When his last visitor had gone, Eisenhower would dictate letters and do more paper work until 6:00 P.M. Eisenhower once said, "No daily schedule of appointments can give a full timetable — or even a faint indication — of the President's responsibilities."

Which of the above schedules resembles President Reagan's work day the most?

section review

1. What is the purpose of the Executive Office of the President?
2. List three functions of the OMB.
3. What do the budget increases between 1970 and 1980 reflect?
4. What problems can arise if Presidents surround themselves only with people who agree with them or with people who are afraid to disagree?
5. What is the major function of the President as discussed in this chapter?

CHAPTER SUMMARY

21

Government and the management of government have become more complex each year. The task of managing a federal bureaucracy of political appointees, civil servants, and aides numbering more than 5 million is a massive undertaking. The Executive Office of the President alone has a staff of over 5,000 people, including 600 aides working within the White House. Lower-level bureaucrats are generally civil service workers whose jobs are unaffected by a change of administration.

The modern presidency has been characterized by a growth in the number of personnel, a rise in White House staff influence and a decline in Cabinet influence, an increase in presidential suspicion of the bureaucracy, and a willingness for special groups to be represented on the White House staff.

The President's personal style determines the organizational structure of the White House. Three approaches to organizational leadership—competitive, formalistic, and collegial—typify twentieth-century Presidents.

Cabinet influence has declined because of the members' conflicting loyalties to the President and their own departments. White House aides are now involved in many areas formerly the domain of Cabinet members—foreign and military policy, domestic policy and legislative programs, and budget and economic policy—as well as congressional relations, press and public relations, and personnel and management matters. Too strong a dependence on the White House staff may isolate a President from outside communication and lead to bad decisions and grievous mistakes.

REVIEW QUESTIONS

1. Why is it difficult for a President to effect major changes during a term in office?
2. Why do Presidents prefer White House aides to Cabinet members in carrying out their programs? Do you think this is a good idea? Why or why not? Be very specific about your reasons.
3. Which of the three approaches to organizational leadership do you think is the best? Explain.
4. What are the most significant political decisions made by the President?
5. Why are presidential decisions in the areas of foreign and military policy the most difficult?

ACTIVITIES FOR REVIEW

activity 1   Prepare a wall chart showing the structure and areas of responsibility of the National Security Council.

activity 2   Research proposals for reorganization of the executive branch. How many proposals can you find? How many have been implemented, fully or in part? Which do you think would be the most effective? Why? Report your findings and recommendations to the class.

activity 3   Read reports of the Watergate scandal, which resulted in the resignation of President Nixon. To what extent did the White House staff organizational structure contribute to the President's fall? Do you think the President could have avoided this problem and his threatened impeachment by using a different administrative structure? Explain.

political science DICTIONARY

Brain Trust—Franklin Roosevelt's group of unpaid advisers.   p. 395

generalists—presidential staff members who gather information and serve as trouble shooters.   p. 403

Kitchen Cabinet—Andrew Jackson's informal group of advisers.   p. 395

UNIT SUMMARY

The Constitution says little about the office of President, and yet it has become one of the most powerful offices in the world. The powers and responsibilities of the presidency have been greatly expanded. Some fear that the executive now overshadows the legislative and judicial branches sufficiently to upset the system of checks and balances.

Constitutional requirements for presidential candidacy are few. The candidate must be at least 35 years old, a citizen by birth, and a resident of the United States for at least 14 years. A candidate must also possess practical qualifications, such as the ability to get elected and to provide leadership in office.

The President derives power from a variety of sources. Some of the power is inherent in the President's roles as chief of state, commander in chief, chief executive, chief legislator, director of foreign, domestic, and economic policy, and party leader.

The President's management role has become larger and more complex as the government has grown, and the responsibilities and power of the presidency have become increasingly complex. In recent years Presidents have come to rely more and more on White House aides with personal loyalty to the President to manage all aspects of the President's program.

Bibliography

Allison, Graham T. *Essence of Decision: Explaining the Cuban Missile Crises.* Waltham: Little, Brown, and Company, 1971.

Barber, James D. *The Presidential Character—Predicting Performances in the White House.* Englewood Cliffs: Prentice Hall, 1977.

Burns, James M. *Roosevelt: The Lion and the Fox.* New York: Harcourt Brace, Jovanovich, Inc., 1956.

Cronin, Thomas E. *The State of the Presidency.* Massachusetts: Little, Brown, and Company, 1975.

Ehrlichman, John. *The Company.* New York: Simon and Schuster, 1976.

Review questions

1. List the eight essential political tasks of the President.
2. What effect do you think continued expansion of the power of the President and the White House staff could have on the concept of separation of powers and the system of checks and balances?
3. Since the mid-1950's, many political observers have argued that there is a need for an appointed Assistant President who could take some of the pressures off the President. Would you favor such a plan? Why or why not?

Skills questions

Based on the charts in Unit 6, answer the following questions:

1. Trace the steps in selecting delegates to a national convention. When is Election Day? What body is responsible for the final selection of the President?
2. Write the names of the departments that are responsible for providing the following:
   a. food stamps
   b. relief from natural disasters
   c. cultural exchanges
   d. job training
   e. mortgage insurance
   f. census information
   g. overseas troops and military bases
   h. firearms control
3. Define the formalistic, competitive, and collegial approaches to organizational leadership. Using the information in the chart, which of these approaches do you think is best? Explain.

Activities

activity 1   Read about the Cuban missile crisis, or see the film *The Missiles of October.* Analyze President Kennedy's organizational style, and report on its strengths and weaknesses.

activity 2   Research the organizational style of a President who interests you. Biographies are a good source of information. Present your analysis to the class.

activity 3   Learn as much as you can about the role of a particular White House aide, such as Sherman Adams, H. R. Haldeman, or John Ehrlichman. How much power did this nonelected aide possess? How much of the President's power was delegated to the aide? Evaluate the benefits and costs of this solution to the problem of handling the massive responsibilities of the presidency.

UNIT 7

PAULA STERN

In 1978 Paula Stern became a United States international trade commissioner. The commission is an independent, impartial, fact-finding government agency that deals with matters of international trade and tariffs. Created in 1916, the Commission's activities include: determining whether domestic industries are being seriously injured by increased imports; taking action to counteract unfair trade practices in import trade; determining whether domestic industries are being injured by the importation and sale of articles at less than fair value; providing the President, Congress, other government agencies, and the public with technical information and advice on trade and tariff matters; conducting studies on trade and tariff issues relating to U.S. foreign trade; and assisting in the development of uniform statistical data to develop comparability among export, import, and domestic production statistics. A commissioner's term lasts for nine years.

Stern has an extensive educational background. She received her B.A. from Goucher College in 1967 and an M.A. in regional studies from Harvard University in 1969. In addition Stern has an M.A. (1970), M.A.L.D. (1970), and Ph.D. (1976) in international affairs from the Fletcher School of Law and Diplomacy. She is married and has one son.

In 1972 Stern started her career in government as a legislative assistant to Senator Gaylord Nelson. (D-WI). She became Senator Nelson's senior legislative assistant in 1976 and served as a policy analyst on matters related to the State Department for the Carter-Mondale transition team. Stern was an international affairs fellow with the Council on Foreign Relations from late 1977 to late 1978.

Stern has worked in many areas. She has written numerous articles on domestic affairs, international trade, foreign policy, and the women's movement. Between 1975 and 1976 she was a guest scholar at the Brookings Institute where she worked on a book, *Water's Edge: Domestic Politics and the Making of American Foreign Policy.* Stern is listed in the 1979 edition of *Outstanding Young Women of America.* She also serves on the board of directors of the Inter-American Foundation, an independent government corporation that supports and stimulates social change in Latin America and the Caribbean.

THE EXECUTIVE BRANCH (Part II)

OVERVIEW

■ The federal bureaucracy has grown rapidly in size and power.

■ A bureaucracy is a group of nonelective officials characterized by specialization of function, hierarchy, job security, informal channels of communication and influence, and incrementalism.

■ The merit system protects most federal jobs from political pressure by emphasizing ability and guaranteeing tenure.

■ The civil service today is characterized by stable size, diverse composition, competitive salaries and benefits, concentration of minority-group members and women at the subprofessional level, and a high rate of turnover.

■ The federal bureaucracy has been criticized as resisting change, being biased in favor of Democratic party policies, producing overlapping and poorly coordinated programs, and being too client-oriented and narrowly specialized.

■ Reform proposals focus on greater responsiveness and accountability.

■ Independent regulatory commissions are responsible for the regulation of interstate commerce. Their authority covers all areas of American economic life.

22

Bureaucrats and Bureaucracy

The federal bureaucracy is sufficiently large and independent of control that it can be considered a fourth branch of government. It consists of 13 executive departments, scores of independent agencies, and several government corporations. Each of these departments, agencies, and corporations is subdivided into bureaus (offices). Bureaus, in turn, are subdivided into smaller units. This pattern of organization is known as a hierarchy. Except for the handful of organizations that are responsible only to Congress or to the Supreme Court, all federal agencies are part of the executive bureaucracy.

Agencies perform specialized functions and often overlap one another. Frequently, two or more agencies operating in the same area will attempt to coordinate their programs. Presidents are interested in coordination but are often frustrated in achieving it.

The civil service system fills federal jobs on the basis of merit. Career civil servants (bureaucrats) come from varied backgrounds and spend most of their adult lives working for the federal government. Bureaucrats tend to develop special ties with the groups served by their agencies. Despite their alliances with special-interest groups, bureaucrats do solve problems—such as improving school reading levels—and do not merely respond to political pressures and demands.

CHAPTER PREVIEW

1. THE FEDERAL BUREAUCRACY
2. CHARACTERISTICS OF BUREAUCRACY
3. THE CIVIL SERVICE
4. CRITICISMS AND SUGGESTED REFORMS

1. THE FEDERAL BUREAUCRACY

The dictionary lists three definitions of "bureaucracy":

1. a body of nonelective government officials;

2. government characterized by the specialization of functions, fixed rules, and a hierarchy of authority; and

3. a system of administration marked by status and red tape.

The federal bureaucracy fits all these definitions. It is composed of government officials who are not elected. Those at the top are political appointees, whereas the others are hired through the civil service system. There are countless bureaus that perform specific and specialized functions. The bureaus are ranked in a hierarchy. The President and the Cabinet secretaries are at the top of the hierarchy, followed by the politically appointed sub-Cabinet officials, then the bureau chiefs, who are career civil servants, and so on down the line. The federal bureaucracy is often criticized for its lack of coordination, its duplication of efforts, its inefficiency, and its issuance of directives that produce red tape.

Functions. The bureaucracy carries out the federal government's policies and programs. It consists of almost 3 million civilian employees, making the federal government the largest single employer in the United States. The Cabinet departments employ 1.7 million people. And 120 federal agencies employ the remainder.

Washington is the center of the government, but only 13 percent of all federal employees work in the nation's capital. The

Postal workers make up a very large percentage of federal employees.

rest, including most postal employees, work throughout the country. The Postal Service alone accounts for almost 600,000 employees, the Veterans Administration employs 200,000, and the Department of Agriculture employs 86,000. Astronauts, scientists who test dangerous drugs, clerks who process Social Security checks, and national park rangers are all bureaucrats. One observer recently described the bureaucracy as "the glue that holds our society together."

Top bureaucrats—Cabinet secretaries and the heads of major agencies—recommend policies and programs to the President. The administration of these policies is the job of the career employees—the middle- and the lower-level bureaucrats.

The bureaucracy in the United States is the largest and the most complex in the world. Bureaucrats are the core of American government. Without career bureaucrats the government would be a collection of generals without armies.

Bureaucrats are asked to do thousands of different jobs. They deliver mail, inspect food, build highways, and license television channels. On the state and local levels, government bureaucrats set standards for buildings, register automobiles, decide what rates can be charged for gas, electricity, and telephone service, and certify births, marriages, and deaths. Virtually every human activity is affected in some way by bureaucrats and the rules that they apply.

All large organizations are bureaucracies—churches, businesses, labor unions, universities. Bureaucracy reflects the bigness and the complexity of modern society. It is an

Bureaucrats are responsible for certifying births.

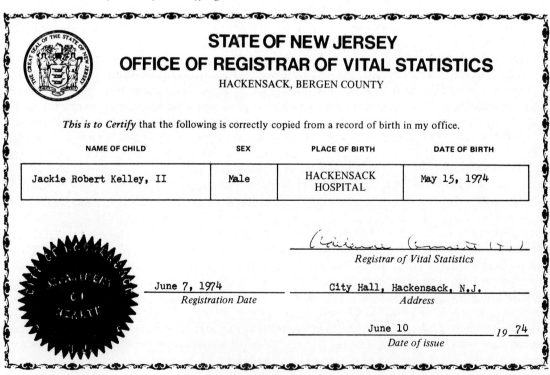

orderly way of organizing people to carry out the programs of a large organization.

Uniqueness. The federal bureaucracy is different from other large organizations in a number of ways. First and foremost, its scope of activities is very broad—ranging all the way from delivering mail to probing outer space, from researching the causes of heart disease to printing paper money (and later burning it when it wears out). The federal bureaucracy differs from other large bureaucracies in other important ways. The American people—not a board of directors—elect the head of the federal bureaucracy. The President's term is much shorter than the length of service of the average bureaucrat. The "board of directors" of the federal bureaucracy is the Congress, which consists of 535 members (senators and representatives) who issue broad rules (laws), supply money (appropriations), and provide publicity (hearings and investigations). Finally, people who disagree with the decisions made by bureaucrats take their complaints not to the top executives or to the board of directors but to a group of judges (federal courts).

There is one other major difference. Employees of other large organizations can be fired. Most federal bureaucrats are secure in their jobs until they retire.

What kinds of problems do bureaucrats face? How representative are they of the people whom they serve? These and other questions will be discussed in this chapter.

Size of the Bureaucracy. The vast majority of the 2.7 million federal bureaucrats are employed in regional and local offices around the country—and, in some cases, around the world. These employees are sometimes referred to as members of the field service. Local post offices and armed forces recruiting centers are part of the field service. To promote coordination, efforts have been made to concentrate federal offices in a small number of regional centers. In spite of this effort, most large cities have several federal offices—each reporting to regional and national offices.

The federal civil service has actually decreased in recent years. There are two reasons for this development. First, many aspects of federal policy have been delegated to people who perform services and spend federal money but are not employed by the federal government. Instead, they sign contracts with the federal bureaucracy. Such people include suppliers of goods and services to the Defense Department, university officials and faculty, hospital administrators, and the directors of government-supported private corporations like COMSAT (the Communications Satellite Corporation, which transmits telephone conversations and television programs to all parts of the world by space satellites).

These private suppliers prefer to enter into contracts with the bureaucracy because that relationship provides maximum financial support with a minimum of bureaucratic restrictions.

Almost half of the civilian employees of the federal bureaucracy work for defense agencies, including the army, the navy, and the air force. However, the Defense Department relies very heavily on outside contractors for defense production, weapons design and development, aerospace equipment, and scientific research.

The second reason for the decrease in the size of the federal bureaucracy is that the federal government and state and local governments now share a number of responsibilities for federal programs, especially those developed by the departments of Health and Human Services (HHS), Housing and Urban Development (HUD), and Transportation. Many state, city, and county agencies are supported almost entirely with federal funds and devote much of their time implementing the programs financed by federal

Pictured here is the Manned Spacecraft Center in Houston, Texas. What figure is shown on the TV screen?

grants. All state and local agencies using federal funds must hire employees on a merit system—as the federal government does—to ensure equal job opportunities for all qualified applicants. There are approximately 13 million employees at state and local levels of government. Bureaucrats, including employees of federal, state, and local government, represent 16 percent of the working population in the United States.

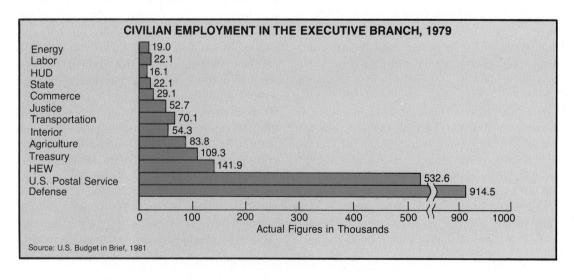

CIVILIAN EMPLOYMENT IN THE EXECUTIVE BRANCH, 1979

Department	Figure
Energy	19.0
Labor	22.1
HUD	16.1
State	22.1
Commerce	29.1
Justice	52.7
Transportation	70.1
Interior	54.3
Agriculture	83.8
Treasury	109.3
HEW	141.9
U.S. Postal Service	532.6
Defense	914.5

Actual Figures in Thousands

Source: U.S. Budget in Brief, 1981

section review

1. What is the function of the nation's federal bureaucracy?
2. How is the federal bureaucracy different from other large organizations?
3. Why has the bureaucracy decreased in size?

2. CHARACTERISTICS OF BUREAUCRACY

Governments of modern industrialized societies employ large numbers of people in complex organizations and use procedures and techniques known only to people who have special training. Bureaucracy developed in response to the needs of complex organizations for skillful, efficient, administration.

All bureaucracies have at least five characteristics:

1. *Specialization of function, or division of labor.* Each position has specific tasks assigned to it, regardless of the individual who holds the job.

2. *Hierarchy, or fixed lines of command.* Departments, bureaus, and subdivisions are organized in a pyramid, with each lower office supervised by a higher office. Decisions flow downward from the top to be put in effect below. Information flows upward from below (or from the field) and forms the basis for policies and decisions made at the upper levels.

3. *Job security, or career employment.* This guarantee attracts people to work for the organization and promotes loyalty to its goals. At the federal level civil service employees are recruited and promoted on the basis of merit (qualifications and competence).

4. *Formal channels of communication and influence.* Relationships are structured according to status within the hierarchy and are formal—and thus impersonal.

5. *Incrementalism, or gradual change.* Bureaucrats move one step at a time (by increments) and adjust programs, rather than restructure or overturn them. Incrementalism avoids the confusion, dislocation, and shifts in personnel that usually accompany more rapid change. The price of this approach may be excessive caution, adherence to obsolete methods, and unwillingness to experiment.

As the most important characteristics of the federal bureaucracy, specialization and hierarchy require further consideration.

Specialization. A basic function of bureaucracy is to introduce specialized or technical knowledge into the policy-making process. Specialized knowledge may lead a bureaucrat to be overenthusiastic about his or her specialty. The wise political leader knows that navy bureaucrats are committed to ships, air force bureaucrats to jets, missiles, and bombs, and army experts to conventional ground forces. Only top administrators who are responsible for many programs have enough general knowledge and information to understand how programs fit together.

Specialization tends to create bureaucratic subdivisions that outlive their usefulness. For example, the National Screw Thread Commission was created during the First World War to standardize the threads of screws. In 1939 it was reorganized into the Interdepartmental Screw Thread Committee and lasted for another 25 years.

Another consequence of specialization is the overlapping of functions among agencies. There are, for example, 13 different drug abuse programs that are administered by various departments. Coordination is needed to prevent these several programs from duplicating one another or from working at cross purposes. Coordination can be achieved in two ways—from above and *laterally* (at the same level).

Bureaus operating in closely connected

The Defense Department relies on outside contractors to build tanks and other equipment. Pictured here is a Detroit tank plant.

areas may be grouped under an assistant secretary who coordinates their activities from above. Assistant secretaries are, in turn, grouped under a secretary who coordinates their activities. Coordination between agencies of two different departments can be

effected by the two secretaries concerned. Coordination among the major executive departments rests with the President.

Under a system of lateral coordination, an interagency or interdepartmental coordinating committee is formed. Officials of comparable authority or rank in their respective agencies meet to exchange information. They also make an attempt to avoid duplication of effort. Sometimes an order from above (issued by the President or the secretary) will give one agency primary responsibility in a particular area. But it will require it to "clear" any policy recommendation with other agencies involved in the same area. The agency with primary responsibility will often make changes in its proposals to accommodate the views of the other agencies involved.

Hierarchy. The more employees there are and the more complex their jobs, the more highly organized an agency will be. A person may work for the Library, Planning, and Development branch of the Division of Library Programs of the Bureau of Libraries and Educational Technology of the Department of Education. This high degree of separation into smaller and smaller units evolves over a long period of time as tasks become more complex.

At the top, or department level, of the bureaucracy, the secretary's administrative responsibilities are generally shared with a deputy secretary, or undersecretary. Several assistant secretaries oversee the major programs. Secretaries also have various staff assistants who help them in planning, budgeting, public relations, and other staff functions.

Departments are divided into bureaus staffed by civil servants. Generally, bureau chiefs are chosen by the President from the highest rank of the civil service. Bureaus are commonly divided according to function— for example, the Bureau of Libraries and Education Technology of the Department of Education. Sometimes, they are divided on the basis of *clientele*—the group served—for example, the Bureau of Indian Affairs of the Interior Department.

The military services and the Foreign Service are organized somewhat differently.

They are hierarchical—for they consist of generals, admirals, and ambassadors at the top and second lieutenants, ensigns, and third secretaries at the bottom. But they are not highly specialized. Leadership is based on general knowledge and broad experience—not on specialization, which is regarded as a narrowing influence. As a result, most officers in the military and foreign services are able to perform in many capacities but lack the specific competence of an expert. Lack of specialization may place them at a disadvantage in dealing with the rest of the government bureaucracy, which values specialized knowledge.

Bureaucrats' Backgrounds. In their social origins, religions, education, occupations, race, and ethnic backgrounds, bureaucrats are more representative of the American people than are political appointees and members of Congress.

Diverse social backgrounds and experience affect bureaucratic decisions. For example, suppose that three people in the Program Planning and Evaluation Bureau of the Office of Education are asked to suggest programs for improving education in high schools. One is Black and formerly taught in an inner-city high school close to where she was born. The second is White and used to teach high school in the comfortable suburb where he grew up. The third is a former professor at Harvard. These people are likely to propose very different programs.

Most bureaucrats have one thing in common with each other but not with the rest of the American people. They have spent most of their adult lives in one department of the federal government.

The typical bureaucrat is a White male, aged 40, who comes from a lower-middle-class family. He is a graduate of a large state university and has taken some post-graduate training. He has served in only two bureaus in his department and has worked his way up through the lower ranks. He has spent several

FORREST J. GERARD, FORMER ASSISTANT SECRETARY OF THE INTERIOR FOR INDIAN AFFAIRS

In 1977 Forrest J. Gerard, a member of the Blackfoot Indian tribe, became the first assistant secretary of the interior for Indian affairs. Born January 15, 1925, in Browning, Montana, Gerard grew up on a ranch on the Blackfoot reservation. The youngest of eight children, he attended public schools in Browning. After graduation from high school in 1943, he joined the Army Air Corps and won the Air Medal for participating in 35 B-24 combat missions over southeastern Europe.

As chief of the Bureau of Indian Affairs (BIA), Forrest Gerard headed the largest subdivision within the Interior Department, accounting for a fourth of its budget and personnel. Previously, the official in charge of Indian affairs was a commissioner, who reported to an assistant secretary. With the upgrading of the post, Forrest Gerard reported directly to the Interior secretary and took part in all departmental policy decisions. This change reflects a growing concern within the Department of the Interior for its "special trust and responsibility to American Indians."

One of the critical areas that the assistant secretary must oversee is the identification of possible solutions to the bitter controversy over Indian water rights in the West. In 1908 the Supreme Court ruled in *Winters* v. *United States* that Native Americans have the right to all the water they need from water that originates, underlays, borders, or flows across reservation land. In spite of this legal victory, however, Native Americans were still, 70 years later, fighting for their water rights in many areas of the Southwest. In that region, where water is scarce, Native Americans have not benefited from the many projects — dams, reservoirs, canals, and irrigation ditches — built by the federal government. These projects, which determined where and how much water would be made available, often favored other interest groups. The need for a fair plan for water distribution remains pressing. The problem is complex. In one area as many as four different tribes have claims upon a river whose water supply is already dwindling because of industrial and urban development.

The options formulated by Forrest Gerard to help relieve this conflict were an important part of the Carter administration's national water policy.

years in the field office where he now has an executive post. He is cautious, is unimaginative in his approach to his job, and is careful to avoid controversy. He has mastered the art of compromise and accommodation. He is content with existing policies and undertakes new initiatives only when they cannot be avoided. He is likely to remain where he is until he retires. He is dedicated to his particular aspect of government activity and probably knows more about it than anyone else does.

section review

1. List five characteristics of bureaucracies.
2. What is the disadvantage of specialization in bureaucratic subdivisions?
3. How are bureau chiefs generally chosen?
4. Describe the typical bureaucrat.

3. THE CIVIL SERVICE

Eighty-eight percent of all federal employees are career civil servants. They carry out all government programs and provide continuity from one administration to the next. Their role is to provide the specialized knowledge and competence needed to administer government services.

History of the Civil Service. Under our early Presidents, ability was one of the primary requirements for appointment to federal office. When Washington made his several hundred appointments, he set out to choose "such persons alone . . . as shall be the best qualified." John Adams insisted on competence and found enough suitable people among supporters of his party, the Fed-

eralists. When Jefferson became President in 1801, he turned out most of Adams' Federalists to make room for his own Democratic-Republicans. But he spoke of "due participation" in government by both political parties.

Andrew Jackson, who became President in 1829, immediately dismissed about 10 percent of the 10,000 employees in the civil service. His opponents charged him with introducing a "spoils system" although Jackson called it rotation in office. Jackson feared the bureaucracy. He believed that no one could hold office for any length of time without becoming corrupt.

"Due participation" and "rotation in office" was advantageous in that it involved ordinary people in government. It also

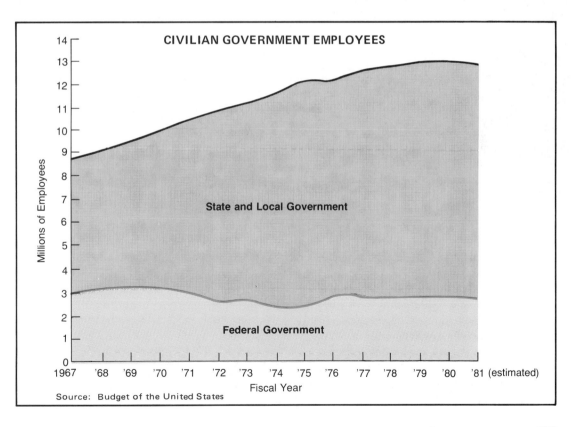

CIVILIAN GOVERNMENT EMPLOYEES

State and Local Government

Federal Government

Millions of Employees

1967 '68 '69 '70 '71 '72 '73 '74 '75 '76 '77 '78 '79 '80 '81 (estimated)

Fiscal Year

Source: Budget of the United States

strengthened the party in power and made the government more responsible to the people.

As the federal government grew bigger and more complex, the spoils system increasingly became the way that government appointees were chosen. Every change in administration swept Washington, D.C., clean. Many talented people were dismissed. Political power was very often in the hands of officeholders who owed their jobs to the President's party. Huge profits could be made on public contracts, and several officeholders were implicated in bribery and scandal.

Concerned citizens organized the National Civil Service Reform League. Public opinion was aroused further in 1881, when President James A. Garfield was assassinated by a disappointed office seeker. In 1883 the Pendleton Act established the basic outlines of the federal civil service system. The act created the Civil Service Commission, composed of three members serving overlapping six-year terms. They are appointed by the President with the Senate's consent. No more than two of them may belong to the same political party.

The Merit System. The Pendleton Act placed certain employees under a new classified service that people could enter by passing competitive examinations. This form of selection came to be called the *merit system*. Congress assigned 10 percent of federal employees to the classified service but authorized the President to expand its ranks. The largest expansion was accomplished by President Theodore Roosevelt. He had headed the Civil Service Commission. Although not all federal employees come under the jurisdiction of the Civil Service Commission (now known as the Office of Personnel Management), almost all career federal employees are covered today by the merit system.

The central principles of the merit sys-

tem are the following:

1. Government employees are selected and promoted on the basis of their abilities and skills.

2. All applicants are treated equally, without regard to race, sex, creed, national origin, or political affiliation.

3. Employees receive fair and adequate salaries. Those who do the same work receive the same salary.

4. Employees are protected from partisan political pressures.

5. Employees are prohibited from using their official positions in partisan politics.

The original purpose of the merit system was to take politics out of public employment. Civil servants were to be dismissed only because of incompetence, inefficiency, or illegal activity. This guaranteed that politics would not enter the picture. The merit system thus helps to ensure honest and effective government.

The Office of Personnel Management (OPM). The Office of Personnel Management (formerly the Civil Service Commission) prevents arbitrary and unfair personnel practices. It institutes standard salary and promotion policies among the various departments and agencies. Bureaucrats must work closely with the OPM in staffing their agencies. The OPM has about 7,000 employees who help to recruit, examine, and appoint government workers. It advertises for new employees throughout the nation (especially in post offices), prepares and administers written examinations (usually true-false, matching, and multiple choice questions) in most major cities, and compiles a register of people who pass the tests. A score of 70 is a passing grade, and veterans are given an extra five-point preference.

To become a court stenographer, you must first take a civil service exam. A score of 70 is a passing grade, and veterans are given a five-point bonus.

Trends in the Civil Service. *Salaries and fringe benefits.* Salaries at all but the top levels are competitive with those in the private sector. In 1981 the lowest starting salary was $7,960 (GS-1 pay grade), and the highest starting salary was $58,500 (GS-18 level). Fringe benefits are also competitive and in-clude a generous retirement program.

Minorities and Women. Although the proportion of Blacks employed in the civil service is higher than in the overall work force, Blacks are underrepresented at the higher levels of the bureaucracy. Women are similarly underrepresented. In spite of the affirmative-action programs, Blacks, Hispanics, and women are concentrated at subprofessional levels of the civil service.

Turnover. Although most federal employees are in the career civil service, nearly 20 percent resign, retire, or otherwise leave government service each year. They are replaced, of course, by new employees.

Restrictions on Political Activity. Congress and the Office of Personnel Management restrict the partisan political activities of government employees. They may not actively take part in campaigns for public office or serve as delegates to party conventions. Nor may they collect funds from others for a party or a candidate—although they may personally contribute to whomever they choose. These restrictions against partisan political activity were set forth in the Hatch Act of 1939. A second Hatch Act in 1940 extended the same restrictions to state and local employees whose salaries are paid wholly or in part by federal funds.

section review

1. What was the spoils system?
2. Why was the Pendleton Act created?
3. List three of the functions of the Office of Personnel Management.
4. How is the political activity of government employees restricted?

4. CRITICISMS AND SUGGESTED REFORMS

Among the most common and justified criticisms leveled at the federal bureaucracy are the following:

1. Bureaucrats resist new ideas and change.

2. Bureaucrats are supposed to be politically neutral so that they can carry out government activites, regardless of which party is in power. However, most bureaucrats are Democrats who share the philosophy of the Democratic party regarding government intervention in the economy, public welfare, and generous government spending.

3. Programs overlap and are poorly coordinated. A poor widow with children might be eligible for Aid to Dependent Children, food stamps, housing assistance, employment counseling, free day care centers and legal services. But for each of these services she would have to go to a different agency.

4. Some bureaucracies are excessively concerned with their clients and may lose sight of the public interest.

5. Many bureaucrats have narrow interests and fail to conceive of policies, programs, and priorities in broader perspectives.

6. There are few opportunities for entry into the highest ranks of the career bureaucracy by qualified outsiders. Also, there is no extraordinary route to the top of the career bureaucracy for any exceptionally qualified insiders.

Proposed Reforms. Several proposals for reform of the bureaucracy are being considered. President Reagan is especially eager to reorganize the government. The aim of reorganization is to increase the bureaucracy's accountability to the President and the President's control over the bureaucracy. A second goal of reorganization is to enable the President to coordinate or eliminate overlapping functions. As we have discussed, major reorganization plans often run into trouble in Congress. Congressional committees and private interest groups resist any reorganization that could break the connections that they have established with particular agencies and bureaus.

Another proposed reform to make the bureaucracy more manageable is *sunset leg-*

islation. Under such legislation each agency is chartered for a certain number of years. At the end of that time, each agency is terminated, unless Congress can be persuaded that there are good reasons to continue it.

A third set of reforms aims at more careful control over government spending. In recent years defense contractors have vastly exceeded their original bids for developing and producing military equipment. A closer monitoring of major spending programs could avoid cost overruns. Moreover, the expenditures of the intelligence agencies are top secret—not even the members of the Appropriations committees know exactly what these agencies spend. Recent adverse publicity about their operations has led many people to call for strict supervision of their activities and spending.

Another proposal to control federal spending is *zero-based budgeting.* Instead of comparing the current year's budget against that of the preceding year, zero-based budgeting forces each agency to justify every dollar requested. If adopted, this budgeting system would force each agency and Congress to consider whether or not a program is necessary and if there might be new and better ways of achieving the same purpose. The answer, "We have always done it this way," would no longer be sufficient to justify continuing certain governmental programs or policies.

Certain reforms propose to make government more responsive to the people. Reformers have suggested that the ombudsman system be adopted by the federal government. For example, an ombudsman would help an elderly person to find out why his or her Social Security check was not delivered. A poor widow with children would similarly be helped to apply for the various federal services to which she is entitled.

The Carter administration directed that all government regulations and letters be written in understandable English rather than in legal terms. Before any regulation is issued, the public must have an opportunity to comment on it. Before it is made final, the agency head must approve it and the author must sign his or her name to the regulation. This directive was made to increase both responsiveness and accountability.

QUOTES from famous people

"Government is a trust, and the officers of the government are trustees; and both the trust and the trustees are created for the benefit of the people."

Henry Clay

President Carter also urged civil service reform to speed the retirement or dismissal of civil servants who no longer perform any useful function. For this plan to work, and to ensure the continuation of high morale with the bureaucracy, the average employee must be convinced that his or her job is secure.

section review

1. What are two criticisms of the nation's federal bureaucracy?
2. What are some proposals to reform the federal bureaucracy?
3. Explain what is meant by a zero-based budget.
4. Why should bureaucrats be politically neutral? Are most bureaucrats neutral?
5. What is meant by sunset legislation?
6. Why did Carter's administration direct that all government regulations be written in understandable English?
7. What types of situations have prompted the call for reform in government spending?

CHAPTER SUMMARY

22

The federal bureaucracy is sufficiently large and independent of control by the President or Congress to be considered a fourth branch of government.

A bureaucracy is a group of nonelective officials within a system characterized by specialization of function, inflexible rules, hierarchy of authority, job security, informal channels of communication and influence, and incrementalism. The system is noted for its officialism and red tape.

Bureaucrats come from diverse social and professional backgrounds. The majority, however, have spent most of their careers in one bureau of the federal government; all have college degrees, and most of them do not come from wealthy families.

The typical bureaucrat is a White male, age 40, from a lower-middle-class family. He has a college degree and has worked in one or two bureaus in his department. He has risen in the hierarchy through caution, avoidance of controversy, and lack of imagination.

In the early years of the Republic, all federal employees were appointed by the President. Concern about political favoritism and the assassination of President Garfield led to the passage of the Pendleton Act, which established a merit system for career employees, administered by the Office of Personnel Management (formerly the Civil Service Commission). The Hatch Act restricts partisan political activities of government employees.

Civil service today is characterized by its stable size, diverse composition, competitive salaries and benefits, concentration of minorities and women at subprofessional levels, and high rate of turnover.

The federal bureaucracy has been criticized for the following reasons: 1) It is resistant to innovation and change. 2) It is philosophically committed to Democratic party policies. 3) Its programs overlap and are poorly coordinated. 4) It is often overly client-oriented. 5) It is too narrowly specialized. 6) It is a closed system with no route to the top for qualified individuals.

Several proposals for reform are being considered that focus on increasing the responsiveness and accountability of the bureaucracy.

REVIEW QUESTIONS

1. Do you agree that bureaucracy is "the glue that holds our society together"? Why or why not? Give specific examples to support your position.

2. Reread the description of the typical bureaucrat. Do you think the traits of bureaucrats add to or detract from the effectiveness of the federal bureaucracy?

3. If you could change the federal bureaucracy in

any way, what would you change? Why? How would you go about instituting this change?

4. The Hatch Act restricts partisan political activities of federal employees. Some see this as a means of protecting the workers; others view it as a denial of their rights as citizens. Do you think federal employees should be able to participate in party politics? Why or why not?

5. Jefferson and Jackson argued that rotation of bureaucrats prevented corruption and allowed the average worker greater opportunity to participate in government, thus making the government more effective and responsive. Do you agree? Why or why not?

ACTIVITIES FOR REVIEW

activity 1   Select a career in which you are interested. Research it in terms of working conditions, training or education requirements, opportunities for advancement, salary, fringe benefits, vacation, and retirement. Are jobs in this field available in both the private sector and government? Compare and contrast the options in these two areas.

activity 2   Prepare a wall chart showing all federal agencies that deal with some aspect of a particular problem (education, health care, welfare, etc.). Show how the agencies overlap and interact.

activity 3   Prepare a report on the growth of the civil service in the United States.

political science DICTIONARY

clientele—the people served by bureaucracies.   p. 423

division of labor—specialization of function; each worker is assigned specific tasks.   p. 421

fixed lines of command—the organization of departments, bureaus, and subdivisions in a pyramid, with each lower office supervised by a higher office.   p. 421

zero-based budgeting—proposed bureaucratic system in which agencies would account for every dollar they request instead of basing the current year's budget on that of the preceding year.   p. 429

23

Bureaucrats and Public Policy

The growth of Cabinet departments, independent agencies, and government corporations can be traced to the growth of industrialization that occurred during the nineteenth century and the Great Depression that brought the New Deal to power in Washington. The economic crisis of the 1930's not only increased the government's role in regulating the economy but also justified its actions in providing goods and services to promote the general welfare.

Congress delegates to the executive branch discretion to interpret and apply laws. Because of their continuity in office and their specialized knowledge, career bureaucrats draft the directives, rules, and regulations that constitute the most important stage in the policy-making process. Their superiors, the Cabinet and sub-Cabinet secretaries, usually approve the recommendations of their subordinates because they respect the knowledge that career bureaucrats have acquired during their tenure in the federal bureaucracy.

When the President seeks—through the preparation of the budget and through reorganization plans—to make the bureaucracy more accountable to the Chief Executive, career bureaucrats seek support from their allies in Congress and from the clients that their bureaus serve. The life of a career bureaucrat is marked by conflicting loyalties—to the President, who is the Chief Executive of the federal bureaucracy; to Congress, which appropriates funds and delegates policy-making authority; and to client groups, with whom the career bureaucrat shares a number of interests and concerns.

CHAPTER PREVIEW

1. THE EXPANDING FEDERAL BUREAUCRACY
2. CHECKS AND BALANCES: BUREAUCRATIC ACCOUNTABILITY
3. BUREAU PROGRAMS AND CLIENT GROUPS

1. THE EXPANDING FEDERAL BUREAUCRACY

Multiplication of federal agencies is a twentieth-century phenomenon. In earlier times the President and the executive departments—such as State, Treasury, and Justice—made up the entire executive branch of government. In 1802, there were only 3,000 civilian government employees, including about 1,000 postmasters. The federal government consisted of the Departments of State, Treasury, War (army), Navy, and the Post Office. The attorney general had no staff and operated out of his own home.

Growth of Agencies. As the country grew, these original departments also grew. The attorney general acquired a staff, and the Post Office received Cabinet status. Only two executive departments were added in the nineteenth century. They were the Department of the Interior (1849), which dealt with westward expansion and Indian affairs, and the Department of Agriculture (1862), which served the needs of farmers. The Civil Service Commission (1883) and the Interstate Commerce Commission (1887) were the only other major agencies of government established in that century.

QUOTES from famous people

"They are not meant to be governing agencies except in some marginal way. They are and were meant to be agencies of representation. They were, in other words, set up not to govern but to be governed."

Theodore Lowi

John R. Block, U.S. Secretary of Agriculture, is very aware of the problems facing farmers. He is shown here on his farm in Illinois prior to his appointment.

Massive industrial and financial expansion, the corresponding demand for government regulation, and the rise of labor organizations led to the formation of two new Cabinet departments at the beginning of the twentieth century—Commerce (1903) and Labor (1913)—and two important regulatory authorities—the Federal Reserve Board (1913) and the Federal Trade Commission (1914).

New Deal Agencies. The multiplication of government agencies entered its most expansive period with the beginning of the New Deal in 1933. Government grew to meet the economic emergency. No Cabinet department was created, although existing departments were given many new responsibilities. FDR's preference, however, was to establish independent agencies to take care of new government functions. Most of those agencies operated under the President's firm control, not under the control of a Cabinet secretary.

Independent Agencies. The independent agencies are misnamed. They are independent of the Cabinet departments but not of the President or Congress. Most of these agencies are headed by one person. That person is appointed by and is responsible to the President.

ACTION includes the Peace Corps, Vista, and other voluntary service organizations. The Environmental Protection Agency (EPA) deals with the control of air and water pollution, solid waste disposal, and a variety of other environmental matters. The National Aeronautics and Space Administration (NASA) builds rockets and space ships and explores

Peace Corps workers dish out food for hungry children in India. The Peace Corps is part of ACTION, which is an independent agency.

STRUCTURE OF THE FEDERAL BUREAUCRACY

THE PRESIDENT

Executive Office of the President (partial listing)

White House Staff
Office of Management and Budget
Council of Economic Advisers

Council on Environmental Quality
National Security Council
Domestic Policy Staff

THE CABINET

State	Defense	Commerce	Justice
Labor	Interior	Treasury	Energy
Agriculture	Housing and Urban Development	Health and Human Services	
Transportation		Education	

THE BUREAUCRACY

Independent Agencies, Regulatory Commissions and Other Offices

ACTION
Advisory Comm. on Intergovernmental Relations
American Battle Monuments Comm.
Civil Aeronautics Board
Consumer Product Safety Comm.
Energy Research and Development Admin.
Environmental Protection Agency
Equal Employment Opportunity Comm.
Export-Import Bank of U.S.
Federal Communications Commission
Federal Deposit Insurance Corporation
Federal Election Commission
Federal Energy Administration
Federal Power Commission
Federal Reserve System
Federal Trade Commission
General Services Administration
Indian Claims Commission
Interstate Commerce Commission
National Aeronautics and Space Admin.
Veterans Administration

National Foundation on the Arts and the Humanities
National Labor Relations Board
National Mediation Board
National Science Foundation
Nuclear Regulatory Commission
Occupational Safety and Health Review Commission
Overseas Private Investment Corp.
Panama Canal Company
Securities and Exchange Commission
Selective Service System
Small Business Administration
Tennessee Valley Authority
U.S. Arms Control and Disarmament Agency
U.S. Civil Service Commission
U.S. Commission on Civil Rights
U.S. Information Agency
U.S. International Trade Commission
U.S. Postal Service

outer space. The Veterans' Administration deals with veterans' affairs and benefits. The General Services Administration (GSA) manages all government buildings, furnishes supplies and equipment, and stores government records. The Small Business Administration (SBA) makes loans to small businesses, advises them about securing government contracts and helps them to adjust to changed economic conditions. The Central Intelligence Agency (CIA) gathers information—sometimes secretly—in matters pertaining to foreign relations and national security.

These agencies are only a few of the 120 examples that could be cited. Some agencies perform multidepartment functions. Most agencies that are designated as commissions are in this category. Others were created to be especially accessible to pressure groups. The Veterans' Administration is a good example. Still others, including most of the New Deal agencies, were formed to meet specific needs. Little thought was given to how they would fit in the organization of the executive branch.

Finally, a number of recent Presidents created new agencies to carry out new programs—the Office of Economic Opportunity (OEO), the Peace Corps, and NASA. The OEO and the Peace Corps were attached to the Executive Office of the President. The main purpose in giving new programs to new agencies is to ensure that such programs will not be restrained by bureaucrats who have fixed ideas about the issues involved.

Government Corporations. The federal government has undertaken economic activities for the general welfare. Government corporations have been established to conduct these activities without regard to politics. They are conducted as though they were private businesses. An act of Congress is required to establish a government corporation. The director and governing board are appointed by the President and confirmed by the Senate. There are now more than 20 government corporations, including the

Postal Service and the Export-Import Bank.

Perhaps the best known example of a government corporation is the Tennessee Valley Authority (TVA). Congress set up the TVA at FDR's urging in 1933. The TVA expressly provided for the "orderly and proper physical, economic, and social development" of the entire region of the Tennessee River valley. This area included 41,000 square miles covering parts of Tennessee, Kentucky, Virginia, North Carolina, Georgia, Alabama, and Mississippi. The TVA's program deals with hydroelectric power, flood control, improved navigation, reforestation, soil conservation, and attracting industry to the area. **Per capita** income has risen enormously in the area since the TVA began providing electric power. The TVA also supplies power for the national atomic energy installation located at Oak Ridge, Tennessee.

The TVA is one of the best-known examples of a government corporation. What does this particular map represent?

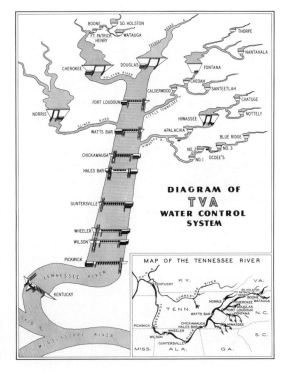

Per capita *means equally to each individual.*

Bureaucratic Policy Making. The bureaucracy is probably the major initiator of public policy. Many proposals for new legislation begin in the bureaucracy. Senior bureaucrats often draft the wording of legislation, testify before committees and subcommittees of Congress, and provide technical information and analysis both to their superiors and to congressional committees. Agency officials often join forces with representatives of interest groups, presidential aides, and congressional leaders to guide bills through Congress.

The bureaucracy does an enormous amount of lawmaking after laws are passed. Congress delegates broad discretion to agency officials to carry out the intent of its laws. Through its interpretations and applications, the bureaucracy determines what those laws mean in practice. For example, a law to control aircraft noise authorizes the federal aviation administrator to "prescribe standards for the measurement of aircraft noise . . . such rules and regulations as he [or she] may find necessary to provide for the control and abatement of aircraft noise and sonic boom."

Another example of bureaucratic policy making can be seen in the former department of HEW's efforts to implement Title IX of the Educational Amendments of 1972. The intent of Congress was to eliminate sex discrimination in all schools and colleges that receive federal funds. How this was to be accomplished was left to the bureaucracy. In 1975 HEW issued regulations that sought to phase out classes "for males only" and "for females only" in coeducational schools. The regulations also called for integrated physical education classes and equal athletic opportunity for both sexes. Such rules have produced great consequences throughout the educational system.

Most bureaucratic policies are not quite as controversial. The less controversial the policy, the more likely it is to be made by people in the middle ranks of a bureau without much review by their superiors. Bureaucrats responsible for such problems as improving children's reading levels are likely to have considerable control over policies and programs in their fields of specialized knowledge.

Once bureaucratic policies are made and imposed, they can be revised by presidential directive, congressional action to clarify legislative intent, and judicial review under the Administrative Procedures Act of 1946.

section review

1. Which two executive departments were added during the nineteenth century?
2. Why may "independent agencies" be misnamed?
3. What is the function of the GSA?
4. How is a government corporation formed?
5. Why was the TVA set up?

2. CHECKS AND BALANCES: BUREAUCRATIC ACCOUNTABILITY

Federal bureaucrats are conscious of the need to justify what they do. They are accountable both to their superiors in the executive branch and to Congress. They are also accountable, in an informal way, to the interest groups with which they deal.

The President and the Bureaucracy. President Johnson once remarked that of the 2.9 million federal employees "on a good day, maybe one hundred are working for the President." Why did the President believe

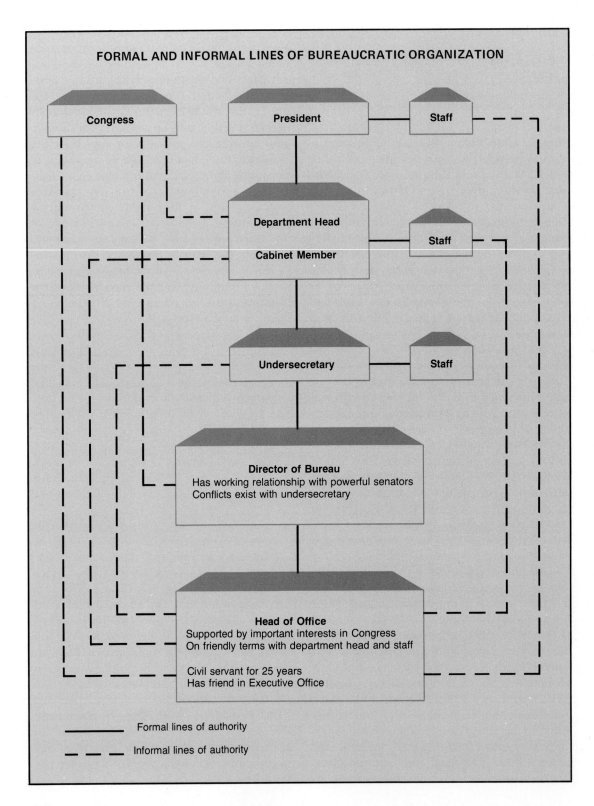

FORMAL AND INFORMAL LINES OF BUREAUCRATIC ORGANIZATION

Congress

President

Staff

Department Head
Cabinet Member

Staff

Undersecretary

Staff

Director of Bureau
Has working relationship with powerful senators
Conflicts exist with undersecretary

Head of Office
Supported by important interests in Congress
On friendly terms with department head and staff

Civil servant for 25 years
Has friend in Executive Office

———— Formal lines of authority

– – – – Informal lines of authority

that the Chief Executive lacks control over the actions and the policies of the federal bureaucracy?

When a new President comes into office, that person is confronted with major policy problems. During the campaign the President probably talked about reorganizing the government. Reorganization may be high on the agenda. But the first thing that the President must do is prepare and submit a revised budget to Congress, which is in the process of holding hearings on the previous President's budget for the coming year.

The new President and department heads have to rely heavily on bureaucrats for the technical knowledge and experience necessary to revise the budget. A pattern of dependence begins to develop that becomes difficult to break. Reorganization plans may be delayed, then modified, and finally abandoned altogether.

Presidents and department heads take office with no preconceived notions about specific policies—that is, how much money should be spent on cancer research, satellite communications, or school lunches. The bureaucracy shapes the agenda for the executive branch. Bureaucrats develop their own policies. By the time policy decisions reach the secretary of the department, bureaucrats have defined problems in their own terms, narrowed the range of possible solutions, and assembled the facts and arguments to justify their recommendations. The secretary sees only the final recommendation and supporting arguments. He or she may never know that alternative proposals have been rejected by the bureaucrats.

Political Appointees. The top policy makers include Cabinet secretaries, sub-Cabinet officials, and the heads of most independent agencies. They are responsible for reconciling policies with the President's objectives. In order to do so, they rely on the bureaucracy for technical information and advice.

Most political appointees below the Cabinet level are selected by department or agency heads. However, their formal appointment comes from the President. Recent Presidents followed the more common pattern of letting department heads choose their own assistants. Membership in the President's party is the usual requirement, together with administrative skills and knowledge of the department's work.

In parliamentary systems like Great Britain's, political appointees are members of the prime minister's party in Parliament. In the course of a political career, a British minister (equivalent to a United States secretary) has served in a variety of posts in several different departments. Most ministers change departments every two or three years. When the opposing party wins an election and takes over the government, former ministers become members of the "shadow government" in Parliament and await their return to power.

In the United States, the most common pattern is for political appointees to be recruited from private life. They usually return to private life at the end of the President's term, if they have not resigned beforehand. Nevertheless, some political appointees have served in several different posts during their lifetimes.

Henry L. Stimson, FDR's secretary of war, had served as secretary of war under Taft, as governor general of the Philippines under Coolidge, and as secretary of state under Hoover. James Schlesinger, Carter's first energy secretary, had previously served as head of the Atomic Energy Commission and as director of the CIA under Nixon and as secretary of defense under Nixon and Ford.

The record for varied service is held by Elliot L. Richardson. Between 1969 and 1980 he served as undersecretary of state, secretary of HEW, secretary of defense, attorney general, ambassador to Great Britain, and secretary of commerce under Ford and Nixon, as well as Carter's ambassador to the UN's Law of the Sea Conference.

ALICE MITCHEL RIVLIN
Director of the Congressional Budget Office

Alice M. Rivlin is the director of the Congressional Budget Office, which was established in 1974. Rivlin, the first person to hold this position, was appointed director in 1975 by the Speaker of the House of Representatives and the President pro tempore of the Senate. In 1979 she was reappointed to a second four-year term.

The Congressional Budget Office was created to give Congress a better overview of the federal budget. This overview helps Congress make overall decisions regarding spending and taxing levels, and the deficit or surplus that these levels incur. The Budget Office is responsible for providing the following: economic forecasting and fiscal policy analysis; monitoring congressional budgetary actions; developing cost estimates for carrying out congressional committee bills; furnishing the House and Senate Budget Committees with an annual report on the budget; and undertaking special studies requested by Congress.

Born in Philadelphia in 1931, Rivlin grew up in Bloomington, Indiana. She graduated from Bryn Mawr College in 1952 and received her doctorate in economics from Radcliffe College in 1958.

Rivlin is an economist, a former senior fellow at the Brookings Institute, and has served as assistant secretary of the Department of Health, Education, and Welfare (HEW). While working for HEW (1966–1969), she played a major role in implementing the planning, programming, budgeting system (PPBS) and introduced the idea of using economic analysis to make departmental decisions. Rivlin also chaired a committee on higher education policy and served as co-chairperson of a panel on social indicators.

Rivlin has written extensively on the federal budget, the economy, social experimentation, the distribution of income, the economics of health and education, and improving decision making. Some of her books include *The Role of the Federal Government in Financing Higher Education* and *Systematic Thinking for Social Action*. She has also co-authored three Brookings volumes on the federal budget entitled *Setting National Priorities*.

The President's Budget. The major tool for making the bureaucracy accountable to the President is the budget. The budget is also the President's main means of setting national priorities and coordinating thousands of government programs.

The budget has a material effect on each unit of the bureaucracy. Through the budget the President and the director of the Office of Management and Budget (OMB) can favor certain programs and phase out others. They can expand certain bureaucratic units and trim down others. Within each department the secretary can exercise control over the bureaucracy through the department's internal budget process.

Most bureau chiefs ask for more money than they think they will get. It is up to the secretary and the President—working through the OMB—to set realistic target figures for each bureau. The main responsibility for evaluating the projected targets falls on the OMB's 60 budget examiners. Most examiners work on the budgets of the same bureaus year after year. They understand both the programs and the capabilities of each bureau. Budget examiners work in the Executive Office of the President, and their primary loyalty is to the Chief Executive rather than to the bureaus.

All those involved in the budget process—the departments' internal budget officers, the OMB's budget examiners, the congressional Budget and Appropriations committees, and the Congressional Budget Office—focus on the changes between the current year's budget and the preceding year's budget.

Most programs increase from year to year once they have been accepted as services to be performed by the government. Marked increases or decreases in the budgets of particular programs or bureaus attract attention. Decreases are likely to make particular bureaucrats unhappy and may cause them to bypass the President and appeal to their friends in Congress.

Large shifts of funds from one set of programs to another happen rarely. With so many people—in Congress as well as in the bureaucracy—committed to the **status quo,** hardly anyone is inclined to ask, "Why do

The late J. Edgar Hoover is shown here visiting the Perkins School for the Blind at Watertown, Massachusetts, in 1963.

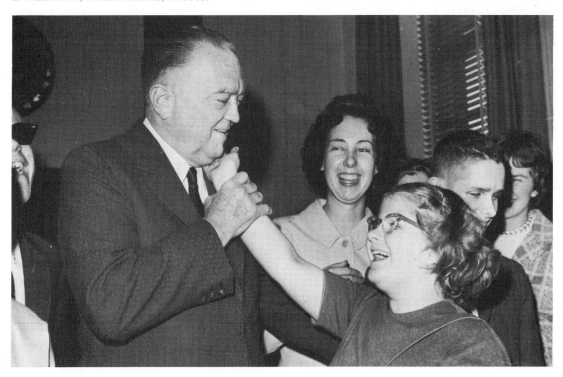

we have this program at all? Does it work at cross-purposes with other federal programs?"

As an example of cross-purposes, HHS and the Federal Trade Commission both have programs to reduce cigarette smoking. But the Department of Agriculture subsidizes tobacco growers. Each program responds to different concerns, and each has its supporters on Capitol Hill.

> **Status quo** means the existing state of affairs.

Reorganization. Recent Presidents have reorganized parts of the executive branch under authority delegated by Congress. Every President has thought of ways to make the bureaucratic structure more effective—and more responsive—to the Chief Executive.

Reorganization proposals tend to succeed when they raise the status of an agency or a number of related agencies by, for example, forming a new Cabinet department. Proposals tend to fail when they lower an agency's status or when they upset existing political arrangements and power balances. The most important of these arrangements involve relationships among the bureaucracy, Congress, and private groups.

Because of bureaucratic resistance to reorganization, the President may choose to create a new agency or try to establish new positions in old agencies and fill them with people dedicated to new programs.

Congress and the Bureaucracy. Congress determines the functions of the bureaucracy and therefore the tasks of career bureaucrats. Congress establishes all agencies (although it has delegated some of its authority to the President) and supports them with money. The General Accounting Office (GAO), an agency of Congress, has broad authority over

government spending. No money can be paid out of the treasury unless the comptroller general (who heads the GAO) certifies the legality of the payment.

Congress continuously reviews the bureaucracy's activities through appropriations hearings and special investigations. Senior members of committees and subcommittees believe that they know more about individual agencies than do the President and the budget examiners. Moreover, they have become acquainted with the heads of various agencies and bureaus through hearings, and shared interests have developed and alliances have been formed. Thus these powerful members of Congress are able to check the President's influence over public policy with influence of their own.

Confirmation hearings for major political appointees are conducted by Senate committees with authority over the policy area involved. No President, for example, is likely to nominate a director of the Veterans' Administration who is unacceptable to the chairperson of the Senate Veterans' Affairs Committee.

Congressional investigations are powerful devices for calling bureaucrats to account for their activities. The CIA, traditionally independent of Congress, was called to account in 1975 by the Senate Special Committtee on Intelligence. Its investigations disclosed that the CIA was involved in a variety of illegal activities. Those disclosures made it easier for Carter to bring the CIA under firmer presidential direction.

Autonomous Bureaus. Because of powerful congressional backing, certain bureaus operate as if they were independent of the President and of their superiors. The Army Corps of Engineers, which builds dams and other public works, is one such bureau. Its chief is authorized to report the bureau's plans for public works to Congress without referring to the President.

The Federal Bureau of Investigation (FBI)

The Army Corps of Engineers, which builds dams and other public works, is an autonomous bureau. What does this mean?

under the leadership of J. Edgar Hoover had many strong supporters in Congress and capitalized on its prestige to enhance its political position. Hoover reported directly to the President rather than to his nominal superior, the attorney general. Since Hoover's death the FBI has come under much closer supervision by the attorney general.

The Bureau of Reclamation in the Department of the Interior is concerned with irrigation projects, flood control, and the construction of dams and hydroelectric power plants. It, too, owes its semi-independent status to powerful supporters in Congress.

Each of these bureaus can call upon congressional supporters to restore funds cut from its budget by the President. Sometimes Congress gives bureaus funds that they have not even asked for.

section review

1. How do bureaucrats help a new President?
2. What is the major tool for making the bureaucracy accountable to the President?
3. Give an example of bureaucracies with cross-purposes.
4. What is the function of the GAO?

3. BUREAU PROGRAMS AND CLIENT GROUPS

In making decisions and in recommending policies, top bureaucrats must try to anticipate the responses of the groups that they serve, the people who work under them, the people whom they work for, their counterparts in other agencies, journalists who cover their departments, interested members of Congress, and the attentive public.

Bureau chiefs usually try to maintain supportive links to key people—congressional committees and client groups. The three elements of this triangle are all interested in protecting and promoting the bureaus' programs.

Multiple Loyalties. Bureaucrats may try to accommodate their superiors' wishes as much as possible, but their actions are influenced by their personalities, backgrounds, alliances, ambitions, and the political context in which they operate.

Bureau chiefs must consider their loyalties when, for example, their individual bureaus, along with all other bureaus, are subject to a 10 percent budget reduction as part of the President's program to curb inflation. The President has a right to expect their loyalty, but so do the people who work with them. Some of them may lose their jobs in the cutback. Bureau chiefs also want to maintain good relations with the people whom their bureaus serve. These people will be hurt by a program cutback. Whom should

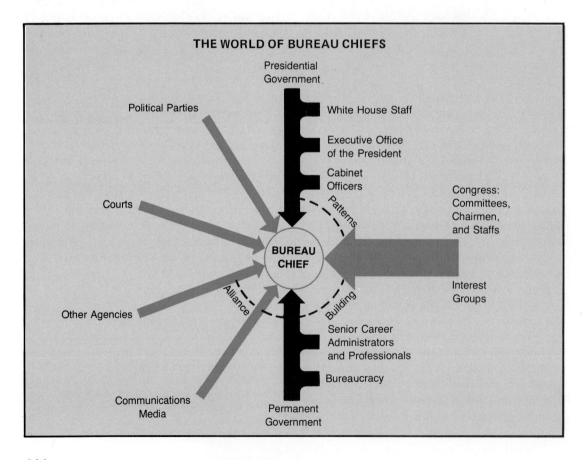

THE WORLD OF BUREAU CHIEFS

Presidential Government

Political Parties

White House Staff

Executive Office of the President

Cabinet Officers

Courts

Patterns

Congress: Committees, Chairmen, and Staffs

BUREAU CHIEF

Other Agencies

Alliance

Building

Interest Groups

Senior Career Administrators and Professionals

Bureaucracy

Communications Media

Permanent Government

they support, therefore? Should they protect their programs and their team by appealing to their friends in Congress? Or should they, as professional administrators, suppport the Chief Executive?

Double Missions. The double mission is not found only in spy thrillers. Bureaucrats sometimes have two missions that work at cross-purposes. For example, the Federal Aviation Agency (FAA) seeks to reduce aircraft noise but also promotes the development of advanced aircraft that may increase such noise.

Meat inspectors often have double (or multiple) missions in protecting both the meat industry and consumers. The problem grows even more complex when the meat industry itself is divided on a particular policy. For example, the Department of Agriculture bureau concerned with meat standards has decided that hamburgers may contain up to 30 percent fat. Meat packers and sellers would be happier if the fat content were raised to 35 percent. Farmers who raise cattle, however, may be having a hard enough time getting a fair price for their beef. Raising the fat content in hamburgers could lower the demand for beef and hence lower the price. Consumers, of course, want as much beef and as little fat as possible.

The bureau usually tries for a *compromise ruling*—one that wholly pleases neither side but gives each side something. As one bureaucrat has observed, "If we can get about equal complaints from all sides, we feel we have probably done a good job on rule making."

Clientelism. A bureau's clientele consists of the people or groups that it serves. For example, farmers constitute the clientele of the Department of Agriculture, and road builders constitute the clientele of the Bureau of Public Roads. Clientele-oriented bureaus or agencies tend to place higher priority on the groups that they serve than on the general public interest. The bureau may believe that its most important contribution to the public interest is to promote the interests of its clientele.

Shared Interests and Associations. Most defense contractors hire retired military officers who seek contracts for their companies from former colleagues in the Defense Department. Some bureaucrats may lean over backward not to favor their friends. Others may tend to give friends whatever benefits they can.

Many bureaucrats in the Office of Education are former teachers and school officials. They share similar backgrounds, training, and professional attitudes with their counterparts in state and county departments of education and local school districts. They are likely to share a common set of values about the goals of education. Bureaucrats are bound to be influenced—or at least reinforced in their attitudes—by day-to-day contacts with the people and groups that they serve.

Shared interests and associations reduce the need for actual lobbying to bring outside views into the bureaucracy. Bureaus always represent those views because they are staffed by people who perceive problems, programs, and policies in much the same way as do the people and groups with whom they deal.

section review

1. Why do bureaucrats have multiple loyalties?
2. What is the double mission of a federal meat inspector?
3. How did shared interests and associations reduce the need for lobbying to bring outside views into the bureaucracy?

CHAPTER SUMMARY

23

The federal bureaucracy has grown at a rapid pace in the twentieth century. In 1802 there were only 3,000 civilian government employees; today there are almost 3 million. The greatest periods of growth came during the Progressive and New Deal eras.

Agencies independent of Cabinet secretaries were created for the following reasons: 1) to perform multidepartmental functions; 2) to protect them from party politics; 3) to make them especially accessible to pressure groups; 4) to meet a specific immediate need; and 5) to carry out new programs unhampered by bureaucrats with fixed ideas about the issue.

Government corporations have been established in certain instances to conduct business activities for the general welfare. The U.S. Postal Service and the Tennessee Valley Authority are the best-known examples.

The bureaucracy, because of its ability to provide technical information and analysis, is probably the major initiator of public policy. Bureaucrats often do the actual writing of proposed legislation. Bureau chiefs are also given wide discretion in interpreting and implementing new laws through regulations. Bureaucrats shape the agenda of the executive branch by developing policy recommendations, which reach the political level already defined and with facts assembled to support them.

The major tool for keeping the bureaucracy accountable to the President is the budget. The President's use of this tool must be extremely skillful, for the budget clearly establishes administrative priorities.

Congress may demand greater accountability from the bureaucracy because it creates the bureaus and votes for bureau appropriations, and because political appointees must be confirmed by the Senate.

Because of powerful congressional backing, certain bureaus are all but independent of the executive branch, in particular, the Army Corps of Engineers and the FBI.

Bureau chiefs have multiple loyalties and objectives, which, because they often conflict, require accommodational rulings. Bureau chiefs are accountable to superiors, employees, and clientele. Satisfying their demands may not always serve the interests of the public.

REVIEW QUESTIONS

1. Federal bureaus are part of the executive branch. Do you think they should be more directly controlled by the President and Cabinet? Why or why not?

2. Some federal agencies, such as the FBI, have

functioned almost autonomously. What are some reasons for their remaining autonomous? What are the dangers of continued autonomy? Explain.

3. Congress has established several government corporations. Should government become involved in areas traditionally in the private sector? Why or why not?

4. If you could reorganize the executive branch of government, how would you change it to meet the needs of the twenty-first century? Be very specific.

ACTIVITIES FOR REVIEW

activity 1   Interview a representative of your local government about the impact of the federal bureaucracy on the operation of your city. Present your findings to the class.

activity 2   Interview a representative of your chamber of commerce or a local businessperson about the impact of federal bureaucratic regulations on small businesses. Present your findings to the class.

activity 3   Interview your area's superintendent of schools about the effect of the federal office of education on your school. Present your findings to the class.

political science DICTIONARY

compromise ruling—an agreement that meets some demands of both sides in a controversy.   p. 445

per capita—equally to each individual.   p. 437

status quo—the existing condition or state of affairs.   p. 442

24

Government as Regulator

The Constitution empowers Congress to regulate commerce. As the American economy grew more complex, Congress found that it lacked the time and the knowledge to assume the sole responsibility for exercising that function. In the nineteenth century certain services, notably transportation (railroads) and communications (telegraph and telephone), were supplied by monopolies. Faced with one source of supply, users of those services began to look to Congress for protection against arbitrarily high rates and prices.

In responding to those needs, Congress began in 1887 to delegate its regulatory authority to a number of commissions and boards. Those bodies were expected to make policies and to issue rules in the public interest. As the economy continued to grow, the work of those independent regulatory commissions (IRC's) expanded. The IRC's were called upon not only to establish regulations for huge industries but also to enforce them, hear complaints, determine awards, approve rate changes, and decide among competing interests and claims.

Government regulation of business is a far cry from the laissez-faire approach of an earlier day. But both policies share the goal of making industry profitable.

CHAPTER PREVIEW

1. STRUCTURE AND POWERS OF REGULATORY COMMISSIONS
2. REGULATORY COMMISSIONS: THE PRESIDENT AND CONGRESS
3. THE INFLUENCE OF REGULATED INDUSTRIES

1. STRUCTURE AND POWERS OF REGULATORY COMMISSIONS

Each regulatory board or commission is headed by a panel of five to eleven members who serve for fixed terms of up to fourteen years. The typical IRC has five or seven commissioners who serve terms of five or seven years.

Commissioners are appointed by the President and confirmed by the Senate. They are to a great extent independent of the President and Congress. Their terms overlap, and usually only one member's term expires in any one year. By law all regulatory commissions are bipartisan—no more than a bare majority (for example, four out of seven) may come from one party. Moreover, unlike most other presidential appointees, they cannot be removed at the President's will. This principle was established in 1935 by the Supreme Court in a case involving a Federal Trade commissioner *(Humphrey's Executor v. U.S.).* These provisions are designed to make IRC's independent of presidential control and political influence. The bipartisan composition of the commissions provides some insurance against abuse of their powers. Commissioners direct staffs of 800 to 2,000 people, including a number of professional economists.

Regulatory boards and commissions issue hundreds, often thousands, of rulings each year. The rulings are generally of two kinds. The first involves universal rules that apply to everyone. For example, "No company may own more than one television station in any city." A universal rule is usually issued after public hearings have been held and those likely to be affected by the rule have testified for or against it. The second kind concerns rules covering particular cases or controversies. For example, which of six companies shall be permitted to operate a TV station in Houston or has an allergy remedy been advertised falsely. Ninety percent of all regulatory matters are resolved informally by the staff without holding formal hearings.

Contrary to the principle of the separation of powers, IRC's show the integration of powers. They have authority to make rules (a legislative function), to enforce rules (an executive function), and to interpret rules in resolving particular cases (a judicial function). Because commissions are not actually courts or legislatures, we say that their functions are *quasi*-legislative and *quasi*-judicial—that is, they are somewhat (quasi) legislative and judicial functions.

Congressional statutes are phrased in broad and general terms. They empower regulatory commissions to elaborate details through rules and regulations. For example, a statute may provide that transportation rates be "just and reasonable," letting the Interstate Commerce Commission set the actual rate structure and issue necessary regulations.

Regulatory commissions exercise quasi-judicial powers when they hold courtlike hearings and settle disputes that affect the specific interests of individual businesses. For example, if a group were to challenge the renewal of a radio station's broadcast license, the Federal Communications Commission would conduct a hearing to determine the merits of the issue and then would decide the case, as a court would. Like lower-court decisions, those of an IRC can be appealed to the federal courts.

Regulatory commissions are seldom free from politics. In the example of six companies competing for a TV license in Houston, five will be disappointed. The decisions made by commissions affect the well-being of major economic interests. Those interests seek to influence decisions and try to get sympathetic people appointed to the commissions and to their staffs.

History of Government Regulation of Business. During the first half of the nineteenth century, commerce was confined to individual states. Hence it was subject to state regulations. States still have primary responsibility for regulating certain industries, such as insurance companies and savings and loan companies. After the Civil War commerce spilled over state boundaries. Then the federal government began to assume responsibility for promoting and regulating commerce and industry.

At first, promotion was more important than regulation. Business leaders were given prime sections of land in order to subsidize railroad expansion, tariffs were enacted to protect young industries, and the police assisted in preventing the growth of unions. These subsidies encouraged arbitrary behavior. Many business leaders came to believe that they were above the law. During the 1870's and 1880's, scandals were fairly common. Some business leaders were implicated in swindles and corrupt deals. While "malefactors of great wealth," as Teddy Roosevelt later called them, enriched themselves, many people, including children, worked long hours in factories and on farms for just enough money to keep alive on. Depressions threw many people out of work. The time was ripe for Congress to respond to the popular demand that government regulate business.

Throughout the 1870's, farmers and merchants demanded federal regulation to control railroad rates. States tried to control rail rates, but in 1886 the Supreme Court prohibited them from regulating the rates of railroads that crossed other states. Public sentiment was turning against railroad "robber barons" like William H. Vanderbilt of the New York Central.

In 1887 Congress passed and the Presi-

Robber barons like William Vanderbilt caused major controversies over railroads in the 1890's.

dent signed into law the Act to Regulate Commerce. In place of narrow case-by-case judicial review, this act introduced permanent daily regulation of the railroads. To supervise railroad management and rates, the act authorized the creation of the Interstate Commerce Commission—an independent, expert, nonpartisan body.

QUOTES from famous people

"The commission, as its functions have now been limited by the courts, is, or can be made, of great use to the railroads. It satisfies the popular clamor for government supervision of the railroads at the same time that the supervision is almost entirely nominal. Further, the older such a commission gets to be, the more inclined it will be found to take the business and railroad view of things. It thus becomes a sort of barrier between the railroads and the people and a sort of protection against hasty and crude legislation hostile to railroad interests."

Richard Olney

Supreme Court Justice Robert H. Jackson once remarked that the rise of the regulatory commissions was "probably the most significant legal trend of the last century." The Interstate Commerce Commission (ICC) became the model for successive commissions that were established to regulate different facets of the nation's economy.

Appointment and Confirmation of Commissioners. Most Presidents check with industry leaders before they appoint or reappoint regulatory commissioners. They rarely appoint anyone to whom industry strongly objects. Few Presidents are willing to risk a

Senate confirmation fight over an IRC member. And no President wants to be considered hostile to business. Therefore they have an incentive to appoint people regarded by industry as "reasonable."

Some commissioners formerly served in the industries that they are expected to regulate. Others are party stalwarts who are willing to "go along" with the majority. Some are lawyers who are interested in profitable future associations with industry.

Sometimes certain appointees resign before the expiration of their terms. They are frustrated by the cautious atmosphere and diffusion of authority that prevail. Most commissioners stay as long as they can—or as long as their political connections and acceptability to industry endure.

The Senate often criticizes IRC nominees. Senators inquire into a nominee's political and economic views and his or her attitude toward the commission's "clients."

Interpreting the Rules. An important function of the IRC's is settling disputes arising from their rules. They judge among conflicting claims much as a court does. Like a court, they receive complaints, hold hearings, listen to witnesses and lawyers, study briefs, and decide cases.

Most of this work is not done by the commissioners but by a hearing examiner (sometimes called an administrative law judge). There are more than 600 hearing examiners in the federal government. Their role was created by Congress to make the work of the IRC's easier and to make decisions as fair and impartial as possible.

A hearing examiner is always a lawyer. He or she presides at public hearings, listens to all testimony, summarizes cases, and recommends a decision. Commissions are thus spared weeks of hearings. They make decisions after listening to summary arguments in behalf of the parties involved. Hearing examiners' decisions can be rejected by the commissioners. However, they are usually accepted.

Regulatory commissions have sometimes been criticized for not acting like judges. Instead, they hold private and informal sessions and are sometimes accused of reaching decisions without hearing sufficient evidence. On the other hand, one of the virtues of administrative judging is that decisions can be reached quickly and informally without the fuss and expense of a court case.

IRC members and staffs are also criticized for mixing too freely with those who appear before them to testify. However, if they did not do so, they might well find themselves accused of regulating without knowing what is really happening.

The Administrative Procedures Act of 1946 was an attempt both to preserve the informality of regulatory decision making and to minimize criticism of it. That act provided for certain procedural safeguards, such as holding more formal hearings and according adequate notice to interested parties. The act also broadened judicial review of IRC decisions by enabling the courts to review the facts—the technical evidence that formed the basis of the commission's decision. Nevertheless, the courts have been reluctant to use their expanded jurisdiction. They have tended to review only those cases in which a commission's judgment is challenged on points of law.

section review

1. What two kinds of rulings are generally issued by the IRC's?
2. What was the purpose of the 1887 Act to Regulate Commerce?
3. Give an example of how regulatory commissions are tied to politics.

2. REGULATORY COMMISSIONS: THE PRESIDENT AND CONGRESS

In theory, the regulatory commissions are independent of the President. In fact, this independence is far from complete.

The President and Regulatory Commissions. A President who is committed, for example, to vigorous protection of the consumer, can exert influence on regulatory commissions. The President can appoint consumer advocates of both parties, exercise some control through the federal budget, and sponsor or oppose particular legislation that affects the scope of a commission's work. If the President sets the tone for consumer protection in addresses to Congress and to the nation, the IRC's will eventually hear and begin to respond. President Eisenhower affected the work of the Interstate Commerce Commission, as well as national transportation policy, when he advocated the multi-billion-dollar interstate highway program in 1956. Apart from its impact on the profits of road builders and highway engineers, the interstate highway program was a huge subsidy to truckers. It brought about a dramatic increase in the amount of freight transported by trucks and a corresponding decrease in rail freight. Ever since the construction of the interstate system, the ICC's rates and regulations have seemed to favor truckers.

Congress and Regulatory Commissions. Most members of Congress are generalists. They lack the time and the specialized knowledge needed to deal with regulatory matters. The setting of fair rates to be charged for freight shipments and the granting of a license to operate a television channel require expert knowledge of those issues. Accordingly, Congress delegates its rule-making authority by statutes to the specialists who head and staff the regulatory commissions.

Both Congress and the Courts recognize the expertise of the IRC's, and this recognition gives commissions wide discretion. However, if a commission abuses its discretion, sooner or later complaints will reach Congress. Each commission operates under acts of Congress, and any IRC decision can be overruled by another act of Congress, although a matter would have to be considered important enough for Congress to assert its power.

Congress can clarify its legislative intent in other ways. It can hold public hearings to investigate the policies and procedures of a regulatory commission. It can also curtail a commission's appropriation.

Regulated companies are important constituents, Congress is unusually sensitive to pressures brought by such constituents and their lobbyists. In the early 1960's President Kennedy concluded that the Interstate Commerce Commission's rules were hurting railroads. He appealed to Congress to overrule the ICC and give railroads more freedom to compete with truckers. The truckers, who were better organized and had more political clout than did the railroads, opposed any change, as did the ICC. Congress rejected the President's appeal.

section review

1. How do Presidents exert influence over regulatory commissions?
2. What power does Congress have over the IRC's?
3. Why does Congress defer to the expertise of the IRC's?

3. THE INFLUENCE OF REGULATED INDUSTRIES

It is difficult to involve oneself in an industry without conceiving of its problems in industry terms. The statutes creating each of the commissions impose the responsibility of maintaining the health of the regulated industries. The consumer is to be protected. But so are the rights of private ownership and the profitability of the regulated industries.

Protecting the Industries. Several regulated industries, including railroads and airlines, have received huge direct subsidies from the government. Lewis Engman, then chairman of the Federal Trade Commission, warned in 1974 that such subsidies were major causes of inflation. On the other hand, saving these businesses saves jobs for hundreds of people.

Regulatory commissions are often accused of having been "captured" by industry-dominated advisory committees. Whether or not this accusation is true, there is little doubt that IRC's attempt to protect the industries that they regulate. They try to set rates that will allow reasonable rates of return on the investments of regulated companies. The Interstate Commerce Commission wants to prevent railroads from losing money. The Civil Aeronautics Board wants to protect the health of the larger airlines.

The personal interests of some IRC officials might foster their sympathy for the industry. The typical official of the Civil Aeronautics Board (CAB) has spent many years dealing with airline problems. His or her career centers on airlines. Many of the people whom he or she talks to each day are involved with the airlines. If the IRC official decides to leave government service, an airline may be his or her next employer. It may be difficult for some IRC employees to keep from developing a special sympathy for this industry and the problems of the people who run it.

Similarly, officials of the Federal Communications Commission are in regular contact with members of the broadcasting industry. Other regulatory officials have like ties with their industries. Often, regulatory officials were recruited from industry in which they acquired useful technical skills. Even more often, officials look forward to jobs in industry that can reward their skills with higher salaries than are available in government. There may well be excessive interaction between the regulators and the regulated, but that interaction may be the nature of the job.

Moreover, it is possible that industries are influenced by regulatory commissions as much as commissions are influenced by industries. With the passage of time, regulated industries seem to grow accustomed to the regulatory climate. Their executives conclude that they would rather deal with the known hazards of regulation than with the unknown hazards of competition. They find themselves defending the regulatory system.

Regulators and regulated interact in *symbiotic* (interdependent) relationships. Where does the consumer fit in? The FCC influences broadcasters, and broadcasters influence the FCC, but who speaks for the viewing public?

Some regulatory commissions appoint staff members to serve as public counsels. The counsel's job is to argue the consumer's point of view at public hearings. He or she develops a case for the consumer's interest in a proposed airline fare increase or in the continuation of railroad passenger services. The intrusion of the consumer's case into the proceedings seems to involve a silent admission that the commissioners do not recognize the public interest that they are sworn to uphold, but that they are trying to give it representation.

QUOTES from famous people

"The politics of regulation is a merry-go-round, on which there is a place for all except consumers. The merry-go-round is propelled by the self-interest of industry that must ride for the preservation of revenues and profits, of the regulators who want to keep their jobs, of members of Congress who need campaign cash, and of White House figures who want business' confidence and use the regulatory agencies for political ends. The interrelationships of self-interest leave no room for consideration of the public interest. . . . Regulation tends to perpetuate the protection of industry and the disregard of the consumer interest. . ."

Louis Kohlmeier

There has been a dramatic rise in the activities of consumer groups such as those led by Ralph Nader. These groups have used publicity and lawsuits to make certain regulatory commissions enforce the law. Consumer advocates have begun to redress the consumer's disadvantage in the regulatory system.

Even without the consumer movement, regulators would still be checked in their official conduct by their professional ethics (as lawyers, economists, scientists), the advice of outside experts, the attitudes of members of Congress, the President, interest groups, and political parties, among others. In the long run these informal checks may be the most effective.

Federal regulatory commissions are potentially the most powerful units in our national government. This stems from the far-reaching effects of the decisions and actions that they initiate and enforce. Almost every interest group in America falls under the regulatory domain of some government agency. For example, labor unions are subject to regulatory action by the National Labor Relations Board; farmers have a regulatory relationship with the Department of Agriculture.

When the Consumer Product Safety Commission (CPSC), an independent regulatory agency, was created, the largest of all interest groups — the American consumer — was provided with a regulatory agency into which a different type of perspective could be injected. In October 1972 Congress passed the Consumer Product Safety Act, which authorized the establishment of the CPSC, in response to the rise in consumer awareness of product-related injuries.

The mission of the CPSC as defined by the act is 1) to protect the public against unreasonable risk of injury associated with consumer products; 2) to assist consumers in evaluating the comparative safety of consumer products; 3) to develop uniform safety standards for consumer products and to minimize conflicting state and local regulations; and 4) to promote research and investigation into the causes and the prevention of product-related deaths, illnesses, and injuries.

Rules and regulations have been established by the CPSC to give the business community the responsibility for the public welfare and the guidelines to safeguard it. Public and private interest groups continuously appear before the commission to deliver presentations that support their particular perspectives. As a rule, consumer groups insist upon greater federal regulation, whereas industry presents reasons that a standard either should not be implemented or should be softened by the commission. The regulatory dilemma begins when the federal agency is confronted with a situation in which a product could pose a substantial hazard. A product ban would ultimately force companies out of business.

The controversy over tris, the children's sleepwear flame retardant, epitomizes this dilemma. After the government instructed sleepwear manufacturers to make their products flame retardant, the chemical tris was used to comply with the government's demands. A few years later, tris was proved in many tests to be a carcinogen — a substance that causes cancer.

In the interest of safety the CPSC in April 1977 banned tris-treated garments and instituted an immediate recall. The questions that arose were obvious: Who was at fault, and who should absorb the economic loss?

Citizens and consumer groups may petition the CPSC for the issuance, amendment, or revocation of a decision or action regarding a consumer product. The CPSC's Office of Public Participation has been created to provide for, among other things, funding of public participation in agency proceedings. The encouragement of greater public interest in the regulatory process should instill a better understanding of the problems that face the American government.

OUR NATION'S REGULATORS: A CASE STUDY OF THE CONSUMER PRODUCT SAFETY COMMISSION BY THADDEUS GARRETT, JR. (FORMER COMMISSIONER)

Editorial Cartoon by Dan Dowling, Courtesy of
Field Newspaper Syndicate

'You Are Not Allowed in the Cockpit!'

What ideas are expressed by this cartoon? Do you agree or disagree?

Interstate Commerce Commission. The 1887 Act to Regulate Commerce, which set up the Interstate Commerce Commission, resulted from a struggle between the railroads and their consumers. Farmers and other rail users protested against gross overcharging by the railroads. The ICC was charged with establishing rules for "just and reasonable" rates and administering the law's prohibition against rate discrimination and other unfair railroad practices. They did this by appealing to the courts. These appeals rarely succeeded until many years later, when the ICC's powers were strengthened.

In 1890 Congress passed the Sherman Antitrust Act. It was the first of several acts that were directed toward keeping prices reasonable and reflecting public reaction against unfair financial dealings and monop-

olistic practices in big business. Antitrust suits are the responsibility of the antitrust division of the Justice Department. They are brought in federal courts against **monopolies** and **trusts.**

> A **monopoly** occurs when a single person or group has exclusive control of a product or service, with resulting power over prices and competition.
>
> A **trust** is a group of several firms or businesses that unite for the purpose of controlling production and prices.

Although the Act to Regulate Commerce did not specifically authorize the ICC to foster rate competition among railroads, the commission announced in 1907 that "competition between railways is the established policy of the nation." The ICC's interest in rate competition soon conflicted with its responsibility to keep railroads profitable. The latter won out. The commission's work became much more complex when its authority was extended to cover interstate motor carriers (trucks and buses) and most carriers operating interstate on lakes, rivers, and coastlines.

The ICC consists of eleven members who serve overlapping seven-year terms. Like all regulatory commissioners, they are nominated by the President and confirmed by the Senate. No more than six members may be of the same political party. The ICC has a staff of 1,900, including economists, lawyers, and investigators.

The ICC sets rates for all carriers of people and goods. If rates are too low, the carrier either loses money or cuts back its service to consumers. If rates are too high, shippers will either make consumers pay more of the transportation costs involved in their purchases or will seek a cheaper carrier—for example, trucks instead of railways.

Before a carrier begins operations or

extends an existing route, it must secure from the ICC a "certificate of public convenience and necessity." This provision helps to eliminate duplications of service. Carriers may not abandon established routes or services without ICC consent. In 1980, by an act of Congress, the trucking industry was deregulated and removed from ICC rate and route control.

The decline of railroads. The ICC sometimes fixes bus and truck rates higher than necessary to make ailing railroads more competitive. The railroads argue that truckers offer unfair competition. The government subsidizes them by building and maintaining the nation's highways, whereas railroads must provide and maintain their own tracks. Truckers contend that they repay their subsidies through gasoline taxes.

Except for a few suburban commuter lines, rail passenger services are quite unprofitable. The ICC requires railroads to continue passenger services wherever possible as part of their responsibility to furnish reasonable service to the public. Railroads normally do not raise passenger rates, for they will lose passengers to planes, buses, and carpools. Faced with this dilemma, most railroads subsidize passenger services with their profits from freight traffic.

Each year, as the squeeze gets tighter, more passenger trains are dropped. Fifty years ago there were 20,000 passenger trains linking American cities and towns. Today, there are 200, many of which are now operated through a large federal subsidy by a semipublic corporation called Amtrak. Amtrak is governed by a fifteen-member board, of whom eight are appointed by the President. Currently, it requires an annual subsidy from Congress of $500 million. As for rail freight business, although it is still profitable, it has declined from 75 percent of all freight shipments in 1930 to less than 40 percent today.

The government undermined the railroads by its huge subsidies of highways and airlines. Confronted now by resulting intolerable levels of congestion and air pollution, the federal government has finally begun to respond to the situation by subsidizing urban mass transit and passenger trains. It remains to be seen whether such help will prove to be too little and too late.

The Federal Trade Commission. In 1914 Congress passed the Clayton Antitrust Act to complement the Sherman Act. The new act gave the government more power to combat monopolies and other business practices that restrained trade and competition. At the same time Congress established the Federal Trade Commission, five members serving staggered seven-year terms, to enforce the Clayton Act and to prevent "unfair methods of competition" and "deceptive practices" in interstate commerce. The main mission of the FTC involves protecting businesses against the unfair practices of their competitors.

The FTC undertakes investigations on its own initiative, on complaints filed by business firms against competitors, and on complaints filed by consumer groups. If the law has been violated, the FTC orders the offending business to "cease and desist" from the offense upon penalty of law.

During the past two decades, Congress has given the FTC additional authority. The FTC has interpreted its authority to include protecting consumers from fraud, dangerous products, and deceptive advertising.

Some examples of FTC prohibitions are:

Deceptive advertising. After an investigation the FTC charged a leading retailer with "bait and switch" advertising. In this instance a customer is lured into a store by an ad for a certain brand of product. The customer is informed that the advertised brand is not available. A more expensive one is offered in its place. The retailer charged in this case

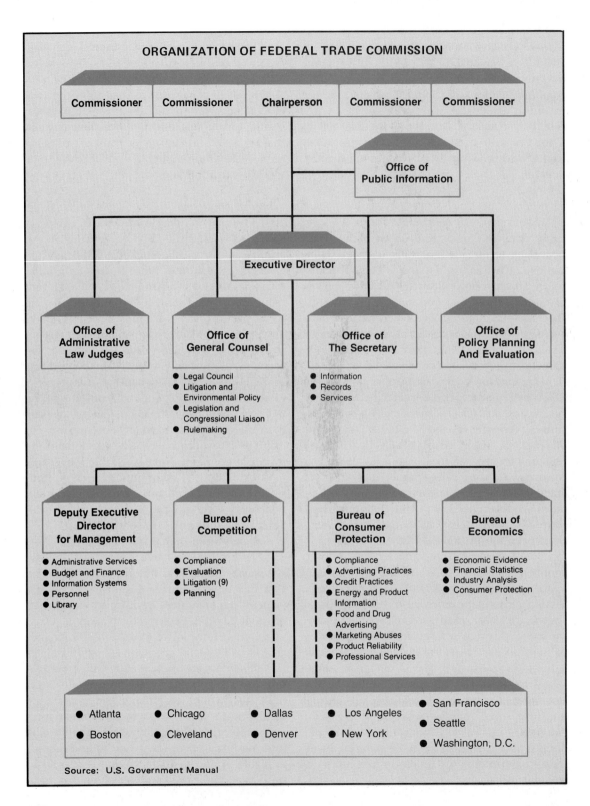

ORGANIZATION OF FEDERAL TRADE COMMISSION

| Commissioner | Commissioner | Chairperson | Commissioner | Commissioner |

Office of Public Information

Executive Director

Office of Administrative Law Judges

Office of General Counsel
- Legal Council
- Litigation and Environmental Policy
- Legislation and Congressional Liaison
- Rulemaking

Office of The Secretary
- Information
- Records
- Services

Office of Policy Planning And Evaluation

Deputy Executive Director for Management
- Administrative Services
- Budget and Finance
- Information Systems
- Personnel
- Library

Bureau of Competition
- Compliance
- Evaluation
- Litigation (9)
- Planning

Bureau of Consumer Protection
- Compliance
- Advertising Practices
- Credit Practices
- Energy and Product Information
- Food and Drug Advertising
- Marketing Abuses
- Product Reliability
- Professional Services

Bureau of Economics
- Economic Evidence
- Financial Statistics
- Industry Analysis
- Consumer Protection

- Atlanta
- Boston
- Chicago
- Cleveland
- Dallas
- Denver
- Los Angeles
- New York
- San Francisco
- Seattle
- Washington, D.C.

Source: U.S. Government Manual

agreed to discontinue the practice. Charges of deceptive advertising have also been leveled against producers of certain common-cold remedies and certain breakfast cereals.

Dangerous products. Under its statutory authority to regulate advertising, the commission has tried to protect consumers from the dangers of cigarette smoking. In 1964, the Surgeon General released a report concluding that cigarette smoking is a serious health hazard. The FTC then ordered all cigarette manufacturers to put on all cigarette packs and in all ads the warning, "Cigarette smoking is dangerous to health and may cause death from cancer and other diseases."

Tobacco is an important agricultural product in several states, and the tobacco industry has powerful friends in Congress. Congress intervened and substituted the mild warning, "Cigarette smoking may be hazardous to your health." In 1967 the FTC reported to Congress that this warning had not affected consumption. In that same year the Federal Communications Commission (FCC) invoked its fairness doctrine to require that broadcasters make time available to antismoking groups who sought to explain the health hazards of smoking.

The antismoking commercials may have contributed to arousing consumer pressure. In 1970 Congress banned all cigarette advertising from radio and television, strengthened the language on the warning of cigarette packs, and returned to the FTC the authority that it had taken away six years earlier—authority to issue health-related regulations for the cigarette industry.

Ad substantiation. The FTC requires all major industries to file data with the commission. This is done so that the commission may verify their advertising claims concerning safety, effectiveness, quality, and comparative prices. A firm that cannot back up its claims is liable to a charge of false advertising.

Let's fight air pollution.

✝ Your Lung Association cares about every breath you take.
The 'Christmas Seal' People.

Posters are often used to warn the public about topics from air pollution to smoking.

Truth in packaging. The FTC requires manufacturers and sellers to package products in such a way that consumers will be able to read the contents of a package and determine the unit price of any product.

Truth in lending. The FTC shares responsibility with the Federal Reserve Board for protecting consumers from misleading advertisements about the rates of interest charged on mortgages, bank loans, and purchases made on credit.

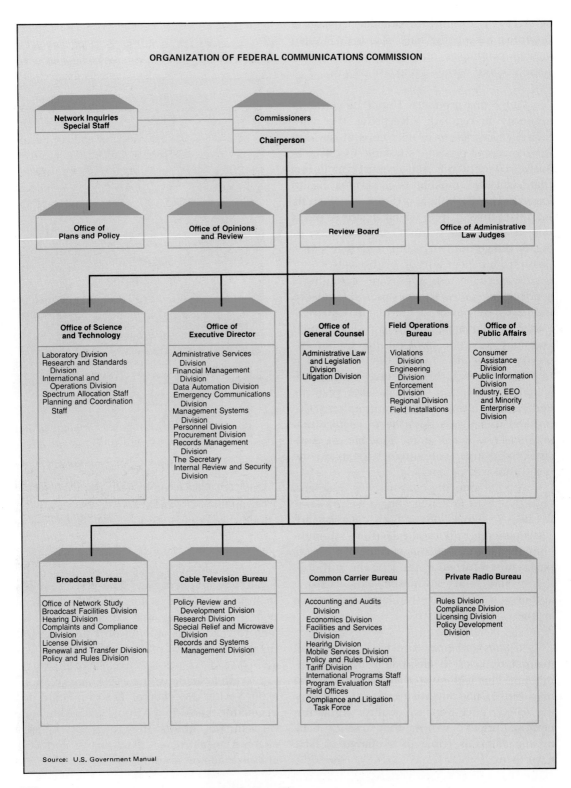

ORGANIZATION OF FEDERAL COMMUNICATIONS COMMISSION

Network Inquiries Special Staff

Commissioners

Chairperson

Office of Plans and Policy

Office of Opinions and Review

Review Board

Office of Administrative Law Judges

Office of Science and Technology

Laboratory Division
Research and Standards Division
International and Operations Division
Spectrum Allocation Staff
Planning and Coordination Staff

Office of Executive Director

Administrative Services Division
Financial Management Division
Data Automation Division
Emergency Communications Division
Management Systems Division
Personnel Division
Procurement Division
Records Management Division
The Secretary
Internal Review and Security Division

Office of General Counsel

Administrative Law and Legislation Division
Litigation Division

Field Operations Bureau

Violations Division
Engineering Division
Enforcement Division
Regional Division
Field Installations

Office of Public Affairs

Consumer Assistance Division
Public Information Division
Industry, EEO and Minority Enterprise Division

Broadcast Bureau

Office of Network Study
Broadcast Facilities Division
Hearing Division
Complaints and Compliance Division
License Division
Renewal and Transfer Division
Policy and Rules Division

Cable Television Bureau

Policy Review and Development Division
Research Division
Special Relief and Microwave Division
Records and Systems Management Division

Common Carrier Bureau

Accounting and Audits Division
Economics Division
Facilities and Services Division
Hearing Division
Mobile Services Division
Policy and Rules Division
Tariff Division
International Programs Staff
Program Evaluation Staff
Field Offices
Compliance and Litigation Task Force

Private Radio Bureau

Rules Division
Compliance Division
Licensing Division
Policy Development Division

Source: U.S. Government Manual

The Federal Communications Commission. In most other countries governments own and operate radio and television. In the United States, Congress has established a system of private broadcasting subject to general regulation by the Federal Communications Commission.

The FCC was created by the Communications Act of 1934. Its seven members serve overlapping seven-year terms. The FCC regulates telephone, telegraph, and cable services, as well as broadcasting. But regulating nonbroadcast communications systems is relatively routine. They are required to provide adequate service at fair and reasonable rates. Changes in interstate rates require FCC approval. A substantial portion of telephone and telegraph service is local and is subject to state regulation.

Most of the FCC's work involves radio and television. The airwaves are not confined within state lines, and therefore all radio and television operations are subject to federal regulation. All radio and television operators and stations must be licensed by the FCC before they can go on the air. Operators are granted licenses after passing FCC examinations. Stations are licensed after investigations have been conducted and public hearings have been held. Licensees are obliged to use public airwaves in the public interest. Station licenses are valid for three years and are renewable at the FCC's discretion. Until recently renewals were almost automatic.

The law directs the commission to assign frequencies, channels, and power among states and localities in a way that results in "a fair and efficient and equitable distribution of service." These broad terms are, of course, subject to the FCC's interpretation.

The assignment of a TV channel places substantial economic benefits on the receiver and is often a highly political decision. The FCC is likely to be pressured not only by broadcasting interests but by Congress. Stations can support or oppose a candidate. They can also offer news coverage. In addition, several members of Congress have financial interests in broadcasting. The resulting pressure on the commission can be considerable.

The FCC cannot afford to be insensitive to Congress, which provides its funds, grants its authority, and can curtail its power at any time. Several years ago FCC officials acknowledged that the status of members of Congress as directors or stockholders of broadcast license applicants was a factor favoring the granting of a license.

The Communications Act of 1934 stipulates that the FCC may not do certain things. Congress has specifically denied it the authority to regulate rates charged to advertisers, to censor what is broadcast, and to interfere with the right of free speech. Neither the act nor the Constitution prevents the commission from refusing to renew a license if it concludes that a licensee has not served the public interest.

The FCC issues licenses to operators of radio and TV equipment before they can go on the air.

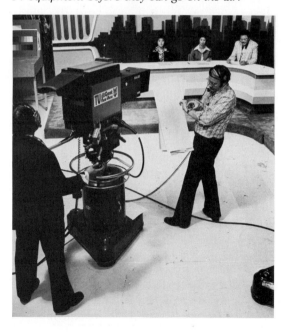

License renewals and challenges. In reviewing applications for license renewals, the commission may consider the content of the broadcaster's past programs to determine whether the public interest has been served. In 1968 the biases of a Mississippi television station in reporting race relations and civil rights were factors in the FCC's decision not to renew the station's license.

During that same year the commission launched a broad study of ownership patterns in the broadcasting industry. As a matter of policy, the commission discourages concentration of media ownership (newspaper, television, and radio) in any single community. Because one Boston TV station was owned by a major Boston newspaper, the FCC transferred the station's license to a citizens' group. Over the past decade citizens' groups have challenged licensees in several cities. The main effect of these challenges has been to make licensees more conscious of serving the public interest. They no longer take their renewals for granted.

The fairness doctrine. Without attempting to regulate the content of programs, the FCC imposes rules designed to ensure fair coverage of events. Congress and the commission have adopted the fairness doctrine, under which licensees that cover issues of public importance must reflect different viewpoints. If a program presents only one side of an issue, the station must provide free time, if necessary, for the other party to present an opposing view. When a person is personally attacked on a program by anyone—whether connected to the station or not—the station must notify that person and offer an opportunity to respond. If the station makes editorial statements or endorses candidates, it must give opponents the right to reply.

In upholding the fairness doctrine against a broadcaster's challenge, Supreme Court Justice Byron White said, "It is the rights of viewers and listeners, not the right of the broadcasters, which is paramount."

Equal time. The FCC is responsible for enforcing Congress' requirement that if a station makes time available to one candidate for public office, it must offer opposing candidates equal time. In presidential campaigns this requirement presents problems. If two major candidates are featured in a debate, candidates of many minor parties can request equal time and, by virtue of the number of parties involved, could dominate the airwaves for a considerable period of time. Because of this possibility, the networks have refused to broadcast debates or other joint appearances by the presidential candidates of the two major parties.

In 1960 Congress suspended the equal-time provision, enabling the major television networks to sponsor the four Kennedy–Nixon debates. Suspensions have not been enacted since 1960. The Reagan–Anderson and Carter–Reagan debates of 1980 were made possible by a 1975 FCC ruling that the equal-time requirement applies only to debates sponsored by stations or networks and held in broadcast studios. Accordingly, the 1980 debates were sponsored by the League of Women Voters. The television networks covered the debates as they would cover any major news event. Minor-party complaints were rejected by the courts.

Broadcasters have recently become skilled at avoiding the equal-time requirement in important election campaigns by using the news interview format. News coverage is not subject to the equal-time rule.

Television is a powerful medium. The TV set glows in the average home for 5 hours and 45 minutes each day. By the age of 65, the average American will have watched TV for roughly 9 full years of his or her life. The FCC may well be giving the public an important service by policing broadcasters and making them more conscious of their obligations to serve the public.

The Securities and Exchange Commission. Many Americans invest money in the stocks and bonds (securities) of business corporations. The Securities and Exchange Commission was created in 1934 to oversee the buying and selling of securities and to provide minimum protection for investors. The SEC is composed of five members who serve overlapping five-year terms. Like many other regulatory commissions, the 1,700-member staff contains many economists, lawyers, and accountants.

To protect investors against fraud and misrepresentation in the securities field, the SEC is empowered by Congress to require full disclosure of all information relating to the issuance of new securities. Such information relates to the company's assets, its owners and directors, and what percentage of company stock is owned by each. All securities listed on the nation's several securities exchanges (for example, the New York Stock Exchange) must be registered with the SEC. Large companies not listed on these exchanges but sold over the counter must also conform with the SEC's requirements for disclosure.

A separate and much smaller regulatory commission—the Commodities Futures Trading Commission—regulates the buying and selling of various agricultural products, timber, and metals before those items actually reach the market. These transactions are known as *futures trading*. The Commodities Futures Trading Commission works to prevent fraudulent trading practices, including price manipulation, attempts to corner a market, and the spreading of false information about crops.

The National Labor Relations Board. The National Labor Relations Board (NLRB) was created by Congress to carry out the provisions of the National Labor Relations Act of 1935. That act recognized the right of employees (whose work has an impact on interstate commerce) to "organize and bargain collectively through representatives of their own choosing." It was left to the NLRB to determine the rights of employers, the definition of unfair labor practices, the rights of nonunion employees, the scope of collective bargaining, and many other policy matters. The NLRB is a regulatory commission composed of five (originally three) members, who serve overlapping five-year terms.

Labor's basic struggle involved the right to organize. Individual actions rarely had an effect on unfair or unhealthy labor policies. During the nineteenth century, unions were viewed with suspicion. Organized efforts to obtain higher wages and better working conditions were sometimes prosecuted as conspiracies. State legislatures had held trade unions to be lawful, but the courts had reduced the effect of that right by legalizing a number of anti-union strategies. One of the most notorious practices in many industries was the *yellow dog contract*. Under the yellow dog contract, as a condition of employment, a worker had to promise not to join a union. On the basis of yellow dog contracts, the courts prohibited labor organizers from attempting to unionize workers who had signed the contracts. Employers also frequently used labor spies and company police to sort out and blacklist union sympathizers. These actions were repeatedly upheld by the courts. Court *injunctions* (orders preventing an act that would injure the personal or property rights of another) were obtained to prevent or end strikes.

Despite these restrictions unions grew in number and political power. In 1932 the labor movement secured the passage of the Norris-La Guardia Act, which made yellow dog contracts unenforceable in federal courts. The act curtailed the use of injunctions in labor disputes and recognized the right of a worker to join a union, to organize others, and to strike. By that time unions had also secured federal regulation of matters such as wages, hours, and working conditions.

The National Labor Relations Act of 1935 was a turning point for the labor movement.

It not only established the right of workers to organize and bargain collectively but also required employers to bargain with unions favored by a majority of their employees and prohibited employers from committing various "unfair labor practices." The NLRB was given two broad responsibilities. The first was to conduct elections among employees to determine which, if any, union they chose to *bargain collectively* (negotiate) for them with employers. (If collective bargaining is successful, employers and workers agree on a contract that sets forth wages, hours, and benefits for a specified period of time. If an agreement is not reached through collective bargaining, a strike usually follows.) The second responsibility of the NLRB was to enforce the provisions of the act outlawing unfair labor practices.

The act made five kinds of action unfair: 1) interfering with workers in their attempts to organize unions or bargain collectively; 2) supporting *company unions* (unions set up and dominated by employers); 3) discriminating against union members in favor of nonunion members; 4) firing or penalizing an employee for union membership or activity; 5) refusing to bargain with union representatives.

Charges of unfair labor practices are investigated by regional officers of the NLRB. Formal complaints may result from such investigations. Trial examiners hold hearings on formal complaints of unfair labor practices and on other disputes within the NLRB's jurisdiction. The hearing examiners then submit reports to the NLRB in Washington.

Many people believed that the National Labor Relations Act was stacked in favor of labor. They demanded that certain union practices be outlawed as "unfair labor practices." One such practice was *featherbedding*. Labor-saving devices reduced the number of workers needed to perform a particular job, but some unions demanded that the original number of workers be paid, even if they had nothing to do. Another such practice was the

These people demonstrated in support of the United Mine Workers, who had been on strike for over three months in 1978.

closed shop—a contract with an employer under which only union members can be hired.

After World War II, labor excesses and a wave of strikes throughout many industries turned public opinion against labor and brought demands in Congress for a law that would treat labor and management equitably. The result was the Labor-Management Relations Act of 1947, commonly called the Taft-Hartley Act.

Applying to all industries affecting interstate commerce, the act 1) outlaws the closed shop and permits the *union shop*—under which new employees must join the union within a stated time after being hired—

ELEANOR HOLMES NORTON, Former Head of the Equal Employment Opportunity Commission

In 1977 President Carter chose Eleanor Holmes Norton to head the Equal Employment Opportunity Commission. Norton viewed her appointment as "a logical progression in my own professional commitment to civil rights." That professional commitment is extensive.

During the 1960's Eleanor Norton spent five years on the staff of the American Civil Liberties Union. In those years she specialized in First Amendment cases. At the same time she was demonstrating for civil rights, she was representing such clients as Governor George Wallace of Alabama and individual members of the Ku Klux Klan. As she explains, "If people like George Wallace are denied free expression, the same thing can happen to Black people. Black people understand this. No Black person ever said to me, 'Sister, how come you're representing George Wallace?' They know how come." She has stated that "almost every social change in the twentieth century" has stemmed from the First Amendment.

Eleanor Holmes Norton considers herself a feminist and requested that she be referred to as "chair," rather than "chairman," in her position. In discussing discrimination against women, she has said, "Blacks have felt it [discrimination] only in the last several hundred years, but for women it has been throughout history."

In 1970 Mayor John Lindsay of New York City appointed Eleanor Norton chair of the New York City Commission on Human Rights. Her agency was reputedly one of the best run in the city. Even some of the businesses under investigation by the commission conceded that she was both efficient and fair. Her achievements were so impressive that New York's next mayor, Abraham Beame, asked her in 1974 to stay on for a second term.

In accepting President Carter's offer to head the Equal Employment Opportunity Commission, Eleanor Holmes Norton took on a backlog of more than 130,000 cases and, consequently, an agency characterized by low morale and internal division. Norton, however, known for her persistence and drive, feels that "overall, the EEOC's problems lend themselves to repair." Of the problem of equal employment opportunity in general, Norton says, "I would emphasize that progress is achieved only by continuing to push. It probably will be a long time before a major employer — government or private — can sit back and enjoy real approval from women and minorities."

only if a majority of the workers agree to its establishment and if state law does not forbid it; 2) outlaws *jurisdictional strikes* (strikes arising from disputes between unions), *secondary boycotts* (strikes to prevent one employer from doing business with another employer who is involved in a labor dispute), spending by unions to influence federal elec-

tions, excessive union dues, and strikes by federal employees; 3) makes it an unfair labor practice for unions to refuse to bargain with employers; 4) outlaws featherbedding; 5) allows the use of an injunction to halt a strike for 80 days if the President determines that such a strike could endanger the national health or safety.

The National Labor Relations Act of 1935 and the Taft-Hartley Act of 1947 give the NLRB most of its authority.

The only other major act administered in part by the NLRB is the Labor-Management Reporting and Disclosure Act of 1959. The chief purpose of this act was to make union records and activities public. Detailed financial reports must be filed with the secretary of labor. This act was passed to prevent fraud in union elections, the misuse of union funds, and the falsification of union records. Elections are required at least every three years for local union officers and at least every five years for national union officers.

The 1959 act contains a union bill of rights that grants union members the right to vote in union elections by secret ballot, to speak up at union meetings, to obtain open hearings in disciplinary cases, and to sue union officers in federal courts.

The Civil Aeronautics Board. The Civil Aeronautics Board (CAB) was created in 1938 to regulate and promote domestic air transportation. Its five members serve overlapping six-year terms. The CAB staff includes over 600 economists, accountants, and lawyers.

The CAB is responsible for assigning routes to the nation's commercial air carriers and for supervising their rates and services. It also determines charges for carrying airmail and administers a program of federal subsidies to sustain certain airlines that operate at a loss. In general, the aircraft industry is generously subsidized for both military and civilian purposes. One of the board's five major responsibilities is subsidizing the aircraft industry, because it has greatly contributed to the military potential of the country.

A second responsibility of the CAB is to maintain a regular network of air routes uniting the nation's cities and towns. This responsibility involves a subsidy for unprofitable local and regional airlines. If the airlines were left entirely to their own devices, they might retain only the most used —and most profitable—"trunk" routes, such as New York to Los Angeles and Washington to Chicago.

The CAB's third responsibility involves expediting the development of new transport aircraft. Like the first, this objective has a military, as well as a civilian, purpose.

A fourth responsibility concerns the CAB's maximizing the safety of air travel by keeping the industry economically stable. If the industry were to sustain heavy losses, it might well cut back on safety measures.

Finally, the CAB tries to keep air fares stable and to restrict price discrimination—although military personnel and families are sometimes given special fare reductions.

Beginning in 1978, the CAB led all other federal agencies in the growing trend toward de-regulation. De-regulating the airline industry means that airlines can change basic fares without CAB approval. Airlines have also been encouraged to expand their routes with few restrictions. Less regulation is expected to lead to more competition within the airline industry and to more air travel by the general public.

The Federal Reserve Board. In many nations the government owns a central bank that determines monetary policy. The United States had two such central banks that lasted for twenty years each. The first Bank of the United States operated from 1791 to 1811. The second Bank of the United States operated from 1816 to 1836. Between 1836 and 1863 state banks controlled the money system. They issued notes that often could not be cashed in.

In 1863 Congress authorized the chartering of national banks that were privately owned corporations and had no direct ties to one another. Money could not be transferred quickly from one bank to another to meet a sudden increase in withdrawals by depositors. During the financial crises of 1893 and 1907, these banks restricted their currency loads and issued fewer notes when there was an increase in money being borrowed. To furnish an **elastic** currency and to coordinate the national banks, Congress in 1913 established the federal reserve system.

> **Elasticity** in the supply of currency is provided by issuing more currency when borrowing is heavy and reducing the issue of currency when demands shrink.

The country is divided into 12 federal reserve districts. A federal reserve bank is located in a major city in each of the districts: Boston, New York, Philadelphia, Cleveland, Richmond, Atlanta, Chicago, St. Louis, Minneapolis, Kansas City, Dallas, and San Francisco. If you look at a dollar bill, you will see at the top that it is a federal reserve note and that it was issued by one of the 12 federal reserve banks. The letter *A* indicates that it was issued by the federal reserve bank in Boston, *B* indicates New York, and so on.

Each federal reserve bank is headed by a nine-member board of directors. Six members are elected by the member banks (three bankers and three other business leaders). The other three members, appointed by the federal reserve's board of governors in Washington, represent the public.

Each federal reserve bank is owned by member banks. All national banks are required to join the system. State banks are also permitted to do so. Today 5,700 of the nation's 14,000 banks are members of the system. These banks handle 85 percent of total deposits.

Board of governors. A seven-member board of governors supervises the federal reserve system. Each member is appointed by the President, with the consent of the Senate, for a 14-year term. The President designates the chairman, who serves a 4-year term. Each member serves a single term, and one member retires every second year. No two members of the board come from the same federal reserve district.

The board of governors supervises the operations of the federal reserve banks and member banks and determines general monetary and credit policies for the nation.

The board of governors affects the flow of money by tightening or loosening credit. It can do this in a number of ways.

1. *The reserve requirement.* The board requires each member bank to *reserve* (deposit) a certain percentage of its funds with its federal reserve bank. By varying the percentage required, the board can expand or restrict the lending potential of member banks. When **inflation** threatens, the board can depress the economy by raising member banks' reserve requirements. Thereby it reduces the cash that they have available for lending. This reduction brings about a "tight money" condition. This means that people borrow less and spend less. When the economy is depressed, the board relaxes its reserve requirements to make more money available for business growth and personal spending.

> **Inflation** is an economic condition in which the price level is increased and the value of money in terms of purchasing power is decreased.

2. *Rediscounting.* The board also controls the amount of credit available by raising and lowering the *rediscount rate.* When a member bank makes a loan, the borrower gives the bank a note. The bank may then rediscount (borrow on) this note from the federal reserve bank and thus receive cash with which to make additional loans. The board of governors sets the interest that member banks pay on such loans—the rediscount rate. If the rediscount rate is low, member banks will be encouraged to make more loans. If the rate is high, loans become more costly, and there is less borrowing and spending.

3. *Open market operations.* The Open Market Committee is composed of all members of the board of governors and five representatives of the federal reserve banks. This committee controls the buying and selling of government securities. If more credit is needed, the committee authorizes the federal reserve banks to buy government securities on the open market, thereby putting more money into the economy. Selling government securities held by federal reserve banks will absorb funds from other investment channels.

4. *Federal reserve notes.* Each federal reserve bank issues paper currency—federal reserve notes—under the board of governor's supervision. This currency is *legal tender,* which means that it must be accepted by a creditor when tendered (presented) in payment for money owed. The board's power to increase or decrease the amount of money in circulation powerfully affects the economy. More money means more spending and more business activity; less money means less spending and reduced business activity.

5. *Margin requirements.* The board controls the amount of credit that may be extended by brokerage houses to investors to purchase securities. Such credit is based on the value of securities bought by the investor. Under a 50-percent margin requirement, for example, an investor needs to pay for only half of the value of securities purchased. The other half is borrowed "on margin" from the brokerage house. To curb inflation, the board may raise margin requirements, thereby reducing credit available in order to increase the prices of securities. To stimulate the economy the board may lower margin requirements.

Through all these strategies the board of governors of the federal reserve system vitally affects the economy.

Other central bank functions. The federal reserve banks serve as depositories for government funds. They clear checks and transfer funds among member banks, buy and sell government securities, and may, in an economic emergency, lend money directly to businesses.

Accountability. The federal reserve system is deliberately isolated from influence by the President. Its members' 14-year terms are obviously much longer than the tenure of any President. Even the chairman's 4-year term expires in the middle of a presidential term. In early 1978, for example, President Carter named a new federal reserve board chairman to replace a chairman who had been appointed by President Nixon in 1974.

Aside from Senate confirmation, Congress exercises little control over the federal reserve board. Unlike other regulatory commissions, the federal reserve system is paid for by member banks and does not depend on congressional appropriations.

When the federal reserve board was established, no one expected it to become a policy-making institution with major responsibility for maintaining a stable economy. The board often has to make a choice between fighting inflation, which may cause unemployment, and stimulating employment at the risk of creating inflation. The United States is probably the only country in which the central banking authorities can disagree with the rest of the government and make their policies prevail.

section review

1. What was the purpose of the Labor-Management Reporting and Disclosure Act of 1959?
2. List six major regulatory commissions. Describe the function of each one.
3. What is one example of an FTC prohibition?
4. Why was the Securities and Exchange Commission created?

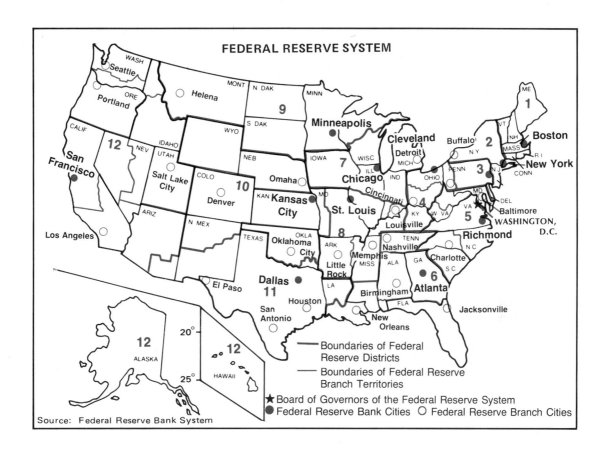

FEDERAL RESERVE SYSTEM

Boundaries of Federal Reserve Districts
Boundaries of Federal Reserve Branch Territories
★ Board of Governors of the Federal Reserve System
● Federal Reserve Bank Cities   ○ Federal Reserve Branch Cities

Source: Federal Reserve Bank System

These men are shown trimming the edges of one-dollar bills.

CHAPTER SUMMARY

24

The Constitution grants Congress the power to regulate interstate commerce. By 1887 the nation's economy had grown so large and complex that Congress began to establish regulatory commissions to make rules and policies in the public interest. The power and responsibilities of independent regulatory commissions have expanded with the economy. The commissions issue rules for large industries, enforce those rules, hear complaints, determine awards, approve rate changes, and decide among competing interests and claims. They combine legislative, executive, and judicial functions. They regulate almost every area of American economic life.

Commissioners are appointed to meet the needs of both industry and the public. If these needs conflict, industry usually wins because it is better organized to make its political influence felt. Commissioners in daily contact with representatives of industry are generally more sympathetic to their viewpoint than to the less clearly stated views of the public.

There are eight major regulatory commissions. Among them are the Interstate Commerce Commission, Federal Trade Commission, Federal Power Commission, Securities and Exchange Commission, National Labor Relations Board, Civil Aeronautics Board, and the Federal Reserve Board. Together they exercise great authority over transportation of people and goods by airplane, railroad, ship, truck, bus, pipeline, and barge; communication by telephone, telegraph, radio, and television; generation and distribution of electric power; water resources and flood control; interstate transportation of natural gas; labor-management relations; and banking practices, monetary policies, and trading of securities.

REVIEW QUESTIONS

Which regulatory agency would you contact in each of the following cases?

1. You believe that the elimination of passenger train service in your area is improper.
2. You believe that a mouthwash company's claim that their product prevents colds is misleading.
3. You believe that you have been overcharged interest on your department store charge account.
4. You have been denied time on a local television station to answer what you believe to be a biased presentation of a controversial issue.
5. You believe that your local gas company is overcharging its customers.
6. You have been denied a promotion because of your union activities.

ACTIVITIES FOR REVIEW

activity 1   Report on the work of one of the eight regulatory commissions described in this chapter.

activity 2   Stage a classroom debate or forum on the following issue: RESOLVED, that the nation's railroads (or airlines, or telephone service, etc.) be nationalized.

political science DICTIONARY

closed shop—a plant where only union members may be hired.   p. 464

company union—an organization of employees dominated by the employer.   p. 464

elastic currency—under the federal reserve system, currency issued by banks in amounts determined by the demand for loans.   p. 467

featherbedding—forcing an employer to use more workers than the job actually requires.   p. 464

futures trading—the buying and selling of commodities or stock before the product reaches the market.   p. 463

inflation—an economic condition in which prices increase and purchasing power decreases.   p. 467

jurisdictional strike—a strike arising from a dispute between two unions over which one has the right to represent the workers.   p. 465

monopoly—exclusive control, by a single person or group, of a product or service, with resulting power over prices and competition.   p. 456

secondary boycott—a strike to prevent one employer from doing business with another employer who is involved in a labor dispute.   p. 465

trust—a group of firms or businesses that unite for the purpose of controlling production and prices.   p. 456

union shop—a plant that may hire both union and nonunion workers but may retain nonunion workers only if they agree to join the union within a given period.   p. 464

yellow dog contract—an agreement signed by an employee promising not to join a union.   p. 463

UNIT SUMMARY

The size, independence, and power of the federal bureaucracy have led some observers to call it the fourth branch of American government. All bureaucracies are characterized by specialization of function, hierarchy, job security, informal channels of communication and influence, and incrementalism.

The Pendleton Act established a merit system for employees of the federal government that emphasizes ability rather than political favoritism. The Hatch Act further protected government employees from political pressure by restricting partisan political activities.

Criticisms of and proposals to reform the federal bureaucracy focus on increasing its responsiveness and accountability.

Congress has delegated to independent regulatory commissions much of its constitutional power to regulate interstate commerce. These commissions have integrated legislative, executive, and judicial functions. They monitor and regulate almost all areas of American economic life.

Bibliography

Cory, William L. *Politics and the Regulatory Agencies.* New York: McGraw-Hill, 1967.

Congressional Quarterly Weekly Report.

Government Printing Office. *The U.S. Budget in Brief* (published annually).

United States Government Organization Manual (published annually).

Kohlmeier, Louis M., Jr. *The Regulators.* New York: Harper and Row, 1969.

Nadel, Mark, and Francis Rourke, "Bureaucracies," *Handbook of Political Science*, Vol. 5. Reading, Mass: Addison-Wesley, 1975.

Wildavsky, Aaron. *The Politics of the Budgetary Process* (2nd edition). Cambridge: Little, Brown and Company, 1974.

Review questions

1. What factors have tended to increase the size and power of the federal bureaucracy? Do you favor this trend? Explain.
2. Most of the day-to-day operation of government is in the hands of nonelective bureaucrats who can only be removed for serious cause. What dangers might this pose for a democracy? What safeguards exist? What additional safeguards do you think should be established? Explain.
3. If you could change the basic structure of the executive branch, how would you structure it to maximize efficiency, effectiveness, responsiveness, and accountability?
4. Do you think some of the authority granted to the IRC's could be more effectively executed by the Executive Office of the President or some other body, such as the President and his or her Cabinet? Explain.

Skills questions

Based on the charts in Unit 7, answer the following questions:
1. Which executive department employs the greatest number of civilians? How many civilians were employed by the state and local governments in 1972? 1981? Give specific reasons for the federal government's decreased employment of civilians from 1972 to the present.
2. Where do formal lines of authority exist under bureaucratic organization?
3. Describe the relationship between Congress and the director of a bureau and between Congress and the head of an office.
4. Outline the structure of the Federal Communications Commission.
5. To which federal reserve district does your state belong? In what city is the federal reserve bank for your district?

Activities

activity 1

Develop a position paper recommending specific reorganization proposals to the President.

activity 2

You have just been appointed to the Cabinet by a newly elected President. On your first day in office, you are asked by the President for recommendations to improve the efficiency and communication in your department. How do you begin? Select a department and try to analyze the various independent agencies that should be placed under your departmental umbrella. Present your recommendations to the class.

activity 3

You have just been elected President of the United States and need to appoint several new commissioners. What criteria would you establish for selecting appointees?

UNIT
8

SAMUEL R. PIERCE, JR.

Samuel R. Pierce, Jr. was appointed Secretary of Housing and Urban Development (HUD) in early 1981. He is the only Black in President Reagan's Cabinet.

PEOPLE IN
POLITICS

Pierce was born in Glenn Cove, New York, in 1922. He received his A.B. degree in 1947 from Cornell University. In his junior year he was made a member of the Phi Beta Kappa scholastic honorary society. Pierce also received his J.D. degree in 1949 from Cornell Law University and his LL.M in Taxation in 1952 from the New York University School of Law. Between 1957 and 1958 Pierce did postgraduate work as a Ford Foundation Fellow at Yale Law School. He received an honorary Doctor in Laws (LL.D) from New York University in 1972. He is married and has one daughter.

Although Pierce had no previous housing experience when he was appointed, he was well known as an extremely intelligent and poised attorney with a broad background in government. His previous government jobs included: assistant district attorney for New York County, assistant undersecretary of Labor, counsel to the Judiciary Subcommittee on Antitrust of the U.S. House of Representatives, and general counsel of the U.S. Treasury Department during the Nixon administration.

From 1961 to the present, excluding the time he worked in the Treasury Department, Pierce has been in private law practice. He is known for his fairness and even temperament.

Pierce has always been a hard worker. He was the first Black to hold the following positions: assistant to the undersecretary of Labor, a partner in a major New York Law firm, a member of the board of a major American corporation, and general counsel to the Treasury Department.

Upon taking office Pierce pledged to take care of those in need. He opposed the Reagan administration's belief that housing assistance be denied to localities that enforce rent controls. Pierce believes that the federal government should not interfere with local rent-control laws or threaten to withhold aid if municipalities keep rent controls. He stated that "local governments should be able to make their own rules with respect to rent controls . . . we ought not tell local governments what to do."

THE EXECUTIVE BRANCH (Part III)

OVERVIEW

■ There are 13 executive departments: State; Defense; Treasury; Justice; Interior; Agriculture; Commerce; Labor; Health and Human Services; Education; Housing and Urban Development; Transportation; and Energy.

■ The original departments — State, Defense, Treasury, and Justice — fulfill essential governmental functions.

■ The special interest departments — Agriculture, Commerce, and Labor — are advocates for special economic groups.

■ The Interior Department has retained its unique position as protector of the nation's natural resources and wildlife.

■ The new service departments—HHS, HUD, Education, Transportation, and Energy—are particularly concerned with the needs of a modern, urban, industrial society.

■ Each department is headed by a secretary, who serves as a member of the President's Cabinet. (The Justice Department is headed by the attorney general.)

■ Several agencies — the FBI, CIA, and Environmental Protection Agency — have independent status, although they are closely allied in purpose and function with the established departments.

25

The Original Departments

Although the Constitution did not establish the executive departments, President George Washington appointed four officers shortly after assuming office. The four officers were the secretary of state, the secretary of the treasury, the secretary of war, and the attorney general. These officers and their few assistants carried out the new government's essential functions—dealing with foreign countries, promoting the general welfare (through taxing and spending), providing for the common defense, and administering justice. Today government has grown. These four departments not only perform their original functions, but also direct the other essential affairs of government.

CHAPTER PREVIEW

1. THE DEPARTMENT OF STATE
2. THE DEPARTMENT OF DEFENSE
3. THE DEPARTMENT OF THE TREASURY
4. THE DEPARTMENT OF JUSTICE

1. THE DEPARTMENT OF STATE

The United States has two overriding foreign policy objectives: to maintain national security and to achieve peaceful relations with all countries. In pursuit of the first

objective, the United States has built up a vast storehouse of military and nuclear weapons. In pursuit of the second, the United States has sought **detente** with the Soviet Union, communications on diplomatic levels with China and Cuba, a halt of the arms race, and cooperation and trade with all nations. The

United States has been forced to pursue both objectives at once because the world is made of sovereign nations, each pursuing its own interests.

Detente is an easing of strained relations and political tensions between nations.

After a generation of cold war and a number of unpopular interventions—notably in the Dominican Republic and Indochina—we seem to be evolving new attitudes about the nature of foreign policy.

Since the end of World War II, Western Europe—with its strong and interdependent economies—and Japan—with its highly developed technology—have become our partners in world trade. African and Asian countries have severed their colonial ties. They have sought to benefit from the continuing efforts of the United States and the Soviet Union to gain their allegiance.

Some situations do not lead to hope for a brighter future. Tensions continue in our relations with the Soviet Union. The demand for majority rule in South Africa has generated hostile racial feelings. The Third World countries of Africa, Asia, Latin America, and the states of the Middle East that do not produce oil continue to call for restructuring of the international economic order. World energy needs are rapidly increasing, and resources are becoming scarce. Imbalances in the distribution and consumption of food could lead to widespread hunger unless the United States and other food-producing nations create bold and far-reaching means for redistribution.

America's foreign policy is the sum of its individual policies in the areas of national security, arms control, international trade, aid to developing nations, energy needs and countless other areas. Developing policies in most of these areas is the main job of the State Department.

The Secretary of State. Every government has a state department or foreign office to handle its relations with other countries. In the United States the Department of State was the first executive department to be created by George Washington in 1789. As a result the secretary of state takes precedence over all other Cabinet members.

The President's chief adviser on foreign policy is usually the secretary of state. Many important people—including Thomas Jefferson, James Madison, James Monroe, Daniel Webster, Henry Clay, Charles Evans Hughes, and George Marshall—have held this office. Several foreign policies or programs have been named for the secretaries who fashioned them. For example, the Marshall Plan gave billions of dollars to war-torn Western Europe to finance its recovery after World War II.

Foreign policy is an arena in which the President plays a primary role. Officially the secretary of state helps the President make foreign policy decisions. In practice the President makes only the most important decisions. On many lesser matters the secretary of state develops foreign policy with his or her staff and then secures the President's approval.

Some secretaries of state have exerted more influence than have others. The degree of influence depends on the President's style and preferences. Foreign policy decisions are so numerous that every secretary of state plays an important role.

The secretary directs a department composed of more than 30,000 employees, including many in posts abroad. The responsibilities of the secretary include:
1. receiving visits from foreign diplomats;
2. attending international conferences;
3. heading the United States delegation to the United Nations on special occasions;
4. making key statements on foreign policy;
5. appearing before congressional committees, especially the House Committee on International Relations and the Senate Com-

Alexander M. Haig, Secretary of State, is shown attending the first Cabinet meeting of President Reagan.

mittee on Foreign Relations, to explain the administration's policies;

6. visiting foreign countries to talk with government leaders and help bring about international settlements, as Secretaries Kissinger and Vance did in the Middle East;

7. exchanging views with American ambassadors to foreign countries.

The secretary's relations with Congress are very critical. Without congressional confidence and support, the administration's foreign policies may be blocked. For example, Congress might refuse to appropriate military aid to a country in line with the administration's promises.

The Routine Conduct of Foreign Affairs. Diplomats and other personnel of the State Department represent American interests to foreign governments. They also report political developments in the rest of the world to the various agencies and desks of the State Department. These reports are analyzed and are sometimes used to shape new policies and put them into effect.

In the day-to-day conduct of foreign relations, the State Department performs three functions:

1. to inform the White House about international developments;

2. to transmit official communications to foreign leaders and ambassadors;

3. to conduct negotiations with foreign governments.

One example of the last function is that an American company may not negotiate a contract with the Soviet Union without State Department approval.

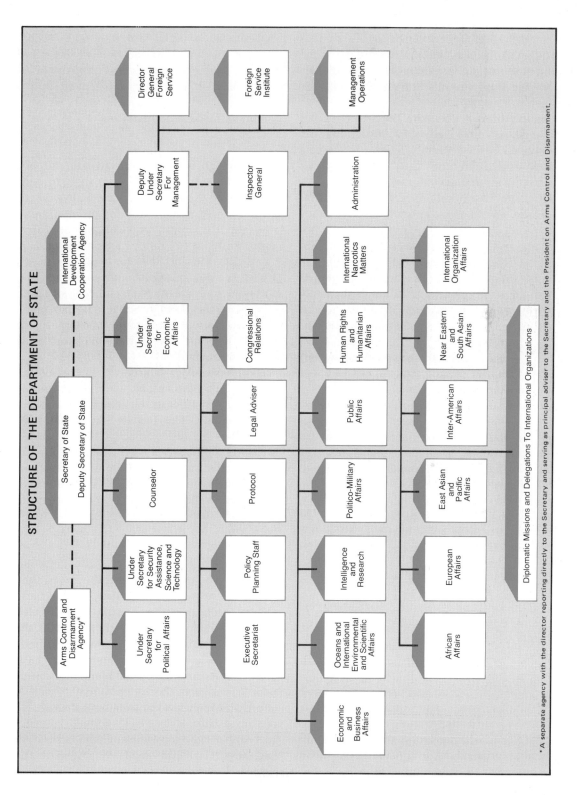

STRUCTURE OF THE DEPARTMENT OF STATE

Secretary of State
Deputy Secretary of State

International Development Cooperation Agency

Arms Control and Disarmament Agency*

Under Secretary for Political Affairs

Under Secretary for Security Assistance, Science and Technology

Counselor

Under Secretary for Economic Affairs

Deputy Under Secretary For Management

Inspector General

Director General Foreign Service

Foreign Service Institute

Management Operations

Executive Secretariat

Policy Planning Staff

Protocol

Legal Adviser

Congressional Relations

Administration

International Narcotics Matters

Human Rights and Humanitarian Affairs

Public Affairs

Oceans and International Environmental and Scientific Affairs

Intelligence and Research

Politico-Military Affairs

Economic and Business Affairs

African Affairs

European Affairs

East Asian and Pacific Affairs

Inter-American Affairs

Near Eastern and South Asian Affairs

International Organization Affairs

Diplomatic Missions and Delegations To International Organizations

*A separate agency with the director reporting directly to the Secretary and serving as principal adviser to the Secretary and the President on Arms Control and Disarmament.

The State Department has the smallest budget of any Cabinet department. Its budget and staff size are less than one percent of the Defense Department's budget and staff size.

Organization. The State Department's policy-making and advisory functions are managed by the secretary, a deputy secretary, three undersecretaries, and a deputy undersecretary for management who supervises the department's operations. Other top officials include several assistant secretaries, a policy-planning staff that formulates long-range programs, and an executive secretariat that coordinates the transmission of information to policy makers. The executive secretariat maintains the operations center. This center, which is the department's crisis room, contains the department's elaborate communications network.

The State Department's daily operations are organized along functional and geographic lines. Eleven bureaus are responsible for functional activities: international organizations affairs, economic and business affairs, oceans and international environmental and scientific affairs, intelligence and research, public affairs, politico-military affairs, protocol, congressional relations, legal advice, human rights and humanitarian affairs, and international narcotics matters.

The five geographic bureaus in the State Department that cover specific regions are: inter-American affairs, European affairs, East Asian and Pacific affairs, Near Eastern and South Asian affairs, and African affairs. These regional bureaus are divided into offices for each country. Those offices are further divided into about 500 desks, operated by officials who are knowledgeable about the specific functions in each country.

The State Department has more assistant secretaries than any other department. Whereas most departments are organized vertically into a hierarchy, the State Department is organized *horizontally*. This means that officials of equal rank have equal status. Indeed, this type of organization causes inefficiency and encourages the breakup of responsibility. It creates a department that is top-heavy, with 40 percent of each bureau's members being administrators.

The Foreign Service. By law, custom, and tradition every nation has the right to send and receive diplomatic representatives. Even before the American war for independence was won, the Continental Congress sent Benjamin Franklin to France as its minister.

Today the United States maintains nearly 300 embassies, missions, and consular posts abroad, which are staffed by more than 13,000 officers of the Foreign Service. It also maintains permanent diplomatic missions to the United Nations, NATO, the OAS, and other international bodies.

Ambassadors. Almost all embassies are headed by ambassadors, who are appointed by the President with the advice and consent of the Senate. The United States maintains embassies in approximately 140 countries. Missions to countries with which the United States does not have diplomatic relations are headed by ministers, chiefs of missions, or diplomatic officers. Until recently most ambassadors were political appointees. Today more than two thirds are career Foreign Service officers.

During the early years of the Republic, ambassadors (or ministers, as they were then called) were people of unusual stature and ability, such as John Adams, Thomas Jefferson, and James Monroe. For most of the nineteenth century, however, top diplomatic posts were given as rewards to the large contributors to presidential campaigns. Such people also had the independent means to afford the high level entertainment expected of ambassadors.

Ambassadors represent the President and report to the President through the secretary of state. Under international law American embassy grounds are considered United States soil. They may not be entered or violated in any way by the police or troops of the host country. Moreover, ambassadors and other Foreign Service officers have *diplomatic immunity*—they are not subject to the jurisdictions of their host countries and may not be taxed or arrested. If a diplomat commits a crime, he or she may be returned to the United States for prosecution. However, if diplomatic immunity is waived, the accused person is then turned over to the host country for prosecution.

QUOTES from famous people

"Observe good faith and justice toward all nations. Cultivate peace and harmony with all."

George Washington

The Foreign Service Today. Foreign Service officers are the United States representatives abroad. Their main duties involve carrying out the foreign policy directives of the secretary of state, gathering and relaying information about their host countries, protecting Americans and American interests in foreign countries, and performing various tasks for government agencies. The Foreign Service officers corps is an elite body of 3,500 men and women. These people are specially trained to serve any place in the world. Appointment to the Foreign Service officers corps is made on the basis of a highly competitive set of written and oral examinations.

Since most officers are male and come from similar social backgrounds, the Foreign Service has been criticized for its inadequate representation of society. However, the Foreign Service is trying to broaden its base of recruitment to include more racial and ethnic groups and women.

Passports. Passports, which are valid for five years, are issued by the State Department's passport office to all American citizens before they travel abroad. International law and treaties entitle passport holders to receive safe protection in the countries they visit. Foreign visitors to the United States are entitled to the same protection.

Consular Service. The United States maintains about 170 consular offices in principal cities throughout the world. Consular officials promote American trade, shipping, navigation, and commercial interests. They also help American travelers who encounter legal and financial problems.

The United States and International Organizations. The United States not only belongs to more than 200 international organizations, but it also sends representatives to major international conferences. These organizations and conferences are part of the American diplomatic effort.

The United Nations. The United States maintains a permanent diplomatic mission at the United Nations in New York City. This mission is headed by an ambassador who coordinates the activities of our many delegates to the various divisions of the United Nations.

Within the State Department, the Bureau of International Organization Affairs plays a major role in developing the policies that our United Nations delegations pursue. It also coordinates those policies with other concerned federal agencies, instructs and advises our delegates, and informs the public about the U.N.

The United States uses the U.N. for diplomatic discussions—especially with representatives of the Third World. The United States has also used the United Nations to

The U.S. State Department helps to bring about international settlements. Members of the Rhodesian Patriotic Front meet with American officials to discuss the growing problems in South Africa (1978).

start international programs on the laws of the sea, economic development, population problems, supplies of energy, and environmental concerns.

Other U.S. Agencies. Four independent agencies should be considered, not only because they are primarily concerned with foreign policy, but also because they coordinate their work with the State Department.

The four agencies are the International Development Cooperation Agency (IDCA), the Agency for International and Cultural Exchange (AICE), the Arms Control and Disarmament Agency (ACDA), and the Central Intelligence Agency (CIA).

The International Development Cooperation Agency (IDCA). Although the headquarters for the International Development Cooperation Agency is in the State Department, it operates with a large degree of independence.

The staff, which consists of 10,000 people, administers economic, technical assistance, and military aid programs to other countries.

Since World War II the United States has provided more than $300 billion in foreign aid. In the 1950's our focus shifted from economic aid to military aid. The mix between economic and military aid is now about equal.

Foreign aid has never been a popular program in Congress. Critics charge that too much aid is directed to friendly governments, some of which suppress their people. Aid programs often impose the condition that the recipient country must buy American products. This provision has provoked criticism.

Aid programs have sometimes been used to manipulate foreign governments. For example, aid to Chile was an issue that caused much dissension in the early 1970's. The

United States cut off almost all economic aid to the Marxist Allende government in 1970. But it continued to finance the Chilean military. At the same time the CIA funded other anti-Allende groups. The Chilean military eventually overthrew Allende and took over the Chilean government in a bloody **coup d'état.**

> A **coup d'état** is a sudden and decisive measure in politics, especially one effecting a change of government illegally or by force.

Those who resent such uses of foreign aid may still support aid programs that provide humanitarian assistance and disaster relief. The United States spends $1 billion a year on no-strings-attached assistance to developing countries. This aid is given through such international organizations as the United Nations and the World Bank.

One aid program with many more friends than critics is the U.S. Peace Corps. Peace Corps volunteers work in 70 developing countries, sharing their skills in such fields as engineering, education, agriculture, and community development.

The Agency for International and Cultural Exchange. In 1978 the AICE was formed when President Carter combined the United States Information Agency with the State Department's Bureau of Education and Cultural Affairs. This agency operates under the direction of the secretary of state and the National Security Council. AICE staff serve in countries in which the United States maintains embassies. AICE staffs are under the authority of those countries' American ambassadors.

AICE operates the Voice of America, which broadcasts news and feature programs about America in 40 languages. Some of these broadcasts are beamed to Soviet bloc nations.

AICE also publishes 66 magazines in 27 languages and finances the production and distribution of books and films. Its 200 overseas libraries are used by 20 million people each year.

The Arms Control and Disarmament Agency. The Arms Control and Disarmament Agency (ACDA), officially independent, is located in the State Department. ACDA's director reports to the secretary of state and the President about arms-control negotiations. Created by Congress in 1961 to deal with a wide range of arms-control problems, ACDA conducts research, briefs arms-control negotiators, and participates in arms-control discussions. ACDA drafted the 1963 Nuclear Test Ban Treaty, secured the hot-line communication system between Moscow and Washington, and helped formulate the Antarctic Treaty, the Nuclear Nonproliferation Treaty, and the Outer Space Treaty.

For 20 years the United States and the Soviet Union have been negotiating to halt the arms race. Since 1969 these negotiations have been conducted through the strategic arms limitations talks (SALT). The first round of SALT lasted 18 months. During this time the United States and the Soviet Union agreed by treaty to limit their stockpiles of defensive **antiballistic missiles** to 200. They also agreed to limit their offensive missile forces for a five-year period.

> **Antiballistic missiles** are special missiles that are launched against approaching enemy missiles.

In 1974 the leaders of the United States and the Soviet Union signed additional agreements banning underground nuclear tests. SALT talks have continued, but U.S. Senate leaders are cautious about further SALT treaties.

ACDA has been a major participant in SALT and in negotiations on detente. ACDA's plans are often rejected by the government—especially the Defense Department. In 1975

Congress gave ACDA the new and important role of determining the impact of new weapons systems on the arms race. In this role the ACDA was to evaluate this impact while weapons systems were still in early stages of development. If a weapons system seemed to conflict with the objective of arms control, development might be halted.

The Central Intelligence Agency. Several federal agencies carry out intelligence work, including units of the State, Defense, and Energy departments. The Energy Department's intelligence staff focuses on international development of nuclear energy. The FBI, the National Security Agency (which works on code-breaking and electronic communications systems), and the CIA are responsible for various aspects of internal and external security.

The CIA, created in 1947, gathers and analyzes information flowing into various parts of the government from all over the world. Its intelligence-gathering activities include *covert,* or secret, operations in foreign posts. It has helped depose governments in Iran (1954), Chile (1971), and Guatemala (1954), and it organized the Bay of Pigs invasion of Cuba (1961).

The CIA organized and trained anti-communist forces in Southeast Asia before the United States intervened in Vietnam. During the war, however, the CIA's advice was often more meaningful than that of other presidential advisers. For example, it questioned U.S. policy in Southeast Asia, which was based on the *domino theory.* This theory held that if one country fell to aggression, the surrounding countries would also fall. The CIA also argued unsuccessfully that bombing North Vietnam would merely stiffen the will of the people to resist.

The CIA, whose headquarters are in a Virginia suburb, employs more than 16,000 people. Its operating funds, which are about $2 billion each year, are hidden in the federal budget. They are mostly under various categories of Defense Department spending.

As head of the U.S. foreign intelligence community, the CIA director oversees research, military intelligence operations, spy satellites, and air reconnaissance activities, which may cost as much as six to ten billion dollars annually.

The CIA is responsible to the National Security Council. It supplies the President with regular intelligence briefings. It also advises the NSC on sensitive and secret foreign policy and national security matters. The CIA has its own overseas career service, and in some nations the local CIA chief has had more personnel, public funds, and influence than the United States ambassador.

Critics charge that the CIA's activities amount to the execution of covert foreign policy that is protected from public scrutiny and congressional control. Sometimes it is even protected from presidential control. The President and congressional leaders have pledged to oversee CIA activities more closely in the future.

section review

1. What are the two United States foreign policy objectives?
2. What is the primary function of the secretary of state? Who is the present secretary of state?
3. Define the concept of diplomatic immunity.
4. Why is the CIA receiving so much criticism and public scrutiny?
5. Describe how the CIA's advice was meaningful during the Vietnam War.

2. THE DEPARTMENT OF DEFENSE

In eighteenth-century America one of the most important reasons for forming the central government was to "provide for the common defense." The President, as commander

Here is an aerial view of the Pentagon.

in chief of the armed forces, decides when to use military power. The President, Congress, the National Security Council, and the State Department make foreign and national security policy. But the day-to-day work of developing and administering the nation's military power and defense programs is the job of the Department of Defense.

Civilian Control over the Military. The framers of the Constitution recognized that military domination did not mix with democratic government. They gave the ultimate military powers to the President and Congress. As commander in chief, the President commissions all officers with the Senate's consent. Congress makes the rules governing the armed forces. It may also support armies, "but no appropriation of money to that use shall be for a longer term than two years." Congress also determines the size of the military services, their pay, their equipment, and their weapons. A congressional statute requires that the secretary of defense and the secretaries of the army, navy, and air force be civilians. At President Truman's urging Congress did make one exception. It allowed General of the Army George C. Marshall—who had served as secretary of state—to become secretary of defense in 1950.

In spite of constitutional and statutory powers, Congress has not found it easy to control the military. Military leaders control the flow of information to Congress. President

Eisenhower criticized the military for gaining "unwarranted influence" by joining forces with defense contractors. Similarly, critics argue today that such an alliance promotes unnecessary weapons systems and prevents closing down unnecessary and costly military bases around the world.

There is no doubt that Congress has the power to control defense spending. But leading members of Congress—particularly those on the Armed Services Committees—have supported military leaders and have encouraged expansion of their responsibilities.

Organization of the Defense Department. The Defense Department spent over $130 billion in fiscal year 1980. It expects to continue spending at about that same level, not counting the cost of inflation. Its headquarters, the Pentagon, contains the office of the secretary of defense and of generals and admirals who do not command troops, ships, or bases.

Before 1947 there were two separate military departments—War and Navy. The War Department was one of the original Cabinet departments. The Navy Department was created nine years later in 1798. Problems of coordination during World War II prompted demands that the two departments be combined into one. In 1947 Congress made the air force a separate unit from the army and placed the three military services—army, navy, and air force—and each one's civilian secretary under the control of the secretary of defense. In 1958 President Eisenhower—a former five-star general—urged Congress to appropriate all funds to the secretary of defense rather than to the three military services. He also urged that the secretary's control be expanded to cover the military services. Congress reorganized the Defense Department. But they refused to appropriate funds for the military services through the secretary of defense. Moreover, Congress continued to allow the joint chiefs of staff and the service secretaries to testify independently before congressional committees.

Centralization of Authority. Robert McNamara, the secretary of defense under Presidents Kennedy and Johnson, instituted several important changes in the organization of the Defense Department. With strong support from the White House, Secretary McNamara and his team of civilian economists and analysts coordinated the functions of the three services. He created unified military commands and used such techniques as systems analysis and program budgeting to evaluate weapons and allocate funds among the various services and commands. Secretary McNamara also overruled admirals and generals when he thought their reasons for advocating military strategies were unsound.

When President Nixon took office, he granted the three service secretaries more authority to shape their budgets. He also gave military leaders stronger roles in making budget and weapons decisions.

Public reaction against operations in Vietnam prompted Congress to scrutinize military proposals more carefully. Military leaders, however, remain prominent in shaping defense policy.

In 1981 President Reagan named Caspar W. Weinberger Secretary of Defense. Weinberger held top state positions when Reagan was governor of California. He had also served as director of the Office of Management and Budget and as Secretary of HEW under President Nixon

The Secretary of Defense and Foreign Policy. Because the position as head of defense is critical, the secretary of defense often influences foreign issues. This influence is further extended by the secretary's membership in several interdepartmental policy groups, the most important of which is the National Security Council.

A deputy secretary, the three service secretaries, several assistant secretaries, and the director of defense research and engineering assist the secretary in managing the Defense Department.

The Joint Chiefs of Staff. The Joint Chiefs of Staff are the principal military advisers to the President, the National Security Council, and the secretary of defense. The JCS is composed of the army chief of staff, the chief of naval operations, the air force chief of staff, the marine corps commandant, and a chairperson who is a ranking general or admiral. They are appointed by the President with the consent of the Senate for two-year terms. They may be reappointed only once.

The joint chiefs shape military strategy, coordinate supply and training programs, review personnel requirements, and recommend the formation of unified commands to the secretary of defense.

The joint chiefs have tended to endorse the spending proposals recommended by each service. During the Vietnamese War, the JCS rarely opposed the recommendations of field commanders. Such action limited their usefulness to the President as military advisers.

The three services. The army, navy, and air force are each headed by a civilian secretary. His or her principal military adviser is the chief of staff of the respective military service. Chiefs of staff have direct command responsibilities over military operations and units.

The army is responsible for all landbased military operations. By 1980 the army was a volunteer force of about 800,000 officers and soldiers.

The navy is responsible for sea warfare and defense. As an additional responsibility it transports troops and aircraft for the army and air force. It also operates submarines armed with nuclear weapons, which patrol waters throughout the world. The navy consists of about 550,000 officers and sailors.

The marine corps is actually a unit of the navy. It is headed by a commandant who is responsible to the secretary of the navy. The corps, which consists of about 200,000, is known for its high morale and courage.

The air force is responsible for military air operations. It numbers about 560,000

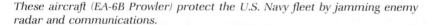

These aircraft (EA-6B Prowler) protect the U.S. Navy fleet by jamming enemy radar and communications.

officers and enlisted personnel. The air force defends the United States against air attacks, carries out aerial reconnaissance missions, and operates the nation's offensive and defensive missiles. Thus the air force is the nation's first defense against surprise attacks.

Air force planes are armed with weapons of enormous destructive power. It is the Defense Department's responsibility to ensure that those weapons are used only at the President's command.

section review

1. What exception was made to the congressional statute requiring the secretaries of defense, army, navy, and air force to be civilians?
2. List the changes in the Department of Defense instituted by Robert McNamara.
3. Describe the functions of the joint chiefs.

3. THE DEPARTMENT OF THE TREASURY

The federal budget for 1980 exceeded $600 billion. Most of this money came from taxes, and the rest was borrowed. The job of collecting taxes, and borrowing and disbursing money belongs to the Treasury Department.

The Treasury Department was one of the original departments set up in 1789. Alexander Hamilton, the first secretary of the treasury, was by far the most influential member of George Washington's Cabinet.

The Secretary of the Treasury. Today the secretary of the treasury supervises a department of 130,000 people. The secretary is concerned with shaping national economic and **fiscal** policy. In recent years the secretary has become the government's primary

representative in financial and trade negotiations with other countries. Such negotiations involve American loans to foreign governments, tariff negotiations, monetary agreements, sustaining of the international value of the dollar, and other matters related to international payments and trade.

Fiscal policies are those policies dealing with government taxing and spending.

Revenue Collection. *Customs duties*—taxes on imported goods—were the main source of federal revenue until the latter part of the nineteenth century. These duties are collected by the Treasury Department's Customs Service, which supervises and inspects articles brought into the country at *ports of entry*—major seaports, airports, and border stations. The Customs Service inspects cargo, determines the value of merchandise, and works with the coast guard to prevent smuggling.

Today most of the nation's revenue comes from taxes collected by the Internal Revenue Service (IRS). Fifty-eight district directors operate field offices throughout the country. All taxes are sent to these district offices. In 1980 the Internal Revenue Service took in over $500 billion a year at a cost of less than 50 cents for each $100 collected.

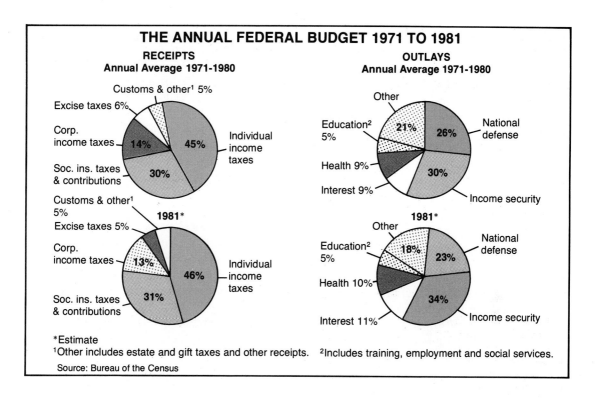

THE ANNUAL FEDERAL BUDGET 1971 TO 1981

RECEIPTS
Annual Average 1971-1980

OUTLAYS
Annual Average 1971-1980

Customs & other[1] 5%
Excise taxes 6%
Corp. income taxes — 14%
Soc. ins. taxes & contributions — 30%
Individual income taxes 45%

Other
Education[2] 5%
Health 9%
Interest 9%
Other 21%
National defense 26%
Income security 30%

Customs & other[1] 5%
Excise taxes 5%
Corp. income taxes — 13%
Soc. ins. taxes & contributions — 31%
1981*
Individual income taxes 46%

1981*
Other
Education[2] 5%
Health 10%
Interest 11%
Other 18%
National defense 23%
Income security 34%

*Estimate
[1]Other includes estate and gift taxes and other receipts. [2]Includes training, employment and social services.
Source: Bureau of the Census

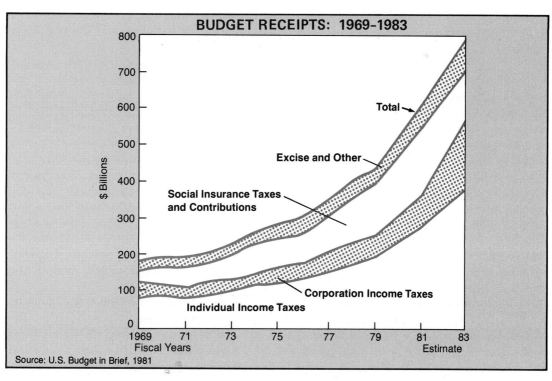

BUDGET RECEIPTS: 1969–1983

$ Billions

Total
Excise and Other
Social Insurance Taxes and Contributions
Corporation Income Taxes
Individual Income Taxes

1969 71 73 75 77 79 81 83
Fiscal Years   Estimate

Source: U.S. Budget in Brief, 1981

Federal taxes come from the following sources:

1. *Personal income taxes.* These taxes provide more than 40 percent of the federal government's revenue. People with high incomes are scheduled to pay larger percentages of their income in taxes than are people who earn lower incomes. Loopholes, or *tax shelters*, enable millionaires to pay about the same proportion of their incomes in taxes as those earning middle incomes of $25,000.
(Internal revenue agents curb cheating by examining records, inspecting bank accounts, and auditing a percentage of all returns. Audits generally require taxpayers to present proof of all claimed deductions. Failure to report all taxable income is a crime punishable by a fine and/or imprisonment, plus the penalty of paying 50 percent of the amount not reported.)
Income tax rates may be raised or lowered to stimulate or restrain economic activity.

2. *Corporate income taxes.* These taxes account for 16 percent of the government's revenue.

3. *Social Security taxes.* This tax is the second largest source of federal revenue. Social Security taxes raise over 31 percent of all federal revenues. Social Security payments account for approximately 22.2 percent of all federal spending. By 1981 every taxpayer paid 6.65 percent of gross income, up to a maximum of $29,700, into the Social Security system. By 1987 all individuals are scheduled to pay 7.15 percent, up to a maximum income of $42,600.
(Most Social Security taxes are deducted from employees' paychecks. Employers must then match all employees' Social Security payments. Because the rate of taxation is uniform for all taxpayers, low-income people pay larger portions of their incomes into Social Security than do people who earn higher incomes.)

4. *Excise taxes.* These taxes provide about 6 percent of the total federal revenue each year. They are levied on such luxury items and services as liquor, tobacco, gasoline, and air travel.

5. *Other sources.* Other taxes include customs duties, which yield about $5 billion, and estate taxes—taxes levied on the property that deceased individuals pass on.

The Fiscal Service. The Fiscal Service accounts for the receipts and expenditures of all federal money. It contains the Office of the Treasurer of the United States, who is responsible for receiving, depositing, and disbursing all public money.

The Fiscal Service also supervises the nation's debt transactions. In 1900 the federal government spent $500 million for goods and services. The United States government now spends 1,000 times the amount that it spent in 1900. It now spends more each year than it did in all the years that elapsed between the founding of the Republic and the beginning of World War II.

A balanced budget means that spending equals income. The federal government has not had a balanced budget in several years. Spending has exceeded income, and the balance has been made up by borrowing money. This borrowed money constitutes the public debt—a sum that grows larger each year.

The public debt exceeds $900 billion, most of which was incurred in fighting wars—World War I, World War II, the Korean War, and the Vietnamese War. The two biggest items for which we incur debt today are national defense and social security. Together they absorb two thirds of the debt of the federal government.

The government borrows money from its citizens. The Constitution gives Congress the authority to borrow money on the credit of the United States. Congress has authorized the Treasury Department to sell securities to

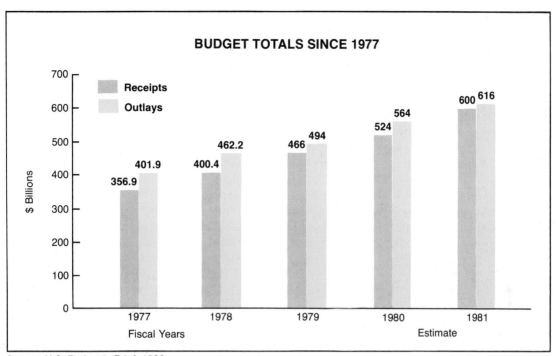

BUDGET TOTALS SINCE 1977

Source: U.S. Budget in Brief, 1980

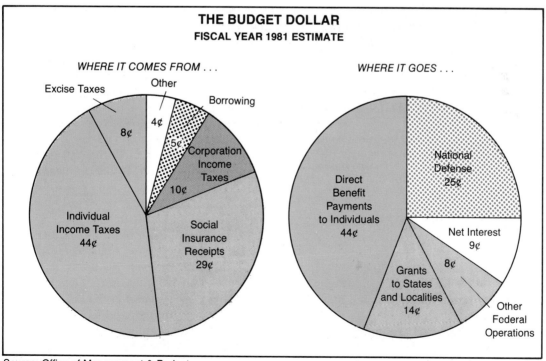

THE BUDGET DOLLAR

FISCAL YEAR 1981 ESTIMATE

Source: Office of Management & Budget

banks, corporations, and private citizens. These securities include long-term bonds and short-term treasury notes. Because the government guarantees its securities, they are bought by banks and investment companies. In times of inflation, the government—through the federal reserve system—increases its sale of securities. This increase withdraws money from the economy and decreases private spending, thus reducing inflation.

The government also borrows by selling Series EE saving bonds. Such bonds pay 8 percent interest—a better rate than most banks pay. They *mature*, or are redeemable, in nine years.

The Currency System. Acting through Congress, the Treasury Department, and the federal reserve system, the federal government controls the economy by manufacturing money, regulating the value of money, and controlling the amount of credit.

◆ *QUOTES* from famous people

"Money is, with propriety, considered as the vital principle of the body politic; as that which sustains its life and motion, and enables it to perform its most essential functions."

Alexander Hamilton

Manufacturing money is relatively simple. The Treasury Department's Bureau of Engraving and Printing uses carefully designed plates and special paper and ink to print paper currency. The bureau also man-

ufactures the equivalent of millions of dollars in bonds, notes, postage stamps, and food coupons each week. All paper currency is circulated through federal reserve banks.

Another treasury unit, the Bureau of the Mint, operates United States mints in Philadelphia, Denver, and San Francisco. These mints manufacture all coins, which make up about 5 percent of the country's cash. The Bureau of the Mint also operates a gold depository at Fort Knox, Kentucky, and a silver depository at West Point, New York.

Coins, especially the old silver dollar, used to contain almost their stated value of metal. At one time much paper currency was redeemable in gold and silver. As late as 1974 certain dollar bills, called silver certificates, might be redeemed for silver through the treasury.

Today coins contain only a fraction of their value in metal, and the actual value of paper money is nothing. How does the government maintain the value of its currency and coins?

Until the end of the nineteenth century, gold and silver coins—with metal values approximating the stated value of the coins—circulated side-by-side. As the value of silver declined and the value of gold rose, debtors preferred to pay their debts in silver, and creditors preferred to be paid in gold. Odd as it may seem now, the silver versus gold debate was a strong national issue during the last quarter of the nineteenth century. Democrats supported silver, and Republicans supported gold.

The Gold Standard. The Gold Standard Act of 1900 settled the issue. Gold was made the standard against which all coins and currency were to be measured. The Treasury Department and national banks were required to store enough gold to back all coins and currency in circulation.

During the depression people lost con-

Silver and paper currency can no longer be redeemed for gold. Can you tell which federal reserve district this dollar came from?

fidence in the value of currency and began to hoard gold. To protect the nation's economy, the Roosevelt administration, in cooperation with Congress, adopted restrictive policies during the early days of the New Deal (1933–34). Silver and paper currency were no longer redeemable for gold. Gold coins were no longer made, and the ones in circulation were recalled. Private transactions in gold were forbidden. Except for the gold that is in jewelry, dental fillings, and a few other things, the federal government owned all the gold in the United States.

Currency is now comprised of about $12 billion in gold and about $90 billion in paper currency. All U.S. currency (federal reserve notes) and coins are legal tender and may not be redeemed for gold or silver. Because gold is traded freely in the international metal markets, Americans have been allowed since 1975 to buy and store as much gold as they wish.

The Value of the Dollar. During the 1970's the value of the dollar declined substantially in relation to the value of other nations' money. This is because the United States spends more abroad—in trade, aid, tourism, and military forces—than it receives in payments for exports. This imbalance results in a balance of payments deficit. Other nations, notably West Germany and Japan, have surplus balances of payments, which increase the value of their money in international markets.

Because our nation's economic health depends on the dollar's value, the secretary of the treasury's top priority is to formulate policies that will maintain and—if possible—increase that value.

The Secret Service. The Secret Service was established in 1865. Its original function was to combat counterfeiters of U.S. currency. Although it still performs that function, the Secret Service is best known today for protecting the President of the United States. The Secret Service's staff and duties were expanded after President Kennedy's assassination in 1963. Today, in addition to protecting the President, the Secret Service protects the President's family, the Vice-President and his family, the President-elect and his family, any former Presidents and their spouses or widows, major presidential candidates, and any visiting foreign leaders.

section review

1. List the primary sources of federal taxes.
2. What agency is given the responsibility for collecting the nation's revenue?
3. How are Social Security taxes obtained by the government?
4. Explain how the Roosevelt administration protected the nation's economy.

4. THE DEPARTMENT OF JUSTICE

One of the principal responsibilities of government is to provide justice for its citizens. Some people think of justice in terms of preventing crimes and catching criminals. But prosecuting people accused of committing federal crimes is only a small part of the Justice Department's work. The administration of justice mostly involves noncriminal matters and special categories of crimes—such as evading taxes, creating monopolies, polluting the air, and depriving people of their civil rights.

The Justice Department prosecutes people (and corporations) who violate federal laws and regulations. It also defends the government against claims brought by individuals and states. The importance of the case and the court in which it is heard determine whether the prosecuting or defending will be done by the attorney general, the solicitor general, Department of Justice attorneys, or several hundred United States attorneys and assistant attorneys who operate throughout the country.

The Attorney General. Since the Justice Department was not established until 1870, the early attorneys general had no department or staff. The original responsibilities of the attorney general were to give legal advice to the President and other government officials and to represent the United States in court.

Today the attorney general has other duties. He or she presides over the department's six divisions (each headed by an assistant attorney general) and bureaus, oversees the federal prison system, and implements immigration and naturalization laws. The attorney general also plays a role in choosing federal judges and U.S. attorneys.

The Solicitor General. The solicitor general, who is the third highest-ranking officer in the Justice Department (after the attorney general and the deputy attorney general), is the government's chief lawyer. The solicitor general and his or her staff of lawyers represent the United States before the Supreme Court. When the government loses a case in the federal district courts or the court of appeals, the solicitor general decides whether to appeal the decision to a higher federal court—the court of appeals or the Supreme Court.

The Six Divisions. The Justice Department's work is divided into six divisions, each headed by an assistant attorney general.

The Antitrust Division. This division brings suit against monopolies, price fixers, and other alleged violators of antitrust laws. In effect it makes antitrust policy by deciding whether to prosecute apparent violators.

The antitrust division consists of about 320 lawyers who prepare government cases in an effort to protect the competitive economic system. Potentially illegal corporate practices are brought to the division's attention by competitors, suppliers, and consumers.

The Civil Division This division represents the United States in most noncriminal cases to which the federal government is a party. It handles damage suits against the United States and represents the executive departments and agencies when their rules or procedures are challenged by private individuals or groups.

The Criminal Division This division pros-

STRUCTURE OF THE DEPARTMENT OF JUSTICE

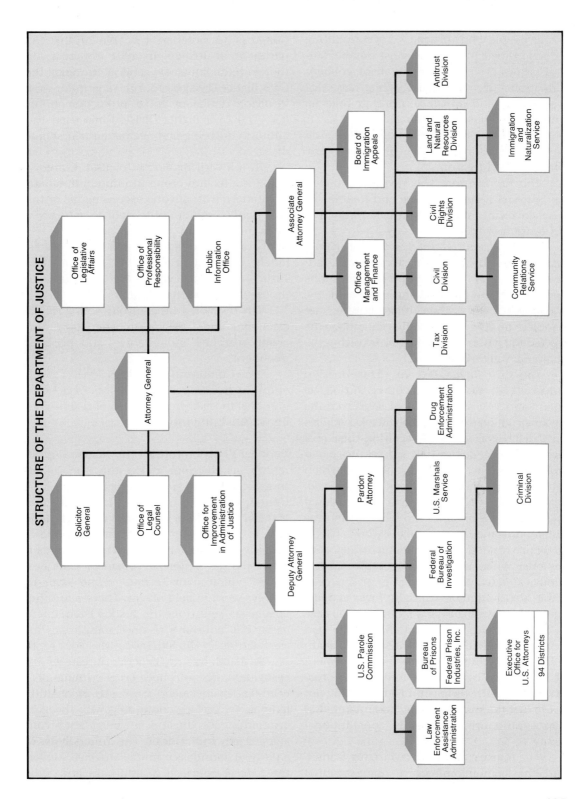

ecutes people who are accused of committing federal crimes. Among the most notable federal crimes are counterfeiting, bank robbery, kidnapping, election fraud, selling narcotics, transporting individuals across state lines for immoral purposes, crossing state lines to avoid prosecution, bribery of federal officials, *perjury*, or testifying falsely in federal proceedings, and treason.

The Tax Division. This division counsels the Internal Revenue Service and handles all cases involving internal revenue laws, such as tax evasion or fraud.

The Land and Natural Resources Division. This division deals with cases involving federal lands and their resources. Questions concerning land titles, oil and mineral leases, water rights, and private timber cuttings are handled by this division. It also represents the federal government in cases involving the affairs of Native Americans.

The Civil Rights Division. This division enforces civil rights laws in courts. During the 1940's and 1950's, remnants of laws from the Reconstruction era were the Black people's only defense against not receiving their civil rights in court. Before 1964 federal juries had to be selected according to state rules, which often worked against the Black people. Proof that a person's civil rights had been violated was difficult to obtain. Even when proof was obtained, some district judges were unsympathetic, making it still difficult to get convictions. When sentences were given, they rarely extended beyond a year in prison, even if the "deprivation of civil rights" was actually the murder of a Black person. In the 1945 case of *Screws* v. *U.S.*, a Georgia sheriff who had beaten a handcuffed Black prisoner to death went free. This was because the Department of Justice, having no legal authority to prosecute cases involving murder, could not prove that the sheriff actually had intended to deprive the prisoner of his constitutional rights.

The murder of several civil rights leaders and the bombing of many homes forced Congress to broaden the role of the Department of Justice. In 1964 Congress authorized the attorney general (through the Civil Rights Division) to intervene in any suit involving denial of equal protection of the law. The Civil Rights Division has used this authority to bring suit against certain school districts.

In the Civil Rights Act of 1964, Congress made it a federal crime to injure, intimidate, or interfere with anyone exercising his or her civil rights, including the right to vote, serve on a jury, attend a public school, or use public accommodations, such as restrooms, hotels, and restaurants. The Department of Justice acts only when the state fails to prosecute civil rights offenders.

The division's cases involve voting rights, election frauds, racial discrimination, unlawful searches and seizures, and prisoner treatment.

The Community Relations Service, a unit of the Justice Department, assists local communities in resolving disputes of discrimination against minority groups.

Federal Prosecutions. The Justice Department's six divisions direct the work of attorneys' staffs in each division. There is a United States attorney based in Washington, D.C., for each of the 91 judicial districts of the federal courts system. Each district also has a United States marshal who makes arrests, takes charge of federal prisoners, and executes federal court orders. Some staff attorneys work in field offices. These and other specialists sent from the Justice Department assist U.S. attorneys in developing cases for prosecution in the federal courts.

Assisted by the Federal Bureau of Investigation, U.S. attorneys bring criminal proceedings against people accused of violating federal law. Before continuing with the government's case, the attorney must first obtain a grand jury **indictment.** The United States is a party to countless criminal and civil suits in the federal courts. U.S. attorneys and their staffs often operate in the *trial court* (the federal district court where the case is heard first), whereas attorneys from the six divisions operate in the court of appeals. Justice department attorneys participate in approximately half of the cases heard by the Supreme Court.

An **indictment** is a formal accusation brought by a grand jury, charging a person with the commission of a crime. The accusation does not involve the determination of the accused person's guilt or innocence regarding the crime.

The Immigration and Naturalization Service. The Immigration and Naturalization Service implements federal immigration laws. Under these laws a total of 170,000 immigrants may be admitted to the United States each year. Wives, husbands, unmarried minor children, and parents of American citizens may immigrate to this country under separate provisions of the law.

Immigrants must qualify under one of several preference classes, which give first consideration to relatives of American citizens and permanent residents. Members of professions—such as doctors, lawyers, and educators—and others with special talents or skills also are given preference.

Congress may create special categories of preference for refugees, as it did in the case of the South Vietnamese in 1975 and the Cubans in 1980.

Any person who comes to the United

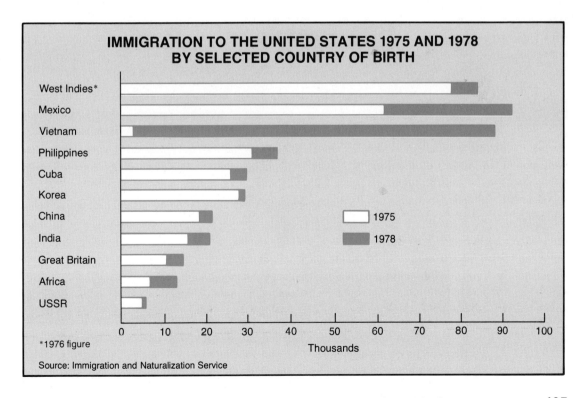

IMMIGRATION TO THE UNITED STATES 1975 AND 1978
BY SELECTED COUNTRY OF BIRTH

*1976 figure

Thousands

Source: Immigration and Naturalization Service

Congress can create special categories of preference for refugees. These Cuban refugees were admitted to the U.S. in 1980.

States as an immigrant is entitled to become a naturalized citizen after residing in the United States for five years. Federal judges and most state judges are empowered to administer the examinations and oaths involved in the naturalization process.

Federal Prisons.   The Justice Department's Bureau of Prisons is responsible for the custody of all people convicted of federal crimes and sentenced to prison by federal courts. The federal prison system is comprised of six maximum-security penitentiaries, several less rigorous penal institutions—including four work camps—and minimum-security facilities. In these minimum-security facilities, inmates may leave for short periods to work or to visit their families.

The Board of Parole grants or revokes paroles involving federal prisoners and supervises those who have been released on parole. Paroles are rarely granted before a prisoner has served one third of his or her sentence.

The pardon attorney is the Justice Department official who recommends pardons or the reduction of sentences to the President on behalf of persons convicted of federal crimes.

The Federal Bureau of Investigation.   The FBI investigates all violations of federal law not assigned to other federal agencies (such as the Internal Revenue Service, the Customs Bureau, and the Secret Service). It investigates all federal crimes except counterfeiting and violations of postal, customs, tax, and narcotics laws.

The FBI's headquarters, which are in a massive building apart from the Justice Department, contain the latest equipment for detecting crime. The FBI's high technology laboratory and fingerprinting resources are available to all law-enforcement agencies. The FBI works closely with state and local police and maintains a national police academy that provides advanced training to law-enforce-

ment personnel. President Carter had sought to strengthen the authority of the attorney general over the FBI. But it may take some years to overcome the FBI's tradition of self-government.

The Law Enforcement Assistance Administration.   The LEAA was established under the Omnibus Crime Control Act of 1968. Its main functions are to fund crime prevention efforts made by state and local law-enforcement authorities and to sponsor research on the causes and the prevention of crime.

LEAA funds are spent in various ways. Some pay for police equipment—such as squad cars, helicopters, weapons, and computers. Other funds are used to train police, upgrade jails, and sponsor citizens' crime-prevention units.

The Drug Enforcement Administration. The Drug Enforcement Administration enforces federal narcotics laws. Narcotics agents are trained to search for illegal drugs at all points of entry. They work closely with the coast guard, the Customs Bureau, and other law-enforcement agencies.

Narcotics such as heroin are *addictive* (habit-forming). Many addicts commit crimes to support their habits. One out of every eight federal prisoners is a narcotics violator—mainly a manufacturer, importer, or seller of illegal drugs.

section review

1. Into what six categories is the Justice Department's work divided?
2. Who is the government's chief lawyer?
3. How did the murder of several civil rights leaders broaden the function of the Justice Department?
4. How many judicial districts are there in the federal court system?
5. What is the function of the Board of Parole?
6. What is the function of the Drug Enforcement Administration?

CHAPTER SUMMARY

25

George Washington established a Cabinet of four advisers to assist him in the essential functions of government: foreign relations, defense and national security, national finance, and the administration of justice. A full department was created to handle three of these areas. Only the administration of justice was assigned to a single person: the attorney general.

As the government and the society grew and became more complex, additional departments were created, and the four original departments grew in size and function.

The major goals of foreign policy are to maintain national security and to achieve peaceful relations with all countries. The foreign policy of the United States is conducted by the President, the secretary of state, and numerous State Department personnel.

The United States sends representatives to major international conferences and participates in more than 200 world organizations, including the United Nations and its various agencies.

The Central Intelligence Agency (CIA) is responsible directly to the President and the National Security Council; its budget is classified but is included in various parts of the Defense Department budget.

The day-to-day work of developing and administering the nation's military and defense programs is the job of the Defense Department. The Founders firmly believed that the military must be under the control of and subject to civilian authority. Congress enacted laws that require the secretary of defense and the secretaries of the armed forces to be civilians.

The Defense Department administers the single largest U.S. budget category. Because of foreign policy objectives of national security, the secretary of defense has a strong voice in shaping that policy. The armed services are all under the supervision of the secretary of defense.

The task of collecting taxes, borrowing money, and paying money out belongs to the Treasury Department. Revenue sources include customs duties, income taxes, social security taxes, and excise taxes.

The Justice Department prosecutes individuals who violate federal laws and regulations, and defends the government against claims brought by individuals and states. The attorney general is the chief legal adviser in the nation.

REVIEW QUESTIONS

1. The two major objectives of American foreign policy imply war and peace. Are these goals in conflict? Why must both be pursued at the same time?

2. The Defense Department has a budget of money

and personnel 100 times greater than the State Department. Do you agree with this allocation of resources? Why or why not?

3. The secretary of defense and the secretaries of the army, navy, and air force must, by law, be civilians. Why is this a requirement? Do you agree with this limitation? Why or why not?

4. Why has there been increasing pressure to bring the CIA under closer supervision by the President and Congress?

ACTIVITIES FOR REVIEW

activity 1   Stage a classroom debate or forum on the following issue: RESOLVED, that the space program should be abandoned (or expanded).

activity 2   Invite a local attorney, public defender, or judge to speak to your class on justice in a democracy.

activity 3   Invite a federal law enforcement officer to discuss the opportunities and problems of federal law enforcement as a career.

political science DICTIONARY

antiballistic missiles—special missiles launched against approaching enemy missiles.	p. 483
coup d'état—a sudden and decisive measure in politics effecting a change in government, illegally or by force.	p. 483
customs duties—taxes on imported goods.	p. 488
detente—literally, "the relaxation of tensions"; an easing of strained relations and political tensions between nations.	p. 477
diplomatic immunity—exemption of ambassadors and other foreign service officers from the jurisdictions of their host countries.	p. 481
domino theory—the theory that if one country is the victim of aggression, neighboring countries will also fall.	p. 484
fiscal policies—policies that deal with government taxing and spending.	p. 488
indictment—a formal accusation brought by a grand jury, charging a person with the commission of a crime but making no determination of guilt or innocence.	p. 497
perjury—the criminal offense of making false statements under oath.	p. 496

26

The Special Interest Departments

The Departments of Agriculture, Commerce, and Labor were formed in the late nineteenth and early twentieth centuries to meet the special needs of farmers, business people, and workers. As it established each of these departments, Congress recognized that the particular group involved had grown strong enough to be entitled to a separate voice in American government. Originally designed to provide a variety of services to each of these communities, each department has become an advocate of the group that it serves.

CHAPTER PREVIEW

1. THE DEPARTMENT OF AGRICULTURE
2. THE COMMERCE DEPARTMENT
3. THE DEPARTMENT OF LABOR

1. THE DEPARTMENT OF AGRICULTURE

At the beginning of the American Republic, the majority of people lived on farms. Thomas Jefferson was a farmer as well as a statesman. The nation's expansion westward in the nineteenth century was motivated largely by a search for new lands to farm. Until the beginning of the twentieth century, a majority of Americans were farmers.

Northern farmers were the Republican party's major constituency in the national elections of 1856 and 1860. Mindful of this allegiance, members of the first Republican

Congress, which took office in 1861, decided to give recognition to farmers. In 1862 Congress created an independent executive department to supervise agriculture; passed the Homestead Act, which granted 160-acre parcels of federal land to people who agreed to settle and farm the land; and passed the Morrill Act, which granted land to the states to establish agricultural colleges.

In 1889 Congress enlarged the department and gave it Cabinet status. The department set up agricultural research stations, undertook conservation and *reclamation* (irrigation of arid lands) projects, and encouraged marketing through farm cooperatives.

During the depression crop prices fell drastically. Farmers tried to grow even more produce, with the result that prices dropped still further. Many farmers were unable to meet mortgage payments and lost their farms.

The Development of National Farm Policy. To relieve the plight of the farmer, FDR sought to restrict production and thereby increase prices. The main instruments that authorized this policy were the Agricultural Adjustment Acts (AAA) of 1933 and 1938. Farmers who reduced production were paid a subsidy. In 1936 the Supreme Court declared the AAA of 1933 unconstitutional because of one of its tax features, but the program had raised farm prices more than 60 percent during the three years that it had been in operation.

The second AAA (1938) removed the illegal tax feature and restored the subsidy program. It provided for storing surpluses that would be used during future shortages—in effect paying the farmers in advance for the eventual sale of crops stored in government granaries and warehouses.

World War II brought an increased demand for farm products, and farmers needed incentives to increase production rather than to limit it. The government's strategy involved guaranteeing minimum prices for certain crops. If farmers could not get better prices on the open market, they could sell their

The federal government has developed many plans to help stabilize agriculture.

crops to the government at the supported price. Most prices stayed above the support level, for the security of promised supports encouraged production.

Over the years the federal government has developed a number of strategies to stabilize farm prices, sustain farmers' incomes, and achieve a balance between supply and demand. The most important strategies are the following.

1. *Acreage allotments.* Experts in the department's Agricultural Stabilization and Conservation Service estimate the probable demand in a given year for supported crops such as cotton, wheat, and rice. They also determine the number of acres needed to produce the required amount. The national acreage is then allotted to individual farms by state and county committees composed of representatives elected by the farmers. To offset a wheat surplus and falling wheat prices in 1977, this procedure was used to reduce wheat acreage by 20 percent in 1978.

2. *Marketing quotas.* If a given crop is overproduced and a collapse in price seems likely, farmers producing this crop may vote in a national referendum to set a marketing quota. This procedure requires a two-thirds vote before a quota can be established. Each farmer is allotted a quota and pays a penalty for exceeding it. Overproduction has not been a problem in recent years, and therefore quotas have not been used.

3. *Price supports.* The price-support system of World War II has been modified. Congress now sets target prices for the most important staple crops—cotton, wheat, rice, and feed grains. Target prices are below market levels but are significantly higher than prices obtained in the 1960's. Subsidies are paid only if overproduction drops market prices below target levels.

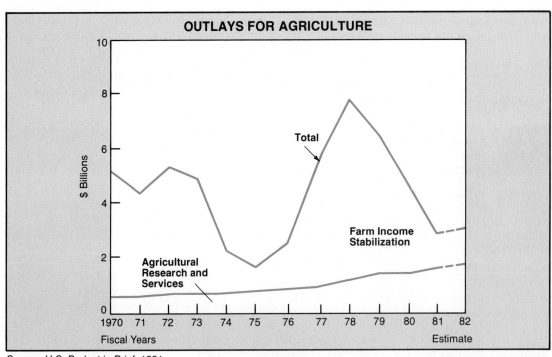

Source: U.S. Budget in Brief, 1981

JOHN RUSLING BLOCK

In December 1980, President Reagan nominated John R. Block to be Secretary of Argiculture. He was confirmed by the Senate in January 1981. Block was born in the rural community of Galesburg, Illinois in 1935. He graduated from the U.S. Military Academy at West Point in 1957 and completed his army service as an infantry officer in 1960. Block is married and has three children.

Block brings to this position firsthand knowledge of the problems facing the agricultural community. This is because he has spent most of his life dealing with farms and farming problems. In 1960 he took control of the family farm in Gilson, Illinois and expanded it from 300 acres and 600 hogs to 3,000 acres and 6,000 animals. His dedication and expertise has helped him to win many awards including the Jaycees Outstanding Young Farmer Award in 1969, the Cooperative Extension Service's Meritorious Service Award for outstanding contribution to Illinois agriculture, and the Governor's Outstanding Achievement Award. Block has been active in many farm organizations. He was a board member of the Illinois Farm Bureau, a trustee of the Farm Foundation, President of the Mid-America International Agri-Trade Council, and chairman of an eleven-state farm summit. The farm summit involved leaders of all major farm organizations.

In 1977 Block became Director of the Illinois Department of Argriculture. His job has enabled him to get not only domestic agricultural experience but also international experience. Block got his start in international agriculture when he represented Illinois at the annual food show in West Germany. There he met with agricultural attachés from several Western European nations. Since then he has also been to other countries such as Japan, China, and Taiwan, as a member of agricultural export teams. Block also led a "people-to-people" fact-finding mission to the Soviet Union, Poland, Hungary, Austria, and Switzerland in 1980.

Block describes himself as a free-market man who believes that the best guarantee of high farm income is high prices for farm goods. He supports maximum trade and exports and was opposed to President Carter's limiting of grain shipments to the Soviet Union.

Block made several significant comments at his committee hearing before being confirmed as Secretary of Agriculture. He stated that programs to protect farm land from erosion and conversion to nonfarm uses should be carried out at the local level, with the federal government providing leadership and some money for the states. Block also stated at the hearing that federal restrictions on the amount that farmers plant, such as the Carter administration's "normal crop acreage" regulations, are generally undersirable.

In his new position Block promised to aggressively promote the sale of American farm goods abroad. He believes that strong export markets would boost farmers' earnings and strengthen the whole U.S. economy. Block pledged to be a strong voice for agriculture in the Reagan administration.

For other crops, support prices are set (by Congress or by the secretary of agriculture) at levels high enough to make the purchasing power of farmers approximately equal to that of city dwellers. This concept of equality is called *parity.*

4. *Conservation payments.* These grants, administered by the Soil Conservation Service, are made to farmers who conserve their soil by periodically retiring lands from agricultural production.

5. *Food for the needy.* The department's Food and Nutrition Service distributes free food— often surplus agricultural commodities—to homes for juveniles, mental hospitals, and other institutions. The service also provides food for the needy through the food stamp program and the school lunch program.

Food stamps are now made available free to 20.4 million people who fall below the poverty line—people in the lowest income bracket. Recipients may use food stamps in place of money to obtain food at most retail stores. In 1981 the program cost $9.7 billion.

Under the school lunch program, the Department of Agriculture subsidizes nonprofit, nutritionally rich school lunches served in both public and private schools. These lunches are provided free or at nominal cost.

The net effect of these programs is the maintenance of a stable national market either by reduction of supply (acreage allotments, marketing quotas, payments for conservation) or by increase of demand (price supports and food assistance programs).

Research Activites. Most of the Department of Agriculture's scientific research is conducted by the Agricultural Research Service (ARS). Its scientists have controlled and eradicated agricultural pests and animal diseases. They have also experimented with seeds and plants to develop stronger strains of various crops. ARS scientists have developed better methods of storing food,

and ARS engineers have improved various kinds of farm machinery.

The Agricultural Research Service enforces various laws through plant, animal, and meat inspection and by regulation of the use of pesticides. The service works through its large research center at Beltsville, Maryland, and through experimental stations across the country.

The Cooperative State Research Service is a federal-state network of agricultural experimental stations that conduct experiments on various aspects of farm technology and marketing.

Conservation Activities and Support Services. The Department of Agriculture's Forest Service and Soil Conservation Service are directly engaged in conserving two great natural resources—earth and forests.

Forests afford wildlife protection, collect rainfall, and prevent floods and soil erosion. Before 147 million acres of forest were set aside for conservation under the Forest Service, huge amounts of timber were haphazardly cut for fuel and construction. Today the Forest Service allows selective logging of mature trees but promotes the growth of younger trees and the planting of new trees.

The Forest Service maintains a number of experimental stations that conduct studies of various aspects of forestry. Most of its 154 national forests offer recreational facilities for public use.

Three hundred million acres of the United States are no longer fertile because of soil erosion. The Soil Conservation Service was established in 1935 to assist farmers in organizing soil conservation districts. There are more than 3,000 such districts in the United States. One function of the Soil Conservation Service is to promote the planting of trees to serve as windbreaks in areas where high winds often sweep away the topsoil.

The Rural Electrification Administration (REA) has brought electricity to more than half of the nation's farms since its creation in

1935. Since its beginnings, REA has loaned over $13.9 billion for rural electrification that serves 9 million homes and has also loaned more than $3.6 billion to bring telephone service to over 4.5 million subscribers.

The Farmers' Home Administration insures loans to small farmers for a variety of purposes including the purchase of family farms, farm improvement and repairs, and the purchase of equipment and supplies.

Marketing Activities The Agriculture Department began its market news reports in 1915. It has continued the service ever since. Current reports, distributed by the Agricultural Marketing Service through 220 field offices, furnishes farmers with information on prices, supply, and crop and market conditions for all major agricultural products. The market news reaches farmers through the press, radio and television reports, and printed bulletins. The information helps farmers to decide what and how much to plant.

The Federal Crop Insurance Corporation insures a large number of farmers against crop losses from causes beyond their control. These causes include such conditions as adverse weather, agricultural pests, and plant diseases.

Farm Problems in the 1970's. Farmers produced large surpluses during the 1950's and early 1960's. But various food assistance programs for the needy and the "food for peace" program to relieve famine and hunger abroad used up those surpluses. By 1981 there appeared to be a balance between supply and demand. Increased foreign demand for food and grain has created occasional shortages that could grow more acute if farmers reduce production in their determination to receive higher prices.

Despite the existence of numerous aid and loan programs, the small farm is gradually disappearing. The most successful farms are large. They use more capital, more

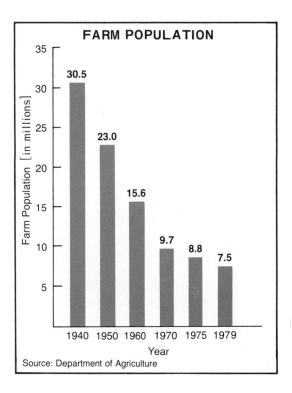

FARM POPULATION

Source: Department of Agriculture

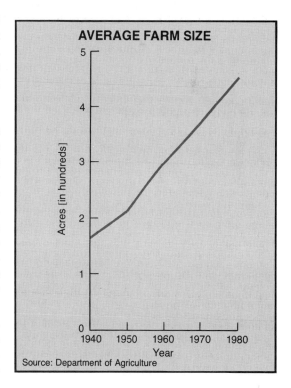

AVERAGE FARM SIZE

Source: Department of Agriculture

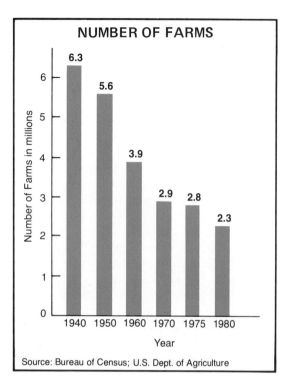

NUMBER OF FARMS

Number of Farms in millions

6.3 — 1940
5.6 — 1950
3.9 — 1960
2.9 — 1970
2.8 — 1975
2.3 — 1980

Year

Source: Bureau of Census; U.S. Dept. of Agriculture

In the suburbs one person in sixteen is poor. In the cities, one person in eight is poor; in rural areas, including all farm communities, one person out of every four is poor.

Migrant farm workers—who move from

These goats were released on the Capitol grounds by farmers in March of 1978. The farmers were protesting low farm prices.

land, more technology, and proportionately less labor than do small or medium-sized farms. One third of all farms produce 90 percent of all food and fibers; by contrast, half of all farms produce only 6 percent of the nation's farm products. Thousands of hard working farm owners earn so little that they fall below the established poverty line.

Federal subsidies tend to widen this inequality. Subsidies are geared to levels of production. The more a farm produces, the more its owner can receive in price supports. Similarly, the more land a farmer takes out of production, the more he or she can receive in conservation payments and other subsidies.

In 1973 Congress placed a limit of $20,000 a year on the amount of money that any farmer can receive for each price-supported crop. Even under this limit a large farmer with five supported crops could receive as much as $100,000.

place to place as the harvest season for each crop arrives—contribute materially to these poverty statistics. According to federal standards, the one million migrant farm workers constitute the most economically and socially deprived group in America. Only through massive strikes have some migrant workers been able to establish their rights to form unions and negotiate contracts.

The majority of farmers have not shared in the nation's economic growth. Many farm communities cannot afford adequate schools, fire protection, and sanitation. Many farmers' homes and buildings are deteriorating, and their children are leaving to seek jobs in crowded urban areas. Many small farmers are selling their farms and moving into mobile homes.

The federal government and the Department of Agriculture seem powerless to reverse these trends. It appears that future farm production in America will be directed by increasingly fewer farmers operating much larger farms.

section review

1. Define the term "reclamation."
2. What government incentive was offered during World War II to get farmers to increase production?
3. What important strategies have been developed by the federal government to stabilize farm prices, sustain farmers' incomes, and achieve a balance between supply and demand?
4. Which of the above strategies are you in favor of? Cite reasons for your answer.
5. Define the concept of conservation payments.
6. How has the REA helped farmers?
7. Describe some of the functions of the Agricultural Research Service.
8. Why do federal subsidies tend to widen inequalities among farmers?
9. What is a migrant farm worker?

2. THE COMMERCE DEPARTMENT

In 1903 Congress created the Department of Commerce and Labor in recognition of the importance of the business and labor communities in the nation's economic life. Ten years later Congress made the labor section into a separate department.

The Department of Commerce is committed to promoting the nation's economic development within the framework of the competitive, free enterprise system.

The Commerce Department provides numerous services for business, and its secretary serves as an advocate for the business community's interests within the government. The secretary manages a department of 31,000 employees.

The Commerce Department assists business in numerous ways. For example, its Social and Economic Statistics Administration reports on both domestic and international business activities and prospects. Other major units of the Commerce Department include the Census Bureau, the National Bureau of Standards, the Patent and Trademark Office, the National Oceanic and Atmospheric Administration, and the Maritime Administration. Each of these units will be examined separately.

The Census Bureau.   The Census Bureau is one of a few government agencies that arose from a constitutional mandate. Article 1, Section 2, Clause 3, of the Constitution requires an "enumeration" of the nation's population every ten years. These *decennial* (every ten years) enumerations form the basis for apportioning seats in the House of Representatives among the several states—states with increasing populations tend to gain seats, whereas those with declining populations often lose seats. The nation's population has grown from 4 million when the first census was taken in 1790, to 220 million.

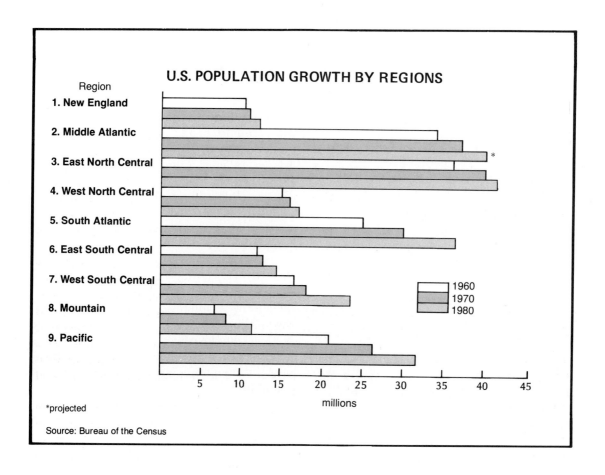

U.S. POPULATION GROWTH BY REGIONS

Region
1. New England
2. Middle Atlantic
3. East North Central
4. West North Central
5. South Atlantic
6. East South Central
7. West South Central
8. Mountain
9. Pacific

1960
1970
1980

5   10   15   20   25   30   35   40   45
millions

*projected

Source: Bureau of the Census

The first 12 censuses were taken by temporary agencies that terminated once each census was completed. In 1902 Congress established the Census Bureau as a permanent agency.

The Census Bureau may be the greatest fact-gathering agency in the world. The facts that it gathers are used in many ways. These data supply business executives with important information on business and farming trends, average incomes, employment figures, and statistics on housing and home ownership. School boards learn how many children in their communities will soon be of school age and can plan accordingly. These examples are only a few of the countless applications that can be made of census data.

During 1980 some 38,000 local government units received more than $70 billion for 120 federal programs. These funds were allocated according to population counts made by the Census Bureau.

The bureau estimates that people with low incomes and members of minority groups are significantly undercounted—they tend to be less responsive to census takers and may be wary of the government's asking questions about their incomes and occupations. The most important result of this undercounting is that communities with large numbers of low income people and minorities lose federal funds to which they would otherwise be entitled.

The Census Bureau encountered many problems in gathering its data for the 1980 census. These problems included people's desire for privacy, changes in residence, complicated forms, and difficulty in locating illegal aliens.

The Census Bureau has always kept its information confidential and contends that the social and economic uses of such information outweigh personal sensitivities. Many still felt that the government had no right to ask them about income, race, age, occupation, and education.

Moreover, many did not fill in and return forms as requested. Census takers had to visit these homes to obtain the needed information. This was a very time consuming and costly operation.

Census costs have risen drastically. The 1970 census cost $225 million, whereas the 1980 census cost $920 million. During the 1980 census the bureau employed 203,000 people.

In 1976 Congress authorized the Census Bureau to take a national census every five years beginning in 1985. This doubling of the number of censuses will add materially to the bureau's expense. Congress, however, believes that the expense is justified by the wide uses that are made of census information and the need for such information to be as up-to-date as possible.

The National Bureau of Standards. The National Bureau of Standards, like the Census Bureau, derives its function from the Constitution. Article 1, Section 8, Clause 5, authorizes Congress to "fix the standards of weights and measures." The National Bureau of Standards, established in 1901, has developed all national standards of measurement. The bureau conducts technical and scientific research, analyzes the properties of chemical compounds, and measures mass, light, electrical energy, nuclear energy, time, space, sound, volume, temperature, and other physical phenomena.

The Patent and Trademark Office. A third unit of the Commerce Department—the Patent and Trademark Office—is authorized under the Constitution, which empowers Congress to guarantee to authors and inventors, for a limited period, "the exclusive right to their respective writings and discoveries."

A patent confers the right of exclusive use and sale of an invention for 17 years. Before issuing a patent, the Patent Office searches its records for other inventions in the same field in order to make sure that earlier patents are not infringed upon. It also judges whether an invention conforms with the Patent Office's standard of originality and usefulness.

Because of their anticompetitive nature and the possibility of monopoly inherent in them, patents are not issued lightly on request. When a patent is infringed upon or challenged, the patent holder may defend his or her rights in a federal district court. Granville T. Woods, a Black inventor, filed and won two suits against the Edison Company by proving that he had earlier rights to inventions claimed by Thomas Edison.

Since 1789 more than 4 million patents have been issued. Early patents were issued for Eli Whitney's cotton gin and Robert Fulton's steamboat. Thomas Edison patented more than a thousand of his inventions. Alexander Graham Bell received a patent for his telephone.

The Patent and Trademark Office also registers trademarks. Trademarks are distinctive words or symbols used to identify producers of marketable goods. Trademarks are registered for 20 years and may be renewed continually.

The National Oceanic and Atmospheric Administration. The National Oceanic and Atmospheric Administration (NOAA) combines two Commerce Department units—the Coast and Geodetic Survey and the National Weather Bureau.

NOAA offers an excellent example of government involvement in science. Its activities include the following: hurricane modification research; sea and weather prediction; charting the nation's waters and coastal areas to produce navigation maps; operating environmental satellites; weather modification research and technological development; establishing fisheries, marine sanctuaries, and other uses of coastal areas; and oceanographic research.

NOAA's weather service bases its forecasts on information channeled from hundreds of field stations. Its services are used by farmers, fruit growers, pilots, fishers,

Weather conditions affect the livelihoods of all farmers. How was this corn field affected by weather?

carriers of perishable freight, building contractors, and many others. Weather substantially affects their lives and livelihoods. Weather predictions enable them to take appropriate action. Flood and hurricane warnings enable local officials and citizens to protect themselves and their property.

The Coast and Geodetic Survey's maps and charts are used in aviation, engineering, and navigation. The survey also conducts research on the nature, location, and force of earthquakes.

NOAA has established a broad network of field offices, laboratories, ocean based research vessels, and observatories across the United States, its surrounding oceans, and at United States bases in Antarctica.

The Maritime Administration. The Maritime Administration subsidizes the American merchant marine with several hundred million dollars a year. The subsidy is based on considerations of national security: In wartime these ships function as naval supply units, carrying essential cargoes. In theory, loans and subsidies to ship builders guarantee that ships will be available for wartime use.

The Maritime Administration has a close relationship with the maritime industry and the Seafarers' Union. These groups resisted President Johnson's attempt to transfer the Maritime Administration into the new Department of Transportation in 1967. Apparently they were satisfied with the Commerce Department's treatment of the Maritime Administration and feared that the new secretary of transportation would seek to impose greater control.

The merchant marine could not meet foreign competition without federal subsidies. Foreign ships are built and operated much more economically than are those of the American merchant marine. Congressional critics of the subsidy program contend that it discourages competition and doubles the costs of ships: All subsidized merchant ships must be built in the United States rather than abroad.

Congressional critics resisted the combined efforts of the maritime industry, the Seafarers' Union, the House Committee on Merchant Marine and Fisheries, and President Carter to require that preference be given to United States oil tankers. Such protectionist measures, even if successful, would have merely slowed the steady decline of the United States merchant marine and increased the price of imported oil that has quadrupled since 1973. American shippers have long preferred to ship their cargoes on cheaper foreign vessels and tankers.

The Maritime Administration keeps more than 1,000 obsolete vessels in a reserve fleet for emergency use. It also operates the United States Merchant Marine Academy at King's Point, New York, to train new officers.

The Federal Maritime Commission is an independent regulatory agency that regulates the rates, services, and employment practices of American shippers engaged in interstate and foreign commerce.

Other Commerce Department Agencies. The Economic Development Administration makes loans and grants to economically distressed communities under the terms of the Public Works and Economic Development Act of 1965. It helps to combat unemployment in depressed areas and funds state and local economic development programs.

The Office of Minority Business Enterprise promotes businesses operated by minority group members. The office acts as a clearing house for information considered useful to minority business people.

The United States Travel Service conducts a large promotional campaign to attract foreign tourists and visitors to this country. During the 1970's the value of the dollar declined in world markets relative to Western European and Japanese currencies, increasing the value of foreign currencies spent in this country by foreign visitors.

section review

1. How does the Commerce Department assist business?
2. Define the term "decennial."
3. Which three bureaus are mandated by the Constitution of the United States?
4. List five examples of government involvement in science.

3. THE DEPARTMENT OF LABOR

The importance of industrial workers in the United States economy was recognized by Congress in 1884 when it established the Bureau of Labor in the Interior Department. Organized labor was in its formative stages in the 1870's and 1880's. By 1913, when the Department of Labor was created, the power of organized labor was beginning to be felt. By creating a Cabinet-level department, Congress acknowledged that labor was entitled to its own advocate in the inner circles of government.

The Department of Labor has more than 22,000 employees. It is the fourth largest department. It promotes the welfare of all American workers. The Department of Labor has no direct role in labor–management disputes, but the secretary of labor has often acted as a mediator and conciliator in such disputes, particularly when they produce far-reaching effects on the nation's economy.

The Labor Department's four main agencies are the Occupational Safety and Health Administration, the Bureau of Labor Statistics, the Employment Standards Administration, and the Employment and Training Administration.

The Occupational Safety and Health Administration (OSHA). OSHA, the first comprehensive federal industrial safety program, was created by the Occupational Safety and Health Act of 1970. The act empowers the secretary of labor to set and enforce safety and health standards for workers of all companies engaged in interstate commerce. The secretary is also authorized to seek a court order to close a plant when he or she concludes that its continued operation would endanger the lives of workers.

The labor movement resisted an alternative plan proposed by employers' groups and the Nixon administration under which two independent regulatory commissions would be established—one to set occupational safety and health standards and the other to enforce them. Labor and a majority of Congress believed that such regulatory agencies could be captured by the industries that they were supposed to regulate.

The act did create a Safety and Health Review Commission within the Labor Department to hear appeals on orders issued by the secretary. The three members of this commission are appointed by the President with the consent of the Senate.

Consumer advocates had long urged strong federal controls over industrial safety and health. Many workers' lives have been shortened because they (and their employers) unknowingly used substances that seemed harmless but were actually dangerous when used over a long period of time. Some of these substances are not assimilated and cause cancer and lung disease after several years.

Many industrial accidents occur because

Ignoring safety precautions can be dangerous to your health.

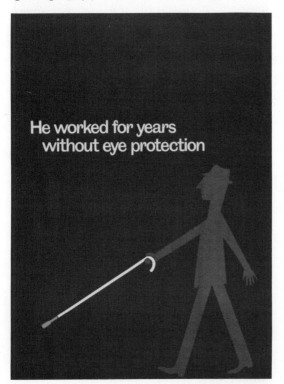

He worked for years without eye protection

OOPS! loose clothing again

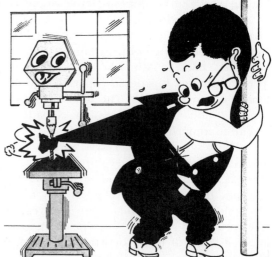

workers ignore safety requirements—such as wearing helmets—and employers are lax in enforcing them.

OSHA conducts thousands of inspections of workplaces to determine whether its standards are being met. Thirty-three states have occupational health and safety agencies that cooperate with OSHA to enforce federal standards (or state standards if they are stricter than federal standards).

The Bureau of Labor Statistics. The Bureau of Labor Statistics is the nation's main fact-gathering organization involved in the area of labor economics. It gathers and publishes statistical information on levels of employment, wages, prices, and costs. The all-important consumer price index, which most people use to measure the purchasing power of the dollar, is published by the Bureau of Labor Statistics. This index and other bureau studies of changing wholesale and retail prices are measures of the cost of living and the state of the United States economy.

The bureau also publishes information on hours of work, productivity, labor–management disputes, and industrial accidents. Its surveys of employee benefits—such as health insurance and pension plans—are useful in collective bargaining between labor and management.

The bureau also surveys employment trends to determine what kinds of occupations are most needed. These surveys are helpful to young people entering the job market.

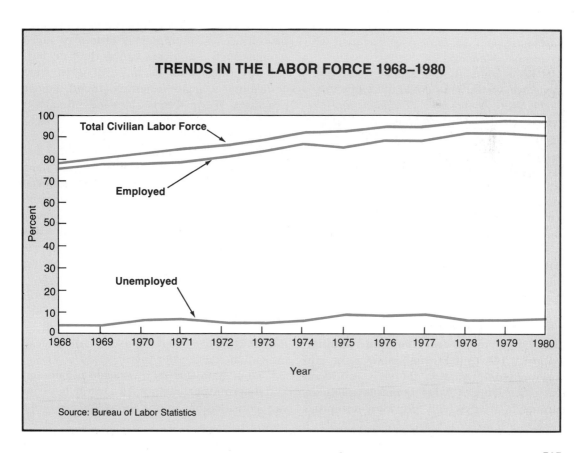

TRENDS IN THE LABOR FORCE 1968–1980

Source: Bureau of Labor Statistics

The Employment Standards Administration. The most important unit of the Employment Standards Administration is its Wage and Hour Division. This division implements the original and amended provisions of the Fair Labor Standards Act of 1938. The act sets minimum wages and maximum hours for all people whose work affects interstate commerce. Most American workers are covered by its provisions.

The minimum wage, which was $.25 an hour in 1938, was increased to $3.35 as of January 1, 1981.

The Fair Labor Standards Act also prohibits employers from hiring people under 16. Exceptions are newspaper delivery, farm work, acting, and employment in family concerns.

The Wage and Hour Division also administers laws designed to end job discrimination. The most notable of these laws is the Equal Pay Act of 1963, which requires that women be paid the same wages as men who do comparable work.

Other units of the Employment Standards Adminstration include the following:

1. *The Office of Workers' Compensation Programs*, which provides injury and accident benefits to those covered by federal workers' compensation laws.

2. *The Office of Federal Contract Compliance*, which is responsible for ensuring that federal contractors comply with the antidiscrimination requirements of the Civil Rights Act of 1964.

3. *The Women's Bureau*, which is concerned with the welfare, working conditions, and employment opportunities of all working women.

The Employment and Training Administration. The unit of the Employment and Training Administration that has produced the widest impact is the Unemployment Insurance Service which provides minimum incomes for a limited time to unemployed workers.

Unemployment compensation was one of several welfare programs established by the Social Security Act of 1935. It was designed especially to alleviate widespread misery that accompanies a depressed economy. Compensation is available only for involuntary unemployment brought about by a number of conditions—automation, bad weather, seasonal shifts in consumer needs, or the closing of a plant or a base.

The unemployment compensation program was intended for people who are willing and able to work. Other welfare programs (administered by the Department of Health and Human Services) provide income assistance for those who cannot work because of old age, sickness, or disability.

The unemployment insurance system is operated jointly by the federal and state governments. Congress has imposed a federal payroll tax on all employers of four or more people. Such employers can deduct on federal tax returns all or most of what they contribute to state unemployment benefit programs. The proceeds of the federal payroll tax are redistributed to the states to help cover their unemployment payouts.

Federal funds also underwrite the administrative costs of state unemployment programs, which enables the federal government to impose certain minimum standards, such as prompt payment and impartial hearings on appeal from claimants who are denied compensation.

Three fourths of the American working population is covered by public unemployment insurance. Those not covered include most farm workers, domestic workers, self-employed people, and employees of firms that have fewer than four workers (unless individual states cover them).

Each state sets its own scale of benefits and determines eligibility. As a result, benefits vary considerably among the states.

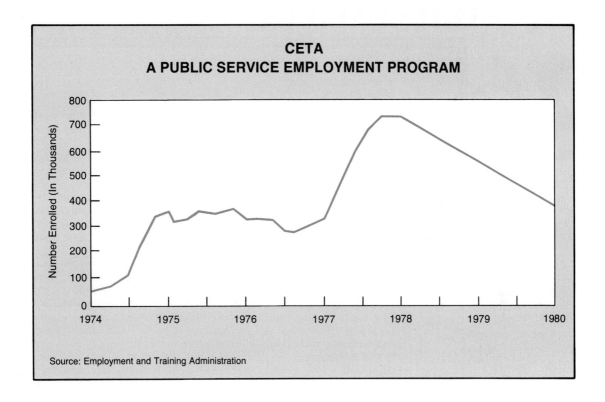

**CETA
A PUBLIC SERVICE EMPLOYMENT PROGRAM**

Number Enrolled (In Thousands)

800
700
600
500
400
300
200
100
0

1974   1975   1976   1977   1978   1979   1980

Source: Employment and Training Administration

Congress now provides federal funds to extend the period of unemployment benefits when unemployment rates rise above a certain level (currently 6.5 percent of the labor force). The Department of Labor's Manpower Administration coordinates efforts among the states to place jobless workers.

Other Labor Department Agencies. The Office of Comprehensive Economic Development is an agency in the Labor Department which was created by the Comprehensive Employment and Training Act of 1973 (CETA). This office administers a variety of grant programs to fund public service jobs (often known as CETA jobs) at state and local levels. The purpose of these programs and jobs is to relieve unemployment in communities that are the most severely affected by unemployment.

The Office of Comprehensive Economic Development also runs the Job Corps. The Job Corps provides two years of job training and related work experience for youths who are considered disadvantaged.

The United States Employment Service funds all state efforts to maintain a network of local employment offices. These offices seek to match workers with jobs in local areas.

section review

1. What are the four main agencies of the Labor Department?
2. When are employers permitted to hire people under age 16?
3. Who is covered by unemployment insurance?
4. Under what conditions is unemployment insurance available?

CHAPTER SUMMARY

26

The Departments of Agriculture, Commerce, and Labor were formed to meet the special needs of farmers, business, and labor. Each department has become an advocate for the group it serves.

The Department of Agriculture has grown since its creation in 1862 from an agency to assist farmers in improving farming techniques to a major advocate of federal policies designed to stabilize farm prices, sustain farmers' incomes, and achieve a balance between supply and demand. Acreage allotments, marketing quotas, price supports, and conservation payments have all been used to achieve these objectives. These programs have been only marginally successful and have resulted in the gradual disappearance of the small farm.

The Commerce Department provides numerous services for business, and its secretary serves as an advocate for the business community's interests within the government. The major units of the Commerce Department are the Social and Economic Statistics Administration, Bureau of the Census, National Bureau of Standards, Patent and Trademark Office, National Oceanic and Atmospheric Administration, and Maritime Administration.

The Department of Labor promotes the welfare, working conditions, and employment opportunities of all American workers. Four major agencies—OSHA, the Bureau of Labor Statistics, the Employment Standards Administration, and the Employment and Training Administration—gather information, provide inspections, and seek to improve the health, safety, and security of American workers.

The establishment of special-interest, Cabinet-level departments reflects the growing concern for the economic well-being of the nation.

REVIEW QUESTIONS

1. Why are small farms gradually disappearing? Is the decline in the number of small farms a threat to the democratic way of life? Why or why not?
2. Why are low-income and minority groups less likely to be counted in a census? What effect might this fact have on the accuracy of the census? on federal aid programs?
3. Do you think the federal government should continue to subsidize the merchant marine? Why or why not?

4. Why does the federal government subsidize agriculture? Do you think these are sufficient reasons? Why or why not? What are some other alternatives?

5. The federal government provides low-interest loans, subsidies, and insurance to farmers, businesses, and persons who are unemployed. Do you think this is the proper role of government? Why or why not? What are some other alternatives?

ACTIVITIES FOR REVIEW

activity 1   Prepare a wall chart illustrating on one side how government assists business and on the other how it regulates business.

activity 2   Research the origins and present-day functions of a major labor union.

activity 3   Interview a local labor representative (government or union), and try to determine the current status and needs of workers in your community. Report your findings and recommendations to the class.

political science DICTIONARY

decennial—every ten years.   p. 509
parity—system of regulating prices of farm commodities through government price   p. 506
    supports to give farmers purchasing power approximately equal to that of city
    dwellers.

27 *The Interior Department and the EPA*

The Interior Department has never represented special interests in the sense that the Agriculture, Commerce, and Labor departments do. During its first fifty years, the Interior Department did champion the special interests of western settlers (and subordinated those of Native Americans). More recently, however, its special interests have involved the conservation of resources, as well as the welfare of Native Americans. Conservation of natural resources, of course, benefits the entire population and generations to come.

The Interior Department is not like the departments that perform essential government functions (State, Defense, Treasury, and Justice), nor does it resemble the new service departments (HHS, HUD, Education, Transportation, and Energy). It is treated separately because much of its work—and the work of the Environmental Protection Agency, which will also be examined—serves a different element of society: future generations.

CHAPTER PREVIEW

1. THE DEPARTMENT OF THE INTERIOR
2. THE ENVIRONMENTAL PROTECTION AGENCY

1. THE DEPARTMENT OF THE INTERIOR

When the first European settlers came to this country, they found a land incredibly rich in natural resources. The country was plentiful with lakes and rivers, forests, and plains, minerals, and wild life. The soil was rich, the air was pure, and the water was clear and sweet. Native Americans had been responsible managers of this country, taking only what they needed for food, clothing, and shelter.

Over the last 150 years, these natural treasures have been plundered in the name of expansion, development, and growth. Today much of our soil is eroded, many of our lakes and rivers are polluted with industrial wastes, and most of the air around the cities has been made impure by exhausts from automobiles and industry. Many of our natural resources are in short supply, including underground water, oil deposits, wildlife, and timberlands.

Few people in the national government recognized the need to conserve resources before Theodore Roosevelt became President in 1901. Using presidential powers to the fullest, Theodore Roosevelt set aside huge tracts of western land for conservation as national parks, national forests, and wildlife refuges.

Today many conservation activities are centered in the Department of the Interior. There are notable exceptions. The Department of Agriculture is in charge of soil conservation and the Forest Service. The Department of Energy is responsible for energy conservation, and the Environmental Protection Agency controls water and air pollution. But most of the nation's public land, the

Our national parks and forests are enjoyed by people and animals alike. This national forest in Oregon serves as a popular swimming, fishing, and camping site for many Americans.

water and mineral resources, and the fish and wildlife are conserved and managed by the Interior Department.

Congress created the Interior Department in 1849. It began as a catchall department, performing functions that could not logically be given to the existing departments. Interior has always had jurisdiction over public lands, Native American affairs, and federal mining regulations. At various times it has supervised federal pensions, United States patents, public buildings, the census, United States marshals, and public institutions in the District of Columbia.

Over time the department became the government's voice for the special interests of western states and territories. Most public lands were located in the less settled west. So also were Native Americans, who were enemies of the department throughout the nineteenth century.

The department has jurisdiction over 540 million acres of land in the United States and its territories. It is responsible for the welfare of 400,000 Native Americans living on reservations and 200,000 people living in American territories in the Caribbean and the South Pacific.

The most important activities of the Interior Department are those administered by the Bureau of Land Management, the Bureau of Indian affairs, the National Park Service, and the Bureau of Reclamation.

The Bureau of Land Management. The federal domain is only a fraction of what it once was. To encourage the settlement of the west, much public land was granted or sold cheaply to homesteaders. Large grants of land were given to railroads to stimulate their expansion and to the states to support public colleges and to build roads and canals.

The Bureau of Land Management today has jurisdiction over 370 million acres of public land, mostly in the western states. Some of these lands are leased to miners and ranchers. Timber is harvested by private in-

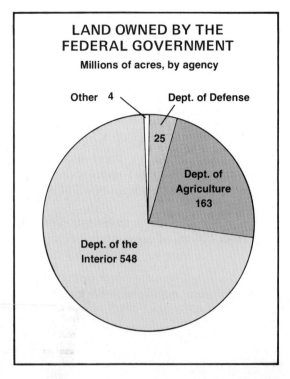

LAND OWNED BY THE FEDERAL GOVERNMENT

Millions of acres, by agency

Other 4

Dept. of Defense

25

Dept. of Agriculture 163

Dept. of the Interior 548

dustry under the Bureau of Land Management's supervision. This bureau also sets aside certain public lands for recreational use.

The BLM is actively engaged in soil conservation, wildlife preservation, and the development of water resources. The Outer Continental Shelf Act of 1953 gave it control over all lands which were farther than 3 miles from shore and which were beneath shallow water (the continental shelf). Submerged land within 3 miles of the shore belongs to the adjacent states. The Submerged Lands Act of 1953 made two exceptions to this rule by giving Texas and Florida control over submerged lands that extended 102 miles into the Gulf of Mexico.

The Atlantic shelf extends as far as 250 miles, and the Gulf of Mexico shelf extends 140 miles. Some of these underwater lands contain oil and natural gas. The BLM has leased a number of these underwater sites to oil and gas companies.

Congress, following the practice of several foreign countries, passed legislation giving the United States exclusive fishing rights within 200 miles of its coastline.

The Bureau of Indian Affairs. By an act of Congress, Native Americans are American citizens. Native Americans living outside reservations have all the rights and obligations of other citizens. Those living on reservations have the right to vote (if 18 or over). In many other respects, however, they are subject to special rules and regulations. These rules and regulations are issued by the Bureau of Indian Affairs (BIA).

The policy of the United States government has undergone several changes. At first the government regarded Native American tribes as foreign and sought to deal with them by treaty. Later, as the interests of

TERRITORY OCCUPIED BY NATIVE AMERICANS

Federal and State Reservations

Source: Bureau of Indian Affairs; Bureau of Census

Native Americans—living undisturbed on their own lands—conflicted with those of western settlers, they were treated as enemies. Aided by the army, the settlers overcame their enemy and claimed most of the lands. Many treaties were violated, and Native Americans were sent to reservations. These reservations were in arid territory hundreds of miles from the Native Americans' original homes.

In the 1870's the government's policy entered a new stage. Native Americans were to be Americanized and integrated into American society. Individuals were granted plots of land in partial compensation for the lands taken from them. But many were swindled out of their new property. Embittered and despairing, many Native Americans returned to their reservations.

In 1933 policy shifted again. The objective was to promote the unique life and culture of Native Americans—particularly those living on reservations. Today about a third of 900,000 Native Americans live on 252 government reservations.

The Bureau of Indian Affairs helps Native Americans use their lands and resources efficiently. It also provides Native Americans with schools and health and welfare services. A special system of courts, run by Native Americans, settles disputes and regulates other relations on the reservations.

A long history of disadvantages, especially less than adequate schools, has deprived Native Americans of equal opportunities in jobs and education. Government studies show that Native Americans are at the bottom of the economic ladder, have exceptionally high rates of unemployment, and are chronically poor.

President Carter and the secretary of the interior have acknowledged the government's special responsibility to Native Americans. Since that acknowledgment the department has taken small but symbolic steps toward correcting the plight of Native Americans. The Bureau of Indian Affairs is now the largest unit of the Interior Department, accounting for 25 percent of its budget and personnel.

A Native American heads the Bureau of Indian Affairs. Five other executive-level posts in the Interior Department are held by Native Americans. Time will show whether these steps foreshadow an improvement in the lives of Native Americans.

The National Park Service. By executive order President Theodore Roosevelt designated that huge tracts of western land be preserved as national parks. Eventually Congress endorsed his plan. In 1916 Congress set up the National Park Service to coordinate and preserve all national parks and monuments administered by the Interior Department. In preserving these parks and monuments, the service is to see that they are left "unimpaired for the enjoyment of future generations."

The national parks system contains 77 million acres of parks, monuments, and recreation areas, and other scenic and historic properties. This system extends from the rugged beauty of Point Reyes National Seashore in California to the unspoiled wilderness of Acadia National Park in Maine. It includes such scenic wonders as Yellowstone's Old Faithful geyser, Yosemite's giant waterfalls, the towering peaks of Mt. McKinley in Alaska and Mt. Rainier in Washington, and the Grand Canyon. Park users include campers, skiers, hikers, naturalists, and visitors from all over the world.

Park rangers try to prevent forest fires and stream pollution. They also try to safeguard plant and animal life, including herds of elk, moose, caribou, big-horn sheep, bear, and bison.

The Bureau of Outdoor Recreation promotes recreational uses of federal land and helps state and local agencies develop recreational facilities. It also administers the National Scenic Rivers System, which saves parts of several rivers in their natural states.

The Fish and Wildlife Service is responsible for preserving and increasing the nation's fish and wildlife. It maintains over 100 fish hatcheries and 350 wildlife refuges, which cover 30 million acres.

In 1980 President Carter signed a bill placing almost 100 million acres of Alaska—more than 90 percent of that state—under federal protection as national parks, national forests, wildlife refuges, and scenic rivers.

The Bureau of Reclamation. For half the year farmers and ranchers in many western states depend on water brought from hundreds of miles away by aqueducts, canals, and other large irrigation systems. The Reclamation Service (now Bureau) was created by the Reclamation Act of 1902 to develop and store waters for the *reclamation* (irrigation) of arid western lands.

The bureau's dams and other engineering projects furnish water to nearly a quarter of the country's irrigated farmland. These large dams serve many purposes. They furnish hydroelectric power, control floods, improve navigation, and provide irrigation.

The best known of the bureau's large dams is Hoover Dam, which was completed in 1936. The Hoover Dam created Lake Mead, the largest artificial lake in the Western Hemisphere. Lake Mead's storage and controlled release of water prevent flooding on the lower reaches of the Colorado River. Lake Mead also irrigates the Imperial Valley

This is an aerial view of Boulder Dam, also known as Hoover Dam. Lake Mead is visible in the background.

of California, which provides a significant amount of the nation's fruits and vegetables.

Hoover Dam is one part of the Boulder Canyon project. The entire system irrigates large sections of Arizona, New Mexico, and southern California. It also provides water for the entire Los Angeles metropolitan area.

The Grand Coulee Dam is another engineering achievement of the Bureau of Reclamation. This dam controls water in the Columbia River basin, which extends through large parts of Washington, Oregon, Idaho, and Montana. Water stored by the Grand Coulee Dam can reclaim more than a million acres of uncultivated land.

In addition to providing irrigation and flood control, the Grand Coulee and other huge dams along the Columbia River provide inexpensive hydroelectric power for the Pacific Northwest. The Bonneville Power Administration markets all hydroelectric power produced at federal projects on the Columbia River, in other parts of Oregon, in Washington, in northern Idaho, and in western Montana.

The Bonneville Power Administration, together with four smaller power agencies, was transferred to the Department of Energy in 1977.

Office of Territorial Affairs. The federal government has the inherent power to acquire territory. President Thomas Jefferson demonstrated this power when he purchased Louisiana in 1803.

The Constitution empowers Congress to make "all needful rules and regulations respecting . . . territory . . . belonging to the United States."

Congress has delegated this power to the department's Office of Territorial Affairs. That office promotes development and self-government in United States territories—specifically Guam, the Virgin Islands, American Samoa, and the trust territory of the Pacific islands. The trust territory was captured from Japan during the World War II

period and is administered by trusteeship from the United Nations.

Other Agencies. The Bureau of Mines tries to protect the environment and public interest by encouraging mine practices that neither scar the surface of the earth nor weaken its subsurface. It conducts extensive research on the nation's mineral deposits and on mine explosions. By doing research on mine explosions, the bureau hopes to reduce the risk of such disasters.

The Mining Enforcement and Safety Administration was established in 1973 to enforce several acts of Congress which were related to health and safety. This unit has extensive powers to inspect and investigate mines and to impose fines for health and safety violations. Its efforts are directed toward eliminating health hazards and reducing the risk of mine accidents.

section review

1. Why was the Interior Department created?
2. What are the most important activities of the Interior Department?
3. Discuss two functions of the Bureau of Land Management.
4. Name the largest artificial lake in the Western Hemisphere.

2. THE ENVIRONMENTAL PROTECTION AGENCY

For most of this century, the Department of the Interior was the principal instrument of government for protecting our natural resources. In the late 1960's a movement began to take shape—generally among younger people—to protect the environment. The environmental protection movement has been concerned not only with preserving land and wildlife in their unspoiled states but

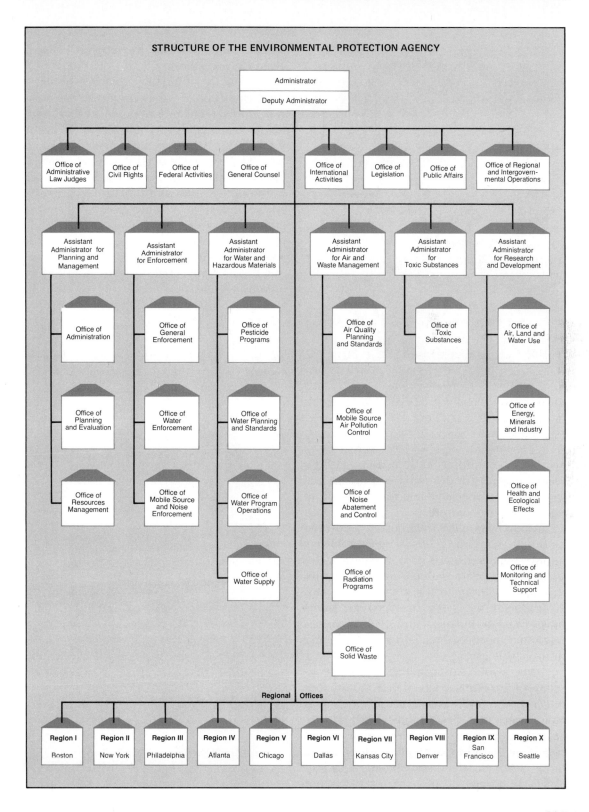

STRUCTURE OF THE ENVIRONMENTAL PROTECTION AGENCY

Administrator

Deputy Administrator

Office of Administrative Law Judges

Office of Civil Rights

Office of Federal Activities

Office of General Counsel

Office of International Activities

Office of Legislation

Office of Public Affairs

Office of Regional and Intergovern- mental Operations

Assistant Administrator for Planning and Management

Assistant Administrator for Enforcement

Assistant Administrator for Water and Hazardous Materials

Assistant Administrator for Air and Waste Management

Assistant Administrator for Toxic Substances

Assistant Administrator for Research and Development

Office of Administration

Office of General Enforcement

Office of Pesticide Programs

Office of Air Quality Planning and Standards

Office of Toxic Substances

Office of Air, Land and Water Use

Office of Planning and Evaluation

Office of Water Enforcement

Office of Water Planning and Standards

Office of Mobile Source Air Pollution Control

Office of Energy, Minerals and Industry

Office of Resources Management

Office of Mobile Source and Noise Enforcement

Office of Water Program Operations

Office of Noise Abatement and Control

Office of Health and Ecological Effects

Office of Water Supply

Office of Radiation Programs

Office of Monitoring and Technical Support

Office of Solid Waste

Regional Offices

Region I	Region II	Region III	Region IV	Region V	Region VI	Region VII	Region VIII	Region IX	Region X
Boston	New York	Philadelphia	Atlanta	Chicago	Dallas	Kansas City	Denver	San Francisco	Seattle

27. The Interior Department and the Environmental Protection Agency   **527**

"MY HOOK DISSOLVED."

© 1970, Maudlin, *Chicago Sun Times*

always easy to make the choice between clean air and jobs.

When the interstate highway system—the largest public works project in history—was undertaken, most people focused only on its benefits: speed and convenience in transporting people by automobile and goods by truck. We have learned that highways have increased air and noise pollution, disrupted communities, and contributed to the energy crisis. Today we require pollution control devices, subsidize urban mass transit, try to restore railroads, and advocate the electric automobile—with federal funds—and hope that these counter-measures will not produce unforeseen costs.

The Environmental Protection Agency

The federal government, through the EPA, spends millions of dollars in detecting and controlling noise pollution.

also with reclaiming and protecting those resources that are degraded by our modern way of life—especially the water we drink and the air we breathe.

Modern industry, technology, and agriculture have improved our standards of living and the quality of our lives in many ways. But they have also done serious—and sometimes irreparable—harm to the environment. Our environment has been damaged by smog, noise, oil spills, chemical and nuclear wastes, random timber cutting, strip mining, and unrecyclable garbage.

One would suppose that anyone conscious of this damage would be committed to repairing it. But environmental protection often comes into direct conflict with growth. Factories operating at narrow margins of profit may have to close if they are forced to meet clean air standards. When a factory closes, hundreds of jobs are lost. It is not

was created in 1970 as an independent agency responsible for enforcing federal laws and regulations. It was not placed in the Interior Department, partly because new agencies do better on their own and partly because its purpose could conflict with the development plans of agencies of the Interior Department—notably, those of the Bureau of Reclamation.

EPA's mission is to control and reduce pollution of air in the areas of water, solid wastes, pesticides, noise, and radiation. It enforces several provisions of the National Environmental Policy Act of 1969, which require the directors of all federal projects to submit environmental impact statements.

Water Pollution. The federal government uses both punishment and reward in dealing with water pollution. On the one hand, those who release pollutants into interstate waters may be fined and jailed, and those responsible for oil spills must pay the cleaning costs involved. On the other hand, the Clean Water Restoration Act of 1966 and the Water Quality Improvement Act of 1970 make federal funds available for water quality control projects and the construction of local sewage treatment plants.

Air Pollution. The control and abatement of air pollution used to be the responsibility of the Department of Health, Education, and Welfare because of the adverse effects of pollution on health. Jurisdiction was transferred to the EPA in 1970.

The Air Quality Control Act of 1967 requires local areas to adopt and implement regional air quality standards under federal supervision and to authorize federal regulation of automobile emissions. Auto emissions have been estimated to cause more than half of all air pollution. The act also funds air quality research directed toward the improvement of state and local air pollution control efforts.

The Clean Air Act Amendments of 1977

Many American factories are our greatest air polluters. This Texas factory burns discarded automobile batteries.

require that all automobiles sold in the United States after 1983 must emit 90 percent less carbon monoxide, hydrocarbons, and nitrogen oxide than did the 1970 models. The law permits manufacturers to petition for delay, and they have done so—citing substantial technical difficulties in complying with the law. The combined influence of automobile manufacturers and the United Auto Workers has been successfully exerted on Congress to effect postponements. Not surprisingly, jobs have been given preference over clean air. President Reagan has pledged to continue this preference.

section review

1. What are the concerns of the environmental protection movement?
2. Describe the areas over which EPA has control.
3. List the requirements of the 1977 Clean Air Act Amendments.

CHAPTER SUMMARY

27

The Interior Department is unique in that, unlike other Cabinet-level departments, its focus is primarily on the future rather than on immediate problems. Most of the nation's public lands, water and mineral resources, and fish and wildlife are conserved and managed by the Interior Department.

Conservation of natural resources benefits the entire population, present and future. It also often conflicts with other goals of the government, such as economic growth and full employment.

The most important divisions of the Interior Department are the Bureau of Land Management, the Bureau of Indian Affairs, the National Park Service, and the Bureau of Reclamation.

The Environmental Protection Agency was created in 1970 as an independent agency. It is concerned with many of the same problems as the Interior Department. The EPA was created as an independent agency, partly because new agencies are more effective initially, and partly because its attitudes toward growth and development could conflict with the development plans of other Interior agencies.

REVIEW QUESTIONS

1. Why do the authors believe that the mission of the Interior Department is fundamentally different from that of other executive departments? Do you agree? Explain.

2. Although the federal domain today is only a fraction of what it once was, the federal government has recently purchased or claimed large parcels of land for parks and recreation areas. Do you favor this trend? Explain.

3. Many nations, including the United States, have extended their territorial limits in the last decade to distances as great as 400 miles out into the ocean. What are the reasons for this extension? What problems might arise from such expansion?

4. The Bureau of Indian Affairs administers laws related to Native Americans. Since 1924 Native Americans have been citizens of the United States. Do you think there is any reason for the continued existence of the Bureau of Indian Affairs? Why or why not? Give examples to support your view.

5. When economic growth and potential air and water pollution restrictions are in conflict, which do you think should take precedence? Why?

6. What measures do you think the federal government should take to conserve our natural resources? Why do you think these measures would be effective?

ACTIVITIES FOR REVIEW

activity 1 Stage a classroom debate or forum on the following issue: RESOLVED, that the internal combustion-driven automobile should be outlawed for its waste of vital natural resources and its contribution to air pollution.

activity 2 Prepare an environmental impact report on some proposed development in your community. Present your findings to the appropriate agency.

activity 3 Review reports of the Law of the Seas Conference. Prepare recommendations for changes in United States policies based on the agreements reached.

activity 4 Write a concise essay describing the role of the Environmental Protection Agency in your locale.

activity 5 In your notebooks, prepare a chart listing the agencies of the Department of Interior and outlining the responsibilities of each agency.

activity 6 Do research on the activities of the Bureau of Indian Affairs in your state. Discuss the steps that have been taken during the past year to aid the Native Americans in your state and the reactions of the Native Americans to these efforts.

activity 7 As part of a selected group of students, interview a representative from an industrial plant in your area. Find out how the company plans to control and reduce its pollution of air and water. Report the group's findings to the class.

political science
DICTIONARY

reclamation—reclaiming waste, desert, marsh, or submerged land for cultivation or other use. p. 525

28

The New Service Departments

Between 1913, when the Department of Labor was separated from the Department of Commerce, and 1953—40 years of growing federal activity—no new Cabinet departments were created. Since 1953, however, Congress has established four departments: Health, Education, and Welfare; Housing and Urban Development; Transportation; and Energy. (In 1979, Congress divided HEW into two departments—Health and Human Services, and Education.) Unlike the departments covered in the last two chapters, these departments do not serve particular occupational groups or geographical regions. They were formed to serve the needs of industrial and urbanized society.

CHAPTER PREVIEW

1. THE DEPARTMENT OF HEALTH AND HUMAN SERVICES
2. THE DEPARTMENT OF EDUCATION
3. THE DEPARTMENT OF HOUSING AND URBAN DEVELOPMENT
4. THE DEPARTMENT OF TRANSPORATION
5. THE DEPARTMENT OF ENERGY

1. THE DEPARTMENT OF HEALTH AND HUMAN SERVICES

Imagine that all human beings before being born had the option of taking out a low-cost insurance policy guaranteeing them care and support if they are born with mental or physical handicaps, or if they become poor or sick for long periods of time, or if they lose their parents when young or are without children when old. How many people do you think would take out an insurance policy of this kind? Probably most people would, assuming the cost were reasonable enough. The cost of that "insurance policy" is, in effect, the annual budget of the Department of Health and Human Services (HHS).

HHS was created in 1979 when Education became a separate cabinet department. Earlier, the two departments had been the Department of Health, Education, and Welfare, which was created in 1953. HHS spends over $130 billion and has over 155,000 employees. HHS's principal agencies are the Social Security Administration, the Office of Human Development, the Public Health Service, and the Food and Drug Administration.

The Social Security Administration. During the depression of the 1930's, 18 million people—including children, the elderly, and the unemployed—were completely dependent on public aid programs. At FDR's urging, Congress set aside billions of dollars for welfare and for public works projects to provide employment.

The Social Security Act of 1935 provided a comprehensive program of social welfare. It established the Unemployment Compensation System, administered by the Department of Labor, and the Old-Age Survivors and Disabilities Insurance Program—known as social security—administered today by HHS's Social Security Administration.

All employed persons in the United States—except federal government workers, who are covered by the civil service retirement system—are now covered by social security. The program provides minimum incomes to those who retire after the age of 62 or who become permanently disabled. It also provides benefits for a retired or disabled worker's dependents and survivors.

By contributing a percentage of their annual earnings to social security, individuals are entitled to receive these monetary benefits. In 1980 over 100 million people made

contributions to social security, and benefits were paid to about 40 million people.

The social security program is financed by taxes paid by all employees and matched in equal amounts by their employers. Self-employed persons contribute to the social security program by paying annual self-employment taxes.

Income Security Programs. All HHS welfare programs involving payments of money to individuals are now consolidated in the Social Security Administration. The largest of these programs is called Aid to Families with Dependent Children (AFDC). Under this program federal funds are distributed by the states to families who demonstrate need.

Under the Supplemental Security Income program, inaugurated in 1974, Congress guaranteed minimum incomes, as a matter of right, to all Americans over age 65 who were not covered by social security and to all disabled or blind people of any age. The amount of these benefits changes from year to year. In 1981 this program provided benefits for 4.2 million people at a cost of $6.9 billion.

This program, financed out of general treasury funds, replaced federally assisted state programs that benefited those same groups. Supplemental security income, for the first time, acknowledged the federal government's legal obligation to provide a minimum income for millions of Americans.

Health Care Financing. Those covered by the social security program are also entitled to subsidized health care after the age of 65. This program, known as *medicare*, was established by Congress in 1965 and was operated by the Social Security Administration until 1977. In that year, medicare was taken over by a new HHS unit, the Health Care Financing Administration. Medicare covers the major portion of hospitalization and nursing home care for more than 24 million elderly people. By paying a small monthly fee, these same people are covered for the major portion of their doctor's bills.

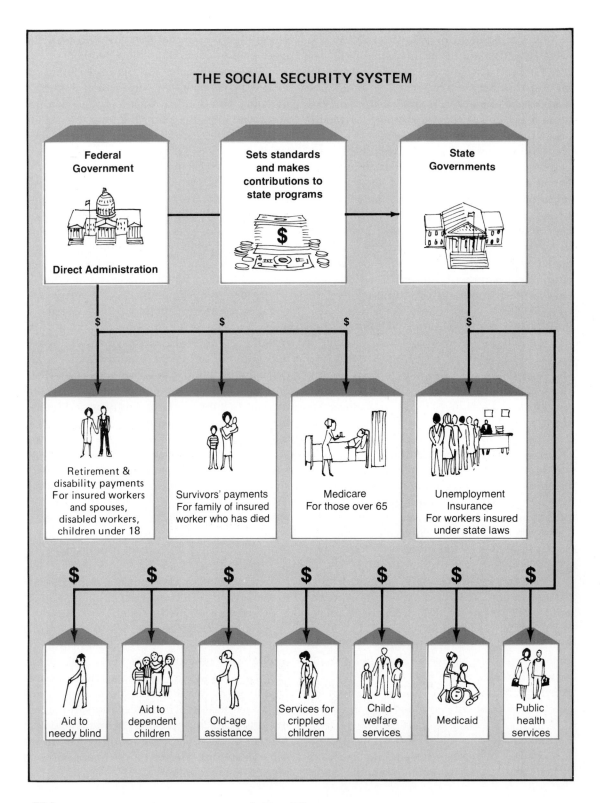

THE SOCIAL SECURITY SYSTEM

Federal Government

Direct Administration

Sets standards and makes contributions to state programs

$

State Governments

Retirement & disability payments
For insured workers and spouses, disabled workers, children under 18

Survivors' payments
For family of insured worker who has died

Medicare
For those over 65

Unemployment Insurance
For workers insured under state laws

Aid to needy blind

Aid to dependent children

Old-age assistance

Services for crippled children

Child-welfare services

Medicaid

Public health services

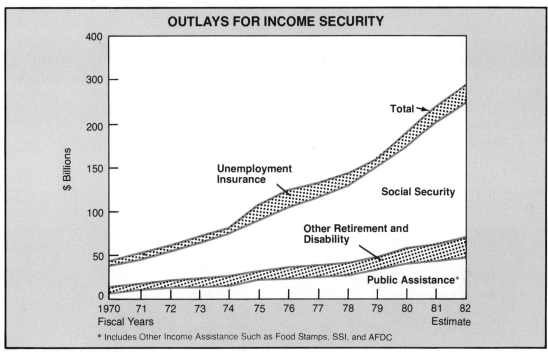

Source: U.S. Budget in Brief, 1981

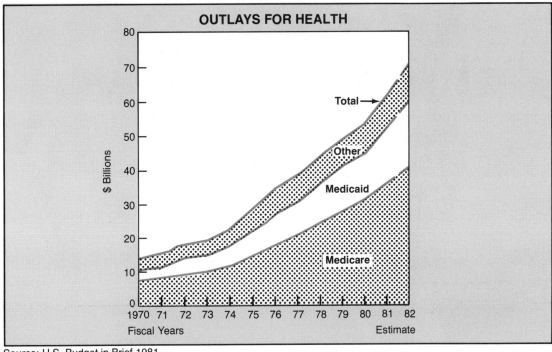

Source: U.S. Budget in Brief 1981

The Health Care Financing Administration also administers a second medical and hospital care program called *medicaid*. Medicaid is a federal grant program to help states provide medical care for all needy and disabled people under the age of 65 and also for "medically indigent" people who have only enough money to take care of their families' needs for food, clothing, and shelter but have nothing for medical expenses. More than 10 million people now benefit from the medicaid program.

QUOTES from famous people

"If a free society cannot help the many who are poor, it cannot save the few who are rich."

John Kennedy

The government provides medical care for those people who cannot afford doctor and hospital expenses.

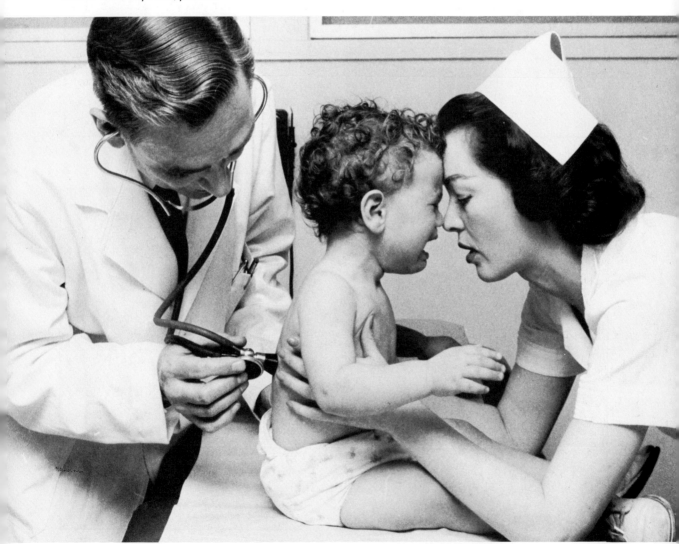

The Office of Human Development. Since 1977 most of HHS's social welfare programs have been administered by its Office of Human Development. This office is the successor of the Social Rehabilitation Service. The Office of Human Development administers most of HHS's programs designed to aid needy people in ways other than the direct payment of money. These programs involve grants-in-aid to the states to operate programs under federal standards. Some examples of the services provided under these programs are

—child care for needy working mothers;
—vocational rehabilitation for the handicapped;
—the Headstart education and care program for young children from low-income families;
—home care for the needy elderly;
—rehabilitation programs for delinquent youth;
—adoption and foster care services; and
—programs to aid the blind.

Welfare Reform. In 1971 President Nixon proposed doing away with virtually all welfare programs and instead providing a guaranteed minimum income for all families in America. This program of income maintenance—called the Family Assistance Plan—was never enacted, but welfare reform has been high on the agenda of every HHS secretary. Most proposals resemble the Nixon plan rather than the present patchwork of diverse and overlapping welfare programs.

In 1977 HEW Secretary Joseph Califano proposed a combination of public service jobs and cash benefits in place of existing welfare programs. His proposal would have elimi-

Many people have received financial assistance through the food stamp program. This program has enabled millions of Americans to buy food necessary for a good diet.

YOU'RE IN GOOD COMPANY

MILLIONS OF AMERICANS USE **USDA FOOD STAMPS**

PA-922
Food and Nutrition Service
U.S. Department of Agriculture

nated the AFDC program, the SSI program, and the food stamp program (administered by the Department of Agriculture).

This new plan would have created 1.4 million public service jobs and have provided a minimum of $4,200 for those not able to work or to find work. An estimated 32 million Americans would have been eligible for cash benefits. The annual cost of this program would have been $31 billion—little more than the cost of the welfare system. Thus far Congress has preferred to make minor adjustments in the present system rather than to undertake far-reaching welfare reform.

The Public Health Service. The Public Health Service administers most of the federal government's health activities. Its Health Services and Mental Health Administration operates the National Communicable Disease Center in Atlanta, Georgia. The center conducts programs throughout the country to prevent and control infectious diseases. It also cooperates with foreign governments and international organizations.

The National Institute of Health (NIH) operates as the research unit of the Public Health Service. The NIH exercises considerable independence, and its annual budget

The federal government allocates funds to the states for the vocational rehabilitation of the physically handicapped.

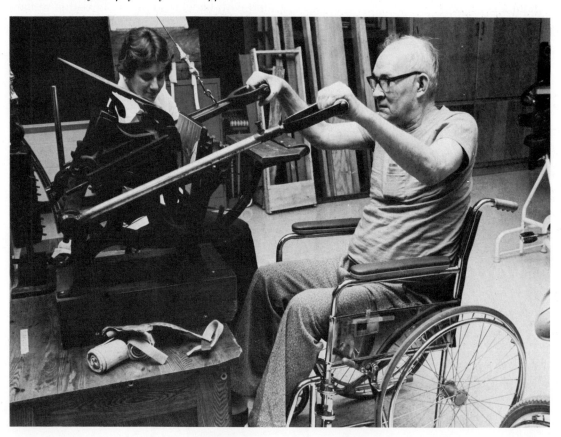

has often been larger than the budget of the parent Public Health Service. At its Medical Research Center in Bethesda, Maryland, and through research grants to institutions around the country, the NIH conducts research in all fields of health and medicine. These fields include environmental health, neurological (brain) disorders, child development, arthritis, heart disease, cancer, infectious diseases, and aging. The NIH spends more than $2 billion annually to support this research.

The National Institute of Mental Health (NIMH) is a separate unit of the Public Health Service. The NIMH conducts research in the area of mental health and defects. It administers a broad program of grants to states, individual scientists, and institutions engaged in mental health research.

The Food and Drug Administration. Currently a semiautonomous unit of the Public Health Service, the Food and Drug Administration (FDA) originated with the Pure Food and Drug Act of 1906. The FDA's objective is to protect the American people against hazards connected with foods, drugs, cosmetics, household cleaning compounds, pesticides, and a broad variety of other products in general use.

The FDA tries to protect people from hazards connected with food, drugs, and other products. Their labs test chemicals in these products to determine whether or not they are harmful.

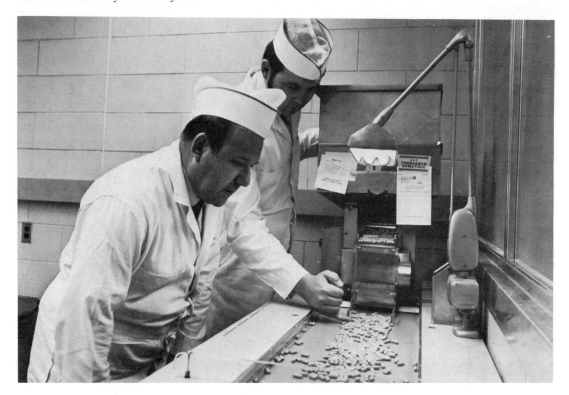

SHIRLEY MOUNT HUFSTEDLER

Shirley M. Hufstedler was born in Denver in 1925. She received her B.A. in business administration from the University of New Mexico in 1945 and her Bachelor of Law degree from Standford University in 1949. Hufstedler has received honorary Doctorates of Law from several colleges and universities.

She has authored numerous articles and books on such subjects as equal justice, privacy issues, and improving the organization of the judiciary. Some of her pieces have won her awards and honors from various publishers and legal organizations. The Los Angeles Times named her Woman of the Year in 1968.

Before taking up law, Hufstedler worked as a teacher, a secretary, and a salesperson. Her career in law began in 1950 when she became a lawyer. Hufstedler practiced law in Los Angeles until 1960. She was appointed to fill an unexpired term as judge in the Los Angeles County Superior Court in 1961. In 1962 she was elected to a full term. In 1966 Hufstedler was appointed an Associate Justice of the California Court of Appeals.

Hufstedler has served as trustee or advisor to many colleges and universities. She has also been a member of the faculty of the Appellate Judges Seminar at the Institute for Judicial Administration and a member of the law faculty at the Salzberg Seminar in American Studies.

In 1968 Hufstedler became a circuit court judge on the U.S. Court of Appeals. She was the highest-ranking woman judge in the country. This was a roving assignment—her post in the Ninth Circuit of the Federal Court took her from Los Angeles through nine states and Guam.

Her extensive traveling gave Hufstedler an overview of the court system, and she became a well-known spokesperson for court reform. One of her complaints was that it is simply too expensive for most people to bring a civil lawsuit to court. No one can afford a civil lawsuit today, the judge has said, "except the rich, the nearly rich, or the person seriously injured by a well-insured defendant." She has spoken and written widely on the need for simplifying the system. "If we are to give people access to the courts, we must create some tribunal the general public can afford to use," she has said.

When Hufstedler was a circuit court judge on the U.S. Court of Appeals, it was often predicted that she would be a trailblazer in an even higher office—in the Supreme Court or the Cabinet. Hufstedler accomplished this in 1979 when she became Secretary of the Department of Education. The department, formed to improve students' declining literacy scores, was created when the Department of Health, Education, and Welfare split.

Upon taking office Hufstedler's main chore was to set up a working department. She was able to do this one month ahead of schedule and $9 million below the estimated cost. As secretary, Hufstedler had to deal with problems of budget, organization, legislation, and regulation. Perhaps one of her most important contributions was her ability to cut some of the red tape involved in the internal regulatory process. Hufstedler held this position until January 1981.

Native American classrooms, such as the one pictured above, receive aid from the federal government.

The FDA conducts its research and investigations in Washington, D.C., and in field offices, laboratories, and inspection stations. Under FDA regulations foods, drugs, and other products found to be dangerous or to misrepresent the facts must be removed from the market. Also, labels must describe the ingredients in every package. New drugs must first be approved by the FDA before they can be sold to the public.

Most of the FDA's records are available for public inspection by consumer advocates and other interested individuals.

section review

1. What is the objective of the FDA?
2. How is the social security system financed?
3. Name the two medical programs administered by the Health Care Financing Administration.

4. What is the National Institute of Health?

2. THE DEPARTMENT OF EDUCATION

The Department of Education was created in 1979 when HEW was split. The new department was formed in response to education groups demanding more recognition.

Public education is primarily the responsibility of states and local governments. States and localities spend over $130 billion a year on public education. During the academic year, every fourth person in America is enrolled in a school or college. More than 34 million people attend elementary schools, 16 million attend high schools, and 10 million are enrolled in colleges or universities.

The national government has long provided for education of Native Americans, resi-

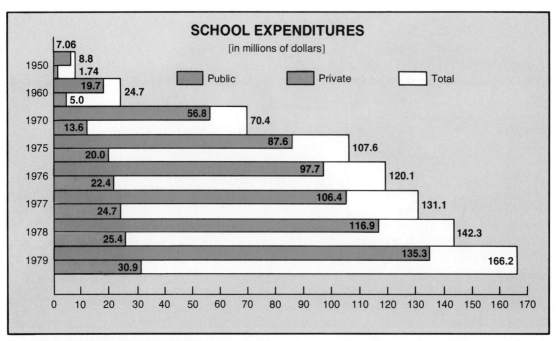

SCHOOL EXPENDITURES

[in millions of dollars]

Public　　　Private　　　Total

Year	Public	Private	Total
1950	7.06	1.74	8.8
1960	19.7	5.0	24.7
1970	56.8	13.6	70.4
1975	87.6	20.0	107.6
1976	97.7	22.4	120.1
1977	106.4	24.7	131.1
1978	116.9	25.4	142.3
1979	135.3	30.9	166.2

0　10　20　30　40　50　60　70　80　90　100　110　120　130　140　150　160　170

Source: National Center for Educational Statistics

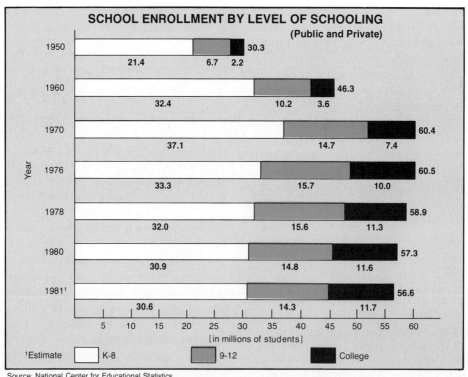

SCHOOL ENROLLMENT BY LEVEL OF SCHOOLING

(Public and Private)

Year	K-8	9-12	College	Total
1950	21.4	6.7	2.2	30.3
1960	32.4	10.2	3.6	46.3
1970	37.1	14.7	7.4	60.4
1976	33.3	15.7	10.0	60.5
1978	32.0	15.6	11.3	58.9
1980	30.9	14.8	11.6	57.3
1981[1]	30.6	14.3	11.7	56.6

5　10　15　20　25　30　35　40　45　50　55　60

[in millions of students]

[1]Estimate　　K-8　　　9-12　　　College

Source: National Center for Educational Statistics

dents of the District of Columbia, and other residents of federal territories. Aside from these special cases, the federal government played a small role in educational matters until the 1960's. In that decade record school and college enrollments—from the post-World War II spurt in population—overtaxed state and local resources. The federal government responded to this situation with a massive infusion of federal aid.

Federal Grant Programs. Federal educational funds have also been provided for groups with special problems, including the mentally and physically handicapped, those with learning disabilities or emotional disturbances, and those from low-income communities whose inadequate school facilities deprive them of equal educational opportunities. Veterans are given special educational

help, as are school districts that contain military or other federal installations. The federal government also maintains overseas schools for military dependents.

The Department of Education administers most of these federal grant programs. The secretary of education—who is expected to be familiar with educational administration—heads the department. He or she is a presidential appointee subject to Senate confirmation. The first secretary of education was Shirley M. Hufstedler, a former federal Court of Appeals judge.

The most significant aid-to-education programs established by Congress in recent years include the National Defense Education Act (NDEA) of 1958 and 1964 and the Elementary and Secondary Education Act (ESEA) of 1965.

The NDEA originally provided grants and loans to improve the teaching of science,

This speech therapy class shows children practicing basic sounds. Do you know of any federally-funded programs for the learning disabled in your community?

mathematics, and languages at all levels of education and supported needy college students in those fields. Today the NDEA program covers most of the humanities and social sciences and is a major source of federal support for many colleges.

The ESEA has allocated more than $1 billion to school districts with large numbers of low-income families to compensate for the low tax base and low school budgets in those districts compared with districts that have wealthier populations. With the ESEA Congress for the first time provided general public school support rather than support for specific programs and activities.

In 1940 the federal government accounted for only a tiny fraction (1.8 percent) of total educational spending. Today federal funds represent almost 15 percent of all such spending. In recent years federal funds have been withheld from states and school districts until they have complied with court rulings on school desegregation.

Certain state courts, notably the California supreme court, have required school districts to equalize the amounts spent on each student. These courts have held that students in wealthy school districts receive better education than do others. Students in wealthy districts are able to benefit from the latest in educational equipment and new textbooks. Students in poorer districts are often forced to share old textbooks because there are not enough to go around. This situation deprives the others of equal educational opportunity.

section review

1. When and why did the federal government become involved in educational funding?
2. Why have federal funds been withheld from some states and school districts?
3. Why has the ESEA heavily funded school districts with large numbers of low-income families?

3. THE DEPARTMENT OF HOUSING AND URBAN DEVELOPMENT

Today more than three fourths of all Americans live in urban areas—mostly in large cities of over 50,000 people.

Most domestic problems are city based, including poor housing, rising crime rates, overcrowded schools, inadequate solid waste disposal, air pollution, and general urban decay. The Department of Housing and Urban Development (HUD) was created by Congress in 1965 to deal with these frustrating problems comprehensively.

The Secretary of HUD. The Housing and Urban Development Act of 1965 empowers the secretary of HUD to coordinate all federal activities relating to housing and urban development. Various Presidents have looked to the secretary for advice on all urban programs—including those administered by other federal departments and agencies.

Blacks, who are even more heavily concentrated in large cities than is the rest of the population, have been in the forefront in providing leadership to HUD. The first secretary, Robert C. Weaver, was the first Black to hold Cabinet office. Samuel R. Pierce, Jr., Reagan's first HUD secretary, is also Black.

HUD contains more than 16,000 employees and administers several federal grant programs. Unlike most federal aid programs, which are administered through state agencies, a substantial portion of HUD's aid money is distributed directly to cities.

The largest such program is the community development block grant program under which $12.5 billion was distributed to cities by 1980. Community development block grant funds are targeted to relieve blight in the aging cities of the Northeast and the industrial Midwest. Cities have fairly wide discretion in how they spend these funds to

After a decade of championing the rights of small neighborhoods within big cities, Gino Baroni, a Catholic priest, was appointed assistant secretary of HUD for neighborhoods, voluntary associations, and consumer protection. It was a new post, established in 1977, and it might have been designed for Monsignor Baroni. It signalled the government's recognition of his pet cause — the neighborhood movement.

"America is not a melting pot," Baroni has said. "It's the most ethnically, racially, culturally, regionally diverse country in the world." Baroni believes in preserving the differences that give each neighborhood its unique character. "We literally destroy neighborhoods in order to save them, by urban renewal and by the highway program." Baroni's special goal was to alter these government policies.

The son of Italian immigrants, Baroni was raised in Acosta, Pennsylvania. "I grew up as an assimilationist," he remembers. "I knew more about Henry Ford, John D. Rockefeller, and Andrew Carnegie than I did about myself. I was going to be one of them, not a coal miner like my old man." Baroni was ordained in 1956. His commitment to social action led him to various causes. He helped set up a credit union for factory workers in Altoona, Pennsylvania. He was roughed up in a civil rights march in Alabama. He helped Blacks rehabilitate an inner-city area in Washington, D.C. He sheltered antiwar protesters during the Vietnam era.

Gradually his work in the cities led him to conclude that one sector being overlooked was that of White ethnic minorities. He believed that they could be a force for social change, but that they felt alienated from liberals and in conflict with the Blacks with whom they shared their inner-city neighborhoods. Baroni's remedy was to find "convergent issues," so that Blacks and Whites within communities could unite in common causes. In 1970 he founded the National Center for Urban Ethnic Affairs, to try to channel money from government grants to local community groups.

In his new post at HUD, one of Baroni's goals was to halt redlining—the practice by banks of denying mortgages to owners of property in declining neighborhoods. Baroni wanted the government to put pressure on financial institutions to make it easier for people to reinvest in older sections of cities. He also wanted his department's temporary Neighborhood Commission to keep reviewing the impact of federal programs, so that those which do not help neighborhoods could be changed. "There's never been a federal policy that respected neighborhoods," Baroni has noted. His job is to speak up on behalf of this basic urban unit.

Baroni has said that his experience in the church stands him in good stead. "I come from the world's largest bureaucracy," he points out, smiling. "It's all the art of discovering what's possible."

Baroni's $50,000-a-year post was the highest in the U.S. government ever accorded a Catholic priest. Baroni's dual mission was clear to him. "Poverty," he has said, "is a spiritual problem because it denies what a person needs to carry on a creative life."

Poor housing and high crime rates are the source of many domestic problems. Many people are even unable to afford rehabilitated housing.

relieve this blight and decay. In a number of cases, however, HUD has conditioned community development block grants on a city's acceptance of housing for low-income minorities.

Federal Housing Programs. Franklin D. Roosevelt spoke of "one third of a nation ill-clothed, ill-housed, and ill-fed." Since the depression the federal government has helped Americans to rent and to buy decent housing.

The Federal Housing Administration. The Federal Housing Administration (FHA) insures mortgages, making it possible for many middle-income families to buy homes. The FHA guarantees banks and other lending institutions against losses on loans made to build, buy, rent, or improve homes. Most homes insured by the FHA contain from one to four families. Approximately one fourth of all homes built recently in the United States are financed with FHA help. FHA-insured mortgages are financed at lower-than-market interest rates and may be repaid over a period of 30 years.

The FHA is the modern successor to several long-term, low-interest loan and loan-guarantee programs operated by the federal government during the 1930's and 1940's to prevent foreclosures and to stimulate home building.

By guaranteeing the savings accounts of depositors in banks and in savings and loan associations (through the Federal Deposit

Insurance Corporation and the Federal Savings and Loan Insurance Corporation), the government has helped these institutions to provide billions of dollars in mortgage loans.

The Housing Assistance Administration. Since 1937 the federal government has operated a low-rent public housing program that today provides housing for 2.5 million people. HUD's Housing Assistance Administration makes long-term, low-interest loans to local housing authorities to help them build low-rent housing.

The Housing Assistance Administration also helps low-income families by paying a portion of their rent directly to landlords. The amount of this payment—called a *rent subsidy* or *rent supplement*—varies according to each family's income.

These programs have been partly successful. Tenants in public housing projects are often robbed or burglarized, usually because their buildings have not been constructed with security in mind, which makes them very vulnerable to such crime. Also,

communities tend to resist the construction of public housing projects, fearing reduction in their property values and increased crime rates. Rent subsidies have been successful in enabling poor families to afford better housing, but they do not expand the total number of housing units available.

In the 1960's and the 1970's, many city-based industries moved to the suburbs. As a result the cities lost many jobs. HUD has tried to move industrial workers nearer to these jobs—mainly by trying to bring low-income housing to the suburbs.

HUD has increased its enforcement of fair housing laws and provides low-cost financing to builders of low-income housing in the suburbs. Despite these efforts suburban residents have often been successful in preventing public housing—frequently by requiring that a public referendum be held before a public housing project is accepted.

Because of these obstacles several HUD officials now advocate replacing public housing construction and rent subsidies with *housing allowances*—that is, direct payments

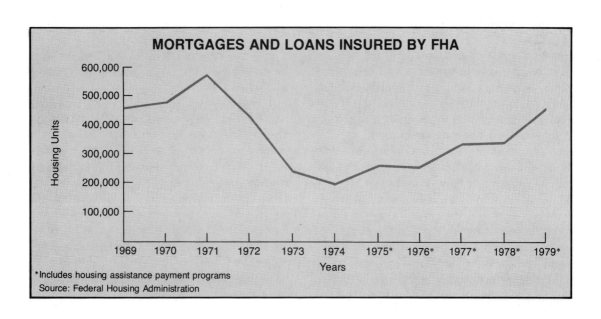

MORTGAGES AND LOANS INSURED BY FHA

*Includes housing assistance payment programs
Source: Federal Housing Administration

to the poor to enable them to compete for housing in the open market. If people had more money to spend on housing, builders would be induced to supply this new market.

The Renewal Assistance Administration. The Renewal Assistance Administration (RAA) manages HUD's urban renewal programs. These programs aid slum clearance and help to rebuild inner-city business and residential areas. The RAA helps to relocate and subsidize families uprooted by urban renewal projects.

Urban renewal has produced some successes, but it has destroyed more housing than it has created. Moreover, most of the poor who used to live in the renewed areas cannot afford to rent or buy the rehabilitated housing units.

The Model Cities Administration. The Model Cities Administration implements the Model Cities Program, conceived in 1966 by President Johnson as a coordinated attack on blighted neighborhoods. Through the Demonstration Cities and Metropolitan Development Act of 1966 and subsequent appropriations, Congress and HUD invited cities to submit proposals for model cities planning grants.

Of the 200 proposals submitted, 63 planning grants were awarded. The Model Cities Administration required recipients of planning grants to involve residents of the targeted neighborhoods in planning all projects. This is called *citizen participation.*

Almost all of these plans were eventually approved and—within the limits of the $1.2 billion appropriated by Congress for the program—the "model cities" received funds necessary to carry out their plans. Typical model cities projects have included community centers, teenage counseling programs, neighborhood health facilities, intracity bus services, rehabilitated housing, and new parks.

Despite these housing and urban renewal programs, most poor people today still live in crowded, deteriorating inner-city housing. These families are plagued by crime, vandalism, delinquency, drug addiction, and broken homes. HUD's primary goal in the late 1970's was to enable inner-city dwellers to move to better neighborhoods where they would have access to better jobs, better schools, and a better quality of life.

Like HEW's welfare programs, HUD's programs make it possible for the costs of metropolitan area poverty to be borne by the nation as a whole rather than by individual cities, which are often least able to afford remedies.

section review

1. Why are community development block grant funds issued?
2. How are FHA rates different from market rates? Why was the FHA instituted?
3. Define the concept of rent subsidy.

4. THE DEPARTMENT OF TRANSPORTATION

The federal government has been involved with transportation since the early nineteenth century. Lands west of the Mississippi River were opened to settlement through government-sponsored trails, wagon roads, and railroads. These facilities enabled factory and farm products to be transported to markets. All forms of transportation have remained in private hands, subject to public regulation.

The Department of Transportation (DOT) was created by Congress in 1967. Like the

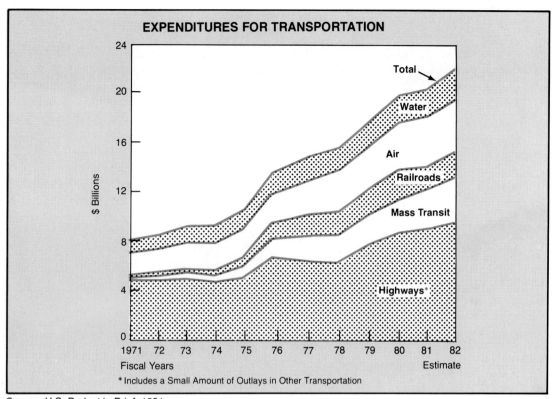

EXPENDITURES FOR TRANSPORTATION

Total

Water

Air

Railroads

Mass Transit

Highways*

1971 72 73 74 75 76 77 78 79 80 81 82

Fiscal Years

Estimate

* Includes a Small Amount of Outlays in Other Transportation

$ Billions

Source: U.S. Budget in Brief, 1981

other departments in this chapter, DOT brought together many agencies and functions formerly lodged elsewhere in the government.

DOT employs over 72,000 people. Americans pay over $200 billion per year for all forms of transporatation—air, rail, and automobiles. The major agencies within DOT reflect these various forms of transportation. They include the Federal Aviation Administration, the Federal Railroad Administration, and the Federal Highway Administration.

The Federal Aviation Administration. Civil air transportation in the United States is controlled by two federal agencies: the Civil Aeronautics Board (CAB), which is an in-

dependent regulatory commission, and DOT's Federal Aviation Administration (FAA).

The FAA, first established in 1958 as an independent agency, licenses all civilian pilots and aircraft. It manages a nationwide air traffic control system and operates control towers at all of the nation's major airports. The FAA sponsors research leading to more advanced aircraft and distributes federal grants-in-aid to local governments for airport construction. It also imposes noise standards for all aircraft and safety regulations for all air traffic.

The National Transportation Safety Board, an independent federal agency, investigates the causes of all accidents in the United States that involve civilian aircraft.

Our nationwide air traffic control system is regulated by the Federal Aviation Administration.

The Federal Railroad Administration. Until the creation of the Federal Railroad Administration (FRA) as part of DOT in 1967, the Interstate Commerce Commission (ICC) had exclusive federal control over railroads. The ICC still regulates railroad rates and schedules. But the FRA now administers all safety rules for railroads and oil pipelines.

An important subunit of the FRA is the Office of High-speed Ground Transportation. Through research and demonstration projects, this office seeks to recover the high-speed rail technology that was lost when railroads began to decline in the late 1920's. Japan's experience in transporting people and goods by rail at speeds of over 300 miles per hour has proved especially helpful to this office.

The Federal Highway Administration. In America today there are almost 160 million motor vehicles traveling on more than 3.9 million miles of roads and streets. There is an average of one car for every two people in the

United States, and almost everyone old enough to drive has a license.

Until the mass production of automobiles, road building and maintenance were the responsibilities of state and local government. States and localities still spend more money today on roads than on anything else except education.

The Federal Highway Administration was created as part of DOT in 1967. It assumed the functions of the Commerce Department's Bureau of Public Roads and is the nation's main road-building agency. Its principal function is to administer the federal highway program.

The Federal Aid Highway Act of 1956 launched the largest public works program in history—the 42,500-mile interstate highway system. This system, which is almost completed, will cost a total of $109 billion. The federal government is paying for 90 percent of the bill, with the states providing the remaining 10 percent on a 9:1 matching formula. The states also receive $3 billion a year (on a 7:3 federal-state matching ratio) to improve more than 800,000 miles of primary and secondary roads in the federal network.

The Federal Highway Administration also constructs and maintains roads on federally owned lands (for example, roads in national parks and forests) and promotes highway safety.

The National Traffic Safety Administration. Together with the Federal Highway Administration, the National Highway Traffic Safety Administration, its companion DOT agency, has required automobile manufacturers to install numerous safety devices to prevent and reduce highway accidents. For example, all automobiles manufactured after 1983 must have air bags.

The National Highway Traffic Safety Administration has required automobile manufacturers to recall 12.5 million vehicles to remedy manufacturing defects. This unit is also responsible for imposing strict fuel econ-omy standards for new cars. Because of its regulations, auto makers are developing engines for heavy cars that use a gallon of gasoline for more than 20 miles.

The Urban Mass Transportation Administration. The Urban Mass Transportation Administration (UMTA) was created as a DOT agency in 1968 to administer federal grants-in-aid and loans to cities to develop and improve mass transit facilities. Rapid transit bus and subway systems within metropolitan areas have been developed and expanded with UMTA funds.

The main thrust of the urban mass transit program is to get people within metropolitan areas to use public transit facilities instead of their own cars. Mass transit has numerous advantages over transportation by private automobile: It reduces pollution, relieves traffic congestion, and shifts city resources and investment away from urban expressways and downtown parking facilities. As more people become frustrated by rush hour traffic and parking problems, subways and buses should become an increasingly attractive alternative.

UMTA's annual funding level is about $2 billion. Mass transit advocates in Congress have attempted, thus far unsuccessfully, to increase this funding with revenues from the federal gasoline tax. Truckers and road builders oppose this proposal, arguing that all gasoline tax revenues are needed for highway maintenance.

QUOTES
from famous people

"The prosperity of commerce is now perceived and acknowledged by all enlightened statesmen to be the most useful as well as the most productive source of national wealth, and has accordingly become a primary object of their political cares."

Alexander Hamilton

San Francisco's automated trains make up one of the nation's most modern mass transportation systems.

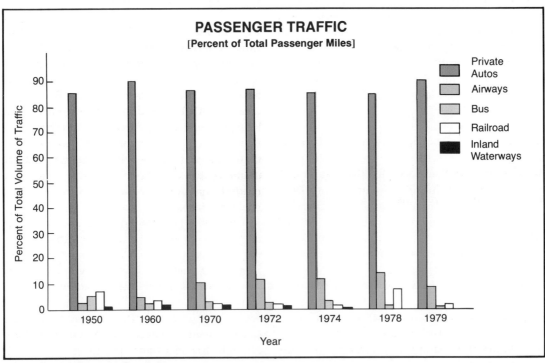

PASSENGER TRAFFIC
[Percent of Total Passenger Miles]

Percent of Total Volume of Traffic

Private Autos
Airways
Bus
Railroad
Inland Waterways

Year

Source: Interstate Commerce Commission

The United States Coast Guard. The coast guard is a branch of the U.S. armed forces and operates as part of the navy in wartime. In peacetime, however, it operates under DOT's jurisdiction. The coast guard contains 39,000 people, including an officer corps trained at the United States Coast Guard Academy in New London, Connecticut. The coast guard was officially established in 1915 as part of the Treasury Department, although its predecessors date to the beginning of the Republic.

The coast guard patrols all waters under the jurisdiction of the United States. It patrols 12,000 miles of coastline to prevent piracy and smuggling. The coast guard aids all persons in distress in coastal waters and on adjacent high seas. It carries out search and rescue operations with the aid of its own ships, planes, lifeboat stations, and radio and radar communications.

The coast guard operates lighthouses, buoys, foghorns, and other navigational aids. It inspects vessels for seaworthiness, imposes safety standards, and helps to clear Alaskan icebound channels. Its six permanent ocean stations provide weather information, conduct oceanographic research, and help to navigate ships and aircraft.

section review

1. What are the advantages of mass transit over private automobile transportation?
2. What are the responsibilities of the coast guard?

5. THE DEPARTMENT OF ENERGY

Before the Industrial Revolution ushered in the age of machines, people depended on fairly simple and readily available sources of energy. Wood fires supplied heat and fuel for cooking. Transportation by wagon, cart, or carriage depended on horsepower. Plows were usually driven by cattle and oxen. Candles and oil lamps provided light. Waterwheels used currents of water for turning machinery, as in flour mills and sawmills. Windmills used wind currents for the same purpose. And human energy was in continual use.

As technology advanced, machinery became more complex. The turbine and dynamo were supplemented by internal combustion engines. Wood, animals, and wind were supplemented with *fossil fuels*—that is, materials stored in the earth from earlier geologic periods. The most commonly used fossil fuels are oil, coal, and natural gas. These fuels power engines and heating systems that in turn power heavier machinery. When water-generated energy, or *hydroelectric power*, is not readily available, these fuels are used to generate electricity.

Energy Supply and Demand. Before 1972 most Americans took energy for granted. The nation's energy resources were assumed to be limitless. Many homes were built without insulation. It was more expensive to insulate than to switch on the gas, oil, or electric heater—even though most of the heat was lost. Several scientists began to measure the country's energy resources against its increasing consumption of energy and concluded that America would eventually face shortages—especially in oil.

By 1972 government officials, scientists, and business leaders perceived that an energy problem existed. Their concerns were more than justified. In January 1973 oil and gas shortages forced the closing of schools, factories, and plants in many cities. That summer thousands of service stations went out of business because they could not get enough gas. Gasoline pump prices nearly doubled. Many people waited in long lines for a few gallons of gasoline. Virtually all Americans felt the "energy crunch."

The shortages of 1973—1974 resulted from the decision of the oil-producing Arab nations to suspend oil exports to the United States and Western Europe and to quadruple the price of oil. Although this situation eased somewhat after 1974, prices remain very high.

Industrial nations demand more energy than is available. Large automobiles, television, major appliances, central heating, and air-conditioning all consume great amounts of energy. The United States has less than 6 percent of the world's population but consumes one third of the world's total production of energy. Unless America reduces its rate of consumption, it will require twice as much energy in 1990 as it consumes today. Increased supply may be available from Arab oil producers but only at exorbitant prices.

The Federal Energy Administration. Congress established the Federal Energy Administration (FEA) in 1974 to ensure that the nation's supplies of energy would meet its needs in the future. To cope with the energy problem, the country must reduce demand and increase supply.

Experts estimate that 30 percent of America's energy is wasted through inefficient use. Strict conservation measures and more energy-efficient engines could greatly reduce the demand for resources. If voluntary measures are not effective, gas rationing and taxes to limit energy use may well be imposed.

Increasing the supply of energy will require the development of alternative sources such as solar and nuclear power. An economical way may also be developed to extract the vast amount of oil embedded in rock (oil shale) throughout the western half of the country.

The Energy Supply and Environmental Coordination Act of 1974 allowed the FEA to order industries to use coal instead of gas and oil where the use of coal would not significantly damage the environment. Coal, however, often causes serious air pollution. The law required the Environmental Protection Agency to approve all FEA-ordered conversions to coal.

Atomic and Nuclear Energy. During World War II the United States developed atomic energy. This new form of energy was first applied destructively. Two atomic bombs devastated the Japanese cities of Hiroshima and Nagasaki and killed or maimed many of their people. The Atomic Energy Commission, created in 1946, was charged not only with building and stockpiling atomic bombs but also with developing peaceful uses of the atom.

One such use has been the development of nuclear power as a source of electricity. Environmentalists frequently oppose the construction of nuclear power plants because they produce radioactive wastes that are extremely difficult to dispose of. They also charge that nuclear plants destroy marine life in adjacent bodies of water. Nevertheless, energy planners expect 1,000 nuclear power plants to be in operation by the year 2000.

In 1974 Congress replaced the Atomic Energy Commission with two bodies—the Energy Research and Development Administration (ERDA) and the Nuclear Regulatory Commission (NRC). ERDA inherited the AEC's developmental function. The NRC assumed the AEC's regulatory responsibilities. These responsibilities include the licensing of nuclear power plants, supervising the safety of nuclear reactors, and imposing safeguards on nuclear materials.

ERDA, a unit of the Department of Energy since 1977, was charged with developing all possible energy sources. It is involved in nuclear fission and fusion, the conversion of coal into liquid and gas, and the development of power from the sun, winds, tides, and ocean currents as well as nuclear sources. In

Pictured here is the San Onofre nuclear generating station.

this and other research, ERDA works through grants and contracts with universities, research institutions, and industry.

Because nuclear power plants are controversial and doubts remain about their safety, the NRC and DOE may be involved in public debate over nuclear policy for some time.

Scope of the Department of Energy. DOE, which began operations on October 1, 1977, has over 20,000 employees and a budget of $10 billion. The new department absorbed all powers, programs, and employees of the FEA, ERDA, and the Federal Power Commission. These three agencies were abolished.

Congress refused President Carter's request to grant the secretary of energy power over energy prices. Instead Congress created a five-member Federal Energy Regulatory Commission. The new commission was given independent authority comparable with that of other regulatory commissions, but it operates within DOE.

The commission has the power to set natural gas, oil, and wholesale electricity prices. Nuclear power rates are regulated by the Nuclear Regulatory Commission, which is completely separate from DOE. The secretary of NRC can issue oil-pricing rules on his or her own authority, however, if the President declares the existence of a national emergency requiring immediate action. In such cases, oil-pricing decisions could be vetoed by either house of Congress within 15 days.

The Federal Energy Regulatory Commission interacts with the secretary in ways that are uncharacteristic of other regulatory commissions: Congress has authorized the secretary to propose commission actions, to intervene in any commission proceedings, and to set reasonable time limits for commission decisions.

Several functions lodged elsewhere in the government have now been assumed by DOE. For example, DOE has taken over responsibility for

—oil-pipeline rate regulation from the ICC;

—oil reserves from the navy;

—energy-saving standards in new buildings from HUD;

—voluntary energy conservation from the Department of Commerce;

—gathering and disseminating data relating

ENERGY: THE GROWING FEDERAL ROLE

Fuel shortages have been plaguing the U.S. for many years. The deterioration of relations with oil-exporting nations has shown how ill-prepared the federal government is to deal with fuel shortages. To alleviate America's dependence on foreign oil, several energy-related programs have been implemented.

One significant piece of energy legislation, passed by Congress in 1979, was a "windfall" profits tax. This is a tax on oil company profits that result from decontrol of oil prices. Profits from this tax are to be used to research the development of synthetic fuels. Other energy-related programs include: the Energy Mobilization Board (E.M.B.), which acts in place of state and local agencies that fail to speed the construction of energy projects; and a gasoline-rationing scheme whereby federal conservation controls could be imposed on any state if there were more than an 8 percent drop in gasoline supplies.

Many are looking to another source for future energy—the sun. Two weeks of sunshine contain as much potential energy as all the known reserves of coal, oil, and gas in the world. The Council on Environmental Quality predicts that solar power could meet 25 percent of U.S. energy needs by the year 2000. The Department of Energy, however, has given only half-hearted support to solar research and development.

Oil companies seem to regard the growth of solar energy as inevitable. Therefore many companies are buying up smaller solar companies. This worries some solar advocates, who note that the majority of technological innovations and breakthroughs come from small and independent inventors, rather than from corporate laboratories.

Despite the resistance of the Energy Department, Congress has recently enacted laws that make federal loans available to small solar businesses, require new military housing to be solar-powered, and support the development of inexpensive, mass-produced solar technology. By enacting such laws, Congress may be more responsive than the executive branch to the wants and needs of the American people.

These people are gathered at a Sun Day exhibit (April 1978). The purpose of this exhibit was to discover ways to use solar energy.

to coal from the Department of the Interior's Bureau of Mines; and
—marketing electric power from the Department of the Interior's public power administrations.

DOE and the Department of the Interior share responsibility for leasing federally owned oil, natural gas, and coal reserves. (The Department of the Interior formerly had sole jurisdiction in this area.) The terms of such leases are to be set by DOE.

An important new unit of DOE is the Energy Information Administration. This unit is charged with developing a unified energy data-collection program. It evaluates each energy company's revenues, profits, and costs resulting from energy-related operations.

The Office of Energy Research is responsible for administering DOE's research and development programs and for advising the secretary on those matters.

DOE has overall responsibility for setting energy production goals for the nation. If another energy crisis looms, the nation will look to DOE to conserve all available resources and to help prevent serious economic harm.

section review

1. How did the 1973-1974 suspension of oil exports by Arab nations affect the American people?
2. Why do environmentalists protest the construction of nuclear power plants?
3. What powers can the Federal Energy Regulatory Commission exercise?

CHAPTER SUMMARY

28

In 1953 Congress created the Department of Health, Education, and Welfare. (In 1979 it became the Department of Health and Human Services.) It was only the first of a variety of new executive departments. In the succeeding 27 years, four additional departments were established: Housing and Urban Development, Transportation, Energy, and Education. Each of these departments was formed to meet the needs of the industrial urbanized society that America has become in the second half of the twentieth century.

Most of the social welfare programs and social services are administered by the Department of Health and Human Services: social security, income security, health care and research, and aid to the needy and handicapped. These multibillion-dollar programs attempt to improve the quality of life for all Americans.

As more and more Americans have moved to urban areas (more than three fourths), domestic problems and solutions have come to be city-based. HUD, a comprehensive, Cabinet-level department created in 1965, reflects this change in the nature of American society. HUD administers and coordinates all federal activities related to housing and urban development. Programs to assist Americans with housing date back to the 1930's Federal Housing Administration, which insured home loans. The scope of federal activities in housing has been broadened to include home loans, the building of low-rent housing, rent subsidies for low-income families, urban redevelopment, and relocation of families displaced by urban renewal programs.

The Department of Transportation was created in 1967 to coordinate the development of an efficient transportation system, using a variety of modes of transport. Three agencies—FAA, FRA, and the Federal Highway Administration—were brought together under the secretary of transportation.

The Department of Education, created in 1979, administers all federal programs aiding elementary, secondary, and higher education.

The Department of Energy has overall responsibility for setting energy production goals for the nation. Its task is twofold: to reduce energy consumption and demand, and to increase sources of energy supply.

REVIEW QUESTIONS

1. Should all income security programs require that applicants demonstrate need (as AFDC does)? Why or why not?
2. Should the U.S. establish a national health insurance program? Why or why not?
3. In 1971 President Nixon proposed replacing existing welfare programs with a guaranteed minimum income. Do you favor such a proposal? Why or why not? What other alternatives can you suggest?

4. Because of relocation of urban businesses to suburbs, cities have declined in population and quality. What programs does the federal government now have to help cities cope with the resultant problems?

5. Why is federal funding now being used for urban mass transit? Do you favor such use of federal funds? Why or why not? What other alternatives can you suggest?

6. How do the purposes of the Departments of HHS, HUD, Transporation, Education, and Energy complement each other? What factors might cause them to come into conflict with each other? with other executive agencies?

ACTIVITIES FOR REVIEW

activity 1   Prepare a report on welfare programs in your community. Cite contributions and shortcomings of the programs. What recommendations would you propose to make the system more effective in reaching the goals for which these programs were established?

activity 2   Prepare a position statement on the need for national health insurance. Present your recommendations to the class.

activity 3   Prepare a report on the benefits and hazards of nuclear power as an alternative energy source.

activity 4   Prepare a wall chart comparing and contrasting various energy sources in terms of availability, cleanliness, health hazards, ratio of mass to energy supplied, etc.

political science DICTIONARY

housing allowances—direct payments to the poor by the federal government, to allow them to compete for housing in the open market.   p. 548

Medicaid—a federal grant program to help states provide medical care for all needy disabled people under the age of 65 who cannot pay medical expenses.   p. 536

rent subsidy—the portion of rent payment made by the federal government to landlords of low-income families; also known as rent supplement.   p. 547

UNIT SUMMARY

President George Washington established a Cabinet of advisers to assist him in the day-to-day operations of the government. He appointed four men to assist him in the essential operations of government. Since 1789 the four advisers have grown to thousands. There are 13 executive departments, each headed by a secretary with a large staff, working in a wide variety of areas the first President probably never even imagined.

The executive departments may be divided into four categories: original or essential government operations, special interests, public and human services, and conservation. These departments reflect the changes that have occurred in the years of growth and change since the nation was founded.

All governments have some equivalent ministers or advisers in the areas of essential government services: state, defense, treasury, and justice.

During America's Industrial Revolution, the special and growing needs of farmers, business people, and workers created a demand for individual departments to serve their interests. The Agriculture, Commerce, and Labor departments were established as each of these groups organized politically and found the need and the opportunity to voice their concerns to the federal government.

The Interior Department is the most flexible of the executive departments. It has been concerned with land use and Native American life from its inception. It has changed its central focus, however. In the early days of the Republic, Interior's concerns were those of an expanding nation—homesteading and Indian relations. Today, conservation and preservation of the land and natural resources are central.

The "new" departments, all established since 1953, reflect the nation's change from an agrarian to an industrial urbanized society. HHS, HUD, Transportation, Energy, and Education are all concerned with problems of a modern urban industrial society.

Bibliography

Downs, Anthony. *Opening up the Suburbs: An Urban Strategy for America.* New Haven: Yale University Press, 1973.

Halperin, Morton H. *Bureaucratic Politics and Foreign Policy.* Washington, D.C.: Brookings Institution, 1974.

Kennedy, Edward. *In Critical Condition: The Crises in America's Health Care.* New York: Pocket Books, Inc., 1972.

Review questions

1. Describe the chronological and functional development of Cabinet-level departments. How do the departments in each category reflect the times in which they were formed?
2. Some people argue that since many of the daily operations of government are handled by the heads of the executive departments, these officials should be elected rather than appointed. Do you agree? Why or why not?
3. Should advocates for such special-interest groups as farmers, business, and labor be part of the executive branch of government? Why or why not?
4. What criteria should be used in selecting Cabinet members? Should the same criteria be used for all departments? Should preference be given to career employees within the individual departments? Explain.

Skills questions

Based on the charts, graphs, and maps in this unit, answer the following questions:

1. Based on the graph titled Budget Receipts: 1969–1983, what conclusions can you draw? Compare the percent of income taxes paid by individuals and corporations in 1977. Do you agree or disagree with this system?
2. What was the total budget outlay for fiscal year 1981? Which two sources received the least amount of federal outlays?
3. Over what department does the attorney general have jurisdiction?
4. Between what two years will there be a substantial decrease in outlays for farm income stabilization? Write an essay explaining the agricultural conditions in the United States between 1974 and 1978.
5. Compare the graphs on pages 507 and 508. What conclusions can you draw?

Activities

activity 1
Stage a classroom debate or forum on the following issue: RESOLVED, that all executive department heads should be career employees rather than political appointees.

activity 2
Research the historical circumstances that led to the creation of one of the executive departments. Prepare a report for the class.

activity 3
As secretary of labor, you find yourself in conflict with the director of the Environmental Protection Agency over automobile emission controls. What steps might you take to resolve the conflict?

UNIT 9

LOUIS D. BRANDEIS

Louis D. Brandeis was one of the most famous American judges. He served on the Supreme Court of the United States from 1916 to 1939.

Born in Louisville, Kentucky, in 1856, Brandeis decided at an early age to become a lawyer. He graduated from Harvard Law School in 1877. Brandeis practiced law continuously from 1878 to 1916 until he was appointed to the United States Supreme Court by President Woodrow Wilson.

Although he never held any public office prior to his nomination to the Supreme Court, Brandeis earned a national reputation as the "public-interest lawyer" of his generation. He served as unpaid counsel for the people in defending the constitutionality of laws regulating wages and hours in Oregon, Illinois, Ohio, and California. As people's attorney, he successfully argued before the Interstate Commerce Commission against railroad rate increases and opposed monopoly of transportation in New England. Throughout his life Brandeis fought bigness. He opposed big government as well as big business.

As a lawyer, Brandeis originated the "Brandeis brief" — a careful and exhaustive factual analysis of the impact of law on social conditions, such as public health, safety, and welfare. Brandeis believed strongly in the "living law." By this he meant that the law must relate to existing conditions in the lives of ordinary men and women. Accordingly, he relied on social statistics and facts rather than abstract legal principles in writing his briefs.

Many of Justice Brandeis' opinions were ahead of the times. His most famous dissents were later adopted as majority opinions of the Court. Joining him in many of these dissents was Justice Oliver Wendell Holmes, Jr. Together they championed the constitutional rights of free speech, free assembly, and freedom from such unreasonable invasions of privacy as wiretapping.

After Brandeis' death in 1941, Dean Acheson, his former law clerk and later secretary of state, declared that Brandeis' "faith in the human mind, and in the will and capacity of people to grasp the truth, never wavered."

THE JUDICIAL BRANCH

OVERVIEW

■ Article 3 of the U.S. Constitution established the judicial power of the United States.

■ Article 6, Section 2 of the U.S. Constitution established the laws and treaties made in pursuance of the Constitution as the Supreme Law of the Land and, thus, provides the basis for judicial review.

■ The power of judicial review by the Supreme Court makes it the final arbiter of what Congress, the executive, and the states may lawfully do.

■ The federal judiciary is divided into three layers: district courts, appellate courts, and the Supreme Court.

■ Courts apply law to the facts through an orderly procedure according to established rules of evidence.

■ Ninety district courts hear most of the federal cases. District (trial) courts have original jurisdiction.

■ Eleven Courts of Appeals (circuit courts) review lower court decisions when they are appealed for improper procedures, admission of illegal evidence, or interpretation of law or the constitutionality on which the trial court based its decision.

■ All matters before the courts must be real cases and the complainant must have standing.

■ Constitutional special courts are the court of claims, customs court, court of customs and patent appeals.

■ Legislative special courts are the court of military appeals, tax court, and courts in the U.S. territories and the District of Columbia.

29

The Federal Judiciary

Article 3 of the Constitution vests the judicial power of the United States in ". . . one Supreme Court, and in such inferior Courts as the Congress may . . . establish." Congress has established district and circuit courts and various special courts. With the Supreme Court these courts constitute the federal judiciary. The judiciary is the branch of the government that has the authority to interpret and apply the law.

This chapter will explore various kinds of law that govern decisions made by federal judges. It will examine the structure and the jurisdiction of the federal courts and the kinds of cases that come before them. It will also focus on what kinds of people become federal judges and how they are appointed. It will examine the impact of federal court decisions on public policy and survey the people and the institutions that compose the federal court system. This chapter will conclude with a review of the special federal courts that exercise jurisdiction over particular subjects, such as taxes, patents, and military matters.

CHAPTER PREVIEW

1. LAW AND JUDGES
2. FEDERAL COURT STRUCTURE
3. APPOINTMENT OF FEDERAL JUDGES
4. ADMINISTERING THE FEDERAL COURT SYSTEM
5. SPECIAL FEDERAL COURTS

1. LAW AND JUDGES

Most court cases involve two elements—facts and law. It is up to the parties in all cases—plaintiff and defendant in **civil** cases, prosecutor and defendant in **criminal** cases—and their witnesses and lawyers to establish the facts. Judges ensure that cases proceed in an orderly way according to established rules of evidence. The judge's main job, however, is to apply the law to the facts. Many cases, including most criminal cases, are governed by particular statutes. The judge must interpret and apply the proper statutes to the case under consideration.

Some cases require judges to interpret and apply a particular provision of the Constitution. Judges avoid interpreting the Constitution if they can find any other law that would provide a basis for reaching a just result. If not, the judge will interpret the

A defense attorney questions a witness during a murder trial. The court stenographer is in the foreground.

constitutional provision in light of past decisions made by the Supreme Court that deal with that provision.

> **Civil cases** are private disputes in which the plaintiff generally seeks money or property from the defendant.
>
> **Criminal cases** involve persons accused of committing crimes. Those found guilty generally are fined or go to prison.

If a case is not based on a constitutional provision and there is no statute involved, judges must apply common law. *Common law* is the law made by judges in America and England over the last eight centuries. It originated from the decisions made by judges who traveled the English countryside to settle disputes in each community according to its own standards.

In time, these local standards came to be accepted throughout England and were applied in colonial America. Each case decided according to common law guides all future cases that involve similar facts. Applying past decisions to reach decisions in similar cases is commonly known as the rule of *precedent.*

Each state has developed common law in individual ways. Louisiana is the one exception. It applies a modified civil code used by the French colonial government before Louisiana was purchased. Disputes in federal court often require the judge to refer to the law of the state where the dispute arose. But if there is no applicable statute, a federal judge will consult the state court decisions of the states involved, which are part of its common law.

In certain cases federal judges apply equity in place of law. *Equity* consists of rules that are applied when the law offers no suitable remedy. For example, a woman may want to prevent her former husband from visiting her. It may be difficult for her to prove

injury and claim damages arising from those visits, but she wants to stop the visits immediately. Her remedy is to seek a court **injunction**—the most common form of equitable relief—ordering her former husband to stop visiting her. If the husband ignores the injunction, he risks a court-imposed penalty.

> An **injunction** is a court order that prohibits certain actions.

Besides constitutional law, statutory law, common law, and equity, federal cases can also involve a relatively new body of principles and precedents called *administrative law.* Federal judges are asked to determine whether federal administrators have acted within the scope of their authority in making particular rules and whether those rules are fundamentally fair.

The Adversary System. American court proceedings are essentially contests beween two lawyers. Both lawyers provide judges and juries with information that enables them to make judgments in court cases. Lawyers present the strongest case they can on behalf of the plaintiff and the defendant.

The adversary system is based on the theory that the truth emerges when each side presents its case as strongly as possible. The parties in dispute are like fighters in a ring. The judge resembles the referee. There can be no decision and no winner until the lawyers have contested one another.

section review

1. Define civil cases.
2. Describe the evolution of common law.
3. When is equity used in court cases?

2. FEDERAL COURT STRUCTURE

Except for a few special courts, the federal judiciary consists of three layers in a hierarchy. At the bottom are the district courts—one for each of 90 districts in the United States and one for Puerto Rico. Each of these district courts has from one to 27 judges, depending on the number of cases heard. Each state has at least one district and may have as many as four. There are 516 federal district judges, including 117 judgeships created by Congress in 1978. All judges are appointed by the President with the consent of the Senate. They hold office for life, depending on good behavior.

District courts are courts of original jurisdiction (that is, trial courts) for both criminal and civil cases. District judges preside over both kinds of cases. In criminal cases district courts regularly use grand juries to determine whether the prosecution has enough evidence to bring an indictment (accusation) against an accused person. *Petit juries*, or trial juries, try civil and criminal cases in which the defendant requests a trial by jury.

All other cases are tried by the judge alone. In special cases involving reapportionment, civil rights, and antitrust actions, Congress has provided for hearings by three-judge district court panels whose decisions can be appealed directly to the Supreme Court.

The middle layer of the federal court system is composed of 11 courts of appeals. The United States is divided into 11 judicial circuits, and each circuit has a court of appeals. The states and territories are grouped in 11 circuits. The District of Columbia—because it is the place of origin of many appeals involving federal agencies—constitutes a separate circuit. By 1981 there were 132 appeals court judges.

U.S. courts of appeals have *appellate jurisdiction*. This means that they hear appeals from the district courts within their circuits. They also hear appeals from the legal decisions of federal departments, agencies, and regulatory commissions. Cases are usually heard by three-judge panels. An important case, however, may be decided by all the appeals judges of the circuit sitting together.

The Supreme Court is the top layer of the federal judiciary. It has both original and appellate jurisdiction. Very few cases arise under its original jurisdiction—namely, cases

Cases involving maritime law are handled by the federal courts.

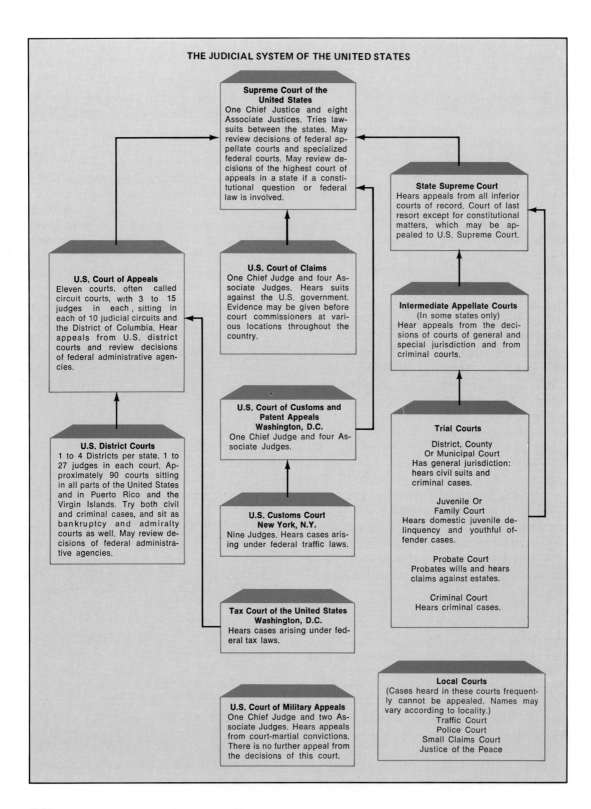

THE JUDICIAL SYSTEM OF THE UNITED STATES

Supreme Court of the United States
One Chief Justice and eight Associate Justices. Tries lawsuits between the states. May review decisions of federal appellate courts and specialized federal courts. May review decisions of the highest court of appeals in a state if a constitutional question or federal law is involved.

State Supreme Court
Hears appeals from all inferior courts of record. Court of last resort except for constitutional matters, which may be appealed to U.S. Supreme Court.

U.S. Court of Appeals
Eleven courts, often called circuit courts, with 3 to 15 judges in each, sitting in each of 10 judicial circuits and the District of Columbia. Hear appeals from U.S. district courts and review decisions of federal administrative agencies.

U.S. Court of Claims
One Chief Judge and four Associate Judges. Hears suits against the U.S. government. Evidence may be given before court commissioners at various locations throughout the country.

Intermediate Appellate Courts
(In some states only)
Hear appeals from the decisions of courts of general and special jurisdiction and from criminal courts.

U.S. District Courts
1 to 4 Districts per state. 1 to 27 judges in each court. Approximately 90 courts sitting in all parts of the United States and in Puerto Rico and the Virgin Islands. Try both civil and criminal cases, and sit as bankruptcy and admiralty courts as well. May review decisions of federal administrative agencies.

U.S. Court of Customs and Patent Appeals Washington, D.C.
One Chief Judge and four Associate Judges.

Trial Courts

District, County Or Municipal Court
Has general jurisdiction: hears civil suits and criminal cases.

Juvenile Or Family Court
Hears domestic juvenile delinquency and youthful offender cases.

Probate Court
Probates wills and hears claims against estates.

Criminal Court
Hears criminal cases.

U.S. Customs Court New York, N.Y.
Nine Judges. Hears cases arising under federal traffic laws.

Tax Court of the United States Washington, D.C.
Hears cases arising under federal tax laws.

Local Courts
(Cases heard in these courts frequently cannot be appealed. Names may vary according to locality.)
Traffic Court
Police Court
Small Claims Court
Justice of the Peace

U.S. Court of Military Appeals
One Chief Judge and two Associate Judges. Hears appeals from court-martial convictions. There is no further appeal from the decisions of this court.

involving ambassadors and foreign diplomats and disputes between two states or between a state and the federal government.

All other cases involve the Supreme Court's appellate jurisdiction. The Supreme Court concentrates on interpreting the law for the guidance of lower courts. Much of its time is devoted to settling conflicts between two or more courts of appeals regarding the meaning of federal statutes.

The Supreme Court also supervises the federal court system by prescribing procedural rules for conducting court business. Besides its supervisory responsibility, the Supreme Court is the only court that is empowered to review state court decisions on issues arising under the Constitution.

Jurisdiction of the Federal Courts. In addition to the original jurisdiction of the Supreme Court, Article 3 of the Constitution extends the "judicial power" of the United States to four kinds of cases:
1. cases involving the Constitution, laws, and treaties of the United States;
2. cases pertaining to admiralty and maritime law;
3. controversies to which the United States is a party; and
4. controversies between citizens of different states.

Federal district courts and courts of appeals—as well as the Supreme Court—have jurisdiction over these cases.

Civil and Criminal Cases. Most federal court decisions involve civil cases. Such cases usually concern disputes in which one party claims damages against another party for some harm suffered. If the case invokes the jurisdiction of the federal courts because the plaintiff and the defendant are citizens of different states (diverse citizenship), the federal court usually applies the law of the state in which the alleged harm occurred. These cases are called *diversity of citizenship* cases. Federal courts will hear such cases only

when the amount in dispute exceeds $10,000.

Other civil cases in the federal courts usually involve federal questions—disputes claiming some right under the Constitution or federal statutes. For example, a small company may sue a large company for attempting to monopolize an industry. This violates the provisions of the federal antitrust laws. The federal government may sue a private citizen or a corporation for civil violations of the law or for damage to government property. The federal government may also be a defendant in civil suits involving tax or personal injury claims.

Criminal cases involve the commission of an act that Congress has made a federal crime and for which it has provided punishment. Defendants in federal criminal cases are protected not only by the Bill of Rights but also by those guarantees enumerated by the Supreme Court in recent years, including the right to counsel at public expense.

Despite these rights, most defendants plead guilty. To secure a guilty plea and thereby avoid the time, expense, and uncertainty of a jury trial, the United States attorney or members of his or her staff, who prosecute cases for the government in the district courts, may agree with the defendant's lawyer to plead the defendant guilty to a less serious charge. A "less serious charge" usually means an offense that carries a lower maximum sentence. (This negotiation between the prosecutor and the defendant's lawyer is called *plea bargaining.)*

The Case or Controversy Requirement. Federal judges decide only those issues that arise from actual disputes or real controversies between parties or—in a criminal case—after an individual has been charged with a crime. A contrived suit to test the constitutionality of a law may be thrown out of court if the contrivance is discovered. Such a case, involving no dispute between two parties, would amount to a "friendly suit,"

Would an accident of this nature prompt the victim to file a civil suit? How would he be justified in doing so?

which is contrary to the adversary system. Moreover, one cannot merely challenge the constitutionality of a criminal law unless one is actually willing to violate the law and risk going to jail.

In addition to the case requirement, a person may bring suit in a federal court only if he or she has sustained or is in danger of sustaining a direct and substantial injury. This requirement of *standing* confers eligibility to sue. Thus a factory worker whose health is impaired by toxic fumes produced by the factory in which he or she works may have standing to sue, but a member of the surrounding community who breathes air contaminated by such fumes may not have standing.

Recently Congress and the Supreme Court have broadened the standing require-

ment to permit court challenges on behalf of protecting the environment or the consumer, known as *class-action suits*. The National Environmental Protection Act of 1969 and various civil rights statutes prohibiting discrimination in employment are among several laws that enable whole classes of people to sue in federal courts.

section review

1. What kinds of cases are tried in district courts?
2. Define the term "appellate jurisdiction."
3. What is a diverse citizenship case? When do federal courts hear such a case?
4. Explain the concept of plea bargaining. How is it used in court?

3. APPOINTMENT OF FEDERAL JUDGES

Because federal judges hold office for life, a President, through judicial appointments, can leave a mark on the judiciary long after leaving office.

For example, between his defeat in November 1800 and Jefferson's inauguration in March 1801, John Adams did all that he could to entrench fellow Federalists in federal judgeships—some of them ("midnight judges") especially created for that purpose on the eve of Adams' departure from office. Among others, he appointed Secretary of State John Marshall to be Chief Justice of the United States; Marshall served for 34 years.

The Jeffersonians were unable to impeach Adams' judges, but by using Congress' constitutional authority to determine the structure and the jurisdiction of the federal courts, they did abolish the circuit courts that the Federalist Congress created before it left office.

The Influence of Politics. When Franklin Roosevelt entered the White House after 12 years of Republican control, he found that 90 percent of all federal judges were Republicans. During his presidency FDR appointed 203 Democrats and 8 Republicans to the federal bench. Truman appointed 129 Democrats and 13 Republicans.

Eisenhower, continuing the partisan selection process, appointed 11 Democrats and 176 Republicans. Kennedy, Johnson, Nixon, Ford, and Carter followed the same partisan tradition. Kennedy appointed no Republicans to his first 85 judicial vacancies, and none of President Carter's first 31 choices was a Republican.

Partisan selection does not guarantee that a judge will serve the President or the party's interest. John Sirica, a Republican, was named to the federal bench by Dwight Eisenhower, a Republican President, in 1957.

NUMBER OF FEDERAL JUDGES APPOINTED AS POLITICAL PATRONAGE		
	Democrats	Republicans
Roosevelt	203	8
Truman	129	13
Eisenhower	11	176
Kennedy	113	11
Johnson	170	11
Nixon	18	220
Ford	12	51
*Carter	31	6

*as of May 1, 1978

Federal judge John Sirica did not play partisan politics in the Watergate incident.

Even so, Sirica's legal standards led him to expose and punish those responsible for the Watergate coverup. His decisions in turn contributed to the resignation of a Republican President.

The Influence of Senators. When either or both of the senators from the state in which a federal district judge is to be appointed are of the President's party, one or both senators submit a list of prospective candidates to the Justice Department. The deputy attorney general usually selects from the list the person whom the Justice De-

J. SKELLY WRIGHT

James Skelly Wright, currently a judge in the U.S. Court of Appeals for the District of Columbia circuit, is a liberal southerner who has been in the center of controversy for the past 20 years. He was born in New Orleans in 1911, and he later taught high school there. It was in New Orleans that he first attained nationwide prominence when, as U.S. district court judge for eastern Louisiana, he ordered the city's schools to integrate in 1960. This was the first court-ordered racial integration in the Deep South. In response to his decree, 100 White citizens marched into the state capitol behind a coffin bearing the blackened, singed effigy of Judge Wright. Wright was forced to accept round-the-clock police protection. A segregationist governor guided the state legislature through a special session, passing numerous resolutions aimed at getting around Wright's edict, but Wright countered every new law with a restraining order, and he finally enjoined the governor and the entire legislature from interfering with integration.

When Wright left New Orleans in 1962 to serve in a higher post in Washington, D.C., he expressed sadness that New Orleans had failed to educate its people "to the social change of the twentieth century." He emphasized his belief that the Constitution should be interpreted not in reference to the time it was written but rather "in reference to the present, or better still, the future." In 1967 Wright once again made headlines, in a case involving integration of the Washington, D.C., school system. In a city with a 93 percent Black enrollment (surrounded by suburbs with a reverse ratio of Whites), Wright ruled that de facto segregation (caused by housing) was unconstitutional, thus paving the way for later court-ordered busing.

Wright has always insisted, "The Bill of Rights protects all of us or none of us." His experience in the Washington courts has convinced him that "crime in the streets is primarily slum-produced crime." Of his concern for the rights of accused persons he has written, "A government that provides a police state for its poor so that the rest of us can breathe the fresh air of freedom is not long for this twentieth-century world."

Wright once said that he would be "unpredictable" as a judge, and in the 1970's his rulings were for stricter regulations on strip mining, but against them on air pollution. This confused environmentalists, but it proved, as "Newsweek" said, that "whatever his personal views, he has scrupulously followed the letter and spirit of the law."

partment prefers and sends his or her name to the President, who then nominates the candidate.

The rule of senatorial courtesy makes it almost impossible for the President to gain Senate confirmation if senators from the President's party oppose the Chief Executive's appointments of district judges within their states. When neither senator from the state belongs to the President's party or when a vacancy appears on the court of appeals, the Justice Department's discretion is much greater. A judicial circuit covers several states, and no senator can play more than an advisory role.

The Influence of the Bar. Lawyers in big city law firms are often reluctant to give up their lucrative practices for the relatively modest income of a federal judge. Studies of the background of federal judges show that they tend to come from small towns, varied practices, and small law firms. They are likely also to have served as district attorneys or in some other law-connected public offices.

Lawyer politicians, lawyers with varied, general practices, and lawyers with criminal law experience may have more understanding of the cases that a federal judge confronts than do corporate lawyers. But the American Bar Association's Committee on the Federal Judiciary, which rates the qualifications of nominees as "exceptionally well qualified," "well qualified," "qualified," or "not qualified," is more likely to give its top rating to corporate trial lawyers.

Presidents need not follow the American Bar Association recommendation. They may prefer to give more weight to party service, strong senatorial backing, or the need for more women or minority-group members on the federal bench. Presidents Eisenhower and Nixon pledged not to nominate candidates whom the bar committee rejected. Other Presidents have been unwilling to make that commitment but have hesitated to nominate anyone rated "not qualified."

Removal of Federal Judges. Because they hold office under the Constitution during good behavior, federal judges remain on the bench until they resign, retire, die, or are impeached. Only four federal judges have ever been removed from office after impeachment trials in the Senate. Charges of impeachment were voted by the House of Representatives against five others, but none was convicted by the Senate.

Judges' Salaries. Congress sets salaries for all federal officials, including judges. In practice the President's salary recommendations take effect unless Congress rejects them. In 1981 district court judges received $67,100, court of appeals judges received $70,900, associate justices of the Supreme Court earned $81,300, and the Chief Justice was paid $92,400.

SALARIES OF FEDERAL JUDGES*			
Court	Number of Judges	Term of Office	Salary
Supreme Court	9	Life	$88,700**
Court of Appeals	97	Life	70,900
District Courts	403	Life	67,100
Court of Claims	7	Life	70,900
Customs Court	9	Life	67,100
Court of Customs and Patent Appeals	5	Life	70,900
Tax Court of U.S.	16	12 years	67,100
Court of Military Appeals	3	15 years	70,900

*As of 1981   **Chief Justice's salary is $92,400

Judges of the customs and tax courts earn the same salaries as those paid to district court judges. Judges of the court of military appeals, the court of customs and patent appeals, and the court of claims receive the same compensation as that given to court of appeals judges.

Judges who have served for at least ten years may retire at age 70 and receive their full salaries for the rest of their lives. They may also retire at full salary at age 65 if they have served 15 years on the federal bench. This generous retirement program was instituted in 1937 to induce aging, anti-New Deal judges to retire so that FDR could choose younger justices more likely to uphold his programs.

Judges as Lawmakers. Since the school desegregation case of 1954, the federal courts have become involved in a broad range of decisions that affect public policy. Federal courts have become involved in countless areas of public policy that seemed beyond their scope a generation ago—for example, education, school admissions, personnel management, construction, hiring, promotion, advertising, and the location of power plants, highways, and trails.

Judges make law every time they interpret and apply statutes in concrete situations. Like administrators, federal judges give meaning to such broad statutory terms as "reasonable care," "safe working conditions," and "environmental harm." Congress

Suits charging discrimination in employment are in the jurisdiction of federal courts.

equal employment opportunity is the law

igualdad de oportunidad en el empleo es la ley

Private Industry, State, and Local Government

Title VII of the Civil Rights Act of 1964, as amended, prohibits job discrimination because of race, color, religion, sex or national origin.

Applicants to and employees of private employers, state/local governments, and public/private educational institutions are protected. Also covered are employment agencies, labor unions and apprenticeship programs. Any person who believes he or she has been discriminated against should contact immediately

The U. S. Equal Employment Opportunity Commission (EEOC)

Industrias Privadas, Gobiernos Locales y Estatales

El Título VII de la Ley de Derechos Civiles de 1964 enmendado, prohíbe la discriminación en el empleo por razón de raza, color, religión, sexo o nacionalidad de origen.

La ley protege a los empleados y solicitantes de empleo en empresas privadas, gobiernos estatales y locales e instituciones educacionales públicas y privadas. También abarca las agencias de empleo, sindicatos de trabajadores y programas de aprendizaje. Cualquier persona, tanto hombre como mujer, que crea que ha sido objeto de discriminación debe escribir inmediatamente a

The U. S. Equal Employment Opportunity

as well as state and local legislatures use broad terms because legislators cannot predict every situation to which their laws will apply.

Moreover, the Constitution contains a host of general terms, such as "due process of law," "equal protection of the laws," and "unreasonable searches and seizures." Judges cannot avoid making law every time they seek to apply these terms to the cases that they are hearing.

All judges make laws in different ways. Each judge brings his or her knowledge, background, practical experience, and personal beliefs to bear on every interpretation of a law that he or she makes. Judges may or may not give equal respect to both sides. Some judges regularly take the side of one of the adversaries; for example, they all sympathize with labor in labor-management disputes. Other judges always take the management viewpoint. Many judges are liberal— or *broad constructionists* of the Constitution—in some areas and conservative—or *strict constructionists,*—in other areas.

QUOTES from famous people

"The interpretation of the laws is the proper and peculiar province of the Courts. A Constitution is, in fact, and must be regarded by the judges as, a fundamental law. It therefore belongs to them to ascertain its meaning as well as the meaning of any particular act proceeding from the legislative body. If there should happen to be an irreconcilable variance between the two, that·which has the superior obligation and validity ought, of course, to be preferred; or, in other words, the Constitution ought to be preferred to the statute, the intention of the people to the intention of their agents."

Alexander Hamilton

section review

1. What is the influence of politics in the selection of federal judges?
2. How can the American Bar Association influence the nomination of judges?
3. What is the term of office for federal judges? How can they be removed from office?
4. Why was a retirement program for federal judges instituted? What are the provisions of the program?
5. What is meant by "broad constructionist"?

4. ADMINISTERING THE FEDERAL COURT SYSTEM

The judicial branch has always operated with very little staff and support services. Each federal court has a clerk who keeps all court records and employs deputy clerks, stenographers, and bailiffs (who maintain order in each courtroom). Every district court also has a United States marshal, who is a presidential appointee. The marshal and his or her deputies make arrests in federal criminal cases, maintain custody over accused persons, protect jurors, serve legal papers, and carry out all orders of the court.

Each district court usually has one or more United States magistrates (called commissioners in some districts). United States magistrates are special officers appointed by the district judge. Magistrates must be trained lawyers and must serve for four or eight years. They issue search and arrest warrants, determine whether there is enough evidence to hold accused persons for indictment, and try minor criminal cases.

Other district court officers include one or more **referees** and **probation officers.** The chief judge of the district usually acts as the administrative manager of the court and its personnel.

U.S. marshals escort Patty Hearst (center), an alleged member of a group of militant radicals, to court during her trial for bank robbery.

the district courts. United States attorneys are appointed by the President with the consent of the Senate to four-year terms. Senatorial courtesy also plays a strong role in the nomination process. United States attorneys have considerable power, and these posts often lead to higher office. United States attorneys are officials of the Department of Justice and are responsible to the attorney general.

Besides prosecuting persons accused of federal crimes, United States attorneys initiate civil suits on behalf of the federal government and defend the government when suits are brought against it in district courts.

Arranging Court Workloads. The 11 courts of appeals are generally responsible for the work of the district courts within their geographic areas. The judges of each court of appeals constitute a judicial council that assigns work among the several district courts and may restrict assignments of particular judges who seem too old or disabled to carry out the work (but who refuse to retire).

The chief judge of each court of appeals calls an annual conference of all the judges in the circuit to plan the year's work schedule.

Referees are persons, usually lawyers, appointed by the court to conduct hearings on particular matters (principally bankruptcy proceedings) and to report their findings to the court.

Probation officers are officers of the court who supervise persons who have been released early from their terms in prison because of good behavior.

Earlier it was noted that the United States attorney for each district and his or her staff are responsible for prosecuting cases in

The Judicial Conference of the United States. The Chief Justice of the United States administers the federal court system. The Chief Justice presides over the judicial conference of the United States, which is composed of the chief judge of each of the 11 circuit courts of appeals plus one district judge from each circuit. The conference recommends rules of procedure to be followed by the federal courts. These rules become effective unless rejected by either house of Congress.

The director of the Administrative Office of the United States Courts assists the judicial conference with the business and finances of the federal court system.

section review

1. Describe the duties of United States marshals and magistrates.
2. How do United States attorneys obtain their jobs? What are their responsibilities?
3. What is the composition of the judicial conference of the United States? What is its function?

5. SPECIAL FEDERAL COURTS

In addition to the federal district courts and the courts of appeals, which have general jurisdiction over federal, civil, and criminal matters, Congress has used its power (under Article 3 of the Constitution) to establish three special courts—the court of claims, the customs court, and the court of customs and patent appeals.

The seven-judge court of claims has jurisdiction over all damage suits brought against the United States. The court sits in Washington but sends commissioners to take evidence all over the country.

The customs court consists of nine judges who hear disputes involving the administration of the tariff laws. Most of its cases review decisions made by officials in the Treasury Department's Customs Bureau. This court works in panels of three judges and tries cases in major port cities such as New York and San Francisco.

Decisions made by the customs court may be appealed to the five-member court of customs and patent appeals, which also reviews patent and trademark decisions of the

Patent Office and rulings of the United States Tariff Commission concerning unfair import practices.

Like other federal judges, the judges of these three special courts are appointed for life.

Legislative Courts. Congress has also created various courts to carry out legislative powers (Article 1 of the Constitution) rather than judicial powers (Article 3). Judges of these "legislative" courts are appointed for fixed terms rather than for life.

Courts in this category include:

1. the U.S. court of military appeals, composed of three civilian judges who are appointed to 15-year terms by the President with the consent of the Senate. This court reviews court martial convictions and applies military law. Military courts grant accused persons many of the due process rights granted by the Constitution.

2. the tax court, which hears appeals in civil suits involving the tax laws. This court consists of 16 judges who are appointed for 12-year terms by the President with the consent of the Senate.

3. courts in United States territories and the District of Columbia that deal with matters of local jurisdiction. These courts function like state courts rather than federal courts.

section review

1. What special courts were established under the Constitution? Describe the jurisdiction of each court.
2. List the courts created through the legislative powers of Congress.
3. What is the term of office for judges of the legislative courts?

CHAPTER SUMMARY

29

Article 3 of the U.S. Constitution vests the judicial power of the United States in "one Supreme Court and in such inferior courts as the Congress may . . . establish."

The major job of all courts is to apply law to the facts through an orderly procedure and established rules of evidence. Federal courts consider cases involving 1) the Constitution or federal statutes, 2) common law, 3) equity, or 4) administrative law. American justice is based on an adversary system: a belief that truth emerges when each side presents its case as vigorously as possible.

There are three layers in the federal judicial system: ninety district courts, eleven courts of appeals, and the Supreme Court. The Supreme Court interprets law for future guidance of the lower courts, prescribes procedural rules, and supervises the work of all federal courts.

The Constitution extends the judicial power of the United States to four kinds of cases: 1) cases arising under the Constitution, laws, and treaties of the United States; 2) cases under admiralty and maritime law; 3) controversies to which the United States is a party; 4) controversies between citizens of different states. Most federal court time is spent on civil, rather than criminal, cases.

All matters before the courts must meet two requirements: 1) be real cases, i.e., arise from actual disputes or controversies between parties, and 2) the complainant must have standing, i.e., suffer direct and substantial injury. Recent statutes and court decisions have broadened the standing requirement to allow challenges on behalf of the environment or the consumer. These are called class actions.

In addition to the three major levels of federal courts, the Constitution names three special courts: court of claims, customs court, and court of customs and patent appeals.

Three other courts handle cases arising from the exercise of particular congressional powers: court of military appeals, tax court, and courts in U.S. territories and the District of Columbia.

REVIEW QUESTIONS

1. What is the main job of a judge?
2. To what extent do the federal courts make law?
3. What is a real case? Why do courts hear only those controversies that involve real cases?
4. What is a class action suit? Why have class action suits been permitted more often in recent years? Do you think they should be? Why or why not?
5. Some judges are "broad" constructionists; others are "strict" constructionists. What is the basic difference between these two interpretations? Which do you think is more appropriate? Why?
6. What courts did Congress create?

ACTIVITIES FOR REVIEW

activity 1   Research a recent example of a class action suit. What are the basic elements of the case? What are the main arguments of the respective sides? How was the case decided? On what basis? Do you agree with the decision? Why or why not?

activity 2   Prepare a wall chart illustrating the organization of and types of cases handled by the federal judiciary.

activity 3   Research various court-related careers such as those of bailiff, court reporter, clerk. Prepare a job description including responsibilities, opportunities for advancement, training required, salary and fringe benefits. Explain why you would or would not be interested in court-related employment.

political science DICTIONARY

administrative law—a body of principles and precedents used in federal cases.   p. 566

appellate jurisdiction—authority of U.S. courts of appeals to hear appeals from the district courts within their circuits.   p. 567

broad constructionists—judges who favor a liberal interpretation of the Constitution when deciding a case.   p. 575

civil cases—private disputes in which the plaintiff seeks money or property from the defendant.   p. 566

common law—law made by judges rather than legislatures. It is based on earlier decisions by the courts.   p. 566

equity—a body of rules applied when the law offers no remedy.   p. 566

injunction—a court order that prohibits certain actions.   p. 566

precedent—an action that serves as a guide for later similar actions.   p. 566

probation officers—officers of the court who supervise prisoners released on parole.   p. 576

referees—persons, usually lawyers, appointed by the court to conduct hearings on particular matters.   p. 576

strict constructionists—judges who favor a conservative interpretation of the Constitution when deciding a case.   p. 575

30

The Supreme Court and the Justices

The United States Supreme Court is the highest court in the land. It has the power to correct legal errors made by lower federal courts. The Supreme Court also has the power of judicial review—the power to declare the laws of Congress and the actions of the executive branch unconstitutional. Congress can reverse the Supreme Court's interpretation of the Constitution only by constitutional amendment. The power of judicial review extends to state and local governments as well.

Today the Court has become the defender of civil liberties, economic freedoms, and civil rights. By announcing national interpretations of federal laws to guide lower courts, the Supreme Court participates in lawmaking in almost every area of public policy from free speech to welfare rights.

CHAPTER PREVIEW

1. THE COURT AND THE CONSTITUTION
2. CHECKS AND BALANCES
3. THE SELECTION OF SUPREME COURT JUSTICES
4. THE SUPREME COURT AND PUBLIC POLICY

1. THE COURT AND THE CONSTITUTION

The Constitution's framers sought to make the national government supreme over the states. The supremacy clause in Article 6 of the Constitution states, "This Constitution, and the laws of the United States which shall be made in pursuance thereof . . . shall be the supreme law of the land; and the judges in every state shall be bound thereby, anything in the Constitution or laws of any state to the contrary notwithstanding."

The only court mentioned in the Constitution is the Supreme Court. The framers believed that the Supreme Court was necessary to maintain national supremacy, to interpret national laws, and to resolve controversies among the states. The absence of such judicial power was one of the major weaknesses of the central government under the Articles of Confederation.

Marbury v. Madison. The case of *Marbury v. Madison* originated as a footnote to the struggle between the Federalists and the Jeffersonians. Before leaving the presidency John Adams sought to protect the country against Jeffersonian democracy by establishing as many new judicial posts as possible and filling them with Federalists. To one such post—as a justice of the peace for the District of Columbia—he appointed William Marbury.

Adams' Secretary of State, John Marshall—who had been appointed and confirmed as Chief Justice of the United States—continued to serve as head of the State Department until the night before Jefferson's inauguration. Adams had signed commissions for the new judges, and Marshall had sealed and delivered all but a few. Marbury's was one of the few commissions that had not been delivered when the new Secretary of State, James Madison, took office.

Madison refused to deliver the commissions. Marbury petitioned the United States Supreme Court for a *writ of mandamus*—that is, a court order instructing that a specific act or duty be carried out—in this case an order compelling Secretary of State Madison to deliver his commission. In the Judiciary Act of 1789, Congress had authorized the Supreme Court to issue such writs.

The Supreme Court was in a quandary. If Chief Justice Marshall issued the writ, it would almost certainly be ignored, and the authority of the highest Court would be undermined.

John Marshall served as Chief Justice of the Supreme Court during the years 1801–1835.

The Court declared that Marbury was entitled to his commission and asserted that a writ of mandamus was the appropriate way to compel delivery. Then came the surprise twist: Chief Justice Marshall said that the Court lacked the authority to issue writs of mandamus. Congress had acted unconstitutionally in trying to give the court such authority. In so doing, said Marshall, Congress had sought to expand the Court's original jurisdiction, which was fixed in the Constitution.

This decision left the Jeffersonians helpless. The decision required no writ that they could ignore. They could not attack the Courts for usurping power—on the surface the Court appeared to have given up some of its power. In giving up the negligible power to issue writs of mandamus, however, the Supreme Court asserted the enormous power to declare an act of Congress unconstitutional.

No other act of Congress was declared unconstitutional during Marshall's years as Chief Justice, nor indeed was any act declared unconstitutional until the Dred Scott case in 1857. But the precedent of judicial review had been established. Marshall's reasoning—that the Supreme Court had the constitutional authority to interpret the Constitution—was firmly planted into the nation's consciousness.

Marshall's court did find more than one state law unconstitutional. The power to invalidate state law seems inherent in the idea of a strong national government. Justice Oliver Wendell Holmes observed many years later, "I do not think the United States would come to an end if we lost our power to declare an act of Congress void. I do think the Union would be imperiled if we could not make that declaration as to the laws of the several states."

The Supreme Court's power of judicial review enables it to maintain boundaries among the three branches of the federal government and between the nation and the states. The Supreme Court has tried to use its power of judicial review very carefully. Justice Louis Brandeis asserted that the Court does not consider whether a law is constitutional unless there are no other grounds for deciding the case.

The slave Dred Scott sued for his freedom in 1846. The Supreme Court ruled that as a slave Scott was not a U.S. citizen and therefore not entitled to sue. Do you remember the other circumstances in the Dred Scott case?

QUOTES from famous people

"It is not the habit of the Courts to decide questions of a constitutional nature unless absolutely necessary to a decision of the case . . . the Court will not pass upon a constitutional question, although properly presented by the record, if there is also present some other ground upon which the case may be disposed of."

Justice Louis Brandeis

Legislative Review. Most of the Supreme Court's time is spent in deciding what the language of a particular law means rather than in reviewing its constitutionality. Many congressional statutes covering a whole range of public policies—including labor relations, economic regulations, social welfare, and environmental protection—are reviewed by the Supreme Court. The Court's interpretations and applications of these laws have a profound effect on public policy, as will be seen later.

section review

1. Why did the framers of the Constitution establish a Supreme Court?
2. Define "writ of mandamus." In the case of *Marbury* v. *Madison*, what was Chief Justice Marshall's opinion on the writ?
3. In reviewing legislation, what takes up most of the Supreme Court's time?

2. CHECKS AND BALANCES

To carry out its decisions the Supreme Court must rely on the cooperation of other actors in the political process. When the Court's decisions do not receive popular support, officials can blunt the force of these decisions. If the Court is out of step with the people, lower federal courts may try to apply the Court's rulings in the narrowest possible way. Congress may consider overruling a Court decision by constitutional amendment. The President may try to change the Court's direction by filling vacancies with people whose views differ from those of the existing majority of judges.

Congress and the Supreme Court. Congress can check the Supreme Court in four ways. These checks have been used very rarely, for none is easy to accomplish. Congress can propose a constitutional amendment to overrule the Court's interpretation of the Constitution; it can change the Court's size and jurisdiction; the Senate can reject the President's Supreme Court nominees; and Congress can impeach members of the Supreme Court.

No Supreme Court justice has ever been convicted on impeachment charges. Associate Justice Samuel Chase was impeached by the House of Representatives in 1804 for alleged political bias. He was narrowly acquitted by the Senate, and he remained on the Court for the rest of his life. His acquittal by the Senate discouraged further attempts to impeach justices for political reasons.

The Court has been overruled only once by constitutional amendment. The Court had declared the income tax unconstitutional. Through the Sixteenth Amendment Congress established its power to levy such taxes.

The Constitution authorizes Congress to determine the size and the jurisdiction of the Supreme Court. Theoretically Congress could reduce the Court to two members (the Constitution speaks only of Supreme Court "judges") or it could expand its membership. Expansion of the Court's membership to 15 was what FDR proposed and Congress rejected in 1937.

Over the course of American history, the Court has had as few as five members and as many as ten. In 1866 Congress reduced the size of the Court from nine to seven members to prevent President Andrew Johnson from filling two vacancies. The previous size was restored during the Grant administration in 1869 and has remained at nine members.

Congress determines the Supreme Court's *appellate jurisdiction*—that is, the kinds of appeals from lower federal courts that the Supreme Court may hear. Theoretically Congress could withdraw all of the Supreme Court's appellate jurisdiction. The Court's jurisdiction was last limited in 1869 when Congress made its Reconstruction Acts unreviewable by the Supreme Court.

During Senate confirmation hearings on a Supreme Court nomination, groups opposing a nominee's views have ample opportunity to discredit that person. If many senators agree, they will be receptive to evidence of inadequacy. In 1969, when President Nixon nominated Judge Clement Haynsworth to fill a Supreme Court vacancy, the Senate had not rejected a Supreme Court nominee in 39 years. The Senate refused to confirm Haynsworth because of objections made by labor and civil rights groups and questions raised about certain financial transactions.

Approval of Nixon's second nominee,

Clement Haynsworth, President Nixon's appointee to the Supreme Court, was rejected by the Senate in 1969.

Judge Harrold Carswell, was then thought to be assured. The Senate had never rejected two nominees in succession. But the same labor and civil rights groups objected, and proved that Carswell had drawn up the charter for a racially segregated club. Carswell's nomination was not helped when one of his Senate supporters observed that Carswell might have been mediocre but asserted that "there are a lot of mediocre judges and people and lawyers. They are entitled to a little representation, aren't they?" A majority of senators disagreed, and Carswell, too, was rejected.

The President and the Supreme Court. In 1795 a group of land speculators bribed the Georgia legislature to give them Cherokee land from which much of Alabama was formed. After Alabama was admitted as a state, the Cherokees brought a suit in federal court to nullify the action of the Georgia legislature.

When the case came before the Supreme Court, Chief Justice Marshall ordered that the

The Navahos will not be displaced. They expect to achieve higher economic status because rich natural resources have been discovered on their lands.

land be returned to the Cherokees. President Andrew Jackson reportedly said, "John Marshall has made his order. Now let him enforce it." Political realities as well as the government's policy of displacing Native Americans to Oklahoma caused the Supreme Court's order to be ignored.

Relations between the President and the Supreme Court are usually not so quarrelsome. The Court is politically sensitive, and most Presidents are unwilling to provoke constitutional crises.

Because Supreme Court justices hold office for life, some are likely to reflect the views of past political eras. A President's primary device for changing the probable

PATRICIA M. WALD

Patricia M. Wald became a judge on the U.S. Circuit Court of Appeals for the District of Columbia in 1979. This court hears most appeals from district courts and federal administrative agencies; it also reviews the decisions of some agencies.

Wald was born in Torrington, Connecticut in 1928. She is married and has five children. Wald graduated Phi Beta Kappa from the Connecticut College for Women in 1948, and Yale Law School in 1951.

After graduation from law school Wald started to establish her career. Her first law-related job was that of law clerk for Judge Jerome Frank, U.S. Court of Appeals for the Second Circuit, in 1951. Slowly she started to move up—she was an associate, an attorney, and prior to her new position she was Assistant Attorney General for Legislative Affairs in the Department of Justice. She held many other positions as well in the course of her career. She was a member of the National Conference on Bail and Criminal Justice (1963), the President's Commission on Law Enforcement and Administration of Criminal Justice (1966), Co-Director of the Ford Foundation Drug Abuse Research Project (1970), and Director of Office of Policy and Issues for Sargent Shriver's vice-presidential campaign in 1972.

Wald has written extensively on many legal problems, especially on problems dealing with juvenile rights. Her first publication was in 1964; she co-authored *Bail in the United States.* Her other writings include *New Vistas for the Juvenile Court* (1968), *Law and the Grievances of the Poor* (1969), *Dealing with Drug Abuse—A Report to the Ford Foundation* (1972), *The Right to Education* (1974), *Advocacy for the Mentally Retarded Offender* (1975), and *The Politics of Mental Health Advocacy in the United States* (1978).

Wald is outspoken on many controversial issues. Many Republicans and conservatives opposed her nomination because they felt that her views on the rights of children, the mentally ill, and other oppressed groups were too liberal. In spite of this, however, the Senate confirmed her nomination to the U.S. Circuit Court of Appeals by a vote of 77–21.

direction of the Court is to fill slots with people whose views are compatible with the President's own views.

On the average there is a Supreme Court vacancy every 22 months. Before the end of his third year in office, President Nixon had named four members to the Supreme Court. He had campaigned in 1968 against the judicial activism of Chief Justice Earl Warren's Court and was soon able to carry out his promise to appoint strict constructionists to the Court.

Unlike most Presidents, FDR had to wait more than four years before appointing his first Supreme Court justice. During those four years the Supreme Court—reflecting the previous generation's commitment to laissez-faire—overturned one major New Deal law after another. FDR confronted the challenge by attempting to expand the Court to 15 members. Had Congress acquiesced, the President's six appointees could have allied with the Court's three broad constructionists to produce a new majority.

FDR's court-packing plan provoked a storm of protest. But the controversy lessened when a series of retirements enabled the President to change the direction of the Court. Even before he made his first appointment, the threat of expanding the Court's size seemed to persuade two "swing" justices to join the three broad constructionists in upholding New Deal legislation.

section review

1. How can lower courts check the Supreme Court's decisions?
2. How can Congress check the Supreme Court's decisions?
3. Who determines the size of the Supreme Court?
4. What is meant by "Congress can determine the Supreme Court's appellate jurisdiction"?
5. What can a President do to change the direction of the Court?

3. THE SELECTION OF SUPREME COURT JUSTICES

Politics has always governed Supreme Court appointments. Political selections can have a far-reaching effect: Although the Federalists won their only national victory in 1796, Federalist Chief Justice John Marshall continued to lead the Supreme Court until his death in 1835.

Marshall's successor, Roger B. Taney, served almost 29 years and expressed the views of his political generation—states' rights, in contrast to Marshall's nationalism. Even though the union was threatened with secession and his health had declined, Taney remained on the bench to prevent Lincoln from nominating a Republican. Taney died toward the end of the Civil War, and Lincoln appointed Salmon P. Chase—an extreme abolitionist—as his successor.

William O. Douglas, who served on the Supreme Court for 36 years, was appointed by FDR in 1939. He served for 30 years after the death of the President who appointed him.

Partly because Supreme Court justices can represent a President for many years after that President leaves office, most Chief Executives have regarded Supreme Court nominations as one of their major prerogatives. When a Supreme Court seat becomes vacant, the President is besieged with recommendations. But the Chief Executive usually asks the attorney general to prepare a list of candidates.

Characteristics of Supreme Court Nominees. Characteristics that Presidents and attorneys general usually look for in Supreme Court nominees are membership in the President's party; membership in the President's Cabinet; present or past service in the Department of Justice; distinguished judicial service; high status in the legal profession; and ability to balance the Court's geographic, racial, and religious composition.

Few candidates will possess all of these characteristics. Some Presidents may consider one or two especially important and the others not important at all. Except for his nomination of Chief Justice Earl Warren, whose support had helped him to win the presidential nomination, President Eisenhower appointed sitting judges to the Supreme Court.

By contrast, the first of President Lyndon Johnson's two nominees was his old friend and close adviser Abe Fortas, who had never held judicial office. His second nominee, Thurgood Marshall, was Black and a former civil rights lawyer whom Johnson had elevated to the federal bench and then made

Thurgood Marshall was appointed to the Supreme Court by President Lyndon Johnson in 1967. He is shown here (center) in 1954 with George Hayes (left) and James Nabrit after the three attorneys won the **Brown** v. **Board of Education** *case, in which segregation was ruled unconstitutional.*

solicitor general. Johnson wanted to be remembered as the first President to appoint Blacks both to his Cabinet and to the Supreme Court.

In selecting Supreme Court justices, most Presidents choose nominees whose political values are similar to their own. But the Supreme Court justices, however, are independent and may behave in ways different from what anyone might have expected. All judges are bound by the ethics of the legal profession and the traditions of the bench that require them to judge each case according to precedent. Thus no judge can give free reign to his or her political values. Justices can be persuaded by the arguments of their colleagues and are likely to vote with those whose judicial temperaments resemble their own.

A President may believe that a nominee shares similar attitudes on a number of issues, but it is impossible to predict what the nominee's views will be on the many diverse issues that come before the Court. A justice may agree with the President, for example, on law and order but differ on school busing or welfare rights.

Political analysts have concluded that Presidents have guessed wrong about one time in four. Their nominees did not behave as they expected. President Eisenhower, an advocate of judicial restraint, nominated Chief Justice Earl Warren, who led the most activist Court in recent history. Many "reliable" justices have voted against the Presidents who appointed them. Chief Justice Chase disappointed Lincoln, Justice Oliver Wendell Holmes disagreed with Theodore Roosevelt, and two of Truman's appointees held his wartime steel seizure policies to be unconstitutional.

Judicial Experience. About half of the justices who have been appointed to the Supreme Court have had judicial experience, although only a quarter of them had been judges for five years or more. Many distinguished justices, including ones like John Marshall, Roger Taney, Charles Evans Hughes, Louis Brandeis, Harlan Fiske Stone, Felix Frankfurter, and Earl Warren, had no judicial experience when they were appointed.

There is no reason to believe that judicial experience or even the long practice of law produces abler justices. Most judges deal with specific and technical legal questions, and most lawyers tend to specialize in single areas of the law. By contrast, the Supreme Court deals with an extremely broad range of important public issues and policies. Broad political experience and understanding of public policy may be more helpful than extensive judicial experience. The "ideal" justice is probably one who has both.

The Lawyers' Monopoly. Although the Constitution does not specify that Supreme Court justices must be lawyers, only lawyers have been selected to fill these positions. The process of narrowing the selection is usually entrusted to the attorney general, who is a lawyer. The attorney general often consults with a committee of the American Bar Association, an organization of and for lawyers. Supreme Court nominees must be approved by the Senate Judiciary Committee, which is composed solely of lawyers.

Once justices are appointed, their work is monopolized by lawyers. Only lawyers present arguments before the Supreme Court, and virtually all the materials that justices draw on in writing their opinions—law review articles, legal briefs, and Court decisions—are prepared by lawyers. The opinions themselves are written in legal language and are directed toward a legal audience. Unlike executive and legislative power, the judicial power of the United States is wielded exclusively by lawyers.

The Justices' Backgrounds. Justice Felix Frankfurter once observed that a Supreme Court justice "brings his whole experience, his training, his outlook, his social, intellec-

tual, and moral environment with him when he takes a seat on the Supreme Bench." What kinds of people are appointed to the Court?

Justices are wealthier, better educated, and more socially prominent than are other public servants. As lawyers and judges, they are likely to have earned large incomes. All Supreme Court justices have been male, and all but one have been White. The vast majority have come from middle- or upper-income families. Over 85 percent of Supreme Court justices have been Protestants of English descent.

Frequently other members of Supreme Court justices' families have been active in politics. Before their appointments to the Court, almost all justices held political positions in one of the three branches of the federal government or served as state executives, legislators, or judges.

Just as their political experience helps justices to understand the other branches of government, their shared educational and legal experience gives them a sense of community with the legal profession.

Judicial Attitudes. Most justices have judicial attitudes that consist of a mixture of political outlook and constitutional philosophy. The terms "strict constructionist" and "broad constructionist" express two judicial attitudes. Strict constructionists interpret the Constitution more narrowly, exercise judicial power more modestly, and are less likely than are broad constructionists to interfere with the other two branches of government.

A traditional way of classifying judicial attitudes is to label them conservative or liberal. In general strict constructionists tend to be conservative, and broad constructionists tend to be liberal. But the classification can be misleading. Felix Frankfurter, for example, was an economic and social liberal and a strong supporter of FDR and the New Deal. On the Court, however, he was the model of a strict constructionist.

CHIEF JUSTICES OF THE UNITED STATES

JUSTICE	AGE ON TAKING OFFICE	STATE FROM WHICH APPOINTED	PRESIDENT BY WHOM APPOINTED	YEARS OF SERVICE	DIED
John Jay	44	New York	Washington	1789–1795	1829
John Rutledge[1,2]	55	South Carolina	Washington	1795	1800
Oliver Ellsworth	51	Connecticut	Washington	1796–1800	1807
John Marshall	46	Virginia	John Adams	1801–1835	1835
Roger B. Taney	59	Maryland	Jackson	1836–1864	1864
Salmon P. Chase	56	Ohio	Lincoln	1864–1873	1873
Morrison R. Waite	58	Ohio	Grant	1874–1888	1888
Melville W. Fuller	55	Illinois	Cleveland	1888–1910	1910
Edward D. White[2]	65	Louisiana	Taft	1910–1921	1921
William Howard Taft	64	Connecticut	Harding	1921–1930	1930
Charles Evans Hughes[2]	68	New York	Hoover	1930–1941	1948
Harlan F. Stone[2]	69	New York	F. D. Roosevelt	1941–1946	1946
Fred M. Vinson	56	Kentucky	Truman	1946–1953	1953
Earl Warren	62	California	Eisenhower	1953–1969	1974
Warren E. Burger	61	District of Columbia	Nixon	1969–	–

[1] While Congress was not in session, Rutledge was appointed by President Washington on July 1, 1795. He presided over the August 1795 term of the Supreme Court. The Senate refused confirmation of his appointment on December 15, 1795.

[2] The following four men served as associate justices before being appointed Chief Justice: John Rutledge, 1789–1791; Edward White, 1894–1910; Charles E. Hughes, 1910–1916; and Harlan Stone, 1925–1941. Rutledge was appointed as associate justice in 1789, but resigned a year and a half later, having attended no sessions of the Court. Hughes resigned as associate justice in 1916 in order to seek the presidency. White and Stone were associate justices when appointed Chief Justice.

Judicial attitudes seem to differ when individual freedom clashes with the power of government. Some justices consistently side with individuals, others with the government. Similarly, some of the justices reveal consistently probusiness attitudes, whereas others consistently side with government, labor, consumers, public-interest groups, or private citizens.

Justices identify with one of the two major political parties, usually, although not always, the party of the President who appointed them. Sometimes the development of a judicial attitude changes a justice's political identity.

Earl Warren, a three-term Republican governor of California, a Republican vice-presidential candidate, and an appointee of a Republican President had so changed during his 16 years on the Supreme Court that he tried to retire in time to give a Democratic President (Lyndon Johnson) the opportunity to appoint his successor.

Like Taney and many others who tried to plan their retirements, Earl Warren was unsuccessful. The Senate refused to confirm the person who was nominated to replace him, and Warren agreed to postpone his retirement for a year so that the Court could continue at full strength. The result was that Warren's successor, Warren Burger, was appointed by a Republican President after all. Regardless of their political identities, Supreme Court justices are expected to avoid all partisan activity once they become members of the Supreme Court.

section review

1. What characteristics do Presidents look for in Supreme Court nominees?
2. Who was the first Black to be appointed to the Supreme Court?
3. What single profession has a virtual monopoly on judgeships? Do you agree or disagree with this practice?

4. THE SUPREME COURT AND PUBLIC POLICY

When the Court engages in judicial review, it makes political decisions and affects public policy. It also influences policy when it interprets and applies acts of Congress. Like Congress and the President, the Court is political. Justices make conscious political choices. The main measure of their effectiveness is whether they make decisions that are widely supported.

Certain groups have participated in the policy-making process mainly through court actions—lawsuits. Lawsuits were the main access to policy making for the civil rights movement until the mid-1960's. The remarkable consequence of judicial review is that a law passed by Congress and signed by the President can be nullified at the behest of a single individual or an otherwise powerless minority. For these people a federal lawsuit replaces legislation as an instrument for participating in public policy.

The Court's policies have never been far behind or far ahead of those preferred by a majority of the people. The Court played a major role in shaping economic and social policy during the era of "judicial supremacy" from the 1890's to the late 1930's. Its defense of free enterprise affirmed rather than negated the general political attitudes of that era. Similarly the Court's defense of equal rights for minority groups during the 1950's and 1960's received popular support.

Civil Rights.   The Supreme Court has played a very small role in interpreting most laws and a very large role in reviewing a few. For many years the Supreme Court made most of the decisions in the area of civil rights. The Supreme Court's activities on behalf of Black Americans probably constitute its most significant contribution to American public policy in the post-World War II years.

In 1896 the Supreme Court's decision in *Plessy* v. *Ferguson* gave segregation the legitimacy of constitutional law. The Court's notion of "separate but equal" endured for nearly 60 years. Segregation in restaurants, train stations, hotels, public transportation, and schools was given a solid legal justification.

The landmark 1954 decision in *Brown* v. *Board of Education* reversed the Plessy ruling and declared that "separate is inherently unequal." The Court found that school segregation by race generates in young people a "feeling of inferiority as to their status in the community that may affect their hearts and minds in a way unlikely ever to be undone." Accordingly the Court held that segregation in public schools was an unconstitutional denial of equal protection that must end.

By 1954 a majority of Americans were opposed to legally enforced segregation. But Congress and the President were unwilling to exercise political leadership. The Supreme Court was willing to exercise such leadership. It was also ready to repair the damage that its predecessors had done 58 years before, and to remove the cloak of legitimacy that it had lent to racial segregation. It was only after the Court took its stand on this critical issue of public policy that Congress and the executive branch began to move toward racial equality.

In 1954 the Supreme Court ruled segregation unconstitutional. Prior to this ruling, Blacks were segregated in many public places.

Rights of Accused Persons. The Constitution grants to all persons, especially to those accused of crimes, the following rights: protection against unreasonable searches and seizures (Fourth Amendment); protection against being tried twice for the same offense (Fifth Amendment); the right not to be a witness against oneself (Fifth Amendment); trial by jury (Sixth Amendment); the assistance of counsel in criminal proceedings (Sixth Amendment); protection against cruel and unusual punishments (Eighth Amendment); and protection against the taking of life, liberty, or property without due process of law (Fifth and Fourteenth Amendments).

The Supreme Court has been particularly successful in protecting the rights of accused persons. Until the 1960's the Court largely confined itself to federal criminal law enforcement and imposed rigorous procedural standards on the lower federal courts. It guaranteed defense counsel to those too poor to hire their own, refused to admit illegally obtained evidence at trials, and insisted that prisoners be brought before a judge promptly rather than held secretly by the police.

The first intrusion into state criminal procedures came in the early 1940's when the Court required states to provide all accused persons with a "fair trial." It began to reverse state convictions resulting from trials that violated fundamental freedoms, or *ordered liberties.*

Many states did not comply, and so the Court moved from the fair trial concept to the *selective incorporation* doctrine. This

CONSTITUTIONAL RIGHTS OF AN ARRESTEE

You are under arrest.

You have the right to remain silent. You are not required to say anything to us at any time or to answer any questions. Anything you say can be used against you in court.

You have the right to talk to a lawyer for advice before we question you and to have him or her with you during questioning.

If you cannot afford a lawyer and want one, a lawyer will be provided for you.

If you want to answer questions now without a lawyer present, you will still have the right to stop answering at any time. You also have the right to stop answering until you talk with a lawyer.

---

doctrine imposed on the states several protections of the Bill of Rights by reasoning that the words "due process" in the Fourteenth Amendment could be defined in terms of the Bill of Rights. Therefore those protections were binding on the states. Today virtually all of the rights guaranteed in the Bill of Rights must be accorded to the accused in criminal cases prosecuted by the states.

Judicial Activism and Self-restraint. For 16 years, 1953–1969, the Warren Court played an activist role in the nation's politics. It confronted such controversial issues as race relations, religion in the schools, free speech, the rights of accused persons, voting rights, and reapportionment.

Except for the unanimous decisions in the area of school desegregation, two principal advocates of judicial self-restraint—Justices Frankfurter and Harlan—dissented from most of the controversial decisions in which they took part. Justice Frankfurter expressed his attitude of judicial self-restraint in a famous dissent: "As a member of this Court I am not justified in writing my private notions of policy into the Constitution, no matter how deeply I may cherish them."

Advocates of judicial self-restraint argue that nonelected justices who serve for life and are not responsible to the people should not overrule elected officials except under grave

threats to the Constitution. Legislators and executives should be responsible for determining public policy.

Activists believe that political choice is inherent in judicial decision making and that justices should consciously exercise their power to achieve social justice. Moreover, according to them, the role of the Court in defending constitutional rights is what the framers of the Constitution prescribed—a check on momentary majorities which otherwise would violate the rights and freedoms of minorities.

QUOTES from famous people

"My analysis of the judicial process comes to this . . . : Logic and history, and custom and utility, and the accepted standards of right conduct, are the forces which . . . shape the conduct of the law. Which of these forces will dominate in any case must depend largely on the comparative importance or value of the social interest that will thereby be promoted or impaired. . . . If you ask how [a judge] is to know when one interest outweighs another, I can only answer that he must get his knowledge just as the legislator gets it: . . . from life itself."

Justice Benjamin Cardozo

Many people take a middle position in this debate. They believe that the Supreme Court should interfere as little as possible with economic and social legislation but should not show the same restraint when laws restrict civil rights and liberties. The Constitution does not prohibit social and economic experiments, which can always be reversed. The Constitution does prohibit restrictions on basic liberties, and such restrictions are not easily removed.

The Supreme Court seems to be moving away from activism, but its new directions are not yet clear.

Decisions of the Burger Court. Although less activist than the Warren Court of the 1950's and 1960's, the Burger Court has not avoided controversial issues. By a seven-to-two margin, it declared state antiabortion laws unconstitutional. Two of President Nixon's strict constructionists voted with the majority in that case.

As noted earlier, the Burger Court accepted the case involving Nixon's Watergate tapes and decided against the President with remarkable speed. The Court also reviewed the "Pentagon Papers" case, upheld the newspapers' right to publish those papers,

Pictured are the justices in the Burger Court (1980). Seated, left to right, are Bryon R. White, William J. Brennan, Jr., Chief Justice Warren R. Burger, Potter Stewart, and Thurgood Marshall; standing, left to right, are William H. Rehnquist, Harry A. Blackmun, Lewis F. Powell, and John P. Stevens.

In 1977 people protested having Black students bused to their schools. School desegregation through busing has long been a topic for court rulings.

and rejected the Nixon administration's argument that "publication . . . violated national security."

In the school busing controversy, the Burger Court tried to avoid extreme positions. It favored busing within a community but blocked lower-court decisions seeking to create multiple-county school districts in which suburban White students could be integrated with central-city Black students.

During the 1970's the Court has asserted several constitutional rights never recognized before—the right to travel abroad and the absolute right to citizenship held by people born in the United States. The Court has also affirmed the right of qualified applicants to receive welfare benefits.

The most recently announced constitutional freedom is the right to privacy. This right has been used to restrain state interference with birth control and abortion. The right to privacy may be extended to protect private citizens against government wiretapping and surveillance which has steadily increased through modern technology.

The Supreme Court's 1976-77 decisions highlight the Burger Court's contradictions. The Court seemed to favor vigorous law enforcement but struck down capital punishment. It upheld abortion but permitted states to refuse medicaid assistance to pay for that procedure. It favored equal treatment for both sexes but approved income protection plans that excluded pregnancy.

In other actions the Court has generally upheld the discretionary power of federal administrative agencies and commissions. For example, the Environmental Protection Agency has been sustained in its regulation of pollutants. The broadened power exercised by the Labor Department's Occupational Safety and Health Administration has also been upheld.

The Burger Court's gradual movement away from judicial activism can be observed in its decision upholding a state's power to withhold medicaid funds for abortions. The Court stated: "We leave entirely free the federal government and the states through the normal processes of democracy to provide the necessary funding. The issues present policy decisions of the widest concern. They should be resolved by representatives of the people, not by this Court." (*Beal* v. *Doe,* 1977.)

The late Justice Frankfurter, the principal advocate of judicial self-restraint, would have approved.

The role of the Supreme Court in American government is very important. The Supreme Court acts as a national conscience, ensuring that justice is done.

In 1974, the Supreme Court ordered President Nixon to surrender White House tapes.

section review

1. What idea did the Supreme Court decision in *Plessy* v. *Ferguson* legitimize? How did this decision affect schools?
2. What decision was made by the Court in 1954 in the case of *Brown* v. *Board of Education*?
3. List the rights guaranteed by the Constitution to accused persons.
4. What arguments have been offered by advocates of judicial self-restraint?
5. Who is the present Chief Justice of the Supreme Court?

CHAPTER SUMMARY

30

The Supreme Court is the highest court in the land. It has the power to review all decisions made by lower federal courts and those state court decisions involving the U.S. Constitution. The Supreme Court also has the power of judicial review—the power to declare laws of Congress and actions of the executive branch unconstitutional.

Congress can check the Supreme Court in three major ways: 1) it can propose a Constitutional amendment; 2) it can change the Court's size and jurisdiction; and 3) the Senate can reject the President's Supreme Court nominees.

The typical justice is a White male lawyer from a politically active middle- or upper-class family. He is generally Protestant and of British descent and is wealthier, better educated, and more socially prominent than other public servants.

The qualities most Presidents look for in nominees are leadership in the President's party; membership in the Cabinet; distinguished judicial service; high status in the legal profession; and geographic, racial, ethnic, or religious origins that provide a balance for the Court.

Most Presidents' top priority nominee is a person with similar political values. The ideal justice is probably one who has both wide experience in the law and broad knowledge of politics and society. Supreme Court justices are expected to avoid all partisan activity once they are on the Court.

Justices have a "judicial attitude"—a mixture of political outlook and constitutional philosophy. Strict constructionists interpret the Constitution more narrowly, exercise judicial power more modestly, and are less likely to interfere with the other two branches of government than are broad constructionists.

The Supreme Court has been particularly successful in fashioning government policy to protect the rights of accused persons. It guarantees defense counsel to those too poor to hire their own, refuses to admit illegally obtained evidence at trials, and insists that prisoners be promptly brought before a judge.

REVIEW QUESTIONS

1. What is the relationship between the Supreme Court and the other two branches of the federal government?
2. What did the Founders consider to be the most important function of the federal courts?
3. If you were asked to nominate a federal judge, what qualities would you look for? Would you look for any different qualities in a Supreme Court justice than in a lower court judge? Which ones? Why?
4. What is the relationship between judicial attitudes and Court decisions?

ACTIVITIES FOR REVIEW

activity 1   Research the life of one of the Chief Justices of the Supreme Court. How does he match the "typical" Supreme Court Justice? In what ways does he differ? Why was he appointed? Did his behavior as a Justice seem consistent with the reasons he was appointed—that is, did he behave as expected? Present your findings to the class.

activity 2   Review the case of *Brown* v. *Board of Education of Topeka, Kansas* (1954). What was the basis for the Court's ruling? How was this case a landmark change in the role of the Supreme Court in policy making? Present your findings to the class.

activity 3   Research some issues that you feel the Supreme Court will have to review and make decisions on in the near future. Construct a chart based on these issues and list information under the following headings: ISSUE, IMPORTANT DATES, PEOPLE INVOLVED, POSSIBLE DECISION, EFFECT OF THAT POSSIBLE DECISION.

political science DICTIONARY

ordered liberties—in constitutional law, the concept that due process includes certain minimum standards that are fundamental freedoms.   p. 591

selective incorporation—a doctrine that forces the states to accord to accused persons the protections guaranteed by the Bill of Rights.   p. 592

writ of mandamus—a court order for a specific act or duty to be carried out.   p. 581

31

The Supreme Court at Work

The Supreme Court is both imposing and informal. Its large building contains 16 Greek columns. Its courtroom is relatively small but impressive with its long bench behind which the nine justices sit in black robes in individually designed black leather armchairs.

The Court's proceedings follow a prescribed ritual. Lawyers and reporters await important decisions that are announced on special days and are filled with references to the Constitution, precedents, and the intent of the framers of the Constitution.

The Supreme Court is also informal. This is evident when lawyers present their arguments. The justices lean back in their chairs, often interrupt lawyers with questions, and sometimes converse among themselves. The role of oral argument will be examined later in this chapter.

CHAPTER PREVIEW

1. CHOOSING CASES
2. THE COURT'S WORKLOAD
3. THE POWER OF THE CHIEF JUSTICE
4. IMPLEMENTING THE COURT'S DECISIONS

1. CHOOSING CASES

Aside from the few and infrequent cases that can be brought directly to the Supreme Court (under its original jurisdiction), the vast majority of cases reach the Court on appeal. If either party in a civil case, or the defendant in a criminal case, is dissatisfied with the verdict

The U.S. Supreme Court, located in Washington, D.C., seats nine justices appointed by the President.

of a trial court, he or she can appeal the case to a higher court.

In an appeal the Court does not review the facts of the case. Rather, it examines the record of the trial court to see if any legal error was made in the procedures followed, in the evidence presented, or in any interpre-

tation of law or of the Constitution on which the trial court based its decision.

After a case has been considered by the highest court of a state or by the court of appeals in the federal system, the only appeal that remains is to the Supreme Court. With a few exceptions the Supreme Court chooses

31. The Supreme Court at Work   **599**

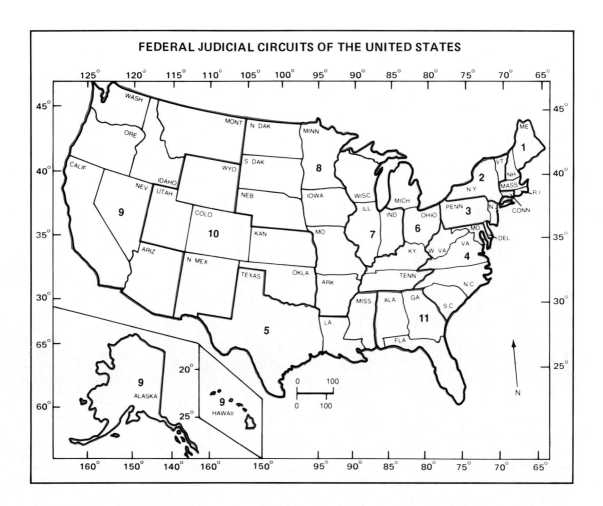

FEDERAL JUDICIAL CIRCUITS OF THE UNITED STATES

the cases that it wishes to hear. The party appealing the case applies to the Supreme Court for a **writ of certiorari,** from the Latin "we wish to be informed." At least four of the nine justices must vote to grant cert, as it is commonly called.

> A **writ of certiorari** is an order issued by a higher court to a lower court to send the record of a case for review.

During a typical term the Supreme Court receives about 5,000 petitions for review and grants fewer than 200 of them. Generally the Court chooses cases of broad national significance. A case may involve a basic constitutional principle, an important question of federal law, or a conflict between state and federal law.

The Supreme Court is likely to choose cases in which two or more of the 11 federal courts of appeals have interpreted the same federal law in different ways. One of the Supreme Court's responsibilities is to ensure uniformity in the application of federal laws.

QUOTES from famous people

"The real strength of the position of the Court is probably in its indispensability to government under a written Constitution. It is difficult to see how the provisions of the 150-year-old document can have much vitality if there is not some permanent institution to translate them into current commands and to see to their contemporary application."

Justice Robert H. Jackson

The Supreme Court is required to hear appeals from lower-court decisions that declare an act of Congress unconstitutional. It must also review decisions of the highest state court if that court has declared a federal law or a treaty unconstitutional or if the state court has upheld state law against the losing party's claim that it is contrary to federal law or to the Constitution.

In general the Supreme Court reviews only those state court decisions that involve constitutional issues. Such decisions often arise from criminal prosecutions in which the defendant claims that a state law is unconstitutional or that the procedures followed in investigating, arresting, or trying him or her are unconstitutional.

During the 1970's a number of Supreme Court decisions have involved state and local antipornography laws. Cases have been appealed by booksellers and film exhibitors who were sentenced to prison for violating the law. The Supreme Court is not interested in justifying pornography. But it is interested in determining whether an antipornography law itself conforms with constitutional protections of free speech and due process.

Denying Review. Ninety-five percent of petitions for Supreme Court review are denied either because the case raises no nationally

Clarence Gideon made his petition to the Supreme Court in a handwritten note on prison stationery. Gideon's case was argued in the Supreme Court by Abe Fortas, who later became a justice of the Supreme Court.

significant issue or because the lower-court decisions seem adequate. Sometimes the Court refuses to review a case because the issue is politically charged. The issue may be the subject of heated political debate elsewhere in the government, and the Court would prefer to wait for tempers to cool. The Court may also be so divided on the issue that it cannot take a stand. When the Court refuses to review a case, the lower-court decision stands.

Per Curiam Decisions. More than half of the Supreme Court's decisions are in the

THE LEGAL AID SOCIETY

"You can't call a lawyer . . . . if you haven't got a dime." The Legal Aid Society once (to encourage contributions) ran an ad campaign in New York City's subways with this as its message, thus summing up the society's purpose: to provide free legal help for those who cannot afford to pay for it.

The Legal Aid Society, which serves New York City, was originally founded in 1876 as a charitable organization to help German immigrants. Within a short time, it had extended its services to help anyone in need. It is now "the largest private law office in the world"; it is still an independent organization and not (as many people think) a government agency.

The Civil Division handles a variety of problems — landlord-tenant disputes, immigration and naturalization, bankruptcy, social welfare benefits, and consumer cases. A person who needs help in such matters generally goes to a Legal Aid office, shows that he or she is eligible because his or her income is below a certain level, and is assigned a lawyer. The society also sends out lawyers to visit the elderly and the mentally ill in homes and institutions.

There is another class of people without the money to hire legal help — and that is children. The society has a Juvenile Rights Division, which defends about 90 percent of all persons accused of juvenile delinquency in New York City and which also acts as law guardians to represent the rights of children who are involved in neglect proceedings.

The Criminal Defense Division represents poor people accused of crimes and visits jails to handle appeals cases. Since most people who commit crimes are poor people, the division handles nearly 70 percent of all criminal defense work in New York City.

Since the 1960's, the U.S. Supreme Court has held in several cases that a person accused of a crime must have a defense counsel provided for him or her at government expense if he or she cannot afford to hire one. In most cities there are public defenders — attorneys who are directly employed by the local government and who are assigned to needy criminal defendants. But in New York City (and in a few other cities), the local government does not have a public defender system. Instead, the city has a contract with the Legal Aid Society to "buy" its services — New York City provides funds and designates the Legal Aid Society as principal defender of the poor in criminal cases.

The Legal Aid Society in New York City is the oldest and biggest agency of its kind. There are some 1,600 other Legal Aid Societies in cities across the country; most of these handle only civil cases.

form of brief orders—that is, *per curiam decisions*—that usually return cases to lower courts for reconsideration in light of recent Court decisions.

Each Supreme Court opinion, of course, sets a precedent to be used by all state and federal judges in deciding similar cases. Sometimes, however, the Court must repeat an earlier ruling in order to make its point clear. Otherwise lower-court judges who disagree with a particular decision may leap on any ambiguous point to reach a contrary decision. These per curiam orders, together with the announcement of the Supreme Court's opinions, help the Court to oversee the work of the federal judiciary as well as to ensure judicial uniformity.

The Case or Controversy Requirement. As was noted in the last chapter, the Supreme Court acts only when confronted with a real case or live controversy. Many doctors believed that state antiabortion statutes infringed on their rights to practice medicine. But the Supreme Court would not review any state court challenge of these laws until a doctor actually performed an abortion and was prosecuted for it.

Political Questions. Political questions are issues that at any given time the Court regards as outside its province. Such issues are politically sensitive and affect the fundamental powers of Congress, the President, or the states. Questions cease to be political when the Court decides to confront the issue.

The question of state legislative reapportionment was designated a political question, but in 1962 the Court decided to assume jurisdiction over the matter. Its reapportionment decisions have fundamentally altered the allocation of electoral power throughout the country. Political questions include most issues of foreign policy and national security.

section review

1. What is a writ of certiorari? How can a writ of cert be granted?
2. Under what conditions does the Supreme Court refuse to review a case?
3. What is a per curiam decision?
4. What is a political question?
5. Which state court decisions does the Supreme Court review?

2. THE COURT'S WORKLOAD

The Supreme Court's workload is extremely heavy. In 1980 the Court reviewed almost three times as many cases as it did in 1960. Per curiam decisions have more than tripled in the last decade, and each decision is based on a review of the case by each justice. During the same 20-year period, written opinions based on oral agruments have increased by 50 percent—from about 120 to about 180 per year.

With almost 5,000 petitions to consider each term, deciding what cases to decide could absorb most of the justices' time. The Court has only a small administrative staff to help it with this paperwork. It considers social and economic issues of enormous complexity without research staffs, field services, or special consultants.

Justices are expected to do their own work. Each justice has two or three law clerks, recent law school graduates who have compiled outstanding records. Most law clerks served as editors of their school's law reviews and are experienced in legal research and writing. The clerks play a major role in reviewing cert petitions and in flagging cases that the Court should review.

The Court's Schedule. Each Supreme Court term runs from early October to late June. During the summer, when the Court is not "sitting," justices and their clerks devote time to reviewing cert petitions. During the term justices hear oral arguments for two weeks (Mondays through Thursdays). They then recess for two weeks to write and circulate their views on these arguments. On days when the Court hears oral arguments, justices read *opinions* (that is, case decisions) that they have prepared for previous cases. On Fridays they meet in conference.

Briefs and Oral Arguments. Among other things, the adversary (opponent) system saves time. Lawyers for each party prepare written *briefs*—that is, papers that present in considerable detail factual and legal arguments and refute their adversary's arguments. The briefs often contain hundreds of pages, including excerpts from precedents and other historical material.

In addition to the briefs submitted by the parties, the Court often receives *amicus curiae* (friend of the Court) *briefs*—that is, those submitted by interested groups or government agencies. This device enables the Department of Justice, for example, to represent the government when a suit between two parties questions the constitutionality of an act of Congress.

Adversary briefs and amicus briefs are the principal devices used to influence the Court. Cases involving major constitutional issues such as equal rights often generate dozens of amicus briefs.

Briefs save the Court the time and the expense of conducting extensive research. Justices rely heavily on the adversaries' briefs—and occasionally on an argument raised in an amicus brief—in preparing their opinions.

The oral argument attempts to summarize the brief. As a rule each party has one hour to present its case, and the time limit is strictly enforced. Lawyers stand at lecterns that contain two lights: the white light flashes five minutes before time is up; when the red light goes on, the lawyer must stop, even in the middle of a sentence.

Oral arguments tend to focus on the policy impact of the Court's decision. Facts and arguments presented to the Court may not be very different from those that the party would present to a congressional committee in support of favorable legislation. Justices frequently interrupt to ask questions. Sometimes they attempt to persuade each other by questioning and arguing with the lawyer.

In oral arguments a lawyer who has considerable experience arguing cases before the Supreme Court has an advantage over a lawyer who is making his or her first appearance.

QUOTES from famous people

"There is hardly a political question in the United States that does not sooner or later turn into a judicial one."

Alexis de Tocqueville

The Conference. Each Friday the Supreme Court meets to discuss and dispose of cases. These conferences begin at 10:00 in the morning and sometimes continue until 6:00 in the evening, with a half-hour break for lunch. The conference room is a large, oak-paneled chamber, with one side lined with books from floor to ceiling. Only the justices are present at the conferences.

The Chief Justice presides and speaks first on each case that is to be discussed. These opening remarks, summarizing the important points, can set the tone for the remaining discussion. The justices express their views in order of seniority. They then

The nine justices meet in the privacy of this room to discuss and dispose of cases.

take a preliminary vote in reverse order of seniority: The most recent justice votes first, and the Chief Justice votes last.

After the vote is taken, the Chief Justice, if in the majority, decides who writes the opinion of the Court. If the Chief Justice votes with the minority, the senior justice among the majority assigns the opinion.

section review

1. Describe the duties of a law clerk.
2. Explain the legal purpose of briefs. How are they used in the Supreme Court?
3. What is the procedure for disposing of a case? Does the seniority of justices play a role? Explain.

3. THE POWER OF THE CHIEF JUSTICE

The prerogatives of the Chief Justice enable that person to lead the Court and influence the other justices in a number of ways:

1. The Chief Justice presides in open court and lends the personal dignity of the position to the Court's proceedings.

2. By speaking first on each case considered at the conference, the Chief Justice compels those who speak afterward to address the points that have been raised.

3. When a vote is close, the prerogative of voting last may give the Chief Justice some room to maneuver. If the other justices are evenly divided, the Chief Justice's vote will determine the outcome of the case. If one justice takes no part in the case and the vote is four to three, the Chief Justice's vote determines whether the Court will speak with a decisive five-to-three opinion or whether the decision of the lower court will stand.

4. By choosing the opinion writer, the Chief Justice can usually determine how the opinion will be written. Having listened to the arguments, the Chief Justice knows what points each justice would emphasize and whether that justice would deal narrowly or broadly with the issues. The Chief Justice often writes the opinions on important cases personally or assigns them to the justice whose views come closest to the Chief Justice's own.

Chief Justices vary in style. Chief Justice Hughes ran the conferences like a stern schoolmaster, exercising tight control over the discussion. Chief Justice Stone, his successor, let discussion wander freely. Chief Justice Warren focused on achieving as much unanimity as he could. The unanimous opinion in the school desegregation cases was a monument to Warren's leadership and skills of persuasion. Chief Justice Burger has de-

Chief Justice Harlan Stone served from 1941–1946.

voted considerable energy to reforming the bar and the federal judiciary.

Supreme Court Opinions. Today a typical opinion of the Supreme Court contains the majority's opinion—called the *opinion of the Court*—together with one or more concurring and/or dissenting opinions.

The justice assigned to write the opinion of the Court is faced with the task of building the strongest majority possible. The other justices voting in the majority may have done so for entirely different reasons. The opinion writer must hold the majority together and try to win over the dissenters. The greater the Court's majority, the more impact its decision will have. Assisted by the opinion writer's law clerks, who often write sections of an opinion under the justice's direction, the justice drafts an opinion and circulates it among the other justices.

Sometimes the other justices will suggest only minor changes or accept the opinion as written. At other times the circulation of the draft presents an opportunity to bargain and compromise. One or more of the justices may persuade the opinion writer by forceful reasoning. On several occasions the assigned opinion writer has reported back that additional study or a colleague's arguments have changed the drafter's opinion.

Shortly after Harlan Fiske Stone became a justice, he was the lone dissenter in a particular case. Stone bombarded the opinion writer, Chief Justice William H. Taft, with several law review articles supporting his view and asked for reconsideration of the case. Taft's opinion was circulated some time later with the following note attached: "Dear Brethren: I think we made a mistake in this case and have written the opinion the other way. Hope you will agree. W.H.T." Everyone did agree, and the new opinion was unanimous.

Other justices may demand that an argument be included as the price for going along. Sometimes a justice will circulate a concurring or a dissenting opinion primarily to persuade the other justices. If the opinion writer and the initial majority justices anticipate public criticism, they may be especially willing to compromise to achieve a larger majority.

For these reasons opinions of the Court often contain vague and inconsistent arguments that bear some resemblance to congressional committee reports on controversial legislation. This should not be too surprising, for the Court often reflects the same clashes of values that Congress does.

In recent years many major constitutional issues have been decided by five-to-

QUOTES from famous people

"The truth is that the law is the highest form of compromise between competing interests. . . . When judges do not agree, it is a sign that they are dealing with problems on which society itself is divided. It is the democratic way to express dissident views. Judges are to be honored rather than criticized for following that tradition, for proclaiming their articles of faith so that all may read."

Justice William O. Douglas

four or six-to-three majorities. Moreover, some of the justices voting with the majority have often written individual concurring opinions in which they have reached the same result for different reasons. This diversity of opinions gives some clue about the clash of judicial attitudes.

Sometimes the justices seek to present a united front. Between 1954—when *Brown* v. *Board of Education* was decided—and 1970, all Supreme Court decisions on school desegregation were unanimous. The justices recognized that any wavering on this crucial issue would invite evasion of the Court's ruling.

Decisions that are not unanimous almost always contain at least one dissenting opinion. In the past some justices wrote "I dissent" and offered no further comment. Today dissenters feel obligated to state their reasons. When justices do not agree, dissents usually reflect divisions within society. A powerful dissent can impress the other justices, the lower courts, and the legal community. In time many dissents have become majority opinions.

The Supreme Court's Audience. Opinions serve to communicate the Court's constitutional views to a variety of constituencies, including lower-court judges, the President, Congress, the bureaucracy, and the legal community. The contents of opinions are carefully studied, reported on in the press, and analyzed in law reviews.

Many opinions contain signals to the bench and to the bar. When an opinion states that "nothing in this opinion is intended to prevent . . ." lawyers and judges are expected to follow the direction or take advantage of the loophole. When the Court states that "in the absence of action by Congress . . ." it is suggesting that Congress act.

Sometimes the Court forces Congress to take action by construing a law so narrowly that the law becomes ineffective. The Court generally respects constitutional boundaries and tries not to antagonize Congress. If a majority of the Court believes that a law violates the Constitution, it may choose to move one step at a time—first narrowing the law's application, then restricting its effect, and finally invalidating it. This gradual approach is designed to promote congressional acquiescence.

section review

1. How can the Chief Justice of the Supreme Court influence discussion in the conference?
2. How can the Chief Justice determine how the Court's opinion will be written?
3. What is meant by "the opinion of the Court"?
4. Why do justices seek to present a unanimous decision on crucial social issues?

Ed Fisher *Saturday Review* Jan. 21, 1967 p. 25 © 1967

"Some Of Us Are Getting Mighty Sick Of These Masterful Dissents Of Yours, Bodgsly!"

4. IMPLEMENTING THE COURT'S DECISIONS

The Court has no power to enforce its decisions. Nearly every decision ends with a *remand*—that is, an order to a lower court or to a government agency to carry out the Court's ruling. Any follow-up work—such as preparing school desegregation plans or reapportioning state legislative districts—is usually done by lower federal courts. For political reasons and because of its lack of enforcement machinery, the Court leaves the implementation of its policies to judges (federal and state) at the site of origin.

Federal and state courts can give effect to Supreme Court decisions in specific cases, but they may encounter difficulty in making people obey a series of Court decisions. Systematic enforcement often requires the cooperation of other branches of government,

James Meredith (center) is shown returning from federal court with his lawyer, Constance Motley, who is now a federal court judge in New York. Meredith became the first Black to attend the University of Mississippi.

including the Justice Department, United States attorneys, and state and local officials.

The hardest decisions to implement are those that require the cooperation of law enforcement officials throughout the country. For example, a Court decision requiring a new standard for police arrests relies on the compliance of thousands of police officials. These officials are instructed and guided by chiefs of police, local prosecutors, and state attorneys general. The Supreme Court may have to encourage the process of compliance by freeing convicted persons whose procedural rights have been violated.

In general, decisions that require action only by the federal executive branch are implemented immediately. By contrast, the Supreme Court's decision outlawing prayers

in the public schools remains widely unenforced. When the decision was announced, many schools voluntarily discontinued Bible reading and prayers. Some school officials tried to circumvent the decision by reading the prayer delivered in Congress each day and printed in the *Congressional Record*. Other school officials simply ignored the decision, and few local prosecutors interfered.

Confronted with what they believed to be a choice between God and the Court, the resisters continued to pray, encouraged by congressional advocacy of a constitutional amendment that would have overruled the Court's decision. The proposed amendment has since been abandoned. Because the average citizen respects the law, the Court's pronouncements rarely give rise to widespread resistance as did the school prayer decision.

The "Finality" of Decisions. Chief Justice Charles Evans Hughes once observed, "the Constitution means what the judges say it means." The power of judicial review makes the Supreme Court the final authority on the Constitution. But Supreme Court decisions—even those pertaining to the meaning of the Constitution—are rarely final. As times change, the Court's constitutional interpretations change.

section review

1. Define the term "remand."
2. Why are decisions requiring the cooperation of local law enforcement officials difficult to implement?
3. Why are Supreme Court decisions rarely final?

CHAPTER SUMMARY

31

The power of judicial review makes the Supreme Court the final authority on the Constitution. Supreme Court decisions are rarely final, however. As times and circumstances change, the Court's constitutional interpretations change with them. A number of factors may change the Court's opinion: 1) the Court may reverse its earlier decision; 2) the Court may change personnel through new presidential appointments; 3) Congress may pass a similar law with minor changes; 4) the Court's decision may be ignored or not enforced; or 5) the Constitution may be amended.

The Supreme Court chooses the cases it wishes to hear: cases of broad national significance, involving a basic constitutional principle, an important question of federal law, or a conflict between state and federal law. It is also likely to choose cases on which two or more federal appeals courts have given differing opinions. One of the Court's main tasks is to ensure national uniformity in the application of federal law.

The Supreme Court is required 1) to hear appeals from lower court decisions that declare an act of Congress unconstitutional; 2) to review decisions of a highest state court that declare a national law or treaty unconstitutional; or 3) to hear a case in which a state court has upheld state law against a claim that it is contrary to federal law or the U.S. Constitution.

The Supreme Court agrees to hear only 5 percent of the cases brought to it. When the Court refuses to review a case, the lower court's decision stands. Each Supreme Court decision sets a precedent to be used by all state and federal judges in deciding similar cases.

The Chief Justice may influence other members of the Court because that official 1) presides in open court and is viewed as the spokesperson for the Court; 2) speaks first on each case, thus compelling others to address the issues raised; 3) votes last and may influence close votes; and 4) chooses the opinion writer.

The Court has no enforcement personnel and does not implement its own decisions. Systematic enforcement often requires the cooperation of other branches of government. The hardest decisions to implement are those that require the cooperation of law enforcement officials throughout the country.

REVIEW QUESTIONS

1. Chief Justice Charles Evans Hughes once observed, "The Constitution means what the judges say it means." Do you agree with Hughes? Do you think this philosophy is appropriate in a democracy? Explain.

2. Supreme Court justices may decide cases narrowly on the law or broadly on social mores. Which do you think is better? Why?

3. What principles do judges apply in reaching decisions? What factors seem to influence judges?

4. What factors may influence Supreme Court justices to change their opinions?

5. List the four ways the Chief Justice can influ-

ence the other justices.

6. What is the typical yearly calendar of a Supreme Court justice?

ACTIVITIES FOR REVIEW

activity 1   Review the cases of *Plessy* v. *Ferguson* and *Brown* v. *Board of Education*. What was the majority opinion in each case? How do you explain the change in the Court's opinion? What factors seem to have been involved?

activity 2   Read about the Warren Court in your school library. Why was it considered an activist Court? How effective was it in changing the social fabric? Explain. Prepare a report to share with the class.

political science DICTIONARY

amicus curiae—"friend of the court," whose function is to give information to the court on some matter of law which is in doubt.   p. 604

opinion of the Court—the opinion of the majority of Supreme Court justices, usually written by one justice.   p. 606

per curiam decision—an opinion by the Court, which expresses its decision in the case.   p. 603

remand—an order to a lower court or government agency to carry out a court's ruling.   p. 608

writ of certiorari—an order issued by a higher court to a lower court to send the record of a case for review.   p. 600

UNIT SUMMARY

The U.S. Constitution provides for the judicial powers of the United States to be vested in a Supreme Court and "in such inferior courts as Congress may . . . establish."

From that simple delegation of power, a major institution has grown to protect and preserve individual liberties from what some of the Founders considered the excesses of the majority.

The federal judiciary consists of constitutional courts and special courts.

The typical justice of the Supreme Court is a White male lawyer from a politically active upper- or middle-class family. He is wealthier, better educated, and more socially prominent than other public servants.

Presidents seek candidates who share their political philosophy. Other important qualities are leadership in the President's party; governmental experience; high status in the legal profession; and the background to balance the racial, ethnic, geographic, and religious composition of the Court.

The Supreme Court hears only 5 percent of the cases brought to it. The cases it selects are those that require a clear judicial precedent for lower courts to follow.

The Chief Justice of the Supreme Court may be very influential. His personal style may well determine the nature of the Court under his leadership.

Enforcement of judicial decisions depends on the cooperation of other federal agencies as well as of state and local law enforcement officers. The Court must be sensitive to the feelings of the country or its decisions may be ignored and, therefore, not enforced.

Bibliography

Abraham, Henry, *Freedom and the Court.* New York: Oxford, 1977.

Mason, Alphens T., *Brandeis: A Free Man's Life.* New York: Viking, 1946.

McCloskey, Robert G., *The Modern Supreme Court.* Cambridge: Harvard University Press, 1972.

Murphy, Walter F., and C. Herman Pritchett, eds. *Courts, Judges and Politics: An Introduction to the Judicial Process*, 3rd edition. New York: Random House, Inc., 1979.

Schmidhauser, John R. and Larry L. Berg, *The Supreme Court and Congress: Conflict and Interaction* Riverside: Free Press, 1972.

Schubert, Glendon, *Judicial Policy-Making: The Political Role of the Courts*, rev. ed. Glenview: Scott, Foresman, 1974.

Review questions

1. How do decisions of the Supreme Court affect the daily lives of Americans?
2. What are some major current issues involving law and the federal courts?
3. When the President vetoes a bill passed by Congress, the veto may be overridden by a two-thirds majority of both houses. Decisions of the Supreme Court may not be overridden. Would you favor a Constitutional amendment empowering Congress to override a Supreme Court "veto" in the same way that they may override a presidential veto? Why or why not?
4. Would you favor increasing the funding of the Supreme Court to provide a larger staff to prepare unbiased briefs rather than continuing the current dependence on partisan briefs and "friends of the court" briefs? Explain.

Skills questions

Using the charts in this unit, answer the following questions:
1. Which court reviews decisions made by the U.S. Court of Appeals?
2. Which courts under the judicial system make appeals directly to the U.S. Supreme Court?
3. What trial courts exist under the state structure? What is the function of each court?
4. How many years did the following people serve as Chief Justice? John Marshall, Roger Taney, Earl Warren. Name the President who appointed them to their post.
5. Outline the rights of an arrested person.
6. Which state court would handle the following cases? a) An industrial plant is charged with polluting a river. b) A 14-year-old is arrested for reckless driving. (Give reasons for your answers.)

Activities

activity 1

"The interpretation of the laws is the proper and peculiar province of the Courts. A Constitution is, in fact, and must be regarded by the judges as a fundamental law. It therefore belongs to them to ascertain its meaning as well as the meaning of any particular act proceeding from the legislative body. If there should happen to be an irreconcilable variance between the two, that which has the superior obligation and validity ought, of course, to be preferred; or, in other words, the Constitution ought to be preferred to the statute, the intention of the people to the intention of their agents." Alexander Hamilton, *The Federalist*, No. 78

How has this philosophy of the Founders been continued by the Supreme Court using the power of judicial review?

activity 2

"It is not the habit of the Courts to decide questions of a constitutional nature unless absolutely necessary to a decision of the case. . . . The Court will not pass upon a constitutional question although properly presented by the record, if there is also present some other ground upon which the case may be disposed of." Justice Louis Brandeis, concurring in *Ashwander* v. *TVA* (1936)

Write a short essay illustrating the practice of this philosophy by justices of the Supreme Court.

activity 3

Prepare wall charts labeled "Landmark Decisions of the Supreme Court: Civil Rights" and "Landmark Decisions of the Supreme Court: Rights of the Accused." Research the development of these concepts through Supreme Court decisions since 1789.

UNIT 10

TONY AMSTERDAM

PEOPLE IN
POLITICS

Anthony (Tony) G. Amsterdam, a Stanford Law School professor, is one of the nation's ranking experts in criminal law and civil rights. He devotes his energies equally to the classroom and the courtroom. In both he has pioneered in new directions.

After graduation from the University of Pennsylvania Law School, he was as interested in pursuing a career in art history as he was in becoming a lawyer (he had worked on a graduate degree in art history while in law school). But a year's clerkship with Justice Felix Frankfurter of the Supreme Court confirmed his commitment to the law. His assignments for Frankfurter forced him to examine the workings of the nation's criminal justice system.

After a year and a half with the United States Attorney's office in Washington, D.C., Amsterdam turned to teaching law in order to practice law and to reform the criminal justice system. Since the 1960's he has worked closely with almost every law-related civil rights organization in the country. He has never accepted a fee for any of his work.

Professor Amsterdam is best known for his efforts to abolish capital punishment. In the early days of the campaign to challenge the death penalty, he helped direct a study of rape convictions in southern states. He was the chief architect and leading strategist of a plan to block all executions already scheduled while presenting arguments in the Supreme Court to get capital punishment judicially abolished.

Amsterdam's deep concern for humanity is revealed in these words: ". . . what I would like to see is a completely open society. What I mean by that is that every individual born into a society should have the greatest opportunity the society can give him to fulfill his own potential, his aspirations, his own instincts—to make of himself a complete and full human being."

CIVIL LIBERTIES AND CIVIL RIGHTS

OVERVIEW

UNIT
CONTENT

■ Most of our civil liberties are guaranteed by the Bill of Rights.

■ The Bill of Rights protects individual liberties and the rights of the accused in criminal proceedings.

■ The First Amendment guarantees freedom of religion, freedom of speech, freedom of the press, the right of peaceful assembly, and the right to petition.

■ The Fourth Amendment prohibits "unreasonable search and seizure." Usually the police must have a warrant issued by a judge.

■ The Fifth Amendment protects citizens from loss of "life, liberty, or property without due process of law," self-incrimination, and double jeopardy.

■ The Sixth Amendment guarantees a speedy and public trial, the right to legal counsel, and the right of the accused to cross-examine the persons who are accusing.

■ The Eighth Amendment bars setting excessive bail and inflicting "cruel and unusual punishment."

■ The Fourteenth Amendment defines citizenship and guarantees the "equal protection of the laws."

32

The First Amendment

The Supreme Court does not use a single doctrine or set of rules to interpret the First Amendment. Instead it uses various doctrines to interpret different sections. What accounts for the different approaches? Different sections of the amendment pose different problems. For example, freedom of the press and freedom of religion protect different kinds of rights. There are 51 court systems in the United States—one federal and 50 state. The cases on First Amendment rights originate in both state and federal courts. Since each court handles these cases at the trial level, procedures for interpreting this amendment have become complex.

This chapter will examine the Supreme Court's analyses of the First Amendment. Decisions on speech which advocate violations of the law are quite different from those on obscenity and religion. Before 1964 defamation—publicly discrediting a person—was controlled mainly by state law. The law on defamation has now been nationalized. This was done through the Supreme Court's interpretation of the First Amendment.

In this chapter historical information is presented and the rules that apply to each section of the First Amendment are analyzed. Such information and analyses will help you evaluate fights over First Amendment rights.

CHAPTER PREVIEW

1. HISTORICAL OVERVIEW OF THE BILL OF RIGHTS
2. FREEDOM OF SPEECH AND ASSOCIATION
3. FREEDOM OF THE PRESS
4. FREEDOM OF RELIGION

1. HISTORICAL OVERVIEW OF THE BILL OF RIGHTS

Most American civil rights and liberties are guaranteed in the Bill of Rights—the first ten amendments to the Constitution. Several states ratified the Constitution only on the condition that a bill of rights would be proposed by the new government. The first Congress proposed the amendments in the fall of 1789, but the necessary ratification by three fourths of the states was not completed until December 1791.

The idea that the Bill of Rights should limit state action was rejected in the early days of the nation. For example, the Supreme Court case of *Barron* v. *Baltimore* in 1833 held that the Fifth Amendment provisions on **eminent domain** applies only to actions of the federal government. This case established a precedent on applying the Bill of Rights to the states. The decision lasted until after the Civil War.

> **Eminent domain** is the right of a state to force a property owner to sell property when it is needed for public use.

Refusal to extend the Bill of Rights to the states caused many citizens to be deprived of their rights. For example, in a federal court it was illegal to try someone who did not have legal representation. However, until 1963 if an accused person lacked the resources to hire a lawyer, a state had no obligation to provide one.

In 1868 the Fourteenth Amendment was

The Fourteenth Amendment protects citizens by guarantee of fundamental liberties. Accused persons have the right of counsel.

adopted. Under this amendment no state could make or enforce any law that would abridge "the privileges or immunities of citizens of the United States; nor . . . deprive any person of life, liberty, or property without due process of law; nor deny to any person within its jurisdiction the equal protection of the laws."

Gradually after 1868 the Supreme Court declared that some of the liberties set forth in the Bill of Rights were fundamental rights of citizenship. These rights were to be protected against state **infringement.** On a case-by-case basis over the years, the Court used the Fourteenth Amendment's due process clause to force the states to apply the protections guaranteed under the Bill of Rights. Today almost all guarantees in the Bill of Rights limit the actions of both federal and state governments. The only two amendments not yet applicable to states are those on the right to a grand jury proceeding in criminal cases (part of the Fifth Amendment) and the right to a jury trial in civil cases (Seventh Amendment).

Infringement is a breach or invasion of some legal right.

Attempts to regulate free expression have generally been concentrated in two areas: restrictions on the content of what is spoken and published and restrictions on the means of communication.

section review

1. Define the term "eminent domain."
2. How are the states restricted by the Fourteenth Amendment?
3. The guarantees in the Bill of Rights limit the actions of what governments?

2. FREEDOM OF SPEECH AND ASSOCIATION

Although the framers of the First Amendment regarded freedom of speech as a fundamental right, they said little about its exact meaning. However, during the eighteenth century, freedom of speech did have a definite popular meaning—the right of people to discuss public affairs without restriction. When the Alien and Sedition Acts of 1798 severely limited freedom of speech, they were vigorously opposed by many groups. These acts were eventually abolished. From the early 1800's until the 1920's, protection of speech was marked both by periods of relative freedom and by periods of restraint in which federal or state actions limited free expression.

The Supreme Court's first major decision on freedom of speech came after World War I. Since that time there have been many other decisions. These decisions have evolved into guidelines for determining what type of speech is protected.

Freedom of speech has been interpreted by the Supreme Court as freedom of expression. Thus freedom of expression includes many kinds of actions or conduct. However, not all conduct undertaken to communicate expression is automatically protected by the First Amendment.

QUOTES from famous people

"To justify suppression of free speech there must be reasonable ground to fear that serious evil will result if free speech is practiced. There must be reasonable ground to believe that the danger apprehended is imminent. There must be reasonable ground to believe that the evil to be prevented is a serious one."

Justice Brandeis

The framers of the Constitution believed that "consent of the governed" should be based on full and free discussion.

Conduct Within the Scope of Freedom of Expression. If there is an important state or federal government interest independent of the expression aspects of the conduct, the conduct may be regulated. For example, a prohibition on draft-card burning was upheld because the federal government had an independent interest in a smoothly functioning draft system (*U.S.* v. *O'Brien*, 1968). However, a prohibition on students wearing black arm bands in schools to protest the Vietnamese War was not upheld. This was because the school board (a unit of local government) had no independent regulatory interest. Its only interest was in prohibiting expression (*Tinker* v. *Des Moines School District*, 1969).

Content Regulation. Attempts at regulation of free expression have generally been in two areas: restrictions on the *content* of what was spoken or published, and restriction on the *means* of communications.

Advocacy of Violation of Law. Contests over freedom of speech have erupted during wartime and in postwar periods when there was public concern about disloyalty and subversion. Individuals who urged violation of the draft laws and the violent overthrow of the government were targets of both state and federal action. Since World War I the Supreme Court has developed a complex series of tests to determine whether advocating

The law permits nonviolent demonstrations by groups such as the Ku Klux Klan, who are shown picketing in this picture.

violation of law is protected by the First Amendment. Many of these cases have involved individuals who belonged to groups such as the Communist party and the Ku Klux Klan. These cases have provided some of the most controversial interpretations of the meaning of freedom of expression.

In 1919 the Supreme Court announced its first rule in the following series of cases: 1) *Schenck* v. *U.S.* (1919), 2) *Debs* v. *U.S.* (1919), 3) *Abrams* v. *U.S.* (1919), 4) *Gitlow* v. *New York* (1925), 5) *Whitney* v. *California* (1927). Under this rule conduct, speech, and writing advocating the forceful overthrow of the government were punishable. Moreover, the Court declared that such punishment did not violate First Amendment guarantees of free expression.

The rule did not focus on speech but rather on the results of speech. If language was used solely to incite to action, the speech might be punished. Thus protection rested on the evaluation of whether a speech might cause a forbidden result. The evaluators were typically juries that assessed the circumstances under which the speech was made and speculated about the risks created by the speech. The test, as enunciated by the Court, became known as the Holmes-Brandeis "clear and present danger" test. Supreme Court interpretations have replaced this test.

In *Dennis* v. *U.S.* (1951), *Yates* v. *U.S.* (1957), and *Brandenburg* v. *Ohio* (1969), the Court refined the "clear and present danger" test. The cases of Dennis and Yates involved members of the Communist party who were indicted under the Smith Act, a federal criminal statute. This act provided for the registration and fingerprinting of alien residents. It also made it unlawful 1) to advocate or teach the forceful overthrow of any government in the United States, 2) to belong to any group advocating such actions, 3) to conspire with others to achieve such an end.

Dennis v. *U.S.* The defendants in the Dennis case were charged with conspiracy to advocate the violent overthrow of the government of the United States and with organizing the Communist party to undertake that action. At the trial little evidence was introduced to prove that any defendant had advocated a specific act of violence or that the Communist party had plans for a revolution. In fact the government proved its case primarily by demonstrating that the Communist party was committed to violent revolution and that the defendants were the major officers of the party.

The Supreme Court only considered whether the Smith Act was constitutional. It did not consider whether evidence against the defendants upheld their convictions. The

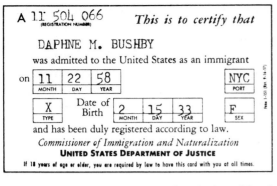

A 11 504 066
(REGISTRATION NUMBER)

This is to certify that

DAPHNE M. BUSHBY

was admitted to the United States as an immigrant

on | 11 | 22 | 58 | | NYC |
    | MONTH | DAY | YEAR | | PORT |

| X | Date of | 2 | 15 | 33 | | F |
| TYPE | Birth | MONTH | DAY | YEAR | | SEX |

and has been duly registered according to law.

Commissioner of Immigration and Naturalization
UNITED STATES DEPARTMENT OF JUSTICE

If 18 years of age or older, you are required by law to have this card with you at all times.

Here is an alien registration card, issued to all legal foreign residents when entering the United States.

Supreme Court stated that the "clear and present danger" test was the correct one to use. However, it did not require that any proof of an immediate danger be necessary in order to punish. The Court sustained the convictions of the defendants and upheld the constitutionality of the Smith Act.

Yates v. *U.S.* After the Dennis case the government began prosecuting the second-level leadership of the Communist party. The first of these cases to reach the Supreme Court was *Yates* v. *U.S.* The charges and the proof against the defendants were similar to those in the Dennis case. But unlike its approach to the Dennis case, the Court considered all the issues. It even considered evidence used earlier to convict the defendants.

The Court's conclusions in the Yates case were very different from those in the Dennis case. As in the Dennis case the Court held that the First Amendment did not require the government to prove that the Communist party constituted a danger to the government. But it did hold that a violation of the Smith Act required proof that a defendant had advocated a specific unlawful act as opposed to a political idea. By declaring that the government could not win by merely showing that a defendant was a member or official of the Communist party, which believed in the

Marxist doctrine of revolution, the Court reversed the defendants' convictions.

Scales v. *U.S.* Four years later in *Scales* v. *U.S.*, the Court interpreted another section of the Smith Act. This section imposed penalties against knowingly being a member of an organization that advocated the violent overthrow of the United States government. The Court insisted, as it had in the Yates case, that no one could be convicted if the organization's only advocacy was that of a political idea and not incitement to illegal action. Thus a person could be convicted of being a member of such a group only if all the following criteria were met: 1) the group must advocate the forceful overthrow of the government in a way not protected under the Constitution, 2) the person must be an active member of the group advocating such an overthrow, 3) the person must have knowledge that what he or she is advocating is not protected under the Constitution, and 4) the individual must be committed to the group's illegal aims.

Brandenburg v. *U.S.* Building on its decisions in the Yates and Scales cases, the Court produced in 1969 its clearest interpretation of the protection that the First Amendment provides for advocating violation of law. This view is in force today. In the Brandenburg case the Court addressed the question of imminency—the immediate likelihood or threat of violence. It declared that the probability of harm would no longer be the primary factor for limiting speech. Only the language of the speaker would be used to determine the imminence of violence. Thus a government may not "forbid or proscribe advocacy of the use of force or of law violation except where such advocacy is directed to inciting or producing imminent lawless action and is likely to incite or produce such action." Thus the courts must distinguish between advocacy of violation of law and direct incitement to imminent lawless action. The focus of the prosecutors must be confined to the speaker's words, not speculation

RIGHTS GUARANTEED BY THE DUE PROCESS CLAUSE OF THE FOURTEENTH AMENDMENT

AMENDMENT	SPECIFIC RIGHT	APPLICATION TO STATES	CASE
First	freedom of religion	yes	**Cantwell** v. **Connecticut** (1940) 310 U.S. 296
First	free speech	yes	**Gitlow** v. **New York** (1925) 268 U.S. 652
First	free press	yes	**Near** v. **Minnesota** (1931) 283 U.S. 697
First	freedom of assembly	yes	**De Jonge** v. **Oregon** (1937) 299 U.S. 1937
Second	right to bear arms	no	
Third	no quartering of soldiers	---	(no cases decided)
Fourth	no unreasonable search and seizure	yes	**Mapp** v. **Ohio** (1961) 367 U.S. 643
Fifth	indictment by grand jury	no	
Fifth	no double jeopardy	yes	**Benton** v. **Maryland** (1969) 395 U.S. 784
Fifth	no self-incrimination	yes	**Malloy** v. **Hogan** (1964) 378 U.S. 1
Fifth	due process	yes	(Fourteenth Amendment contains same language)
Fifth	no taking of property without compensation	yes	(Fourteenth Amendment contains same language)
Sixth	speedy trial	yes	**Klopfer** v. **North Carolina** (1967) 386 U.S. 723
Sixth	public trial	yes	**In re Oliver** (1948) 333 U.S. 257
Sixth	trial by jury	yes	**Duncan** v. **Louisiana** (1968) 391 U.S. 145
Sixth	impartial tribunal	yes	**Tumey** v. **Ohio** (1927) 273 U.S. 510
Sixth	right to be informed of the charge	yes	**Cole** v. **Arkansas** (1948) 333 U.S. 196
Sixth	confrontation and cross-examination	yes	**Pointer** v. **Texas** (1965) 380 U.S. 400
Sixth	right to obtain witnesses	yes	**Washington** v. **Texas** (1967) 388 U.S. 214
Sixth	assistance of counsel	yes	**Gideon** v. **Wainwright** (1963) 372 U.S. 335
Seventh	trial by jury (civil cases)	no	
Eighth	no excessive bail	---	(no cases decided)
Eighth	no cruel and unusual punishment	yes	**Robinson** v. **California** (1962) 370 U.S. 660

about whether violence might have occurred.

Obscenity. A second major area of content regulation deals with obscenity. But controlling obscenity involves considerations different from those involved in controlling advocacy of violation of law. There is considerable disagreement over the suppression or limitation of materials considered obscene in the United States. Some believe there is no such thing as obscenity because it endangers neither the public's safety nor an individual's welfare. Obscenity simply offends the majority's views, and such an offense is not sufficient enough cause to ban something. The Supreme Court and a majority of the American public, however, have not accepted this viewpoint.

The Supreme Court has had great difficulty deciding on a workable definition of obscenity and on the standards by which materials should be judged as obscene. The Court has reversed itself several times in the last two decades. As a result almost every obscenity conviction is appealed to the Court.

In 1969 the Court decided that punishing for private possession of obscene materials (*Stanley* v. *Georgia*) violated the First Amendment. Nevertheless, Congress may ban the sale and movement of obscene materials in foreign and interstate commerce. It may also ban their sale and movement through the mail (*U.S.* v. *Orito,* 1973). Such distribution may be a crime even if it involves willing adults (*U.S.* v. *Reidel,* 1971). Further, the exhibition of obscene materials in places of public accommodations, which include theaters for adults only, may also be a crime (*Paris Adult Theatre* v. *Slaton,* 1973.)

The current definition of obscenity is found in *Miller* v. *California* (1973). To be deemed obscene, the material must first be considered as a whole by "the average person applying contemporary community standards." It must then obtain affirmative answers to three extremely vague questions. These three questions deal with what is considered acceptable or unacceptable sexual writings, displays, art, or pictures. These questions can be interpreted in different ways by different individuals or groups.

However, the definition given above creates problems. The standards for obscenity in small towns are now different from those in such metropolitan areas as Los Angeles and New York City. This situation is especially difficult for film makers, publishers, and prosecutors because small towns do not give advance notice of what they consider to be obscene. Consequently, there have been a series of trials involving magazine publishers in town after town across the country. And these decisions have raised the question again of whether a general right should be limited by the standards of a specific area.

Another problem is that applicable state laws and local ordinances are not always specific about the conduct they prohibit. Some local lawmakers have complained that to describe explicit conduct considered to be obscene, the law itself would have to be obscene. Such vagueness often enhances juries' problems, since juries do not have limitless discretion in deciding what is obviously offensive. Appellate courts, when necessary, conduct independent reviews of constitutional claims to ensure that prohibited materials depict or describe patently offensive and obscene sexual materials (*Jenkins* v. *Georgia,* 1974). Nevertheless, major obscenity cases usually reach the Supreme Court, which continues to have varied views on what it considers obscene.

A third problem is that every trial is marked by testimony from opposing experts who pronounce the artistic value of a given work. Consequently, juries and judges in obscenity cases have been cast in the role of literary and film critics.

Defamation. Another major area of content regulation involves defamation. There are two kinds of defamation: libel (printed statements) and slander (spoken statements). For a statement to be considered defamatory, it must lower the reputation of the person to whom it refers, or it must deter others from associating with that person.

Since Congress has never passed a national law dealing with this kind of content regulation, defamation is governed by 50 sets of state laws. Moreover, most lawsuits involving defamation have not been criminal actions in which a state punished an individual for libeling or slandering another individual or a group. Instead they have been civil actions in which an individual sued another to collect damages.

Not until 1964 in the *New York Times Co.* v. *Sullivan* case did the Supreme Court examine the constitutional aspects of the civil law on libel. This case and several subsequent cases changed the law on libel at the state level.

As a result of the *New York Times* case and other cases, rules for recovering damages depend on who the plaintiff is and who the defendant is. These rules are:

1. If the plaintiff is a public official and the defendant is a member of the press or the broadcast media, freedom of speech and of the press bars a plaintiff from winning a civil libel case against the defendant who criticized the plaintiff's official conduct. This rule does not apply, however, if the plaintiff can prove malice.

To prove malice an official must show either that the defamatory material was known to be false at the time it was published or that it was published with reckless disregard to its truth or falsity. To prove reckless disregard, an official would have to prove that the defendant had serious doubts about the truthfulness of the material but despite these doubts the defendant published the material.

The *New York Times* rule also applies to libel actions by public figures if the defendants are members of the press or the broadcast media (*Curtis Publishing Co.* v. *Butts*, and *Associated Press* v. *Walker*, 1967).

A citizen becomes a public figure in one of two ways. The first way is by achieving "general fame or notoriety in the community and pervasive involvement in the affairs of society." The second way is by either voluntarily injecting himself or herself or by voluntarily being drawn into a controversy.

2. If the plaintiff is a private citizen and the defendant is a member of the press or the broadcast media, the first rule does not apply in the same way. In this situation a plaintiff may win a libel case only if he or she shows that the defendant was negligent, deliberate, or reckless in his or her behavior. If it is proved that the defendant was negligent, then the plaintiff must also prove that he or she suffered actual damage. If it is proved that the defendant was reckless, then the plaintiff may recover damages without proving that he or she was hurt in any way. The plaintiff may also be able to obtain punitive damages against the defendant.

3. If the plaintiff is a private citizen and the defendant is not a member of the news media, the rules above do not apply. In such a situation the plaintiff must show that the defendant intentionally or negligently published the defamatory statement. In some states the plaintiff must prove actual damages to reputation (for example, loss of employment or business). In other states, however, damages are presumed—that is, injury to the plaintiff is presumed simply because the statement was published. Thus juries may award substantial sums of money for supposed damage to reputation without any proof that such harm actually occurred.

Other Kinds Of Content Regulation. *Fighting Words.* The First Amendment does not protect situations in which fighting words are used. Such words are most often intended as a personal insult to the person addressed, and by their utterance they tend to provoke an immediate breach of the peace. Usually fighting words can be regulated under narrowly written or narrowly interpreted statutes covering "breach of the peace" or "disorderly conduct." In *Chaplinsky* v. *New Hampshire* (1942), the Supreme Court upheld the conviction of a man who denounced another man on a public sidewalk. This conviction was upheld under a breach of peace statute. The Court's rationale in this and similar cases was that the slight social value of fighting words was outweighed by the public interest in order.

But the fact that certain words are viewed by some as offensive, unpatriotic, disrespectful, or defiant does not make them fighting words. For example, the Supreme Court overturned the conviction under a California law of one young man. The conviction had been based on a law that prohibited "maliciously and willfully disturbing the peace or quiet of any neighborhood or person . . . by . . . offensive conduct." The defendant had been tried for wearing in a courthouse corridor a jacket bearing a term of abuse against the draft. The Court's decision was that the state government was punishing the defendant for words, not conduct. Furthermore, the Court held that the term was not erotic (and therefore not covered under obscenity rules). Nor was it considered to be directed as a personal insult to any person (*Cohen* v. *California*, 1971).

The Court also struck down a similar federal law. That law made it a crime to engage in a theatrical production while wearing an army uniform if the acting "tended to discredit" the armed forces. An actor, the Court stated, has a constitutional right to freedom of speech, "including the right openly to criticize the government during a dramatic performance" (*Schacht* v. *U.S.*, 1970).

Overbroad and Vague Laws. Often a state or the federal government passes a law regulating expression and association, only a portion of which is not protected by the First Amendment. According to the Court such laws tend to produce a "chilling effect" on the exercise of free expression and association.

A statute may be overbroad because it is written in vague or imprecise language. In such a case people of common intelligence must guess at what the statute means. For example, a state oath that affirms, "I have not and will not lend aid, support, advice, counsel, or influence to the Communist party" was held to be unconstitutional because it was vague. The oath's prohibitions might have applied to anyone who had ever supported a cause or a candidate also supported by the Communist party (*Cramp* v. *Board of Public Instruction*, 1961).

Another unconstitutionally vague law involved a local ordinance. This ordinance made it a crime "for three or more persons to assemble on any of the sidewalks and there conduct themselves in a manner annoying to persons passing by." The ordinance was nullified by the court for being vague as well as for violating the First Amendment right of association. It contained "an obvious invitation to discriminatory enforcement" against those whose association was "annoying" to others because of their ideas or physical appearance (*Coates* v. *Cincinnati*, 1971).

Prior Restraint. A state or the federal government has the power to punish some kinds of speeches once they have been made. However, it may not prevent a speech from being delivered or material from being published beforehand. In most situations a government may not establish a system of censorship to regulate what may be spoken or published. In the case of *Near* v. *Minnesota* (1931), the Supreme Court struck down a Minnesota law prohibiting the publication of "malicious, scandalous, and defamatory" periodicals. Such attempts to regulate in advance are called prior restraints.

Historically, prior restraints have taken place when an official government censor had to approve in advance the publication of a newspaper or book; otherwise publication was illegal. When in doubt most censors said no. Many of the cases that came before the Supreme Court involved newspaper reporting and fair trials.

Some people consider prior restraints on speech and publication to be the most serious and the least tolerable infringement of First Amendment rights. But there are a few extraordinary circumstances in which prior restraint is allowed. Certain information may be censored during wartime. The Supreme Court has suggested in *Nebraska Press Association* v. *Stuart* (1976) that an injunction against the reporting of criminal proceedings may be issued 1) if there is a clear threat to the fairness of the trial, 2) if such a threat is posed by the actual publicity to be restrained, 3) if less restrictive alternatives are unavailable. In this case the Court did not uphold an injunction issued by a judge that prohibited media reportage.

Another area in which certain forms of censorship and prior restraints have been upheld is obscenity. But this has occurred only when the censorship system contained adequate procedural and judicial safeguards. An example of this was when a state law, which permitted an injunction against further distribution of a publication found to be obscene after a full judicial hearing, was upheld (*Kingsley Books, Inc.* v. *Brown*, 1957).

There may be no large-scale seizures of allegedly obscene books and films without a full adversary hearing and a judicial determination of obscenity (*Heller* v. *New York*, 1973). Informal sanctions by a state agency, which have the effect of a prior restraint, are also unconstitutional. Thus a state commission on juvenile delinquency may not informally recommend to book distributors that they ban objectionable books for youths and then fol-

low those recommendations with such measures as threats of court action or visits from the police to stop their sale (*Bantam Books, Inc.* v. *Sullivan*, 1963).

The Court has upheld censorship systems for movies on the basis that "films differ from other forms of expression" and that the time delays inherent in censorship do not constitute too great a burden. Nonetheless, movie-censorship systems must meet the following requirements: 1) the standards for denying a license or permit to show a movie must be narrowly drawn, 2) the censor must promptly seek an injunction from the appropriate court to stop the showing if he or she does not want to issue a permit, 3) the censor must bear the burden in an injunction hearing of proving that the movie does not warrant First Amendment protection, 4) the court must rule promptly on whether to grant the injunction.

A troublesome area of prior restraint involves state secrets. If a government stamps material "secret" or "confidential," citizens of the state or nation may be denied information necessary for an adequate discussion and debate of current government policies. If a newspaper obtains some of these secrets, may the government prevent their publication on the grounds that publication would harm national security?

This question arose in the "Pentagon Papers" case, which is officially known as *New York Times* v. *United States* (1971). In this case Daniel Ellsberg had taken a set of classified documents from the Department of Defense. The *New York Times* and the *Washington Post* had been preparing to publish parts of these documents. However, the government had obtained a court injunction ordering them to stop publication. The Supreme Court held that the order was not justified, although the six justices who had voted to overturn the lower court's order voiced different reasons for lifting the publication ban.

Daniel Ellsberg leaked the Pentagon papers. Should the government prevent the publication of secret information?

Two justices declared that any court order that prohibited the press from publishing violated the First Amendment. Another justice said that the government should prove that publication of the classified documents would harm national security. Until there was such proof, an interim prohibition on publishing violated the First Amendment. Three other justices maintained that Congress might authorize judicial restraints against the press if the case involved national security. But since this case did not, the court order was not justified. Thus in one case the Court did uphold the publishing of state secrets; however, its reasons for doing so were diverse.

Broadcasting. Radio and TV broadcasting are closely regulated, and such regulation does not violate First Amendment Rights (*NBC* v. *U.S.*, 1943). Because there is a limited number of radio and TV frequencies available, broadcasters have both special privileges and special responsibilities. They must devote broadcast time to matters of public interest, and they must cover a broad range of programs. Under the fairness doctrine the Supreme Court upheld orders by the Federal Communications Commission (FCC) requiring radio stations to offer free broadcast time to opponents of political candidates, to those who opposed the views endorsed by the station, and to any person who had been attacked during a broadcast (*Red Lion Broadcasting* v. *FCC*, 1969). But the Supreme Court also declared that radio and TV stations do not have to accept paid political ads (*CBS, Inc.* v. *Democratic National Committee*, 1973).

Newspapers are treated very differently from radio and television. They are normally free of federal and state regulation. For example, in *Miami Herald Publishing Co.* v. *Tornillo* (1974), the Supreme Court struck down a Florida statute that granted political candidates the right to equal newspaper space to reply to a newspaper's criticism. The Court said that attempts to regulate the content of newspapers violated freedom of the press.

Regulation of the Means of Communication. In the previous sections we learned that the content of certain types of speech may be controlled constitutionally. But regulation and control of the manner of speech are involved with parades, handbills, picketing, and similar public demonstrations. There are also problems of regulation when speech involves a hostile audience.

The public may not be denied all access to public places historically associated with the exercise of First Amendment rights.

Streets, sidewalks, and parks are in this category (*Hague* v. *CIO*, 1939). Also in this category are public schools (*Tinker* v. *Des Moines School District*, 1969) and grounds surrounding a statehouse (*Edwards* v. *South Carolina*, 1963).

Still, other kinds of public property may be completely closed to activities that exercise First Amendment rights. Included in this category are areas not open to the general public and areas in which the exercise of free speech would interfere with normal use of the property. In this category are 1) jailhouse grounds (*Adderley* v. *Florida*, 1967), 2) areas immediately surrounding courthouses in which trials are being held (*Cox* v. *Louisiana*, 1965), and 3) military bases (*Greer* v. *Spock*, 1976).

Public places in which First Amendment rights may be exercised are subject to reasonable regulations as to time, place, and manner. Examples of permissible and impermissible regulations include the following:

1. *Handbills.* A government may not bar the distribution of handbills. Nor may it require that handbills always be identified by including the author's name and address. Such disclosure produces a "chilling effect" on the right of free speech.

2. *Picketing.* Picketing may be barred if it will obstruct the free entrance to and exit from public buildings.

3. *Door-to-door solicitation.* A government may not ban all knocking at doors or ringing of bells to distribute handbills. This is because an unreceptive home owner can protect his or her privacy by posting a "No Solicitors" sign.

The government may require a permit or a license to use public streets, sidewalks, and parks for meetings, speeches, and demonstrations. However, the permit or license must specify the time, place, manner, duration, and fees involved in such use. In issuing these permits and licenses, the government may not give the licensing official (for example, a mayor or a police chief) unlimited discretion to decide who may receive them. The government must set clearly defined standards. For example, an ordinance requiring that individuals obtain a permit to use a sound truck on a public street, which did not establish any standard for granting or denying the permit, was found to be unconstitutional (*Saia* v. *N.Y.*, 1948). Another ordinance, one that gave local officials the right to deny parade permits based on their predictions about its effects on the community's welfare or morals, was also found to be unconstitutional (*Shuttlesworth* v. *Birmingham*, 1969). And an ordinance making it a crime for any person to stand about or loiter on a street after being requested to move by the police was also held to be unconstitutional. This was because the ordinance did not provide standards about what conduct was prohibited. Instead, the ordinance left such determination to the police officer on the beat (*Shuttlesworth* v. *Birmingham*, 1969).

The Hostile Audience Problem. Do the police have a duty to ensure a person's right to speak by restraining a noisy, objecting audience, or should a potential threat to public safety be avoided by silencing the speaker? Speech is often challenging. Frequently it produces conditions of unrest, anger, and hostility. The two cases below illustrate the Court's views on cases involving hostile audiences.

Feiner v. *New York* (1951). Irving Feiner, an army veteran attending a university in Syracuse, New York, used a loudspeaker to address a crowd of people on a Syracuse street. He called the President "a bum," the American Legion "a Nazi Gestapo," and the mayor "a champagne-sipping bum." He also

The First Amendment protects a citizen's right to distribute handbills that do not identify the author and place of publication.

urged Blacks to "rise up in arms and fight" for their rights. Some members of the crowd, which had gathered around him, grew restless. When Feiner was asked to stop speaking by two officers, he refused to do so. Feiner's subsequent arrest and conviction for disorderly conduct were upheld by the Supreme Court.

Edwards v. *South Carolina* (1963). Black high school and college students protested discrimination against Blacks by parading around the South Carolina statehouse. Within a few hours 200 to 300 hostile onlookers had gathered. The police advised the demonstrators to disperse within 15 minutes or they would be arrested. Almost 200 students who refused to disperse were arrested and con-

victed of breaching the peace. The Supreme Court reversed the convictions on the ground that demonstrators may not be punished merely because the views they expressed "were sufficiently opposed to the views of the majority of the community to attract a crowd and necessitate police protection."

section review

1. During the eighteenth century, what was the popular meaning of "freedom of speech"?
2. When is a statement considered defamatory? What are the two kinds of defamation?

3. What kind of conduct is protected by the First Amendment?

4. What was the Supreme Court's decision in the case of *Miami Herald Publishing Co.* v. *Tornillo* (1974)?

5. Give two examples of how the exercise of First Amendment rights may be regulated with regard to time, place, and manner.

3. FREEDOM OF THE PRESS

Most provisions of the Bill of Rights protect specific liberties or individual rights. But the First Amendment's freedom of the press clause protects the publishing business. This is the only organized private business given specific protection under the Constitution.

When analyzing the content regulations in the previous section, we examined the problems of prior restraint and we noted that such restraints were often aimed at the press. But there have been attempts to limit the press in other ways. Judges have sometimes held newspapers in contempt of court and subjected them to fines for criticizing their conduct as judges. Such convictions have been struck down by the Supreme Court (*Bridges* v. *California*, 1941).

Most cases involving the press have dealt with prior restraints or prohibitions against publishing. One particular form of prior restraint has presented unusual problems. Often the Court must balance the guarantees of both the First Amendment right to freedom of the press and the Sixth Amendment right to a fair and impartial trial for the accused. Although such cases have been few, those few have posed complex questions. Should the press be limited in its right to report information about the accused and that person's trial proceedings? In *Sheppard* v. *Maxwell* (1966), the Court ordered the defendant released after ruling that his trial had been turned into a "carnival atmosphere" by reporters who had

"free reign" in the courtroom during the trial. In *Gannett* v. *DePasquale* (1979) the Court ruled that judges have the right to close pre-trial hearings to the press. Most often, however, the Court has struck down attempts by trial courts to limit reporting of their proceedings (*Nebraska Press Association* v. *Stuart*, 1976). In 1980 the Court held that the press has the "right of access" to criminal trials.

section review

1. What is the only organized private business given specific protection under the Constitution? Do you agree or disagree with this guaranteed protection? Give at least three reasons.

2. Which types of cases involving the press and prior restraint have presented the court with the most problems?

4. FREEDOM OF RELIGION

The freedom of religion clause of the First Amendment contains two sections. One section prohibits the "establishment of religion," and the other section prohibits the passing of any law that would prevent "free exercise" of religion. Even though these provisions protect overlapping rights, you will examine them separately.

Conflicts involving the establishment clause have developed frequently in the context of public schools. These controversies have focused on the separation between church and state. First, may the government (state or federal) provide assistance to activities conducted by religious organizations? For example, may the government give financial aid to parochial schools or their students? Second, may religious matters intrude into government activities? For example, may prayers and Bible reading be conducted in the schools?

These Hassidic Jewish children board a bus to go to their own private school.

The free exercise clause has raised questions about applying general state regulations. May orthodox Jews or Seventh Day Adventists—whose day of rest is Saturday—refuse to observe a Sunday-closing law?

The Establishment Clause. A government action will not violate the establishment clause 1) if it has a secular purpose, 2) if it produces a principal effect that neither advances nor inhibits religion, or 3) if it does not cause the government to become excessively entangled with religion (*Lemon* v. *Kurtzman*, 1971). Nonetheless, application of this test involves matters of degree.

The constitutionality of dispensing financial benefits to church-related institutions is a large part of the controversy over the establishment clause. In *Everson* v. *Board of Education* (1947), the Court held that aid primarily intended to benefit the pupils rather than the schools was acceptable. Con-

sequently, a state might provide busing for parochial school students. However, a state may not reimburse parents for a percentage of the tuition they paid to these nonpublic schools (*Committee for Public Education* v. *Nyquist*, 1973).

Some aid may be given directly to church-related institutions without violating the test. For example, state and federal governments may give direct grants to church-related private colleges so long as the grants are not used for religious purposes (*Roemer* v. *Maryland Board of Public Works*, 1976; *Tilton* v. *Richardson*, 1971). However, in the Tilton case the Court voided a section of the 1963 Federal Higher Education Facilities Act. This section allowed colleges to use federally financed buildings for religious purposes after 20 years. The Court maintained that such use would advance religion.

Grants to parochial schools for the salaries of teachers of secular subjects also have been held to violate the establishment clause. Since parochial schools greatly emphasize religious teaching, the government would have to continually check that teachers paid with public funds were not teaching religion (*Lemon* v. *Kurtzman*, 1971). Such involvement would be considered an "excessive entanglement."

States may not give public funds to parochial schools to repair facilities or to administer tests. According to the Court such uses of public funds could advance religion. However, public funds may legally be used to provide church schools with secular textbooks. Such books mainly benefit schools rather than churches.

Another issue involved in the relations between church and state concerns religion in the public schools. This issue has caused at least as much controversy as the one over public aid to private schools. The three major areas of controversy concern Bible reading and praying in schools, the teaching of religion and/or evolution, and allowing the

As a result of a Supreme Court ruling, Amish children are exempt from mandatory attendance in public schools.

students time off from public school classes to obtain religious instruction.

Prayer and the Bible. In 1962 and 1963 the Court struck down laws in New York, Pennsylvania, and Maryland, which required or allowed schools to open classes with prayers or Bible reading. These rulings were one of the most controversial decisions made by the Court in recent years, and serious attempts to overturn them by constitutional amendment have failed.

Evolution and Religion. Some of the most impassioned debates have concerned the teaching of evolution in the schools. The Scopes trial of 1925 in Tennessee was a well-publicized event. John Scopes, a teacher in Dayton, Tennessee, defied a state law that

made the teaching of evolution illegal. William Jennings Bryan acted for the prosecution and Clarence Darrow represented the defense. Scopes was convicted. However, because an appeals court upheld the law but voided the penalties applied to Scopes, the matter went no further. It was not until 43 years later that a similar case, *Epperson* v. *Arkansas* (1968), reached the Supreme Court. This time the court struck down an Arkansas statute forbidding the teaching of evolution in the schools. In this decision the Court held the state "had no legitimate interest in protecting any or all religions from views distasteful to them." Religion and the Bible, the Court added, might be taught if they were "presented objectively" from a "literary and historic viewpoint," and if they were part of a secular education program.

Learned Hand was born on January 27, 1872, in Albany, New York. Hand graduated summa cum laude from Harvard University in 1893 and was elected to Phi Beta Kappa. He earned an M.A. degree with honors in philosophy in 1894 and received his LL.B degree with honors from the Harvard Law School in 1896. Hand was descended from a long line of legal people — Hand's grandfather, Augustus Hand, was a justice of the New York state supreme court. His father, Samuel Hand, was a leading New York lawyer with the reputation of having argued more cases before the New York state court of appeals than any other lawyer of his time. His uncles, Clifford and Richard Hand, were also distinguished attorneys, and his cousin, Augustus N. Hand, was a U.S. district court judge.

Hand began his career as a law clerk for Marcus T. Hun of Albany and then worked with several prestigious law firms. In 1909 Hand was appointed by President Taft to serve as a judge for the southern district of New York. During his 15 years with the district court, he rendered 637 opinions that encompassed all boundaries of the law. In 1924 President Coolidge named Judge Hand to the bench of the U.S. Court of Appeals for the Second Judicial Circuit, a lifetime appointment. Hand became the senior judge of this court in 1939 and served in that capacity until his retirement in 1951. A federal judge longer than anyone else in U.S. history, Hand rendered close to 3,000 opinions and was considered first and foremost among American judges.

One of Hand's most important decisions involved the Associated Press. The federal government charged that the Associated Press was monopolistic in its distribution of the news. Hand believed that the Associated Press acted as a by-law of the association because it permitted its members to veto admission of competing papers. According to Hand, this practice constituted a monopolistic practice under provisions of the Sherman Antitrust Law.

Another notable decision rendered by Judge Hand was **Sheldon** v. **Metro-Goldwyn Pictures**. This case involved a novel, a play, and a film based on an actual incident. It was brought before the court to determine if the film was based on the facts of the incident, which was of public record, or on the novel and play written by Sheldon. In Hand's opinion, which required lengthy and critical evaluation into the subject of creative expression, the motion picture company had made unfair use of the novelist's copyright by using the events in his book. To members of the legal profession, his opinion in this case ranks as one of the foremost examples of judicial style.

Learned Hand felt that liberty was something found in "the hearts of men and women; when it dies there, no constitution, no law, no court can help it." He further stated that "the spirit of liberty is the spirit which seeks to understand the minds of other men and women" and considered each of his cases as a "new intellectual pursuit of freedom." Judge Hand, utilizing the traditional privilege, sat on the federal bench following his retirement until his death in New York City on August 18, 1961.

Federal and state government funds may not be used for church-related activities. Funds may be used to purchase nonreligious textbooks.

Released Time. Most states allow students to be released from public school to attend religious classes. The Court struck down laws on released time when they involved the use of public facilities (*McCollum* v. *Board of Education*, 1948). However, laws involving nonpublic accommodations were upheld (*Zorach* v. *Clausen*, 1953). In other words, released time is permissible for religious education in private facilities.

The Free Exercise Clause. When ruling on laws that violate the free exercise clause, the Supreme Court has distinguished between laws that interfere with religious beliefs and ones that interfere with conduct. The free-dom to hold religious beliefs is absolute, and the government may not force anyone to accept a particular creed (*Cantwell* v. *Connecticut*, 1940). Consequently, a state regulation requiring all public school students to salute the flag and recite the pledge of allegiance is unconstitutional (*West Virginia Board of Education* v. *Barnette*, 1943). This is because state governments may not force children to participate in ceremonies their religions forbid.

But not all conduct connected with religious beliefs is protected by the free exercise clause. A "direct" burden on the exercise of religion results when a law makes the conduct demanded by an individual's religion illegal. An "indirect" burden does not make a religious duty illegal; but it makes it more difficult for an individual to carry out religious obligations.

When analyzing both direct and indirect burdens on the exercise of religion, the Court balances the burden on the individual's religious obligations against the state or federal government's interest in passing the law. It also reviews alternative ways for the government to achieve its objective without imposing so large a burden on religion.

The following cases are examples of direct burdens on religious freedom.

Reynolds v. U.S. (1878). In this case the Court upheld a law making polygamy illegal, even though the Mormon religion at that time permitted it. The Court ruled that the state had an important interest in protecting the children of marriages, and this interest outweighed the burden on religion.

Prince v. Massachusetts (1944). In this case the Court upheld a state law, which had been applied to the children of Jehovah's Witnesses whose religion required the children to sell religious literature. The Court ruled that the state's interest in protecting the enforcement of a child labor law, which would prevent the children from selling the religious literature, outweighed the burden on religion.

Gillette v. United States (1971). The Court upheld an act of Congress exempting from military service only those "conscientious objectors" who opposed war in any form. Opposers of only particular wars might not obtain the exemption.

Wisconsin v. Yoder (1972). The Court made an exception to the state's compulsory school laws for children of members of the Amish sect. (Usually the Court makes no such exception on religious grounds.) The Court

ruled that the group's long-established life style of self-sufficiency was essential to its faith and would be "threatened by exposure of their children to modern education."

The following cases are examples of indirect burdens on religious freedom.

Braunfeld v. Brown (1961). In this case the Court held that a Sunday-closing law applied to orthodox Jews.

Johnson v. Robison (1974). In this case the Court held that denying veterans' educational benefits to conscientious objectors who performed alternative civilian service did not impose a burden on the free exercise of religion.

Sherbert v. Verner (1963). In this case the Court struck down a state unemployment compensation rule requiring that Seventh Day Adventists accept work on Saturday, their Sabbath, or lose benefits.

Murdock v. Pennsylvania (1946). In this case the Court struck down a vendor's license tax that was applied to people whose religion required the selling of religious literature. The Court ruled that the state's interest in obtaining money could be satisfied by other sources.

section review

1. Under what three conditions will a government action not violate the establishment clause?
2. What restrictions are placed on church-run schools that receive federal and state grants?
3. Explain what is meant by direct and indirect burdens on religious freedom.
4. Cite four examples of court cases that involved indirect burdens on religious freedom.
5. Cite three examples of court cases that involved direct burdens on religious freedom.

CHAPTER SUMMARY

32

Most of our civil liberties are guaranteed by the Bill of Rights. Several states ratified the Constitution only on condition that a bill of rights be adopted by the new government. Before the Civil War, the Bill of Rights was applied only to federal actions. Refusal to extend its application to the states caused many citizens to be deprived of their rights. Since the ratification of the Fourteenth Amendment in 1868, the courts have expanded application of the Bill of Rights to actions of both the federal and state governments.

The First Amendment guarantees freedom of religion, speech, and the press, the right of peaceful assembly, and the right of petition. Freedom of speech has been defined by the Supreme Court as freedom of expression. Attempts to regulate free expression have generally been in two areas: restrictions on the content of what is spoken and published, and restrictions on the means of communication.

Three major areas of content restriction are advocacy of violation of law, obscenity, and defamation (including slander and libel). "Fighting words", overbroad and vague laws, prior restraint, national security, and broadcasting are other areas in which the courts have developed guidelines for the protection of both individual rights and the welfare of society.

REVIEW QUESTIONS

1. Why was the Bill of Rights considered essential by some states before they would ratify the Constitution?
2. How has the court defined freedom of speech? Under what conditions may free expression be regulated?
3. What is the Holmes-Brandeis "clear and present danger" test? Could you apply that test to the American Nazi party parades in Skokie, Illinois? Cite reasons for your answers.
4. What criteria were established in *Scales* v. *U.S.*? Apply these criteria to the Skokie incident.

Would the city of Skokie be permitted to prevent the parade? Explain.
5. How do libel and slander laws limit freedom of speech? freedom of the press?
6. Define prior restraint. Under what conditions do you think prior restraint should be permitted? Explain.
7. When can an injunction be issued against the reporting of criminal proceedings?
8. Define direct and indirect burdens on religious freedom. Cite one case as an example of each burden.

ACTIVITIES FOR REVIEW

activity 1   Stage a classroom debate or forum on the following issue: RESOLVED, that freedom of the press does not apply to people who advocate the overthrow of the government.

activity 2   Research the facts in the case of *Tinker* v. *Des Moines School District.* With other students in your class, prepare and present a role play of the incidents in the case.

activity 3   Research the policy of civil disobedience advocated by Martin Luther King, Jr. Prepare a report entitled "Civil Disobedience and First Amendment Rights" for presentation to the class.

activity 4   Prepare a version of the First Amendment rewritten in your own words. Try to get people to sign a petition in support of the ideas expressed. Report to the class the number who signed or refused to sign, and report the comments of all those surveyed.

political science DICTIONARY

eminent domain—the right of a government to force a property owner to sell property when it is needed for public use.   p. 617

infringement—a breach or invasion of some legal right.   p. 618

prior restraint—an attempt to regulate in advance.   p. 625

33

The Rights of an Accused Person

This chapter explores what rights a person accused of a crime possesses under the Fourth, Fifth, Sixth, and Eighth amendments. According to the Bill of Rights, when an individual is subjected to sanctions by the government, he or she has certain rights associated with "due process of law" or fair procedure. However, as with First Amendment rights, the interpretation of these rights has generated much controversy. The focus of the continuing dispute is the issue of how careful the state must be in protecting a criminal defendant's rights.

Those who criticize the Supreme Court argue that its decisions have hampered the police. They contend that the Court is "soft" on criminals. Those who support its decisions maintain that the Court is protecting all citizens' rights from infringement by the government.

These opposing views reflect conflicting attitudes toward our criminal justice system. Herbert Packer has labeled these two views the "crime control model" and the "due process model." Professor Packer considers the crime control model an assembly line and the due process model an obstacle course.

As you study the materials in this chapter, try to decide whether the criminal justice system is more like an assembly line or an obstacle course.

CHAPTER PREVIEW

1. PRETRIAL RIGHTS AND LIMITATIONS
2. RIGHTS DURING AND AFTER THE TRIAL
3. JUVENILE RIGHTS

1. PRETRIAL RIGHTS AND LIMITATIONS

Arrests and Other Detentions. Any arrest or other detention is considered a "seizure" and must meet the Fourth Amendment's prohibition against unreasonable searches and seizures. The kind of detention and the circumstances surrounding it determine the scope of constitutional protection. An arrest is different from a "stop-and-frisk" method of detention.

For an arrest to be valid the Constitution requires **probable cause.** Probable cause is established when there is evidence (detailed information) testifying to the reason(s) the arresting officer was convinced that the person arrested had committed—or was in the process of committing—a crime. The requirement of probable cause applies to arrests made with or without a warrant.

An officer may frisk an individual believed to be carrying a concealed weapon.

> **Probable cause** is reasonable grounds for suspicion supported by evidence.

Arrests with a Warrant. An arrest warrant is a paper usually issued by a judge. The person requesting the warrant—usually a police officer—must present to the judge facts sufficient to prove that there is probable cause that the person to be arrested has committed a crime.

Arrests Without a Warrant. Arrests can be made without warrants. Generally speaking, a police officer or private citizen may arrest someone who is committing or attempting to commit a crime in his or her presence. Police officers also have the right to arrest persons who they have reasonable cause to believe have committed crimes outside the presence of an officer.

An arrest that is made with an invalid arrest warrant may be valid. If the prosecutor can demonstrate that the arresting officer had probable cause at the time of the arrest, then the arrest is considered valid.

The Supreme Court has not decided if it is permissible to arrest a person (when probable cause exists) without a warrant in his or her own home, especially when there is time to get an arrest warrant. But if the police are in "hot pursuit" of a suspect who returns to his or her home, they may enter the premises and arrest the person without a warrant (*U.S. v. Santana*, 1976).

However, under federal law and under the laws of some states, the police must announce their presence and purpose before they can use force to enter a home to make an arrest. The arrest is illegal if no announcement is made. But there are a few exceptions to the announcement rule. An announcement is not necessary 1) if it would place the officer(s) in danger, 2) if it would increase the possibility of escape, or 3) if it would permit the destruction of evidence.

Detention of an individual may be justified as reasonable under the Fourth Amendment without showing probable cause to arrest. If a police officer believes that criminal activity is afoot, the officer may detain and question a person. He or she may also "frisk" or "pat down" the person's outer clothing for a weapon (*Terry* v. *Ohio*, 1968). Although a warrant is not required for such an investigation, the officer must have some objective basis for believing that criminal activity is in progress. The officer's personal observations or a reliable informant's tip satisfies the requirement.

Searches and Seizures. The Fourth and Fourteenth amendments limit searches and seizures by both federal and state governments. Four major questions must be asked. 1) Was the police activity a search or a seizure? 2) Was a search warrant required? If so, did the police obtain a valid one? 3) Did the circumstances justify a search without a warrant? 4) What was the proper scope of the search, and did the police stay within that scope?

The general rule requires the police to obtain a warrant for a search even though they have probable cause to proceed with the search. However, they may search without a warrant if the search constitutes an exception to the rule. Nevertheless, the courts are stricter about warrantless searches than they are about warrantless arrests.

A search is any governmental interference with an individual's reasonable and justifiable expectation of privacy. A seizure involves a governmental exertion of control over a person or a thing. A search occurs whenever or wherever the person involved is entitled to expect privacy. The place may be either private or public. An individual's privacy is violated and an illegal search occurs when, for example, the police bug a public telephone booth without a warrant (*Katz* v. *U.S.*, 1967). And an illegal search occurs when the police use a peephole in the ceiling of a public restroom to observe activity in the stalls.

But a search does not occur when a person has no legitimate expectation of privacy. Thus objects in plain view may be seized without a warrant if the police have a right to be there. For example, if an officer patrolling a street sees a car with stolen license plates parked in an individual's driveway, he or she may search and seize the car. The officer saw the car from a site (a public sidewalk) that he or she had a right to inhabit. But if the officer had entered the driveway and opened the garage door in order to see the car, then his or her actions would constitute a search in violation of the Fourth Amendment for no warrant had been obtained to authorize the search.

Searches with a Warrant. There are five requirements for a valid search warrant. First, a search warrant must be issued by a judge. A search warrant issued by a state's chief investigator and prosecutor has been held to be invalid (*Coolidge* v. *New Hampshire*, 1971).

Second, the search warrant must be based on probable cause. Probable cause is established when the facts are given to a judge and he or she concludes by independent evaluation that criminal evidence may be found in a certain spot. The information given to the judge cannot be merely the conclusions of the police officer. Probable cause is not established when the only information that the judge obtains from the police is that they have "reliable information" from a "credible person" that the defendant has committed a crime (*Aquilar* v. *Texas*, 1964). The police may present information to a judge that they obtained from an informant, but in this situation they must show that the informant is reliable.

Search warrants must be issued by a judge in order to be valid.

Third, the warrant must be specific. It must describe in detail the things to be seized and the place to be searched. For example, a specific apartment must be identified, not merely an apartment building.

Fourth, the warrant must be served in a valid way. Unless special permission is obtained, the search warrant must be served during daylight hours. And it must be served within a limited period of time after it is issued, for example, within ten days. (Arrest warrants, however, are usually valid indefinitely.) Unless special circumstances exist (see the discussion under arrests), police officers must announce themselves when serving a warrant.

Fifth, a search and seizure must not exceed the scope of the warrant. The warrant cannot be used by the police for a "fishing expedition." For example, the police cannot search a detached garage if the warrant specifies the house as the only place to be searched. And the search must be limited to finding the things described in the warrant. However, the police may seize evidence that is in plain view during a valid search.

Searches Without a Warrant. The following are six situations involving special factors under which a search without a warrant is justified:

1. *Consent.* An individual may consent to a search. But for such a search to be upheld, it must be shown that the person consenting had the authority to consent, that the consent was voluntary, and that the search did

not go beyond the scope of the consent given. A landlord has no authority to consent to a search of a tenant's house or apartment (*Stoner* v. *California*, 1964). But if two persons share an apartment, either can consent to a search of the areas that they share (living room, kitchen, and so on). However, neither can consent to the search of areas reserved for the other's exclusive use (*U.S.* v. *Matlock*, 1974).

There is no valid consent if the police falsely assert that they have legal authority to search and, as a result, prevail on an individual to give consent. Nor is there valid consent if the police trick an individual into admitting them (for example, by posing as repairers) and then conduct an unwarranted search. (*Gouled* v. *U.S.*, 1921). A person in custody may consent to a search, but the government must show that such consent was voluntary (*U.S.* v. *Watson*, 1976).

2. *Searches incident to a valid arrest.* If a person has been legally arrested, the police may conduct a search of the person and the areas within immediate reach. But the search must be conducted only to protect the police from danger (for example, if police officers think that the suspect is armed) and to prevent the destruction of evidence.

3. *Searches incident to "stop and frisk."* A search of a person detained but not arrested is valid if it is limited to a frisk to determine if the person is armed. If a weapon is found, it is admissible as evidence in a charge of carrying a concealed weapon. State and lower federal courts have held that other evidence obtained during a frisk is admissible in court, but the Supreme Court has not ruled on this issue.

4. *Searches in "hot pursuit."* If the police are in hot pursuit of a suspect, they may enter a building or a house without a warrant to search for the suspect. Any evidence that they see in plain view may be seized and used in court.

5. *Automobile searches.* There are three situations in which the police may search a

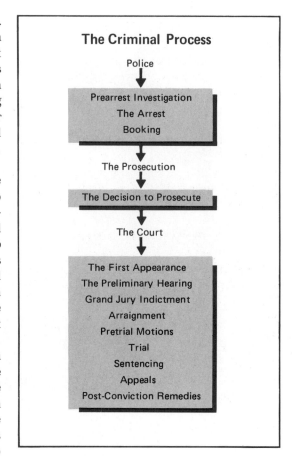

The Criminal Process

Police

↓

Prearrest Investigation
The Arrest
Booking

↓

The Prosecution

↓

The Decision to Prosecute

↓

The Court

↓

The First Appearance
The Preliminary Hearing
Grand Jury Indictment
Arraignment
Pretrial Motions
Trial
Sentencing
Appeals
Post-Conviction Remedies

vehicle without a warrant.

(a) Auto "no time." If the police have probable cause to think that items in a car will be removed before they can obtain a warrant, they may search a vehicle that they temporarily stopped on a highway. In *Chambers* v. *Maroney* (1970) the Supreme Court upheld the legality of searching a car at a police station a few hours after the driver had been stopped. The Court ruled that because the police had probable cause to stop the suspect's car and to arrest him for robbery, they also had probable cause to search the car without a warrant. The fact that they searched later at the police station did not negate probable cause or require them to obtain a search warrant.

(b) Impounded vehicles. Whenever the

police have impounded a car, they may make an inventory of the car's contents without a warrant. Such a search protects the owner's property, protects the police against a charge that the property was taken while the car was impounded, and protects against the possibility that others may find firearms (*South Dakota* v. *Opperman*, 1976).

(c) Public safety. If a car has been towed to a private garage, the police may search it if they believe the search necessary to protect the public, that is, if they believe that the car contains firearms (*Cady* v. *Dombrowski*, 1973).

6. *Emergency searches.* A major exception to the warrant rule involves situations in which the police believe that delaying a search would permit the removal or the destruction of evidence or would endanger the police or others. In such circumstances the police may search without a warrant.

Electronic surveillance through the use of wiretapping and bugging has presented the Supreme Court with difficult problems in interpreting protection under the Fourth Amendment. In 1928, in *Olmstead* v. *U.S.*, the Supreme Court upheld a bootlegger's conviction obtained with a warrantless wiretap on the ground that the recording of the calls had taken place outside the bootlegger's home. But 39 years later, in *Katz* v. *U.S.* (1967), the Court overturned the conviction of a man who had been bugged by the FBI when he used a telephone booth for illegal betting. The Court said that the Fourth Amendment protected persons as well as places and that Katz had the right to expect privacy in the booth.

Today a warrant authorizing a wiretap or other electronic surveillance must meet the following requirements. There must be a showing of probable cause. The persons to be listened to must be named. The nature of the conversations to be bugged must be described. The tap must be limited to a specified period of time. The police must return to the court to show what conversations were intercepted.

The Exclusionary Rule. Until the *exclusionary rule* was adopted in the federal courts (*C. Weeks* v. *U.S.*, 1914) and in state courts (*Mapp* v. *Ohio*, 1961), an individual had no remedy if he or she was searched and evidence was seized in violation of protections provided by the Fourth Amendment. The exclusionary rule prohibits the prosecutor from using such illegally obtained evidence in a criminal trial. The rule requires the courts to exclude the evidence illegally seized as well as any other evidence that is obtained later as the direct or indirect result of an illegal search or arrest. However, if the police can prove that the later evidence is not connected to the earlier illegally seized evidence, such later evidence will be admissible in court.

Illegally seized evidence is not admissable in a criminal court trial. What is your opinion regarding this rule?

The purpose of the rule is to prevent police misconduct. But critics argue that a guilty person should not be allowed to profit from a police officer's violation of the Constitution and be freed for that reason. Supporters of the rule argue that all other procedures have completely failed to secure compliance with the constitutional provisions on the part of police officers. Consequently, when illegally seized evidence was admitted, the courts were "required to participate in, and in effect condone, the lawless activities of law enforcement officers."

The Supreme Court under the leadership of Chief Justice Warren Burger has limited the applications of the exclusionary rule. For example, even though illegally seized evidence cannot be used at a trial, it may be used for the very limited purpose of impeaching the credibility of a defendant if he or she chooses to testify at his or her trial (*Harris* v. *New York*, 1971).

Confessions and Incriminating Statements. The Supreme Court has ruled that the Fifth Amendment prevents the use of any involuntary or coerced confession in the federal courts (*Brown* v. *U.S.*, 1897). This rule applies to the states (*Malloy* v. *Hogan*, 1964).

What is an involuntary or a coerced statement? The key element involves determining whether the suspect's confession was voluntarily made. In evaluating the voluntary nature of a statement, a trial court analyzes factors such as the age, intelligence, and experience of the accused as well as the methods employed by the police in obtaining the confession, for example, the length of time the person was detained or the method of interrogation that was used. The Supreme Court threw out the conviction of a man who had a history of emotional instability because he was questioned without interruption for eight hours and was encouraged to confess by a friend who followed police instructions (*Spano* v. *N.Y.*, 1959). The promise of benefits or leniency makes a confession involuntary in

most states. The use of fraud, trickery, or force also makes a confession involuntary.

An involuntary or *coerced confession* cannot be used against the accused for any purpose. If such a confession is used in a trial, the conviction of the accused upon appeal will be reversed automatically.

Voluntary Statements. Even if a confession or some other incriminating statement were made voluntarily, it could be excluded from a criminal trial if some constitutional right of the accused had been violated by the police in obtaining the statement. The rules for the admission of voluntary statements involve the following:

1. *Escobedo Rule.* If a confession or an incriminating statement is obtained from the accused while he or she is denied the Sixth Amendment right to counsel, the confession or statement must be excluded in a state or a federal criminal trial (*Escobedo* v. *Illinois*, 1964). But the right to counsel does not apply until formal charges have been filed. Thus if an accused person claims the right to consult a lawyer before the filing of formal charges, such a claim must be based on the Fifth Amendment privilege against self-incrimination (*Kirby* v. *Illinois*, 1972).

2. *Miranda Rule.* In *Miranda* v. *Arizona* (1966) the Supreme Court ruled that a confession obtained during a custodial interrogation, held either before or after formal charges had been filed, cannot be admitted in a criminal trial unless certain safeguards are observed. For example, the police must inform a suspect a) that he or she has the right to remain silent, b) that anything he or she says may be used against him or her, and c) that he or she has the right to talk with a lawyer (either one hired by the accused or appointed by the court if the accused is poor) at the time of the interrogation.

The concept of being in police custody is broadly interpreted. It includes many situations other than the questioning of a suspect at the police station. The questioning of a

Accused persons may not be coerced into confessing. All statements must be made voluntarily.

person in his or her bedroom after arrest requires that the Miranda warnings be given (*Orozco* v. *Texas*, 1969). If a suspect is already in jail, he or she cannot be questioned about a different, unrelated crime without being informed of his or her rights under Miranda (*Mathis* v. *U.S.*, 1968).

The Miranda rule does not apply when the police are conducting on-the-scene questioning or pursuing general fact finding. Similarly, the rule does not apply to statements made to a person who is not a police officer. The police cannot put a disguised officer in a cell with a suspect and pump him or her for information; in that situation the Miranda rules would apply.

Once a suspect has been given the Miranda warnings, he or she may waive the right to remain silent and may talk to the police. But the Supreme Court has ruled that the prosecution must prove that such a waiver was made voluntarily. Even though a suspect has begun to talk after waiving his or her rights, he or she may later assert the right to remain silent. Further attempts to question the suspect can take place only after a significant period of time has passed and new Miranda warnings have been given.

3. *Massiah Rule.* Because the Sixth Amendment right to counsel applies once formal charges are made, any statement obtained from an accused after formal charges are filed is not admissible unless the suspect's lawyer was present (*Massiah* v. *U.S.*, 1964).

Disguised police officers may not be put in cells with suspects to gain information.

4. *McNabb-Mallory Rule.* This rule applies only to federal criminal trials. The Supreme Court has held that statements made by a suspect while in detention but before being charged must be excluded during the trial if unnecessary delays were encountered in charging him or her (*McNabb* v. *U.S.*, 1943; *Mallory* v. *U.S.*, 1957). This court ruling has been modified by statute. Today only statements made more than six hours after an arrest in which no formal charges have been filed are excluded as evidence.

Both the Escobedo and Miranda rules have been modified in their application to federal criminal trials. The balance of the required warnings does not automatically exclude incriminating statements. Instead, the test for admissibility is voluntariness. Failure to warn the suspect of his or her rights is one factor in determining voluntariness.

Pretrial Identifications and Line-ups. There is no right to counsel at police line-ups that are held before a suspect is charged formally with a crime (*Kirby* v. *Illinois*, 1972). But once a suspect is charged, he or she has the right to have a lawyer present at a line-up (*U.S.* v. *Wade*, 1967). The Wade ruling has been changed by law. Now, even if a suspect's lawyer is not present at a line-up after formal charges have been filed the eyewitness identification is admissible at the trial.

There is no right to counsel in other kinds of identification proceedings. An accused has no right to have his or her lawyer present when blood, handwriting, or voice samples are taken.

Even though a suspect is not entitled to have counsel present during most pretrial identifications, the procedure used for identifications must be fair. In judging whether a procedure is fair, the court examines the conditions surrounding a witness' ability to view the suspect at the time of the crime, the accuracy of any preliminary description that was given by a witness, the length of time that elapsed between the crime and the identification, and whether the suspect was present alone or with others during the identification procedure.

It must be noted that the Fifth Amendment right against self-incrimination extends only to an accused person's testimony. Thus Fifth Amendment rights are not violated when the police take blood or handwriting samples, make the accused appear before witnesses for possible identification, take fingerprints, make the accused repeat certain words or gestures, or make him or her give voice samples.

The fingerprint method is an infallible means of identification. Why?

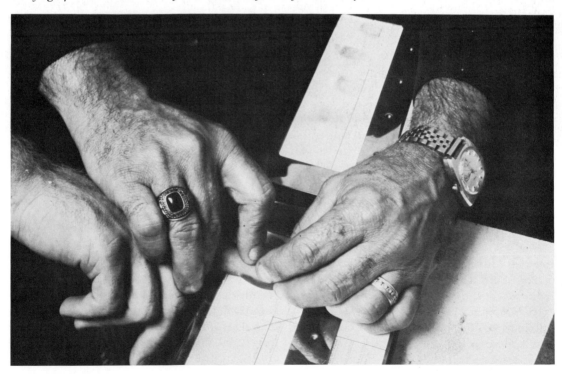

Speed. Most states and the federal government are required by law or court rulings to bring a suspect before a judge promptly. These rules or laws are not "constitutional rules." However, if a suspect can prove that the prosecutor deliberately delayed the filing of formal charges, guarantees of due process may require that the charges against the suspect be dismissed.

Bail. The Eighth Amendment prohibits excessive bail. The general rule for bail (*Stack* v. *Boyle*, 1951) requires that it bear some relation to the gravity of the offense. Its major purpose is to ensure that the accused will appear for trial. The rule stipulates that bail should not be set so high that it prevents the accused from securing liberty in order to prepare a defense. Nor should it be used in such a way that it promotes discrimination on the basis of wealth. The Supreme Court has not decided whether this provision applies to the states. But many states have banned excessive bail.

Speedy Trial. The Sixth Amendment requires that accused persons shall enjoy the right to speedy and public trials. This right extends to criminal trials in state courts. The right may be waived, but such a waiver must be made voluntarily. Whenever the government, federal or state, is charged with denying a speedy trial, the courts will examine the following factors: the duration of the delay, the reasons for the delay, and the disadvantage resulting to the accused because of the delay. Whenever the right to a speedy trial is denied, the only remedy is the dismissal of the charges.

Pretrial Publicity. The due-process clauses of the Fifth and Fourteenth amendments require that the accused be given a fair trial by an impartial jury. This right is denied if publicity before or during a trial creates an atmosphere that will prevent a jury from

CRUEL — BUT FAR FROM UNUSUAL!

considering the evidence impartially and objectively. For example, the Supreme Court overturned a conviction for murder because despite promises to decide the case only on the evidence presented, 8 of 12 jurors decided that the accused was guilty on the basis of beliefs formed before the trial (*Irvin* v. *Dowd*, 1961).

Born April 11, 1862, in Glens Falls, New York, Charles Evans Hughes graduated from high school at the age of 13 and entered Colgate University at the age of 14. After two years Hughes transferred to Brown University, where he earned his A.B. degree in 1881 with honors and was elected to Phi Beta Kappa. Hughes received his LL.B. from the Columbia University Law School in 1884 with highest honors. He was admitted to the bar during the same year and began his career with the law firm of Chamberlain, Carter and Hornblower. He left the firm in 1891 due to failing health, taught law at Cornell University for two years, and then returned to practice.

Hughes was elected governor of New York in 1907 and served two terms in office. As governor, he recommended passage of a child labor bill, prompted passage of a workmen's compensation bill, and sponsored and put through reforms in insurance company regulations. In 1910 Governor Hughes resigned his post to accept an appointment as an associate justice of the U.S. Supreme Court, and he soon became one of the court's most prominent members.

In 1916 Hughes resigned from the Court in order to run for the office of President against Woodrow Wilson. During his campaign, Hughes, against the advice of other politicians, made a tour of the country. Although his speeches were earnest, well-written, and honest, they were not the speeches of an experienced practicing politician who knew how to appeal to the electorate. Thus, Hughes was labeled "animated feather duster" and "the human icicle," a reputation that followed him around the country. He lost the election by a very narrow margin. Following his defeat, Hughes returned to the practice of law.

In 1921 Mr. Hughes was appointed secretary of state under President Harding. During his term of office, Secretary Hughes was able to conclude more than 50 treaties with foreign nations. He reestablished friendly relations with South America and successfully negotiated the treaties that resulted from the 1921–1922 Washington Conference on disarmament, which he headed.

Hughes was reappointed to the Supreme Court by President Hoover in 1930, this time as Chief Justice. The historic decisions of the Hughes Court include upholding an Illinois statute forbidding the employment of children under the age of 16, upholding a California statute forbidding the employment of women for more than an eight-hour day or a forty-eight hour week, upholding an act of Congress limiting the hours of work on interstate railroads, and the 1941 ruling that Blacks were entitled to railroad accomodations equal to that of Whites. Hughes was noted for a number of opinions. One, about a Minnesota "gag" law, was a forthright defense of the freedom of the press; another, in a California case in which a woman was convicted for waving a red flag, stated that free political discussion was essential if the government was to remain responsive to the will of the people. Hughes upheld the rights of railway clerks to form their own labor union in yet another decision. Chief Justice Hughes resigned his post on June 2, 1941, because of failing health and died on August 27, 1948, with the distinction of being the greatest Chief Justice since John Marshall.

CHARLES EVANS HUGHES

Prosecution Evidence. In a criminal case the prosecution must give evidence favorable to the accused prior to the trial if the accused makes a specific request for it and if the evidence is likely to influence the outcome of the trial. Failure to turn over such evidence is a violation of due process.

Competency. An accused person's right to due process is also violated if he or she is tried, sentenced, or punished while incompetent. A defendant is competent when he or she understands the proceedings against him or her and can assist in the defense (by working with the lawyer).

Grand Jury Indictment. The Fifth Amendment requires that in all proceedings involving a federal felony a grand-jury hearing be held and an indictment be issued unless the right is waived. This right, however, does not apply to the states. The function of the grand jury is to decide whether the evidence presented to it warrants the filing of a formal charge. Although it hears evidence from the prosecutor, a grand jury has the power to obtain other evidence.

In place of the grand jury, most states use a process called *information*. In this process, the accused person is brought before a judge to plead to the charges. If he or she pleads not guilty, the judge holds a preliminary examination to determine whether or not a crime has been committed and whether there is probable cause to believe that the accused person committed the crime. If the judge decides that there is enough evidence, the suspect is detained until the prosecutor files an information—the formal charge.

section review

1. Why is probable cause a valid requirement for making an arrest?

2. What are the exceptions to the announcement rule? Do you agree or disagree with these exceptions? Why?
3. What is the Miranda rule? List the safeguards that must be observed.
4. Which constitutional amendment guarantees the right to counsel? When is it not necessary for a suspect to have a lawyer present?
5. What factors are examined when the government is charged with denying a speedy trial?

2. RIGHTS DURING AND AFTER THE TRIAL

Right to Counsel. As previously discussed, every person accused of a crime has a right to be represented by a lawyer. The Supreme Court has ruled that this right extends to "every critical stage" of the proceedings against the accused.

Critical stages include the trial itself, interrogations while the accused is under arrest or after the accused has been formally charged, any appearance before the court in which a plea is entered or a defense is presented, a preliminary hearing, and sentencing. It does not include grand-jury hearings, or prison discipline, and does not apply to minor crimes. (But if conviction for an offense—either a felony or a misdemeanor—would entail imprisonment, the right to counsel applies.)

If a defendant is denied the right to counsel at the time of the trial, at the time that he or she is required to plead to the charge, or at the time of sentencing, then the exclusive remedy is the automatic reversal of any conviction (*Ferguson* v. *Georgia*, 1961). An individual can waive the right to counsel, but such a waiver must be made voluntarily and intelligently.

The Right to a Public Trial and a Trial by Jury. The Sixth Amendment assures the accused of a speedy and a public trial. This right extends to state courts through the Fourteenth Amendment.

The Sixth Amendment guarantees the accused the right to a trial by a jury of his or her peers. This right also extends to state court proceedings. But a jury of 12 is not required. The Supreme Court has upheld the legality of a jury composed of six persons in all but capital cases (*Williams* v. *Florida*, 1970). But the Court has not stipulated the minimum number for a jury.

Federal criminal cases require a unanimous jury verdict, but this requirement is not binding on the states. In noncapital cases the Court has upheld the validity of a less than unanimous jury verdict—9 of 12 (*Apodaca* v. *Oregon*, 1972).

However, the right to a jury trial applies only to serious offenses. If the punishment authorized by law is a prison term of more than six months, the offense is considered serious.

The right to a trial may be waived, but it must be waived voluntarily and intelligently.

Jurors must be selected from a cross-section of the community. Jury service cannot be restricted to certain groups. Three groups that historically had been excluded from jury service—Blacks, women, and Mexican Americans—are now members of jury pools.

The Right to a Fair and Impartial Trial. A jury composed of people who believe that the suspect is guilty before the trial begins, prejudicial publicity, prejudicial associations with jurors (deputy sheriffs who are key prosecution witnesses cannot be the guards for jurors during a trial—*Turner* v. *Louisiana*, 1965), mob violence, inflammatory evidence, knowing use of false testimony by the prosecution, or compelling a defendant to appear for trial in prison clothes are all grounds for reversing a conviction.

The Right to Confront Witnesses and the Right to Obtain Witnesses. If an accused person is to have a fair trial, he or she must be tried only on evidence presented in court. He or she must be able to cross-examine the witnesses. The accused must be able to introduce his or her own witnesses. If necessary, he or she must be able to use the power of the court to compel witnesses who possess evidence favorable to him or her to testify.

The Sixth Amendment right to confront witnesses extends to state criminal proceedings. The right of confrontation means that the accused must be permitted to cross-examine all witnesses who testify against him or her during the trial. This right is violated when the confession of a codefendant is introduced against the accused. The codefendant cannot be compelled to take the stand since he or she also possesses the right against self-incrimination. Therefore, the defendant cannot cross-examine him or her regarding the confession (*Burton* v. *U.S.*, 1968).

The Sixth Amendment expressly provides that an accused person has the right to force witnesses favorable to him or her to appear in court. This right also extends to state court proceedings. This right has been interpreted to mean that the accused has the right to present a defense. For example, when a defendant offered evidence that another witness had made an oral confession to the crime and the trial court excluded this evidence, the Supreme Court held that the exclusion violated the defendant's right to present a defense (*Chambers* v. *Mississippi*, 1973).

Privilege Against Self-incrimination. The Fifth Amendment mandates that no person "shall be compelled in any criminal case to be a witness against himself." This privilege against self-incrimination guarantees that a defendant does not have to take the stand in a trial. At any other point in the criminal process, an accused person does not have to make any statement that would tend to incriminate him or her. (See the discussion under Confessions and Incriminating Statements.) This privilege has been extended to state courts by the Fourteenth Amendment's due-process clause. This right protects not only testimony, but it extends to documents or records that are testimonial in nature (*U.S. v. White*, 1944).

This privilege also extends to a person who is a witness (not the accused) in any judicial or official hearing, investigation, or inquiry. Any question that tends to incriminate a witness by implicating him or her directly or indirectly in the commission of a crime does not have to be answered. But the privilege protects against the possibility of prosecution; and if a witness is granted immunity from prosecution, he or she must answer the questions.

If either a defendant or a witness claims the privilege and refuses to testify, no one in the proceedings may make a negative comment about claiming the privilege.

Limitations on Guilty Pleas. Whenever a defendant pleads guilty to a crime, the records must clearly show that the plea was made voluntarily and that the defendant understood its consequences. Courts are careful about guilty pleas, for such pleas waive the privilege against self-incrimination, trial by jury, and confrontation of witnesses. For example, in federal court proceedings, the judge must question the defendant to determine whether the plea was made voluntarily and whether there were solid grounds for such a plea.

Double Jeopardy. The Fifth Amendment states that no person can be put twice "in jeopardy of life or limb." This strange phrasing comes from the medieval custom of hanging, drawing, and quartering as well as cutting off various parts (limbs) of criminals. The law stated simply means that once a person has been tried for a crime, he or she cannot be tried again for that same crime.This is the case no matter what new evidence is produced in the future.

QUOTES from famous people

"The value system that underlies the Crime Control Model is based on the proposition that the repression of criminal conduct is by far the most important function to be performed by the criminal process. . . . In order to achieve this high purpose, the Crime Control Model requires that primary attention be paid to the efficiency with which the criminal process operates to screen suspects, determine guilt, and secure appropriate dispositions of persons convicted of crime. . . . The image that comes to mind is an assembly-line conveyor belt down which moves an endless stream of cases, never stopping, carrying the cases to workers who stand at fixed stations and who perform on each case as it comes by the same small but essential operation that brings it closer to being a finished product, or . . . a closed file. . . . If the Crime Control Model resembles an assembly line, the Due Process Model looks very much like an obstacle course. Each of its successive stages is designed to present formidable impediments to carrying the accused any further along in the process. . . . The Due Process Model insists on the prevention and elimination of mistakes to the extent possible."

Herbert L. Packer

Double jeopardy does not mean that someone cannot appear twice in court for the same act. This can occur under the following four circumstances:

1. A single act may violate laws in different jurisdictions. For example, those accused of murder or violence against civil rights protestors in the 1960's were often acquitted of murder in a state court but then convicted in a federal court of violating individuals' civil rights.

2. A single act may involve more than one crime in the same jurisdiction. An example is a robbery involving both force and the use of an illegal weapon.

3. If a trial ends in a *hung jury* (a jury that cannot agree) or in a mistrial, the case may be retried.

4. If a case is appealed to a higher court, the proceedings in that court are not considered a new trial.

Protections against double jeopardy were held to extend to the states by the Fourteenth Amendment in *Benton* v. *Maryland*, 1969.

Cruel and Unusual Punishment. The Eighth Amendment prohibits "cruel and unusual punishment." This prohibition also applies to the states.

The Supreme Court has never defined what kinds of punishment were cruel and unusual. Consequently, judges have had to make this determination on a case-by-case basis. One approach to this problem is to determine if the punishment fits the crime. A 12-year imprisonment in irons at hard labor for falsifying public records was held to be excessive and therefore cruel and unusual (*Weems* v. *U.S.*, 1910).

A second approach involves examining the nature of the punishment itself, regardless of the crime involved. The Court held that Congress could not strip an army deserter of his citizenship. Making a person stateless is too cruel a punishment for any crime (*Trop* v. *Dulles*, 1958).

Recently the death penalty has provoked great controversy in regard to cruel and unusual punishment. In 1972, in *Furman* v. *Georgia*, the Court ruled that the penalty itself was not cruel, but under existing laws it was applied unevenly (therefore unusual). In effect, the death penalty violated the equal-protection clause because it was applied only to some prisoners, most of whom were Black.

Thirty-five states passed new death penalty laws after the Furman decision. Those laws fell into two classes: mandatory laws that ordered death automatically for certain categories of offenses and two-stage laws that provided for, first, the establishment of guilt or innocence and then a proceeding providing for punishment. In 1976 the Court was faced with reviewing 63 different cases from six states. It overturned all the mandatory laws (*Woodson* v. *North Carolina*, *Roberts* v. *Louisiana*) as "unduly harsh and unworkably rigid" but upheld the two-stage laws. The debate over the constitutionality and the applicability of the death penalty will continue to be a major issue.

Capital punishment is a controversial issue in America. What are your views on the death penalty?

Procedural Rights. Whenever a sentence is imposed on a defendant or probation is revoked, the defendant has the right to seek the aid of counsel.

In certain kinds of postconviction proceedings, an individual has the right to a hearing and to confront any witnesses who may be questioned. For example, if additional facts are required in order to determine a sentence, a defendant has the right to cross-examine any witness who testifies (*Specht* v. *Patterson*, 1967).

Prison inmates have the right of reasonable access to the court system. If inmates are denied the right to an attorney while in prison (for example, because they cannot pay for one), then they have the right to consult with other inmates on legal matters (*Johnson* v. *Avery*, 1969).

If the federal or a state government provides that everyone may appeal a conviction, then poor defendants must receive the help of lawyers appointed by the courts (*Douglas* v. *California*, 1963). But this right to counsel

Many prison libraries help inmates familiarize themselves with the law and prepare their own defense.

does not extend beyond the first appeal (*Ross* v. *Moffit*, 1974).

The due-process clauses of the Fifth and Fourteenth amendments and the equal-protection clause of the Fourteenth Amendment require that on an appeal a defendant must be given a free transcript of the trial court proceedings or that the state must "find some other means of affording adequate and effective appellate review to *indigent* (needy) defendants" (*Griffin* v. *Illinois*, 1956).

section review

1. What guarantees are given an accused person under the Sixth Amendment?
2. What constitutes a "serious offense"?
3. Why should an accused be able to cross-examine a witness?
4. Under what circumstances can an accused be brought to court twice on the same charge?

3. JUVENILE RIGHTS

Throughout most of our history, juveniles have been denied the rights guaranteed to adults by the Bill of Rights. In treating juvenile offenders the emphasis has been on correction and rehabilitation rather than punishment and deterrence. This philosophy requires that juvenile courts operate in place of the parent and not formally prosecute juveniles.

But the treatment of juveniles has varied widely across the country with the result that "the child receives the worst of both worlds; . . . he gets neither the protection accorded to adults nor the . . . care and . . . treatment postulated for children." (Justice Fortas in *Kent* v. *U.S.*, 1966).

In extending some of the Bill of Rights' guarantees to juveniles, the Supreme Court has held that the Fourteenth Amendment does demand "the essentials of due process and fair treatment." In the Gault decision of 1967, the Court extended the following guarantees to juveniles in state court proceedings:

1. The right to written notice of the court proceedings and charges and time to prepare a defense.
2. The right to counsel; poor juveniles must have court-appointed attorneys.
3. The right to confront and cross-examine witnesses.
4. The right to claim the privilege against self-incrimination.

Since the Gault decision, the Supreme Court has extended the protections of juveniles in state court proceedings. If a juvenile is charged with an act that would constitute a crime if committed by an adult, guilt must be established by proof beyond a reasonable doubt. Finding a juvenile guilty by evidence that leaves a reasonable doubt violates due process and fair treatment.

Whenever a juvenile is involved in a *delinquency hearing*—a hearing that determines whether the juvenile is a delinquent—he or she is put in jeopardy. Consequently, the juvenile cannot be brought to trial as an adult for the same offense. To do so would be to put the juvenile in double jeopardy in violation of the Fifth Amendment (*Breed* v. *Jones*, 1975). If the juvenile court wants to treat the juvenile as an adult, it must transfer the juvenile to the jurisdiction of the adult court before it makes any determination that the juvenile is guilty of the crime.

A juvenile cannot be declared delinquent without a hearing. The Supreme Court has held, however, that due process does not require a jury trial in a delinquency hearing.

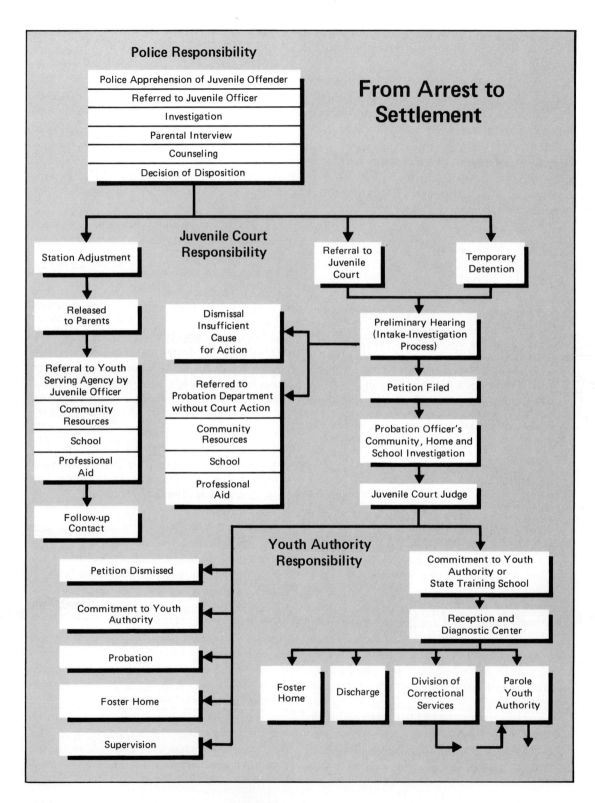

Police Responsibility

Police Apprehension of Juvenile Offender

Referred to Juvenile Officer

Investigation

Parental Interview

Counseling

Decision of Disposition

From Arrest to Settlement

Juvenile Court Responsibility

Station Adjustment

Referral to Juvenile Court

Temporary Detention

Released to Parents

Dismissal Insufficient Cause for Action

Preliminary Hearing (Intake-Investigation Process)

Referral to Youth Serving Agency by Juvenile Officer

Community Resources

School

Professional Aid

Referred to Probation Department without Court Action

Community Resources

School

Professional Aid

Petition Filed

Probation Officer's Community, Home and School Investigation

Juvenile Court Judge

Follow-up Contact

Youth Authority Responsibility

Petition Dismissed

Commitment to Youth Authority or State Training School

Commitment to Youth Authority

Reception and Diagnostic Center

Probation

Foster Home

Foster Home

Discharge

Division of Correctional Services

Parole Youth Authority

Supervision

EARL WARREN

Earl Warren was born March 19, 1891, in Los Angeles, California, and grew up in Bakersfield, California. He received his LL.B. degree in 1912 and his J.D. degree in 1914 from the University of California at Berkeley. Warren was admitted to the California bar in March 1914, beginning his law career in San Francisco. His career was interrupted when he was drafted into the army during World War I.

After the war, Warren held offices as the Oakland deputy city attorney and as deputy and district attorneys for Alameda County. As district attorney, Warren was a "new broom in a sensational cleanup campaign," as stated in **Saturday Evening Post**. He cleared up race track gambling "practically singlehanded," waged war against racketeers, harassed the Ku Klux Klan, and swept the mayor of Oakland and all but one member of the Oakland city council out of office.

Warren's political career then took him to state offices. He served as attorney general for the state of California from 1939 to 1943. In 1942 he was elected governor of California, and was reelected in 1946 and 1950. During this period he was successful in reducing taxes in the state and further expanded state services. In 1948 Warren ran unsuccessfully for Vice-President of the United States on the Thomas E. Dewey ticket. Then, in 1953, Warren resigned as governor when President Dwight D. Eisenhower appointed him Chief Justice of the U.S. Supreme Court.

During Warren's tenure, the court dealt with a multitude of critical issues. The most important decisions involved civil rights questions. Despite his early reputation as a "hard prosecutor" and his support of wartime internment of Japanese-Americans, Warren consistently stood for a broad interpretation of the constitutional protections of the individual. The Warren Court years marked many important historical civil rights decisions, such as the landmark **Brown** v. **Board of Education**. Others include **Perez** v. **Brownell, Trop** v. **Dulles, The United States** v. **Brown,** and the famous **Miranda** v. **Arizona** decision.

In 1963 Chief Justice Warren was persuaded by President Johnson to head the official investigation into the assassination of President John F. Kennedy. The Warren Commission's report was released in 1964.

Warren resigned as Chief Justice in 1968 (effective in 1969), after serving on the Court during a period of unparalleled developments in the area of civil rights. He died in Washington, D.C., on July 9, 1974.

Such a hearing is not a criminal prosecution under the Sixth and Fourteenth amendments. Requiring a jury trial could end the "idealistic prospect of an intimate, informal, protective proceeding" (*McKeiver* v. *Pa.,* 1971).

section review

1. List the guarantees that protect juveniles in state court proceedings.
2. What action must be taken in order to try a juvenile in an adult court?

CHAPTER SUMMARY

33

According to the Bill of Rights, whenever a person is subjected to sanctions by government, he or she has certain rights associated with due process of law or fair procedure. These rights are guaranteed by the Fourth, Fifth, Sixth, Eighth, and Fourteenth amendments.

Three types of legal sources protect a criminal defendant. They are the U.S. and state constitutions, federal and state laws, and judicial rulings of federal and state courts.

During the investigation, probable cause must be established, and generally a warrant is required. Searches and seizures must satisfy specific requirements. The search may not exceed the scope of the warrant. Illegally obtained evidence is excluded from use in a criminal trial.

Under the following circumstances, a search without a warrant is justified: 1) The individual voluntarily consents to the search; 2) the search is incident to a valid arrest; 3) the search is incident to "stop and frisk"; 4) the police are in "hot pursuit" of a suspect; 5) a situation exists in which the police or others might be endangered or evidence destroyed.

Three major court decisions (Escobedo, Miranda, Massiah) during the last ten years have expanded the Bill of Rights' protection of the rights of the accused. Rulings in these cases have made the police more aware of due process procedure in arresting suspects.

The Bill of Rights also guarantees the following pretrial rights: 1) a speedy and public trial; 2) limitations on excessive bail; 3) a fair trial by an impartial jury; 4) presentation of evidence favorable to the accused; 5) determination that the accused is able to understand the legal proceedings.

Following conviction, the Bill of Rights prohibits cruel and unusual punishment and guarantees prisoners access to courts of appeal.

Since 1967, juveniles have been extended some of the Bill of Rights' guarantees, particularly the Fourteenth Amendment's guarantee of due process.

REVIEW QUESTIONS

1. What right of the accused was established in the case of *Escobedo* v. *Illinois?*
2. What procedure does the decision in *Miranda* v. *Arizona* require when a person is arrested or interrogated by police officers? What are exceptions to the Miranda rule?
3. Do you think the American criminal justice system is like an assembly line or an obstacle course? Cite specific reasons for your view.
4. For what kinds of offenses and at what age do you think juveniles should be remanded to adult authorities? Give reasons for each.
5. Can a person be tried twice without being placed in double jeopardy? Explain.
6. Why is a person accused of a crime guaranteed a speedy and public trial by the Constitution?

7. Do you consider the death penalty to be "cruel and unusual" punishment? Why or why not?
8. Under what conditions may a police officer search your car? Is the officer required to present a search warrant?
9. What is a fair trial?

ACTIVITIES FOR REVIEW

activity 1 Prepare a role play illustrating the changes in arrest procedures under the Escobedo and Miranda rules. Present the role play to the class.

activity 2 Research arguments about the use of the death penalty for serious crimes. What are the major arguments of those who claim that the death penalty is "cruel and unusual punishment?" Which of the arguments do you find most persuasive? Why?

activity 3 When a person pleads Fifth Amendment protection against self-incrimination, how can he or she really be protected from conviction? Should people be allowed to plead the Fifth Amendment? Why or why not?

activity 4 Invite a local judge or law enforcement officer to your class to discuss how protection of the rights of the accused person affects his or her role.

political science DICTIONARY

coerced confession—an involuntary confession. p. 644
indigent—needy; poor. p. 655
probable cause—reasonable grounds for suspicion supported by evidence. p. 639

34 *Equal Protection*

The Fourteenth Amendment provides that no state shall deny to any person the "equal protection of the laws." This amendment was written to protect Blacks shortly after the Civil War. Many Supreme Court cases that have invoked this amendment have involved the question of racial practices. But during the 1960's and 1970's, increasing numbers of equal protection cases have involved sex, income, and "reverse discrimination."

The equal protection clause of the Fourteenth Amendment has presented complex problems for state and federal courts that have had to determine whether someone has been discriminated against. What happens when individuals in similar situations are treated differently under the law? The Supreme Court has recognized that classification is a part of law making and that the equal protection clause allows legislators to pass laws that classify people. But when does classification result in discrimination?

CHAPTER PREVIEW

1. EQUAL PROTECTION UNDER THE LAW
2. VIOLATIONS OF THE EQUAL PROTECTION CLAUSE
3. EQUAL PROTECTION AND CITIZENSHIP

1. EQUAL PROTECTION UNDER THE LAW

Two kinds of discrimination may violate the equal protection clause—*de jure* and *de facto*. *De jure* discrimination is intentional discrimination. It has occurred in three ways:

1. A state law, regulation, or judicial order

This picture shows the first Black jury to serve in Houston County, Alabama.

may state that a certain group is to be excluded. A state law that prohibited Blacks from serving on juries was held by the Supreme Court to violate the equal protection clause (*Strauder* v. *West Virginia*, 1880).

2. The application of a state law may constitute de jure discrimination. *Yick Wo* v. *Hopkins* (1886) concerned a San Francisco ordinance that had been applied to deny licenses to Chinese to operate laundries. The Supreme Court found "intentional and purposeful" discrimination. Other situations in which "neutral" laws have been applied in a discriminatory manner include the exclusion of minorities from juries; the enforcement by police of criminal laws against certain groups and not against others; the charging of members of certain groups, not others, with crimes; and uneven sentencing practices.

3. A state law may be found to be discriminatory if the plaintiff is able to prove that the purpose—the motive—for the law is forbidden by the equal protection clause. For example, the Supreme Court found de jure discrimination when the public schools in a certain community were closed in order to avoid racial desegregation (*Griffin* v. *County School Board*, 1964).

De facto discrimination is unintentional discrimination. It occurs most often when the actions of a state government produce a discriminatory effect. De facto discrimination has been an issue in voting cases, school desegregation cases, and cases involving the poor. This kind of discrimination has been charged in an increasing number of equal protection cases.

State Action. The Fourteenth Amendment stipulates that a state cannot deny anyone the equal protection of the laws, but there is no provision in the Constitution that prohibits private discrimination. Thus, before the courts can consider an equal protection case, the plaintiffs must demonstrate that state action is involved. Determining what constitutes state action has presented the courts with major problems.

State action is any action taken by the legislatures, executives, courts, and administrators of a state government. It can include certain actions taken by private individuals or organizations. Whenever an individual or group has performed a task for society that could be classified as a state or public function, the Supreme Court has considered the

At one time it would not have been possible for this man to be a police officer. Can you guess why?

individual or group subject to the Fourteenth and Fifteenth amendments.

For example, the Democratic party of Texas (a private group) did not allow Blacks to vote in its primary elections. Because state law regulates primaries, the Supreme Court held that by conducting the primary the party was performing a state function. Thus, excluding Blacks violated the equal protection clause (*Smith* v. *Allwright*, 1944).

In another case involving political parties in Texas, the Court also found state action. A county political group known as the Jaybirds held elections before the primary and excluded Blacks. The winners of these preprimary elections usually ran unopposed in the Democratic primary and in the general election as well. In effect, the Jaybirds selected the person who would be elected.

Even though the state did not regulate these preprimary elections, the Court found state action and ruled that a violation of the equal protection clause had occurred (*Terry* v. *Adams*, 1953).

State action was also found when a private corporation that owned a particular town forbade the distribution of religious materials in that town. The Supreme Court said that the private corporation acted like a local government in running the town for its employees. The Court ruled that those employees had the same First Amendment rights to receive information as those possessed by citizens in an ordinary town (*Marsh* v. *Alabama*, 1946).

A second major category of state action cases has involved action by private individuals in which there has been "significant state participation." Thus state action was found in the following cases:

1. *Pennsylvania* v. *Board of Trusts*, 1957. Public officials acted as trustees under the provisions of a private will that required racial discrimination.

2. *Burton* v. *Wilmington Parking Authority*, 1961. The owner of a restaurant leased the restaurant space in a publicly owned parking facility and refused to serve Blacks in his restaurant. The Court held that because the city owned and controlled the building from which the restaurant derived benefits for its customers, state action was involved. The city could require the lessor of the space not to practice discrimination.

3. *Shelley* v. *Kraemer*, 1948. The Supreme Court found state action when a state court enforced a racially restrictive housing covenant (agreement). Voluntary adherence to such covenants did not involve state action; but when the courts were used to enforce such covenants, there was state action.

State action also includes the conduct of government officials acting in their official roles—"under color of law"—even though the specific action taken may be forbidden by law. For example, the Supreme Court found state action when a state jury commissioner discriminated against Blacks in selecting jury panels. Such action was already illegal at the time under state and federal law (*Ex parte Virginia*, 1880).

Citizens of company-owned towns have the same First Amendment rights as citizens of ordinary towns.

section review

1. Why was the Fourteenth Amendment written?
2. Explain the difference between de jure and de facto segregation.
3. What is meant by state action? Give an example of a state action.

2. VIOLATIONS OF THE EQUAL PROTECTION CLAUSE

In determining whether a classification is reasonable and does not violate the equal protection clause, the Supreme Court has applied three different tests to legislation.

1. According to the traditional test, as long as the classification is reasonable and "rationally related to the object of the legislation," it will be upheld. This test has given states wide latitude to pass laws that treat groups differently. The test places a great burden on the plaintiff to demonstrate that the classification is "irrational or arbitrary."

2. A stricter test requires that classification

be "substantially related" to the sole purpose of the law. Under this test the law-making body (and not the plaintiff) has the burden of proving that the classification is not only rational but also is a necessary part of an important state objective.

3. According to the strictest test, laws that single out certain groups are "inherently suspect" if they are based on criteria determined "solely by the accident of birth" or if they discriminate against groups of people who have historically been discriminated against. Thus if a law involves a classification based on race, national origin, or alien status, it is suspect. The Supreme Court examines such laws with "strict scrutiny." A substantial relationship between the law and its purpose is not enough. The state must demonstrate a "compelling or overriding" interest in using the classification. If it cannot do so, the classification will be declared unconstitutional. Laws involving classifications based on sex, illegitimacy, income, or age are not considered suspect. They are examined under one of the other two tests.

Race. Classifications involving members of a race are suspect and will almost never be upheld today. This judgment, however, was not always the case. In 1896, in *Plessy* v. *Ferguson*, the Supreme Court said that "separate but equal" facilities did not violate the Constitution; as long as facilities were available for both races, their separation did not deny equal protection of the laws. By 1900 almost all southern and border states had established separate schools and other public facilities and denied Blacks the right to vote.

In 1954 the Supreme Court rejected the "separate but equal" argument. In *Brown* v. *Board of Education of Topeka*, the Court struck down racial segregation in the public schools. It announced general guidelines for invalidating state-created racial segregation in education, voting, public accommodations, transportation, housing, and employment.

Voting. Unit Two examined some of the problems that the courts encountered in improperly apportioned legislative districts. Another area that involved voting and reapportionment was the denial of the vote to Blacks.

In 1898 the Supreme Court in *Williams* v. *Mississippi* upheld discriminatory voting laws when it allowed a Mississippi scheme designed to deny Blacks the right to vote. The scheme established a poll tax, a literacy test, and a residency requirement. Many of the southern states followed Mississippi's lead. They inserted grandfather clauses in their voting laws. Such clauses allowed anyone to vote without taking tests if that person or one of his or her ancestors had voted in 1866 or earlier. All others (which meant all Blacks, for they had not been allowed to vote in 1866) had to pass rigorous tests.

The White primary was also used to deny southern Blacks the right to vote. Whoever won the Democratic primary for an office in a southern state was certain to win the general election. And the Democratic party would not let Blacks vote in such primaries. In a series of cases (see the discussion under State Action) the Supreme Court struck down primaries of this kind.

The use of poll taxes in southern states also kept the poor—Black and White—from voting. In 1965 the Supreme Court held that the poll tax was a "requirement of Negroes and applied in a discriminatory manner" (*Harman* v. *Forssenius*).

A variety of other techniques were used in southern states to keep Blacks from voting. Some states required that an applicant demonstrate knowledge of state laws and the Constitution. The registrar had the power to decide who passed and who did not. Whites were passed, and Blacks, including college graduates, were not.

Some counties in Alabama and Mississippi used voucher systems. In order to register to vote, each applicant had to have a

An Alabama resident fills out a lengthy question-naire as he applies for registration as a voter.

registered voter "vouch" that he or she was a person of good character. Each Black could only vouch for one new voter a year, whereas Whites could vouch for many more. Still other states eliminated the names of Blacks from their voting rolls by rejecting them for "errors" committed in filling out forms.

Finally Congress took action to stop these practices. It passed the 1957 Civil Rights Act that gave the attorney general of the United States the power to institute suits dealing with voting rights. But the powers of the attorney general were not wide enough to take action to prevent all voting discrimination practices.

In 1960 and again in 1965, Congress passed laws that dealt with the subtle and widespread practices that were designed to deny Blacks the vote. The 1965 act permitted federal regulation of voter registration and elections in states where literacy tests (or similar restrictive practices) were in force on November 1, 1964, and where fewer than 50 percent of voting-age residents were registered or had voted in the presidential election of 1964. In *South Carolina* v. *Katzenbach* (1966), the Supreme Court upheld this law.

Most discriminatory voting practices have been eliminated, so that Blacks can now vote almost anywhere in the South.

Education. The field of education is one of the most important arenas in which the struggle against discrimination continues to be waged. But attempts to bring about equality of educational opportunity have presented our society—and especially the courts—with complicated problems.

The dual educational system upheld by the Supreme Court in 1896 was most unequal. White schools always received more money. In 1954, when the Court outlawed separate school systems and ordered school desegregation "with all deliberate speed," some states complied immediately with the Court's ruling. But in many other states there was great resistance. These states tried various tactics to prevent integration of their public schools. The courts became congested with lawsuits demanding that schools be integrated.

Integration moved slowly in the South, for it depended on the filing of lawsuits in school district after school district. The federal government became involved in the integration process after Congress passed several laws that authorized HEW to withhold federal money for education until a school district was integrated. Although this practice was controversial, it became a very effective tool in speeding up integration in the South.

Segregation in schools outside the South has presented even thornier problems in interpreting the equal protection clause. Whereas segregation in the South was de jure discrimination, discrimination in schools elsewhere is de facto. Segregation exists because of residential patterns and the practice of assigning pupils to neighborhood schools.

Discrimination in the sale and rental of housing has resulted in minority groups being concentrated in certain areas in large and small cities alike. For example, over 90 percent of Chicago's Black elementary school students attend schools where Blacks are in the majority. Over 80 percent of Black elementary school students in Los Angeles attend schools where Blacks are in the majority. The figures vary from city to city, but the high concentration of minorities in certain schools is a way of life in all metropolitan areas.

The issue for these school districts to resolve is whether local school boards have the obligation to eliminate segregation resulting from segregative residential patterns. Some courts have said yes; others have said no. The California state supreme court ruled that the city of Pasadena did have an obligation to do away with racial segregation in schools "regardless of its cause." Busing has been the method used most often to balance the racial and ethnic populations in the schools. But as the violence in South Boston revealed, busing is not a popular remedy; and it is opposed bitterly.

The Supreme Court overruled one federal district court's solution to segregated schools. The lower court had ordered Detroit

The racial make-up of the classroom is often the result of de facto or de jure segregation practices.

and 53 surrounding (White) school districts to form a multidistrict plan to integrate the Detroit schools, which were about 64 percent Black. The Supreme Court stated that ". . . it must be shown that racially discriminatory acts of the state or local school districts, or of a single school district, have been a substantial cause of inter-district segregation. . . . Without an inter-district violation and inter-district effect, there is no constitutional wrong calling for an inter-district remedy" (*Milliken et al.* v. *Bradley et al.*, 1974).

Segregated schools in the North will continue to be a major problem well into the 1980's. Segregation, however, is not the only racial problem facing education today. The issue of "reverse discrimination" was raised in the *Bakke* case of 1978. Allen Bakke, a White male, was twice denied entry to the University of California at Davis Medical School. His test scores exceeded the scores of students admitted following standard admissions procedures and the scores of 16 minority students who entered under a special admissions program. Bakke contended that he was excluded from the Medical School on the basis of race.

The Supreme Court ruled that admissions programs cannot use race as a sole criterion; race can, however, be considered as one of many criteria. While rejecting simplistic affirmative action programs, the court claimed that race could and should be taken into account where such a consideration was intended to remedy past injustices or disadvantages.

Housing. Even though the federal government and many states have passed fair housing laws, segregated housing is the rule rather than the exception in the United States today.

For many years the housing industry perpetuated segregated housing patterns. As late as 1950 the code of ethics of the National Association of Real Estate Boards (NAREB) contained this statement: "The realtor should not be instrumental in introducing into a neighborhood a character of property or occupancy, members of any race or nationality, or any individual whose presence will clearly be detrimental to property values in the neighborhood."

Thus, realtors "steered" Whites to one neighborhood and Blacks to another. These practices continue today in both the sale and rental of houses and apartments. Although such practices are outlawed in the states (because of either state laws or the 1968 federal Civil Rights Act), it is very difficult to prove discrimination.

Finding "state action" is complicated because housing involves private persons, groups, or organizations. Private discrimination in buying and selling property to maintain segregated neighborhoods is difficult to detect; and even when it can be detected, it is not always state action.

Employment. Minorities generally get jobs that pay less than do the jobs Whites get. Unemployment among Black youths is more than double the national average for White youths. This figure stayed relatively constant in past years but recently has been increasing.

The gap between the income of Black and White workers has continued to widen. In 1978 the median income of Blacks was $10,879; compared with $18,368 for Whites.

As with housing, state action is difficult to find in order to apply the equal protection clause. State action is readily found when a state government grants contracts or makes loans to private individuals. In such situations a government may require nondiscrimination in a firm's hiring practices.

But when individuals or firms conduct business that has nothing to do with government contracts or loans, state action is harder to find. Thus state and national legislation outlawing job discrimination by both public and private employers has become the

EVERETT McKINLEY DIRKSEN

Everett Dirksen, born on January 4, 1896, in Pekin, Illinois, was the son of German immigrant parents, Johann Frederick and Antje Dirksen. After attending the University of Minnesota in Minneapolis for two years, he joined the United States Army in 1918 and served overseas during World War I. Upon his military discharge in 1919, he returned to Pekin, where he had a varied business career, including managing a dredging company and working in the wholesale bakery business.

In 1927 he was elected to the part-time position of commissioner of finance of Pekin and served in that capacity until 1931. In the April 1930 primaries Dirksen was defeated in his bid for the nomination to run for the United States House of Representatives. However, he was successful in 1932 and was elected to the House. Dirksen was reelected to the House seven times. While serving in the House, he completed his law education at night school in Washington, D.C., and was admitted to the District of Columbia and Illinois bars in 1936. Dirksen was elected to the United States Senate in 1950.

Many politicians have sought distinction with fine clothes. However, Dirksen distinguished himself from his fellows by cultivating a sloppy appearance. He wanted to look like "just folks." He made himself a cartoonist's delight by suggesting that he be sketched as a ragamuffin. To complete his deliberately unkempt appearance, Dirksen would each day make sure his hair was in complete chaos.

Dirksen enjoyed the hobby of remembering people's names and could startle strangers on the street by greeting them by their first names, even remembering where and when they had first met. As the Senate's minority leader, Dirksen made it a point each year to learn the names of the new group of Senate pages.

Dirksen's early Senate years were characterized by his conservative attitude. He backed Robert Taft in 1952 as a presidential candidate, and he usually did not approve of the programs sponsored by the Eisenhower administration. But once he became the Senate minority leader, he cooperated more closely with President Eisenhower.

During the Kennedy administration, Dirksen supported the nuclear test ban treaty but opposed federal medicare for the elderly. When Lyndon Johnson became President, he and Dirksen formed an unusual alliance. It was during the Johnson administration that Dirksen played an important role in formulating the Civil Rights Act of 1964 and the Voting Rights Act of 1965. In 1965 and 1966 he opposed the repeal of federal laws authorizing state right-to-work laws against union shops. In 1966 he refused to allow open occupancy housing legislation to come before the Senate for a vote. However, in 1968 he helped that same bill through Congress. By helping to draft the language of the Civil Rights Acts of the 1960's, he was able to influence their exact legislative direction and intent.

Dirksen will always be remembered for his legislative craftsmanship and his oratory. He died in Washington, D.C., on September 7, 1969.

greatest resource in protecting the rights of minorities.

Discrimination by private employers is prohibited by legislation in 25 states. These laws are enforced most often by state ·administrative agencies that have the power to investigate complaints of discrimination. Because the bulk of the time of these agencies is spent in dealing with complaints (a very long process), they have been unable to devote much of their time and resources to other aspects of discrimination. Most of these agencies are small and underfunded. At best, they have been able to help only modestly in stopping discrimination.

One approach to the problem involves setting up systems of **preferential hiring.** But this practice has provoked controversy. The goal of preferential hiring is to give non-Whites the opportunity to perform in a wide variety of jobs that have been previously denied to them. Preferential hiring usually aids only those who are skilled. And the majority of non-White workers are unskilled or semiskilled individuals who are seldom able to take advantage of preferential hiring programs.

Preferential hiring is the practice of employing minority persons to fill positions previously denied to them.

Sex. The Supreme Court has never held laws discriminating against women suspect (and therefore subject to the Court's test requiring "strict scrutiny" and "compelling interest"). However, in most cases involving sexual discrimination in recent years, the Court has invalidated such laws by using the traditional test. Thus in *Reed* v. *Reed* (1971), the Court struck down a law under the equal protection clause that gave preference to men over women in administering *estates* (income

or property left by people after death). In *Frontiero* v. *Richardson* (1973), the Court struck down a federal law that required married female members of the armed forces (but not married males) to prove their spouses were dependent on them in order to obtain increased allowances. In 1975 (*Weinberger* v. *Wisenfeld*) the Court held that the spouse of a deceased·female wage earner was entitled to receive her Social Security benefits. (Previously only the spouse of a male wage earner had been so entitled.) A law requiring female public school teachers to take extended maternity leave was also struck down (*La Fleur* v. *Cleveland Board of Education*, 1974). In 1979 (*Orr* v. *Orr*) the Court held that a law requiring only men to pay alimony violated equal protection.

A few laws favoring women have been upheld. Thus the Court held that a special property tax exemption for widows but not for widowers was constitutional (*Kahn* v. *Shevin*, 1974).

The attack on laws that discriminate in favor of or against women has been heightened by the battle over the ratification of the equal rights amendment. The proposed Constitutional amendment states:

Section 1. Equality of rights under the law shall not be denied or abridged by the United States or by a state on account of sex.

Section 2. The Congress shall have the power to enforce by appropriate legislation the provisions of this article.

Section 3. This amendment shall take effect two years after the date of final ratification by the states.

Those who argue for the amendment state that discrimination based on sex is still widespread. Special restrictions regarding hours of work exist. Some school districts

What are your feelings about women doing what was once considered men's work?

have two pay schedules—one for men, another for women. Alimony is awarded to ex-wives but rarely to ex-husbands. Women are still prohibited from entering some types of occupations.

Those opposed to the amendment base their objectives on what they claim would be the harmful effects to women workers and on their beliefs of what the traditional role of a woman is. These opponents argue that special labor standards that now give women advantages and protections would be eliminated. All public facilities, including restrooms, would be integrated regardless of sex, they contend. Moreover, men and women are different in many ways and cannot possibly be made equal. Some of these opponents view women as helpers to their husbands. They do not see them as independent individuals. But this view not only restricts the rights of married women, it also ignores the millions of women who are not married and never will marry.

section review

1. What tests have been applied by the Supreme Court to determine if legislation is in violation of the equal protection clause?
2. List four techniques that were used to keep Blacks from voting.
3. Explain what conditions have arisen as a result of de facto segregation in northern cities.
4. Define the concept of preferential hiring.

3. EQUAL PROTECTION AND CITIZENSHIP

No country extends equal rights to and imposes equal responsibilities on all those who live within its borders. The concept of citizenship developed in classical times. A citizen was one who had the full rights and responsibilities of the state. In ancient democracies, such as that of Athens, only some

10 percent of the population were citizens. Young people, criminals, women, slaves, and aliens were denied the privileges of citizenship. Military service and payment of taxes were among the responsibilities.

Throughout the history of the United States, the rights of citizenship have steadily been extended to include Blacks, Native Americans, and women. These groups were once denied full rights. Certain citizens— notably, people under 18 and those in prison —may not vote or hold political office.

Defining Citizenship: The Past. Although the United States is traditionally concerned with citizenship, its Constitution originally contained no definition of the concept. It spoke of citizens "of the United States" and "of the States." As the slavery question became a vexing problem, this ambiguity became serious. The federal government's practice was to grant national citizenship to citizens of individual states. Anyone recognized as a citizen of one of the states automatically became a United States citizen.

But the slave states refused to recognize Black citizens of free states. As the slavery controversy heightened, so did the question of citizenship. The first definition of national citizenship was made by the Supreme Court in *Dred Scott* v. *Sanford* (1857). In this case the Court ruled that Blacks, free or slave, could not be citizens. However, the Dred Scott decision was not accepted by the North, and it quickly became a **dead letter.** After the Civil War, the victorious Republicans defined national citizenship in the first clause of the Fourteenth Amendment (1868): "All persons born or naturalized in the United States, and subject to the jurisdiction thereof, are citizens of the United States and of the State wherein they reside."

> A **dead letter** is a law or ordinance that has lost its force, although it has not formally been repealed or abolished.

Acquiring and Losing Citizenship. There are three ways to acquire citizenship: by birth, inheritance, and naturalization. Only naturalization is mentioned in the Constitution (Article 1, Section 8, clause 4). Exclusive jurisdiction over naturalization is given to Congress.

In the first century of American history, there were no restrictions on immigration and very few on naturalization. But since the late 1800's, the procedures for both have become far more complicated.

Citizenship by Birth. The Fourteenth Amendment defines as American citizens all persons born in the United States and "subject to the jurisdiction thereof." The definition also applies to persons born in United States embassies and **legations** abroad, as well as to those born on any "public vessel" (ship or airplane) of the United States government. Under the principle of extraterritoriality, these locations are considered part of the United States.

Anyone born within the United States is a citizen. In *United States* v. *Wong Kim Ark* (1898) the Supreme Court held that Wong, born in the United States of Chinese parents, was a citizen even though the Chinese Exclusion Act of 1882 forbade the admission of Chinese.

> A **legation** is the residence or office in a foreign country of an official who represents his or her government and has lower rank than an ambassador.

Until 1871 Native Americans were treated as foreigners with whom the American government signed treaties. From 1871 to 1924 Native Americans born to tribal members living on reservations were considered wards of the government. They received citizenship in 1924 by act of Congress.

Citizenship by Inheritance. Congress has recognized that citizenship can be inherited. The present laws on this subject vary according to the status of the parents. If both parents are citizens, the law requires only that one of them must have lived in the United States at some time in order for the child to become automatically a citizen. If one parent is an alien, the citizen parent must have lived in the United States for ten years, including five years after the age of 14, for the child to be born a citizen. The child must live in the United States for five consecutive years between the ages of 14 and 28, or else the child's citizenship will be forfeited.

Loss of Citizenship. Historically, there have been three ways of losing United States citizenship involuntarily: conviction for certain crimes, expatriation, and denaturalization. Today involuntary loss of American citizenship is extremely rare.

Crimes. Conviction for most crimes may result in the loss of some of the privileges of citizenship (such as the right to vote) but not in the loss of citizenship itself. However, certain crimes are punishable by loss of citizenship. Until 1958 desertion from military service in wartime was such a crime. In that year, in *Trop* v. *Dulles*, the Supreme Court held that this law violated the Eighth Amendment (cruel and unusual punishment). And in 1963 the Court ruled that war resisters who left the country to avoid the draft did not automatically lose their citizenship. In *Kennedy* v. *Mendoza-Martinez*, the Court held that this provision violated Article 1, Section 9, of the Constitution, which provided that bills of attainder (punishment without trial) were illegal.

Expatriation. Loss of citizenship through expatriation—leaving one's native country—can be voluntary or involuntary. Expatriation is voluntary when a person is naturalized by a

Wong Shee Chew is a first-generation immigrant from China. Her granddaughter (third generation) was born in the United States.

The Statue of Liberty, a gift from France, has always been a symbolic welcome to immigrants entering the United States via New York Harbor.

foreign state, takes an oath of allegiance to a foreign state, or formally renounces citizenship in the presence of a representative of the attorney general or the State Department. Involuntary expatriation was ended by the Supreme Court in 1967 in *Afroyim* v. *Rusk*. The Court held that the Fourteenth Amendment prevented Congress from revoking someone's citizenship without his or her consent. The case involved a law which provided that persons voting in foreign elections automatically forfeited their citizenship.

Denaturalization. Naturalized citizens can lose their citizenship in several circumstances that do not apply to native-born citizens. Foreign-born citizens can be denaturalized if 1) within five years after naturalization, they join any organization in which membership at the time of naturalization would have been grounds for refusal to grant citizenship, 2) it is proved that fraud was used to obtain citizenship, or 3) it can be shown that the oath of allegiance was taken with "mental reservations." Until 1964 the law

On July 4, 1976, this group of aliens took part in the naturalization ceremonies at Chicago Stadium.

also stated that three year's residence in their country of origin would lead to the automatic denaturalization of foreign-born citizens. But in that year the Supreme Court, in *Schneider v. Rusk*, ruled that Congress had no authority to make this distinction between native-born and naturalized citizens. In one respect, a naturalized citizen remains less privileged than a native-born citizen: Article 2, Section 1, clause 5, of the Constitution prevents a naturalized citizen from becoming President.

The Constitution and Aliens. The liberties in the Constitution are guaranteed not only to United States citizens but to "all persons." Aliens are legally persons and are therefore protected by these guarantees.

However, some rights are guaranteed only to citizens. Therefore, it is legal to restrict noncitizen travel, since the Privileges and Immunities clause of the Constitution (Article 4, Section 2, clause 1) and the Fourteenth Amendment apply only to citizens. The government uses this power in wartime to restrict travel by aliens and in peacetime to prevent some foreigners from traveling to security areas.

The most controversial use of this power, however, extended it to include native-born American citizens as well as aliens. In the second year of World War II, 120,000 people of Japanese descent living on the Pacific Coast were deported to "war relocation camps" inland. Two thirds of these people were native-born citizens, and because of their internment, a great many of them lost most of their assets, usually without proper payment. Remarkably, the Supreme Court in 1944, in *Korematsu* v. *United States*, upheld this forced evacuation as a reasonable measure under wartime conditions. But on the same day, in *ex parte Endo*, it held that establishment of an internee's loyalty—through enlistment in the armed forces, sponsorship by Americans, or the signing of an oath of allegiance—prevented any further restraint being placed upon his or her movements.

Limitations on Liberty. "Self-preservation is the first law of all government." No liberty is absolute. Liberty must be limited by the liberties of others. Supreme Court Justice Oliver Wendell Holmes expressed the limitations of liberty in two famous phrases. In one, where a man claimed the right to swing his fist where he pleased, Holmes said, "His right stopped where the other man's nose began." And in another, he wrote that free speech "would not protect a man in falsely shouting 'Fire!' in a theatre."

When a governmental system is under attack, or in a life and death situation, many liberties are likely to go by the board. One of the longest constitutional arguments in American history has been over the tendency for rights to shrink in war or quasi-war conditions. From the Alien and Sedition Laws passed during the quasi-war with France in 1798, to the violations of civil liberties by the Lincoln administration during the Civil War, to the repression and the "Red scare" during and immediately after World War I, to the forced deportation of Japanese-Americans in World War II, to the violent repression of war resisters during the Vietnam era, it is these moments of perceived foreign and/or domestic danger that have been the testing grounds for the American system of civil liberty. Even after these episodes, historians and the general public have not always been able to agree on what course of action should have been taken. Generally, the courts and the people have tended to err on the side of "safety" in the time of crisis and of "liberty" after it is over.

section review

1. Define expatriation. Some countries permit their citizens to maintain dual citizenship. What is your opinion on this matter?
2. In what way is a naturalized American citizen less privileged than a native-born citizen?
3. List and explain three ways in which a person may become a citizen of the United States.

CHAPTER SUMMARY

34

Citizenship is not defined in the body of the Constitution. The Fourteenth Amendment, ratified in 1868, was primarily intended to make Black former slaves citizens. But because it is the only place where citizenship is actually defined, it has much broader application.

The Fourteenth Amendment provides that no state shall deny to any person the "equal protection of the laws." All laws classify to some extent; the equal protection clause prohibits classifications that are irrational or arbitrary, unrelated to the legitimate purpose of the law, or inherently suspect because they discriminate solely by the accident of birth (i.e., race, nationality, or sex).

Other citizenship rights protected by the Constitution are the right to travel freely from state to state and abroad, the right to personal privacy, and the right to vote.

When a state has granted some residents the right to vote while denying others, such laws have been held to deny equal protection.

The body of the Constitution says little about individual freedoms. The framers who met in Philadelphia were more interested in expanding government power than in limiting it, and it was the opponents of the Constitution who insisted that the document needed a bill of rights. The provisions for individual liberties in the body of the Constitution dealt with treatment of those accused of crimes.

REVIEW QUESTIONS

1. What are two basic types of discrimination? Explain each.
2. Define the categories of "state action."
3. What three tests for violations of the equal protection clause has the Supreme Court applied to legislation?
4. What was the decision in *Plessy* v. *Ferguson?* As a result of this decision, how did southern states treat their Black populations? How did *Brown* v. *Board of Education of Topeka* change that treatment?
5. What is the grandfather clause? How was it used in southern states to prevent Blacks from voting?
6. Define the concept of preferential hiring. Do you think this concept is working? Explain.
7. What factors have made school integration more difficult in northern states than in southern states?
8. What is the purpose of the equal rights amendment? Outline its major provisions.
9. Describe the major steps in the typical naturalization process.

ACTIVITIES FOR REVIEW

activity 1   Prepare a report on changes in civil rights since the 1954 *Brown* v. *Board of Education* decision.

activity 2   Research the proposed equal rights amendment. What are its major provisions? What are the arguments pro and con? Do you favor its ratification? Why or why not?

activity 3   Does your state have laws prohibiting discrimination in housing and employment? What are the major provisions? What agency is responsible for their enforcement?

activity 4   Locate someone in your community who is a naturalized immigrant. Interview that person and write a report on that person's reasons for coming to the United States and the steps that person took to become a citizen.

political science DICTIONARY

dead letter—a law or ordinance that has lost its force, although it has not been formally repealed or abolished.   p. 671

de facto discrimination—unfair treatment or denial of normal privileges to persons because of race, whether supported by law or not; an unintentional condition.   p. 661

de jure discrimination—unfair treatment or denial of normal privileges to persons because of race, as sanctioned by law or encouraged by the acts of people holding political office; intentional discrimination.   p. 660

legation—the residence or office in a foreign country of an official who represents his or her government and has lower rank than an ambassador.   p. 671

preferential hiring—the practice of employing minority group members to fill positions previously denied them.   p. 669

UNIT SUMMARY

UNIT SUMMARY

Most American civil liberties are guaranteed by the Bill of Rights. The First, Fourth, Fifth, Sixth, Eighth, and Fourteenth amendments are most often the basis for judicial decisions in civil or criminal cases.

Most civil cases are based on First Amendment guarantees of freedom of religion, freedom of speech, freedom of the press, the right of peaceful assembly, and the right of petition.

The rights of those accused of crimes are protected by the Fourth, Fifth, Sixth, and Eighth Amendments. No person may be 1) subjected to unreasonable search and seizure, 2) deprived of life, liberty, or property without due process of law, 3) required to testify against himself or herself, 4) tried twice for the same crime, 5) denied a speedy and public trial, 6) denied the right to legal counsel or to face accusers, and 7) subjected to excessive bail or cruel and unusual punishment.

The Fourteenth Amendment defines citizenship and guarantees to all persons the equal protection of the laws.

Bibliography

Clark, Todd. *Fair Trial/Free Press.* Riverside, N.J.: Benziger, Inc., 1976.

Harris, Richard. *Decision.* New York: Dutton, 1971.

Harris, Richard. *Justice: The Crisis of Law, Order and Freedom in America.* New York: Dutton, 1970.

Harris, Richard. *The Fear of Crime.* New York: Praeger, 1969.

Kluger, Richard. *Simple Justice.* New York: Knopf, 1976.

Lawson, Steven. *Black Ballots: Voting Rights in the South, 1944n69.* New York: Columbia Press, 1976.

Lewis, Anthony. *Clarence Earl Gideon and the Supreme Court.* New York: Vintage Sundial Books, 1972.

Lewis, Anthony. *Gideon's Trumpet.* New York: Random House, 1964.

White, G. Edward. *The American Judicial Tradition: Profiles of Leading American Judges.* New York: Oxford University Press, 1976.

Review questions

1. What amendments deal with the rights of the accused?
2. How does the Fourteenth Amendment broaden the scope of the Bill of Rights?
3. Why do you think the body of the Constitution says so little on the subject of individual liberties?
4. What effects have recent Supreme Court decisions discussed in this unit had on protection of the rights of minority group members?
5. Define American citizenship.
6. Should an American citizen be free to travel anywhere in the world at any time? Are there any restrictions that you believe the government should impose? What are they?
7. What three major court decisions recently expanded the Bill of Rights' protection of the rights of the accused?

Skills questions

Using the charts in this unit, answer the following questions:
1. What steps are involved in the criminal process between the time a suspect is booked and appears in court for the first time?
2. List five possible outcomes of a juvenile court case.
3. List four possible ways the case of a youth may be handled when the youth is released from a state training school.
4. What specific right was questioned in the case of *Malloy* v. *Hogan* (1964)?
5. Free press was a specific right questioned in which 1931 case?
6. Was *Mapp* v. *Ohio* (1961) a case that applied to the states?
7. In which specific rights areas have no cases been decided?

Activities

activity 1   Prepare a handbook of student rights and responsibilities for your school.

activity 2   Develop a series of charts or posters illustrating the rights of a person accused of a crime. Try to make them so clear that even a person who cannot read English can understand them.

activity 3   Interview a judge, a prosecutor, a defense attorney or public defender, and a policeman. What is the opinion of each about the Escobedo and Miranda decisions? Is there a difference based on the job of the person interviewed? How have those decisions affected their work? Prepare a report of your findings, and write a short essay stating your position on these decisions.

CONCLUSION
Stability and Change in American Politics

In its immense capacity to accommodate change, the American political system may be one of the wonders of the modern world.

By the time of Andrew Jackson's presidency, the basic style and most of the institutions of modern American government were in effect. It is now some 150 years later, and they still are in effect. There is no other country in the world of which the same statement can be made.

Except during the Civil War, political change has occurred through the electoral process. Elections have peacefully replaced old officials with new ones. Sometimes incumbent politicians have changed their policies to stay in office. Electoral changes have also brought new leadership and new ideas into government through the Chief Executive's power to appoint most top officials.

The pace of change in American politics is normally quite slow. Sometimes, however, the combination of events and strong leadership bring about major changes in a relatively short time.

Although much has changed in America since 1789, the foundations of our government—the Constitution, federalism, the three branches of government, checks and balances—have remained stable and continuous.

At the same time, government is more complex, provides more services, and affects the lives of citizens much more than it did in earlier times. Moreover, the areas affected by government have themselves changed dramatically. The press is one example. The constitutional guarantee of freedom of the press applied to competing small newspapers in the eighteenth and nineteenth century. Today it applies to giant communications systems.

Is change permanent, or does it occur in cycles? Certainly, some kinds of change—such as the swing from activism to non-participation, or from the radical left to the conservative right—seem to occur in cyclical patterns. Consider the 1960's. Some trends of the 1960's have vanished; it is as if they had never occurred. Others, including changes in attitudes toward race, sex, and the rights of women, seem to be permanent. It would not have been possible in the 1960's to predict what features of the political scene would persist.

The "realism" of the Founders was based on an eighteenth-century view of human nature that is out of fashion today. Yet the government they created has served us well. It has continued to enjoy legitimacy and public acceptance, it has peacefully resolved most social conflicts, and it has provided for widespread equality without limiting freedom.

The Founders were aware that human affairs are complicated and not easy to predict, and that the American Republic would be preserved only through active struggle. The continuity of our government did not "just happen." It had to be fought for, not only with arms but also through the democratic participation and devoted effort of America's citizens.

The Declaration of Independence

PREAMBLE

When, in the course of human events, it becomes necessary for one people to dissolve the political bands which have connected them with another, and to assume, among the powers of the earth, the separate and equal station to which the laws of nature and of nature's God entitle them, a decent respect to the opinions of mankind requires that they should declare the causes which impel them to the separation.

NEW PRINCIPLES OF GOVERNMENT

We hold these truths to be self-evident: that all men are created equal, that they are endowed by their Creator with certain unalienable rights, that among these are life, liberty, and the pursuit of happiness.

That, to secure these rights, governments are instituted among men, deriving their just powers from the consent of the governed;

That whenever any form of government becomes destructive of these ends, it is the right of the people to alter or to abolish it, and to institute new government, laying its foundation on such principles, and organizing its powers in such form, as to them shall seem most likely to effect their safety and happiness. Prudence, indeed, will dictate that governments long established should not be changed for light and transient causes; and accordingly all experience hath shown that mankind are more disposed to suffer while evils are sufferable, than to right themselves by abolishing the forms to which they are accustomed. But when a long train of abuses and usurpations, pursuing invariably the same object, evinces a design to reduce them under absolute despotism, it is their right, it is their duty, to throw off such government, and to provide new guards for their future security.

REASONS FOR SEPARATION

Such has been the patient sufferance of these colonies; and such is now the necessity which constrains them to alter their former systems of government. The history of the present king of Great Britain is a history of repeated injuries and usurpations, all having in direct object the establishment of an absolute tyranny over these states. To prove this, let facts be submitted to a candid world.

He has refused his assent to laws the most wholesome and necessary for the public good.

He has forbidden his governors to pass laws of immediate and pressing importance unless suspended in their operation till his assent should be obtained; and when so suspended, he has utterly neglected to attend to them.

He has refused to pass other laws for the accommodation of large districts of people, unless those people would relinquish the right of representation in the legislature, a right inestimable to them, and formidable to tyrants only.

He has called together legislative bodies at places unusual, uncomfortable, and distant from the depository of their public records, for the sole purpose of fatiguing them into compliance with his measures.

He has dissolved representative houses repeatedly, for opposing, with manly firmness, his invasions on the rights of the people.

He has refused, for a long time after such dissolutions, to cause others to be elected; whereby the legislative powers, incapable of annihilation, have returned to the people at large for their exercise; the state remaining, in the mean time, exposed to all the dangers of invasion from without and convulsions within.

He has endeavored to prevent the population of these states; for that purpose obstructing the laws of naturalization of foreigners, refusing to pass others to encourage their migration hither, and raising the conditions of new appropriations of lands.

He has obstructed the administration of justice, by refusing his assent to laws for establishing judiciary powers.

He has made judges dependent on his will alone for the tenure of their offices, and the amount and payment of their salaries.

He has erected a multitude of new offices, and sent hither swarms of officers to harass our people and eat out their substance.

He has kept among us, in times of peace, standing armies, without the consent of our legislature.

He has affected to render the military independent of, and superior to, the civil power.

He has combined with others to subject us to a jurisdiction foreign to our constitution and unacknowledged by our laws, giving his assent to their acts of pretended legislation:

For quartering large bodies of armed troops among us;

For protecting them, by a mock trial, from punishment for any murders which they should commit on the inhabitants of these states;

For cutting off our trade with all parts of the world;

For imposing taxes on us without our consent;

For depriving us, in many cases, of the benefits of trial by jury;

For transporting us beyond seas, to be tried for pretended offenses;

For abolishing the free system of English laws in a neighboring province, establishing therein an arbitrary government, and enlarging its boundaries, so as to render it at once an example and fit instrument for introducing the same absolute rule into these colonies;

For taking away our charters, abolishing our most valuable laws, and altering, fundamentally, the forms of our governments;

For suspending our own legislatures, and declaring themselves invested with power to legislate for us in all cases whatsoever.

He has abdicated government here, by declaring us out of his protection and waging war against us.

He has plundered our seas, ravaged our coasts, burned our towns, and destroyed the lives of our people.

He is at this time transporting large armies of foreign mercenaries to complete the works of death, desolation, and tyranny already begun with circumstances of cruelty and perfidy scarcely paralleled in the most barbarous ages, and totally unworthy the head of a civilized nation.

He has constrained our fellow-citizens, taken captive on the high seas, to bear arms against their country, to become the executioners of their friends and brethren, or to fall themselves by their hands.

He has excited domestic insurrections among us, and has endeavored to bring on the inhabitants of our frontiers the merciless Indian savages, whose known rule of warfare is an undistinguished destruction of all ages, sexes, and conditions.

In every stage of these oppressions we have petitioned for redress in the most humble terms; our repeated petitions have been answered only by repeated injury. A prince whose character is thus marked by every act which may define a tyrant is unfit to be the ruler of a free people.

Nor have we been wanting in attention to our British brethren. We have warned them, from time to time, of attempts by their legislature to extend an unwarrantable jurisdiction over us. We have reminded them of the circumstances of our emigration and settlement here. We have appealed to their native justice and magnanimity; and we have conjured them, by the ties of our common kindred, to disavow these usurpations, which would inevitably interrupt our connections and correspondence. They, too, have been deaf to the voice of justice and of consanguinity. We must, therefore, acquiesce in the necessity which denounces our separation, and hold them, as we hold the rest of mankind, enemies in war, in peace, friends.

We, therefore, the representatives of the United States of America, in General Congress assembled, appealing to the Supreme Judge of the world for the rectitude of our intentions, do, in the name and by authority of the good people of these colonies, solemnly publish and declare, that these united colonies are, and of right ought to be, free and independent states; that they are absolved from all allegiance to the British crown, and that all political connection between them and the state of Great Britain is, and ought to be, totally dissolved; and that, as free and independent states, they have full power to levy war, conclude peace, contract alliances, establish commerce, and to do all other acts and things which independent states may of a right do. And, for the support of this declaration, with a firm reliance on the protection of Divine Providence, we mutually pledge to each other our lives, our fortunes, and our sacred honor.

THE ARTICLES OF CONFEDERATION

Agreed to by Congress November 15, 1777; ratified and in force, March 1, 1781

TO ALL TO WHOM these Presents shall come, we the undersigned Delegates of the States affixed to our Names send greeting. Whereas the Delegates of the United States of America in Congress assembled did on the fifteenth day of November in the Year of our Lord One Thousand Seven Hundred and Seventy seven, and in the Second Year of the Independence of America agree to certain articles of Confederation and perpetual Union between the States of Newhampshire, Massachusetts-bay, Rhodeisland and Providence Plantations, Connecticut, New York, New Jersey, Pennsylvania, Delaware, Maryland, Virginia, North-Carolina, South-Carolina and Georgia in the Words following, viz. "Articles of Confederation and perpetual Union between the states of Newhampshire, Massachusetts-bay, Rhodeisland and Providence Plantations, Connecticut, New-York, New-Jersey, Pennsylvania, Delaware, Maryland, Virginia, North-Carolina, South-Carolina and Georgia.

Art I. The Stile of this confederacy shall be "The United States of America."

Art. II. Each state retains its sovereignty, freedom and independence, and every Power, Jurisdiction and right, which is not by this confederation expressly delegated to the United States, in Congress assembled.

Art. III. The said states hereby severally enter into a firm league of friendship with each other, for their common defence, the security of their Liberties, and their mutual and general welfare, binding themselves to assist each other, against all force offered to, or attacks made upon them, or any of them, on account of religion, sovereignty, trade, or any other pretence whatever.

Art IV. The better to secure and perpetuate mutual friendship and intercourse among the people of the different states in this union, the free inhabitants of each of these states, paupers, vagabonds and fugitives from Justice excepted, shall be entitled to all privileges and immunities of free citizens in the several states; and the people of each state shall have free ingress and regress to and from any other state, and shall enjoy therein all the privileges of trade and commerce, subject to the same duties, impositions and restrictions as the inhabitants thereof respectively, provided that such restriction shall not extend so far as to prevent the removal of property imported into any state, to any other state of which the Owner is an inhabitant; provided also that no imposition, duties or restriction shall be laid by any state, on the property of the united states, or either of them.

If any Person guilty of, or charged with treason, felony, or other high misdemeanor in any state, shall flee from Justice, and be found in any of the united states, he shall upon demand of the Governor or executive power, of the state from which he fled, be delivered up and removed to the state having jurisdiction of his offence.

Full faith and credit shall be given in each of these states to the records, acts and judicial proceedings of the courts and magistrates of every other state.

Art. V. For the more convenient management of the general interests of the united states, delegates shall be annually appointed in such manner as the legislature of each state shall direct, to meet in Congress on the first Monday in November, in every year, with a power reserved to each state, to recal its delegates, or any of them, at any time within the year, and to send others in their stead, for the remainder of the Year.

No state shall be represented in Congress by less than two, nor by more than seven Members; and no person shall be capable of being a delegate for more than three years in any term of six years; nor shall any person, being a delegate, be capable of holding any office under the united states, for which he, or another for his benefit receives any salary, fees or emolument of any kind.

Each state shall maintain its own delegates in a meeting of the states, and while they act as members of the committee of the states.

In determining questions in the united states, in Congress assembled, each state shall have one vote.

Freedom of speech and debate in Congress shall not be impeached or questioned in any Court, or place out of Congress, and the members of congress shall be protected in their persons from arrests and imprisonments, during the time of their going to and from, and attendance on congress, except for treason, felony, or breach of the peace.

Art VI. No state without the Consent of the united states in congress assembled, shall send any embassy to, or receive any embassy from, or enter into any conference, agreement, or alliance or treaty with any King, prince or state; nor shall any person holding any office of profit or trust under the united states, or any of them, accept of any present, emolument, office or title of any kind whatever from any king, prince or foreign state; nor shall the united states in congress assembled, or any of them, grant any title of nobility.

No two or more states shall enter into any treaty, confederation or alliance whatever between them, without the consent of the united states in congress assembled, specifying accurately the purposes for which the same is to be entered into, and how long it shall continue.

No state shall lay any imposts or duties which may interfere with any stipulations in treaties, entered into by the united states in congress assembled, with any king, prince or state, in pursuance of any treaties already proposed by congress, to the courts of France and Spain.

No vessels of war shall be kept up in time of peace by any state, except such number only, as shall be deemed necessary by the united states in congress assembled, for the defence of such state, or its trade; nor shall any body of forces be kept up by any state, in time of peace, except such number only, as in the judgment of the united states, in congress assembled, shall be deemed requisite to garrison the forts necessary for the defence of such state; but every state shall always keep up a well regulated and disciplined militia, sufficiently armed and accoutred, and shall provide and constantly have ready for use, in public stores, a due number of field pieces and tents. and a proper quantity of arms, ammunition and camp equipage.

No state shall engage in any war without the consent of the united states in congress assembled, unless such state be actually invaded by enemies, or shall have received certain advice of a resolution being formed by some nation of Indians to invade such state, and the danger is so imminent as not to admit of a delay, till the united states in congress assembled can be consulted: nor shall any state grant commissions to any ships or vessels of war, nor letters of marque or reprisal, except it be after a declaration of war by the united states in congress assembled, and then only against the kingdom or state and the subjects thereof, against which war has been so declared, and under such regulations as shall be established by the united states in congress assembled, unless such state be infested by pirates, in which case vessels of war may be fitted out for that occasion, and kept so long as the danger shall continue, or until the united states in congress assembled shall determine otherwise.

Art. VII. When land-forces are raised by any state for the common defence, all officers of or under the rank of colonel, shall be appointed by the legislature of each state respectively by whom such forces shall be raised, or in such manner as such state shall direct, and all vacancies shall be filled up by the state which first made the appointment.

Art. VIII. All charges of war, and all other expences that shall be incurred for the common defence or general welfare, and allowed by the united states in congress assembled, shall be defrayed out of a common treasury, which shall be supplied by the several states, in proportion to the value of all land within each state, granted to or surveyed for any Person, as such land and the buildings and improvements thereon shall be estimated according to such mode as the united states in congress assembled, shall from time to time direct and appoint. The taxes for paying that proportion shall be laid and levied by the authority and direction of the legislatures of the several states within the time agreed upon by the united states in congress assembled.

Art. IX. The united states in congress assembled, shall have the sole and exclusive right and power of determining on peace and war, except in the cases mentioned in the sixth article—of sending and receiving ambassadors—entering into treaties and alliances, provided that no treaty of commerce shall be made whereby the legislative power of the respective states shall be restrained from imposing such imposts and duties on foreigners, as their own people are subjected to, or from prohibiting the exportation or importation of any species of goods or commodities whatsoever—of establishing rules for deciding in all cases, what captures on land or water shall be legal, and in what manner prizes taken by land or naval forces in the service of the united states shall be divided or appropriated—of granting letters of marque and reprisal in times of peace—appointing courts for the trial of piracies and felonies committed on the high seas and establishing courts for receiving and determining finally appeals in all cases of captures, provided that no member of congress shall be appointed a judge of any of the said courts.

The united states in congress assembled shall also be the last resort on appeal in all disputes and differences now subsisting or that hereafter may arise between two or more states concerning boundary, jurisdiction or any other cause whatever; which authority shall always be exercised in the manner following. Whenever the legislative or executive authority or lawful agent of any state in controversy with another shall present a petition to congress stating the matter in question and praying for a hearing, notice thereof shall be given by order of congress to the legislative or executive authority of the other state in controversy, and a day assigned for the appearance of the parties by their lawful agents, who shall then be directed to appoint by joint consent, commissioners or judges to constitute a court for hearing and determining the matter in question: but if they cannot agree, congress shall name three persons out of each of the united states, and from the list of such persons each party shall alternately strike out one, the petitioners beginning, until the number shall be reduced to thirteen; and from that number not less than seven, nor more than nine names as congress shall direct, shall in the presence of congress be drawn out by lot, and the persons whose names shall be so drawn or any five of them, shall be commissioners or judges, to hear and finally determine the controversy, so always as a major part of the judges who shall hear the cause shall agree in the determination: and if either party shall neglect to attend at the day appointed, without shewing reasons, which congress shall judge sufficient, or being present shall refuse to strike, the congress shall proceed to nominate three persons out of each state, and the secretary of congress shall strike in behalf of such party absent or refusing; and the judgment and sentence of the court to be appointed, in the manner before prescribed, shall be final and conclusive; and if any of the parties shall refuse to submit to the authority of such court, or to appear to defend their claim or cause, the court shall nevertheless proceed to pronounce sentence, or judgment, which shall in like manner be final and decisive, the judgment or sentence and other proceedings being in either case transmitted to congress, and lodged among the acts of congress for the security of the parties concerned: provided that every commissioner, before he sits in judgment, shall take an oath to be administered by one of the judges of the supreme or superior court of the state, where the cause shall be tried, "well and truly to hear and determine the matter in question, according to the best of his judgment, without favour, affection or hope of reward:" provided also that no state shall be deprived of territory for the benefit of the united states.

All controversies concerning the private right of soil claimed under different grants of two or more states, whose jurisdictions as they may respect such lands, and the states which passed such grants are adjusted, the said grants or either of them being at the same time claimed to have originated antecedent to such settlement of jurisdiction, shall on the petition of either party to the congress of the united states, be finally determined as near as may be in the same manner as is before prescribed for deciding disputes respecting territorial jurisdiction between different states.

The united states in congress assembled shall also have the sole and exclusive right and power of regulating the alloy and value of coin struck by their own authority, or by that of the respective states—fixing the standard of weights and measures throughout the united states.—regulating the trade and managing all affairs with the Indians, not members of any of the states, provided that the legislative right of any state within its own limits be not infringed or violated—estab1ising and regulating post-offices from one state to another, throughout all the united states, and exacting such postage on the papers passing thro' the same as may be requisite to defray the expences of the said office—appointing all officers of the land forces, in the service of the united states, excepting regimental officers.—appointing all the officers of the naval forces, and commissioning all officers whatever in the service of the united states—making rules for the government and regulation of the said land and naval forces, and directing their operations.

The united states in congress assembled shall have authority to appoint a committee, to sit in the recess of congress, to be denominated "A Committee of the States," and to consist of one delegate from each state; and to appoint such other committees and civil officers as may be necessary for managing the general affairs of the united states under their direction—to appoint one of their number to preside, provided that no person be allowed to serve in the office of president more than one year in any term of three years; to ascertain the necessary sums of Money to be raised for the service of the united states, and to appropriate and apply the same for defraying the public expences—to borrow money, or emit bills on the credit of the united states, transmitting every half year to the respective states an account of the sums of money so borrowed or emitted,—to build and equip a navy—to agree upon the number of land forces, and to make requisitions from each state for its quota, in proportion to the number of white inhabitants in such state; which requisition shall be binding, and thereupon the legislature of each state shall appoint the regimental officers, raise the men and cloath, arm and equip them in a soldier like manner, at the expence of the united states, and the officers and men so cloathed, armed and equipped shall march to the place appointed, and within the time agreed on by the united states in congress assembled: But if the united states in congress assembled shall, on consideration of circumstances judge proper that any state should not raise men, or should raise a smaller number than its quota, and that any other state should raise a greater number of men than the quota thereof, such extra number shall be raised, officered, cloathed, armed and equipped in the same manner as the quota of such state, unless the legislature of such state shall judge that such extra number cannot be safely spared out of the same, in which case they shall raise officer, cloath, arm and equip as many of such extra number as they judge can be safely spared. And the officers and men so cloathed, armed and equipped, shall march to the place appointed, and within the time agreed on by the united states in congress assembled.

The united states in congress assembled shall never engage in a war, nor grant letters of marque and reprisal in time of peace, nor enter into any treaties or alliances, nor coin money, nor regulate the value thereof, nor ascertain the sums and expences necessary for the defence and welfare of the united states, or any of them, nor emit bills, nor borrow money on the credit of the united states, nor appropriate money, nor agree upon the number of vessels of war, to be built or purchased, or the number of land or sea forces to be raised, nor appoint a commander in chief of the army or navy, unless nine states assent to the same: nor shall a question on any other point, except for adjourning from day to day be determined, unless by the votes of a majority of the united states in congress assembled.

The congress of the united states shall have power to adjourn to any time within the year, and to any place within the united states, so that no period of adjournment be for a longer duration than the space of six Months, and shall publish the Journal of their proceedings monthly, except such parts thereof relating to treaties, alliances or military operations as in their judgment require secresy; and the yeas and nays of the delegates of each state on any question shall be entered on the Journal, when it is desired by any delegate; and the delegates of a state, or any of them, at his or their request shall be furnished with a transcript of the said Journal, except such parts as are above excepted, to lay before the legislatures of the several states.

Art. X. The committee of the states, or any nine of them, shall be authorised to execute, in the recess of congress, such of the powers of congress as the united states in congress assembled, by the consent of nine states, shall from time to time think expedient to vest them with; provided that no power be delegated to the said committee, for the exercise of which, by the articles of confederation, the voice of nine states in the congress of the united states assembled is requisite.

Art. XI. Canada acceding to this confederation, and joining in the measures of the united states, shall be admitted into, and entitled to all the advantages of this union: but no other colony shall be admitted into the same, unless such admission be agreed to by nine states.

Art. XII. All bills of credit emitted, monies borrowed and debts contracted by, or under the authority of congress, before the assembling of the united states, in pursuance of the present confederation, shall be deemed and considered as a charge against the united states, for payment and satisfaction whereof the said united states, and the public faith are hereby solemnly pledged.

Art. XIII. Every state shall abide by the determinations of the united states in congress assembled, on all questions which by this confederation are submitted to them. And the Articles of this confederation shall be inviolably observed by every state, and the union shall be perpetual; nor shall any alteration at any time hereafter be made in any of them; unless such alteration be agreed to in a congress of the united states, and be afterwards confirmed by the legislatures of every state.

AND WHEREAS it has pleased the Great Governor of the World to incline the hearts of the legislatures we respectively represent in congress, to approve of, and to authorize us to ratify the said articles of confederation and perpetual union, KNOW YE that we the under-signed delegates, by virtue of the power and authority to us given for that purpose, do by these presents, in the name and in behalf of our respective constituents, fully and entirely ratify and confirm each and every of the said articles of the confederation and perpetual union, and all and singular the matters and things therein contained: And we do further solemnly plight and engage the faith of our respective constituents, that they shall abide by the determinations of the united states in congress assembled, on all questions, which by the said confederation are submitted to them. And that the articles thereof shall be inviolably observed by the states we respectively represent, and that the union shall be perpetual. In Witness whereof we have hereunto set our hands in Congress. Done at Philadelphia in the state of Pennsylvania the ninth Day of July in the Year of our Lord one Thousand seven Hundred and Seventy-eight, and in the third year of the independence of America.

PRESIDENTS OF THE UNITED STATES

To the right of each portrait are the President's name,
his age on taking office, terms of office, party affiliation,
the name of the Vice-President, and the name of the President's wife.

1.
George Washington, 57
1789–1797
Federalist
John Adams
Martha Dandridge
　Washington

7.
Andrew Jackson, 61
1829–1837
Democrat
John C. Calhoun
Martin Van Buren
Rachel Donelson Jackson

2.
John Adams, 61
1797–1801
Federalist
Thomas Jefferson
Abigail Smith Adams

8.
Martin Van Buren, 54
1837–1841
Democrat
Richard M. Johnson
Hannah Hoes Van Buren

3.
Thomas Jefferson, 57
1801–1809
Democratic-Republican
Aaron Burr
George Clinton
Martha Wayles Jefferson

9.
*William Henry Harrison, 68
1841–1841
Whig
John Tyler
Anna Symmes Harrison

4.
James Madison, 57
1809–1817
Democratic-Republican
George Clinton
Elbridge Gerry
Dolley Payne Madison

10.
John Tyler, 51
1841–1845
Whig
. . . . .
Julia Gardiner Tyler

5.
James Monroe, 58
1817–1825
Democratic-Republican
Daniel D. Tompkins
Eliza Kortright Monroe

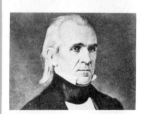

11.
James K. Polk, 49
1845–1849
Democrat
George M. Dallas
Sarah Childress Polk

6.
John Quincy Adams, 57
1825–1829
Democratic-Republican
John C. Calhoun
Louisa Johnson Adams

12.
*Zachary Taylor, 64
1849–1850
Whig
Millard Fillmore
Margaret Smith Taylor

13.
Millard Fillmore, 50
1850–1853
Whig
. . . . .
Abigail Powers Fillmore

20.
**James A. Garfield, 49
1881–1881
Republican
Chester A. Arthur
Lucretia Rudolph Garfield

14.
Franklin Pierce, 48
1853–1857
Democrat
William R. King
Jane Appleton Pierce

21.
Chester A. Arthur, 50
1881–1885
Republican
. . . . .
Ellen Herndon Arthur

15.
James Buchanan, 65
1857–1861
Democrat
John C. Breckinridge
(unmarried)

22.
Grover Cleveland, 47
1885–1889
Democrat
Thomas A. Hendricks
Frances Folsom Cleveland

16.
**Abraham Lincoln, 52
1861–1865
Republican
Hannibal Hamlin
Andrew Johnson
Mary Todd Lincoln

23.
Benjamin Harrison, 55
1889–1893
Republican
Levi P. Morton
Caroline Scott Harrison

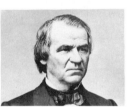

17.
Andrew Johnson, 56
1865–1869
Democrat
. . . . .
Eliza McCardle Johnson

24.
Grover Cleveland, 55
1893–1897
Democrat
Adlai E. Stevenson
Frances Folsom Cleveland

18.
Ulysses S. Grant, 46
1869–1877
Republican
Schuyler Colfax
Henry Wilson
Julia Dent Grant

25.
**William McKinley, 54
1897–1901
Republican
Garret A. Hobart
Theodore Roosevelt
Ida Saxton McKinley

19.
Rutherford B. Hayes, 54
1877–1881
Republican
William A. Wheeler
Lucy Webb Hayes

26.
Theodore Roosevelt, 42
1901–1909
Republican
Charles W. Fairbanks
Edith Carow Roosevelt

689

27.
William H. Taft, 51
1909–1913
Republican
James S. Sherman
Helen Herron Taft

34.
Dwight D. Eisenhower, 62
1953–1961
Republican
Richard M. Nixon
Mamie Doud Eisenhower

28.
Woodrow Wilson, 56
1913–1921
Democrat
Thomas R. Marshall
Edith Bolling Wilson

35.
**John F. Kennedy, 43
1961–1963
Democrat
Lyndon B. Johnson
Jacqueline Bouvier Kennedy

29.
*Warren G. Harding, 55
1921–1923
Republican
Calvin Coolidge
Florence Kling Harding

36.
Lyndon B. Johnson, 55
1963–1969
Democrat
Hubert H. Humphrey
Claudia (Ladybird) Taylor
  Johnson

30.
Calvin Coolidge, 51
1923–1929
Republican
Charles G. Dawes
Grace Goodhue Coolidge

37.
***Richard M. Nixon, 55
1969–1974
Republican
Spiro T. Agnew
Gerald R. Ford
Thelma (Pat) Ryan Nixon

31.
Herbert C. Hoover, 54
1929–1933
Republican
Charles Curtis
Lou Henry Hoover

38.
Gerald R. Ford, 61
1974–1977
Republican
Nelson A. Rockefeller
Elizabeth (Betty) Bloomer
  Ford

32.
*Franklin D. Roosevelt, 51
1933–1945
Democrat
John N. Garner
Henry A. Wallace
Harry S. Truman
Anna Eleanor Roosevelt

39.
James E. Carter, 52
1977–1981
Democrat
Walter F. Mondale
Rosalyn Smith Carter

33.
Harry S. Truman, 60
1945–1953
Democrat
Alben Barkley
Bess Wallace Truman

40.
Ronald W. Reagan, 69
1981—
Republican
George Bush
Nancy Davis Reagan

*died while in office   **assassinated   ***resigned from office

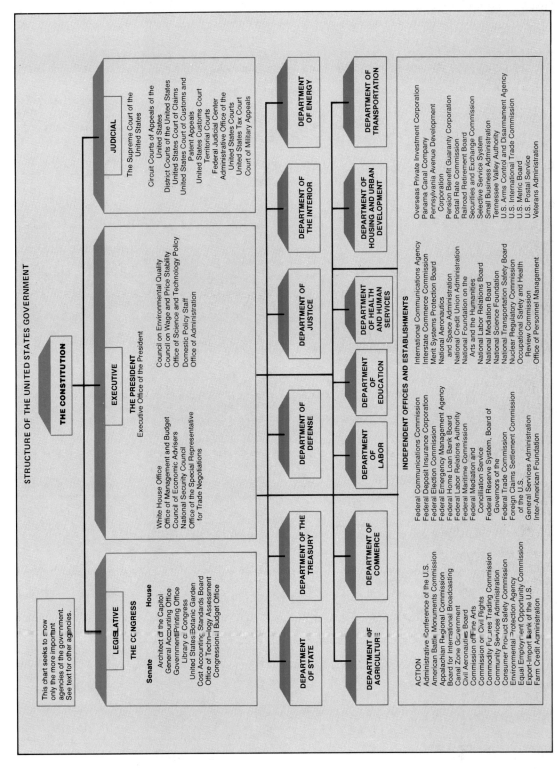

STRUCTURE OF THE UNITED STATES GOVERNMENT

THE CONSTITUTION

LEGISLATIVE
THE CONGRESS

Senate   **House**

Architect of the Capitol
General Accounting Office
Government Printing Office
Library of Congress
United States Botanic Garden
Cost Accounting Standards Board
Office of Technology Assessment
Congressional Budget Office

EXECUTIVE
THE PRESIDENT
Executive Office of the President

White House Office
Office of Management and Budget
Council of Economic Advisers
National Security Council
Office of the Special Representative
for Trade Negotiations

Council on Environmental Quality
Council on Wage and Price Stability
Office of Science and Technology Policy
Domestic Policy Staff
Office of Administration

JUDICIAL

The Supreme Court of the
United States

Circuit Courts of Appeals of the
United States
District Courts of the United States
United States Court of Claims
United States Court of Customs and
Patent Appeals
United States Customs Court
Territorial Courts
Federal Judicial Center
Administrative Office of the
United States Courts
United States Tax Court
Court of Military Appeals

DEPARTMENT OF STATE

DEPARTMENT OF THE TREASURY

DEPARTMENT OF DEFENSE

DEPARTMENT OF JUSTICE

DEPARTMENT OF THE INTERIOR

DEPARTMENT OF ENERGY

DEPARTMENT OF AGRICULTURE

DEPARTMENT OF COMMERCE

DEPARTMENT OF LABOR

DEPARTMENT OF EDUCATION

DEPARTMENT OF HEALTH AND HUMAN SERVICES

DEPARTMENT OF HOUSING AND URBAN DEVELOPMENT

DEPARTMENT OF TRANSPORTATION

INDEPENDENT OFFICES AND ESTABLISHMENTS

ACTION
Administrative Conference of the U.S.
American Battle Monuments Commission
Appalachian Regional Commission
Board for International Broadcasting
Canal Zone Government
Civil Aeronautics Board
Commission of Fine Arts
Commission on Civil Rights
Commodity Futures Trading Commission
Community Services Administration
Consumer Product Safety Commission
Environmental Protection Agency
Equal Employment Opportunity Commission
Export-Import Bank of the U.S.
Farm Credit Administration

Federal Communications Commission
Federal Deposit Insurance Corporation
Federal Election Commission
Federal Emergency Management Agency
Federal Home Loan Bank Board
Federal Labor Relations Authority
Federal Maritime Commission
Federal Mediation and
Conciliation Service
Federal Reserve System, Board of
Governors of the
Federal Trade Commission
Foreign Claims Settlement Commission
of the U.S.
General Services Administration
Inter-American Foundation

International Communications Agency
Interstate Commerce Commission
Merit Systems Protection Board
National Aeronautics
and Space Administration
National Credit Union Administration
National Foundation on the
Arts and the Humanities
National Labor Relations Board
National Mediation Board
National Science Foundation
National Transportation Safety Board
Nuclear Regulatory Commission
Occupational Safety and Health
Review Commission
Office of Personnel Management

Overseas Private Investment Corporation
Panama Canal Company
Pennsylvania Avenue Development
Corporation
Pension Benefit Guaranty Corporation
Postal Rate Commission
Railroad Retirement Board
Securities and Exchange Commission
Selective Service System
Small Business Administration
Tennessee Valley Authority
U.S. Arms Control and Disarmament Agency
U.S. International Trade Commission
U.S. Metric Board
U.S. Postal Service
Veterans Administration

This chart seeks to show
only the more important
agencies of the government.
See text for other agencies.

SENATE STANDING COMMITTEES AND SUBCOMMITTEES

AGRICULTURE, NUTRITION AND FORESTRY	Agriculture Credit and Rural Electrification ● Agricultural Production, Marketing and Stabilization of Prices ● Agricultural Research and General Legislation ● Environment, Soil Conservation, and Forestry ● Foreign Agricultural Policy ● Nutrition ● Rural Development
APPROPRIATIONS	Agriculture and Related Agencies ● Defense ● District of Columbia ● Energy and Water Development ● Foreign Operations ● HUD-Independent Agencies ● Interior ● Labor, Health, Education, and Welfare ● Legislative Branch ● Military Construction ● State, Justice, Commerce, the Judiciary ● Transportation ● Treasury, Postal Service, General Government
ARMED SERVICES	Arms Control ● General Procurement ● Manpower and Personnel ● Military Construction and Stockpiles ● Procurement Policy and Reprogramming ● Research and Development
BANKING, HOUSING AND URBAN AFFAIRS	Consumer Affairs ● Economic Stabilization ● Financial Institutions ● Housing and Urban Affairs ● Insurance ● International Finance ● Rural Housing and Development ● Securities
BUDGET	None
COMMERCE, SCIENCE AND TRANSPORTATION	Aviation ● Communications ● Consumer ● Merchant Marine and Tourism ● Science, Technology, and Space ● Surface Transportation ● Study Group-National Ocean Policy
ENERGY AND NATURAL RESOURCES	Energy Conservation and Supply ● Energy Regulation ● Energy Research and Development ● Energy Resources and Materials Production ● Parks, Recreation, and Renewable Resources
ENVIRONMENT AND PUBLIC WORKS	Environmental Pollution ● Nuclear Regulation ● Regional and Community Development ● Resource Protection ● Transportation ● Water Resources
FINANCE	Energy and Foundations ● Health ● International Trade ● Oversight of the Internal Revenue Service ● Private Pension Plans and Employee Fringe Benefits ● Public Assistance ● Revenue Sharing, Intergovernmental Revenue Impact, and Economic Problems ● Social Security ● Taxation and Debt Management Generally ● Tourism and Sugar ● Unemployment and Related Problems
FOREIGN RELATIONS	African Affairs ● Arms Control, Oceans, International Operations, and Environment ● East Asian and Pacific Affairs ● European Affairs ● International Economic Policy ● Near Eastern and South Asian Affairs ● Western Hemisphere Affairs
GOVERNMENTAL AFFAIRS	Civil Service and General Services ● Energy, Nuclear Proliferation and Federal Services ● Federal Spending Practices and Open Government ● Government Efficiency and the District of Columbia ● Intergovernmental Relations ● Investigations ● Oversight of Government Management
JUDICIARY	Administrative Practice and Procedure ● Antitrust, Monopoly and Business Rights ● Constitution ● Criminal Justice ● Improvements in Judicial Machinery ● Jurisprudence and Governmental Relations ● Limitations of Contracted and Delegated Authority
LABOR AND HUMAN RESOURCES	Aging ● Alcoholism and Drug Abuse ● Child and Human Development ● Education, Arts and Humanities ● Employment, Poverty and Migratory Labor ● Handicapped ● Health and Scientific Research
RULES AND ADMINISTRATION	None
VETERANS' AFFAIRS	None

Source: Congressional Quarterly

HOUSE STANDING COMMITTEES AND SUBCOMMITTEES

AGRICULTURE
Conservation and Credit ● Cotton ● Dairy and Poultry ● Department Investigations, Oversight and Research ● Domestic Marketing, Consumer Relations, and Nutrition ● Family Farms, Rural Development, and Special Studies ● Forests ● Livestock and Grains ● Oilseeds and Rice ● Tobacco

APPROPRIATIONS
Agriculture, Rural Development and Related Agencies ● Defense ● District of Columbia ● Energy and Water Development ● Foreign Operations ● Housing and Urban Development—Independent Agencies ● Interior ● Labor—Health, Education and Welfare ● Legislative ● Military Construction ● State, Justice, Commerce and Judiciary ● Transportation ● Treasury—Postal Service—General Government

ARMED SERVICES
Investigations ● Military Compensation ● Military Installations and Facilities ● Military Personnel ● Procurement and Military Nuclear Systems ● Research and Development ● Seapower and Strategic and Critical Materials ● Special Subcommittee—NATO Standardization, Interoperability, and Readiness

BANKING, FINANCE AND URBAN AFFAIRS
The City ● Consumer Affairs ● Domestic Monetary Policy ● Economic Stabilization ● Financial Institutions Supervision, Regulation and Insurance ● General Oversight and Renegotiation ● Housing and Community Development ● International Development Institutions and Finance ● International Trade, Investment and Monetary Policy

BUDGET
None

DISTRICT OF COLUMBIA
Fiscal Affairs and Health ● Government, Budget and Urban Affairs ● Judiciary, Manpower and Education ● Metropolitan Affairs

EDUCATION AND LABOR
Elementary, Secondary and Vocational Education ● Employment Opportunities ● Health and Safety ● Human Resources ● Labor-Management Relations ● Labor Standards ● Postsecondary Education ● Select Education

FOREIGN AFFAIRS
Africa ● Asian and Pacific Affairs ● Europe and the Middle East ● Inter-American Affairs ● International Economic Policy and Trade ● International Operations ● International Organizations ● International Security and Scientific Affairs

GOVERNMENT OPERATIONS
Commerce, Consumer and Monetary Affairs ● Environment, Energy and Natural Resources ● Government Activities and Transportation ● Government Information and Individual Rights ● Intergovernmental Relations and Human Resources ● Legislation and National Security ● Manpower and Housing

HOUSE ADMINISTRATION
Accounts ● Contracts ● Libraries and Memorials ● Office Systems ● Personnel and Police ● Printing ● Services ● Policy Group—Information and Computers

INTERIOR AND INSULAR AFFAIRS
Energy and the Environment ● Mines and Mining ● National Parks and Insular Affairs ● Oversight/Special Investigations ● Pacific Affairs ● Public Lands ● Water and Power Resources

INTERSTATE AND FOREIGN COMMERCE
Communications ● Consumer Protection and Finance ● Energy and Power ● Health and the Environment ● Oversight and Investigations ● Transportation and Commerce

JUDICIARY
Administrative Law and Governmental Relations ● Civil and Constitutional Rights ● Courts, Civil Liberties and the Administration of Justice ● Crime ● Criminal Justice ● Immigration, Refugees, and International Law ● Monopolies and Commerical Law

MERCHANT MARINE AND FISHERIES
Coast Guard ● Fisheries and Wildlife Conservation and the Environment ● Merchant Marine ● Oceanography ● Panama Canal

POST OFFICE AND CIVIL SERVICE
Census and Population ● Civil Service ● Compensation and Employee Benefits ● Human Resources ● Investigations ● Postal Operations and Services ● Postal Personnel and Modernization

PUBLIC WORKS AND TRANSPORTATION
Aviation ● Economic Development ● Oversight and Review ● Public Buildings and Grounds ● Surface Transportation ● Water Resources

RULES
Legislative Process ● Rules of the House

SCIENCE AND TECHNOLOGY
Energy Development and Applications ● Energy Research and Production ● Investigations and Oversight ● Natural Resources and Environment ● Science, Research and Technology

SMALL BUSINESS
Access to Equity Capital and Business Opportunities ● Antitrust and Restraint of Trade Activities Affecting Small Business ● General Oversight and Minority Enterprise ● Energy, Environment, Safety and Research ● SBA and SBIC Authority and General Small Business Problems ● Special Small Business Problems

STANDARDS OF OFFICIAL CONDUCT
None

VETERANS' AFFAIRS
Compensation, Pension, Insurance, and Memorial Affairs ● Education, Training and Employment ● Housing ● Medical Facilities and Benefits ● Special Investigations

WAYS AND MEANS
Health ● Oversight ● Public Assistance and Unemployment Compensation ● Select Revenue Measures ● Social Security ● Trade

Source: Congressional Quarterly

VOCABULARY INDEX

INDEX

Presidential primary, 179–180
Press, freedom of, 33, 40, 67, 376, 626, 630
Pressure groups, 210–218, 281
  agriculture, 212–213
  business, 211–212
  economic-interest, 211
  labor, 213–214
  lobbying, 216–217
  noneconomic, 214–215
  professional, 213
Price supports, 504, 506
Primary elections, 177–180, 329
Prince v. Massachusetts (1944), 635
Prior restraint, 626–627, 630
Prisons, 499
Privacy, right to, 594, 671
Privileges and immunities, 89, 90
Probable cause, 639, 640, 643
Probation officers, 575–576
Procedural questions, 263
Professional pressure groups, 213
Profit, 14, 18
Progressive Era amendments, 43
Progressive income tax, 153, 274
Progressive movement, 109
Progressive party, 188, 189
Prohibition, 42, 43, 72–73, 74–75
Prohibition (order), 113
Project grants, 162
Proletariat, 16
Property tax, 156–159
Proportional representation, 187
Proportional tax, 153
Proprietary colonies, 24, 25
Public debt, 71, 490
Public Health Service, 311, 538–539
Public opinion, 196–206
  definition of, 196–199
  demonstrations, 201
  editorial comment, 201–202
  formation of, 199–200
  measurement of, 201–206
  polls, 202–206, 238
  position issues, 199
  President and, 364
  self-selected, 202–203
  valence issues, 199
Public Works and Economic
  Development Act of 1965, 513
Puerto Rico, 256
Pulitzer, Joseph, 219
Punishment, cruel and unusual,
  68, 591, 653–654
Pure Food and Drug Act of 1906,
  539
Puritans, 23

Quakers, 23
Quartering Acts, 25

Race relations, 275, 279, 281
Raiding, 178
Railroads, 450–451, 453, 456–457,
  550
Rallying effect, 250
Randolph, Peyton, 43
Rappeport, Michael, 198
Reagan, Nancy, 348
Reagan, Ronald, 172, 297, 348
  appointments by, 362
  background, 352, 354
  bureaucratic reform and, 428
  Bush and, 361
  campaign financing, 360
  electoral college and, 359
  military and, 486
  1980 election, 356
  staff, 397
Reagan-Anderson debates, 462
Reapportionment, 106–107, 290–291, 603, 664
Reasonable discrimination, 90
Reciprocity, 313
Reclamation, 503
Reclamation Act of 1902, 525
Reconstruction amendments, 42,
  228
Red Lion Broadcasting v. FCC, 627
Rediscounting, 468
Redistribution, 274
Redlining, 133
Reed v. Reed (1971), 669
Referees, 575–576
Referendum, 6, 109, 209
Refugees, 497
Regional planning districts, 147–148
Registration, 230, 240
Regressive tax, 153
Regulations, 273, 274
Regulatory commissions, 380,
  448–469
  appointment and confirmation of
    commissioners, 451
  Civil Aeronautics Board, 453,
    466–467, 549
  Congress and, 449, 450, 452–453,
    457, 461, 469
  criticism of, 452, 453
  Federal Communications
    Commission, 449, 454, 459,
    461–463, 627
  Federal Reserve Board, 383, 434,
    467–469
  Federal Trade Commission, 442,
    457, 459, 461
  Interstate Commerce
    Commission, 433, 451–453,
    456–457, 550
  National Labor Relations Board,
    455, 463–466

President and, 449, 452
protection of industries, 453–454
rulings, interpreting, 451–452
rulings, types of, 449
Securities and Exchange
  Commission, 463
structure and powers of,
  449–450
Reid, Ogden, 190
Religion, freedom of, 24, 33, 40, 67,
  631–635
Remand, 608
Renewal Assistance
  Administration (RAA), 548
Rent subsidies, 547
Reorganization Act of 1949, 381
Representative democracy, 6, 8
Representative government, 23,
  24, 39
Republic, 6
Republican party
  national committee, 181
  partisan identification, 190, 192
  predominance, 187
  pressure groups and, 216
  voter registration, 230
  See also Presidential elections
Residency requirements, 229–230,
  234, 664, 671
Revenue sharing, 88, 162, 165
Reynolds v. U.S. (1878), 635
Rhode Island, 24, 28–29, 33, 35, 86,
  91
Ricardo, David, 17
Richardson, Elliot L., 439
Riegle, Donald, 190
Rio Pact, 266
Robber barons, 450
Roberts v. Louisiana (1976), 653
Rockefeller, Nelson A., 76, 187, 294,
  362
Rockefeller, Winthrop, 190
*Roemer v. Maryland Board of
  Public Works* (1976), 631
Roosevelt, Franklin, D., 75, 203,
  258, 355, 375, 546
  advisers, 395
  appointments by, 574
  bureaucracy and, 399–400, 434
  economic policy, 350
  farm policy, 503
  fireside chats, 364
  foreign policy, conduct of, 372,
    373
  Japanese-Americans, confinement
    of, 386
  legislative programs, 354, 382
  1938 congressional elections, 384
  personality, 352
  staff, 392, 394–396
  State of the Union message, 381

710

civil rights legislation and, 232–234
extension of suffrage, 226–228
federal power, 234
literacy tests, 228, 231–234, 664
minimum age, 77, 220, 229, 234
nonvoting, 239–241
poll tax, 76, 84, 228, 664
registration, 230, 240
residency requirements, 229–230, 234, 664, 671
state power, 235–236
Supreme Court and, 229–230, 232, 664–665, 671
White primary, 228, 664
women and, 73, 228
Voting Rights Act of 1965, 228, 233
Voting Rights Act of 1970, 229, 232, 234
Voucher systems, 664–665

Wagner, Robert F., 123
Wald, Patricia, 585
Waldheim, Kurt, 266
Wallace, George, 178, 187, 189, 190, 359
Wallace, Henry, 238
War Department, 433, 486
War of 1812, 256
War Powers Act of 1973, 46, 253, 319, 372
Ward (district) leaders, 183
Warrants, 639, 640–641
Warren, Earl, 586, 587, 588, 589, 606
Washington, George, 32, 35, 47, 90, 256, 348, 349, 481
appointments by, 425
executive departments, creation of, 476, 477
as "great" president, 354
Jay Treaty and, 374
personal style, 375
State of the Union message, 381
Whiskey Rebellion, 370
Washington Conference of 1921–

1922, 258
Washington state
county government, 137
primary elections, 178
regional planning districts, 149
special districts, 147
Water pollution, 529
Water Quality Improvement Act of 1970, 529
Watergate, 253, 292, 299, 316, 363, 368, 376, 572, 593
Watergate Committee, 299, 316
Watkins v. U.S. **(1957),** 319
Weaver, Robert C., 544
Webster, Daniel, 477
Weeks v. U.S. **(1914),** 643
Weems v. U.S. **(1910),** 653
Weinberger v. Wisenfield **(1975),** 669
Welfare, 19, 274, 537–538
West Virginia, 86, 91
West Virginia Board of Education v. Barnette **(1943),** 634
Whig party, 188
Whips, 296
Whiskey Rebellion, 87, 370
White, Byron, 462
White House Staff, 392, 394–397, 402–407
White primary, 228, 664
Whitney, Eli, 511
Whitney v. California **(1927),** 618, 620
Wildavsky, Aaron, 372
Williams v. Florida **(1970),** 651
Williams v. Mississippi **(1898),** 664
Wilson, James, 183
Wilson, Woodrow, 47, 187, 250, 258, 370
Congress and, 350
as "great" president, 354
legislative programs, 46, 381–382
personality, 352
staff, 392
State of the Union message, 381

Versailles Treaty, 374
in World War I, 350
Winters v. United States **(1908),** 424
Wiretapping, 594, 643
Wisconsin
primary elections, 178, 180
regional planning districts, 149
voter registration, 230
Wisconsin v. Yoder **(1972),** 635
Witnesses
right of accused to confront, 651, 654
rights of, 318–319
Women, 465
citizenship and, 12
in Cabinet, 362
in civil service, 427–428
in Congress, 286, 336
sex discrimination, 669
voting, 73, 228
wages, 516
Women's Bureau, 516
Women's movement, 197
Woods, Granville T., 511
Woodson v. North Carolina **(1976),** 653
Woodward, Bob, 219
World Bank, 266, 269
World order through law, 259, 261
World War I, 258, 350
World War II, 258, 351, 370–371
Wyoming, 103

Yates v. U.S. **(1957),** 620, 621
Yellow dog contract, 464
Yick Wo v. Hopkins **(1886),** 661
Yorktown, battle of, 254
Young, Andrew, 265, 362
Young Plan, 258
Yugoslavia, 19

Zenger, Peter, 219–220
Zero-based budgeting, 429
Zoning, 125, 126
Zorach v. Clausen **(1953),** 634

PHOTO CREDITS

Sources have been abbreviated as follows:

Unit 1: xxi—© Dilip Mehta/Contact Press Images. **xxii**—Granger Collection. **3**—© Rick Smolan/Contact Press Images. **5**—Keystone Press Agency. **6**—Camera 5. **7**—Jean-Claude Francolon/Gamma-Liaison. **8**—Sipa/Black Star. **10**—Keystone Press Agency. **12**—Woodfin Camp & Associates. **13**—Sygma. **15**—CP. **18**—Marc Riboud/Magnum Photos. **23**—Pilgrim Hall, Plymouth, Mass. **27**—LC. **28**—Yale University Art Gallery. **31**—NYPL, Emmet Collection. **34**—NYPL, Picture Collection. **41, 43, 44**—CP. **45**—© Rick Smolan/Contact Press Images. **62**—New York Historical Society. **81**—Ad Council. **82**—LC. **83**—*The New York Times.* **88**—UPI.

Unit 2: 102—*Baton Rouge State Times.* **104**—EPA. **105**—Mimi Forsyth/MPPS. **108**—CP. **111**—*Raleigh News & Observer.* **112**—Mimi Forsyth/MPPS. **122**—EPA. **124**—WW. **126**—Magnum Photos. **127**—Stock, Boston. **128**—Magnum Photos. **129**—Hugh Rogers/MPPS. **133**—Taurus Photos. **137**—Don Pasewark. **138**—Mimi Forsyth/MPPS. **142**—EPA. **143**—Mimi Forsyth/MPPS. **146**—Sybil Shelton/MPPS. **153**—Mimi Forsyth/MPPS. **156**—EPA. **161**—UPI.

Unit 3: 170—WW. **173**—*The New Yorker*, Nov. 1, 1976. **176**—Penelope Breese & Lief Skoogfors/Gamma-Liaison. **177**—CP. **179**—Steve Liss/Gamma-Liaison. **181**—UPI. **184**—Ivan Mercado/The News World. **186**—WW. **197**—Mimi Forsyth/MPPS. **198**—WW. **202, 203**—UPI. **204**—WW. **206**—The Gallup Poll. **212**—Paul Conklin/MPPS. **213**—UPI. **214**—The President's Council on Employment of the Handicapped. **218**—National Council to Control Hand Guns. **223**—Ad Council. **227**—CP. **231**—Beryl Goldberg. **232**—LC. **236**—CBS News. **237**—Goldman. **240**—Mimi Forsyth/MPPS.

Unit 4: 246—The World Bank. **251, 252**—UPI. **255**—WW. **259**—U.S. Coast Guard Photo. **260**—UPI. **261**—WW. **264**—Brian F. Alpert/Keystone Press Agency. **265**—WW. **272**—USDA Photos. **275**—New York Historical Society. **276**—UPI. **277, 278**—WW. **279**—© Rick Smolan/Contact Press Images.

Unit 5: 286—Office of Nancy Kassebaum. **289**—Herbert Lanks/Black Star. **292, 294**—UPI. **297, 306**—WW. **308**—UPI. **311**—Nour David/News Photos Worldwide. **312**—Office of Barbara Milkulski. **317**—WW. **318** (top)—Robert Phillips/Black Star. **318** (bot)—UPI. **320**—WW. **323**—Teresa Zabala/*The New York Times.* **325**—© Diane Mara Henry, 1978. **329**—Duane Howell/*The Denver Post.* **330, 334** (top)—WW.

Unit 6: 346—WW. **349**—© 1981 Fred Ward/Black Star. **350**—WW. **355**—Acme Photos. **361**—UPI. **365**—© 1981 Dennis Brack/Black Star. **369**—WW. **371**—FDR Library. **373**—UPI. **375**—WW. **388**—WW. **389** (left)—Harris & Ewing © 1908. **389** (right)—CP. **393**—Don Hesse/*St. Louis Globe Democrat.* **398**—WW. **400**—USDA. **402**—WW. **405**—*The New York Times.* **407**—UPI. **414**—Courtesy of Paula Stern. **417**—HRW Photo By Lonny Kalfus. **420**—NASA.

Unit 7: 422—Andrew Sacks/EPA. **424**—Bureau of Indian Affairs. **427**—John J. Lipinot © 1978/Black Star. **433**—Illinois Dept. of Agriculture. **434**—Peace Corps. **436**—Tennessee Valley Authority. **440**—Congressional Budget Office. **441**—UPI. **443**—U.S. Army Corps of Engineers. **450**—CP. **459**—American Lung Association. **461**—Andrew Sacks/EPA. **464**—WW. **469**—UPI.

Unit 8: 474—WW. **478**—Nour David/News Photos Worldwide. **484**—Sygma. **485**—American Airlines. **487**—Grumman Aerospace Corporation. **493**—Bureau of Engraving & Printing. **498**—© Dan Miller 1980/Woodfin Camp & Associates. **503**—Daniel S. Brody/EPA. **505, 508**—WW. **512**—UPI. **514**—National Safety Council. **521** (left)—UPI. **521** (right)—Oregon State Highway Department. **525**—WW. **528** (bot)—**529**—US Environmental Protection Agency. **537**—U.S. Dept. of Agriculture. **538**—U.S. Dept. of Health, Education and Welfare. **539**—Food & Drug Administration. **540**—WW. **541**—© Michal Heron 1979/Woodfin Camp & Associates. **543**—© Van Bucher/Photo Researchers. **545**—U.S. Dept. of Housing and Urban Development. **546**—George Malave/Stock, Boston. **550**—© Betty Medsger. **552, 555**—WW. **557**—A. Pierce Bounds/Uniphoto.

Unit 9: 562, 565, 567—UPI. **570**—© Donald Dietz/Stock, Boston. **571**—WW. **574**—Equal Employment Opportunity Commission. **576**—WW. **583**—Bettmann Archive. **584** (top)—UPI. **585** (bot)—Jim McHugh/Sygma. **585**—Office of Patricia Wald. **587**—WW. **591**—Magnum Photos. **593**—U.S. Supreme Court Historical Society. **594**—Stock, Boston. **595**—UPI. **599**—MPPS. **605**—U.S. Supreme Court Historical Society. **606**—WW. **609**—UPI.

Unit 10: 614—News and Publication Service, Stanford University. **617**—Bob Adelman. **619**—Beryl Goldberg. **620**—Bruce Hosking/Uniphoto. **627**—UPI. **629**—Beryl Goldberg. **631**—© Leonard Freed/Magnum. **632**—Srickler/MPPS. **633**—WW. **634**—Sybil Shelton/MPPS. **639, 641**—Spring 3100, Police Department of the City of New York. **645**—© Michael Philip Mannheim/Photo Researchers. **646**—Peter Karas. **647**—Robin Forbes/Image Bank. **649**—UPI. **653, 654, 656, 661**—WW. **662**—Joe Favale/Boston Police Department. **663, 665**—WW. **666**—Stock, Boston. **668**—WW. **670**—HRW Photo by Sally Andersen-Bruce. **672**—Ginger Chih. **673**—Port Authority of New York. **674**—WW.

PRESIDENTS OF THE UNITED STATES: 688 from top to bottom—The White House; Essex Institute; Granger Collection; Bowdoin College Museum of Fine Arts; New York City Hall Gallery; Metropolitan Museum of Art; LC; LC; LC. **689**—Chicago Historical Society; LC; LC; LC; LC; LC; LC; LC; LC; LC; Clinedinst Studio; LC. **690**—LC; LC; LC; LC; LC; LC; Harry S. Truman Library; General Services Administration; WW; Lyndon B. Johnson Library; Holt, Rinehart and Winston; WW; The White House; Richard Evans/Gamma-Liaison.

Cover Photo by Reginald Wickham.